Lecture Notes of the Institute for Computer Sciences, Social Informatics and Telecommunications Engineering 98

Pinyi Ren   Chao Zhang   Xin Liu   Pei Liu
Song Ci (Eds.)

Wireless Internet

6th International ICST Conference, WICON 2011
Xi'an, China, October 19-21, 2011
Revised Selected Papers

 Springer

Volume Editors

Pinyi Ren
Chao Zhang
Xi'an Jiaotong University
Xianning West Road 28
Xi'an, 710049 Shaanxi, China
E-mail: {pyren; chaozhang}@mail.xjtu.edu.cn

Xin Liu
University of California
3013 Kemper Hall, Davis, CA 95616, USA
E-mail: liu@cs.ucdavis.edu

Pei Liu
Polytechnic Institute of New York University
6 Metrotech Center, New York, NY 11201, USA
E-mail: pliu@poly.edu

Song Ci
University of Nebraska-Lincoln
200B Peter Kiewit Institute, Omaha, NE 68588, USA
E-mail: sci@engr.unl.edu

ISSN 1867-8211   e-ISSN 1867-822X
ISBN 978-3-642-30492-7   e-ISBN 978-3-642-30493-4
DOI 10.1007/978-3-642-30493-4

Springer Heidelberg Dordrecht London New York

Library of Congress Control Number: 2012938532

CR Subject Classification (1998): C.2, H.4, I.2, H.3, F.1, K.6.5

Typesetting: Camera-ready by author, data conversion by Scientific Publishing Services, Chennai, India

Printed on acid-free paper

Springer is part of Springer Science+Business Media (www.springer.com)

Preface

The 2011 6th International ICST Conference on Wireless Internet (WICON)was successfully held in Xi'an, China, during October 19–21, 2011. This year's conference continued its tradition of being the premier forum for presentation of results on cutting-edge research in telecommunications and networking, bringing together international researchers and practitioners for discussions on the latest developments in information and communication technologies. The conference attracted 55 international registrants from about ten countries in Asia Pacific, North America, and Europe.

The Technical Program Committee (TPC) did an outstanding job in organizing a diverse technical program consisting of three tracks that covered a broad range of research areas in information and communication technologies. Under the excellent leadership of the General Chair, Pinyi Ren, and TPC Co-chairs, the Track Chairs and TPC members handled the reviews of about 100 papers submitted through the open call with 3 reviews per paper on average. From these open submissions, 55 papers were presented in 10 technical sessions. Based on the reviews, the TPC selected one paper for the "Best Paper Award," and one paper co-authored by students for the "Best Student Paper Award." Several journal special issues collecting extended versions of selected best papers from the technical program are being organized. We anticipate that this body of work will provide important references to the technical community.

The technical program featured two outstanding keynote speakers: John Thompson from the University of Edinburgh, "Green Radio for Energy-Efficient Wireless Communications," and Jiro Katto from Waseda University, "Multimedia Transport Technologies over Wired/Wireless Networks." A gala banquet was held on the evening of 20 October, during which the best paper awards were presented. The banquet featured a musical performance by several students from Xi'an Jiaotong University, which was very much appreciated by the attendees.

The success of any conference depends on many hard-working people. The TPC Chairs, Xin Liu, Pei Liu, and Song Ci, did an outstanding job in organizing the technical program. Many thanks to the four Track Chairs, Xiang Chen (PHY Track), Jun Cai (MAC Track), Zhou Su (Network Track), and Zhen Ji (Service/Application Track) for handling the reviews and selection of the WICON papers. I would also like to express my appreciation to the following contributors for their support and dedication during the organizational process of WICON 2011: ICST Executive Director, Csaba A. Szabo, Steering Committee, Imrich Chlamtac (Chair), Xudong Wang, Hsiao-Hwa Chen, Mahmoud Daneshmand,

Sponsorship Chair, Jiangguo Deng, Publication Chair, Chao Zhang, Publicity Chair, Qinghe Du, Web Chair, Gangming Lv, and Conference Coordinator, Aza Swedin for their excellent work. Special thanks are given to Fan Li, the Local Arrangements Chair, for his excellent job in arranging the venue and handling many other logistics. This conference was organized under the sponsorship of ICST and the technical sponsorships of EAI. The corporate patronage of Huawei and NSFC is gratefully acknowledged.

Pinyi Ren

Conference Organization

General Chair

Pinyi Ren   Xi'an Jiaotong University, China

Technical Program Co-chairs

Xin Liu   University of California, USA
Pei Liu   Polytechnic Institute of New York University, USA
Song Ci   University of Nebraska-Lincoln, USA

Steering Committee

Imrich Chlamtac (Chair)   Create-Net, Italy
Xudong Wang   TeraNovi Technologies, Inc., USA
                          Shanghai Jiao Tong University
Hsiao-Hwa Chen   National Cheng Kung University, Taiwan
Mahmoud Daneshmand   AT&T Labs, USA

PHY Track Chair

Xiang Chen   Tsinghua University, China

MAC Track Chair

Jun Cai   University of Manitoba, Canada

Network Track Chair

Zhou Su   Waseda University, Japan

Service/Application Track Chair

Zhen Ji   Shenzhen University, China

Publicity Chair

Qinghe Du   Texas A&M University, USA

Publication Chair

Chao Zhang   Xi'an Jiaotong University, China

Local Arrangements Chair

Fan Li   Xi'an Jiaotong University, China

Web Chair

Gangming Lv   Xi'an Jiaotong University, China

Sponsorship Chair

Jianguo Deng   Xi'an Jiaotong University, China

Technical Program Committee

PHY Track

Ove Edfors	Lund University, Sweden
Oliver Holland	King's College London, UK
Wei Chen	Tsinghua University, China
Jun-ichi Takada	Tokyo Institute of Technology, Japan
Yan Zhang	Simula Research Laboratory, Norway
Weiyu Xu	Cornell University, USA
Tsung-Hui Chang	National Tsinghua University, Taiwan
Jianwen Chen	UCLA, USA
Guanding Yu	Zhejiang University, China
Weimin Wu	Huazhong University of Science and Technology, China
Bin Tian	Xidian University, China
Yang Yang	Texas A&M University, USA
Zheng Ma	Southwest Jiaotong University, China
Qimei Cui	Beijing University of Posts and Telecommunications, China
Ben Slimance	KTH, Sweden
John Thompson	University of Edinburgh, UK
Jing Xu	Shanghai Research Center for Wireless Communications, China
Paul D. Mitchell	University of York, USA

MAC Track

Baoxian Zhang	Chinese Academy of Science, China
Dalei Wu	University of Nebraska-Lincoln, USA
Dongmei Zhao	McMaster University, Canada

Haojin Zhu	Shanghai Jiaotong University, China
Jiming Chen	Zhejiang University, China
Jinho Choi	Swansea University, UK
Kui Ren	Illinois Institute of Technology, USA
Lin Chen	University of Paris-Sud 11, France
Lingyang Song	Peking University, China
Ping Wang	Nanyang Technological University, Singapore
Sangheon Pack	Korea University, Korea
Song Wei	University of New Brunswick, Canada
Thomas Kunz	Carleton University, Canada
Weiwei Wang	Fujitsu, Japan
Xinbing Wang	Shanghai Jiaotong University, China
Xingpeng Mao	Herbin Institute of Technology, China
Yixin Jiang	Tsinghua University, China

Network Track

Ahmed H. Zahran	University College Cork, Ireland
Chunyi Song	National Institute of Information and Communications
Eric Renault	TELECOM & Management Sud Paris, France
Hongbo Shi	Yokohama National University, Japan
Jen-Wen Ding	National Kaohsiung University of Applied Sciences, Taiwan
Jun Wu	Waseda University, Japan
Kashif Sharif	University of North Carolina at Charlotte, USA
Rongtao Xu	Beijing Jiaotong University, China
Seong-eun Yoo	Daegu University, Korea
Wanqing Tu	Glyndwr University, UK
Xia Yang	Nanyang Technological University, Singapore
Yu Chen	State University of New York - Binghamton, USA
Zhongren Cao	University of California, San Diego, USA

Table of Contents

PHY Track

Network and Application Track

Hardware Track

Optimal Joint Subcarrier Assignment and Power Allocation for Multi-user Video Streaming over OFDMA Downlink Systems

Fan Li, Pinyi Ren, and Qinghe Du

School of Electronic and Information Engineering,
Xi'an Jiaotong University, Xi'an, China
{lifan,pyren,duqinghe}@mail.xjtu.edu.cn

Abstract. In this paper, we present a cross-layer design for multi-user video streaming over OFDMA (orthogonal frequency-division multiple-access) downlink systems, based on the joint optimization of subcarrier assignment and power allocation. The objective is to maximize the received video quality of all the users subject to the network resource constraint. With the optimal joint subcarrier assignment and power allocation, the proposed scheme can maximally satisfy the requirements of the packet scheduling from the higher layer. Employing the Lagrange dual decomposition method, we can obtain the global optimal solution to the optimization problem. Simulation results show that the proposed algorithm has superior performance compared to the existing alternatives.

Keywords: resource allocation, OFDMA, multi-user, optimization, lagrange dual decomposition.

1   Introduction

The demand for video transmission over wireless networks is growing dramatically. Video transmission is characterized not only by a large amount of required data-rate, but also by a significant variability of the data-rate over time. The requirements are becoming aggravating if multiple users request video streams from a single access point, which serves a given wireless cell. In the multi-user scenario, the packet scheduling for different packets of different users will incur different video qualities, due to the various video contents. Therefore, the decision of packet scheduling is important for the end-to-end video qualities. The wireless resource allocation should satisfy the requirements of packet scheduling from the higher layer.

It is really a challenge for the video transmission over wireless networks, due to the time-varying nature and the scarcity of the wireless resources. Moreover, advanced wireless access technique should be studied for the multi-user video transmission. The Orthogonal Frequency Division Multiple Access (OFDMA) is such an advanced technique. OFDMA can provide great flexibility for subcarrier assignment to maximize the system capacity and the spectral efficiency. Therefore, the problem for

P. Ren et al. (Eds.): WICON 2011, LNICST 98, pp. 1–11, 2012.
© Institute for Computer Sciences, Social Informatics and Telecommunications Engineering 2012

video transmission over OFDMA networks is how to manage the wireless resources to satisfy the requirements of packet scheduling by using effective subcarrier assignment and power distribution.

Packet scheduling for video transmission and subcarrier allocation for data transmission are both well-studied topics. The problem of dynamic subcarrier allocation for OFDMA systems is also well investigated [1]-[2]. The methods of adaptive subcarrier assignment focus on improving the data throughput and the spectrum efficiency, and guaranteeing the fairness among users as well. These methods in [1]-[2], however, are only available for data transmission, and cannot be directly applied to video applications. The increase of the throughput or the spectrum efficiency does not always correspond to the improvement of received video quality.

A lot of works have focused on the problem of real-time video transmission over OFDMA systems in recent years. By jointly considering the video content and channel condition, references [3] and [4] investigate the determination of the video encoding modes and the design of the transmission policy. These methods, however, are not applicable to the transmission for the pre-coded video streams, for which the video streams have been pre-encoded elsewhere. Therefore, video encoding parameters cannot dynamically change according to the variation of the wireless channel.

Many schemes for the transmission of pre-coded, non-scalable video are also proposed [5]-[11]. In [8], a cross-layer design for video transmission for OFDMA systems is proposed. Based on the distortion analysis for video applications, the subcarrier assignment policy is selected from a preset policy domain in order to maximize the video quality. However, the subcarrier assignment and power allocation were not mentioned in these schemes, and the improvements of the video quality are thus limited. In [9], the video quality, which is modeled as a function of video bit rate, is maximized using a piecewise continuous objective function. Therein, the maximization of the objective function is achieved by optimally allocating the wireless resources. However, the continuous objective functions proposed in [9] are not fit for video transmission. In the applications of packet switching, the packet, rather than the bit, is the unit for decoding. If a packet is not completely received, it would be fully dropped in the lower layers, such as the link layer in redundancy check. In [10], a stepwise scheme is presented, where the contribution of each packet to the video quality is measured by a gradient function. With this in mind, the packet which contributes most to video quality is scheduled in priority, and then the resources are allocated. The stepwise scheme is not optimal, because the packet with the largest contribution to video quality may consume over-many wireless resources. In our previous work in [11], we proposed a cross-layer packet scheduling algorithm in order to maximize video qualities. However, the wireless resource allocation is not considered.

In this paper, an optimal resource allocation scheme for pre-coded multi-user video transmission over OFDMA networks is presented. By optimal joint subcarrier assignment and power allocation, the proposed scheme can maximally satisfy the requirements of the packet scheduling from the higher layer. The goal of the scheme is to maximize the video quality over all video users.

The rest of the paper is organized as follows. In Section 2, we outline the presented system architecture and formulate the problem. Section 3 proposes the optimal resource allocation scheme. Section 4 describes the simulation model and gives the results. Finally, conclusions are drawn in Section 5.

2   System Overview and Problem Formulation

We consider an application scenario where a BS delivers video streams to K MUs located within its cell. The BS receives video streams from a media server via the backbone network, which is of high bandwidth and lossless. The media server stores the pre-coded video sequences. All MUs are assumed to share the same network resources but request different video streams. All connections communicate with the BS using a combination of TDM and OFDMA.

The major issues for the end-to-end video transmission include packet scheduling and wireless resource allocation. The former deals with the problem that which packet of which user should be transmitted in priority. While the latter decides that which subcarrier in which OFDM symbol is employed for packet transmission. There have already existed the optimization methods for packet scheduling and wireless resource allocation, respectively. However, the joint consideration of the two for optimizing the end-to-end video quality is still open.

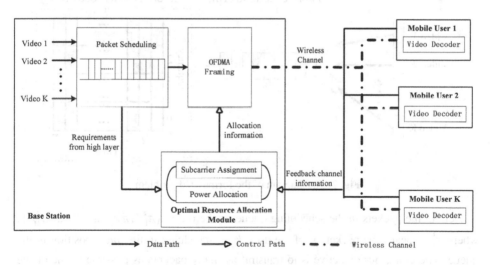

Fig. 1. The cross-layer design model of an OFDMA system

2.1   System Architecture

Fig. 1 depicts the system framework. Once a video stream is requested by a MU, the packets are transmitted over a backbone network to the video queue in the BS. In the queue, the video packets are scheduled by the scheduling schemes in order to guarantee the video qualities and the delay requirements. Meanwhile, the channel state information (CSI) is supposed to be ideally estimated by the MUs and sent to the Optimal Resource Allocation Module through the feedback channel. Note that the subcarriers suffer different channel responses for different users. Therefore, at a specific time, the CSI is a two-dimension matrix, in which the row and the column represent users and subcarriers, respectively. Then, the resource allocation scheme will be employed by jointly assigning the subcarriers and allocating the power. The OFDMA frames are formed as the optimal decision. At the receiver, each MU extracts its own information from the OFDMA frame. Then, the video are decoded and displayed.

2.2   Problem Formulation

To maximize the end-to-end video qualities of all users, we should adopt the effective packet scheduling algorithm and the wireless resource allocation scheme, as shown in Fig. 2. The packet scheduling algorithm deals with the optimized order of packets, considering the video contents, the error concealments algorithm, and the channel conditions. Then, the wireless resource allocation scheme works to satisfy all the users' rate requirements by the scheduling order. In this paper, we focus on the issue of the resource allocation for the scheduled packets, which is in the box in Fig. 2.

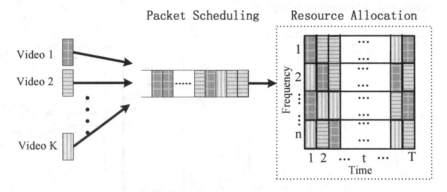

Fig. 2. The diagram of the formulated problem

Denote the packets in the scheduling queue as the order $\{\pi_1^{k,j}, \pi_2^{k,j}, ..., \pi_m^{k,j}, ..., \pi_M^{k,j}\}$, where $\pi_m^{k,j}$ means the packet j of the user k is scheduled in the mth position in the queue. Therefore, our objective is to transmit as many packets as possible in the queue according to the scheduling order. Mathematically, the problem can be formulated by

$$find \ M_a = \max m \tag{1}$$

s.t.

$$\sum_{m=1}^{M_a} R_k(m) \le W \cdot \sum_{n=1}^{N} s_{k,n} \log_2(1 + p_{k,n} \cdot \alpha_{k,n}) \tag{2}$$

$$\sum_{k=1}^{K}\sum_{n=1}^{N} s_{k,n} p_{k,n} \leq P_{total} \tag{3}$$

$$p_{k,n} \geq 0 \tag{4}$$

$$s_{k,n} \in \{0,1\} \tag{5}$$

$$\sum_{k=1}^{K} s_{k,n} = 1 \tag{6}$$

where $R_k(m)$ is the size of the packet in the mth position in the queue of user k. $a_{k,n}$ and W are given as

$$\alpha_{k,n} = h_{k,n}^2 / (N_0 \cdot B / N) \tag{7}$$

$$W = tm \cdot (B / N) \tag{8}$$

Note that constraint (2) guarantees that the resources assigned to the user k should be sufficient to transfer the selected packets to be transmitted. (3) constrains that the consumed total power can not exceed the maximum power limit P_{total}. Constraint (5) denotes $s_{k,n} \in \{0,1\}$ as the binary variable for subcarrier assignment, where $s_{k,n} = 1$ represents subcarrier n is assigned to user k and $s_{k,n} = 0$ otherwise. Next, we will propose the optimal solution of the problem.

3   Optimal Resource Allocation

In this section, the optimal resource allocation scheme is proposed to estimate how many packets can be successfully transmitted given the scheduling decision.

3.1   How Many Packets Can Be Transmitted

Restricted by the scheduling queue order, the wireless resource should be allocated according to the requirements of all users.

The video packets firstly are sorted by the contribution for the video quality in descending order. The packet with higher contribution for the video quality is scheduled in priority. Then, the optimal power distribution is employed to transmit the queued video packets. Compared the optimal power to the available power, the number of the packets which can be transmitted is estimated by adopting the dichotomy.

3.2   Can Be Transmitted for Given Packet Numbers

This subsection will estimate whether the given packets can be successfully transmitted, under the restriction of the wireless resource. For the given packets of all users, we propose an optimal resource allocation scheme for the subcarrier assignment and the power allocation as the following optimization problem:

$$P_{used} = \min_{\{\mathbf{p},\mathbf{s}\}} \sum_{i=1}^{N} \sum_{j=1}^{K} s_{k,n} p_{k,n} \qquad (9)$$

$$s.t. \quad \text{Eq.}(2)(4)(5)(6)$$

Here, P_{used} is the minimum power needed to transmit the given packets. If P_{used} is less than the total power P_{total} which the base station can provide, the given packets can be successfully transmitted. To solve the optimization problem, we obtain the globally optimal solution by employing the Lagrange dual decomposition method.

The Lagrangian of the problem is defined over domain ξ as

$$L(\mathbf{p},\mathbf{s},\boldsymbol{\beta}) = \sum_{n=1}^{N} \sum_{k=1}^{K} s_{n,k} \cdot p_{n,k} - \sum_{k=1}^{K} \beta_k \left(W \cdot \sum_{n=1}^{N} s_{n,k} \cdot \log_2\left(1 + p_{n,k}\alpha_{n,k}\right) - R_k \right) \qquad (10)$$

where the domain ξ is defined as the set of all non-negative $p_{n,k}$ such that for each n, only one $p_{n,k}$ is positive for all users. Then, the Largrange dual function is

$$g(\boldsymbol{\beta}) = \min_{\{p_{k,n}, s_{k,n}\} \in \xi} L(\mathbf{p},\mathbf{s},\boldsymbol{\beta}) \qquad (11)$$

Eq.(10) suggests that the maximization of L can be decomposed into the following N independent optimization problems

$$g'(\boldsymbol{\beta}) = \min_{\{p_{k,n}\} \in \xi} \left\{ \sum_{k=1}^{K} p_{k,n} - W \cdot \sum_{k=1}^{K} \beta_k \log_2\left(1 + p_{k,n}\alpha_{k,n}\right) \right\} \qquad (12)$$

for $n = 1,...,N$. Then, the Lagrange dual function becomes

$$g(\boldsymbol{\beta}) = \sum_{n=1}^{N} g'_n(\boldsymbol{\beta}) + \sum_{k=1}^{K} \beta_k \cdot R_k \qquad (13)$$

With a fixed $\boldsymbol{\beta}$, the object of the minimization in (12) is a concave function of $p_{k,n}$. By taking the derivative of this object regarding $p_{k,n}$, the next optimality condition, which minimize $g'(\boldsymbol{\beta})$, is obtained as

$$p_{k,n}(\boldsymbol{\beta}) = \left(\frac{W \cdot \beta_n}{\ln 2} - \frac{1}{\alpha_{k,n}} \right)^+ \qquad (14)$$

where $(x)^+ = \max(0,x)$. Substituting (14) into (12), we can rewrite (12) as

$$g'_n(\boldsymbol{\beta}) = \sum_{k=1}^{K} \left(\left(\frac{W \cdot \beta_n}{\ln 2} - \frac{1}{\alpha_{k,n}} \right)^+ - W \cdot \beta_k \log_2\left(1 + \left(\frac{W \cdot \beta_n}{\ln 2} - \frac{1}{\alpha_{k,n}} \right)^+ \alpha_{k,n} \right) \right) \qquad (15)$$

By computing all K possible user assignments for subcarrier n, the optimal subcarrier allocation to minimize $g(\boldsymbol{\beta})$ can be obtained as

$$s_{n,k} = \begin{cases} 1, & k = \arg\min_{k} \left(\left(\frac{W \cdot \beta_n}{\ln 2} - \frac{1}{\alpha_{k,n}} \right)^+ - W \cdot \beta_k \log_2 \left(1 + \left(\frac{W \cdot \beta_n}{\ln 2} - \frac{1}{\alpha_{k,n}} \right)^+ \alpha_{k,n} \right) \right) \\ 0, & \text{otherelse} \end{cases} \quad (16)$$

Through the above analysis about optimal power allocation and subcarrier assignment at a given dual point β, the following task of the optimization problem is to iteratively search the optimal value of dual point. This leads to the optimization problem expressed as

$$\max g(\beta), \, s.t. \, \beta \geq 0 \quad (17)$$

The dual problem (17) is a convex optimization problem, even though the primal problem (9) is not convex. Hence, a subgradient method can be used to maximize $g(\beta)$ subject to $\beta \geq 0$. In this paper, we define $\Delta \beta^l = (\Delta \beta_1^l, \Delta \beta_2^l, \cdots, \Delta \beta_K^l)$ as the gradient of the $g(\beta)$ at the dual point β^l, where l indicates the number of the iteration. $\Delta \beta^l$ can be obtained as follows:

$$\Delta \beta^{l-1} = W \cdot \sum_{n=1}^{N} s_{n,k}(\beta^{l-1}) \cdot \log_2 \left(1 + p_{n,k}(\beta^{l-1}) \alpha_{n,k} \right) - R_k \quad (18)$$

In the $l-th$ iteration, $\Delta \beta^l$ is updated by the following formula:

$$\Delta \beta^l = \beta^{l-1} + \varepsilon^l \Delta \beta^{l-1} \quad (19)$$

Here, ε^l is the step size and its update conforms to the rule:

$$\varepsilon^l = \varepsilon^{l-1} / \sqrt{l} \quad (20)$$

Having solved the optimization (17), we now obtain all the information needed to perform the optimal subcarrier assignment and power allocation.

4   Simulation Results

Six video sequences with varied content (Highway, Foreman, Dancer, Container, Mother & Daughter, and News), in CIF (352*288) format are used for the simulations. The video sequences are encoded in H.264 (JVT reference software, JM 10.2) with a frame rate of 25fps. All frames except the first one are encoded as P frames. To increase the error resilience, 15 random I MBs are inserted into each frame, and constrained intra prediction is used at the encoder. A slice consists of a row of MBs, enabling a good balance between error robustness and compression efficiency. Each video has 1800 frames, in which each sequence is repeated for 6 times. Each video sequence is encoded with a bit rate of 500 kbit/s.

We have six users demanding for six different video sequences and 512 subcarriers to be assigned. The time length of an OFDMA symbol is 4 ms. The total power constraint is 1W, and the total bandwidth is 1 MHz. The wireless channel used in the simulator is modeled as a frequency-selective channel consisting of six independent Rayleigh multipaths. The component of each path is calculated by the Clarke's flat fading model. The relative power values of the six multipath components are [0,-8. 69,-17.37,-26.06,-34.74,-43.43] dB. The power spectral density of AWGN is -70dB.

The simulations are used to verify the performance of the proposed scheme. We compare four methods as follows.

(1) DSA (dynamic subcarrier allocation scheme): the scheme proposed in [2]. The DSA allocates the subcarriers to the user with best channel response in order to optimally maximize the throughput.

(2) SA (stepwise allocation scheme): the scheme for packet scheduling and subcarrier assignment, which is a revised version of the one proposed in [10]. The packet scheduling is first done based on a content-aware utility function, and the subcarriers proceed to be allocated for the selected packet.

(3) SAEP (Stepwise-allocation with equal power scheme): It is similar to SA, except the equal power allocation on each subcarrier.

(4) PROPOSED: the scheme proposed in Section 3. We adopt the packet scheduling scheme proposed in [10] in order to compare with the SA algorithm to express the superiority of the resource allocation algorithm of proposed scheme.

Fig. 3 shows the average PSNR of the received six video streams after transmission over OFDMA networks using the four different schemes. The total available transmit power is 1.1W. It can be seen that the average PSNR of the proposed scheme is 34.5913 dB, whereas those of DSA, SA and SAEP schemes are 28.7623 dB, 31.8023 dB and 29.1850 dB, respectively. The SA scheme separates the packet scheduling from the subcarrier allocation, and thus can not jointly optimize the two aspects. Therefore, the received PSNR of the video users degrades. The DSA scheme only pursues the throughput of the wireless networks, and allocates most wireless resource to the user with better channel condition. However, the higher throughput of the wireless networks does not always mean the higher received video quality. Fig. 4 shows the service rates of the four schemes. We can see the proposed scheme does not achieve the highest service rate despite of its achievability of the highest PSNR. Fig. 5 illustrates the average quality at each frame averaged over all the users for different four schemes. We also see that the performance of the proposed scheme is better than that of the other three counterparts.

Then, the performances of the schemes with various transmit power are simulated. As shown in Fig. 6, we can see that the average PSNR of the proposed scheme is also higher than other alternatives in each condition, although the performances have been improved by every scheme.

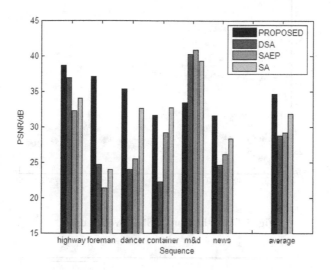

Fig. 3. Average PSNR for each video sequence

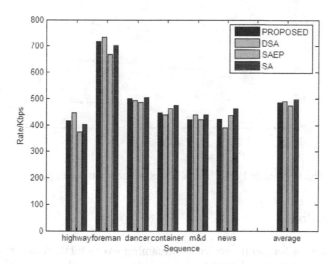

Fig. 4. Transmission rate for each frame

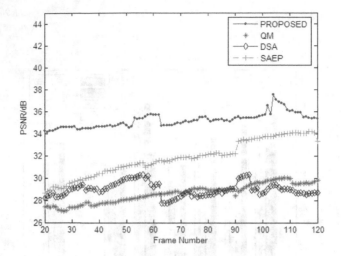

Fig. 5. Frame-by-frame PSNR over all users

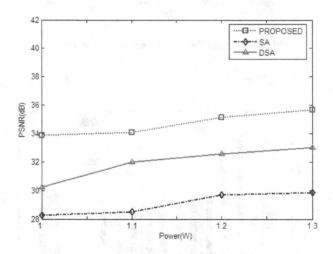

Fig. 6. Average PSNR over all users in various transmit power

5   Conclusion

A cross-layer design for multi-user video streaming over OFDMA downlink systems is present in this paper. Based on the joint optimization of subcarrier assignment and power allocation, the received video quality of all the users is maximized. Employing the Lagrange dual decomposition method, we can obtain the global optimal solution to the optimization problem. Simulation results show that our proposed algorithm outperforms 2.8-5.8 dB to the existing alternatives.

Acknowledgments. This work was supported in part by National Science and Technology Major Project 2010ZX03005-003, National Natural Science Foundation of China 61001095, and National Hi-Tech Research and Development Plan of China under Grant 2009AA01180.

References

1. Biagioni, A., Fantacci, R., Marabissi, D., Tarchi, D.: Adaptive subcarrier allocation schemes for wireless ofdma systems in wimax networks. IEEE Journal on Selected Areas in Communications 27(2), 217–225 (2009)
2. Song, G., Li, Y.: Cross-layer optimization for OFDM wireless networkspart II: algorithm development. IEEE Trans. Commun. 4(2), 625–634 (2005)
3. Zhang, R., Regunathan, S.L., Rose, K.: Video encoding with optimal Inter/Intra-mode switching for packet loss resilience. IEEE J. Select. Areas Commun. 18, 966–976 (2000)
4. He, Z., Cai, J., Chen, C.W.: Joint source channel rate-distortion analysis for adaptive mode selection and rate control in wireless video coding. IEEE Trans. Circuits Sys. Video Technol. 12(6), 511–523 (2002)
5. Chan, C., Bambos, N., Wee, S., Apostolopoulos, J.: Scheduling algorithms for broadcasting media with multiple distortion measures. IEEE Transactions on Wireless Communications 8(8), 4188–4199 (2009)
6. Xu, J., Shen, X., Mark, J.W., Cai, J.: Quasi-optimal channel assignment for real-time video in OFDM wireless systems. IEEE Trans. Wireless Communications 7(4), 1417–1427 (2008)
7. Bokhari, F.A., Yanikomeroglu, H., Wong, W.K., Rahman, M.: Cross-Layer Resource Scheduling for Video Traffic in the Downlink of OFDMA-Based Wireless 4G Networks. EURASIP Journal on Wireless Communications and Networking, 2009, Article ID 212783, 10 pages (2009)
8. Khan, S., Brehmer, J., Kellerer, W., Utschick, W., Steinbach, E.: Application-driven Cross-layer Optimization for Coded OFDMA Systems. In: 9th WPMC 2006, San Diego, USA (September 2006)
9. Shen, C., van der Schaar, M.: Optimal resource allocation for multimedia applications over multiaccess fading channels. IEEE Transactions on Wireless Communications 7(9) (September 2008)
10. Pahalawatta, P., Berry, R., Pappas, T., Katsaggelos, A.: Content-aware resource allocation and packet scheduling for video transmission over wireless networks. IEEE Journal on Selected Areas in Communications 25(4), 749–759 (2007)
11. Li, F., Liu, G., He, L.: Cross-layer Scheduling for Multiuser H.264 Video Transmission over Wireless Networks. IET Communications 4(8), 1012–1025 (2010)

Throughput and Sensing Bandwidth Tradeoff in Cognitive Radio Networks

Wenshan Yin, Pinyi Ren, and Shuangcheng Yan

School of Electronics and Information Engineering
Xi'an Jiaotong University, Xi'an, China 710049
{yws.xjt,yansc}@stu.xjtu.edu.cn, pyren@mail.xjtu.edu.cn

Abstract. Within the sequential sensing and transmission paradigm (SSTP), spectrum sensing over the whole primary user (PU) band always suspends secondary user (SU) data transmission in the sensing interval. Delay incurred by this kind of suspension may be intolerable to delay sensitive SU services. To alleviate this problem, we adopt a parallel sensing and transmission paradigm (PSTP), within which the SU transmits and senses simultaneously. In this paper, we investigate the relationship between the achievable SU throughput and bandwidth allocated for spectrum sensing within the PSTP, under the constraint that the PU is sufficiently protected. We also study the delay improvements of the PSTP over that of the SSTP. Both theoretical analyses and simulation results that there exists an optimal sensing bandwidth that maximizes the achievable SU throughput within the PSTP. Furthermore, compared to the SSTP, the SU delay is reduced by using the PSTP.

Keywords: Delay, throughput, bandwidth, spectrum sensing.

1 Introduction

The rapid developments of wireless systems and services place high pressure on the limited radio spectrum resources. However, field measurements show that most of the licensed primary user (PU) spectrum resources are underutilized [1]. Cognitive radio (CR) has been proposed to alleviate the problem of spectrum scarcity by improving the spectrum utilization [2].

It is required that the unlicensed secondary user (SU) should not cause harmful interference to the licensed PU, which makes the spectrum sensing function one of the key technologies in the implementation of CR [3]. To provide sufficient protection to the PU, it is required that the probability of detection be no smaller than a prescribed value within the sensing interval [4]. Under this constraint, when the SU receives weak PU signal, the probability of false alarm may be high, which always lead to low spectrum utilization. Further more, shadowing and fading generally degrades the performance of spectrum sensing [5].

Abundant works on spectrum sensing are carried out within the sequential sensing and transmission paradigm (SSTP) over the whole PU band. Authors in

P. Ren et al. (Eds.): WICON 2011, LNICST 98, pp. 12–22, 2012.

[6] derived the optimal spectrum sensing time that maximizes the achievable SU throughput. To improve achievable SU throughput [7], the SU transmits when the channel states between SU transceivers are good, and sense the PU activity otherwise. To improve spectrum utilization [8], the SU adaptively chooses the sensing action based on historical information. The maximum channel throughput both of the PU and SU systems are derived in [9]. A new spectrum sharing scheme based on spectrum sensing is proposed in [10]. The SU transmits with a high rate when the PU is detected to be present, and transmits with a low rate otherwise. Lots of works on spectrum sensing are also based on the parallel sensing and transmission paradigm (PSTP), within which the PU band is divided into two parts for spectrum sensing and SU transmission, respectively. In [11], the authors reduce the average detection time by fixed relay and variable relays schemes. In [12], a cooperation strategy is introduced to exchange sensing information between SUs and reduce the detection delay.

It is well known within the SSTP over the whole PU spectrum band, the SU must suspend its data transmission in the sensing interval. Although the achievable SU throughput can be maximized under the PU protection constraint [6], the SU generally experiences long data transmission delay. For some time delay sensitive services, transmission delay caused by interruption generally degrades the quality of service (QoS) to the SU. Furthermore, the time interval allocated for spectrum sensing within each frame is quite limited. When the received PU signal strength at the SU receiver is low, the spectrum sensing results are quite unreliable, which results in low achievable SU throughput. Within the PSTP [11] [12], the SU can sense the PU activity and transmit its data simultaneously. Therefore, the SU data transmission delay can be reduced. However, under the PU protection constraint, with a fixed bandwidth allocated for spectrum sensing within a fixed frame, the average achievable throughput of the SU can be low in different wireless environments.

In this paper, we investigate the relationship between the achievable SU throughput and the bandwidth allocated for spectrum sensing within the PSTP. It is shown that the achievable SU throughput is a concave function of the bandwidth allocated for spectrum sensing. Provided that certain protection to PU is guaranteed, the optimal sensing bandwidth that maximizes the SU throughput is derived. We also investigate the SU transmission delay. Compared with the transmission delay within the SSTP, the SU delay is reduced significantly within the PSTP without any loss in the achievable SU throughput. Both simulation and theoretical results show that there is an optimal bandwidth for spectrum sensing that maximizes the SU throughput. Furthermore, the PSTP shows obvious advantage in the SU transmission delay.

This paper is organized as follows. Section 2 presents the system model. In Section 3, the tradeoff between throughput and sensing bandwidth is formulated and analyzed. And in Section 4, simulation results are presented. Finally, brief conclusions are drawn in Section 5.

2 System Model

We consider a CR network within which each SU operates based on the PSTP, which is shown in Fig. 1. The licensed PU band is divided into two parts, over which spectrum sensing and data transmission are carried out simultaneously. The band of width W_s is allocated for exclusive spectrum sensing. In this part of PU band, SU data transmission is forbidden to avoid co-channel interference. The SU transmits frame-by-frame over its data transmission band of width $W - W_s$. The frame duration of the SU signal is T.

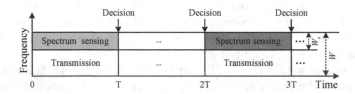

Fig. 1. The parallel sensing and transmission paradigm

Assume without loss of generality that both the PU and SU transmits based on the orthogonal frequency division multiplexing (OFDM) signaling. The sub-carrier distance of the SU signal over its transmission band of width $W - W_s$ is the same as that of the PU signal. Under such an assumption, when the SU simultaneously senses the PU activity and transmits its own data, the out-of-band emission could be neglected, since the transmission process is orthogonal with the sensing process in the frequency domain. The power of the SU signal σ_s^2 is evenly distributed over its transmission bandwidth, with PSD N_s. Then, we have $\sigma_s^2 = N_s (W - W_s)$.

Let H_0 and H_1 be the hypotheses that the PU transmission is inactive and active, respectively. Then, the problem of sensing can be formulated as

$$x[i] = \begin{cases} n[i], & H_0 \\ n[i] + h_p s[i], & H_1 \end{cases} \tag{1}$$

where $i = 1, 2, \cdots, L$, $L = 2TW_s$; $n[i]$ is the zero mean complex additive white Gaussian noise (AWGN) with probability distribution $n[i] \sim CN(0, \sigma_n^2)$, $\sigma_n^2 = N_0 W$, and N_0 is the power spectrum density (PSD) of the AWGN; h_p is the channel gain between the PU transmitter and SU receiver; and $s[i]$ is the PU signal, which is assumed to be a zero mean complex Gaussian process with power σ_p^2 and probability distribution $s[i] \sim CN(0, \sigma_p^2)$ [13]. The power of the PU signal is evenly distributed over its transmission band of width W, with PSD N_p. Therefore, $N_p W = \sigma_p^2$.

The result of spectrum sensing is a binary decision on the presence or absence of the PU signal. To protect the PU from harmful interference, the SU is allowed to transmit only when the PU signal is detected to be absent. When the sensing result indicates that the PU transmission is present, the SU must terminate its transmission until it detects a new spectrum opportunity. Although the SU may stop or restart its transmission when the sensing result claims the presence or absence of the PU signal in the current frame, the spectrum sensing process carries on continuously in the next frame.

3   Throughput and Sensing Bandwidth Tradeoff

As can be seen from Fig. 1, with larger bandwidth allocated for spectrum sensing, the SU can obtain more information on the PU signal and thus better sensing performance. However, the larger the bandwidth allocated for spectrum sensing, the smaller the bandwidth available for SU transmission, which may lead to low achievable SU throughput. Therefore, there exists a tradeoff between the achievable SU throughput and bandwidth allocated for spectrum sensing.

3.1   Secondary User Spectrum Sensing

For discussion purpose, spectrum sensing is performed by the energy detector [14]. The test statistic of the energy detector can be presented as $\Lambda = \frac{1}{\sigma_n^2} \sum_{i=1}^{2TW_s} |x[i]|^2$. According to the central limit theory (CLT), when the product $2TW_s$ is large enough, Λ can be approximated as Gaussian distributed. Under the hypothesis of H_0, $\Lambda|_{H_0} \sim CN(2TW_s, 2TW_s)$. Under the hypothesis of H_1, $\Lambda|_{H_1} \sim CN\left(2TW_s(1+\gamma), 2TW_s(1+\gamma)^2\right)$, where γ is the signal to noise ratio (SNR) of the PU signal received at the SU receiver, which is defined as $\gamma = |h_p|^2 \frac{N_p W_s}{N_0 W_s} = \frac{|h_p|^2 \sigma_p^2}{\sigma_n^2}$.

The probability of detection $P_d(W_s) = \Pr(\Lambda \geq \lambda|H_1)$ and probability of false alarm $P_f(W_s) = \Pr(\Lambda \geq \lambda|H_0)$ are [15]

$$P_f(W_s) = Q\left(\frac{\lambda}{\sqrt{2TW_s}} - \sqrt{2TW_s}\right) \tag{2}$$

$$P_d(W_s) = Q\left(\frac{\lambda}{(1+\gamma)\sqrt{2TW_s}} - \sqrt{2TW_s}\right) \tag{3}$$

where $Q(x) = \frac{1}{\sqrt{2\pi}} \int_x^\infty e^{-t^2/2} dt$, and λ is the sensing threshold.

3.2   Secondary User Data Transmission

In the spectrum sensing process, when $\Lambda \geq \lambda$, the PU is detected to be present; otherwise, the PU is detected to be absent. Once a SU decides that the PU is absent, it tries to access the PU band. Therefore, the SU transmits its data in two cases: the PU transmission is absent, and the SU detected its absence correctly; the PU transmission is present, but the SU missed to detect its presence.

In the first case, only the SU transmits its data over the band of width $W - W_s$. The achievable throughput is

$$C_1(W_s) = (W - W_s)\ln(1 + \Omega_1(W_s)) \tag{4}$$

where $\Omega_1(W_s) = \frac{|h_s|^2 N_s(W-W_s)}{N_0(W-W_s)}$ is the SNR of the SU and h_s is the channel gain between SU transceivers. Since the SU SNR can be represented as $\rho = \frac{|h_s|^2 N_s(W-W_s)}{N_0(W-W_s)}$, $\Omega_1(W_s)$ can be simplified as $\Omega_1(W_s) = \rho$.

In the second case, both the PU and the SU transmit their data. The PU signal is treated as interference at the SU receiver. Therefore, the achievable SU throughput becomes

$$C_2(W_s) = (W - W_s)\ln(1 + \Omega_2(W_s)) \tag{5}$$

where $\Omega_2(W_s) = \frac{|h_s|^2 N_s(W-W_s)}{(N_P|h_p|^2 + N_0)(W-W_s)}$ is the signal to noise-plus-interference ratio (SINR) of the SU. Since $\frac{N_P|h_p|^2(W-W_s)}{N_0(W-W_s)} = \frac{|h_p|^2 N_P W}{N_0 W}$ and $\gamma = |h_p|^2 \frac{N_P W}{N_0 W}$, we have $\Omega_2(W_s) = \frac{\Omega_1(W_s)}{\gamma+1}$. While according to the definition of ρ, $\Omega_2(W_s)$ can be further simplified as $\Omega_2(W_s) = \frac{\rho}{\gamma+1}$.

Let $P(H_0)$ and $P(H_1)$ be the probabilities that the PU is absent and present, respectively. Then, $P(H_0) + P(H_1) = 1$. Consequently, the probabilities of the first case and second case can be respectively presented as $P(H_0)(1 - P_f(W_s))$ and $P(H_1)(1 - P_d(W_s))$. By taking (4) and (5) into account, the total achievable SU throughput can be derived as

$$C(W_s) = P(H_0)(1 - P_f)C_1 + P(H_1)(1 - P_d)C_2 \tag{6}$$

where $P_f = P_f(W_s)$, $C_1 = C_1(W_s)$, $P_d = P_d(W_s)$, and $C_2 = C_2(W_s)$ for presentational simplicity.

3.3   Tradeoff between Throughput and Sensing Bandwidth

For discussion purpose, let $U_1 = P(H_0)\ln(1 + \rho)$ and $U_2 = P(H_1)\ln\left(1 + \frac{\rho}{1+\gamma}\right)$. Then, $C(W_s)$ in (6) can be represented as

$$C(W_s) = \varphi_1(W_s)U_1 + \varphi_2(W_s)U_2 \tag{7}$$

where $\varphi_1(W_s) = (W - W_s)(1 - P_f(W_s))$ and $\varphi_2(W_s) = (W - W_s)(1 - P_d(W_s))$. When the SU transmitter is far away from the SU receiver and close to the PU transmitter, which means that the PU signal strength is much larger than the SU signal strength at the SU receiver, the contribution of the second term on the right hand side of (7) is minimal. However, when the case is opposite, the contribution of the second term becomes dominant.

From the point view of the SU, it is desirable to maximize $C(W_s)$ by choosing the proper sensing bandwidth W_s, i.e.,

$$\max_{0 < W_s < W} C(W_s) = \varphi_1(W_s)U_1 + \varphi_2(W_s)U_2 \tag{8}$$

It can be readily shown that the less the bandwidth allocated for spectrum sensing, the higher the achievable SU throughput.

While from the point view of the PU, it is required that the PU be sufficiently protected. To protect the PU, the $P_d(W_s)$ should not be lower than a prescribed value P_d^{th}, i.e., $P_d(W_s) \geq P_d^{th}$ [4]. The larger the $P_d(W_s)$, the better the PU is protected. As can be seen from (3), the larger the sensing bandwidth W_s, the larger the $P_d(W_s)$. However, larger bandwidth allocated for spectrum sensing will result in lower bandwidth available for SU transmission. Furthermore, as can be seen from (2), the $P_f(W_s)$ also increases with increase of W_s. The larger the $P_f(W_s)$, the lower the spectrum utilization. Therefore, it is only necessary to satisfy the basic requirement on protection, i.e., $P_d(W_s) = P_d^{th}$. Consequently, the optimization problem in (8) can be reformulated as

$$\max_{0 < W_s < W} \quad C(W_s) = \varphi_1(W_s) U_1 + \varphi_2(W_s) U_2$$
$$s.t. \quad P_d(W_s) = P_d^{th} \tag{9}$$

According to (2) and (3), for a given $P_d(W_s)$, the $P_f(W_s)$ in (2) can be presented as

$$P_f(W_s) = Q\left((1+\gamma) Q^{-1}(P_d(W_s)) + \sqrt{2TW_s}\gamma\right) \tag{10}$$

Therefore, by employing (10), the optimization problem in (9) is equivalent to

$$\max_{0 < W_s < W} \quad \hat{C}(W_s) = (W - W_s) f_1(W_s)$$
$$s.t. \quad P_f(W_s) = Q(f_2(W_s)) \tag{11}$$

where $f_1(W_s) = (1 - P_f(W_s)) U_1 + (1 - P_d^{th}) U_2$, and $f_2(W_s) = (1+\gamma) Q^{-1}(P_d^{th}) + \sqrt{2TW_s}\gamma$.

It can be derived that the first partial derivative of $\hat{C}(W_s)$ with respect to W_s is

$$\frac{\partial \hat{C}(W_s)}{\partial W_s} = -f_1(W_s) + (W - W_s)\frac{\partial f_1(W_s)}{\partial W_s} \tag{12}$$

where $\frac{\partial f_1(W_s)}{\partial W_s} = \frac{\gamma U_1}{2}\sqrt{\frac{T}{\pi W_s}}\exp\left\{-\frac{[f_2(W_s)]^2}{2}\right\}$. It can also be derived that the second partial derivative of $\hat{C}(W_s)$ with respect to W_s is

$$\frac{\partial^2 \hat{C}(W_s)}{\partial W_s^2} = -2\frac{\partial f_1(W_s)}{\partial W_s} + (W - W_s)\frac{\partial^2 f_1(W_s)}{\partial W_s^2} \tag{13}$$

where the derivative $\frac{\partial^2 f_1(W_s)}{\partial W_s^2} = -f_3(W_s)\exp\left\{-\frac{[f_2(W_s)]^2}{2}\right\}$ and $f_3(W_s) = \frac{\gamma U_1}{4 W_s}\sqrt{\frac{T}{\pi W_s}}[1 + \sqrt{2TW_s}\gamma f_2(W_s)]$.

It can be seen from the first and second partial derivative of $f_1(W_s)$ that $\partial f_1(W_s)/\partial W_s > 0$, and $\partial^2 f_1(W_s)/\partial W_s^2 < 0$, respectively. Since $W - W_s > 0$, we have

$$\frac{\partial^2 \hat{C}(W_s)}{\partial W_s^2} < 0 \quad for \quad 0 < W_s < W \tag{14}$$

which means that $\hat{C}(W_s)$ is a concave function of the sensing band width W_s over the range $0 < W_s < W$. Therefore, there exists an unique optimal sensing bandwidth $W_s^{opt} \in (0, W)$ that maximizes the SU throughput.

Since $\hat{C}(W_s)$ is a concave function of W_s, we can get the optimal sensing bandwidth W_s^{opt} by setting the first derivative of $\hat{C}(W_s)$ to zero, i.e., $\partial \hat{C}(W_s)/\partial W_s = 0$, or equivalently

$$f_1(W_s) - (W - W_s)\frac{\partial f_1(W_s)}{\partial W_s} = 0 \qquad (15)$$

There is no closed form solution to (15). However, it can be seen from the convexity of $\hat{C}(W_s)$ that $\partial \hat{C}(W_s)/\partial W_s$ is a monotonic function of W_s. Therefore, equation (15) could be solved by the well known bisection search method.

3.4   Secondary User Transmission Delay

Within the PSTP, the SU suspends its transmission in two cases: the PU is present, and the SU correctly detects its presence; the PU is absent, but the SU falsely detects its presence. The average SU transmission delay in the former and later case is $D_1(W_s) = TP_d(W_s)$ and $D_2(W_s) = TP_f(W_s)$, respectively. Since the probability of the first case is $P(H_1)$, and the probability of the second case is $P(H_0)$, the total transmission delay introduced by the PSTP is

$$D(W_s) = P(H_1)D_1(W_s) + P(H_0)D_2(W_s) \qquad (16)$$

Under the PU protection constraint in (9), the transmission delay $D_1(W_s)$ is inevitable, since SU transmission in this case could cause harmful interference to the licensed PU. The transmission delay $D_2(W_s)$ degrades spectrum utilization, which is unnecessary but inevitable, and should be minimized. The total transmission delay $D(W_s)$ is mainly dominated by the first term on the right hand side of (16), although $P(H_0)$ is generally larger than $P(H_1)$.

Under the protection constraint that $P_d(W_s) = P_d^{th}$, the transmission delay $D(W_s)$ in (16) can be transformed to

$$D(W_s) = T\left[P(H_1)P_d^{th} + P(H_0)Q[f_2(W_s)]\right] \qquad (17)$$

It can be seen from (17) that for a given protection constraint P_d^{th} to the PU, the larger the sensing bandwidth W_s, the lower the transmission delay $D(W_s)$. However, the larger the sensing bandwidth, the smaller the bandwidth available for SU data transmission, and thus the lower the achievable SU throughput.

For comparison, the transmission delay within the SSTP [6] under the PU protection constraint can be presented as

$$D(\tau, W) = \tau + \left(P(H_0)P_f(\tau, W) + P(H_1)P_d^{th}\right)(T - \tau) \qquad (18)$$

where $P_f(\tau, W) = Q\left((1 + \gamma)Q^{-1}\left(P_d^{th}\right) + \sqrt{2\tau W}\gamma\right)$ is the probability of false alarm within the SSTP. It has to be pointed out that within the SSTP, data transmission is interrupted with probability one in each sensing interval τ, and the sensing bandwidth is W rather than W_s.

The probability of detection within the SSTP can be presented as $P_d(\tau, W) = Q\left(\frac{\lambda}{(1+\gamma)\sqrt{2\tau W}} - \sqrt{2\tau W}\right)$. It can be shown that when $W_s T = W\tau$, we have $P_f(\tau, W) = P_f(W_s)$ and $P_d(\tau, W) = P_d(W_s)$. Define the relative delay as $\Delta D(\tau, W_s) = D(\tau, W) - D(W_s)$. Then,

$$\Delta D(\tau, W_s) = \tau \left(1 - P(H_0) P_f(W_s) - P(H_1) P_d^{th}\right) \tag{19}$$

For the convenience of discussion, define $p_{00} = 1 - P_f(W_s)$, $p_{01} = P_f(W_s)$, $p_{11} = P_d^{th}$, and $p_{10} = 1 - P_d^{th}$. Then, equation (19) can be transformed into

$$\Delta D(\tau, W_s) = \tau \left(1 - P(H_0) p_{01} - P(H_1) p_{11}\right) \tag{20}$$

Since $\Delta D(\tau, W_s)/\tau = P(H_0) p_{00} + P(H_1) p_{10} > 0$, we have

$$\Delta D(\tau, W_s) > 0 \tag{21}$$

Therefore, if the optimal spectrum sensing time τ^{opt} within the SSTP and the optimal spectrum sensing bandwidth within the PSTP satisfy the condition that $\frac{W_s^{opt}}{W} = \frac{\tau^{opt}}{T}$, we have $P_f(\tau^{opt}, W) = P_f(W_s^{opt})$, $P_d(\tau^{opt}, W) = P_d(W_s^{opt})$, and $\Delta D(\tau^{opt}, W_s^{opt}) > 0$. Thus, the SU transmission delay within the SSTP is reduced compared to that within the PSTP.

4   Simulation Results

In the simulation, we assume that the PU system transmits based on the DVB-T signaling [16]. The bandwidth of the PU is $W = 6MHz$. The number of subcarriers of the the PU signal is 2048. The sampling rate over the spectrum sensing band is the same as the bandwidth allocated for spectrum sensing. The frame duration of the SU is $T = 100ms$. The subcarrier distance of the SU signal is the same as that of the PU signal. The SU SNR ρ is set to be $20dB$. The probability that the PU occupies its licensed channel is 0.3, which means that $P(H_1) = 0.3$, and $P(H_0) = 1 - P(H_1) = 0.7$. The basic protection level to the licensed PU is $P_d^{th} = 0.9$ [4]. Each simulation result is averaged over 5000 realizations.

Figure 2 shows the probability of false alarm $P_f(W_s)$ versus the sensing bandwidth W_s for a given probability of detection $P_d(W_s) = 0.9$. The theoretical probability of false alarm is derived according to (10). It can be seen that simulation results comply with theoretical results very well. It can also be observed that the probability of false alarm decreases monotonically with the increase of PU SNR γ since the SU obtains stronger PU signal. Moreover, the probability of false alarm decreases with the increase of sensing bandwidth W_s. This is mainly because that with the increase of W_s, the SU obtains more information on the PU signal.

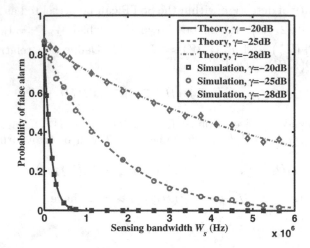

Fig. 2. Probability of false alarm $P_f(W_s)$ within the PSTP

Figure 3 shows the normalized throughput of the SU versus the sensing bandwidth W_s. The normalized throughput of the SU is defined as $C(W_s)/W$. The theoretical normalized SU throughput is derived according to (7). It can be seen that theoretical results are verified by simulation. On the one hand, the optimal sensing bandwidth that achieves the maximum throughput increases with the decrease of PU SNR. On the other hand, the larger the PU SNR γ, the higher the achievable SU throughput. By comparing Fig. 3 with Fig. 2, it can also be seen that lower probability of false alarm does not necessarily results in higher SU throughput. Since simulation results comply with theoretical results, we will only show theoretical results hereafter for simplicity.

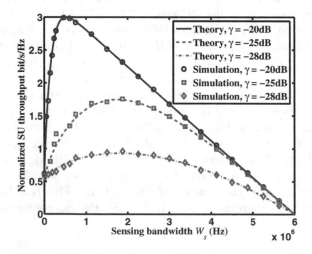

Fig. 3. Normalized SU throughput within the PSTP

Figure 4 compares the average SU transmission delay $D(\tau, W)$ when the optimal spectrum sensing time τ^{opt} is given with $D(W_s)$ when the optimal spectrum sensing bandwidth W_s^{opt} is given. Three conclusions can be drawn from the figure. First, the transmission delay $D(W_s^{opt})$ is generally lower than $D(\tau^{opt}, W)$. Second, the relative delay $\Delta D(\tau^{opt}, W_s^{opt})$ is a concave function of γ. This is mainly because that, when γ is large, the PU can be detected quickly; otherwise, the SU can be considered outside the coverage of the PU and no spectrum sensing function is needed. Third, $\Delta D(\tau^{opt}, W_s^{opt})$ increases with the increase of frame length T. However, the frame length T is dependent on practical consideration.

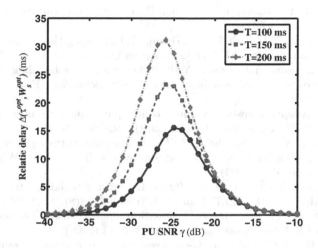

Fig. 4. Relative transmission delay

5   Conclusions

In this paper, we investigated the tradeoff between sensing bandwidth and achievable SU throughput in cognitive radio networks. The investigation is based on a PSTP, within which the licensed PU band is divided into two parts, one part allocated for spectrum sensing and the other part for transmission. We obtained the optimal bandwidth for sensing the PU signal that maximizes the achievable SU throughput, under the constraint that certain protection to the PU is guaranteed. We also showed that compared to the SSTP, the PSTP have advantage in average transmission delay. Simulation results confirmed our analyses.

Acknowledgments. The research reported in this paper (Corresponding Author Pinyi Ren) is supported by the National Hi-Tech Research and Development Plan of China under the Grant 2009AA011801, the National Natural Science Foundation of China under the Grant 60832007, it is also supported by the National Science and Technology Major Project of China under the Grant 2010ZX03005-003.

References

1. FCC, Spectrum policy task force report (November 2002),
   http://www.fcc.gov/sptf/files/SEWGFinalReport-1.pdf
2. FCC, Notice of proposed rule making FCC 04-113: Unlicensed operation in the TV broadcast bands (ET Docket No.04-186) (May 2004),
   http://www.naic.edu/~phil/rfi/fccactions/FCC-04-113A1.pdf
3. Yücek, T., Arslan, H.: A survey of spectrum sensing algorithms for cognitive radio applications. IEEE Commun. Surveys Tuts. 11(1), 116–130 (2009)
4. Zeng, Y.H., Liang, Y.C., Lei, Z., Oh, S.W., Chin, F., Sun, S.: Worldwide regulatory and standardization activities on cognitive radio. In: DySPAN, Singapore, pp. 1–9 (April 2010)
5. Ma, J., Li, G.Y., Juang, B.H.: Signal Processing in Cognitive Radio. IEEE Proc. 97(5), 805–823 (2009)
6. Liang, Y.C., Zeng, Y.H., Peh, E.C.Y., Hoang, A.T.: Sensing-throughput tradeoff for cognitive radio networks. IEEE Trans. Wireless Commun. 7(4), 1326–1337 (2008)
7. Hoang, A.T., Liang, Y.C., Zeng, Y.H.: Adaptive joint scheduling of spectrum sensing and data transmission in cognitive radio networks. IEEE Trans. Commun. 58(1), 235–246 (2010)
8. Choi, K.W.: Adaptive sensing technique to maximize spectrum utilization in cognitive radio. IEEE Trans. Veh. Technol. 59(2), 992–998 (2010)
9. Shen, J., Jiang, T., Liu, S., Zhong, Z.: Maximum channel throughput via cooperative spectrum sensing in cognitive radio networks. IEEE Trans. Wireless Commun. 8(10), 5166–5175 (2009)
10. Kang, X., Liang, Y.C., Garg, H.K., Zhang, L.: Sensing based spectrum sharing in cognitive radio networks. IEEE Trans. Veh. Technol. 58(8), 4649–4654 (2009)
11. Ganesan, G., Li, Y., Bing, B., Li, S.: Spatiotemporal sensing in cognitive radio networks. IEEE J. Sel. Areas Commun. 26(1), 5–12 (2008)
12. Li, H., Dai, H., Li, C.: Collaborative quickest spectrum sensing via random broadcast in cognitive radio systems. IEEE Trans. Wireless Commun. 9(7), 2338–2348 (2010)
13. Yin, W., Ren, P.: A suboptimal spectrum sensing scheme for OFDM signal in cognitive radios. In: Globecom, Miami, pp. 1–6 (December 2010)
14. Urkowitz, H.: Energy detection of unknown deterministic signals. IEEE Proc. 55(4), 523–531 (1967)
15. Proakis, J.G.: Digital Communication, 4th edn., translated by Junli Zhang etc. Publishing House of Electronic Industry (2006)
16. ETSI EN 300 744 V1.6.1, Digital Video Broadcasting (DVB): Framing structure, channel coding and modulation for digital terrestrial television,
    http://www.dvb.org/technology/standards/index.xml

A Common Symbol Timing Offset Synchronization (post FFT) Method for OFDM System

Di Na[*], Ji longli, Yang Ming, and Gao Peng

Radio Institute Academy of Broadcasting Science State
Administration of Radio, Film & Television, Beijing, China

Abstract. As we know, synchronization issues are of great importance in OFDM receiver especially symbol timing offset synchronization. Synchronization errors not only cause inter-symbol interference (ISI) but also introduce inter-carrier interference (ICI) duo to the loss of orthogonally among all sub-carriers. In this paper, we proposed an improved method which can not only get better estimation performance but also decrease computation complexity that never needs any analogy timing loops for better ASIC area cost and power consumption.

Keywords: OFDM, synchronization, symbol timing offset.

1 Introduction

OFDM technique has been used in many audio and video broadcasting systems, because of high-quality video audio services and reliable stability transmission demand. Unfortunately, the OFDM systems are much more sensitive to carrier frequency offset (CFO) and symbol timing offset (STO).Therefore many synchronization algorithms have been proposed to solve these problems, but it has been shown that the performance may be great deteriorated due to synchronization errors [1]. In this paper, we mainly discuss the STO issues, which consist of fine symbol offset and sampling clock offset synchronization method. First, we will discuss a conventional synchronization algorithm [3] based on analogy timing loop. Second, we will introduce an improved method which use scatter pilots to estimate timing and clock offset errors post FFT (Fast Fourier Transform), and use NCO (Numerical Control Oscillator) to realize tracking loop. Simulation results show the improved method has the much better performance as the conventional method in multi-path channels. This method is also more flexible in receiver, because it supports multiply baseband symbol rate by using a fixed sampling frequency DAC (Digital to Analogy Convert).

2 Common Synchronization Procedure

In most OFDM systems, synchronization procedure includes: transmission mode detection, symbol timing synchronization pre FFT, carrier frequency synchronization, symbol timing synchronization post FFT.

---

[*] Corresponding author.

P. Ren et al. (Eds.): WICON 2011, LNICST 98, pp. 23–32, 2012.

Symbol timing synchronization post FFT consists of fine symbol timing offset and sampling clock offset synchronization. Fine symbol timing offset synchronization can estimate residual timing offset after coarse symbol timing synchronization, and adjust FFT windows to proper position. Sampling clock offset leads to sample rob/stuff phenomenon that must be estimated post FFT. It works in the tracking stage and needs a symbol timing tracking loop.

3   Conventional Symbol Timing Synchronization for OFDM System

A symbol timing synchronization method is proposed by Dong Kyu Kim[3] that may be used for OFDM system with two-dimensional (frequency-domain and time-domain) interleaving, and enough pilots. For example the DRM+[2] system has the transmission frame pilot format as shows in figure 1.

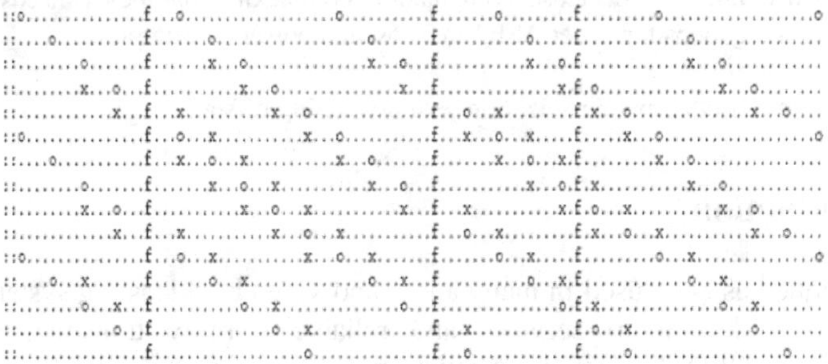

Fig. 1. DRM+ frame structure

Figure 1 shows the frame structure of DRM+ transmission in frequency domain, each OFDM symbol has frequency reference cells character "f", scattered pilots character "o", and FAC(Fast Access Channel) cells character "x". Frequency reference cell is a kind of pilot mainly used for frequency synchronization. The FAC is used to provide information on the channel parameters required for de-multiplex as well as basic service selection information for fast scanning. Scattered pilots (SPs) are used for timing synchronization and channel estimation.

In this method, a joint estimation method based scatter pilots is used. Fine symbol timing offset synchronization can be performed with sampling clock offset synchronization using phase difference between the SPs carriers. Detailed algorithm can be summarized as follows:

1) First, the phase rotation occurred at the k-th subcarrier of the j-th OFDM symbol is

$$\phi_{k,j} = Arg[S\hat{P}_{k,j}SP^*_{k,j}] = 2\pi k \frac{T_d + \Delta t(j)}{T_u} + \phi_0 + 2\pi\Delta f T_{sym} \qquad (1)$$

Where $S\hat{P}_{k,j}$ and $SP^{*}_{k,j}$ are the transmitted and received SP cells indexed with carrier indices k and symbol number j respectively. $Arg[\cdot]$ is the arctangent function. And Td, $\Delta t(j)$, ϕ_0 and Δf are fine symbol timing offset, sampling clock offset, phase offset , frequency offset in the the j-th OFDM symbol, respectively. They are all related to the synchronization errors. T_u, T_s and T_{sym} are the useful data duration, nominal sampling period and the total OFDM symbol duration, respectively. T_{sym} is the sum of the useful data duration and the guard interval. The difference of the phase rotation between $k = k_1$ and $k = k_2$ SP carriers of the j-th symbol is expressed as in (2).

$$\Delta\phi_{k_{2,1}}(j) = \phi_{k_2}(j) - \phi_{k_1}(j) = 2\pi\Delta k \frac{T_d + \Delta t(j)}{T_u} \tag{2}$$

Where Δk is frequency spacing between two scattered pilots carricrs.

2) From (2) the difference of phase rotation between the two scattered pilots in a symbol is the function of the frequency spacing $k_2 - k_1$, the normalized fine symbol timing offset Td/Ts, and the normalized sampling clock offset $\Delta t(j)$/Ts. The synchronization error $\varepsilon_{k_{2,1}}(j)$ is the sum of fine symbol offset and sampling clock offset and can be obtained as (3). The average phase difference can be obtained using all the scattered pilots in one OFDM symbol, as in (4). Then the average phase difference can be divided into an integer part and a fractional part as in (5).

$$\varepsilon_{k_{2,1}}(j) = \frac{T_d + \Delta t(j)}{T_s} = \frac{N}{2\pi} \times \frac{\Delta\phi_{k_{2,1}}(j)}{\Delta k} \tag{3}$$

$$\varepsilon(j) = \frac{1}{L}\sum_{n=0}^{L-1}\varepsilon_{k_{2n+1,2n}}(j) \tag{4}$$

$$\varepsilon(j) = int[\varepsilon(j)] + \{\varepsilon(j) - int[\varepsilon(j)]\} \tag{5}$$

Where L is the carrier number of the SPs in symbol j, N is the length of FFT. int[z] means the largest integer not exceeding z. The value of the integer is the fine symbol timing offset and the value of the fraction can be used for correcting the sampling clock offset.

Figure 2 shows the block diagram of the algorithm. There needs an analog timing loop which uses the fraction part as the input to the phase detector of PLL. The symbol timing offset can be tracked by PLL to adjust ADC's sampling frequency and the FFT widow controller. Thus the ADC sampling clock will be adjusted to output correct sampling frequency and the fine timing offset will also be compensated.

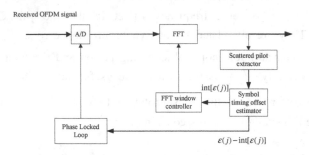

Fig. 2. Block diagram of timing loop

The symbol timing offset synchronization method post FFT for DRM+ has the following drawbacks:

1. It is based on the difference of phase rotations between the two SPs, there are L SPs used in one OFDM symbol, so there will be L-1 estimations of the phase difference according (4). Otherwise, we need calculate L times the phase angle for the arctangent function in one OFDM symbol duration. As we know, in real system or hardware realization, the arctangent function is a class of iterative computations, which needs much processing timing, either for the arctan() look-up table or for the ORDIC algorithm. In DRM+ system, there are 23 SPs in one OFDM symbol for robustness mode A and spectrum occupancy 20kHz [2], and repeated every five symbols, so too much processing time and power consumption are needed. However for mobile reception, the power consumption is a key problem that needs to be considered. In addition, the power characteristic is utilized in the algorithm. It is well known that, power characteristic is much more sensitive to the multi-path fading channels. So the performance of the method is not good under multi-path fading channels.

2. From figure 2, a fine symbol timing tracking loop is combined with sampling synchronization loop. In the method, the symbol timing synchronization which decided the FFT window position can be achieved by adjusting the ADC's sampling frequency and phase and the FFT window controller. However, it needs an analog timing loop which covers some analog components. As we know, analog timing loop is difficult to integrate in ASIC design, which will increase the ASIC area and power consumption. In many OFDM systems, such as ISDB-T [6], there must be at least two sampling rates for reception mode, the ADC's sampling clock must be changed corresponding to the reception mode that means the analog timing loop needs 2 VCOs. It will increase the ASIC area and power consumption.

Taking the above two drawbacks into consideration, more suitable method needs to be developed.

4   The Proposed Method

The above symbol timing synchronization method must calculate a number of arctangent functions in one OFDM symbol and need an analog timing loop to track the symbol timing offset. An improved method which decreases the arctangent functions is proposed based on the method above. At the same time, the symbol timing offset can be tracked by a NCO controlled loop.

The proposed new symbol timing offset synchronization method and tracking loop can be summarized as follows:

1)   The improved method also utilizes the joint operation between fine symbol timing recovery and sampling clock adjustment based on the method above. First, we do the correlation operation between the local and received SPs.

$$\phi_{k,j} = S\hat{P}_{k,j} \cdot SP^*_{k,j} \tag{6}$$

The symbol timing offset is expressed:

$$\varepsilon(j) = \frac{N}{2\pi\Delta k} Arg\left[\frac{\sum_{k=0}^{L-1} Im(\phi_{k+1,j}\phi^*_{k,j})}{\sum_{k=0}^{L-1} Re(\phi_{k+1,j}\phi^*_{k,j})} \right] \tag{7}$$

The integer part of the symbol timing offset is:

$$\varepsilon_i = int[\varepsilon(j)] \tag{8}$$

Where, int⌊z⌋ means the largest integer not exceeding z. The value of the integer ε_i can also be used for estimating the sampling clock offset.

$$\varepsilon_i = int[\varepsilon(j)]\eta(j) = \frac{\varepsilon(j) - \varepsilon(j-1)}{N + N_g} \tag{9}$$

Where Ng is the length of guard interval and η is the relative sampling clock offset. The basic block diagram of improved method is illustrated in the figure 3.

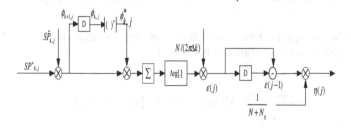

Fig. 3. The block diagram of the improved method

In the figure 3, the received SPs and local SPs are used to estimate the fine symbol timing offset by a series of correlation operation every symbol. The output signal $\varepsilon(j)$ is used to estimate the sampling clock offset by the differential operation every two symbols. The improved method firstly gets the sum of the correlation operation, and then calculates phase angle. This method just needs a calculation for arctangent function every OFDM symbol. Because the phase characteristic is less sensitive to the multi-path channels than power characteristic, so the utilized phase characteristic can get better performance than that of the method proposed by Dong Kyu Kim[3].

2) Since many systems are multimode and have multi-rate. In reception, the ADC input signal should be sampled at a free running clock regardless transmission mode and transmitting rate. In the improved method, we use a differential operation for sampling clock offset estimation, which can be tracked by a NCO controlled interpolation loop as shown in figure 4. For a non-synchronized sampling receiver system, symbol timing loop includes mainly interpolator, and interpolation controller (NCO) and FFT window controller.

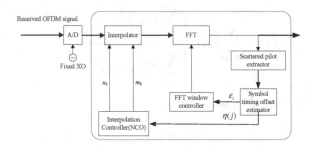

Fig. 4. Block diagram of NCO controlled timing loop

Refer to the figure 4, the ADC input signal is digitized under a fixed XO, which is commonly about 2 times or 4 times upsample. As we know, the fixed XO sampling rate must be converted to the IFFT sampling rate to carry out correct FFT computation. As shown in the figure, an interpolation loop is used for rate conversion and sampling clock offset tracking. The fine symbol timing offset ε_i will be used to feedback to FFT window controller to adjust the FFT start position. While $\eta(j)$ can be used to compensate and track the sampling clock offset through the interpolation loop based NCO.

3) The sampling rate conversion can be realized by interpolation. The interpolating equation can be written as:

$$y(kT_i) = \sum_{I=I_1}^{I_2} x[(m_k - i)T_s]h_I[(i+\mu_k)T_s] \tag{10}$$

Where $h_I(t)$ is the pulse response of interpolating filter, $x(k)$ is input sample, m_k is a base point index and μ_k is the timing offset, $0 \le \mu_k < 1$. The interplant $y(kT_i)$ is computed from (10) using adjacent samples $x(k)$ and I samples of the interpolating filter. The correct set of signal samples is identified by the base point index m_k and the correct set of filter samples is identified by the μ_k.

In consideration of implementation complexity, a Farrow structure polynomial-based filter is more desirable [4]. It can be expressed as:

$$y(k) = \sum_{l=0}^{N} u_k^l v(l), \qquad v(l) = \sum_{i=I_1}^{I_2} b_l(i)x(m_k - i) \tag{11}$$

Where, the coefficients $b_l(i)$ are fixed numbers, independent of μ_k. For a cubic interpolation:

$$y(k) = \left[\{v(3)u_k + v(2)\}u_k + v(1) \right]u_k + v(0) \tag{12}$$

A block diagram for interpolator is shown in figure 5. The cubic interpolator consists of 4 fir branches and 3 multipliers.

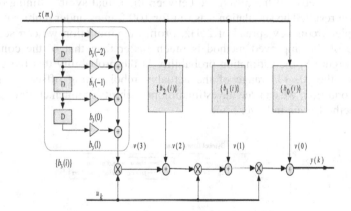

Fig. 5. Farrow structure of cubic interpolator

4)   The interpolation controller determining m_k and μ_k, and making that available to do the interpolate calculation. The necessary control can be provided by a number-controlled oscillator (NCO), m_k and μ_k can be expressed as:

$$m_{k+1} = \text{int}[T_i / T_s + u_k] + m_k \tag{13}$$

$$u_{k+1} = \left[u_k + \frac{T_i}{T_s} \right] \bmod 1$$

(14)

Here T_i is sampling rate after interpolator, T_s is sample rate before interpolator. The structure of the NCO is shown in the figure 6. And $frac[\cdot]$ means get the fractional part. The Interval is mean value and decided by the upsample times.

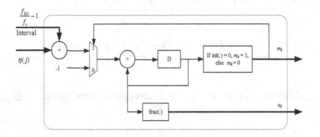

Fig. 6. NCO structure

We evaluate the performance of the proposed symbol timing offset estimation post FFT by computer simulation with the results given in figure 7 and figure 8. In figure 7, the MSE is a metric of the difference between the actual symbol timing offset and the estimation result. The simulation was run for 100 frames under multi-path channel with a Doppler frequency spread of 20Hz. From the simulation we can see that the performance of the improved method is much better than that of the conventional method. In Figure 8, the estimation probability is the probability that the estimation result locates the (0, +1) range of the actual symbol timing offset. At the same simulation condition, we can see the estimation probability is much close to 1 with the improved method, even in lower SNR.

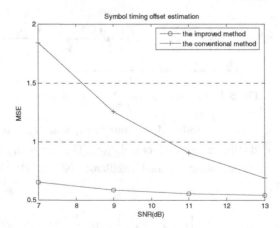

Fig. 7. Performance comparison of the two symbol timing offset synchronization methods

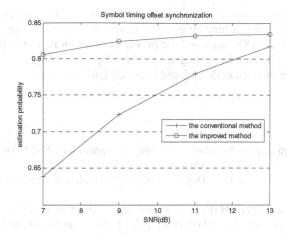

Fig. 8. Estimation probability comparisons of the two methods

5   Conclusion

We have proposed a new symbol timing offset synchronization method with all tracking loop digitally in OFDM reception systems. For the improved and conventional symbol timing offset synchronization methods, some conclusions showed as follows:

(1)   The common ground is that both of them are based on phase difference of the scattered pilots to estimate the symbol timing offset post FFT.

(2)   The key point is the conventional method firstly calculates every phase difference between the two SPs, and then average the estimation. It uses the power characteristic. In fact, we can use the phase characteristic to estimate the offset, which justly need calculate a phase difference.

(3)   The main difference is that they adopt different cost functions for symbol timing offset synchronization and different timing tracking loop to track symbol timing offset.

Compared with the conventional method, the advantages of the improved method are:

(1)   Better estimation performance and lower computation complexity. Simulation results show the improved method has the much better performance as the conventional method in multi-path channels. As far as computation complexity is concerned, the conventional method needs calculate a number of arctangent functions in one OFDM symbol duration. This causes higher computation complexity since arctangent operation is a time-consuming and complex process, and need much more processing timing. The proposed method gets the sum of the correlation operation and justly need calculate an arctangent function.

(2)   Much less resources and good compatibility. The conventional method need an analog timing loop for tracking the symbol timing offset, which increase the ASIC area and the power consumption. The improved method uses an all digitally timing loop and adapt to multi-mode and multi-rate receivers in multimode and multi-rate OFDM systems.

References

1. Santella, G.: A frequency and symbol synchronization system for OFDM signals: Architecture and simulation results. IEEE Trans. On Veh.Technol. 49(l), 254–275 (2000)
2. ETSI ES 201 980 v3.1.1, Digital Radio Mondiale(DRM):System Specification (August 2009)
3. Kim, D.K., Do, S.H., Cho, H.B.: A new joint algorithm of symbol timing recovery and sampling clock adjustment for OFDM systems. IEEE Trans. on Consumer Electronics 44(3), 1142–1149 (1998)
4. Gardner, F.M.: Interpolation in Digital Modems—Part I: Fundamentals. IEEE Transactions on Communications 41(3), 501–507 (1993)
5. Zhao, M.: All digital tracking loop for OFDM system timing, IEEE (2002)
6. ABNT NBR 15606-3, Digital terrestrial television – Data coding and transmission specification for digital broadcasting – Part3 :Data transmission specification (August 2008)

Statistical QoS Driven Power and Rate Allocation over Rayleigh Fading Cognitive Radio Links

Yichen Wang, Pinyi Ren*, and Qinghe Du

School of Electronic and Information Engineering
Xi'an Jiaotong University, P.R. China
wangyichen.0819@stu.xjtu.edu.cn, {pyren,duqinghe}@mail.xjtu.edu.cn

Abstract. In this paper, we propose a statistical Quality-of-Service (QoS) driven power and rate allocation scheme over wireless Rayleigh fading cognitive radio links. Specifically, we consider the scenario that one secondary link coexists with one primary link by sharing particular portions of the spectrum. Our proposed power and rate allocation scheme aims at maximizing the system effective capacity, which can be seen as the maximum arrival rate supported by the secondary link subject to a given statistical delay QoS constraint. In this work, we not only take into account the average transmit and interference power constraints for the secondary link, but also consider the influence from the transmission of the primary link to the effective capacity of the secondary link. Simulation results show that, (1) the effective capacity of the secondary link decreases when the statistical delay QoS constraint becomes stringent; (2) given the QoS constraint, the effective capacity of the secondary link varies with the interference power constraint and the SNR of the primary link.

Keywords: Cognitive radio, power allocation, statistical QoS guarantees, effective capacity.

1 Introduction

Cognitive radio is a promising yet challenging technology to solve wireless-spectrum underutilization problem caused by the traditional static spectrum allocation strategy [1] [2]. Spectrum sharing (underlay) and spectrum access (overlay) are two available methods for the secondary users (SUs) to dynamically utilize the spectrum which belongs to the primary users (PUs). Because the former method allows the SU to use the spectrum occupied by the PUs subject to a interference constraint, which can increase the spectrum utilization more obviously than the latter one, it has attracted a great deal of research attention.

---

* The research reported in this paper (correspondence author: Pinyi Ren) was supported in part by the National Natural Science Foundation of China under Grant No. 60832007 and the National Hi-Tech Research and Development Programme of China under Grant No. 2009AA011801.

P. Ren et al. (Eds.): WICON 2011, LNICST 98, pp. 33–44, 2012.

In the spectrum sharing networks, power and rate allocation is a critical problem to improve the capacity of the secondary link and some researches have been investigated. In this context, [3] and [4] are two fundamental researches. In [3], the optimal power allocation, which aims at maximizing the ergodic capacity of the secondary link over the additive white Gaussian noise (AWGN) channel under a received power constraint, is obtained. [4] considered different fading channel model, derived the corresponding optimal power allocation strategies, and evaluated the corresponding ergodic capacity of the secondary link. Based on the two fundamental researches, some investigations arise in recent years [5]-[10]. In [5] and [6], the authors analyzed the ergodic, outage, and delay-constrained capacities, respectively, and obtained the corresponding power allocation schemes under the block Rayleigh fading channel. In [7], the author considered the ergodic sum capacity of fading cognitive multiple-access and broadcast channels, respectively, and derived the corresponding TDMA structures as well as the power allocation scheme.

In the above researches, Quality of Service (QoS) guarantee related to the queue delay, which is important for the secondary link, is not integrated into the power and rate allocation. Effective capacity, which can be seen as the maximum arrival rate supported by the system, is an efficient tool to guarantee the statistical delay QoS of the system [11] [12]. The authors in [13] and [14] analyzed the effective capacity of the secondary link subject to different transmit and interference power constraints over the fading channel and obtained the corresponding optimal power allocations.

However, in these existing works, the influence of the transmissions implemented by the primary link, which is an important factor for the secondary link, does not take into consideration. In order to overcome the above problem and guarantee the statistical delay QoS for the SU, in this paper we consider the scenario that one secondary link coexists with one primary link by sharing particular portions of the spectrum and propose a statistical Quality-of-Service (QoS) driven power and rate allocation scheme, which aims at maximizing the effective capacity of the secondary link subject to a given statistical delay QoS constraint over the Rayleigh fading channel. We not only take into account the average transmit and interference power constraints for the secondary link, but also consider the influence from the transmissions of the primary link to the effective capacity of the secondary link. Moreover, we also derive the close-form of the optimal power and rate allocation strategy, which can maximize the effective capacity of the secondary link subject to our constraints.

The rest of this paper is organized as follows. Section 2 presents the system model. Section 3 introduces the concept of effective capacity. Section 4 develops the optimal power and rate allocation scheme based on the effective capacity introduced in Section 3. Simulation results are given in Section 5. The paper concludes with Section 6.

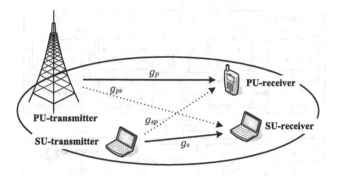

Fig. 1. The scenario that the secondary link coexists with the primary link

2   System Model

We consider the scenario that one secondary link coexists with one primary link by sharing a particular portions of the spectrum, as shown in Fig. 1. Each link consists of one transmitter and one receiver, respectively. The total spectrum bandwidth is denoted by B. The additive noise at the PU and SU receivers are modeled as zero-mean Gaussian random variables with the same variance $N_0 B$, where N_0 denote the noise power spectral density.

We assume that the upper-protocol-layer packets are divided into frames, which have the same time duration denoted by T_f, at the datalink layer, as shown in Fig. 2. The discrete-time channel gains between the PU transmitter and PU receiver, the SU transmitter and SU receiver, the PU transmitter and SU receiver, as well as the SU transmitter and PU receiver are denoted by $g_p[i]$, $g_s[i]$, $g_{ps}[i]$, and $g_{sp}[i]$, respectively, and we define the system channel gain vector denoted by $\mathbf{G}[i] \triangleq [g_s[i], g_p[i], g_{ps}[i], g_{sp}[i]]$, where i is the time index of the frame. We assume that the four channel gains are stationary, ergodic, independent, and block fading processes, which represent that the gains are invariant within a frame, but vary from one frame to another. Moreover, we assume that the channels gains described above all obey the same exponential distribution with mean a, so that their probability density functions (pdf) can be written as:

$$f_x\left(g_x\right) = a e^{-a g_x}, \ g_x \geq 0; \ x \in \{s, p, ps, sp\}. \tag{1}$$

Throughout this paper, we assume that the maximal average transmit power of the SU transmitter is P_{av}, the maximal average interference power that the PU receiver can tolerate is Q_{av}, and the PU transmitter transmits data packets to the PU receiver with the constant transmit power P_{p}. Besides, we assume that the channel state information (CSI) $\mathbf{G}$ can be perfectly estimated by the PU and SU receivers and reliably fed back to the SU transmitter without delay. We also assume that the datalink-layer buffer size of the SU transmitter is infinite.

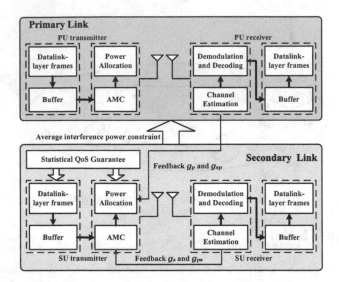

Fig. 2. The system model with statistical QoS guarantee

3   Effective Capacity

Delay QoS guarantee plays a critically important role in the wireless communication systems. However, the deterministic delay QoS guarantee will most likely result in extremely conservative guarantee. For example, in a Rayleigh or Ricean fading channel, the lower bound of the capacity that can be deterministically guaranteed is zero, which implies that the delay QoS guarantee is infinite. This conservative guarantee is clearly useless. Therefore, we need to use the statistical version to satisfy the delay constraint of the system.

The effective capacity, which is first proposed in [11], is an efficient tool to statistically guarantee the delay QoS of the system. The effective capacity is a dual concept of effective bandwidth [15]. In the effective bandwidth theory, the distribution of queue length process $Q(t)$ converges to a random variable $Q(\infty)$, which can be written as

$$-\lim_{x\to\infty} \frac{\log\left(\Pr\left\{Q\left(\infty\right)>y\right\}\right)}{y} = \theta, \qquad (2)$$

where y is the queue length threshold and θ is a critically important role for statistical delay QoS guarantee called QoS exponent. The smaller θ is, the looser the QoS guarantee is, and the larger θ is, the more stringent the QoS guarantee is. inspired by the effective bandwidth, the effective capacity can be defined as the maximum constant arrival rate that a given service service process can support in order to guarantee a QoS requirement specified by θ.

Assume that the sequence $\{R[i], i = 1, 2, \cdots\}$ is a discrete-time stationary and ergodic stochastic service process and the partial sum of the service process is $S[t] \triangleq \sum_{i=1}^{t} R[i]$. Assume that the Gartner-Ellis limit of $S[t]$, which can be expressed as

$$\Lambda_C(\theta) = \lim_{t \to \infty} \frac{1}{t} \log\left(\mathbb{E}\left\{e^{\theta S[t]}\right\}\right),\tag{3}$$

exists and is a convex function which is differentiable for all real θ. Therefore, the effective capacity of the system, denoted by $E_C(\theta)$, is

$$E_C(\theta) \triangleq -\frac{\Lambda_C(-\theta)}{\theta} = -\lim_{t \to \infty} \frac{1}{\theta t} \log\left(\mathbb{E}\left\{e^{-\theta S[t]}\right\}\right),\tag{4}$$

where $\theta > 0$. If the sequence $\{R[i], i = 1, 2, \cdots\}$ is an uncorrelated process, the effective capacity can be reduced to

$$E_C(\theta) = -\frac{1}{\theta} \log\left(\mathbb{E}\left\{e^{-\theta R[i]}\right\}\right).\tag{5}$$

In this paper, we aim at maximizing the effective capacity of the secondary link when the SU transmitter is subject to the given power constraints.

4   Optimal Power and Rate Allocation with Statistical QoS Guarantees

In this section, we will derive the optimal power and rate allocation, which can maximize the effective capacity subject to the average transmit and interference power constraints.

Since the channel power gains, which are g_s, g_p, g_{sp}, and g_{ps}, respectively, have been assumed to be block fading in section 2, the instantaneous service rate $R[i]$ of the secondary link during the frame i is

$$R[i] = T_f B \log_2\left(1 + \frac{g_s[i]\mu(\theta, \mathbf{G}[i]) P_{\text{av}}}{g_{ps}[i] P_p + N_0 B}\right)$$

$$= T_f B \log_2\left(1 + \frac{g_s[i]\mu(\theta, \mathbf{G}[i]) \bar{\gamma}_s}{g_{ps}[i]\bar{\gamma}_p + 1}\right),\tag{6}$$

where $\bar{\gamma}_s$ and $\bar{\gamma}_p$ are the average Signal-to-Noise Ratio (SNR) at the SU and PU transmitters, respectively, and $\mu(\theta, \mathbf{G}[i])$ is the power allocation policy of the secondary link, which are the functions of both QoS exponent θ and system channel gain vector $\mathbf{G}[i]$. In the following discussions, we omit the discrete time-index i for simplicity.

As the SU transmitter must be subject to a upperbounded average transmit power P_{av}, the power allocation policy $\mu(\theta, \mathbf{G}[i])$ need to satisfy

$$\mathbb{E}_\mathbf{G}\{\mu(\theta, \mathbf{G})\} \leq 1.\tag{7}$$

In order to protect the data transmissions of the primary link, the transmit power of the SU transmitter must satisfy the average interference power constraint imposed by the PU receiver, which can be written as

$$\mathbb{E}_{\mathbf{G}}\left\{g_{sp}\mu\left(\theta,\mathbf{G}\right)\right\} \leq \rho, \tag{8}$$

where ρ is the ratio of the average transmit power and average interference power and can be expressed as $\rho = P_{\mathrm{av}}/Q_{\mathrm{av}}$.

Our objective is to maximize the effective capacity of the secondary link subject to the constraints shown in (7) and (8). The mathematical description of our optimization problem can be written as

$$\max_{\mu(\theta,\mathbf{G})} \left\{ -\frac{1}{\theta}\log\left(\mathbb{E}\left\{ e^{-\theta T_f B \log_2\left(1+\frac{g_s\mu(\theta,\mathbf{G})\bar{\gamma}_s}{g_{ps}\bar{\gamma}_p+1}\right)}\right\}\right)\right\},$$

$$\text{s.t.} \begin{cases} E_{\mathbf{G}}\left\{\mu\left(\theta,\mathbf{G}\right)\right\} \leq 1, \\ E_{\mathbf{G}}\left\{g_{sp}\mu\left(\theta,\mathbf{G}\right)\right\} \leq \rho. \end{cases} \tag{9}$$

Because the function $\log(x)$ is a monotonically increasing function of x, the solution to the maximization problem shown in (9) is the same with the one for the minimization problem, which can be expressed as

$$\min_{\mu(\theta,\mathbf{G})} E\left\{\left[1+\frac{g_s\mu(\theta,\mathbf{G})\bar{\gamma}_s}{g_{ps}\bar{\gamma}_p+1}\right]^{-\beta}\right\},$$

$$\text{s.t.} \begin{cases} E_{\mathbf{G}}\left\{\mu\left(\theta,\mathbf{G}\right)\right\} \leq 1, \\ E_{\mathbf{G}}\left\{g_{sp}\mu\left(\theta,\mathbf{G}\right)\right\} \leq \rho, \end{cases} \tag{10}$$

where β is the normalized QoS exponent and can be written as

$$\beta = \frac{\theta T_f B}{\log(2)}. \tag{11}$$

It is clear that the objective function in (10) is strictly convex and the constraints in (7) and (8) are both linear with respect to $\mu\left(\theta,\mathbf{G}\right)$. Therefore, the minimization problem has a unique optimal solution. We try to derive the optimal solution by using the Lagrangian optimization method [17]. The Lagrangian function, denote by $\mathcal{L}\left(\mu\left(\theta,\mathbf{G}\right),\lambda,\xi\right)$, can be expressed as

$$\mathcal{L}\left(\mu\left(\theta,\mathbf{G}\right),\lambda,\xi\right) = E\left\{\left[1+\frac{g_s\mu(\theta,\mathbf{G})\bar{\gamma}_s}{g_{ps}\bar{\gamma}_p+1}\right]^{-\beta}\right\}$$

$$+ \lambda\left[E_{\mathbf{G}}\left\{\mu\left(\theta,\mathbf{G}\right)\right\}-1\right] \tag{12}$$

$$+ \xi\left[E_{\mathbf{G}}\left\{g_{sp}\mu\left(\theta,\mathbf{G}\right)\right\} \leq \rho\right],$$

where λ and ξ are the nonnegative Lagrangian multipliers. Differentiating the Lagrangian function given by (12) and setting the derivative equal to zero, we have

$$\frac{\partial L(\mu(\theta,\mathbf{G}),\lambda,\xi)}{\partial\mu(\theta,\mathbf{G})} = \lambda + \xi g_{sp}$$

$$- \beta\frac{g_s\bar{\gamma}_s}{g_{ps}\bar{\gamma}_p+1}\left[1+\frac{g_s\mu(\theta,\mathbf{G})\bar{\gamma}_s}{g_{ps}\bar{\gamma}_p+1}\right]^{-\beta-1} = 0. \tag{13}$$

Therefore, the optimal power and rate allocation policy, which can maximize the effective capacity of the secondary link, can be expressed as

$$
\mu^{\mathrm{opt}}\left(\theta, \mathbf{G}\right) = \begin{cases} \dfrac{\beta^{\frac{1}{1+\beta}}}{\Gamma^{\frac{\beta}{1+\beta}}\left(\lambda+\xi g_{sp}\right)^{\frac{1}{1+\beta}}} - \dfrac{1}{\Gamma}, & \Gamma\beta \geq \lambda+\xi g_{sp} \\[4mm] 0, & \Gamma\beta < \lambda+\xi g_{sp} \end{cases}
\tag{14}
$$

where Γ is

$$
\Gamma = \frac{g_s\overline{\gamma}_s}{g_{ps}\overline{\gamma}_p + 1}.
\tag{15}
$$

λ and ξ are determined such that the average transmit and interference power, which are shown in (7) and (8), respectively, are equal to 1 and ρ, respectively, i.e.,

$$
\int_{g_s}\int_{g_p}\int_{g_{sp}}\int_{g_{ps}} \mu^{\mathrm{opt}}\left(\theta, \mathbf{G}\right) f_{ps}\left(g_{ps}\right) f_{sp}\left(g_{sp}\right)
$$
$$
f_p\left(g_p\right) f_s\left(g_s\right) dg_{ps}\, dg_{sp}\, dg_p\, dg_s = 1
\tag{16}
$$

and

$$
\int_{g_s}\int_{g_p}\int_{g_{sp}}\int_{g_{ps}} g_{sp}\mu^{\mathrm{opt}}\left(\theta, \mathbf{G}\right) f_{ps}\left(g_{ps}\right) f_{sp}\left(g_{sp}\right)
$$
$$
f_p\left(g_p\right) f_s\left(g_s\right) dg_{ps}dg_{sp}dy_pdg_s - \rho.
\tag{17}
$$

In [12], the author analysis the effective capacity of one wireless fading link, which contains one transmitter and one receiver, and obtained the optimal power and rate adaptive policy. In this fundamental work, the author found that the optimal policy converges to the water-filling and total channel inversion when $\theta \to 0$ and $\theta \to \infty$, respectively. Now we will check whether our derived optimal power and rate allocation policy $\mu\left(\theta, \mathbf{G}\right)$ also has the same property. When $\theta \to 0$, $\mu\left(\theta, \mathbf{G}\right)$ becomes

$$
\lim_{\theta\to 0} \mu^{\mathrm{opt}}\left(\theta, \mathbf{G}\right) = \begin{cases} \frac{1}{\lambda+\xi g_{sp}} - \frac{1}{\Gamma}, & \Gamma \geq \lambda+\xi g_{sp} \\ 0, & \Gamma < \lambda+\xi g_{sp} \end{cases}
\tag{18}
$$

which is just the water-filling formula [16]. When $\theta \to \infty$, we have

$$
\lim_{\theta\to\infty} \mu^{\mathrm{opt}}\left(\theta, \mathbf{G}\right) = 0,
\tag{19}
$$

which is the same conclusion as in [16] that the power allocation of the total channel inversion over Rayleigh fading channel is always zero. Therefore, we can conclude that the optimal power and rate allocation policy also has the same property as described in [12], i.e., when the QoS constraint becomes loose, the optimal power policy of the secondary link converges to the water-filling scheme and the effective capacity equals to the ergodic capacity, on the other hand, when the QoS constraint gets stringent, the optimal policy converges to the total channel inversion scheme and the transmission rate of the secondary is zero.

In our derived optimal power and rate allocation policy, not only the statistical delay QoS constraint is considered, but also the influence from the PU transmitter to the SU receiver is taken into consideration. When $g_{ps} \to 0$, the optimal policy $\mu(\theta, \mathbf{G})$ becomes

$$\lim_{g_{ps} \to 0} \mu^{\mathrm{opt}}(\theta, \mathbf{G}) = \left[\frac{\beta^{\frac{1}{1+\beta}}}{(g_s \bar{\gamma}_s)^{\frac{\beta}{1+\beta}} (\lambda + \xi g_{sp})^{\frac{1}{1+\beta}}} - \frac{1}{g_s \bar{\gamma}_s} \right]^+ \tag{20}$$

which converges to the power allocation scheme obtained in [13]. Moreover, if we assume that $\theta \to 0$ and $g_{ps} \to 0$ simultaneously, our obtained optimal policy becomes

$$\lim_{\substack{\theta \to 0 \\ g_{ps} \to 0}} \mu^{\mathrm{opt}}(\theta, \mathbf{G}) = \begin{cases} \frac{1}{\lambda + \xi g_{sp}} - \frac{1}{g_s \bar{\gamma}_s}, & g_s \bar{\gamma}_s \geq \lambda + \xi g_{sp} \\ 0, & g_s \bar{\gamma}_s < \lambda + \xi g_{sp} \end{cases} \tag{21}$$

which is the same as the power allocation scheme derived in [4] and [6]. Therefore, we can conclude that, if the statistical delay QoS constraint become loose and the channel power gain between the PU transmitter and the SU receiver is small, our derived policy $\mu(\theta, \mathbf{G})$ will maximize the ergodic capacity of the secondary link subject to the average transmit and interference power constraints, and the power policy is only the functions of g_s and g_{sp}, but is unrelated with g_p and g_{ps}.

5   Simulation Results

Observe our optimization problem and the derived optimal power and rate allocation policy, which are shown in (9) and (14), respectively, the maximal average transmit power of the SU transmitter, the transmit power of the PU transmitter, and the maximal average interference power are the critically important parameters that will impact the effective capacity of the secondary link. Therefore, in this section, we will analyze how the effective capacity of the SU link varies with the three parameters mentioned above through simulation. As described in [12], the optimal power allocation policy $\mu^{\mathrm{opt}}(\theta, \mathbf{G})$ depends on the frame duration T_f and the spectrum B through the normalized QoS exponent β. In our simulation, we set the frame duration $T_f = 2$ ms and the bandwidth $B = 10^5$ Hz. The other system parameters are detailed respectively in each of our simulation figures.

First, we evaluate the impact of the maximal average interference power to the normalized effective capacity of the second link, which is defined as the effective capacity divided by T_f and B. In this scenario, we set the average SNR at the SU transmitter $\bar{\gamma}_s = 0$ dB and the SNR at the PU transmitter $\bar{\gamma}_p = 0$, respectively. As describe in (8), the maximal average interference power Q_{av} can be reflected by the normalized average interference coefficient ρ, we vary ρ instead of changing Q_{av}. Fig. 3 presents the normalized effective capacity of the secondary link under different QoS exponents and normalized average interference coefficients. The

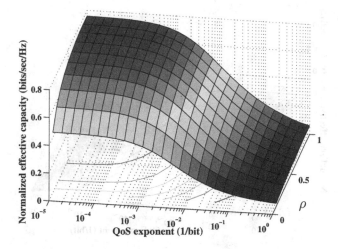

Fig. 3. The effective capacity of the secondary link when the transmit power of the PU transmitter varies

simulation result shows that, under any given normalized average interference coefficient ρ, the normalized effective capacity of the secondary link decreases while increasing the QoS exponent θ, which is the same as the results presented in [12]. Such observation can be explained as, when θ is small, the statistical delay constraint is loose, thus the traffic can be arrived with higher rate, but the statistical delay constraint will get stringent while increasing θ, which results that the secondary link can only support lower traffic arrival rate. The simulation result also shows that, under any given QoS exponent θ, the normalized effective capacity increases as the normalized average interference coefficient ρ increases. The reason for such phenomenon is that, the larger ρ implies that the PU receiver can tolerate more interference power. Therefore, the SU transmitter can use more power for the transmission even when the channel power gain between the SU transmitter and the PU receiver is larger compared with the scenario under smaller ρ, which leads to the improvement of the effective capacity of the SU link.

Second, we analyze the impact of the transmit power of the primary link to the effective capacity of the secondary link. As shown in the Eq. (6), the PU transmit power can be reflected by the SNR $\overline{\gamma}_p$ at the PU transmitter, the larger the transmit power is, the larger $\overline{\gamma}_p$ is. In this scenario, we set the average SNR at the SU transmitter $\overline{\gamma}_s = 0$ dB and the normalized average interference coefficient $\rho = 0.2$. The SNR at the PU transmitter $\overline{\gamma}_p$ varies from 0 dB to 10 dB. Fig. 4 shows the normalized effective capacity of the secondary link under different QoS exponents and SNRs of the PU transmitter. From the simulation result, we can observe the similar phenomenon as shown in Fig. 3, i.e., given the SNR $\overline{\gamma}_p$, the normalized effective capacity decreases as the QoS exponent θ increases. The explanation for this observation is the same with that mentioned above. Moreover, we also find that, given the QoS exponent θ, the normalized

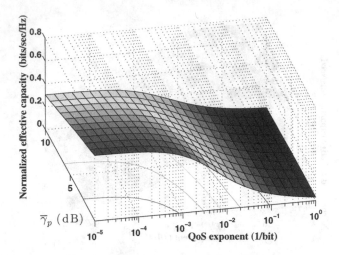

Fig. 4. The effective capacity of the secondary link when the ratio of the maximal interference power and the average transmit power varies

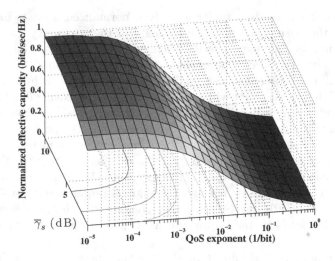

Fig. 5. The effective capacity of the secondary link when the transmit power of the SU transmitter varies

effective capacity of the secondary link decreases when we increase the SNR $\overline{\gamma}_p$. This is because that larger $\overline{\gamma}_p$ implies larger PU transmit power P_p, which will result in a lower signal-to-interference plus noise ratio (SINR) Γ at the SU receiver as shown in Eq. (15). Therefore, under the given channel power gain g_{ps} between the PU transmitter and the SU receiver, the channel capacity and the maximal traffic arrival rate that can be supported by the secondary link will be reduced as $\overline{\gamma}_p$ increases, which lead to the decreasing tendency of the normalized effective capacity.

Finally, we evaluate the impact of the transmit power of the secondary link to its normalized effective capacity. As shown in the Eq. (6), the transmit power used by the secondary link can be reflected by the maximal average SNR $\overline{\gamma}_s$ at the SU transmitter. The larger the transmit power is, the larger $\overline{\gamma}_s$ is. In this scenario, we set the SNR at the PU transmitter $\overline{\gamma}_p = 0$ dB and the normalized average interference coefficient $\rho = 0.5$. The maximal average SNR at the SU transmitter $\overline{\gamma}_s$ varies from 0 dB to 10 dB. Fig. 5 presents the normalized effective capacity of the secondary link under different QoS exponents and maximal average SINRs of the SU transmitter. From the simulation result, we can also find that, under the given $\overline{\gamma}_s$, the normalized effective capacity decreases when the statistical delay QoS constraint becomes stringent, which is the same with the observations shown in Fig. 3 and Fig. 4. From the simulation result, we can also observe that, when we increase the maximal average SINR $\overline{\gamma}_s$, the normalized effective capacity of the secondary link also increases. The reason is that larger $\overline{\gamma}_s$ implies that the SU transmitter uses larger transmit power, which causes a larger SINR Γ as shown in Eq. (15). Therefore, under the given channel power gains g_s and g_{sp} as well as the SNR $\overline{\gamma}_p$, the maximal traffic arrival rate that can be supported by the secondary link will increase as $\overline{\gamma}_s$ increases, which improves the normalized effective capacity. Furthermore, we can also observe that the normalized effective capacity is nearly a constant when $\overline{\gamma}_s \geq 5$ dB. Such phenomenon is caused by the maximal average interference power constraint, which is reflected by ρ. As described in section 2, ρ is the ratio of the maximal average interference power Q_{av} and the maximal average power P_{av}. Since Q_{av} is unchanged in this scenario, a larger P_{av} (or $\overline{\gamma}_s$) will cause a smaller ρ, which represents a more strict interference power constraint. Therefore, although the SU transmitter are allowed to use larger power for its transmission, the maximal average interference power constraint prevents the SU transmitter from utilizing larger power, which keeps the normalized effective capacity of the secondary link nearly the same.

6   Conclusion

In this paper, we proposed a statistical Quality-of-Service (QoS) driven power and rate allocation scheme over wireless Rayleigh fading cognitive radio links in the scenario that one secondary link coexists with one primary link by sharing particular portions of the spectrum. Our derived power and rate allocation policy can maximize the effective capacity of the secondary link subject to both the average transmit power and average interference power constraints. In this work, we also considered the impact of the transmission of the primary link to the secondary link. Simulation results show that: (1) the effective capacity of the secondary link decreases when the statistical delay QoS constraint becomes stringent; (2) given the QoS constraint, the effective capacity of the secondary link increases as the average interference power constraint becomes looser, but decreases when the PU transmit power increases; (3) given the QoS constraint, the effective capacity of the secondary link will be improved with looser average transmit power constraint, but the effective capacity cannot be further increased with continuously increasing the transmit power because the average interference constraint will become more strict when the average interference power is unchanged.

References

1. Mitola, J., Maguire, G.Q.: Cognitive radio: making software radios more personal. IEEE Personal Commun. 6(4), 13–18 (1999)
2. Haykin, S.: Cognitive radio: brain-empowered wireless communications. IEEE J. Selec. Areas Commun. 23(2), 201–220 (2005)
3. Gastpar, M.: On capacity under receive and spatial spectrum-sharing constraints. IEEE Trans. Inf. Theory 53(2), 471–487 (2007)
4. Ghasemi, A., Sousa, E.S.: Fundamental limits of spectrum-sharing in fading environments. IEEE Trans. Wireless Commun. 6(2), 649–658 (2007)
5. Musavian, L., Aissa, S.: Capacity and Power allocation for spectrum-sharing communications in fading channels. IEEE Trans Wireless Commun. 8(1), 148–156 (2009)
6. Kang, X., Liang, Y., Nallanathan, A., Garg, H., Zhang, R.: Optimal power allocation for fading channels in cognitive networks: ergodic capacity and outage capacity. IEEE Trans. Wireless Commun. 8(2), 940–950 (2009)
7. Zhang, R., Cui, S., Liang, Y.: On ergodic sum capacity of fading cognitive multiple-access and broadcast channels. IEEE Trans. Inf. Theory 55(11), 5161–5178 (2009)
8. Kang, X., Zhang, R., Liang, Y., Garg, H.K.: Optimal power allocation strategies for fading cognitive radio channels with primary user outage constraint. IEEE J. Selec. Areas Commun. 29(2), 374–383 (2011)
9. Khoshkholgh, M.G., Navaie, K., Yanikomeroglu, H.: Access strategies for spectrum sharing in fading environment: overlay, underlay, and mixed. IEEE Trans. Mobile Compu. 9(12), 1780–1793 (2010)
10. Kang, X., Garg, H.K., Liang, Y., Zhang, R.: Optimal power allocation for OFDM-based cognitive radio with new primary transmission protection criteria. IEEE Trans. Wireless Commun. 9(6), 2066–2075 (2010)
11. Wu, D., Negi, R.: Effective capacity: a wireless link model for support of Quality of Service. IEEE Trans. Wireless Commun. 2(4), 630–643 (2003)
12. Tang, J., Zhang, X.: Quality-fo-Service driven power and rate adaptation over wireless links. IEEE Trans. wireless Commun. 6(8), 3058–3068 (2007)
13. Musavian, L., Aissa, S.: Effective capacity of delay-constrained cognitive radio in nakagami fading channels. IEEE Trans. Wireless Commun. 9(3), 1054–1062 (2010)
14. Ma, Y., Zhang, H., Yuan, D., Chen, H.: Adaptive power allocation with quality-of-service guarantee in cognitive radio networls. Computer Communications 32(18), 1975–1982 (2009)
15. Chang, C.: Stability, queue length, and delay of deterministic and stochastic queueing neyworks. IEEE Trans. Automatic Control 39(5), 913–931 (1994)
16. Goldsmith, A.J., Varaiya, P.: Capacity of fading channels with channel side information. IEEE Trans. Inf. Theory 43(6), 1986–1992 (1997)
17. Boyd, S., Vandenberghe, L.: Convex Optimization. Cambridge University Press (2004)

Joint Subcarrier and Power Allocation Considering Fairness in OFDM-Based Cognitive Radio Systems

Shuangcheng Yan, Pinyi Ren, and Yu Hong

School of Electronics and Information Engineering
Xi'an Jiaotong University, Xi'an, China 710049
{yansc,hongyu.2046}@stu.xjtu.edu.cn, pyren@mail.xjtu.edu.cn

Abstract. Orthogonal frequency division multiplexing (OFDM) is an attractive modulation candidate for cognitive radio networks. In OFDM-based cognitive radio (CR) networks, effective and reliable subcarrier and power allocation is a challenging problem. And the fairness of resource allocation is another important problem in this network.In this paper, We present a joint subcarrier and power allocation algorithm considering fairness (JSPACF) among secondary users (SUs) for OFDM-based CR networks. In JSPACF, we allocate the subcarriers to SUs in the first step, not only considering the channel gain and the interference introduced to primary users (PUs) by SUs, but also considering proportional fairness among SUs. Then in the second step, we allocate the power to the subcarriers to maximize sum capacity of all SUs with total power constraint and interference constraint, considering proportional fairness among SUs too. Theory analysis and simulation results show that JSPACF can offer the beneficial tradeoff between system performance and fairness, while largely reducing complexity compared to the optimal solution.

Keywords: OFDM, cognitive radio, subcarrier and power allocation, fairness.

With the increasing explosion of wireless communications, available spectrum resource is becoming more and more scarce, which seriously hindered the development of new technologies. However, one of the FCC documents has indicated that many licensed frequency bands are severely underutilized in both the time domain and the spatial domain [1]. The spectrum is extremely under-utilized mostly due to the unreasonable command-and-control spectrum regulation, but not the physical scarcity of spectrum. Cognitive Radio (CR) [2][3] is a promising technology for dynamic spectrum access with the ability of observing the surrounding environment and adapting itself to the change of network environment. In the cognitive radio systems, secondary users (SU) can use the spectrum of primary users (PU) as long as the interference introduced to the PU by SU remains within a tolerable range.

Orthogonal frequency division multiplexing (OFDM) has already been recognized as a potential transmission technology for CR systems, since it has the reconfigurable subcarrier structure that can facilitate adaptive adjustment of

P. Ren et al. (Eds.): WICON 2011, LNICST 98, pp. 45–57, 2012.

parameters, and the Fast Fourier Transform module of its receivers can also be used for the spectrum sensing [4].

In CR system, available resource for SUs include spectrum, power, bit and so on. Resource allocation is a very important problem, because it can Seriously affect the performance of cognitive radio systems. All of the classical algorithms that was proposed to solve the problem in conventional multicarrier systems cannot be applied to the CR systems due to the existence of the two different types of users (PU and SU) where the interference introduced to the PU by SU should be taken into consideration. Recently, there has been a flurry of literatures addressing difference approaches on resource allocation for cognitive networks.The authors in [5] proposed an optimal and two suboptimal power loading algorithms for a downlink transmission scenario using the Lagrange formulation to maximize the downlink capacity of the CR system while keeping the interference induced to only one PU below a pre-specified threshold without the consideration of the total power constraint, and showed that the amount of interference introduced to the PU's band by a CR user's subcarrier depends on the power allocated in that subcarrier as well as the spectral distance between that particular subcarrier and the PU's band. An energy-efficient power allocation scheme is proposed based on a risk-return model in [6]. The authors in [7][8]present two-step resource allocation solution for multiuser based CR systems employing OFDM, separating subcarrier and power allocation, thus reducing the number of variables in the objective function of the optimization problem by half, is a promising method to reduce the complexity.

However these resource allocation algorithms do not consider the fairness among SUs. it is important to maintain fairness among users to avoid severe QoS degradation for users with unfavorable channel conditions. The The author in [9] proposes a joint channel and power allocation algorithm based on fair sharing, and introduces the fairness utility based on the definition of poverty line (PL) to guarantee fairness among SUs. In [10], a two-step resource allocation in multiuser OFDM-based CR systems is proposed, which has similar process with [7][8], but it considers proportional fairness among SUs. In [11], the authors proposed a power loading algorithms that guarantee the fairness of multiple SUs.

In this paper, we propose a joint subcarrier and power allocation algorithm considering fairness among secondary users (SUs) for OFDM-based Cognitive radio networks. In JSPACF, we allocate the subcarriers to SUs first, not only considering the channel gain and the interference introduced to primary users (PUs) by SUs, but also considering proportional fairness among SUs. Then for a given subcarrier assignment, we allocate the power to the subcarriers to maximize sum capacity of all SUs with total power constraint and interference constraint, considering proportional fairness among SUs too. JSPACF can offer the beneficial tradeoff between system performance and fairness, while largely reducing complexity compared to the optimal solution.

The rest of this paper is organized as follows: Section 2 presents the system model. Section 3 formulates JSPACF algorithm that we propose. In Section 4, the simulation result is presented. Finally, we conclude this paper in Section 5.

1   System Model

We consider a typical cellular transmission scenario with a single cell. In this transmission scenario, the CR system coexist with the PUs radio in the same geographical location, and PUs allow SUs to transmit while keeping the interference level low. it is assumed that The available bandwidth for CR transmission is divided into N subcarrier based OFDM system, and the bandwidth for each subcarrier is Δf Hz. there are M SUs, and SUs can use the non-active PU bands provided that the interference introduced to the PU by SU is within the interference threshold. The frequency band has been occupied by the PU (active PU band) is B Hz.

In the transmission scenario considered by us, there are three instantaneous fading gains: between the mth SU's transmitter and receiver for the nth subcarrier denoted as $h_{m,n}$; between the mth SU's transmitter and PU receiver for the nth subcarrier denoted as $g^{sp}_{m,n}$; between PU's transmitter and the mth SU's receiver for the nth subcarrier denoted as $g^{ps}_{m,n}$. In this paper, we assume that these instantaneous fading gains are perfectly known at the SU's transmitter.

In cognitive radio systems, due to the coexistence of PUs and SUs, there are two types of interference. One is introduced by the PUs into the SU's band, and the other is introduced by the SU into the PU's band. Now, we briefly describe the mathematical models for interference between SUs and PUs.

We assume that the signal transmitted on the subcarrier is an ideal Nyquist pulse, according to [12], the power density spectrum of the nth subcarrier can be written as

$$\varphi_{m,n}(f) = p_{m,n}T_s \left(\frac{\sin \pi f T_s}{\pi f T_s} \right)^2 \tag{1}$$

where $p_{m,n}$ is the transmit power in the nth subcarrier for the mth SU and T_s is the symbol duration. Then the interference introduced to the PU band by the the mth SU in the nth subcarrier is

$$I_{m,n}(p_{m,n}) = \left| g^{sp}_{m,n} \right|^2 p_{m,n}T_s \int_{d_n-B/2}^{d_n+B/2} \left(\frac{\sin \pi f T_s}{\pi f T_s} \right)^2 df \tag{2}$$

where d_n is the distance in frequency between the nth subcarrier and the PU band, $K_{m,n}$ denotes the interference factor for the mth SU in the nth subcarrier.

According to [12], the power density spectrum of the PU signal after M-fast Fourier transform (FFT) processing can be expressed as

$$E\{I_N(\omega)\} = \frac{1}{2\pi M} \int_{-\pi}^{\pi} \varphi_{PU}\left(e^{j\omega}\right) \left(\frac{\sin(\omega-\psi)M/2}{\sin(\omega-\psi)/2} \right)^2 d\psi \tag{3}$$

where $\varphi_{PU}\left(e^{j\omega}\right)$ is the power density spectrum of the PU signal, the PU signal has been taken to be an elliptically filtered white noise process with an amplitude P_{PU} [12].

According to [5], the interference introduced to the nth subcarrier by the PU band can be written as

$$J_{m,n}(P_{PU}) = \left| g^{ps}_{m,n} \right|^2 \int_{d_n+\Delta f/2}^{d_n-\Delta f/2} E\{I_N(\omega)\} d\omega \tag{4}$$

According to Shannon capacity formula, the transmission rate for the mth SU in the nth subcarrier is given by

$$r_{m,n} = \Delta f \log_2 \left(1 + \frac{|h_{m,n}|^2 p_{m,n}}{\sigma^2 + J_{m,n}} \right) \tag{5}$$

where σ^2 denotes the additive white Gaussian noise (AWGN) variance (we assume that the noise of each subcarrier is AWGN).

Let $a_{m,n}$ to be a subcarrier allocation indicator, and $a_{m,n} \in \{0,1\}$. if and only if the nth subcarrier is allocated to the mth user, $a_{m,n} = 1$, else $a_{m,n} = 0$. It is assumed that each subcarrier can be used for transmission to at most one user at any given time, so $\sum_{m=1}^{M} a_{m,n} \leq 1$.

Our objective is to maximize the total transmission rate of SUs with total transmit power constraint and interference constraint. Therefore, the optimization problem can be formulated as

$$\max_{a_{m,n}, p_{m,n}} \sum_{m=1}^{M} \sum_{n=1}^{N} a_{m,n} \Delta f \log_2 \left(1 + \frac{|h_{m,n}|^2 p_{m,n}}{\sigma^2 + J_{m,n}} \right) \tag{6}$$

subject to:

$$a_{m,n} \in \{0,1\}$$
$$\sum_{m=1}^{M} a_{m,n} \leq 1, for\ \forall n \in \{1,2,\cdots,N\}$$
$$\sum_{m=1}^{M} \sum_{n=1}^{N} a_{m,n} p_{m,n} \leq P_T \tag{7}$$
$$p_{m,n} \geq 0$$
$$\sum_{m=1}^{M} \sum_{n=1}^{N} a_{m,n} p_{m,n} K_{m,n} \leq I_{th}$$
$$R_1 : R_2 : \cdots\cdots : R_M = \gamma_1 : \gamma_2 : \cdots\cdots : \gamma_M$$

where P_T is the total power constraint, I_{th} is the interference threshold of PU, R_m is the total transmission rate of the mth SU, and $R_m = \sum_{n=1}^{N} a_{m,n} r_{m,n}$, $\{\gamma_1, \gamma_2, \cdots\cdots, \gamma_M\}$ is a set of predetermined constants to ensure proportional fairness [13] amongst SUs.

The fairness index is defined as

$$\zeta = \left(\sum_{m=1}^{M} \frac{R_m}{\gamma_m} \right)^2 / \left(M \sum_{m=1}^{M} \left(\frac{R_m}{\gamma_m} \right)^2 \right) \tag{8}$$

Note that ζ with maximum value of 1 is the greatest fairness case in which all users would achieve the same proportional data rate.

The optimization problem in (6)(7) under multiple constraints is generally very hard to solve because of the uncertain variables $a_{m,n}$ and the continuous variables $p_{m,n}$. Therefore, it is computationally very costly to find the optimal schemes. Moreover, there is always a trade-off between the optimal schemes and the constraints.

2   The JSPACF Algorithm

The author in [7][8][10] have proposed some classic algorithms to solve this optimization problem, they separately find the subcarrier allocation and power allocation solution. Similarly, in JSPACF, we first solve the subcarrier allocation problem, not only considering the channel gain and the interference introduced to primary users (PUs) by SUs, but also considering proportional fairness among SUs. Then for a given subcarrier allocation, we present a suboptimal scheme to solve power allocation problem, considering proportional fairness among SUs too. In the next subsection, we first present the algorithm for subcarrier allocation in JSPACF.

2.1   Subcarrier Allocation

Since the proportion of rates are hardly guaranteed, a rough proportionality is acceptable as long as the capacity is maximized and the algorithm complexity is low. We use the reasonable assumption in [14] that the number of subcarriers assigned to each CR is approximately the same as their rates after power allocation, and thus would roughly satisfy the proportionality constraints. Based on this assumption, the number of allocated subcarriers per CR is accomplished by

$$N_1^{\max} : N_2^{\max} : \cdots\cdots : N_M^{\max} = \gamma_1 : \gamma_2 : \cdots\cdots : \gamma_M \qquad (9)$$

where $N_m^{\max}$ is the maximal number of subcarriers allocated to the mth SU. Since $N_1^{\max} + N_2^{\max} + \cdots\cdots + N_M^{\max} = N$, we can know that

$$N_m^{\max} = \frac{\gamma_m}{\gamma_1 + \gamma_2 + \cdots\cdots + \gamma_M} N \qquad (10)$$

In the subcarrier allocation, we assume that equal power is in all subcarriers. To satisfy the interference constraint and power constraint, the power in all subcarriers is described as

$$p_{eq} = \min \left\{ \frac{P_T}{N}, \frac{I_{th}}{\sum_{m=1}^{M} \sum_{n=1}^{N} K_{m,n}} \right\} \qquad (11)$$

The classical algorithm in many literatures allocate subcarriers according to channel gain, such that the subcarriers are allocated to the SU who has the best channel gain. But in the subcarrier allocation algorithm we propose, the subcarriers are allocated to the SU who has the best channel gain and produces least interference to PU. We define Ω_N as the set of the subcarriers that have not been allocated to SU, Ω_M as the set of SU who requires subcarriers, N_m is the number of subcarriers allocated to the mth SU, and $N_m \leq N_m^{\max}$, Φ_m is the set of the subcarriers allocated to the mth SU. The proposed subcarrier allocation algorithm is as follows.

(a) Initialization
   Set $\Omega_N = \{1, 2, \cdots, N\}$, $\Omega_M = \{1, 2, \cdots, M\}$, $N_m = 0, a_{m,n} = 0$, and $\Phi_m = \varphi, R_m = 0, \forall m, \forall n$

(b) For $m = 1$ to M

$n = \arg\max_{n \in \Omega_N} \frac{|h_{m,n}|}{K_{m,n}}$

$a_{m,n} = 1$

$\Omega_N = \Omega_N - \{n\}$

$N_m = N_m + 1$

$\Phi_m = \Phi_m + \{n\}$

$R_m = r_{m,n}$

(c) While $\Omega_N \neq \phi$

$m = \arg\min_{m \in \Omega_M} \frac{R_m}{\gamma_m}$

$if\ N_m < N_m^{\max}$

$n = \arg\max_{n \in \Omega_N} \frac{|h_{m,n}|}{K_{m,n}}$

$a_{m,n} = 1$

$\Omega_N = \Omega_N - \{n\}$

$N_m = N_m + 1$

$\Phi_m = \Phi_m + \{n\}$

$R_m = R_m + r_{m,n}$

$else\ \ \Omega_M = \Omega_M - \{m\}$

From this algorithm, we can know $\Phi_1 \cup \Phi_2 \cup \cdots \cup \Phi_M = \{1, 2, \cdots, N\}$. our subcarrier allocation algorithm assigns roughly the proportional number of subcarriers to each CR according to the proportional fairness, thus improving fairness amongst SUs. Furthermore, this algorithm is suboptimal in a sense that equal power has been assumed in all subcarriers, however the complexity of the algorithm is low. Now, in the next subsection we introduce the power allocation scheme in JSPACF for a given subcarrier assignment.

2.2   Power Allocation

The power allocation in JSPACF consider interference constraint and total power constraint. Using Lagrange multiplier, we can get

$$G = \sum_{m=1}^{M} \sum_{n=1}^{N} a_{m,n} \log\left(1 + H_{m,n} p_{m,n}\right) - \alpha \left(\sum_{m=1}^{M} \sum_{n=1}^{N} a_{m,n} p_{m,n} - P_T \right)$$
$$- \beta \left(\sum_{m=1}^{M} \sum_{n=1}^{N} a_{m,n} p_{m,n} K_{m,n} - I_{th} \right) \tag{12}$$

where α and β are Lagrangian multipliers, $H_{m,n} = \frac{|h_{m,n}|^2}{\sigma^2 + J_{m,n}}$. We differentiate (12) with respect to $p_{m,n}$ and set each derivative to zero to obtain

$$\frac{a_{m,n} H_{m,n}}{1 + H_{m,n} p_{m,n}} - \alpha a_{m,n} - \beta a_{m,n} K_{m,n} = 0 \tag{13}$$

Then, it can be derived that

$$p_{m,n} = \left[\frac{1}{\alpha + \beta K_{m,n}} - \frac{1}{H_{m,n}} \right]^{+} \tag{14}$$

where $[x]^{+} = \max(x, 0)$, α and β are determined by

$$\alpha \left(\sum_{m=1}^{M} \sum_{n=1}^{N} a_{m,n} p_{m,n} - P_T \right) = 0 \qquad (15)$$

$$\beta \left(\sum_{m=1}^{M} \sum_{n=1}^{N} a_{m,n} p_{m,n} K_{m,n} - I_{th} \right) = 0 \qquad (16)$$

Solving for the more than one Lagrangian multiplier is computational complex. Of course, these multipliers can be found numerically using ellipsoid or interior point method, but its complexity is very high. The high computational complexity makes this solution unsuitable for practical application, so we propose a low complexity power allocation algorithm.

If the interference constraint is ignored in (7). Similarly, we use Lagrange multiplier, when the total transmission capacity is maximized, the power of the mth SU in the nth subcarrier is given by

$$p_{m,n}^1 = \left[\frac{1}{\alpha} - \frac{1}{H_{m,n}} \right]^+ \qquad (17)$$

where α is determined by

$$\sum_{m=1}^{M} \sum_{n=1}^{N} a_{m,n} p_{m,n}^1 = \sum_{m=1}^{M} \sum_{n \in \Phi_m} \left[\frac{1}{\alpha} - \frac{1}{H_{m,n}} \right]^+ = P_T \qquad (18)$$

Consequently,we can get

$$\alpha = \frac{N}{P_T + \sum_{m=1}^{M} \sum_{n \in \Phi_m} \frac{1}{H_{m,n}}} \qquad (19)$$

It is obvious that if the summation of the interference to PU under only the total power constraint is lower than or equal the interference constraint, i.e. $\sum_{m=1}^{M} \sum_{n=1}^{N} a_{m,n} p_{m,n}^1 K_{m,n} \leq I_{th}$, then (17) (19) will be the optimal solution with a given subcarrier assignment under the given total transmit power constraint and interference constraint.

Similarly, If the total power constraint is ignored in (7). we use Lagrange multiplier, the power of the mth SU in the nth subcarrier is given by

$$p_{m,n}^2 = \left[\frac{1}{\beta K_{m,n}} - \frac{1}{H_{m,n}} \right]^+ \qquad (20)$$

where β is determined by

$$\sum_{m=1}^{M} \sum_{n=1}^{N} a_{m,n} K_{m,n} \left[\frac{1}{\beta K_{m,n}} - \frac{1}{H_{m,n}} \right]^+ = I_{th} \qquad (21)$$

Therefore,we can get

$$\beta = \frac{N}{I_{th} + \sum_{m=1}^{M} \sum_{n \in \Phi_m} \frac{K_{m,n}}{H_{m,n}}} \qquad (22)$$

Similarly, if the summation of the allocated power under only the interference constraint is lower than or equal the available total power budget,, i.e. $\sum_{m=1}^{M} \sum_{n=1}^{N} a_{m,n} p_{m,n}^2 \leq P_T$, then (20)- (22) will also be the optimal solution with a given subcarrier assignment under the given total transmit power constraint and interference constraint.

It is assumed that P_T^{re} is the left available total power, I_{th}^{re} is the left interference constraint, Ω is the set of SU who need to be allocated power again, M^{re} is the number of SU who need to be allocated power again. The power allocation in JSPACF is described as follows.

1. Initialization
   Set $\Omega = \{1, 2, \cdots, M\}, M^{re} = M, P_T^{re} = P_T, I_{th}^{re} = I_{th}, p_{m,n} = 0, \forall m, \forall n$
2. while $M^{re} > 0$
   (a) Ignore the interference constraint, there are M^{re} SUs, through equations (17)(19), we get the power of the mth SU in the nth subcarrier $p_{m,n}^1$ only with the total power constraint P_T^{re}, if $\sum_{m \in \Omega} \sum_{n \in \Phi_m} a_{m,n} p_{m,n}^1 K_{m,n} \leq I_{th}^{re}$, the solution is found and $p_{m,n} = p_{m,n}^1$, else continue.
   (b) Ignore the total power constraint, there are M^{re} SUs, through equations (20)(22), we get the power of the mth SU in the nth subcarrier $p_{m,n}^2$ only with the interference constraint I_{th}^{re}, if $\sum_{m \in \Omega} \sum_{n \in \Phi_m} a_{m,n} p_{m,n}^2 \leq P_T^{re}$, the solution is found and $p_{m,n} = p_{m,n}^2$, else continue.
   (c) Set $p_{m,n} = \min \left(p_{m,n}^1, p_{m,n}^2 \right)$, calculate the transmission rate of the mth SU R_m through $R_m = \sum_{n=1}^{N} a_{m,n} r_{m,n}$.
   (d) Find m that satisfies $\frac{R_m}{\gamma_m} \geq \frac{R_i}{\gamma_i}$ for all $i \in \Omega$, for the found m, assign:
   $$\Omega = \Omega - \{m\}$$
   $$I_{th}^{re} = I_{th}^{re} - \sum_{n \in \Phi_m} a_{m,n} p_{m,n} K_{m,n}$$
   $$P_T^{re} = P_T^{re} - \sum_{n \in \Phi_m} a_{m,n} p_{m,n}$$
   $$M^{re} = M^{re} - 1$$

2.3   Complexity Analysis

For the optimization problem in (6)(7), if we use exhaustive search algorithm to find the optimal solution, there are M^N methods for subcarrier allocation. For a given subcarrier assignment, the complexity of the optimal power allocation algorithm is $O\left(N^3\right)$, so the complexity of the optimal solution in the optimization problem (6)(7) is $O\left(M^N N^3\right)$, which is very high. For JSPACF, the complexity of subcarrier allocation is $O\left(N\right)$, the complexity of power allocation is $O\left(MN \log N\right)$, so the total complexity of JSPACF is $O\left(MN \log N + N\right)$, which is much lower than the complexity of the optimal scheme.

3 Simulation Results

In the numerical results presented in this section, we assume the value of M and N to be 5 and 20 respectively, i.e., there are 5 SUs and 20 subcarriers. We assume the value of T_s to be 4 μs, and Δf ,B have been assigned the value of 0.3125MHz, 5MHz respectively. The channel noise is assumed to be AWGN, the value of σ^2 is assumed to be 10^{-6}. The value of amplitude P_{PU} is assumed to be 0.01W. The channel gains $h_{m,n}$,$g_{m,n}^{sp}$, and $g_{m,n}^{ps}$ are assumed to be Rayleigh fading with an average channel power gain equal to 1. For the proportional fairness,we assume that $\gamma_1 : \gamma_2 : \gamma_3 : \gamma_4 : \gamma_5 = 3 : 4 : 4 : 4 : 5$, so $R_1 : R_2 : R_3 : R_4 : R_5 \approx 3 : 4 : 4 : 4 : 5$. As is shown in table 1.

Table 1. Parameter Values

Parameter	M	N	T_s	Δf	B	σ^2	P_{PU}
Values	5	20	4 μs	$0.3125MHz$	$5MHz$	10^{-6}	$0.01W$

3.1 Subcarrier Allocation

The results of Subcarrier allocation is shown in Fig. 1. In simulation, it is assumed that the interference constraint of PU is 4mW, the total power constraint of SUs is 1W. there are 5 SUs and 20 subcarrier, $N_1^{\max} : N_2^{\max} : N_3^{\max} : N_4^{\max} : N_5^{\max} = \gamma_1 : \gamma_2 : \gamma_3 : \gamma_4 : \gamma_5$, so we can know that $N_1^{\max} = 3$, $N_2^{\max} = 4$, $N_3^{\max} = 4$, $N_4^{\max} = 4$, $N_5^{\max} = 5$. As is shown in Fig. 1, the subcarrier allocated to SU1 is 3, the subcarrier allocated to SU2 is 4, the subcarrier allocated to SU3 is 4, the subcarrier allocated to SU4 is 4, the subcarrier allocated to SU5 is 5, this is the same as the theory and it approximately guarantees proportional fairness among SUs, which is also shown in the simulation of fairness.

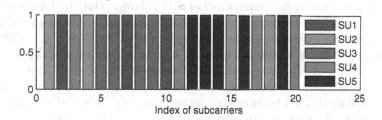

Fig. 1. The results of subcarrier allocation among SUs in JSPACF

3.2 Comparisons of Achievable Maximum Transmission Data Rates

In Fig. 2, we plot the achievable transmission rate of SUs versus the total power constraint of SUs for the optimal algorithm, JSPACF algorithm , and the classical resource allocation algorithm. In Fig. 2, the interference constraint of PU is fixed and is equal to 1mW. The relationship between the achievable transmission rate of SUs and interference constraint for the optimal algorithm, JSPACF algorithm , and the classical resource allocation algorithm, is shown in Fig. 3. In Fig. 3, the total power constraint of SUs is fixed and is equal to 2W. Here, by the classical resource allocation algorithm we mean the algorithm described in [7]. the classical resource allocation algorithm has not guaranteed the fairness among SUs. there is two steps in the classical resource allocation algorithm, the first step is subcarrier allocation for SUs, the second step is power allocation, which is optimal power allocation algorithm for a given subcarrier assignment.

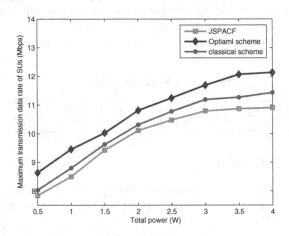

Fig. 2. The relationship between transmission rates of SUs and total power constraint

As shown in Fig. 2, In the same interference constraint of PU, the total transmission rate of SUs increases with the total power constraint of SUs increasing for different schemes under consideration, which is the same with the theory. The power allocated to every subcarrier is more when the total power constraint is larger, so the total transmission rates of SUs is larger. But the total transmission rates of SUs don't increase and are almost unchanged when the total power constraint increase to certain range. This is because with such a given interference constraint, the total power constraint is the main factor affecting the total transmission rates of SUs when the total power constraint is small, but when the total power constraint is increasing to certain range, the total transmission rates of SUs are mainly limited by interference threshold of primary users, and almost have nothing to do with the total power constraint. The system reach to the maximum total power that can be used to keep the interference to the primary user below the prescribed threshold. In the same interference threshold, the optimal scheme achieves the highest transmission rate for secondary users. It can be noted that the capacity achieved using JSPACF is close to that achieved using the optimal algorithm with a good reduction in the computational complexity. At the same time, the transmission rate that can be achieved using JSPACF is also close to that achieve by the classical algorithm. As mentioned before, there is two steps in the classical resource allocation algorithm, the complexity of the first step is $O(N)$, the complexity of the second step is $O(N^3)$, so the

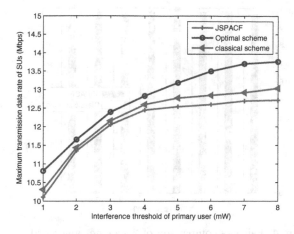

Fig. 3. The relationship between transmission rates of SUs and interference constraint

complexity of the classical resource allocation algorithm is $O\left(N^3 + N\right)$, which is higher than the complexity of JSPACF.

As shown in Fig. 3, In the same total power constraint of SUs, the total transmission rate of SUs increases with the interference constraint of SUs increasing for different schemes under consideration. The power allocated to every subcarrier is more when the interference constraint is larger as long as the total power of SUs is not beyond total power constraint, so the total transmission rates of SUs is larger. But the total transmission rates of SUs don't increase and are almost unchanged when the interference constraint increase to certain range. This is because the interference constraint is the main factor affecting the total transmission rates of SUs when the interference threshold is small, but the total transmission rates of SUs are mainly limited by the total power constraint, and almost have nothing to do with the interference threshold when the interference threshold is increasing to certain range.

3.3 Comparisons of Fairness

The comparison of fairness index versus two algorithms (JSPACF and the classical algorithm) can be seen from Fig. 4. From Fig. 4, we can see that JSPACF significantly improves fairness compared to the the classical algorithm, and the fairness index of JSPACF is very close to 1 (maximum value of 1 is the greatest fairness), so all SUs can almost achieve the same proportional data rate in JSPACF. This is due to the fact that the subcarrier allocation and the power allocation in JSPACF are all considering the proportional fairness, so as to improve fairness among the SUs. As mentioned before, the transmission rate that can be achieved using JSPACF is a little lower than that achieve by the classical algorithm, so we can know that there is always a trade-off between the performance and the fairness among SUs.

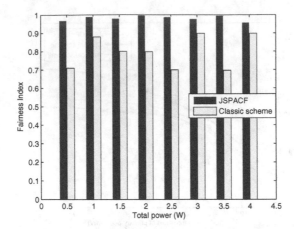

Fig. 4. Fairness comparison of 2 schemes among SUs

4   Conclusion

In this paper, we investigate the resource (subcarrier and power) allocation algorithm in the cellular transmission scenario with a single cell for OFDM-based cognitive radio systems, our objective is maximize the transmission data rate of secondary users, and We have augmented the optimization formulation of this problem by taking into account the fairness among SUs. we propose a joint subcarrier and power allocation algorithm considering fairness among secondary users (SUs) for OFDM-based Cognitive radio networks. In JSPACF, we allocate the subcarriers to SUs in the first step, not only considering the channel gain and the interference introduced to primary users (PUs) by SUs, but also considering proportional fairness among SUs. Then in the second step, we allocate the power to the subcarriers to maximize sum capacity of all SUs with total power constraint and interference constraint, considering proportional fairness among SUs too. Theory analysis and simulation results show that JSPACF can offer the beneficial tradeoff between system performance and fairness, while largely reducing complexity compared to the optimal solution.

Acknowledgments. The paper is supported by the National Hi-Tech Research and Development Plan of China under the Grant 2009AA011801, the National Natural Science Foundation of China under the Grant 60832007, and the National Science and Technology Major Project of China under the Grant 2010ZX03005-003.

References

1. Federal Communications Commission Spectrum Policy Task Force, FCC Report of the Spectrum Efficiency Working Group (November 2002)
2. Haykin, S.: Cognitive radio: Brain-Empowered Wireless Communications. IEEE Journal on Selected Areas in Communications 23(2), 201–220 (2005)

3. Zhao, Q., Sadler, B.: A survey of dynamic spectrum access: signal processing, networking, and regulatory policy. IEEE Signal Processing Magazine 55(5),
   2294–2309 (2007)
4. Keller, T., Hanzo, L.: Multicarrier modulation: a convenient framework for time-
   frequency processing in wireless communications. Proc. IEEE 88(5), 611–640 (2000)
5. Bansal, G., Hossain, M.J., Bhargava, V.K.: Optimal and Suboptimal Power Allocation Schemes for OFDM-based Cognitive Radio Systems. IEEE Transactions on
   Wireless Communication 7(11), Part 2, 4710–4718 (2008)
6. Hasan, Z., Bansal, G., Hossain, E.: Energy-Efficient Power Allocation in OFDM-
   Based Cognitive Radio Systems: A Risk-Return Model. IEEE Transactions on
   Wireless Communication, 6078–6088 (July 2009)
7. Bansal, G., Hasan, Z., Hossain, M.J., et al.: Subcarrier and Power Adaptation
   for Multiuser OFDM-based Cognitive Radio Systems. In: National Conference on
   Communications, Chennai, India (January 2010)
8. Shaat, M., Bader, F.: A Two-Step Resource Allocation Algorithm in Multicarrier
   Based Cognitive Radio Systems. In: IEEE Communications Society Subject Matter
   Experts for Publication in the WCNC 2010 (February 2010)
9. Lin, Y.Q., Zhu, Q.: Joint Power and Channel Allocation Based on Fair Sharing
   in Cognitive Radio System. In: International Conference on Wireless Communications, Networking and Mobile Computing, Beijing, China, pp. 1573–1576 (September 2009)
10. Mao, X., Si, P., Ji, H., et al.: A two-step resource allocation in multiuser OFDM-
    based cognitive radio systems. In: 7th ISWCS, pp. 996–1000 (2010)
11. Tang, L., Wang, H., Chen, Q.: Subcarrier and power allocation for OFDM-based
    cognitive radio networks. In: IEEE ICCTA, Beijing, China, pp. 457–461 (October
    2009)
12. Weiss, T., Hillenbrand, J., Krohn, A., Jondral, F.K.: Mutual interference in
    OFDM-based spectrum pooling systems. In: IEEE VTC Proc., Milan, Italy, vol. 4,
    pp. 1873–1877 (May 2004)
13. Shen, Z.K., Andrews, J.G., Evans, B.L.: Adaptive resource allocation in multiuser
    OFDM systems with proportional rate constraints. IEEE Transactions on Wireless
    Communications, 2726–2737 (November 2005)
14. Shum, K.W., Leung, K.K., Sung, C.W.: Convergence of iterative waterfilling al-
    gorithm for gaussian interference channels. IEEE Journal on Selected Areas in
    Communications 25(6), 1091–1100 (2007)

Analysis and Implementation of a Precise Paging Mode in Co-LAC for 2G/3G Convergence Core Networks with Path Diversity

Yu Su and Xian Feng

School of Marine Engineering, Northwestern Polytechnical University
Xi'an 710072, China
sy906@hotmail.com

Abstract. Nowadays the 2G/3G interoperability has been enabled over the real networks. However, as there are many 2G/3G borders in the same area, especially in the same location, too much extra network traffic is caused by paging signals and location updates within the 2G and 3G networks. In this paper, we propose a new method to reduce the traffic of both paging signal and update messages by path diversity. Theoretical analysis is shown and implementation results are also given.

Keywords: Precise paging, Update message, Path diversity.

1   Introduction

In the early phase of TD core network construction, macro coverage and indoor coverage have not been optimized. When 2G/3G interoperability is enabled on the network, there are many 2G/3G borders in the same area, especially in the same location area (LA). As a result, a great number of location updates and paging signals occur between 2G and 3G networks [1]-[4].

Users are unreachable during location update. Therefore, the voice call completion rate of the TD network decreases badly, and user experience is also affected. It is possible to set location area codes (LACs) of 2G and 3G networks uniformly in areas in which this problem is rather severe to enable co-routing. In this manner, terminals in idle state do not perform immediate routing area update after cell reselection within the same routing area. Terminals initiate routing area update only when the network side initiates paging or terminals initiate services. This can reduce routing area update signaling caused by reselection. In the actual networking, however, when the core network performs paging based on LACs, paging messages are delivered over the 2G and 3G networks concurrently. Extra invalid paging messages bring paging congestion on the 2G network and radio side of the TD network, therefore affecting the paging success ratio.

As a result, in this paper we determine to adopt precise paging mode based on co-LAC for 2G/3G to meet network requirements and improve user experience. We make an analysis of the reduction of paging signals and update messages by path diversity. And the implementation is also done, where the results prove the efficiency of our proposal.

P. Ren et al. (Eds.): WICON 2011, LNICST 98, pp. 58–66, 2012.

2   Concept and Principle

2.1   Concept of LAC

On a cell-based mobile communications network, a great number of base transceiver stations (BTSs) are deployed, and mobile stations are not fixed. When mobile users are in the service area regardless of where they move, the mobile communications network must perform the switching control function to implement location update (registration), cross-cell handover, and automatic roaming. The following figure shows the definition of areas in a GSM network.

An LA can consist of one or several cells (or BTS areas). To call a mobile station, all the BTSs in the same LA can send paging signals concurrently.

The identity of an LA is referred to as location area identity (LAI). An LAI consists of three parts: mobile country code (MCC), which is of three numbers and identifies the country to which a mobile user belongs; mobile network code (MNC), which identifies the mobile network to which a mobile user belongs; LAC, which identifies an LA on a GSM Public Land Mobile Network (PLMN). The LAC is the most important portion of an LAI. Therefore, an LA is often referred to as an LAC, and co-LAC means co-LA.

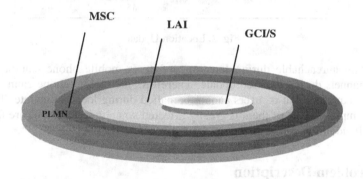

Fig. 1. Areas in a GSM network

2.2   Concept of Location Update

Due to MS mobility, it is important to locate an MS. Only after the current location of an MS is known, connection to the called MS can be set up.

Roaming refers to the feature that a mobile user requests changing of the connection to the cell and network during movement. Location update refers to changing of an LA during roaming and LA confirmation. A mobile switching center (MSC) does not need to be informed of movement within the same LA but movement between cells of different LAs. Location update is primarily composed of the following:

When an MS detects that its LAI is to be updated, the MS sets up a connection with the MSC/visitor location register (VLR) proactively. Then, the MS sends a request, and data on the VLR is updated. If the LAI belongs to different MSCs/VLRs, data on the home location register (HLR) also needs to be updated. After update, the connection between the MS and the BTS is released.

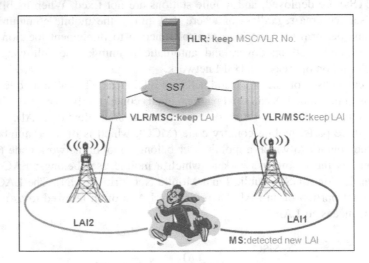

Fig. 2. Location Update

Users are unreachable during location update (a mobile phone cannot listen on paging channels during location update. Therefore, the mobile phone cannot respond to paging requests), that is, users cannot be called during location update. Therefore, the call completion rate of them is greatly affected when their locations are frequently updated. In addition, communications are badly affected.

3   Problem Description

3.1   Problems of Update Message

1) Different LACs for 2G/3G

As shown in the preceding figure, in the scenario of different LACs for 2G/3G, the chance of TD-to-GSM cell reselection is limited in the area covered by the TD network continuously. Therefore, location update messages for the GSM network do not increase significantly. TD cells are preferred. Therefore, the chance of GSM-to-TD cell reselection is also limited. Consequently, location update messages for the TD network do not increase significantly, either.

At the coverage edge of the TD network, dual-mode terminal users who enter TD network coverage all initiate location update and register with the TD network because TD cells are preferred. Users who leave the TD network need to initiate location update on the GSM network and register with the GSM network. Compared with GSM and TD networks, location updates increase greatly at the TD network border.

The GSM network provides an extensive coverage, and GSM users seldom need to switch to the TD network. During the early phase of the TD network, there is a big gap between the coverage of the TD network and that of the GSM network, and TD users often need to reselect cells or switch to the GSM network. In this case, location updates occur. Especially in the same geographical area where different LAs are used for GSM and TD, TD users are more likely to reselect cells or switch to the GSM network. Therefore, a great number of location updates occur.

Paging to users is performed on the basis of LAs on the GSM or TD network. LAs are set separately. Therefore, the TD network is responsible for only paging users who really register with the TD network. Users are unreachable during location update. A mobile phone cannot respond to paging messages during location update. Therefore, in the preceding scenario in which location updates increase, the voice call completion rate of the TD network decreases badly, and user experience is also affected. Therefore, the solution of co-LAC for 2G/3G needs to be introduced to solve this problem.

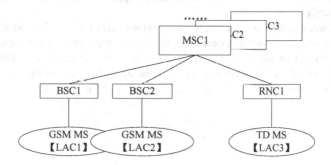

Fig. 3. Different LACs for 2G/3G

2) Co-LAC for 2G/3G

See the preceding figure. At the coverage edge and areas without coverage or weak coverage of the TD network, dual-mode terminal users who enter the TD network coverage initiate inter-RAT cell reselection and select the TD network. This is because the TD network is preferred. The core network, however, is not informed of the reselection. Users who leave the TD network also initiate inter-RAT cell reselection and reselect the GSM network. The core network is not informed of the reselection either.

Advantages of co-LAC: When a user performs cell reselection between 2G and 3G wireless systems, the user does not need to initiate location update to the core network. This is because the LAC does not change and the core network does not need to be informed of LAI change. In addition, the delay of system reselection is very short. Therefore, the possibility that paging and system reselection (including location update) occur concurrently can be minimized. In this manner, the paging success ratio increases and the completion rate of calls can be improved.

There are three types of location updates: normal location updates (cross-LA), periodical location updates, and International Mobile Subscriber Identity (IMSI) attachment (corresponding to the process of terminal power-on). In the case of co-LAC for GSM and TD networks, the number of periodical location updates and IMSI attachments do not change greatly. This is because mobile phones complete these two types of location updates within their own networks. The major change is that normal location updates decrease. This is because in the same LAC, location updates do not occur just because a TD user reselects cells or switches to the GSM network due to weak signals or insufficient coverage. This also excludes the possibility of call drop due to location update. In the early phase of TD network construction, this can greatly improve the service experience of TD users.

Because the LAC is shared, when the core network pages a piece of user equipment (UE), the core network needs to perform paging over the entire LA, including the coverage areas of both TD and GSM networks.

The GSM network needs to serve users who register with the TD network. Although these paging messages are not responded to, they occupy the paging channels of the GSM network. Considering the small number of users in the early phase of the TD network, the impact on the GSM network is limited after co-LAC deployment. With the increase in the number of TD users, the paging capability of the GSM network may decrease inevitably.

The TD network needs to serve users who register with the GSM network. Although these paging messages are not responded to, they occupy the paging channels of the TD network. The impact to the TD network is great because the number of GSM users is multiple times that of the TD network. To prevent invalid paging in the scenario of co-LAC, the solution of precise paging for co-LAC needs to be introduced.

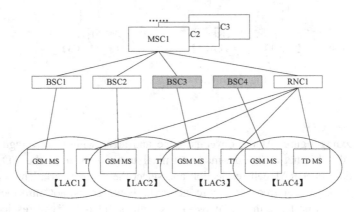

Fig. 4. Co-LAC for 2G/3G

3.2   Problems of Paging Signal

When a mobile phone performs location update in a co-LAC area, the core network obtains parameters of the mobile phone, including classmark1 and classmark3, and saves the parameters to the data area of the VLR.

During paging delivery in the LA for the mobile phone, the MSC determines whether the mobile phone is a GSM-only one. If yes, the paging is sent to only the BSC in Fig.5.

If the mobile phone is not a GSM-only one or the terminal type is not reported, the MSC sends paging to both the BSC and the RNC concurrently in Fig.6.

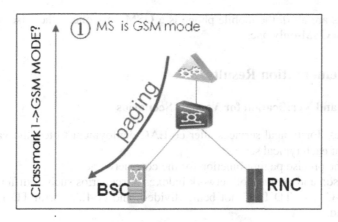

Fig. 5. Conventional method for paging signal

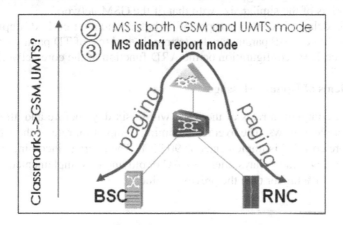

Fig. 6. Proposal to determine the type of a mobile phone

During location update, the MSC obtains the revision level from classmark1 in the location update message sent from the mobile phone. Revision level is a two-bit parameter. When its value is 01 (GSM PHASE 1) or 10 (GSM PHASE 2), the mobile phone is a GSM-only one.

When its value is not 01 (GSM PHASE 1) or 10 (GSM PHASE 2), you can determine the mobile phone type based on the following parameters in classmark3 reported by the mobile phone. If the mobile phone does not report classmark 3, the MSC can send the classmark update message to obtain this parameter proactively.

UMTS FDD Radio Access Technology Capability
CDMA 2000 Radio Access Technology Capability
UMTS 3.84 Mcps TDD Radio Access Technology Capability
UMTS 1.28 Mcps TDD Radio Access Technology Capability

The preceding parameters represent a special 3G radio access technology. If the preceding bits are 1, the mobile phone supports this radio access technology. If the preceding bits are all 0, the mobile phone is a GSM-only one. Otherwise, the mobile phone is not a GSM-only one.

4   Implementation Results

4.1   Tests and Verification for Various Scenarios

Regression test for typical services after co-LAC deployment to test the validity and consistency of each typical service

Test of the precise paging function for the core network

Comparison and analysis of network indexes in scenarios such as different LACs, co-LAC with TD LAC not being divided, and co-LAC with TD LAC being divided.

The LA of a TD network is greater than that of a GSM network. LA division refers to dividing a large LA into several smaller LAs so that the LA of the TD network is of the similar size with that of the GSM network.

Change in delay of 2G/3G interoperability before and after co-LAC deployment

Compatibility of PBP parameters for terminals, and test of TD paging capacity

Effect of co-LAC configuration on the ARD function of the core network

4.2   Problems of Update Message

The incoming completion rates of the RNC within six days before and after co-LAC deployment are as follows. The average incoming completion rate of the RNC within six days before co-LAC is implemented is 90.92%. The average incoming completion rate of the RNC within six days after co-LAC deployment is implemented is 93.06%. This value is 2.14% higher than the previous value

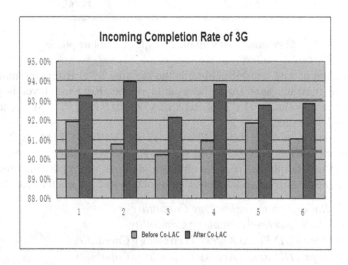

Fig. 7. Incoming completion rates of the RNC within six days before and after co-LAC

The paging success rates in the entire region in four scenarios within six days are collected. The preceding data indicates: The average paging success rate in the entire region within six days is 95.74% in scenario 1, 97.26% in scenario 2, 95.32% in scenario, and 96.46% in scenario 4.The success rate in scenario 2 is 1.5% higher than that in scenario 1. The success rate in scenario 2 is 0.8% higher than that in scenario 4.

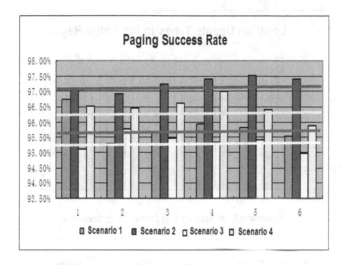

Fig. 8. Paging success rates in the entire region

The success rates of location update in the entire region in four scenarios within six days are all higher than 97%.

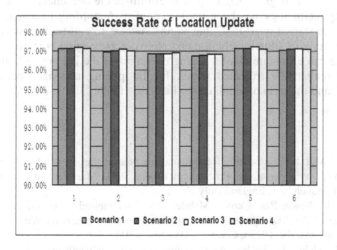

Fig. 9. Success rates of location update

Times of location update in the entire region in four scenarios within six days are collected. The average value is 3094353 times in scenario 1, 2887721 times in scenario

2, 3102822 times in scenario 3, and 3048604 times in scenario 4. The number of location update times in the entire region in scenario 2 is the smallest, which is 160883 (about 5.3%) smaller than that in scenario 4, 206632 (about 6.7%) smaller than that in scenario 1, and 215101 (6.9%) smaller than that in scenario 3.

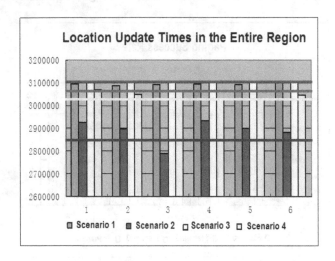

Fig. 10. Times of location update in the entire region

5   Conclusions

The proposed precise paging technology can eliminate the bottleneck of co-LAC. The precise paging technology has been implemented o. According to actual test, when precise paging is started in co-LAC, the paging success rate of the live network is not affected. The study of situations before and after precise paging is started shows that precise paging can eliminate invalid paging messages of the 2G network upon the 3G network and realize the expected target. Invalid paging messages decrease from 78432 to 705, and the ratio of valid paging increases to 48.23% from 47%.

References

[1] Hacklin, F., Marxt, C.: Assessing R&D management strategies for wireless applications in a converging environment. In: Proceedings of The R&D Management Conference 2003 (RADMA), Manchester, England (July 2003)
[2] Koljonen, T.: Nokia Res. Center, Mobile system technologies beyond current 3G. In: Proceedings of the 2001 Symposium on Applications and the Internet-Workshops (SAINT 2001 Workshops), San Diego, CA, USA (January 2001)
[3] Nguyen, T., Mehra, P., Zakhor, A.: Path diversity and bandwidthallocation for multimedia streaming. In: Proceedings of ICME 2003, (July 2003); Elissa, K.: Title of paper if known (unpublished)
[4] Wang, Y., Panwar, S., Lin, S., Mao, S.: Wireless video transportusing path diversity multiple description vs layered coding. In: Proceedings of IEEE ICIP (2002)

Peak-to-Average Power-Ratio Reduction Scheme Employing Fountain Codes

Juan Zhou, Ying Shen, and Youxi Tang

National Key Lab of Science and Technol. on Commun.,
University of Electronic Science and Technology of China
Chengdu, China
{zhoujuan06,shenying,tangyx}@uestc.edu.cn

Abstract. New peak-to-average power-ratio (PAPR) reduction scheme for multiuser CDMA systems are developed by employing fountain codes. In the proposed scheme, the transmission data is encoded by the fountain code. The encoded data is discarded at the transmitter if the PAPR exceeds the specified threshold, and at the same time another encoded data will be created. In consequence, the PAPR is dominated below the threshold. From the simulation methods, we find that the proposed scheme can reduce the PAPR with no degradation on the performance.

Keywords: PAPR, fountain codes, reduction.

1 Introduction

The multiuser DS/CDMA (Direct Sequence Code Division Multiple Access) wireless systems are known to show high capacities and good performances against the time dispersion effects of multipath propagation [1][2]. However, envelope fluctuations and peak-to-average power-ratio (PAPR) of multiuser CDMA signals can be very high when we combine a large number of signals with different spreading codes. A number of approaches have been proposed to deal with the PAPR problem. These techniques include amplitude clipping [3], clipping and filtering [4], coding[5], and so on. These techniques achieve PAPR reduction at the expense of transmit signal power increase, bit error rate (BER) increase, data rate loss, and so on. In this paper, we propose a new scheme to reduce the PAPR without loss in receiver performance, transmit signal power or data rate.

In the proposed scheme, the fountain code is employed to implement the PAPR reduction. As mentioned in [6][7], the key feature of fountain codes is their so-called rateless property: an arbitrary number of code symbols can be generated from a given set of information symbols. The rateless property means that a transmitter can simply transmit code symbols until each receiver has enough unerased symbols to recover the associated information symbols. Here in this paper, we make use of this feature to generate enough encoded data satisfying the PAPR requirement. We first determine the PAPR threshold and encode rate. If the PAPR of the encoded data exceed the

P. Ren et al. (Eds.): WICON 2011, LNICST 98, pp. 67–72, 2012.

PAPR threshold, then the encoded data is discarded, otherwise, is reserved for transmission. This process persists until the reserved transmit data are enough to meet the specified encode rate. As a result of the application of fountain codes, the PAPR reduction is restricted under the PAPR threshold.

The rest of this paper is organized as follows. The system model is introduced in Section 2. The proposed PAPR reduction scheme employing fountain codes is studied in Section 3 and Section 4 provides numerical results. Finally in Section 5 we present the conclusion.

2   System Model

In this new PAPR reduction scheme, the system model contains two parts: the transmitter and receiver. Since the receiver is the same as the conventional receiver, as depicted in Fig. 1, we emphasis on the transmitter in this paper.

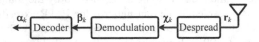

Fig. 1. Receiver of User k

Consider a multiuser CDMA transmitter with K users data to be transmitted as illustrated in Fig. 2 where the FC represents the frame controller and CS denotes that the PAPR of the data is compared with the PAPR threshold and then saved if lower than the PAPR threshold.

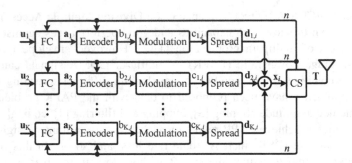

Fig. 2. Multiuser CDMA Transmitter. (FC represents frame controller. CS denotes that the PAPR of the data is compared with the PAPR threshold and then saved if lower than the PAPR threshold)

As for user k ($k=1,2,...,K$), the pth frame from the FC is $\mathbf{a}_{k,p} = \left[a_{k,p,1}, a_{k,p,2}, \cdots, a_{k,p,q}\right]_{1\times q}$, where q is the number of bits in a frame. The frame data is first encoded by fountain coded, which is given as

$$b_{k,p,i} = \mathbf{a}_{k,p} \mathbf{G}_i .$$ (1)

where $\mathbf{G}$ is the $q \times w$ generation matrix of fountain codes, and $\mathbf{G}_i$ is the ith row of $\mathbf{G}$. After BPSK modulation, we get

$$c_{k,p,i} = 1 - 2b_{k,p,i} .$$ (2)

The modulated data is then spread

$$\mathbf{d}_{k,p,i} = c_{k,p,i} \mathbf{\Psi}_k .$$ (3)

where $\mathbf{\Psi}_k = \left[\psi_{k,1}, \psi_{k,2}, \cdots, \psi_{k,N} \right]_{1 \times N}$ is thespreading code for user k and N is the length of the spreading code. Summing up the data of all the users, we have

$$\mathbf{x}_{p,i} = \sum_{k=1}^{K} \mathbf{d}_{k,p,i} = \left[x_{p,i,1}, x_{p,i,2}, \cdots, x_{p,i,N} \right]_{1 \times N} .$$ (4)

The PAPR of $\mathbf{x}_{p,i}$ is calculated and compared with the given PAPR threshold $PAPR_t$. If $PAPR_{\mathbf{x},p,i} \leq PAPR_t$, the number of qualified data should be increased and $\mathbf{T}_{p,m+1} = \mathbf{x}_{p,i}$ is saved for transmitting. Otherwise, keep the value of m and delete $\mathbf{x}_{p,i}$. For simplicity, we assume the delete position i will be broadcast to all the users. The change of m corresponding to each case can be expressed as

$$m = \begin{cases} m+1 & \text{if} \quad PAPR_{\mathbf{x},p,i} \leq PAPR_t \\ m & \text{if} \quad PAPR_{\mathbf{x},p,i} > PAPR_t \end{cases} .$$ (5)

m is feedback to determine the work of the frame controller and fountain encoder. If the m reaches the specified number M, the frame controller will chose next frame $\mathbf{a}_{k,p+1}$ data to process, meanwhile, the encoder will stop the encoding work on the present frame and all the saved data $\mathbf{T} = [\mathbf{T}_{p,1}, \mathbf{T}_{p,2}, ..., \mathbf{T}_{p,N}]$ are transmitted immediately. Here, the number M is determined by the coding rate r and frame length q, that is $M=q/r$. Otherwise, the encoder will do the fountain coding on the present frame $\mathbf{a}_{k,p}$. The detail on the implementation of PAPR reduction scheme will be described later in Section 3.

3 Proposed PAPR Reduction Scheme

In this section, the new PAPR reduction scheme employing fountain codes is presented. According to system requirement, we first predetermined the PAPR threshold $PAPR_t$, the coding rate r, the required number of qualified data M, and the frame length q. Then under the system model described in Section 2, the proposed scheme is summarized as follows:

1) *Initialization.* Get new frames $\mathbf{a}_{k,p}$ (k=1,2,...,K) for all the users, and let the qualified data number counter m=0, the encoder time number counter i=0.

2) *Encoding of fountain codes, BPSK modulation, spread, and summing up to get* $\mathbf{x}_{p,i}$, *give by eqn. (4).*

3) *PAPR calculation.* The PAPR of $\mathbf{x}_{p,i}$ can be calculated as

$$PAPR_{\mathbf{x},p,i}(dB) = 10 \, \log_{10} \left(\frac{\max_{j=1,2,\cdots,N} \left\{ \left| x_{p,i,j} \right|^2 \right\}}{E \left| \mathbf{x}_{p,i} \right|^2} \right). \tag{6}$$

where $E\left[\left| \mathbf{x}_{p,i} \right|^2 \right] = \sum_{j=1}^{N} \left| x_{p,i,j} \right|^2 \Big/ N$

4) *PAPR comparison.* Compare $PAPR_{\mathbf{x},p,i}$ with the PAPR threshold $PAPR_t$, and

   a) If $PAPR_{\mathbf{x},p,i} \le PAPR_t$: It denotes the PAPR of the data fulfilling the system requirement. We first let m=m+1, and then save the data $\mathbf{T}_{p,m+1} = \mathbf{x}_{p,i}$.

     • If m=M, meaning the saved data num is enough, $\mathbf{T} = [\mathbf{T}_{p,1}, \mathbf{T}_{p,2}, ..., \mathbf{T}_{p,N}]$ are transmitted immediately and the positions for the deletion data are broadcast. At the same time, frame controller and encoder get the information that the processing on the present frame is completed. The encoder stops the encoding work on the present frame. The frame controller gets the next frame, let p=p+1 and return to step 1).

     • If m<M, meaning the saved data num is not enough, the encoding num $i=i+1$ and the encoder continues the encoding work on the present frame. The frame controller still keeps the present frame. Return to step 2).

   b) If $PAPR_{\mathbf{x},p,i} > PAPR_t$: It denotes the PAPR is not meeting the requirement. We delete the $\mathbf{x}_{p,i}$, and record the delete position i. The encoding num i=i+1 and the encoder continues the encoding work on the present frame. The frame controller still keeps the present frame. Return to step 2).

This proposed PAPR reduction scheme benefits the communication system in several ways: i) Reducing the PAPR effectively. ii) No performance degradation due to PAPR reduction. iii) The receiver of user is the same as before.

4   Simulation Results

In this section, we present simulation results of the proposed scheme. Consider a network of K=16 users, the coding rate r=1/2, the required number of qualified data M=20, and the frame length q=10.

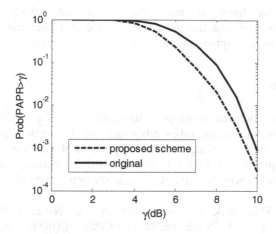

Fig. 3. CCDF plot of proposed PAPR reduction scheme

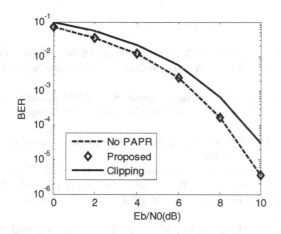

Fig. 4. BER of multiple CDMA signals. "No PAPR" represents no PAPR reduction on the signals. "Proposed" means that the proposed PAPR reduction scheme is performed on the signals. "Clipping" denotes the conventional clipping PAPR reduction is executed on the signals.

Fig. 3 depicts the complementary cumulative distribution function (CCDF) of the proposed PAPR reduction scheme. In the simulation, the baseband samples are deleted if the amplitude is larger than the threshold. Here the threshold is assumed to be 6.4. From this figure we can find that the scheme can reduce the PAPR effectively. The choice of the threshold is a matter of convenience, other thresholds can be applied according to the system requirement.

Fig. 4 depicts the bit error rate (BER) performance comparison between the proposed scheme and the conventional clipping scheme. In the simulation, the amplitude threshold for clipping method is the same as that of the proposed scheme. From Fig. 4, we can see that the proposed scheme does not impact the system performance, whereas, the clipping method declines the performance.

5   Conclusion

In this paper, a new scheme employing fountain codes for PAPR reduction is proposed. The proposed scheme takes advantage of the rateless property of the fountain codes, and delete the samples if the amplitudes of which are larger than the threshold. In consequence, the PAPR is reduced with no performance degradation. Meanwhile, the proposed scheme will not increase the complexity of the receiver.

Acknowledgment. This work was supported by the National Natural Science Foundation of China (No.U1035002/L05, No.60832007, No.60901018, No.61001087, and No.60902027).

References

1. Viterbi, A.J.: CDMA: Principles of SS Communication. Addison Wesley (1995)
2. Karim, M.R., Sarraf, M.: W-CDMA and cdma2000 for 3G Mobile Networks. McGraw-Hill (2002)
3. Dinis, R., Gusmao, A.: On the Performance Evaluation of OFDM Transmission Using Clipping Techniques. In: Pro. Veh. Techol. Conf. (VTC), Amsterdam, Netherhnds, pp. 2923–2928 (September 1999)
4. Li, X., Cimini Jr., L.J.: Effect of Clipping and Filtering on the Performance of OFDM. IEEE Commun. Lett. 2, 131–133 (1998)
5. Davis, J.A., Jedwab, J.: Peak-to-Mean Power Control in OFDM, Golay Complementary Sequences, and Reed–Muller Codes. IEEE Trans. Info. Theory 45, 2397–2417 (1999)
6. Luby, M.: LT codes. In: Proc. 43rd Annual IEEE Symp. Foundations Computer Science (FOCS), pp. 271–282 (2002)
7. Byers, J.W., Luby, M., Mitzenmacher, W.: A digital fountain approach to asynchronous reliable multicast. IEEE J. Select. Areas Commun. 20, 1528–1540 (2002)
8. Han, S.H., Lee, J.H.: An overview of peak-to-average power ratio reduction techniques for multicarrier transmission. IEEE Wireless Comm. 12, 56–65 (2005)

Antenna Location Design for Distributed Antenna Systems Based on Timing Acquisition

Tian Xia[1], Chaojin Qing[1,2], Shihai Shao[1], Mintao Zhang[2], and Youxi Tang[1]

[1] National Key Lab of Communications,
University of Electronic Science and Technology of China, Chengdu 610054, China
qingchj@uestc.edu.cn
[2] School of Electrical and Information Engineering,
Xihua University, Chengdu, 610039, China

Abstract. We address the antenna location problem for distributed antenna systems based on timing acquisition in frequency selective channel. Coarse timing estimation is performed for the orthogonal frequency division multiplexing system. The probability of worst case is introduced in terms of the probability of correct detection of each distributed receive antenna. A minimax criterion is proposed to provide the optimal antenna locations in a sense that it offers the best system performance that the probability of worst case is minimized. Simulation results illustrate that the distributed receive antennas should be located symmetrically about the linear cell when the mobile station distribution is uniform. The optimal antenna locations also show robustness to carrier frequency offset.

Keywords: antenna location design, distributed antenna systems, OFDM, minimax criterion.

1   Introduction

Distributed antenna system (DAS) is increasingly gaining interest from academic researchers for its attractive merits such as increased system capacity, lowered transmit power, and enhanced cell coverage [1], [2]. Whether these advantages can be realized is directly affected by antenna locations. In order to achieve the optimal system performance under certain criterion, we need carefully design distributed antennas locations.

In [3], the antenna location design problem was investigated for two transmit antennas in a linear cell to minimize the area averaged bit error probability (AABEP). This work is then extended to a more general scenario called generalized DAS (GDAS) in [4], where the authors proposed a squared distance criterion (SDC) to maximize the cell averaged ergodic capacity. The method proposed in [5] is similar to [3] whereas a circular cell and more than 2 antennas are considered. However, they all assume the timing and frequency synchronization is perfectly accomplished, which is not a trivial task in distributed antenna systems. In synchronization process, timing acquisition is the first and crucial step the receive antenna takes and directly determines the performance of following procedures [6].

P. Ren et al. (Eds.): WICON 2011, LNICST 98, pp. 73–81, 2012.
© Institute for Computer Sciences, Social Informatics and Telecommunications Engineering 2012

This paper deals with distributed antenna location design problem based on timing acquisition for the orthogonal frequency division multiplexing (OFDM) system. The probability of worst case, denoted as P_{WC}, is derived in term of the probability of correct detection of each antenna. Optimal antenna locations can then be obtained by minimizing the probability of worst case P_{WC} for every possible combination of antenna locations. Simulation results show that the optimal antenna locations ought to be located symmetrically about the linear cell center, when the mobile station (MS) distribution is uniform. The optimal antenna locations are also robust for several trial values of carrier frequency offset.

The rest of the paper is organized as follows. Section 2 describes the system model. Section 3 develops the process of timing acquisition. In section 4, the minimax criterion is proposed. Section 5 provides the simulation results. Section 6 concludes this paper.

2   System Model

We consider a linear cell as shown in Fig. 1. The length of the linear cell is R. The distributed receive antenna, denoted as RX_i, is placed at a_i. A MS is at position x.

The OFDM symbol at the output of the inverse fast fourier transform (IFFT) transmitted from the MS is given by

$$x(k) = \frac{1}{\sqrt{N}} \sum_{n=0}^{N-1} X_n e^{j2\pi nk/N}, \quad -N_g \leq k \leq N-1, \tag{1}$$

where N is the total number of subcarriers, X_n represents the data symbol transmitted on the nth subcarrier, and N_g is the length of guard interval, which is designed longer than the maximum channel delay spread to avoid intersymbol interference (ISI). The transmit power is $E\{|x(k)|^2\} = \sigma_s^2$.

We consider a composite channel model, which comprises path loss, shadow fading, and multipath fading. The channel fading coefficient between the MS and RX_i can then be expressed as [4]

$$g_i = \sqrt{\frac{cs_i}{D_i^\alpha}} H_i, \quad i = 1, 2, \tag{2}$$

where c is a constant, s_i is a log-normal random variable representing shadow fading, i.e., $10\log_{10} s_i$ is a zero-mean Gaussian random variable with standard deviation σ_{sh}, α is the path loss exponent, D_i is the effective distance from the MS to RX_i, which is given by [4]

$$D_i = \max\{d_0, d_i\}, \tag{3}$$

where d_i is the distance between the MS and RX_i, d_0 is the minimum allowable value of d_i. Multipath fading H_i can be written as

$$H_i = [h_i(0), h_i(1), \cdots, h_i(l_i), \cdots, h_i(L_i - 1)], \tag{4}$$

where $h_i(l_i)$ is the channel tap and L_i is the duration of channel impulse response.

The signal received by RX_i can be represented as

$$r_i(k) = e^{j2\pi\varepsilon_i k/N} y_i(k) + w_i(k), \tag{5}$$

where

$$y_i(k) = \sum_{l_i=0}^{L_i-1} \sqrt{\frac{cs_i}{D_i^\alpha}} h_i(l_i) x(k - l_i - \tau_i), \tag{6}$$

where ε_i is the frequency offset normalized to the subcarrier spacing, τ_i is the symbol timing offset between the MS and RX_i, and $w_i(k)$ is complex additive white Gaussian noise (AWGN) with zero mean and variance σ_{iw}^2.

Fig. 1. Linear cell layout

3 Timing Acquisition

3.1 Training Symbols

In [7], training symbol is specifically designed for OFDM timing acquisition, which comprise L identical part and have a specific pattern (signs). The identical structure is desirable as it is robust to possible large carrier frequency offset when auto-correlation method is applied. Since training symbol structure is not the major point of this paper and it matters little when cross-correlation approach is employed, we simply select the polyphase codes introduced by CHU [8] as the training symbol for its perfect auto-correlation property.

3.2 Cross-Correlation

The cross-correlation method in [9] is employed. The cross-correlation between the received signal and the training symbol is given by

$$C_i(m) = \sum_{k=0}^{N-1} r_i(k+m)s^*(k)$$
$$= P_i(m) + W_i(m), \quad m \in [0, U - N], \tag{7}$$

where

$$P_i(m) = \sum_{k=0}^{N-1} e^{j2\pi\varepsilon_i k/N} y_i(k+m)s^*(k), \tag{8}$$

$$W_i(m) = \sum_{k=0}^{N-1} w_i(k+m)s^*(k), \tag{9}$$

where U represents the the observation window which is sufficiently long to accommodate at least two symbols with CP, $W_i(m)$ is AWGN with zero mean and variance $N\sigma_{iw}^2$ as $w_i(k+m)s^*(k)$ has the same statistic with $w_i(k+m)$.

3.3 Timing Acquisition

The timing offset estimate can be found by searching the maximum of absolute value $|C_i(m)|$, which is given by

$$\hat{\tau}_i = \arg \max_m |C_i(m)|. \tag{10}$$

Since we consider the ISI channel, the mean of timing estimate might be delayed due to the channel dispersion. Fortunately the cyclic prefix (CP) exists, and the coarse timing estimate can therefore be shifted earlier within the CP range by some samples λ as [7]

$$\hat{\tau}_{ic} = \hat{\tau}_i - \lambda, \tag{11}$$

where λ need be carefully chosen so that the start point of the DFT window will not be distorted by the dispersive channel.

4 Minimax Criterion

The minimax approach [10] is applied to design distributed antenna locations for an unknown MS position. For given distributed antenna locations, there exists a least favorable MS position which lead to the worst system performance. The minimax approach offers the optimal upper bound of the worst system performance by searching for every possible combination of antenna locations. In this section, we first derive the probability of correct detection, then introduce the probability of worst case, and finally obtain the optimal antenna locations.

According to [9], at timing instants other than those having path channels, denoted as m_{NC}, $P_i(m_{NC})$ can be negligible due to the sharp auto-correlation property of $s^*(k)$, then $C_i(m_{NC}) \approx P_i(m_{NC})$ thus $|C_i(m_{NC})|$ a Rayleigh variable. Consider the constant false alarm detection, i.e., the probability of false alarm, denoted as P_{FA}, is assumed a constant, the threshold of RX$_i$ can then be set by [11]

$$\gamma_i = \sqrt{-2N\sigma_{iw}^2 \ln P_{FA}}. \tag{12}$$

With the threshold derived above and the coarse timing estimate obtained in (11), the probability of correct detection P_{Di} can be obtained, which means the maximum of $|C_i(m)|$ must exceed the threshold indicating the signal is coming and the timing offset estimate must also be dropped in the ISI free area. Thus, P_{Di} can be presented as

$$\begin{aligned} P_{Di} &= P\left\{|C_i(\hat{\tau}_i)| > \gamma_i, \; -N_g + L_i \le \hat{\tau}_{ic} \le 0\right\} \\ &= P\left\{|C_i(\hat{\tau}_i)| > \gamma_i\right\} P\left\{-N_g + L_i \le \hat{\tau}_{ic} \le 0\right\}, \end{aligned} \tag{13}$$

and the probability that neither receive antenna correctly detects the signal from the MS, denoted by P_N, can be given by

$$P_N = \prod_{i=1}^{I} \left(1 - P_{Di}(|x - a_i|)\right), \tag{14}$$

which means a miss or error detection occurs. The probability of correct detection P_{Di} here is represented as a function of $|x - a_i|$ which is the distance between the MS and RX$_i$ as illustrated in Fig. 1.

The worst case happens when the probability P_N reaches its maximum in terms of a specific MS position (usually at the cell edge); its probability can be expressed as

$$P_{WC} = \max_x \{p(x)P_N\}, \quad x \in [0, R], \quad (15)$$

where $p(x)$ is the probability density function (PDF) of MS distribution.

Apparently the worst case probability P_{WC} should be made as small as possible to provide the best system performance overall. Then, the antenna location design problem becomes an minimax estimation problem [10] and the optimal antenna location solution can be obtained by

$$\hat{a}_i = \arg \min_{a_i} P_{WC}. \quad (16)$$

Substituting (15) into (16), we obtain

$$\hat{a}_i = \arg \min_{a_i} \left\{ \max_x \{p(x)P_N\} \right\}. \quad (17)$$

Assuming the MS distribution is uniform, hence $p(x)$ is a constant and can be dropped without affecting the optimal solution, then (17) becomes

$$\hat{a}_i = \arg \min_{a_i} \left\{ \max_x P_N \right\}, \quad x, a_i \in [0, R]. \quad (18)$$

5   Simulation Results

The proposed method is investigated by computer simulations. The parameters are depicted in Table. I. The system operates in the ITU-R M.1225 Vehicular test Channel A model [12] with the maximum Doppler shift of 222 Hz which is induced by the MS motion of 120 km/h. The receiver input signal-to-noise ratio (SNR), averaged over multipath fading, is denoted as $\overline{SNR}$, which is a random variable over the shadow fading at a given distance D. The median of $\overline{SNR}$, denoted as ρ, is given by [13]

$$\rho = \frac{c\sigma_s^2}{D^\alpha \sigma_w^2}, \quad (19)$$

where the transmit power σ_s^2 can be adjust according to ρ. D is set to $R/2$.

As long as we find out the probability of worst case for every possible set of antenna locations, the optimal antenna locations can immediately be obtained by searching for its minimum. Fig. 2 shows the probability of worst case P_{WC} versus two receive antenna locations with $\rho = 5$ dB assuming no carrier frequency offset. The curve has exactly two minimum points indicating the optimal antenna locations. It is obtained that two distributed receive antennas ought to be located at 170 m and 830 m, respectively, when the search step is set to 5

Table 1. Simulation Parameters

Parameters	Description
FFT size	128
CP length	16
Carrier Frequency (GHz)	2
Sampling Frequency (MHz)	1.5
Linear cell length (m)	1000
Constant c [4]	$c \cdot 100^{-3.7} = -78\text{dB}$
Minimum distance (m)	20
Noise power (dBm)	-100
Shadowing standard deviation (dB)	8
Path loss exponent	3.7
Probability of false alarm	1×10^{-6}

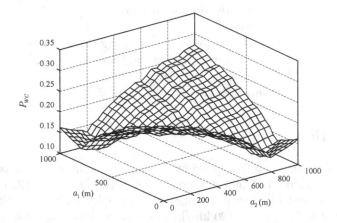

Fig. 2. Probability of worst case versus two receive antenna locations. $\rho = 5$ dB, the search step is 40 m, and carrier frequency offset $\varepsilon = 0$.

m. The curve is also symmetrical about the line $a_1 + a_2 = 1000$, which crosses the two minimum points. Therefore, the distributed antennas should be placed symmetrically about the linear cell center.

Since we employ the cross-correlation method to implement timing acquisition, the effect of carrier frequency offset is concerned. Here we assume that each RX_i has same carrier frequency offset for simplicity. The carrier frequency offset trial values [0, 0.5, 5.6] are evaluated in Fig. 3. The distributed antennas are located at optimal place obtained in Fig. 2. It shows that the carrier frequency offset has little affect on the probability P_N. Thus optimal antenna locations obtained for these carrier frequency offset values are much the same. This result demonstrates robustness to carrier frequency offset as long as which is not very

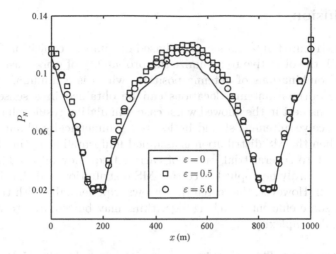

Fig. 3. Probability that neither receive antenna correctly detects the signal versus the MS position. Carrier frequency offset $\varepsilon = 0, 0.5, 5.6$.

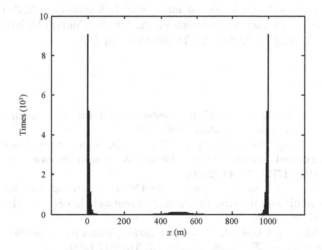

Fig. 4. The times that worst case happens versus the MS position for all combination of antenna locations. Carrier frequency offset $\varepsilon = 0$.

large. It is also observed that the probability P_N has a floor effect when the MS is near the antenna location. This is because the effective distance D_i defined in (3) has a minimum value of 20 m.

Fig. 4 investigate the least favorable MS positions where the worst case happens for all combinations of antenna locations. It shows that the worst case happens either at the cell edges or in the middle of antennas. Both sides of cell edge account for an overwhelming proportion. This is because when the MS is at cell edge, the distance between the MS and the antenna nearest to it, is almost always larger than the distance corresponding to other MS positions.

6   Conclusion

We design distributed antenna locations based on timing acquisition for OFDM systems. With the objective to minimize the probability of worse case among all the possible combinations of antenna position, which is a minimax estimation problem, the optimal antenna locations can be obtained in a sense that the system performs best in the allowed worst case. Simulation results show that the distributed receive antennas should be located symmetrically about the linear cell center when the MS distribution is assumed uniform. The optimal locations are also robust to several trial values of carrier frequency offset. The method can straightforwardly be applied to certain MS distribution and the circular cell scenario as well. However, the search time grows exponentially with the antenna number and some efficient searching algorithms may be required to reduce the computational complexity.

Acknowledgment. This work is supported in part by the National Natural Science Foundation under Grant number 60832007, 60901018, 60902027, U1035002/L05, 61001087, 863 Project under Grant number 2009AA01Z236, the National major projects under Grant number 2010ZX03003–002, 2011ZX03001–006–01, and the Fundamental Research Funds for the Central Universities under Grant number ZYGX2009J008, ZYGX2009J010 of China.

References

1. Zhang, J., Andrews, J.: Distributed antenna systems with randomness. IEEE Trans. Wireless Commun. 7, 3636–3646 (2008)
2. You, X.-H., Wang, D.-M., Sheng, B., Gao, X.-Q., Zhao, X.-S., Chen, M.: Cooperative distributed antenna systems for mobile communications. IEEE Wireless Commun. Mag. 17(3), 35–43 (2010)
3. Shen, Y., Tang, Y., Kong, T., Shao, S.: Optimal antenna location for STBC-OFDM downlink with distributed transmit antennas in linear cells. IEEE Commun. Lett. 11, 387–389 (2007)
4. Wang, X., Zhu, P., Chen, M.: Antenna location design for generalized distributed antenna systems. IEEE Commun. Lett. 13, 315–317 (2009)
5. Han, L., Tang, Y., Shao, S., Wu, T.: On the design of antenna location for OSTBC with distributed transmit antennas in a circular cell. In: Proc. IEEE International Conference on Communications (ICC), Cape Town, South Africa, pp. 1–5 (2010)
6. Morelli, M., Kuo, C.-C., Pun, M.-O.: Synchronization techniques for orthogonal frequency division multiple access (OFDMA): a tutorial review. Proc. IEEE 95, 1394–1427 (2007)
7. Minn, H., Bhargava, V., Letaief, K.: A robust timing and frequency synchronization for OFDM systems. IEEE Trans. Wireless Commun. 2(4), 822–839 (2003)
8. Chu, D.: Polyphase codes with good periodic correlation properties. IEEE Trans. Inform. Theory 18(4), 531–532 (1972)
9. Awoseyila, A., Kasparis, C., Evans, B.: Robust time-domain timing and frequency synchronization for OFDM systems. IEEE Trans. Consumer Electron. 55(2), 391–399 (2009)

10. Verdu, S., Poor, H.: On minimax robustness: a general approach and applications. IEEE Trans. Inform. Theory 30(2), 328–340 (1984)
11. Kay, S.M.: Fundamentals of Statistical Signal Processing: Detection Theory. Prentice-Hall, Upper Saddle River (1998)
12. Guidelines for evaluation of radio transmission technologies for IMT-2000, Recommendation ITU-R M.1225 (1997)
13. Catreux, S., Driessen, P., Greenstein, L.: Data throughputs using multiple-input multiple-output (MIMO) techniques in a noise-limited cellular environment. IEEE Trans. Wireless Commun. 1(2), 226–235 (2002)

A Novel Image Transmission System
Based on Joint Source-Channel Coding

Junhong Chen and Qinyu Zhang

Dept. of Electronic and Information Engineering
Harbin Institute of Technology Shenzhen Graduate School
518055, Shenzhen, China
johnhitsz@gmail.com, zqy@hit.edu.cn

Abstract. A novel joint source/channel image coding algorithm for image transmission system was proposed. The proposed algorithm is based on the best wavelet packet in a rate-distortion sense. Because of the noise in transmission channel, the channel and the channel code information had been introduced to the source image coding. The image coding is based on wavelet packet, and a bit plane coding algorithm have been used for the wavelet packet sub-band coding, so the coded bit streams can be match to UEP transmission by WICP-LDPC code. The simulation results in BSC channel show that, the proposed algorithm is better than the EEP and several other image transmission algorithms.

Keywords: joint source channel coding, best wavelet packet, UEP, image transmission.

1   Introduction

As the development of wireless communications technology, multimedia communications becomes more and more attention. As the most important and most basic technology, image transmission technology has become a hot research topic in recent years. The traditional image transmission system is based on the Shannon separation theorem [1], however, its codec complexity and storage capacity are both demanding, because of these defects, the traditional system is hard to meet in practical applications, especially in wireless communications. However, this issue has inspired the exploration and research of joint source channel coding (JSCC) algorithm. At present, many of the specific image communication system based on JSCC have been proposed [2-6]. There is an important class of JSCC system in those systems is unequal error protection (UEP) system, which divide the source into different parts in accordance with the significance level, when the channel coding implement different error protection. As the channel transmission processing, the sensitivity of the bit error rate the in different types of data is completely different, therefore, the equal error protection (EEP), which take all the information for the same level of error control coding, is a bandwidth waste on the protection of non-essential information, and the protection of critical information has become deficient. Fortunately, the use of UEP is a good way to solve this contradiction.

P. Ren et al. (Eds.): WICON 2011, LNICST 98, pp. 82–90, 2012.

Wavelet image coding is a very successful source coding, it can achieve very good compression ratio. In recent years, many efficient algorithms have been proposed, such as embedded coding algorithm interception (EBCOT) algorithm, which is the core of JEPG2000 algorithm [7,8], and the optimal wavelet packet based image compression algorithm [9-10]. However, these wavelet coding algorithms is designed for the separation system, they can not be effectively bound into the UEP channel coding. Based on the above considerations, a novel image source coding algorithm based on optimal wavelet packet have been proposed, which can be good match for WICP-LDPC channel coding [11]. In Section 2, we present our optimal wavelet packet algorithm. Section 3 formulates our UEP channel coding problem which used WICP-LDPC, and present the system model. Section 4 provides simulation details use the system in Section III. Finally, we conclude the paper in Section 5.

2   WP Image Coding

2.1   Prune Algorithm of the WP

The basic idea of wavelet packets is using the decomposition of non-octave band, to make the given signals select their best base adaptively. There is a general approach for the choice of optimal basis, which is to define a cost function, then look for the full tree to find a sub-tree, which make the global cost function minimum. That means, during the tree-pruning procedure, the cost of a parent sub-band $J(P)$ is compared with the sum of its four children's costs $\Sigma J(C_i)$, as the Fig.1 shows. If the parent's cost is costly, the four sub-branches are retained, and the parent's cost is updated to the sum of its children's costs, otherwise the four sub-branches are pruned. When this tree-pruning procedure reaches the root node, the best sub-tree that minimizes the global cost function is found.

Ramchandran and Vetterli propose a rate-distortion based cost function [9], which is given by

$$J(\lambda) = D + \lambda \cdot R \tag{1}$$

where λ is the quality factor, which controls the tradeoff between the distortion D and the budget bit rate R. The rate-distortion cost function can solve the problem of the best basis selection in a rate-distortion sense. For any given wavelet packet, the decomposition of the leaf node will correspond to the packet sub-band. Assuming that the sub-band can be represented by the $\{B1, B_2, ..., B_m\}$, and because of the additivity between rate and distortion, the global cost function can be represented by

$$J(\lambda) = \sum_{i=1}^{m} (D_i(R_i) + \lambda R_i) \tag{2}$$

where R_i is the sum rate of sub-band B_i, and D_i is the sum distortion of sub-band B_i.

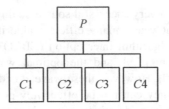

Fig. 1. A branch of the full tree

Then, the optimal wavelet packet pruning algorithm can be presented as follows. In every branch of the tree, if (3) is satisfied, the parent sub-band will be retained; otherwise it is broken down into four child sub-bands. When the tree pruning algorithm reach the root node, as the given λ, it can get the best wavelet packet decomposition and optimal quantization for each sub-band encoding.

$$D_0 + \lambda R_0 \leq \sum_{i=1}^{4} D_i + \lambda R_i \tag{3}$$

In the image transmission system, due to the presence of channel noise, the stream of source compression coding need another channel coding, which increases the total coding rate, and the channel noise increases the total distortion. Assumptions the ratio between increased total code rate and the original rate is σ, then, the global cost function can be represented by

$$J(\lambda) = \sum_{i=1}^{m} (D_i(R_i) + \lambda R_i + D(\sigma)) \tag{4}$$

where, $D(\sigma)$ is the distortion caused by channel noise. Let e be the error of the original code words x from the decoding code words y, that means $e=|x-y|$, then we can get

$$E(e) = (2^{\sigma R_i} - 1)P \tag{5}$$

and

$$E(D(\sigma)) = \frac{\sum \left[(2^{\sigma R_i} - 1)P \right]^2}{n} = \left[(2^{\sigma R_i} - 1)P \right]^2 \tag{6}$$

where, σR_i is the total rate of the sub-band B_i; P is the BER of the noise channel, it is related in noise channel and channel coding. In this paper, we use BSC channel for the simulated channel, and calculate (7) by its channel BER p. For other given noise channel, P can be determined by the specific coding and decoding methods and the noise channel. So in a given error control coding algorithm, we can calculate the P in deferent SNR, and store it in a table, In the actual transmission coding, the encoder will look for the storage table to find the channel coding rate, based on the current channel condition and transmission requirements.

$$D_0 + \lambda R_0 + \left[(2^{\sigma R_0} - 1)P \right]^2 \leq \sum_{i=1}^{4} D_i + \lambda R_i + \left[(2^{\sigma R_i} - 1)P \right]^2 \tag{7}$$

In summary, the choice of optimal wavelet basis is summarized as follows:

- Decompose the input image to a given depth N to form the full decomposition tree.
- For a given , *look for the storage table, find the* σ, P, then populate each node of the full tree with the *equation (7)* over all the rate-distortion pairs of that node.
- Prune the full tree recursively, starting from the leaf nodes to the root node, by making spilt/merge binary decisions. From this step the best basis and the corresponding quantizers are known for the given λ.
- Iterate over λ using bisection search method to meet the target bit rate R.

2.2 Block-partitioning Coding Algorithm

After WP decomposition, each WP sub-band needs a block-partitioning coding to quantize the WP sub-band. Consider a WP sub-band Ω, whose coefficient p located at position (i, j) is denoted by $c_{i,j}$. A sub-block B of Ω is said to be significant with respect to a threshold n, if

$$\max_{(i,j)\in B}\{|c_{i,j}|\} \geq 2^n$$

(8)

otherwise, it is insignificant.

The block-partitioning coding algorithm adopts a bit-plane coding fashion. The main idea is to locate significant coefficients in each bit-plane and encode groups of insignificant coefficients efficiently with a few symbols. To achieve this objective, the coding algorithm tests the significance of a coefficient block first. If the block is significant in current bit-plane n, it is partitioned to find significant coefficient in it, as shown in Fig. 2; otherwise, it is retained for the next bit-plane revisit.

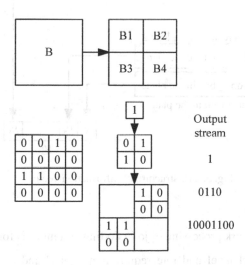

Fig. 2. Partition of a significant coefficient block

3   Transmission System by UEP

3.1   The WIPC-LDPC Coding

Ma and Yuan [11] propose a irregular low-density parity-check (LDPC) code based on weight-increasing parity-check matrix (WIPC), which have an excellent unequal error protection (UEP) performance. With systematic encoding, the important information bits in information sequence could successfully be mapped to the elite bits of an irregular LDPC code. Accordingly, the bit plane coding in section II can be mapped into WIPC-LDPC based on their importance.

Assuming the maximum threshold of the bit plane coding is N, obviously, the plane with threshold N has the highest important level, and with the decrease of the threshold, the importance of the plane will decrease. Thereby, we can select N degrees in the information nodes of WIPC-LDPC, assuming that the numbers of information nodes in each degree are S_1, S_2, $\cdots$, S_N, where, S_N have the highest important level, and S_1 have the lowest level. Then the channel coding processing can be represented as follows:

- Rearrange the bit plane coding streams to construct a new information vector V. Get S_N bits from the plane N, S_{N-1} bits from plane N-1, ..., S_1 bits from plane 1, then arrange them as Fig. 3 shows.
- Encode the information vector V with WIPC-LDPC code.

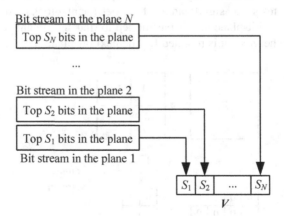

Fig. 3. The structure of information vector

3.2   System Model

As Fig. 4 shows, the work processing of joint coding system is as follows:

- For a given channel and rate requirement, get P and σ by looking for the storage table.

- Prune the WP tree of the source image according to (7) and bit-plane coding.
- Channel encode with WIPC-LDPC.

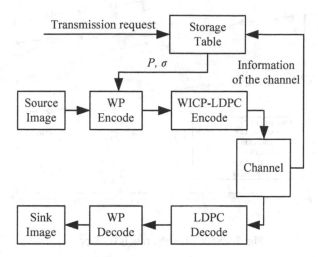

Fig. 4. The joint coding transmission system

4   Simulation

Computer simulations are carried out on BSC channel to assess the performance of the proposed transmission system, using several popular images, *lena*, *barbara* and *goldhill*. The parameters of the selected LDPC code are as follows: the code length is 8192 bits, rate is 0.5 and the column polynomial of the irregular LDPC is

$$\lambda(x) = 0.1322x + 0.124x^2 + 0.3306x^{19} + 0.4132x^{49} \tag{9}$$

The row polynomial is

$$\rho(x) = 0.8678x^{14} + 0.1322x^{15} \tag{10}$$

The elementary transformation of the matrix derived by $\lambda(x)$ can be transformed to a WIPC matrix, and this WIPC-LDPC code has the following properties, the first 4096 bits are parity bits, the followed 2560 bits have the degree of 3, the next 1024 bits have the degree of 20, the final 512 bits have the degree of 50. And the σ of this WIPC-LDPC code is 2, when it is used in error control code on BSC channel. BP decoding algorithm has been used in channel decoding, the number of iterations set to 50.

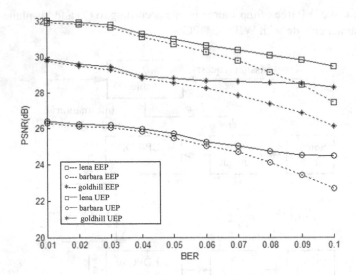

Fig. 5. PSNR when the rate is 0.25bpp

As a comparison test, EEP transmission using general irregular LDPC as channel coding, and its generator polynomial is $\lambda(x)$. Fig. 5 shows the results when the transmission rate is 0.25bpp, and Fig. 6 is 0.5bpp.

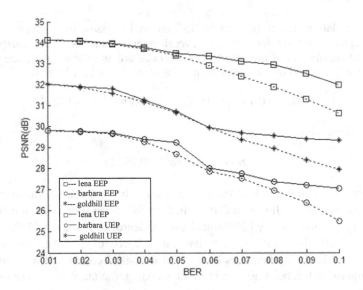

Fig. 6. PSNR when the rate is 0.5bpp

Fig. 5 and Fig. 6 show WIPC-LDPC codes with UEP scheme is significantly better than the general irregular LDPC codes. And with the increase of channel bit error, UEP can gain greater image quality improved. At the same time, compare Fig. 5 and Fig. 6, can be derived that, the advantage of UEP is more obvious when the transmission rate is low. Thus, in poor transmission conditions, low rate and high channel error, the use of UEP transmission can improve the quality of the reconstructed image more obviously.

Table 1 compares the proposed algorithm and the algorithms proposed by Sherwood, Banister and Lan, when the transmission rate is 0.25bpp, while Table 2 is the rate of 0.5bpp. TABLE I and TABLE II show that the proposed joint coding algorithm is generally better than other algorithms.

Table 1. PSNR of the restructure image while rate=0.25bpp

BER		Lena	Barbara	Goldhill
0.1	algorithm in [2]	29.40	24.71	27.69
	algorithm in [3]	30.21	24.25	27.92
	algorithm in [4]	30.68	24.33	28.49
	proposed algorithm	29.44	24.49	28.27
0.03	algorithm in [2]	31.90	26.32	29.16
	algorithm in [3]	32.32	25.99	29.21
	algorithm in [4]	32.74	26.18	29.37
	proposed algorithm	31.77	26.25	29.41

Table 2. PSNR of the restructure image while rate=0.5bpp

BER		Lena	Barbara	Goldhill
0.1	algorithm in [2]	31.10	26.99	28.60
	algorithm in [3]	31.76	26.77	29.89
	algorithm in [4]	32.21	27.31	28.92
	proposed algorithm	31.97	27.03	30.31
0.03	algorithm in [2]	34.15	29.12	31.38
	algorithm in [3]	34.50	29.41	31.50
	algorithm in [4]	34.82	29.30	31.66
	proposed algorithm	34.77	31.10	31.99

5   Conclusion

In this paper, a novel joint source/channel image coding algorithm was proposed based on the best wavelet packet in a rate-distortion sense. Different from other wavelet packet image coding, the channel and the channel code information were introduced to the source coding, so the proposed algorithm could be applied to image transmission. The coding of wavelet packet sub-band used bit plane coding, thereby made the bit streams match to UEP transmission by WICP-LDPC code. The simulation results show that, in poor transmission conditions, low rate and high channel error, the use of UEP transmission can improve the quality of the reconstructed image more obviously. And the proposed joint coding algorithm has better performance than the algorithm proposed by Sherwood, Banister, and Lan.

Acknowledgments. This research was supported by the national natural science foundation of China, No. 61032003.

References

1. Shannon, C.E.: A mathematical theory of communication. The Bell System Technical Journal 27, 379–423 (1948)
2. Sherwood, P.G., Zeger, K.: Progressive image coding for noisy channels. IEEE Signal Process. Lett. 4, 189–191 (1997)
3. Babuster, B., Belzer, B., Fischer, T.: Robust image transmission using JPEG2000 and turbo-codes. IEEE Signal Process. Lett. 9, 117–119 (2002)
4. Lan, C.F., Xiong, Z., Narayanan, K.R.: Source-optimized irregular repeat accumulate codes with inherent unequal error protection capabilities and their application to scalable image transmission. IEEE Trans. Image Process 15, 1740–1750 (2006)
5. Fresia, M., Lavagetto, F.: Determination of optimal distortion-based protection in progressive image transmission: a heuristic approach. IEEE Trans. Image Process 17, 1654–1662 (2008)
6. Pan, X., Banihashemi, A.H., Cuhadar, A.: A fast trellis-based rate-allocation algorithm for robust transmission of progressively coded images over noisy channels. IEEE Trans. Communications 54, 1–6 (2006)
7. Atzori, L.: Transmission of JPEG2000 images over wireless channels with unequal power distribution. IEEE Trans. Consumer Electronics 49, 883–888 (2003)
8. Torki, M., Hajshirmohammadi, A.: Unequal power allocation for transmission of JPEG2000 images over wireless channels. In: Globecom 2009, pp. 3279–3284 (2009)
9. Ramchandran, K., Vetterli, M.: Best wavelet packet bases in a rate-distortion sense. IEEE Trans. Image Process 2, 160–175 (1993)
10. Yang, Y., Xu, C.: A wavelet packet-based rate-distortion optimization algorithm for block partitioning image coding. Science in China Series F: Information Sciences 51, 1039–1054 (2008)
11. Ma, P., Yuan, D.: Reasearch on unequal error protection of irregular LDPC codes. Journal on Communications 26, 132–136 (2005)

Uplink Interference Rejection Combining
for WCDMA Using Multiple Antennas

Zhanghong Hao, Hongzhi Zhao, Taofu Mo, Youxi Tang, and Huiyue Yu

National Key Laboratory of Science and Technology on Communications,
University of Electronic Science and Technology of China, 611731 Chengdu, China
{hzh_0515hzh,lyn,motaofu,tangyx,huiyue1107}@uestc.edu.cn

Abstract. A major limitation to the capacity of WCDMA is multiple access interference (MAI) produced by the other co-channel users. In this paper, a simplified rake receiver with interference rejection combining (IRC) is investigated. The signal transmitted on the control channel is used for channel estimation and weight calculation. Compared to the maximum ratio combining (MRC), IRC can get better MAI rejection. It is a simplified algorithm to be implemented.

Keywords: WCDMA, MAI, IRC, MRC.

1   Introduction

With the development of the 3rd generation wireless communication, WCDMA is coming into the commercial phase in Europe, North America and Asia [1]. It has become the most widely accepted standard of the 3rd wireless communication in the world. However, the interferences including intersymbol interference (ISI) and multiple access interference (MAI) are the key limiting challenges to overcome in the cellular systems of the 3rd generation [2].

The Interference Rejection Combining (IRC) has been proven to mitigate both multipath fading and co-channel interference. The IRC principle has been successful for co-channel and adjacent channel interference (MAI) suppression in 2G and 3G systems [3]. In [4], the relative performance of IRC is studied. The wiener filter with IRC combining in down-link is discussed in [5]. [6] proposed a spatio-temporal rake receiver but the calculation of the covariance matrix of interference and noise is complicated. In [7], the signal received by the antenna (before despreading) is used to calculate the covariance.

Space diversity can significantly improve the performance of wireless communication [8]. In this paper, we propose a more simplified method to calculate the covariance matrix employing multiple antennas. The signal transmitted on the control channel is used to estimate the channel impulse response and reconstruct the desired signal. Expressions for the correlation of interference and noise for a WCDMA uplink with receive diversity are presented in the paper.

P. Ren et al. (Eds.): WICON 2011, LNICST 98, pp. 91–96, 2012.
© Institute for Computer Sciences, Social Informatics and Telecommunications Engineering 2012

2   Data Model

In the WCDMA, the uplink transmission is performed using two types of codes namely scrambling and channelization codes, while scrambling codes are used for device identification, channelization codes are used for channel separation [9]. The uplink spreading is depicted in Fig. 1. There is only one DPDCH (dedicated physical data channel). The I branch is the DPDCH, the Q branch is the DPCCH (dedicated physical control channel). The transmitted signal is modeled as [6].

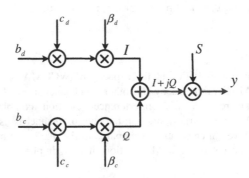

Fig. 1. The spreading of DPDCH and DPCCH

$$y(t) = \beta_d \sqrt{2E_c} \sum_i b_d[i] a_{d,i}(t - iN_d T_c) + j\beta_c \sqrt{2E_c} \sum_i b_c[i] a_{c,i}(t - iN_c T_c).$$ (1)

Where $b_d \in \{-1, +1\}$ is the sequence of bits transmitted on the data channel (DPDCH) and $b_c \in \{-1, +1\}$ is the sequence of bits transmitted on the control channel (DPCCH). The spreading factors for the data channel and the control channel are denoted N_d and N_c. The transmitted energy per chip is related to E_c and the gain factors, β_d and β_c, are used to adjust the power ratio of the data channel and the control channel. T_c is the chip duration. The spreading waveforms are modeled as

$$a_{d,i}(t) = \sum_{n=0}^{N_d-1} c_{d,i}[n] p_s(t - nT_c),$$ (2)

$$a_{c,i}(t) = \sum_{n=0}^{N_c-1} c_{c,i}[n] p_s(t - nT_c).$$ (3)

Where $p_s(t)$ is pulse shape, it is assumed that the pulse is normalized so that $\int |p_s(t)|^2 dt = 1$. The spreading sequences are modeled as

$$c_{d,i}[n] = c_d[n] S[iN_d + n],$$ (4)

$$c_{c,i}[n] = c_c[n]S[iN_c + n].$$ (5)

Where $c_d[i] \in \{-1,+1\}$ and $c_c[i] \in \{-1,+1\}$ are the channelization codes for the data and control channels. $S[i]$ is scrambling code.

The signal $r(t)$ received by the K antennas can be expressed as

$$r(t) = \sum_{l=0}^{L-1} h_l y(t - \tau_l) + \sum_{m=1}^{M} \sum_{l=0}^{L-1} h_{m,l} y_m(t - \tau_{m,l}) + n(t).$$ (6)

The k th element of the $K \times 1$ vector $r(t)$ holds the signal of the k th antenna. L is the resolvable multi-path. h_l is the complex valued coefficient of the l th ray with delay τ_l. M is the number of the interference. $y_m(t)$ is the signal of the m th interference which is modeled as

$$y_m(t) = \beta_d \sqrt{2E_I} \sum_i b_d[i] a_{d,i}(t - iN_d T_c) + j\beta_c \sqrt{2E_I} \sum_i b_c[i] a_{c,i}(t - iN_c T_c).$$ (7)

Where E_I is the energy per chip of the interfering signal.

3   Combining Weights

The received signal of each antenna is descrambled and despreaded, we can get the signal of the control and data channel separately. The rake receiver combines the data channel signals from all antennas and all fingers. We assume that the number of the fingers is L. The output of the l th finger on the k th antenna is simply expressed as

$$r_{k,l}(t) = h_{k,l}(\tau_l) y(t - \tau_l) + u_{k,l}(t).$$ (8)

where $u_{k,l}(t)$ models the overall noise (noise and interference).

For applying the interference rejection combining, we need to calculate the covariance of the interference and noise i.e., $R_{uu} = E[uu^H]$, $u = [u_{1,1}, \cdots u_{k,1}, u_{1,2} \cdots, u_{k,2}, \cdots, u_{k,l}]^T$, $E[\cdot]$ denotes expected value, H denotes conjugate transpose, $(\cdot)^T$ denotes transpose of a matrix.

In this paper, the signal of the control channel is used to estimate the channel impulse response $\hat{h}_{k,l}$ as follows:

$$\hat{h}_{k,l} = \frac{1}{N_c} \sum_{i=1}^{N_c} p^*(i) \tilde{p}_{k,l}(i).$$ (9)

Where $*$ denotes the complex conjugate. $p(i)$ is the pilot symbol. $\tilde{p}_{k,l}(i)$ means the pilot symbols in the received signals on the k th antenna of the l th finger, which is descrambled and despread by the scrambling code and the channelization code for the control channel.

The estimated channel impulse response is used to reconstruct the desired signal, which is subtracted from the received signal of the data channel. The correlation between fingers of different antennas is expressed as

$$R_{ks,lj} = \frac{1}{P \cdot N_d} \sum_{i=0}^{PN_d-1} \left(r_{ll}(i) - \hat{h}_{kl} p(i) \right) \left(r_{sj}(i) - \hat{h}_{sj} p(i) \right)^* \quad k,s=1,\cdots,K \ l,j=1,\cdots,L. \tag{10}$$

where P means the number of symbols in one slot on the data channel.

The covariance is obtained as follows:

$$R_{uu} = \left\{ R_{ks,lj} \right\} \ k,s = 1,\cdots,K \ l,j = 1,\cdots,L . \tag{11}$$

The optimum weights can be expressed as

$$\omega_{IRC}^H = \hat{h}^H R_{uu}^{-1} . \tag{12}$$

where $\hat{h} = \left[\hat{h}_{1,1},\cdots,\hat{h}_{K,1},\hat{h}_{1,2},\cdots,\hat{h}_{K,2},\cdots,\hat{h}_{K,L} \right]^T$.

We compare the IRC receiver with the MRC receiver, which weighting vector can be expressed as

$$\omega_{MRC}^H = \hat{h}^H . \tag{13}$$

4   Simulation Results

To verify the the ability of the IRC receiver to reject the MAI, the IRC receiver using multiple antennas is simulated. The channel coding is not considered. During this simulation, we followed the WCDMA standard. Related simulation parameters can be seen in TABLE I. The channelization code is OVSF (orthogonal variable spreading factor). For simplicity, there are 2 antennas and one-ray Rayleigh distributed channel, the maximum Doppler frequency is 40 Hz. $\beta_c = \beta_d = 1$.

Table 1. WCDMA Simulation Parameter

Item	Parameter
Spreading Code	OVSF
Scrambling Code	Gold code
Modulation	BPSK
Chip Rate (Mcps)	3.84
Spreading Factor of Data Channel	64
Spreading Factor of Control Channel	256

Fig. 2 shows the BER characteristics of both the IRC receiver and MRC receiver with $E_c = E_I$. As can be seen, when there is one interfering user, at the typical BER value of 10^{-3}, IRC gives about 4dB better performance than MRC. When the number of interfering users increases, the difference between IRC and MRC becomes small.

Fig. 3 illustrates the BER as a function of Ec/N0 with different SIR (signal to interference ratio). SIR is defined as $SIR = E_c / ME_I$. In the simulation, there is one interfering user. Fig. 3 demonstrates that the IRC receiver has an excellent performance for combating the effect of MAI. At the BER value of 10^{-2}, SIR=-3dB, the IRC gives about 1 dB better performance than MRC. When SIR=-6dB, the IRC gives about 12dB better performance than MRC.

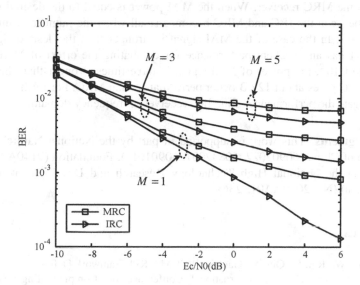

Fig. 2. The BER performance Vs Ec/N0. M : the number of interfering users

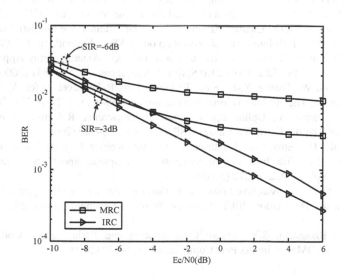

Fig. 3. The BER performance Vs Ec/N0. $SIR = E_c / ME_I$

5   Conclusions

In this paper, the BER performance of IRC receiver and MRC receiver in uplink is evaluated. The signal transmitted on the control channel is used to estimate the channel response and calculate the covariance of the interference and noise. From the simulation results we have seen that the BER performance of IRC receiver is better than that of the MRC receiver. When the MAI power is equal to the desired user, the difference between the IRC and MRC becomes small when the number of interfering users increases. In the case of the MAI signal is stronger than the desired signal, the IRC receiver has an excellent performance for combating the effect of MAI. At the BER value of 10^{-2}, the power of MAI signal is three times stronger than the desired signal, the IRC gives about 12 dB better performance than MRC. For further study, we will investigate the performance of the IRC receiver in frequency domain.

Acknowledgments. This work is supported in part by the National Natural Science Foundation of China (60902027, 60832007, 60901018), Foundation (9140A2103020-9DZ02), and the National High Technology Research and Development of China (863 Program) (No. 2009AA01Z236).

References

1. Ke, X., Li, W., Rui, L., Qiu, X., Guo, S.: WCDMA KPI Framwork Definition Methods and Applications. In: The 2nd International Conference on Computer Engineering and Technology, pp. 471–475 (2010)
2. Ho, Q.-T., Massicotte, D.: VLSI Implementation of an Adaptive Multiuser Detector for Multirate WCDMA Systems. Journal of Signal Processing Systems 61(2), 127–139 (2010)
3. Yu, C.-H., Tirkkonen, O.: Characterization of SINR Uncertainty due to Spatial Interference Variation. In: IEEE 11th International Workshop on SPAWC, Finland, pp. 1–5 (2010)
4. Ylitalo, J., Tiirola, E.: Performance Evaluation of Different Antenna Array Approaches for 3G CDMA Uplink. In: IEEE VTC-2000 Spring Tokyo, Japan, pp. 883–887 (2000)
5. Tsai, T., Soichi, W., Huang, Y.-L., Sato, T.: Down-Link Rake Receiver for WCDMA with Wiener Filter. In: The 5th International Symposium on WPMC, vol. 2, pp. 377–380 (2002)
6. Astély, D., Artamo, A.: Uplink Spatio-Temporal Interference Rejection Combining for WCDMA. In: The IEEE 3rd Workshop on SPAWC, pp. 326–329 (2001)
7. Pajukoski, K., Horneman, K., Nuutirien, J.: On Interference Suppression in DS-CDMA Systems. In: IEEE 7th International Symposium on Spread Spectrum Techniques and Applications, vol. 1, pp. 268–272 (2002)
8. Zhang, X.J., Gong, Y.: Adaptive Power Allocation for Regenerative Relaying with Multipel Antennas at the Destination. IEEE Trans. on Wireless Communications 8(6), 2789–2794 (2009)
9. Saini, D.S., Bhooshan, S.V.: OVSF Code Sharing and Reducing the Code Wastage Capacity in WCDMA. Wireless Pers Commun. 48, 521–529 (2009)

A Simplified Fair Scheduling Algorithm for Multiuser MIMO System

Zhao Shen[1,2,*], Daiyu Fu[2], and Fan Jin[3]

[1] Coll. Elect. Engn., Naval Univ. Engn.,
Wuhan, China
[2] Department of Elect. & Informat. Engn., Huazhong Univ. of Sci. & Technol.,
Wuhan, China
[3] Elect. and Computer Sci. & University of Southampton,
Southampton, England
{clingerlisa,fudaiyu}@gmail.com, fjlg10@ecs.soton.com

Abstract. In this paper, an efficient user scheduling algorithm with fairness is proposed. In the multiuser MIMO system, how to ensure the MIMO multiplexing gain and fairness is a key point. Although the PF algorithm ensures the fairness of the system, the sum-capacity is restricted. We improves the PF algorithm, and achieve a tradeoff between the multiplexing gain and fairness. The simulation results show the proposed algorithm can get the multiplexing gain, ensuring the fairness.

Keywords: Multiuser MIMO, Fairness, Block digonalization, PF, user scheduling.

1 Introduction

In the downlink of multiuser multiple-input multiple-output(MIMO) system, the multiple antennas at the base station allow for spatial multiplexing of transmissions to multiple users in a given time slot and frequency band. When the channel state information(CSI) of all the users is known at the base station, complete multiuser interference precancellation can be performed. The optimal strategy is known as dirty paper coding(DPC)[1], but the implement of which is very difficult. Block diagonalization(BD) is a sub-optimal algorithm, which cancels the multiuser interference using channel inverse[2].

Meanwhile, in the multiuser MIMO system, the user scheduling is a challenging. The exhaust algorithm is the optimal user scheduling algorithm[3], but because of its complexity, the implementation is difficult. The literature[4] proposed a greedy user scheduling algorithm with low complexity, where block diagonalization can maximize the system sum-capacity. The scheduling algorithm

* This work is supported by the National High-Tech. R&D Program of China (863 Program) under Grant No. 2009AA01Z205, and by the National Science Key Special Project of China under Grants No. 2010ZX03003-001,2008ZX03003-004 and 2009ZX03003-007.

P. Ren et al. (Eds.): WICON 2011, LNICST 98, pp. 97–104, 2012.
© Institute for Computer Sciences, Social Informatics and Telecommunications Engineering 2012

based on the channel norm had been proposed in[5][6], a scheduling algorithm based on the channel correlation was proposed in [7]. However, the object of all the algorithms is to achieve the maximum sum-capacity, which tends to select the strong users, often causing unfairness. Proportionally fair(PF) scheduling is a user scheduling algorithm with fairness, but losing the multiplexing gain[8].

In this paper, an efficient user scheduling algorithm with fairness is proposed. Simulation results show that the proposed algorithm can get the multiplexing gain, ensuring the fairness.

The rest of this paper is organized as follows: Section 2 describes the system model. Proposed algorithm with fairness is discussed in Section 3. In the Section 4, simulation results are given, and Section 5 presents some concluding remarks.

In the paper, $(\bullet)^T, (\bullet)^H, |\bullet|, \|\bullet\|$ denote the transpose, conjugate and transpose operation(Hermitian), inner product and Frobenius norm. I means the identity matrix.

2   System Model

We consider the multiuser MIMO downlink system with M transmit antennas at the base station and N receive antennas at the kth user, and there are K users. $H_k \in \mathbb{C}^{N \times M}$ expresses the channel matrix of the kth user. We assume the channel is flat rayleigh fading and independent for different users. Let $S_k \in \mathbb{C}^{r_k \times 1}$ is the kth user's transmit data, $W_k \in \mathbb{C}^{M_T \times r_k}$ is the precoding matrix, when the base station sends data to L users simultaneously, the received signal of the kth user, is given:

$$y_k = H_k \sum_{j=1}^{L} W_j s_j + n_k \tag{1}$$

Where $n_k \in \mathbb{C}^{N \times 1}$ denotes the additive Gaussian noise of the kth user whose elements have zero mean and unit variance. When $K \gg M$, the station need to make user scheduling. Denote the service user set S, the number of the service users is $|S|$, the we get $\max\{|S|\} = M/N$.

3   The Proposed Scheduling Algorithm with Fairness

3.1   The Block Diagonalization (BD) Algorithm

Let us define a $\sum_{j=1, j \neq k}^{K} N \times M$ aggregate channel matrix as:

$$\hat{H}_k = (H_1^T, \ldots, H_{k-1}^T, H_{k+1}^T, \ldots, H_k^T)^T \tag{2}$$

Zero multiuser interference condition requires the precoding matrix W_k of the kth user lies in the null space of $\hat{H}_k$ to have a dimension which is greater than 0. Denote the singular value decomposition(SVD) of $\hat{H}_k$ as:

$$\hat{H}_k = \hat{U}_k(\sum_k \overset{\wedge}{0})(\hat{V}_k^1 \hat{V}_k^0)^H \tag{3}$$

$\sum_k$ is a $r_k \times r_k$ diagonal matrix, containing r_k nonzero singular values of $\hat{H}_k$, $\hat{V}_k^0$ holds the $M - r_k$ right singular vectors and $r_k = rank(\hat{H}_k)$. BD is possible if $M > \max(r_1, r_2, \ldots, r_k)$[2]. With this, the multiuser channel is decoupled into several parallel single user MIMO channel, which is:

$$H_k' = H_k \hat{V}_k^0 \tag{4}$$

Denote the SVD of H_k' as:

$$H_k' = U_k \begin{bmatrix} \Sigma_k & 0 \\ 0 & 0 \end{bmatrix} [V_k^1 V_k^0]^H \tag{5}$$

So the precoding matrix of the kth user is $W_k = \hat{V}_k^0 V_k^1$, with sum power constraint P, the achievable throughput of the block diagonal system is:

$$C_{BD}(S) = \sum_{k \in S} \log |I + H_k W_k Q_k W_k^H H_k^H|$$

$$s.t\, Q_k \geq 0, \sum_{k \in S} Tr(Q_k) \leq P \tag{6}$$

Where Q_k is the power allocation matrix of the kth user.

3.2   The Proposed Scheduling Algorithm

In the Section 2, we assume that $K \gg M$, and user scheduling is required. Considering the fairness, we introduce the PF algorithm first.

The PF algorithm achieves the multiuser diversity and guarantees the fairness. Every slot only one user is scheduled, assume the k^*th user is scheduled at a slot, which satisfies the condition:

$$k^* = \arg \max_{k \in K} \{\frac{R_k(t)}{T_k(t)}\} \tag{7}$$

Where $R_k(t)$ and $T_k(t)$ express the instantaneous rate and average rate of the k^*th user at the tth slot. $T_k(t)$ is updated as following:

$$T_k(t+1) = \begin{cases} (1 - \frac{1}{t_c})^* T_k(t) + \frac{1}{t_c}^* R_k(t), k = k^* \\ (1 - \frac{1}{t_c})^* T_k(t), k \neq k^* \end{cases} \tag{8}$$

t_c is the forgetting factor, t_c is more larger, the update of the $T_k(t)$ is slower, and the fairness of the system is worse.

However, PF just schedules one user at a slot, which loses the multiplexing gain, and can not reflect the advantages of multiple degrees of freedom in the MIMO system. In order to take advantage of the multiplexing gain and guarantees the fairness, we propose a improved PF scheduling algorithm.

First, select a alternative user set $\tilde{S}$, which satisfies $S \leq |\tilde{S}| \leq K$. $\tilde{S}$ is selected as following criterion: sort $\frac{R_k(t)}{T_k(t)}$ in descending order, and choose the front $|\tilde{S}|$ users as the alternative users. $T_k(t)$ is updated as following:

$$T_k(t+1) = \begin{cases} (1 - \frac{1}{t_c})^*T_k(t) + \frac{1}{t_c}{}^*R_k(t), k \in S \\ (1 - \frac{1}{t_c})^*T_k(t), k \notin S \end{cases} \tag{9}$$

When the alternative set is determined, we need select $|S|$ users from the set $\tilde{S}$, in this paper, greedy scheduling is used, and the detail of the proposed algorithm is as following:

a) Determine the alternative set $\tilde{S}$;
b) Initialize the service user set $S = \emptyset$;
c) Initialize the power allocation matrix Ω:
   $\Omega = \frac{P}{M}I_M$, I_M expresses the M-dimensional identity matrix;
d) Select the ith user μ_i from the set $\tilde{S}$:

$$u_i = \arg\max_{j \in \tilde{S}} \det(I + H_j \Omega H_j^H) \tag{10}$$

e) Update the related sets and matrixes:

$$\Omega = \Omega - \Omega H_i^H (I_{m_g} + H_i \Omega H_i^H)^{-1} H_i \Omega \tag{11}$$

$$\tilde{S} = \tilde{S} - \{u_i\}; S = S + \{u_i\} \tag{12}$$

f) Repeat the steps d), e), until M/N users are selected, or other restricted conditions are satisfied.

In the proposed algorithm, the alternative set is determined with fairness, and the object of selecting users from the alternative set is to maximize the sum-capacity of the system. Thus we can get the multiplexing gain as well as the multiuser diversity.

Determining the size of the alternative set is a challenging. The more users in the alternative set, the larger is the sum-capacity, but the worse is the fairness. In the Section 4, we will discuss how to determine the best size of the alternative set.

4   Simulation Results

4.1   The Proposed Scheduling Algorithm Compared with BD and PF

The scheduling algorithms based on the capacity will always select the stronger users, often losing the fairness. Considering the block fading model, the channel matrix is constant every slot. Dividing a block into 1000 slots, every slot user scheduling is done. In the Fig.1 and 2, the probability of users being scheduled is shown.

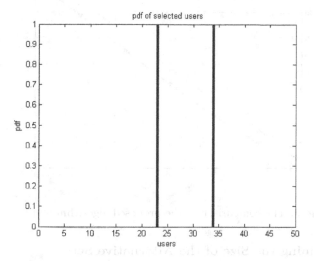

Fig. 1. The probability of users being selected in BD

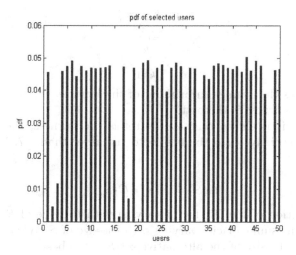

Fig. 2. The probability of users being selected in the proposed algorithm

In the Fig. 1, only user 23 and 34 are scheduled, no resource is allocated to other users. In the Fig. 2, in the proposed algorithm, we combine the PF and BD. When users are scheduled with equal probability, the scheduled probability is 0.04. Actually, the scheduled probability is 0.05, and the fairness is fine. In the Fig. 3, because the proposed algorithm has good fairness, the sum-capacity decreases.

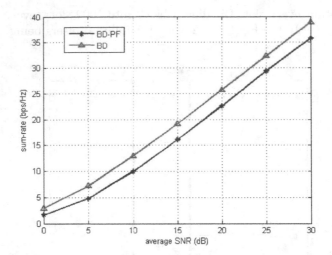

Fig. 3. The comparison of the proposed algorithm and BD

4.2   Determining the Size of the Alternative Set

In order to size of the set $\tilde{S}$, we define the fair factor F[9]:

$$F = \frac{(\sum\limits_{k=1}^{K} x_k)^2}{K \sum\limits_{k=1}^{K} x_k^2} \tag{13}$$

Here, x_k expresses the average throughput of the kth user. F varies from 0 to 1, when $F = 1$, the fairness is the best.

In the Fig. 4, it is shown that the better is the fairness, the worse is the sum-capacity, especially when the fair factor is larger than 0.7. We define the function G:

$$G(\tilde{S}) = F(\tilde{S}) * C(\tilde{S}) \tag{14}$$

$F(\tilde{S})$ is the function of the fair factor varying with the size of $\tilde{S}$, and $C(\tilde{S})$ is the function of the sum-capacity varying with the size of $\tilde{S}$. When $G(\tilde{S})$ has the maximum value, the size of the alternative set $\tilde{S}$ is the best.

In the simulation, the number of the total users is 50, the number of scheduled users is $M/N = 2$, so the size of the alternative set satisfies $2 \le |\tilde{S}| \le 50$.

Fig. 4 shows that the function G is convex, and G has a maximum value, when $|\tilde{S}| = 11$, which is the best size of the alternative set. From the TABEL 1, we see that when the size of the alternative is optimal, the sum-capacity of the system has small decline , but the fairness of the system increases significantly.

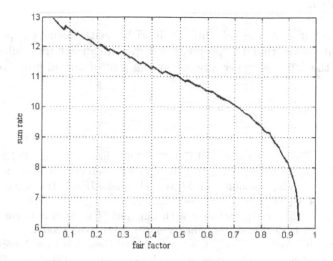

Fig. 4. The variation of the fair factor and sum rate

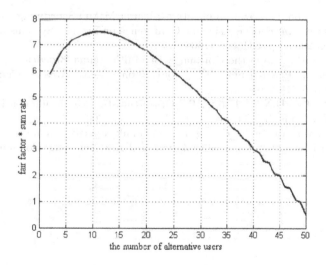

Fig. 5. G varies with the number of alternative users

Table 1. The performance of different sizes of the alternative set

The num of alternative set	2	11 (optional)	30	50
Fair facror	0.9418	0.8310	0.4309	0.0397
Sum-capacity	6.2759	9.1370	10.826	12.93

5 Conclusion

In this paper, an efficient user scheduling algorithm with fairness is proposed. Simulation results show that the proposed algorithm can get the multiplexing gain, ensuring the fairness, especially when the size of the alternative set is optimal.

References

1. Costa, M.: Writing on dirty paper. IEEE Trans. Inf. Theory. 29(5), 439 (2003)
2. Spencer, Q.H., Swindlehurst, A.L., Haardt, M.: Zero-forcing methods for downlink spatial multiplexing in multiuser MIMO channels. IEEE Trans. Signal Process. 52(4), 461–471 (2004)
3. Caire, G., Shamai, S.: On the achievable throughput of a multi-antenna Gussian broadcast channel. IEEE Trans. Inf. Theory 43(7), 1691–1760 (2003)
4. Shen, Z., Chen, R., Andrews, J.G.: Low Complexity User Selection Algorithm for Multiuser MIMO Sysem. IEEE Trans. Signal Process 54(9), 3658–3663 (2006)
5. Shen, Z., Chen, R., Andrews, J.G.: Sum Capacity of Multiuser MIMO Broadcast Channels with Block Diagonalization. In: IEEE International Symposium, vol. 54(9), pp. 886–890 (2006)
6. Xiaojie, Z., Jungwoo, L.: Low Complexity Multiuser MIMO Scheduling with Channel Decomposition. In: Fortieh Asilomar Conference on Signals, Systems and Computers, ACSSC 2006, pp. 641–645 (2006)
7. Yoo, T., Goldsmith, A.: On the Optimality of Multiantenna Broadcast Scheduling Using Zero-Forcing Beamforming. IEEE Journal on Selected Areas in Communications 24(3), 528–541 (2006)
8. Viswanath, P., Tse, D.N.C., Laroia, R.: Opportunistic beamforming using dumb antennas. IEEE Trans. Inf. Theory. 48(6), 1277–1294 (2002)
9. Viswanath, H., Venkatesan, S., Huang, H.: Downlink capacity evaluation of cellular networks with kown-interference cancellation. IEEE J. Sel.Areas Commun. 21(6), 802–811 (2003)

A New Cooperative Spectrum Sensing Scheme for Cognitive Ad-Hoc Networks

Yang Du[1,2], Hongxiang Li[2], Sentang Wu[1], Weiyao Lin[3], and Xudong Wang[4]

[1] School of Automation Science and Electrical Engineering,
Beihang University, Beijing, China
[2] Electrical and Computer Engineering, North Dakota State University, Fargo, ND, USA
[3] Institute of Image Communication and Information Processing,
Shanghai Jiao Tong University, Shanghai, China
[4] TeraNovi Technologies, Inc. USA & Shanghai Jiao Tong University, Shanghai, China

Abstract. As the radio spectrum is becoming more and more crowded, the cognitive radio has recently become a hot research topic to improve the spectrum utilization efficiency. It is well known that the success of cognitive radio depends heavily on fast and efficient spectrum sensing that can be very difficult in practice. Toward this end, this paper introduces a new guard-resident collaborative spectrum sensing topology for a cognitive ad-hoc network. In particular, we classify cognitive nodes as either *resident* or *guard* based on the spectrum neighbor decision and distributed boundary search. The guard nodes sense the spectrum and then inform the resident nodes that are free from spectrum sensing about the environmental changes. The analysis and simulation results show that the proposed algorithm can significantly reduce the total spectrum sensing load and improve the sensing accuracy.

Keywords: cognitive radio, spectrum sensing, ad-hoc, multi-cell, distributed boundary search.

1   Introduction

In order to improve the spectrum utilization, cognitive radio (CR) has recently gained significant attention from the wireless community [1]. In CR, within a tiered access hierarchy, the primary users retain preferential use rights; the secondary users may only use a primary channel when it is identified as unoccupied and must release such a channel whenever a primary user's transmission is detected. As is well known, the success of CR operation depends heavily on fast and efficient spectrum sensing [2]. This seemingly innocuous task can actually be quite difficult in practice due to the large variations in the dynamic range and bandwidth of signals to be detected.

To achieve better performance, people proposed the cooperative spectrum sensing (CSS) concept where each single node collects individual sensing results from its neighbors and combines them to make a better decision [3]. The existing cooperative spectrum sensing research is mostly focused on how to do the combination of sensing

P. Ren et al. (Eds.): WICON 2011, LNICST 98, pp. 105–116, 2012.
© Institute for Computer Sciences, Social Informatics and Telecommunications Engineering 2012

information collected by cooperative cognitive radio users and the optimization of sensing parameters [4, 5]. Paper [6] modeled the CSS problem as a nontransferable coalitional game where the network of CR users could form cooperating coalitions and interact on whether to merge or split based on the comparison relation for improving their spectrum sensing performance. Paper [7] modeled the CSS problem as an evolutionary game where the payoff was defined as the throughput of a secondary user. Paper [8] proposed a fast spectrum sensing algorithm for a large network which required fewer than the total number of cognitive radios in cooperative spectrum sensing while satisfying a given error bound. However, all existing CSS approaches put additional burden on neighboring nodes for constant spectrum sensing. Another major drawback of the existing CSS solutions is that most of them assume the collaborating nodes are subject to the same frequency exposure, few work consider the multi-cell primary network scenario where the neighboring cognitive nodes have exposure to different frequencies, leaving some open issues such as the well known *hidden node problem* [9] still unsolved.

In this paper, we consider a CR ad-hoc network (CRAHN), where the secondary network has ad-hoc connectivity (such as distributed multi-hop communication, self-organizing and dynamic network topology [10]). In CRAHN, the cognitive (ad-hoc) nodes generally have limited computation capability and thus constant spectrum sensing is not a suitable solution. *The key contribution of this paper is we derive a new guard-resident CSS method that can significantly reduce the overall spectrum sensing load without sacrificing the overall performance.*

The rest of the paper is organized as follows: Section 2 provides system model and the assumptions, followed by detailed discussion of the guard-resident CSS algorithms in Section 3. In Section 4, simulation results are presented. Finally, a conclusion is drawn in Section 5.

2   System Model

In this section, we describe the system model and assumptions. Compared to other existing CSS models, our model has two distinct features: (1) the primary network has multiple frequency zones; (2) cognitive nodes have ad-hoc connectivity so that cooperation is not limited to geographic neighbors.

Consider a multi-cell TV broadcasting (or cellular downlink) primary network as shown in Fig. 1, where we assume no frequency reuse for adjacent cells to avoid inter-cell interference. We define a *frequency zone* as an area covered by the same primary transmission. Ideally, cognitive users within the same frequency zone should have the same spectrum sensing results. Fig. 1 shows a three-cell primary network with seven frequency zones. The cognitive users with different densities are randomly distributed over the whole area. For any particular cognitive node, we define its *geometric neighbor as those* who have direct (one hop) connection with the node. Note that a node's geometric neighbors may be located at different frequency zones, which is particularly true for those who are on the cell edge.

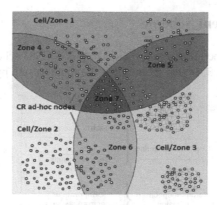

Fig. 1. Multi-cell TV broadcasting primary network

As we mentioned earlier, the benefits (increased sensing accuracy) of the existing CSS methods come at a price (increased sensing load). Furthermore, these methods are problematic for any cell edge cognitive user whose neighbors are from different frequency zones. On the other hand, we realize that cooperation between any two cognitive nodes is possible if they are connected (via single hop or multi-hop) within the same frequency zone, and such cooperation can be used to reduce the overall sensing load and avoid those problems associated with cell edge cognitive users. Toward this end, we propose our new guard-resident CSS scheme. The basic idea is to classify each cognitive node as either *resident* or *guard*, where only the guard nodes sense the spectrum and inform the resident nodes about the environmental changes. As shown by Fig. 2, the polygon formed by the guards becomes a safe zone such that any cognitive node within the safe zone will be free from spectrum sensing.

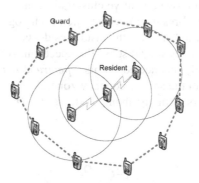

Fig. 2. The guard-resident scheme

In this work, we make the following assumptions: (1) Each CR node has no knowledge about the primary network, but it knows the direction of its geometric neighbor(s), which can be obtained by the positioning devices such as GPS or calculated from some "directional finding" algorithms [11]; (2) The CRAHN has a common control channel (CCC) that is dedicated to coordination and control information exchange among CR users [12].

3   Guard-Resident Scheme

The guard-resident cooperative spectrum sensing (GRCSS) scheme can be illustrated by the flow chart in Fig. 3. In this section, we'll explain it step by step.

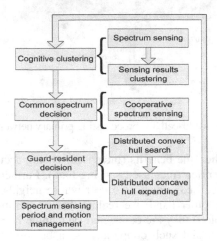

Fig. 3. Guard-resident scheme frame

3.1   Cognitive Clustering

The goal of this step is to divide cognitive users into *clusters* such that nodes within the same cluster are fully connected and located in the same frequency zone. For example, in Fig. 1, there are two cognitive clusters in zone 3. The cognitive cluster is the basic unit to make guard-resident decision, i.e., each cognitive cluster will form a connected guard boundary to "protect" the inside residents.

Initially, all cognitive nodes should sense the spectrum. According to their sensing results, each node is only connected to its *spectrum neighbors,* which are the geometric neighbors within the same frequency zone. As shown in Fig. 4, node *A* has seven geometric neighbors. Among them, node *B*, *C*, *D* and *J* are also spectrum neighbors of *A*.

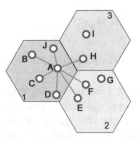

Fig. 4. Geometry neighbors and spectrum neighbors

   Due to the noise and other imperfections, nodes in the same frequency zone may have different sensing results. Then the question is how to decide a node's spectrum neighbors with sensing errors. In this paper we use *cluster analysis* to partitions the cognitive nodes into a certain number of clusters so that the sensing results in the same cluster are similar while those from different clusters are quite different. We aim to maximize both the cluster internal homogeneity and the external separation. Among many clustering algorithms, we choose hierarchical clustering algorithm (HCA) [13] because it doesn't need the prediction of the number of clusters and yields good performance in our cognitive clustering.

   There are two design parameters when applying HCA to our cognitive clustering: one is the *distance* among cognitive nodes and the other is the *threshold* for cutting the hierarchical tree. For example, in Fig. 5, we have a hierarchical tree with three clusters (10, 12, 5, 1, 8, 11, 14), (2, 6, 7, 3) and (4, 9, 13) using the threshold of 0.25. There are no fixed criteria for choosing the distance and the threshold because they depend on the specific application.

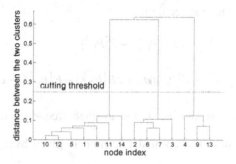

Fig. 5. The dendrogram of a hierarchical tree

   Note that the specific spectrum sensing technique is not the focus of this paper. For the convenience of the discussion, we use energy detection based spectrum sensing (EDSS) technology to illustrate how to define the distance and threshold in HCA. The EDSS approach has the following two hypotheses:

$$\begin{cases} H_0 : Y = N \\ H_1 : Y = S + N \end{cases}.$$
(1)

where Y is the overall sensed signal on a particular frequency channel; S is the primary signal to be detected; N is the additive white Gaussian noise (AWGN).

   Assuming a node has n-1 geometric neighbors and m channels to sense, we use the following n-by-m matrix $X\{x_{ij}\}_{n\times m}$ to denote the sensing results:

$$X = \begin{pmatrix} 1 & 0 & 0 & 1 & 0 & 1 & \cdots & 0 \\ \vdots & \vdots & \vdots & \vdots & \vdots & \vdots & \ddots & \vdots \\ 1 & 1 & 0 & 0 & 1 & 0 & \cdots & 0 \end{pmatrix}_{n\times m}.$$
(2)

where $x_{ij} = 1$ or 0 means the channel j is sensed by node i as available or occupied. In X, each row vector represents the sensing results of a particular node. For any two nodes r and s, we use normalized Hamming distance (NHD) as the distance metric:

$$d_{rs} = \frac{1}{m} \sum_{j=1}^{m} x_{rj} \oplus x_{sj} . \qquad (3)$$

Note that the symbol " $\oplus$ " is the mod operation, which can give erroneous result because each node may have detection errors. For node i, we denote the detection error rate for a particular channel j as $P_E(i, j)$. In order to maximize both the cluster internal homogeneity and the external separation, the *threshold* for cutting the hierarchical tree can't be either too large or too small. We denote the *threshold* as λ_{cut} and it should satisfy $\lambda_{min} < \lambda_{cut} < \lambda_{max}$ .We have derived both λ_{min} and λ_{max} (derivation is omitted due to space limit):

$$\lambda_{min} = 2E\{P_E\}(1 - E\{P_E\}) . \qquad (4)$$

$$\lambda_{max} = (1 - 2E\{P_E\}(1 - E\{P_E\}))d_z + 2E\{P_E\}(1 - E\{P_E\})(1 - d_z) . \qquad (5)$$

where $E\{\cdot\}$ is expectation and d_z is the average frequency diversity rate of two adjacent frequency zones. The optimal threshold is given by $\lambda_{cut} = \frac{1}{2}(\lambda_{min} + \lambda_{max})$. Another question is whether or not we can always find a solution for λ_{cut}. Obviously, λ_{cut} always has a solution if $\lambda_{max} - \lambda_{min} \geq 0$. Plugging above results, we have

$$\lambda_{max} - \lambda_{min} = d_z(2E\{P_E\} - 1)^2 \geq 0 . \qquad (6)$$

Therefore, λ_{cut} always exists.

Once the cognitive clustering is done, cooperative spectrum sensing will be done within each cluster, which includes the common spectrum decision shown in Fig. 3.

3.2   Guard-Resident Decision

The most important step in GRCSS is to make guard-resident decision for each cognitive cluster. Intuitively, the boundary nodes of each group can serve as the guards and "protect" the inside residents. For example, Fig. 6 shows a cognitive cluster where the square and round nodes are marked as guard and residents respectively. It is a concave hull of the CR nodes. However, the challenge is how to determine the boundary nodes considering the ad-hoc nature of the network. A major contribution of this work is that we derive efficient distributed algorithm to find the connected boundary of any arbitrary cognitive cluster.

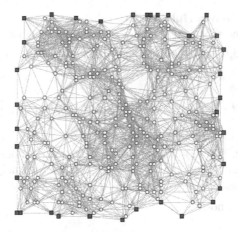

Fig. 6. A simulation of Guard-Resident Decision

Note that in CRAHN, each node can only decide its state (guard or resident) according to the limited local information. Most existing work on concave hull searching is not distributed and needs position information. Paper [14] proposed a distributed boundary search method but it assumed dense node connectivity, which only has limited applications. The distributed boundary search algorithm we present in this paper assumes each node only has its neighbor's direction information, which is represented by the counter-clockwise angle θ from one edge to another (see Fig. 7).

The guard-resident decision contains two steps, the first is distributed convex hull searching aimed to find a rough boundary and the second is distributed concave hull expanding aimed to expand some nodes as the boundary nodes for the final concave hull (Fig. 8).

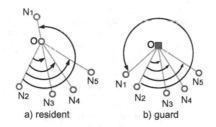

Fig. 7. Guard and resident

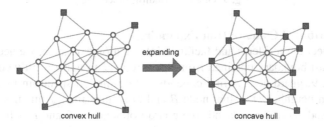

Fig. 8. Distributed boundary search algorithm

3.2.1   Distributed Convex Hull Search

As shown in Fig. 7. The spectrum neighbor of node O is denoted by N_i, i=1, 2, 3...
Select an arbitrary edge ON_j, the counter-clockwise angle from ON_j to ON_i is
$\{\theta_i | i = 1,2,3...\}$, define:

$$\Delta\theta = \min\{\theta_i \cup 2\pi | \pi < \theta_i \le 2\pi\} - \max\{\theta_i \cup 0 | 0 \le \theta_i \le \pi\} \tag{7}$$

Node O is called *guard* (boundary node) if $\Delta\theta > \pi$ (Fig. 7b). Otherwise, it is
resident (interior node, Fig. 7a). The spectrum neighbors that achieve the "min" and
"max" value in (7) are called the *left* and *right* spectrum neighbors of node O
respectively. For example, for the guard node O in Fig. 7b, N_1 and N_5 are its left
and right spectrum neighbors.

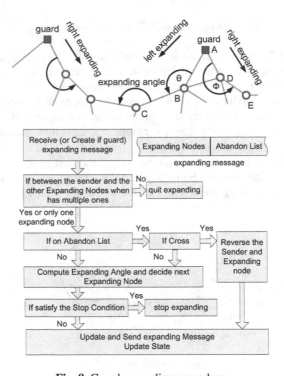

Fig. 9. Guard expanding procedure

3.2.2   Distributed Concave Hull Expanding

To better protect the residents and facilitate information exchange, we need to expand
the rough guard boundary obtained from Section *3.2.1* to make it fully connected. As
shown in Fig. 9, guard node A first expends to both its left spectrum neighbor B and
right spectrum neighbor D so that node B and D change their status from resident to
guard. Then node B further expands the guard boundary to C and E, where node C is

called the *left expanding node* of B (E is the *right expending node* of D). The angel θ and ϕ are called *expanding angles* of the node B and D. The same procedure will continue till a stopping condition is met.

4   Simulation

To evaluate the performance of the proposed GRCSS scheme, we consider a rectangular service area with dimensions 1000m×1000m. There are totally 100 frequency channels. The communication radius of the node is 30m.

4.1   Single Cell Scenario

As shown in Fig. 10, we scatter 500 nodes in a given area. The *SNR* is set as 5db. After running our distributed guard-resident algorithm, overall 82 percent of the nodes become residents (hollow round node) (see Table 1), which means the majority of the nodes are released from constant spectrum sensing.

Table 1. The resident ratio of single cell scenario

Color	red(small group)	red(large group)	total
Guard	23	66	89
Resident	22	389	411
Ratio	49%	85%	82%

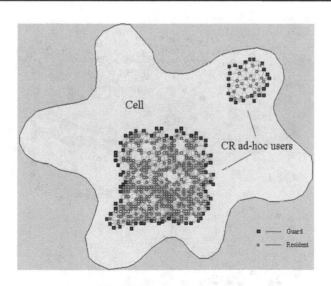

Fig. 10. Single cell scenario

When the detection error rate goes to 40%, we show the result in Fig.11, where many nodes make incorrect clustering decisions.

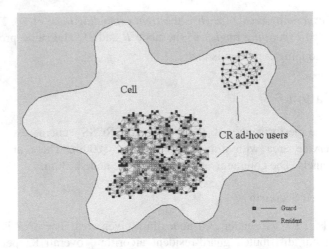

Fig. 11. Clustering error caused by detection error

4.2   Multi-Cell Scenario

As shown in Fig.12, the frequency channels are evenly allocated to three cells with overlap but no frequency reuse. The whole area forms seven different spectrum zones and the NHD between every two adjacent zones equals 0.33; the *SNR* is 5db. We can get the result in Fig. 12 (Different colors denote different sensing results) and Table 2.

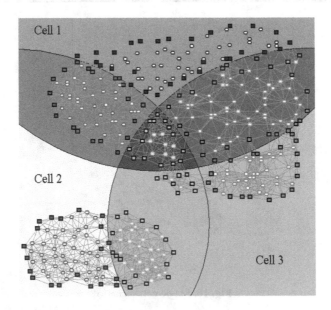

Fig. 12. Multi-cell scenario

Table 2. The resident ratio of multi-cell scenario

Color	purple	blue	cyan	gray	yellow	green	red	total
Guard	20	29	25	15	24	19	21	153
Resident	37	39	54	8	27	31	39	235
Ratio	65%	57%	68%	35%	53%	62%	65%	61%

Obviously, from the computation point of view, larger node density yields better performance. On the other hand, we also want to control the size of the cluster to make sure communications are effective within the same cluster.

5   Conclusion

This paper proposed a new guard-resident cooperative spectrum sensing method based on cluster theory and distributed boundary search. We grouped the nodes into two types: guard nodes and resident nodes. The guard nodes will constantly sense the spectrum and inform the environmental changes to their residents. Within the coherent time period, the area formed by the guards becomes a safe zone and the residents can be free from spectrum sensing. The analysis and simulation results suggest that the proposed scheme can reduce the total sensing load of the CRAHN significantly.

Acknowledgments. This work was supported in part by the National Science Foundation of USA (#1032567), ND NASA EPSCoR (#43500) and in part by the National Science Foundation of China (#61001146).

References

1. Haykin, S.: Cognitive radio: brain-empowered wireless communications. IEEE J. Sel. Areas Commun. 23(2), 201–220 (2005)
2. Ghasemi, A., Sousa, E.S.: Spectrum sensing in cognitive radio networks: requirements, challenges and design trade-offs. IEEE Commun. Mag. 46(4), 32–39 (2008)
3. Cabric, D., Mishra, S.M., Brodersen, R.W.: Implementation issues in spectrum sensing for cognitive radios. In: IEEE 38th Asilomar Conf. Signals Systems, Computers, pp. 772–776 (November 2004)
4. Liang, Y.-C., Zeng, Y., Peh, E., Hoang, A.T.: Sensing-throughput tradeoff for cognitive radio networks. IEEE Trans. Wireless Commun. 7(4), 1326–1337 (2008)
5. Quan, Z., Cui, S., Sayed, A.H.: Optimal Linear Cooperation for Spectrum Sensing in Cognitive Radio Networks. IEEE J. Sel. Topics Signal Process 2(1), 28–40 (2008)
6. Saad, W., Han, Z., Basar, T., Debbah, M., Hjørungnes, A.: Coalition Formation Games for Collaborative Spectrum Sensing. IEEE Trans. Vehicular Technology 60(1), 276–297 (2011)
7. Wang, B., Ray Liu, K.J., Charles Clancy, T.: Evolutionary Cooperative Spectrum Sensing Game: How to Collaborate? IEEE Trans. Commun. 58(3), 890–900 (2010)

8. Zhang, W., Mallik, R.K., Letaief, K.B.: Optimization of Cooperative Spectrum Sensing with Energy Detection in Cognitive Radio Networks. IEEE Trans. Wireless Commun. 8(12), 5761–5766 (2009)
9. Krenik, W., Batra, A.: Cognitive radio techniques for wide area networks. In: Proc. Conf. Design Automation, Anaheim, pp. 409–412 (June 2005)
10. Akyildiz, I.F., et al.: NeXt generation/dynamic spectrum access/ cognitive radio wireless networks: a survey. Computer Networks 50(13), 2127–2159 (2006)
11. Krizman, K.J., Biedka, T.E., Rappaport, T.S.: Wireless Position Location: Fundamentals, implementation strategies and sources of error. In: IEEE 47th Vehicular Technology Conference, vol. 2, pp. 919–923 (May 1997)
12. Akyildiz, I.F., Lee, W.-Y., Chowdhury, K.R.: CRAHNs: Cognitive radio ad hoc networks. Ad Hoc Networks 7(5), 810–835 (2009)
13. Hastie, T., Tibshirani, R., Friedman, J.: Elements of Statistical Learning: Data Mining, Inference and Prediction, 14.3.12 Hierarchical clustering (February 2009)
14. McLurkin, J., Demaine, E.D.: A distributed boundary detection algorithm for Multi-Robot systems. In: IEEE Intelligent RObots and Systems (IROS) (October 2009)

Iterative DS-CDMA Anti-interference Technique Based on Interference Power Cognition

Taofu Mo, Zhanghong Hao, and Youxi Tang

National Key Laboratory of Science and Technology on Comunications
University of Electronic Science and Technology of China
Chengdu, 611731, China
{motaofu,hzh_0515hzh,tangyx}@uestc.edu.cn

Abstract. In the additive white Gaussian noise channel, an iterative anti-interference method based on interference power cognition is proposed, where the interference is broadband digital modulation signal and desired signal is direct sequence spread spectrum(SS) signal. The power ratio of SS signal and interference is detected by cognitive method, and threshold value is calculated meanwhile. After that, the order of iteration is chose based on power ratio and threshold, if the ratio is bigger than threshold, the SS signal is detected first, or vice versa. Result shows the BER performance is improved by using proposed method, the performance is improved from 4e-3 to 1e-4 by using the proposed method, when the spread gain is 63, the SNR is -5dB, and the SIR is -12dB.

Keywords: Spread spectrum signal, Iterative detection, Desired signal, interference cancellation.

1 Introduction

Spread-spectrum systems are naturally resistant to narrowband interference, existing active NBI suppression techniques can be grouped into three basic types: transform-domain techniques1, time-domain cancellation techniques2, and code-aided techniques3. As the name implies, transform-domain techniques operate by transforming the received signal into frequency domain, and masking frequency bands of interference. The basic idea of time-domain techniques is the difference of the time correlation between interference and spread spectrum signal. Reconstruct the interference and subtracted from the received signal to suppress the interference. If we know the spreading code of at least one user of interest, the code-aided techniques can take this advantage for interference cancellation(IC).

As the data rate growing, the bandwidth of the interference becomes wide. The performance of IC techniques mentioned above is deteriorated. The main reason of this phenomenon is these techniques treat the interference as random signal, without using priori information of interference. In this article, we consider the interference is digital modulated signal, which bandwidth is the same as the CDMA signal. An

P. Ren et al. (Eds.): WICON 2011, LNICST 98, pp. 117–124, 2012.

iterative detection based on power cognition4 is proposed: The power ratio of desired signal and interference is cognized for iteration order selection, if the ratio is bigger than the threshold, the CDMA is detected first, then reconstruct the CDMA signal and cancel it from the original signal, after that the interference is detected. On the other side, the ratio is smaller than the threshold, the iteration order is reverse. The threshold is calculated based on spreading code and SNR.

This paper is organized as follows. Section 2 presents system model, including the interference model and receiver model. Section 3 is devoted to the proposed detection method. The results are the subject of Section 4. Section 5 is the conclusion.

2   System Model

2.1   Interference Model

Fig.1. shows the block diagram of transmitter, the desired signal combines with the interference. The desired signal is spread spectrum signal, which is BPSK modulated after spectrum spread. The bandwidth of the interference is the same as the desired signal. BPSK modulation is chosen for interference. With different channel gains, the two signals combine together in receiver. The channel gains are assumed to be constant in detection interval.

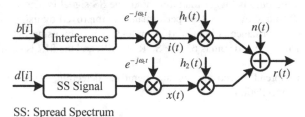

SS: Spread Spectrum

Fig. 1. Interference model

The baseband signal of interference is denoted as $I(t) = \sum_{i=-\infty}^{+\infty} b[i]S_b(t - iT_b)$, where $b[i]$ is the symbol transmitted by co-channel user at i th time slot, $i \in (-\infty, +\infty)$ .The transmitted interference is

$$i(t) = \text{Re}[I(t)e^{-j\omega_c t}] \tag{1}$$

The baseband signal of desired signal is denoted as $X(t) = d(t)c(t)$, where $c(t) = \sum_{i=-\infty}^{+\infty} c(i)P_{T_c}(t - iT_c)$ is the spreading code, the function $P_{T_c}(t)$ is the shape pulse that length is T_c . $d(t) = \sum_{i=-\infty}^{+\infty} d(i)P_T(t - iT)$ is the data symbols, function $P_T(t)$ is the shape pulse that length is T .Data $d(i)$ is encoded and modulated by transmitter, the spread gain is $N = T/T_c$ .The carrier of desired signal is the same as the interference, the transmitted signal is

$$x(t) = \text{Re}[X(t)e^{-j\omega_c t}] \tag{2}$$

Through the different channel, the received signal is

$$r(t) = h_1(t)x(t) + h_2(t)i(t) + n(t) \tag{3}$$

We have $T_c = T_b$ because the bandwidth of the interference and desired signal is the same.

2.2   Receiver Model

Fig.2. shows the block diagram of receiver, the time and frequency synchronization is assumed here. After A/D transform, the received signal $r(t)$ is changed into

$$r(n) = h_1(n)x(n) + h_2(n)i(n) + n(n) \tag{4}$$

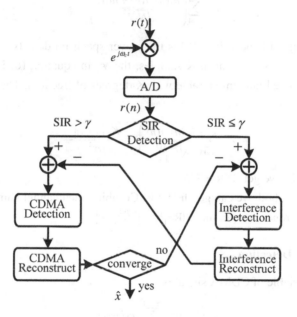

Fig. 2. Receiver model

$h_1(n)$ and $h_2(n)$ are channel gains, which are assumed to be constant in detection interval. The channel gain can be attained by cognitive techniques.

After we get $r(n)$, the SIR is detected by energy detection technique, which is widely used in cognitive radio. The iterative anti-interference process is shown in Fig.2., when the SIR is bigger than threshold γ, we detect the CDMA signal at first, then reconstruct and cancel it from the original received signal $r(n)$, after that, the interference is detected from the cancelled signal. While, when the SIR is smaller than threshold, vice versa. The iteration is combined by detection, reconstruction and cancellation.

3   Cognitive Detection Method

3.1   SIR Detection

We detect the SNR and INR separately, which is the power ratio of desired signal and Gaussian noise, the power ratio of interference and Gaussian noise respectively[4]. When we detect the INR, the desired signal is not transmitted, as equation (3) shown, the received signal is

$$r(t) = h_2(t)i(t) + n(t) \qquad (5)$$

From the continual K samples[5], we get

$$\varepsilon = \sum_{n=1}^{K} \left(\frac{h_2(n) \cdot i(n) + n(n)}{\sqrt{N_0 W}} \right)^2 \qquad (6)$$

The W is the signal bandwidth, N_0 is the power spectrum density. We assume the channel gain $h_2(n)$ is constant in K samples, the ε in equation (6) is a non-central chi-square distributed random variable with K degrees of freedom. The non-centrality parameter is

$$\lambda = \sum_{n=1}^{K} \left(\frac{h_2(n) \cdot i(n)}{\sqrt{N_0 W}} \right)^2 = \frac{K \cdot |h_2(n)|^2}{\sigma^2} \qquad (7)$$

From equation (7), we get $\mathrm{INR} = \lambda / K$.

As the same method, we can get the SNR. Combing the channel gain of the desired signal and interference, we get the $\mathrm{SIR} = |h_1(n)|^2 / |h_2(n)|^2$.

3.2   Iterative Detection

The decision variable of CDMA signal is

$$U(g) = \sum_{l=(g-1)N}^{gN-1} c(l)r(l) \qquad (8)$$

From equation (8), we get the decision value of desired signal $\hat{x}(n) = U(g) / |U(g)|$. Then, reconstruct and cancel the desired signal from original signal $\tilde{r}(n) = r(n) - h_1(n)\hat{x}(n)$. As the bandwidth of interference is same as the CDMA signal, we get interference decision value from the cancelled signal $\hat{i}(n) = \tilde{r}(n) / |\tilde{r}(n)|$.

After that, reconstruct and cancel the interference from original signal $\tilde{r}(n) = r(n) - h_2(n)\hat{i}(n)$. We get the decision variable of desired signal again. This is the process of iteration when the SIR is bigger than threshold. On the other side, the interference is detected at first. When the CDMA signal is convergence, iteration is stopped.

3.3   Threshold

As we show before, the key problem of iteration is the iteration order decision, which is based on the SIR threshold γ. We give a numerical analysis result here.

The SNR is defined as $\text{SNR} = |h_1|^2/\sigma^2$, where the σ^2 is the power of Gaussian noise. The INR is $\text{INR} = |h_2|^2/\sigma^2$. To the interference, there are CDMA signal and Gaussian noise interfere its decision. The joint PDF of CDMA signal and Gaussian noise is[7]

$$f(x) = \frac{1}{2}\left(\frac{1}{\sqrt{2\pi}\sigma}\exp\left(-\frac{(x-h_1)^2}{2\sigma^2}\right) + \frac{1}{\sqrt{2\pi}\sigma}\exp\left(-\frac{(x+h_1)^2}{2\sigma^2}\right)\right) \tag{9}$$

The bit error rate of interference decision is

$$P_e^B = P(X < -h_2) = \int_{-\infty}^{-h_2} f(x)dx \tag{10}$$

Rewrite equation (10) as

$$P_e^B(\text{SNR,INR}) = P\left(X < -\sqrt{\text{INR}}\right) = \int_{-\infty}^{\sqrt{\text{INR}}} f(t)dt \tag{11}$$

Where the $f(t)$ is

$$f(t) = \frac{1}{2\cdot\sqrt{2\pi}}\left\{\exp\left[-\frac{\left(t-\sqrt{\text{SNR}}\right)^2}{2}\right] + \exp\left[-\frac{\left(t+\sqrt{\text{SNR}}\right)^2}{2}\right]\right\} \tag{12}$$

After the interference is detected, we reconstruct and cancel it from the original signal, the desired signal decision variable is

$$\bar{r}(n) = h_1(n)x(n) + h_2(n)\left(i(n) - \hat{i}(n)\right) + n(n) \tag{13}$$

As the error rate of interference is $P_e^B(\text{SNR,INR})$, the CDF of resident interference $i(n) - \hat{i}(n)$ is based on it.

$$\xi(n) = i(n) - \hat{i}(n) = \begin{cases} 0 & 1 - P_e^B \\ +2 & P_e^B/2 \\ -2 & P_e^B/2 \end{cases} \tag{14}$$

From equation (14), we know the mean of resident interference is 0, and variance is $4P_e^B(\text{SNR,INR})|h_2|^2$ [6]. As the dispreading process, the resident interference $\xi(n)$ is transformed into different form, and the new form is also a Gaussian random variable.

The power of dispread CDMA signal is $N|h_1|^2$, then the SIR is

$$\eta = \frac{N|h_1|^2}{4P_e^B(\text{SNR,INR})|h_2|^2 + \sigma^2} \tag{15}$$

We can get the bit error rate of desired signal based on SIR η and error function $Q(x) = \int_x^\infty \exp(-t^2/2)dt \big/ \sqrt{2\pi}$ [6]

$$P_e^C(\text{SNR,INR}) = Q(\text{SNR,INR})$$

$$= Q\left(\sqrt{\frac{N \cdot \text{SNR}}{4P_e^B(\text{SNR,INR}) \cdot \text{INR} + 1}} \right) \tag{16}$$

$$= \frac{1}{\sqrt{2\pi}} \int_{\sqrt{\frac{N \cdot \text{SNR}}{4P_e^B(\text{SNR,INR}) \cdot \text{INR} + 1}}}^\infty \exp\left(-\frac{x^2}{2} \right) dx$$

Derivation calculus for INR, we get the BER peak of desired signal

$$\frac{\partial Q(\text{SNR,INR})}{\partial \text{INR}} = 0 \tag{17}$$

The simplification of equation (17) is

$$f\left(-\sqrt{\text{INR}}\right)\sqrt{\text{INR}} - 2\int_{-\infty}^{\sqrt{\text{INR}}} f(t)dt = 0 \tag{18}$$

When the SNR is determined, we can get the threshold γ form equation (18).

4   Simulation Results

The parameter of simulation is given in Table 1.

Table 1. Simulation parameter

SF: Spread Factor	63
Spread code	m sequence
CDMA data rate(bps)	19.2Kbps
Interference data rate (Kbps)	SF × 19.2
SNR	−8,−5 dB
SIR	−21 ~ 9 dB

With different iteration order, the BER performance is given in Fig.3., when the SNR $= -8, -5$dB. As the figure show, when the SIR is low, the BER performance is better if we detect the interference first. On the other side, when the SIR is high, BER performance is better when we choose to detect the CDMA signal first.

There is a intersection of two different iteration order that is the SIR threshold, which is used for iteration order selection. Fig.4. shows the numerical results of threshold when he SNR $= -8, -5$dB. The SIR threshold are $\gamma = -10.1$dB and -7.7dB respectively, which is the same as the intersections in Fig.3.

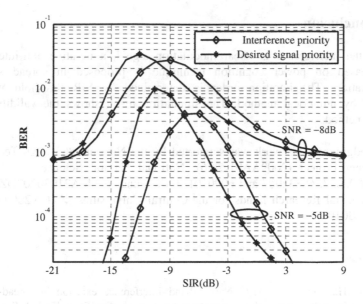

Fig. 3. BER performance of different iterative order when the SNR are −8 and −5 dB

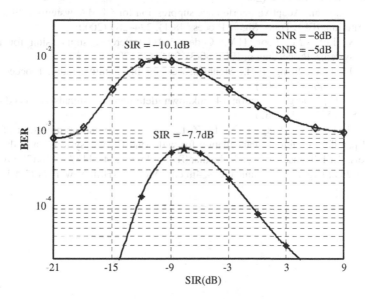

Fig. 4. Numerical results of threshold as the SNR are . −8 . and −5 dB

As we stated before, when the SIR is detected by cognitive technique, and threshold is calculated, the iteration order can be select for better BER performance. When the SNR is −5dB , and SIR is −12dB , the BER is improved from 4e-3 to 1e-4 as we detect the interference at first. On the other side, when the SIR is −3dB , the BER is improved from 1e-3 to 1e-4 as we detect the desired signal at first.

5   Conclusion

Consider the interference is linear modulation signal, a iterative anti-interference method based on power cognition technique is proposed in spread spectrum communication. The iteration order is determined by SIR threshold which is calculated by numerical method. The simulation result shows the validity of the proposed method.

Acknowledgment. This work was supported by the National 863 High Technology Development Project (2009AA01Z236), National Natural Science Foundation of China (60902027, 60832007 and 60901018), the Funds (9140A21030209DZ02), and the Fundamental Research Funds for the Central Universities (ZYGX2009J008 and ZYGX2009J010).

References

1. Li, C.N., Hu, G.R., Liu, M.J.: Narrow-band interference excision in spread-spectrum systems using self-orthogonalizing transform-domain adaptive filter. IEEE J. Select. Areas Commun. 18(3), 403–406 (2000)
2. Nagaraj, S., et al.: Adaptive interference suppression for CDMA systems with a worst-case error criterion. IEEE Trans. Signal Process 48(1), 284–289 (2000)
3. Buzzi, S., Lops, M., Poor, H.V.: Code-aided interference suppression for DS/CDMA overlay systems. Proceeding of IEEE 90(3), 394–435 (2002)
4. Ma, J., Li, G.Y., Juang, B.H.: Signal processing in cognitive radio. Proceedings of the IEEE 97(5), 806–823 (2009)
5. Urkowitz, H.: Energy detection of unknown deterministic signals. Proceedings of the IEEE 55(4), 523–531 (1967)
6. Hu, C.-H., Li, S.-Q., Tang, Y.-X., Li, Z.-L.: Performance and optimization of multistage partial parallel interference cancellation for wideband CDMA systems in multipath fading channels. IEEE Transactions on Vehicular Technology 55(4), 1137–1158 (2006)
7. Proakis, J.G.: Digital Communications, 4th edn. McGraw-Hill, New York (2001)

Outage-Based Optimal Transmit Antenna Location for Distributed Antenna Systems with Selection Transmission

Liang Han, Tian Liu, Shihai Shao, Chaojin Qing, and Youxi Tang

National Key Lab of Science and Technology on Communications,
University of Electronic Science and Technology of China, Chengdu 611731, China
{hanliang,liutian,ssh,qingchj,tangyx}@uestc.edu.cn

Abstract. In this paper, we investigate the optimal transmit antenna location for distributed antenna systems (DAS) with selection transmission in the downlink. Considering the effects of path loss, shadow fading, rayleigh fading and white Gaussian noise, we first derive the approximate cell averaged outage probability at high signal-to-noise ratio (SNR). Then, we obtain the transmit antenna location by minimizing the approximate cell averaged outage probability. Simulation results validate the analytical results and show that DAS with optimized antenna locations offers smaller outage probability over the traditional co-located antenna system (CAS).

Keywords: antenna location, distributed antenna systems, outage probability, selection transmission.

1 Introduction

Distributed antenna system (DAS) was originally introduced by Saleh for coverage improvement in indoor wireless communications[1]. In recent years, DAS has attracted worldwide research interests as a promising technique [2]–[4]. Compared with co-located antenna system (CAS), DAS has many advantages: more independent channel fading, larger system capacity [5][6], shorter access distance, and lower transmission power [7].

In [8], the spectral efficiency of random layout DAS is analyzed and it has been found that the system performance is influenced by the antenna location. In [9], the optimal antenna location for a linear cell is obtained by minimizing the area averaged bit error probability for STBC-OFDM systems. The authors of [10] studied the antenna positioning problem for the uplink of DAS and propose the squared distance criterion. However, there has been little research on the antenna location optimization from the perspective of outage probability.

Our contribution in this paper can be briefly described as follows. First, we derive the approximate outage probability in a circular cell for distributed antenna systems with selection transmission. Second, we obtain the optimal transmit antenna location by minimizing the approximate cell averaged outage probability.

P. Ren et al. (Eds.): WICON 2011, LNICST 98, pp. 125–132, 2012.

The rest of the paper is organized as follows. In section 2, the system model is introduced. In section 3, the expression of approximate cell averaged outage probability is derived and the antenna location is then obtained by minimizing the approximate cell averaged outage probability. Afterward, in section 4, some simulation results are given to demonstrate the analytical results. Finally, section 5 concludes this paper.

The notation used in this paper follows the usual convention. Matrices and vectors are denoted by symbols in boldface. $(\cdot)^T$ and $(\cdot)^H$ are transpose and conjugate transpose of $(\cdot)$, respectively. $E(\cdot)$ is the mathematical expectation of $(\cdot)$.

2 System Model

2.1 Circular Cell Architecture

The circular cell architecture is shown in Fig. 1. In a circular cell of radius R, M_T distributed transmit antennas are connected to a single base station by fibers or coax cables. The polar coordinate for the nth transmit antenna is denoted by (r_n, θ_n), $n = 1, \cdots M_T$. In order to make the analysis tractable, we assume that the transmit antennas are placed uniformly on a circle of radius ρ, i.e.,

$$\begin{cases} r_1 = r_2 = \cdots = r_{M_T} = \rho \\ \theta_n = \frac{2\pi(n-1)}{M_T}, \quad n = 1, 2, \cdots M_T \end{cases} . \tag{1}$$

A mobile station (MS) is assumed to be uniformly distributed in the cell [11], and its polar coordinate is denoted by (r, θ). Thus, the probability density function (PDF) of (r, θ) is given by

$$f(r, \theta) = \frac{r}{\pi R^2}, \quad 0 \le r \le R, 0 \le \theta \le 2\pi. \tag{2}$$

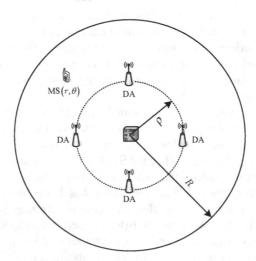

Fig. 1. A circular cell layout of distributed antenna system(DAS)

The distance d_n from the MS to the nth transmit antenna can be calculated as [12]

$$d_n = \sqrt{r^2 + \rho^2 - 2r\rho\cos(\theta - \theta_n)}. \tag{3}$$

2.2 Transmission Strategy

There are many possible strategies to use the distributed transmit antennas for signal transmission. In this paper, we considered one of the most commonly used: selection transmission [5][6]. In selection transmission scheme, only a single distributed antenna module is selected out of all the antennas for transmission by the criterion of minimizing propagation pathloss. When MS is located in the shadow region as shown in Fig. 2, the base station selects the 1st antenna to transmit signals. Selection transmission has gained increasing interest in DAS because it reduces the other-cell interference (OCI) and retains the effects of the spatial diversity.

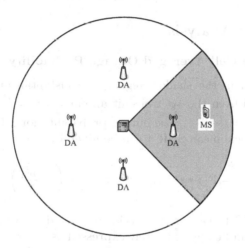

Fig. 2. Selection transmission

2.3 Channel Model

For practical reasons, the MS is assumed to have a single antenna. When MS is located in the shadow region, the received signals can be expressed as

$$r = h_1 x + n \tag{4}$$

where x is the transmitted signal from the 1st distributed antenna with $E[|x|^2] = E_b$, h_1 denotes the fading channel coefficient from the 1st transmit antenna to the MS, n denotes the additive white complex Gaussian noise with zero-mean and variance N_0.

The fading channel coefficient h_1 is modeled as [13]

$$h_1 = \xi_1 \sqrt{L_1 S_1} \tag{5}$$

where ξ_1 is a zero-mean complex Gaussian random variable with unit variance that models the Rayleigh fading, S_1 represents the shadow fading between the 1st transmit antenna and the MS, and L_1 denotes the path loss from the 1st transmit antenna to the MS.

We model S_1 as a log-normal random variable, meaning that $10\log_{10}(S_1)$ is assumed to be normally distributed with zero mean and standard deviation $\sigma_{s,1}$.

L_1 is modeled as the following form

$$L_1 = \frac{c}{d_1^{\alpha}} \tag{6}$$

where c is a constant, α is the path loss exponent.

3   Performance Analysis

3.1   Approximate Cell Averaged Outage Probability

When MS is located in the shadow region, the instantaneous signal-to-noise ratio (SNR) received from the 1st transmit antenna is $\gamma = \frac{E_b S_1 L_1 |\xi_1|^2}{N_0}$ and the local mean SNR is $\bar{\gamma} = \frac{E_b S_1 L_1}{N_0}$. The outage probability for a fixed MS location conditioned on the local mean SNR $\bar{\gamma}$ can be given by

$$P_{out} = \Pr(\gamma < \gamma_{\text{req}} | \bar{\gamma}) = 1 - \exp\left(-\frac{\gamma_{\text{req}}}{\bar{\gamma}}\right) \tag{7}$$

where γ_{req} is the SNR target for the service requested by MS. For large $\bar{\gamma}$, the outage probability can be approximately expressed as [14]

$$P_{out} \approx \frac{\gamma_{\text{req}}}{\bar{\gamma}} \approx \frac{N_0 \gamma_{\text{req}}}{E_b S_1 L_1}. \tag{8}$$

Under the assumption of log-normal distribution for S_1, $\frac{1}{S_1}$ is also a log-normal random variable, i.e., $10\log_{10}\frac{1}{S_1} \sim N\left(0, \sigma_{s,1}^2\right)$. Then equation (8) can be written as

$$\begin{aligned} P_{out} &\approx \exp\left(\frac{\sigma_{s,1}^2 \ln^2 10}{200}\right)\frac{N_0 \gamma_{\text{req}}}{E_b L_1} \\ &\approx \exp\left(\frac{\sigma_{s,1}^2 \ln^2 10}{200}\right)\frac{N_0 \gamma_{\text{req}}}{c E_b} d_1^{\alpha}. \end{aligned} \tag{9}$$

Considering the symmetry of the transmit antenna, the average outage probability of the entire cell is equivalent to the the average outage probability of the shadow region. Then the approximate cell averaged outage probability can be obtained

$$
\begin{aligned}
\bar{P}_{out} &= \mathrm{E_{MS}}\left(P_{out}\right) \\
&= \mathrm{E_{MS}}\left[\exp\left(\frac{\sigma_1^2 \ln^2 10}{200}\right)\frac{N_0 \gamma_{req} d_1^\alpha}{cE_b}\right]. \\
&= \exp\left(\frac{\sigma_1^2 \ln^2 10}{200}\right)\frac{N_0 \gamma_{req}}{cE_b}\mathrm{E_{MS}}\left[d_1^\alpha\right]
\end{aligned}
\tag{10}
$$

3.2 Optimization Problem and Solution

The mathematical model for the optimization problem can be written as

$$
\rho^* = \arg\min_\rho \bar{P}_{out} = \arg\min_\rho \mathrm{E_{MS}}\left[d_1^\alpha\right].
\tag{11}
$$

Form (11), we note that the optimal antenna location depends on the path loss exponent. Without loss of generality, we just consider $\alpha = 2$ and $\alpha = 4$ in this paper. Other path loss exponents can be obtained in the same way.

When $\alpha = 2$, the cell averaged outage probability can be obtained as

$$
\begin{aligned}
\bar{P}_{out} &= \exp\left(\frac{\sigma_{s,1}^2 \ln^2 10}{200}\right)\frac{N_0 \gamma_{req}}{cE_b}\mathrm{E_{MS}}\left[d_1^2\right] \\
&= \exp\left(\frac{\sigma_{s,1}^2 \ln^2 10}{200}\right)\frac{N_0 \gamma_{req}}{cE_b}\frac{N}{\pi R^2}\int_{-\frac{\pi}{M_T}}^{\frac{\pi}{M_T}}\int_0^R r\left(r^2 + \rho^2 - 2r\rho\cos(\theta - \theta_n)\right)dr d\theta. \\
&= \exp\left(\frac{\sigma_{s,1}^2 \ln^2 10}{200}\right)\frac{N_0 \gamma_{req}}{cE_b}\left[\frac{R^2}{2} + \rho^2 - \frac{4\rho R M_T}{3\pi}\sin\left(\frac{\pi}{M_T}\right)\right]
\end{aligned}
\tag{12}
$$

We set the first order derivative of (12) equal to 0, and obtain the optimal antenna location

$$
\rho^* = \frac{2R M_T}{3\pi}\sin\left(\frac{\pi}{M_T}\right).
\tag{13}
$$

When $\alpha = 4$, the cell averaged outage probability can be obtained as

$$
\begin{aligned}
\bar{P}_{out} &= \exp\left(\frac{\sigma_{s,1}^2 \ln^2 10}{200}\right)\frac{N_0 \gamma_{req}}{cE_b}\mathrm{E_{MS}}\left[d_1^4\right] \\
&= \exp\left(\frac{\sigma_{s,1}^2 \ln^2 10}{200}\right)\frac{N_0 \gamma_{req}}{cE_b}\frac{M_T}{\pi R^2}\int_{-\frac{\pi}{M_T}}^{\frac{\pi}{M_T}}\int_0^R r\left(r^2 + \rho^2 - 2r\rho\cos(\theta - \theta_n)\right)^2 dr d\theta \\
&= \exp\left(\frac{\sigma_{s,1}^2 \ln^2 10}{200}\right)\frac{N_0 \gamma_{req}}{cE_b}\frac{M_T}{\pi R^2} \\
&\quad \left\{\frac{R^4}{3} + \rho^4 - \frac{8M_T \sin\left(\frac{\pi}{M_T}\right)R}{3\pi}\rho^3 + \left[\frac{R^2 M_T \sin\left(\frac{2\pi}{M_T}\right)}{2\pi} + 2R^2\right]\rho^2 - \frac{8\rho R^3 M_T \sin\left(\frac{\pi}{M_T}\right)}{5\pi}\right\}
\end{aligned}
\tag{14}
$$

We set the first order derivative of (14) equal to 0, and get

$$
\rho^3 - \frac{2R M_T \sin\left(\frac{\pi}{M_T}\right)}{\pi}\rho^2 + \frac{R^2 M_T \sin\left(\frac{2\pi}{M_T}\right) + 4\pi R^2}{4\pi}\rho - \frac{2R^3 M_T \sin\left(\frac{\pi}{M_T}\right)}{5\pi} = 0.
\tag{15}
$$

According to the formula for finding roots of cubic equations, the real root in the interval $[0, R]$ is just the solution to our optimization problem.

4   Numerical and Simulation Results

In this section, we validate the analytical results by simulations. Some basic simulation parameters are given as follows: $R = 1000$m, $\sigma_{s,1} = 6$dB, $\gamma_{\text{req}} = 10$dB, $N_0 = -100$dBm.

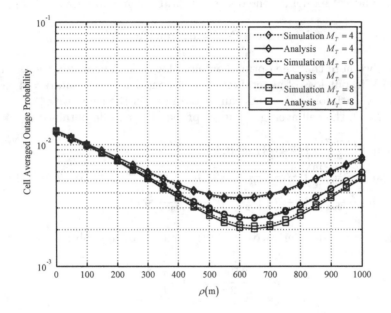

Fig. 3. Cell averaged outage probability versus transmit antenna location when path loss exponent $\alpha = 2$. $R = 1000$m, $\sigma_{s,1} = 6$dB, $\gamma_{\text{req}} = 10$dB, $N_0 = -100$dBm, $E_b = -10$dBm.

Fig. 3 illustrates the cell averaged outage probability versus transmit antenna location when path loss exponent $\alpha = 2$. As shown in Fig. 3, the optimal transmit antenna location is close to $0.6R$ and the simulation results approximately agree with the analytical results.

Fig. 4 shows the cell averaged outage probability versus transmit antenna location when path loss exponent $\alpha = 4$. From Fig. 4, we can observe that the optimal transmit antenna location is close to $0.65R$. It is further proved from Fig. 4 that the simulation results approximately agree with the analytical results.

Both Fig. 3 and Fig. 4 validate the analytical results and show that DAS with optimized antenna locations offers smaller outage probability over the traditional co-located antenna system.

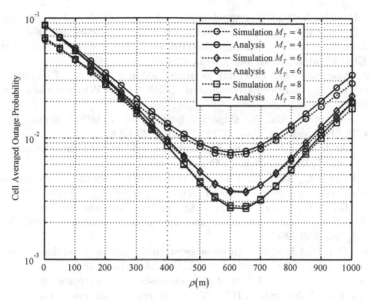

Fig. 4. Cell averaged outage probability versus transmit antenna location when path loss exponent $\alpha = 4$. $R = 1000$m, $\sigma_{s,1} = 6$dB, $\gamma_{\text{req}} = 10$dB, $N_0 = -100$dBm, $E_b = 40$dBm.

5   Conclusion

In this paper, we have derived the approximate cell averaged outage probability for distributed antennas systems with selection transmission in the downlink and obtained the optimal transmit antenna location by minimizing approximate cell averaged outage probability. Simulation results validate the analytical results and show that DAS with optimized antenna locations offers smaller outage probability over the traditional CAS. The research results provide a scheme to determine the location of transmit antennas for the next generation wireless communication networks based on DAS.

Acknowledgment. This work was supported in part by the National major projects (No.2010ZX03003-002,2011ZX03001-006-01), National Natural Science Foundation of China (No.60902027, No.60832007 No.U1035002/L05 and No.60901018), and the Fundamental Research Funds for the Central Universities under Grant number ZYGX2009J008, ZYGX2009J010 of China.

References

1. Saleh, A., Rustako, A., Roman, R.: Distributed antennas for indoor radio communication. IEEE Trans. Commun. 35(12), 1245–1251 (1987)
2. Zhou, S., Zhao, M., Xu, X., Yao, Y.: Distributed wireless communication system: a new architecture for future public wireless access. IEEE Commun. Mag. 41(3), 108–113 (2003)

3. Roh, W., Paulraj, A.: MIMO channel capacity for the distributed antenna systems. In: Proc. IEEE VTC, Vancouver, Canada, pp. 706–709 (February 2002)
4. He, X., Luo, T., Yue, G.: Optimized distributed MIMO for cooperative relay networks. IEEE Commun. Lett. 14(1), 9–11 (2010)
5. Choi, W., Andrews, J.G.: Downlink performance and capacity of distributed antenna systems in a multicell environment. IEEE Trans. Wireless Commun. 6(1), 69–73 (2007)
6. Zhong, C., Wong, K., Jin, S.: Capacity bounds for MIMO Nakagami-m fading channels. IEEE Trans. Sig. Proc. 57(9), 3613–3623 (2009)
7. Zhang, J., Andrews, J.G.: Distributed antenna systems with randomness. IEEE Commun. Lett. 7(9), 3636–3646 (2008)
8. Zhuang, H., Dai, L., Xiao, L., Yao, Y.: Spectral efficiency of distributed antenna system with random antenna layout. Electron. Lett. 39(6), 495–496 (2003)
9. Shen, Y., Tang, Y., Kong, T., Shao, S.: Optimal antenna location for STBC-OFDM downlink with distributed transmit antennas in linear cells. IEEE Commun. Lett. 11(5), 387–389 (2007)
10. Wang, X., Zhu, P., Chen, M.: Antenna location design for generalized distributed antenna systems. IEEE Commun. Lett. 13(5), 315–317 (2009)
11. Mukherjee, S., Avidor, D.: Effect of microdiversity and correlated macrodiversity on outages in a cellular system. IEEE Trans. Wireless Commun. 2(1), 50–58 (2003)
12. Coxeter, H.S.M.: Introduction to Geometry, 2nd edn. Wiley, New York (1969)
13. Stüber, G.L.: Principles of Mobile Communications. Kluwer, New York (2002)
14. Simon, M.K., Alouini, M.-S.: Digital Communications over Fading Channels: A Unified Approach to Performance Analysis. Wiley, New York (2000)

Signal Detection for Joint Distributed Space-Time Coding in Asynchronous Cooperative Cellular Systems[*]

Zhuo Wu, Luodan Liu, and Xin Wang

Key Laboratory of Specialty Fiber Optics and Optical Access Networks,
Shanghai University, China
Information School, Telecommunications, University of Pittsburgh, United States
{zwu,liuluodan}@shu.edu.cn, xiw54@pitt.edu

Abstract. In this paper, a signal detection scheme using parallel interference cancellation (PIC) joint with successive interference cancellation (SIC) is proposed for an asynchronous cooperative cellular system utilizing the efficient joint distributed space-time coding (J-DSTC). Simulation results demonstrate that the proposed scheme outperforms the conventional J-DSTC equalization scheme in suppressing the interference at the destination upon receiving the jointly encoded transmit signals from the relay user using J-DSTC, including the information of both the relay user and the source user. It is also shown to be effective in removing the impact of inter-symbol-interference caused by the imperfect synchronization during the cooperative transmission. Meanwhile, a low structural and computational complexity is retained.

Keywords: parallel interference cancellation, successive interference cancellation, joint DSTC, imperfect synchronization.

1 Introduction

Multiple-input multiple-output (MIMO) techniques have been demonstrated to provide substantial capacity improvements to wireless communication systems, by using multiple antennas at both the transmitter and the receiver [1]. However, it is quite difficult to place multiple antennas in mobile units in cellular communication systems due to the size and cost limits. Cooperative communication technologies are then proposed to generate virtual MIMO arrays by transmitting signals from different locations to obtain the spatial gain [2].

Some cooperative transmit strategies and corresponding interference cancellation algorithms have been proposed [3-4], however, the cooperative nodes are selected only as relays of the source nodes, and are not considered to transmit their own information in these scenarios. To realize the space-time cooperation when considering all users

---

[*] This work was supported in part by the National Natural Science Foundation of China under Grant No.60972055, by Shanghai Educational Development Foundation under Grant No. 09CG40, and by Science and Technology Commission of Shanghai Municipality under Grant 10220710300.

P. Ren et al. (Eds.): WICON 2011, LNICST 98, pp. 133–143, 2012.

transmit both their own information and their cooperative partners' information, distributed space-time coded systems with four transmit phases were introduced in [5], where mobile users transmitted cooperatively and utilized space-time coding in a distributed manner to improve the system performance. By reducing one phase in the cooperative transmission, [6] recently proposed a joint distributed space-time coding (J-DSTC) scheme to improve the transmit efficiency compared to [5], and achieves the same diversity order as [7]. Therefore, we consider a cooperative cellular system using the efficient J-STBC in this paper.

Most prior work on cooperation assumes synchronous communication between the signals transmitted from different cooperating users in the network. However, it is hard to achieve perfect synchronisation in practical systems. So considering J-DSTC in an asynchronous scenario is necessary.   Limited work has been reported in the literature addressing the imperfect synchronization issue for cooperative communications [8-9]. These existing schemes either potentially incur a much higher computational complexity at the receiver, or did not consider the J-STBC transmit strategy.

Therefore, in this paper, we investigate a cellular system applying J-DSTC on the uplink. Each user of the cellular system selects a partner to transmit the combined signals. Signals transmitted from these two cooperating terminals are received asynchronously at BS. Such assumptions, unfortunately, will damage the orthogonality of the J-STBC and meanwhile lead to substantial performance degradation. Therefore, a signal detection scheme using parallel interference cancellation (PIC) [10-11] to remove the inter-symbol-interference (ISI) caused by the imperfect synchronization, jointly with successive interference cancellation (SIC) [12] to suppress the interference upon receiving the jointly encoded transmit signals from the relay user using J-DSTC, including the information of both the relay user and the source user. The proposed scheme is then shown to offer significant system performance improvement compared to that of using the conventional J-STBC equalization scheme [6], and still retains a relatively low structural and computational complexity under quasi-synchronization.

The paper is organized as follows. Section 2 describes the system model and the frame structure of an asynchronous cooperative system. In section 3, the proposed signal detection scheme is described. Simulation results are illustrated in section 4. Finally, conclusions are drawn in section 5.

2   System Model

2.1   System Model

The system model considered in this paper is similar to the system model in [6], in which two mobile users are selected as a group to transmit their information cooperatively to the base station (BS) in a cellular system. They both transmit their information to the same BS with only one antenna equipped on each of them. Both of the mobile users share the same frequency band and each user cannot transmit and receive at the same time. In this paper, four receive antennas are assumed to be equipped at the BS. The structures can be described more specifically in Figure 1.

2.2   Frame Structure

In the cooperative transmission process, each frame is divided into two subframes [6], a listening subframe and a cooperation subframe, as illustrated in Fig.1.

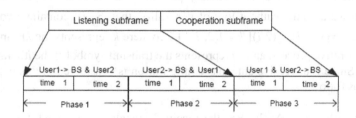

Fig. 1. Frame structure of the cooperation process

In the first phase of the listening subframe, mobile user1 transmits its information to the BS and mobile user2 simultaneously, while in the second phase of the listening subframe, mobile user2 transmits its information to the BS and user1. The cooperation subframe is shared by both user 1 and user2, to relay the information including both their own data and the cooperative partner's data [6].

2.3   Imperfect Synchronization Structure

Because of factors such as different propagation delays, the signals from user1 and user2 will normally arrive at BS at different time instants. As accurate synchronization is difficult or impossible [8, 9], there is normally a timing misalignment of τ between the received versions of these signals. Since a rough synchronization is always required, we assume here that τ is smaller than the symbol period T as shown in Fig.2. It will still cause 'intersymbol interference (ISI)' from neighboring symbols at D, owing to sampling/matched filtering (whatever kind of pulse shaping is used) [10].

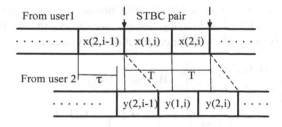

Fig. 2. Time delay (imperfect synchronization) between two users

3   Signal Detection Algorithm

3.1   Signal Model of J-STBC

We assume the interuser channels and the user-destination channels are independent of each other. All channels experience frequency flat fading and are quasi-static, i.e. they are fixed during a subframe and change independently in the next subframe. With the above assumptions, we now consider a discrete time model. In the first phase of the listening subframe, the first user broadcasts the ith pair of the transmitted symbols, $\mathbf{S}_k(i)$, which are selected from equally probable MPSK symbols. To simplify the expression we assume, without loss of generality, that $\mathbf{S}_k(i)$ contains two symbols, e.g. $\mathbf{S}_k(j,i) = [s_k(1,i), s_k(2,i)], k = 1, 2, j = 1, 2$, where k represents the kth mobile user in the cooperative process, and j represents the transmit symbol at the jth transmission time slot. Since four receive antennas configuration is considered in this paper, signal model is as follows.

Listening Subframe. At the BS, the received signals $\mathbf{r}_{k\,\mathrm{B}}(j,i), k = 1, 2, j = 1, 2$ during Phase1 and Phase2 corresponding to the kth user's direct transmission to the base station, are given as $\mathbf{r}_{k\,\mathrm{B}}(j,i) = \mathbf{h}_{k\,\mathrm{B}} \times \mathbf{S}_k(j,i) + \mathbf{n}_{k\,\mathrm{B}}$, where $\mathbf{h}_{k\,\mathrm{B}}$ is the channel gain between the kth user and the BS during the transmission of the listening subframe, and $\mathbf{n}_{k\,\mathrm{B}}$ is the additive Gaussian noise (AWGN) at the receiver. The received signal $\mathbf{r}_{k\,\mathrm{B}}(j,i)$ and the noise can be represented as $\mathbf{r}_{k\,\mathrm{B}} = \begin{bmatrix} r_{k\,\mathrm{B}1}(1), \dots, r_{k\,\mathrm{B}\,n_R}(1) \\ r_{k\,\mathrm{B}1}(2), \dots, r_{k\,\mathrm{B}\,n_R}(2) \end{bmatrix}^T$ and $\mathbf{n}_{k\,\mathrm{B}} = \begin{bmatrix} n_{k\,\mathrm{B}1}(1), \dots, n_{k\,\mathrm{B}\,n_R}(1) \\ n_{k\,\mathrm{B}1}(2), \dots, n_{k\,\mathrm{B}\,n_R}(2) \end{bmatrix}^T$, respectively. Meanwhile, the received signal at the cooperative users can be written respectively as $\mathbf{r}_{u_1 u_2}(j) = h_1 \mathbf{S}_1(j) + \mathbf{n}_1(j)$ and $\mathbf{r}_{u_2 u_1}(j) = h_2 \mathbf{S}_2(j) + \mathbf{n}_2(j)$.

Here $\mathbf{r}_{u_q u_p}(j), q = 1, 2, p = 2, 1, j = 1, 2$ denotes the received signal at the pth user from the qth user during the listening subframe. $h_q, q = 1, 2$ represents the channel gain from the qth user to its partner. $\mathbf{n}_k(j), k = 1, 2$ is the AWGN.

Cooperation Subframe. In the cooperation subframe, both users act as relays and transmit the combination of the relay signals and their own information. The signal arriving at the destination is a linear combination of the signals from both the transmission paths. Without the loss of generality, we can assume that BS is synchronized to user1. The received signal at BS for cooperation subframe can be written as

$$\mathbf{r}(i) = \begin{bmatrix} r_1(1,i), \dots, r_{n_R}(1,i) \\ r_1(2,i), \dots, r_{n_R}(2,i) \end{bmatrix}^T = \mathbf{H}_f \cdot \tilde{\mathbf{S}}(i) + \mathbf{I} + \mathbf{N}$$

$$= \begin{bmatrix} h_{11}, \dots, h_{n_R 1} \\ h_{12}, \dots, h_{n_R 2} \end{bmatrix}^T \times \begin{bmatrix} \tilde{s}_1(1,i), \tilde{s}_1(2,i) \\ \tilde{s}_2(1,i), \tilde{s}_2(2,i) \end{bmatrix} + \mathbf{I} + \begin{bmatrix} n_1(1,i), \dots, n_{n_R}(1,i) \\ n_1(2,i), \dots, n_{n_R}(2,i) \end{bmatrix}^T \tag{1}$$

where $r_m(l,i)$, $l=1,2; m=1...n_R$ represents the received signal of the mth antenna at BS at the lth time slot. h_{mk}, $m=1,\cdots,4; k=1,2$ represents the channel gain between the kth user and the BS during the transmission of the cooperation subframe. The inter-symbol-interference (ISI) generated by the imperfect synchronization, $\mathbf{I}$, is

$$\mathbf{I}(i) = \begin{bmatrix} h_{12}(-1)\tilde{s}_2^*(2,i-1) & h_{22}(-1)\tilde{s}_2^*(2,i-1) & ... & h_{n_R 2}(-1)\tilde{s}_2^*(2,i-1) \\ h_{12}^*(-1)\tilde{s}_2^*(1,i) & h_{22}(-1)\tilde{s}_2^*(1,i) & ... & h_{n_s 2}^*(-1)\tilde{s}_2^*(1,i) \end{bmatrix}^T \tag{2}$$

where $h_{m2}(-1)$ reflects the ISI from the previous symbol at the mth receive antenna and depends upon timing delay τ and the particular pulse shaping waveform used. Its relative strength can then be represented by ratio $\beta \overset{\pm}{=} |h_{m2}|^2 / |h_{m2}(-1)|^2$ (dB).

$\tilde{s}_k(l,i)$ is the combined signal transmitted by the kth user at the lth time slot in the cooperation subframe, which can be described as

$$\tilde{\mathbf{S}}_1(i) = [\tilde{s}_1(1,i), \tilde{s}_1(2,i)] = \tag{3}$$
$$[\sqrt{\alpha_{11}}s_1(1,i) + \sqrt{\alpha_{12}}\sigma_2 r_{u_2 u_1}^*(2,i), \sqrt{\alpha_{11}}s_1(2,i) - \sqrt{\alpha_{12}}\sigma_2 r_{u_2 u_1}^*(1,i)]$$

And

$$\tilde{\mathbf{S}}_2(i) = [\tilde{s}_2(1,i), \tilde{s}_2(2,i)] = \tag{4}$$
$$[\sqrt{\alpha_{22}}s_2(1,i) + \sqrt{\alpha_{21}}\sigma_1 r_{u_1 u_2}^*(2,i), \sqrt{\alpha_{22}}s_2(2,i) - \sqrt{\alpha_{21}}\sigma_1 r_{u_1 u_2}^*(1,i)]$$

where $\alpha_{ij}, i=1,2, j=1,2$ denotes the symbol energy for the ith user's combined signal. $\sigma_i, i=1,2$ is an automatic gain control(AGC) parameter of non-regenerative systems, which is required at the relay mobile in order to prevent $r_{mn}(i)$ from saturating the relay amplifier. Specifically, we constrain the average radiated energy per symbol at the relay mobile to be 1 [5], a good choice is to adopt an AGC that employs

$$\sigma_k = \frac{h_k^*}{|h_k|} \sqrt{\frac{1}{\alpha_k |h_k|^2 + N_k}}, k=1,2 \tag{5}$$

where σ_k is the transmit power in the first and second subframes (from user1 to user2 and from user2 to user1,respectively). N_k represents the noise which has the same properties as $n_{nm}(j,i)$.

At the destination, the received signal in (1) can be rewritten as (6)

$$\mathbf{r}(i) = \mathbf{H} \cdot \begin{bmatrix} s_1(1,i) \\ s_1^*(2,i) \\ s_2(1,i) \\ s_2^*(2,i) \end{bmatrix} + \mathbf{I} + \mathbf{Noise} \tag{6}$$

Where

$$
\mathbf{H} =
\begin{bmatrix}
h_{11}\sqrt{\alpha_{11}} & h_{12}\sqrt{\alpha_{21}}\sigma_1 h_1^* & h_{12}\sqrt{\alpha_{22}} & h_{11}\sqrt{\alpha_{12}}\sigma_2 h_2^* \\
-(h_{12}\sqrt{\alpha_{21}}\sigma_1 h_1^*)^* & (h_{11}\sqrt{\alpha_{11}})^* & -(h_{11}\sqrt{\alpha_{12}}\sigma_2 h_2^*)^* & (h_{12}\sqrt{\alpha_{22}})^* \\
& & \vdots & \\
h_{n_R1}\sqrt{\alpha_{11}} & h_{n_R2}\sqrt{\alpha_{21}}\sigma_1 h_1^* & h_{n_R2}\sqrt{\alpha_{22}} & h_{n_R1}\sqrt{\alpha_{12}}\sigma_2 h_2^* \\
-(h_{n_R2}\sqrt{\alpha_{21}}\sigma_1 h_1^*)^* & (h_{n_R1}\sqrt{\alpha_{11}})^* & -(h_{n_R1}\sqrt{\alpha_{12}}\sigma_2 h_2^*)^* & (h_{n_R2}\sqrt{\alpha_{22}})^*
\end{bmatrix}
\tag{7}
$$

And

$$
\mathbf{Noise} =
\begin{bmatrix}
h_{11}\sqrt{\alpha_{12}}\sigma_2 n_2^*(2,i)+h_{12}\sqrt{\alpha_{21}}\sigma_1 n_1^*(2,i) \\
\left(-h_{11}\sqrt{\alpha_{12}}\sigma_2 n_2^*(1,i)-h_{12}\sqrt{\alpha_{21}}\sigma_1 n_1^*(1,i)\right)^* \\
h_{21}\sqrt{\alpha_{12}}\sigma_2 n_2^*(2,i)+h_{22}\sqrt{\alpha_{21}}\sigma_1 n_1^*(2,i) \\
\left(-h_{21}\sqrt{\alpha_{12}}\sigma_2 n_2^*(1,i)-h_{22}\sqrt{\alpha_{21}}\sigma_1 n_1^*(1,i)\right)^* \\
h_{31}\sqrt{\alpha_{12}}\sigma_2 n_2^*(2,i)+h_{32}\sqrt{\alpha_{21}}\sigma_1 n_1^*(2,i) \\
\left(-h_{31}\sqrt{\alpha_{12}}\sigma_2 n_2^*(1,i)-h_{32}\sqrt{\alpha_{21}}\sigma_1 n_1^*(1,i)\right)^* \\
h_{41}\sqrt{\alpha_{12}}\sigma_2 n_2^*(2,i)+h_{42}\sqrt{\alpha_{21}}\sigma_1 n_1^*(2,i) \\
\left(-h_{41}\sqrt{\alpha_{12}}\sigma_2 n_2^*(1,i)-h_{42}\sqrt{\alpha_{21}}\sigma_1 n_1^*(1,i)\right)^*
\end{bmatrix}
+
\begin{bmatrix}
n_1(1,i) \\
(n_1(2,i))^* \\
n_2(1,i) \\
(n_2(2,i))^* \\
n_3(1,i) \\
(n_3(2,i))^* \\
n_4(1,i) \\
(n_4(2,i))^*
\end{bmatrix}
\tag{8}
$$

Equation (6) can further be expressed as

$$
\mathbf{r} =
\begin{bmatrix}
\mathbf{R}_1 \\
\mathbf{R}_2 \\
\vdots \\
\mathbf{R}_{n_R}
\end{bmatrix}
= \mathbf{H}
\begin{bmatrix}
\mathbf{S}_1 \\
\mathbf{S}_2
\end{bmatrix}
+ \mathbf{I} + \mathbf{Noise} =
\begin{bmatrix}
\mathbf{A}_{11} & \mathbf{A}_{12} \\
\mathbf{A}_{21} & \mathbf{A}_{22} \\
& \vdots \\
\mathbf{A}_{n_R 1} & \mathbf{A}_{n_R 2}
\end{bmatrix}
\begin{bmatrix}
\mathbf{S}_1 \\
\mathbf{S}_2
\end{bmatrix}
+ \mathbf{I} + \mathbf{Noise}
\tag{9}
$$

where $\mathbf{S}_k = \begin{bmatrix} s_k(1,i) \\ (s_k(2,i))^* \end{bmatrix}$, $k \in \{1,2\}$ consists of the two signals transmitted from the kth user and $\mathbf{R}_k = \begin{bmatrix} r_k(1,i) \\ (r_k(2,i))^* \end{bmatrix}$.

Moreover $\mathbf{A}_{kl}$, $k \in \{1, n_R\}$, $l \in \{1,2\}$, is the corresponding channel matrix from the lth user to the kth receive antenna, which have the Alamouti-like structures [13], i.e.,

$$
\mathbf{A}_{kl} =
\begin{bmatrix}
h_{1k}\sqrt{\alpha_{11}} & h_{k2}\sqrt{\alpha_{21}}\sigma_1 h_1^* \\
-(h_{k2}\sqrt{\alpha_{21}}\sigma_1 h_1^*)^* & (-h_{1k}\sqrt{\alpha_{11}})^*
\end{bmatrix}
\text{ for } l=1, \text{ and } \mathbf{A}_{kl} =
\begin{bmatrix}
h_{2k}\sqrt{\alpha_{22}} & h_{k1}\sqrt{\alpha_{12}}\sigma_2 h_2^* \\
-(h_{k1}\sqrt{\alpha_{12}}\sigma_2 h_2^*)^* & (-h_{2k}\sqrt{\alpha_{22}})^*
\end{bmatrix}
$$

for $l=2$.

3.2   SIC Processing

The received signal in (9) can be further written as:

$$\tilde{r}(i) = \mathbf{H} \cdot \mathbf{s}(i) + \mathbf{I} + \mathbf{Noise}$$

$$= \begin{bmatrix} \mathbf{A}_{11}(1) \\ \mathbf{A}_{21}(1) \\ \vdots \\ \mathbf{A}_{n_R 1}(1) \end{bmatrix} s_1(1,i) + \ldots + \begin{bmatrix} \mathbf{A}_{12}(2) \\ \mathbf{A}_{22}(2) \\ \vdots \\ \mathbf{A}_{n_R 2}(2) \end{bmatrix} s_2^*(2,i) + \mathbf{I} + \mathbf{Noise} \tag{10}$$

where $\mathbf{A}_{kl}(x), x \in \{1,2\}$ denotes the xth column of $\mathbf{A}_{kl}$. Rewrite the above equation as

$$\tilde{r}(i) = \mathbf{H}_{11}s_1(1,i) + \mathbf{H}_{12}s_1^*(2,i) + \mathbf{H}_{21}s_2(1,i) + \mathbf{H}_{22}s_2^*(2,i) + \mathbf{I} + \mathbf{Noise} \tag{11}$$

and then the SIC detection can be performed as follows:

The signals that have relatively larger channel power should be decoded before those with smaller power. For convenience, suppose the channel power has the ordering of $\|\mathbf{H}_{11}\|^2 \geq \|\mathbf{H}_{12}\|^2 \geq \|\mathbf{H}_{21}\|^2 \geq \|\mathbf{H}_{22}\|^2$, therefore, we begin with the detection of the first symbol of $\mathbf{s}$, i.e. $s(l) = s_1(1)$ $l = 1$. The other undetected terms, $\mathbf{H}_{12}s_1^*(2), \mathbf{H}_{21}s_2(1), \mathbf{H}_{22}s_2^*(2)$ and Noise are treated as a Gaussian variable with matching mean and variance [7], such that (11) can be approximately expressed as:

$$\tilde{r}(i) = \mathbf{H}_{11}s(l) + \boldsymbol{\eta} \qquad l = 1 \tag{12}$$

where $\boldsymbol{\eta}$ is a zero-mean complex Gaussian random variable with variance

$$\Lambda_1 = E(\mathbf{h}_{2,4}\mathbf{h}_{2,4}^H)|\bar{s}|^2 + \sigma_n^2(\Lambda_{\tilde{N}} \bullet \Lambda_{\tilde{N}}^H) + \sigma_n^2 \mathbf{I}_t + \mathbf{I} \tag{13}$$

Here $|\bar{s}|^2$ represents the average power of the symbols in constellation M. $\mathbf{I}_t$ is a $t \times t$ identity matrix with $t = 2 n_R$. $\Lambda_{\tilde{N}}$ is a $t \times 1$ Matrix, reshaped   from the following:

$$\Lambda_{\tilde{N}t} = \mathbf{H}_f \cdot \tilde{\mathbf{N}}_d = \begin{bmatrix} h_{11}, \ldots, h_{n_R 1} \\ h_{12}, \ldots, h_{n_R 2} \end{bmatrix}^T \cdot \begin{bmatrix} \sqrt{\alpha_{12}}\sigma_2 & -\sqrt{\alpha_{12}}\sigma_2 \\ \sqrt{\alpha_{21}}\sigma_1 & -\sqrt{\alpha_{21}}\sigma_1 \end{bmatrix} \tag{14}$$

All the possible modulated symbols related to $s(l)$ $l = 1$ can be examined by:

$$\tilde{s}(l) = \arg \min_{s(l) \in M} \left\| [\tilde{r} - \mathbf{H}_{11}s(l)]^H \Lambda_1^{-1} [\tilde{r} - \mathbf{H}_{11}s(l)] \right\| \quad l = 1 \tag{15}$$

where the calculation of Λ_1^{-1} can be greatly simplified using the matrix inversion lemma. As a result, $\tilde{s}(l)$ $l = 1$ can be estimated by choosing the smallest value of (15).

In the lth detection, the previously detected symbols can be used to decode the following symbol. Again, the undetected terms should be treated as a Gaussian variable. The following equation can be applied to calculate the probabilities for $\tilde{s}_1^*(2,i)$, $\tilde{s}_2^*(2,i)$ successively:

$$\tilde{s}(l,i) = \arg \min_{s(l)\in M} \left| [\tilde{\mathbf{r}} - \mathbf{H}_{i2}\tilde{s}_i(2,i) - \mathbf{H}_{i1}s_i(1,i)]^H \cdots \right.$$
$$\left. \Lambda_l^{-1} [\tilde{\mathbf{r}} - \mathbf{H}_{i2}\tilde{s}_i(2,i) - \mathbf{H}_{i1}s_i(1,i)] \right| \tag{16}$$

where $\tilde{\mathbf{s}}(l,i) = [\tilde{s}_1(1,i)...\tilde{s}_2(2,i)]$ $l = 1,\cdots,4$ and Λ_l^{-1} can be simplified similarly. The same detection process will be repeated until each pair of the transmitted symbols from each user during the cooperation transmission has been detected. The signals received during the listening subframe still contains valuable information even if the direct transmission fails, therefore should be combined with the detected signals from the cooperation subframe to improve the accuracy of the estimated transmitted symbols from both users. Applying the conventional maximum ratio combining (MRC) method to $\mathbf{r}_{kB}$, and the combined signal can be expressed as

$$\mathbf{g}_1 = [g_1(1) \quad g_1(2)]^T = \mathbf{h}_{1B}^H \mathbf{r}_{1B} + [\tilde{s}_1(1) \quad \tilde{s}_1(2)]^T$$
$$\mathbf{g}_2 = [g_2(1) \quad g_2(2)]^T = \mathbf{h}_{2B}^H \mathbf{r}_{2B} + [\tilde{s}_2(1) \quad \tilde{s}_2(2)]^T \tag{17}$$

Finally, the detected transmitted symbols of the kth user can be obtained by choosing the smallest value from the following:

$$s_k(j) = \arg\{\min_{s_m \in M} |g_k(j) - \lambda s_m|^2\} \quad k = 1,2, j = 1,2 \tag{18}$$

where $\lambda = 1 + |h_{kB1}|^2 + ... + |h_{kBn_R}|^2$.

3.3   PIC Processing Joint with SIC

Since ISI is included in the received signal $\mathbf{r}(i)$ and affects the performance of the SIC processing significantly, we hereby propose to use PIC processing in the signal detection to improve the accuracy of $\mathbf{r}(i)$, and hence improve the performance of the SIC processing. The PIC iteration process, which has been applied to the co-located STBC system [12], can then be used to mitigate the impact of I as follows.

Initialization. $k=0$

— For convenience, we first reshape $\mathbf{r}(i)$ as follows,

$$\mathbf{r}(i) = \begin{bmatrix} r_1(1,i) & r_2(1,i) & \cdots & r_{n_R}(1,i) \\ r_1^*(2,i) & r_2^*(2,i) & \cdots & r_{n_R}^*(2,i) \end{bmatrix}^T \tag{19}$$

— From the received signal $\mathbf{r}(i)$, calculate $\mathbf{r}'^{(0)}(i) = [\mathbf{r}(1,i) - \mathbf{I}(1,i), \mathbf{r}^*(2,i)]^T$, where $\mathbf{r}(j,i), j \in \{1,2\}$ represents the jth row of $\mathbf{r}(i)$ and $\mathbf{I}(j,i)$ represents the jth row of $\mathbf{I}(i)$ in (2).

— Reshape $\mathbf{r}'^{(0)}(i)$ into a 8×1 matrix. Calculate $\tilde{\mathbf{s}}^{(0)}(i)$ using the SIC detector introduced in the above subsection with $\mathbf{r}'^{(0)}(i)$.

Iteration. $k=1, ..., K$

— Reshape $\mathbf{r}(i)$ as the first step in the initialization stage.
— Calculate

$$\mathbf{r}^{'(k)}(i) = [\mathbf{r}(1,i) - \mathbf{I}(1,i), \mathbf{r}^*(2,i) - \mathbf{I}^{(k-1)}(2,i)]^T \tag{20}$$

where $\mathbf{I}^{(k-1)}(2,i) = h_2^*(-1)[s^{(k-1)}(2,i)]^*$.

— Transform $\mathbf{r}^{'(k)}(i)$ into a 8×1 matrix.   Calculate $\tilde{\mathbf{s}}^{(k)}(i)$ by SIC with $\mathbf{r}^{'(k)}(i)$.

For $k = 0$, the computation is the same as the conventional STBC detector. For K iterations, the complexity issue refers to [4]. As normally $K = 2$ or 3, the increase in computational complexity is very moderate.

4   Simulation Results

Simulation results are shown in this section to demonstrate the performance of the proposed signal detection algorithm using PIC jointly with SIC. Four receive antennas are considered to be equipped at the BS. The modulation scheme used is 8PSK, and $\beta = 0$ (dB).

In Fig.3, the BER performance of using the proposed signal detection scheme is compared with that of using the linear filter [6] and with the PIC detector joint with the linear filter [6] under imperfect synchronization, and with that of using the linear filter [6] under perfect synchronization. It can be observed from the figure that our proposed scheme in the asynchronous scenario outperforms the existing linear filter [6] significantly, even when the linear filter is under perfect synchronization, and the PIC detector is very effective in removing the ISI.

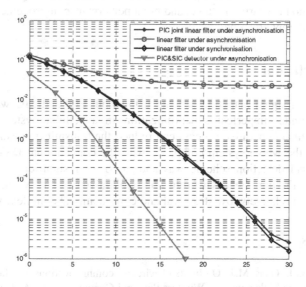

Fig. 3. BER comparisons of PIC joint SIC detector, PIC detector joint linear filter, linear filter detector under asynchronization and linear filter detector under synchronization

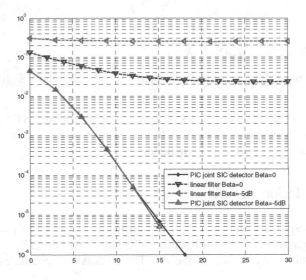

Fig. 4. BER comparison of PIC joint SIC detector and linear filter with different Beta values under imperfect synchronization

Fig.4 shows the BER performance comparisons between the proposed scheme and the existing scheme in [6] under different β values. It is shown that the smaller the β values is, the worse the ISI is caused by the imperfect synchronization during cooperative transmission. While the performance of using the existing linear filter [6] degrades significantly when the β value decreases, the performance of using the proposed signal detection method is nearly the same, and great performance improvement is achieved in the case of different β values.

5   Conclusion

In this paper, a signal detection scheme using both PIC and SIC was proposed for Joint-DSTC under imperfect synchronization in a cellular system. By using the Joint-DSTC, the cooperative process can reduce the transmit frames and improve the efficiency of the whole system compared with the conventional DSTC scheme. The proposed signal detection scheme was shown to offer significant performance improvement for the imperfect synchronized cooperative cellular system using J-DSTC, but still retain a relatively low structural and computational complexity.

References

1. Foschini, G.J., Gans, M.J.: On limits of wireless communications in a fading environment when using multiple antennas. Wireless Personal Communications 6, 311–335 (1998)
2. Sendonaris, A., Erkop, E., Aazhang, B.: User cooperation diversity-Part I: system description. IEEE Trans. Commun. 51, 1927–1938 (2003)

3. Barbarossa, S., Scutari, G.: Distributed space-time coding for multihop networks. In: Proc. IEEE International Conference on Communications, June 20-24, pp. 916–920 (2004)
4. Jing, Y., Jafarkhani, H.: Interference cancellation in distributed space-time coded wireless relay networks. In: Proc. IEEE International Conference on Communications, pp. 740–741 (1987/2009)
5. Laneman, J.N., Wornell, G.W.: Distributed space-time coded protocols for exploiting cooperative diversity in wireless networks. IEEE Trans. Inf. Theory 49(120), 2415–2425 (2003)
6. Xu, J., Choi, J., Seo, J.: Distributed space-time coding and equalization for cooperative cellular communications system. IEEE Trans. Consumer Electron. 54(1), 47–51 (2008)
7. Anghel, P.A., Kaveh, M.: On the performance of distributed space-time coding systems with one and two non-generative relays. IEEE Trans. Wireless Commun. 5(3) (March 2006)
8. Jia, Y., Andrieu, C., Piechocki, R.J., Sandell, M.: Gaussian approximation based mixture reduction for near optimum detection in MIMO systems. IEEE Commun. Lett. 9(11), 997–999 (2005)
9. Li, X.: Space-time coded multi-transmission among distributed transmitters without perfect synchronisation. IEEE Signal Process. Lett. 11(12), 948–951 (2004)
10. Zheng, F.-C., Burr, A.G., Olafsson, S.: PIC detector for distributed space-time block coding under imperfect synchronization. Electronic Letters 43(10), 580–581 (2007)
11. Zheng, F.-C., Burr, A.G.: Signal detection for orthogonal space-time block coding over time-selective fading channels: a PIC approach for the Gi systems. IEEE Trans. Commn. 53(6), 969–972 (2005)
12. Song, L.-Y., Burr, A.G.: Successive Interference Cancelation for Space-Time Block Codes over Time-Selective Channels. IEEE Communication Letters 10(12) (September 2006)
13. Tarokh, V., Jafarkhani, H., Calderbank, R.: Space-Time Block Coding for Wireless Communications: Performance Results. IEEE JSAC 17(3) (March 1999)

Enhanced Algorithm
for MMIB in Distributed MIMO System

Jian Sun, Shidong Zhou, Xibin Xu, Yunzhou Li, and Jing Wang

Tsinghua University of Electronic Engineering Department,
Beijing, China
jsun05@gmail.com

Abstract. Link abstraction model based on MMIB (Mean Mutual Information per Bit) has already been applied to 802.16m-based systems. MMIB performs well in SISO system. However, it will make an inaccurate prediction of BLER if directly applied to Distributed MIMO system. In this paper we propose an enhanced algorithm. Simulations show great improvements compared to the original MMIB algorithms.

Keywords: MIMO, MMIB, AMC, ESINR, Link abstraction model.

1 Introduction

The next generation wireless communication system (4G) requires a data rate of above 1Gbps. Wide bandwidth and high spectral efficiency are applied to achieve such a high rate. As low frequency spectrum resource is valuable, the high frequency band above 6GHz is alternative. However, as frequency increases, coverage ability reduces. To maintain good coverage when users are in any position, distributed base stations can be used. To achieve high spectral efficiency, high order modulations as well as multi-antenna technology are required. Therefore, distributed MIMO technology will be widely used in 4G wireless communication system.

AMC can increase the average throughput, in which modulation order and coding rate adapt to changes of channel capacity. AMC technology needs instantaneous link performance prediction. In recent years, some models have been brought out.

Reference [1] proposed EESM (Exponential Effective SINR Mapping) algorithm. SNR values on all modulation symbols within a coded block are mapped to a value ESINR by an exponential function, and this value corresponds to the only BLER on AWGN channel. One drawback of the algorithm is that the AWGN reference curves are different for different modulation modes. So EESM is not suitable to be used when coded bits are mapped onto multi-modulation types in a coded block.

MIESM (Mutual Information Effect SINR Mapping) algorithm [2] uses the mutual information per received symbol to map BLER. AWGN reference curves with MIESM are independent of modulation types, but only dependent of coding rate. Simulation results show that MIESM algorithm outperforms EESM algorithm.

P. Ren et al. (Eds.): WICON 2011, LNICST 98, pp. 144–153, 2012.

MIESM calculates mutual information on an equivalent "symbol channel", which is constrained by the symbol constellation. However, the channel between encoder and decoder contains modulation and demodulation except the "symbol channel". The non-ideal demodulation algorithm may affect the channel mutual information. An improvement is MMIB (Mean Mutual Information per Bit) algorithm [3]. MMIB calculates MIB on the channel between coding output bits and LLR (Log-Likelihood Ratio) output after demodulation. MMIB which is the average of all MIB values in a coded block is used to correspond to BLER.

MMIB algorithm is accurate in SISO systems. However, in distributed MIMO systems, different data streams may differ in average SNR. As a result, SNR values in a code block will vary much if stream interleaving is used. BLER curves may not coincide with AWGN reference curves. So it is not accurate that predicting BLER according to AWGN reference curves. This paper proposes a modified method based on power function, which makes great improvements compared to the original MMIB algorithm.

This paper is organized as follows. The second section explains the distributed MIMO system model and the link abstract model. The third explains the modified MMIB model. Simulation results are present for verification in the fourth part and a conclusion follows.

2 Distributed MIMO System Model and Link Abstract Model

2.1 Distributed MIMO System Mode

A simulation scenario for distributed MIMO system is presented as follows.

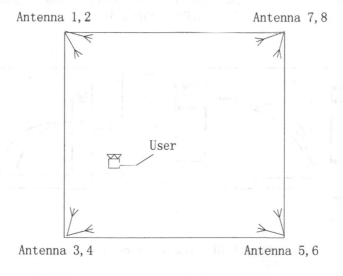

Fig. 1. A simulation scenario distributed MIMO system

Four base stations distribute at the corners of a rectangular channel. Every base station has two antennas. One is vertically polarized, the other is horizontally polarized. So a total of eight antennas achieve the coverage of the whole channel. The user side also has eight antennas, with half wavelength distance between each other. Horizontally polarized antennas and vertically polarized ones are alternately placed.

The whole process in physical layer is shown in Figure 2.

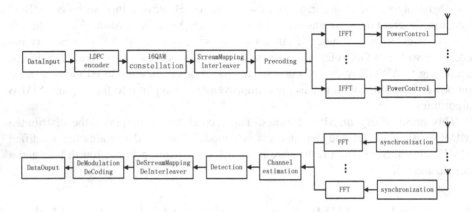

Fig. 2. Physical layer architecture

2.2   Link Abstract Model

The link abstract model is used to predict BLER by detection SNR. The link abstract model based on MMIB is described as follows (Figure 3).

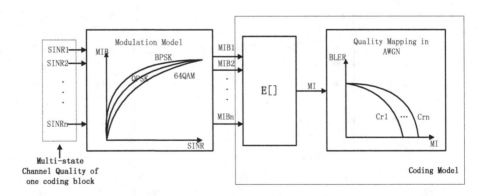

Fig. 3. MMIB based link abstract model

SNRi represents the SINR of the ith modulation symbol in a coded block. The Mutual information per bit (MIB) will be received from SINR-BLER mapping curve which is dependent of modulation order, demodulation algorithm and SINR. The mean mutual information MI will be got by averaging MIB, which can be regarded as the upper capacity bound of the channel between encoder output port and decoder input port. At last, refer to the AWGN link performance curves to obtain the BLER, which is only relevant with code rate.

The differences among link abstract models mainly rest on Modulation models in which mutual information is calculated on different equivalent channel. MIESM uses the "symbol channel". However, a "bit channel" between encoder and decoder is closer to the actual system (Figure 4).

Fig. 4. Bit channel model

Bit channel, composed of three parts of modulation, AWGN channel, demodulation, is an abstract to the actual physical channel. Precise approximation of the actual channel capacity can be got by introducing MIB.

In modulator, every m bits ($b_{i1}, ..., b_{im}$, i=1,...,n, n represents the symbol number in a coded block, m={2,4,6} is the modulation order) are mapped to a modulation symbol . Due to the asymmetry of the modulation map, the mutual information between every bit b_{ij} in a modulation symbol and demodulator output LLR (b_{ij}) may be not equal. So we average the bit mutual information.

$$I_i = \frac{1}{m} \sum_{j=1}^{m} I(b_{ij}, LLR(b_{ij})) \tag{1}$$

The mean mutual information of all symbols over a coded block is

$$MI = \frac{1}{nm} \sum_{i=1}^{n} \sum_{j=1}^{m} I(b_{ij}, LLR(b_{ij})) \tag{2}$$

Mutual information is only dependant on SINR if modulation order is specified. So the formula (2) can be described as

$$MI = \frac{1}{n} \sum_{i=1}^{n} I_i (SINR_i) \tag{3}$$

The mutual information of every bit in a symbol under different SINR can be computed numerically. Then the mean bit mutual information will be got, which can be stored in a table for use. Tables should be built for every modulation order.

3   The Modified MMIB Model in Distributed MIMO System

Reference [3] gives the MMIB model in MIMO system with linear receiver.

$$MI = \frac{1}{nN_t} \sum_{i=1}^{n} \sum_{k=1}^{N_t} I_i^k (SNR_i^k)$$

$$BLER = B_{AWGN} (MI) \tag{4}$$

Where N_t refers to the number of transmitting antennas and n the number of modulation symbols. B_{AWGN} is the mapping function between MI and BLER on AWGN channel.

In distributed MIMO systems, post-detection SINR values may vary much in a coded block due to two factors. One is that user have different distances from different base stations. Since power control may non-ideal, received power of each transmitting antenna may differ. The other is the potential correlation among some base station antennas in the case of numerous data streams. As a result, post-detection SINR may vary among different data streams. For example, SINR distribution in a code block with user in two positions may be as follows.

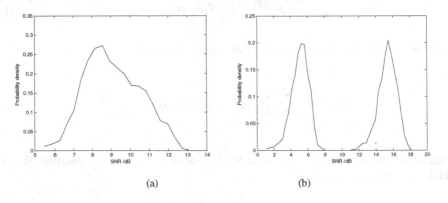

(a)   (b)

Fig. 5. SINR distribution with user in two positions

The left shows the SINR distribution when user is in the center of the channel. We can see that the mapping between MI and BLER coincides with the AWGN reference curve (Fig.6(a) dots represent mapping in actual channel and solid line is AWGN reference curve). The right shows the SINR distribution when user is close to two base stations and far from the other two stations. SINR values of data streams mapping to close stations are high and SINR values of other streams are low. The mapping curve between MI and BLER differ widely from that on AWGN channel (Fig. 6(b)).

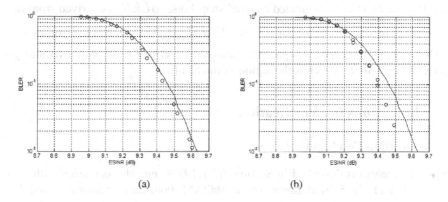

(a)   (b)

Fig. 6. MI and BLER mapping in different positions

The deviation between two curves in Fig. 6(b) results from the great difference between SINR values in a coded block. So we can add a modified function on SINR to make dispersive SINR values intensive. Meanwhile, curves that fit AWGN reference curves well (Fig. 6(a)) might be insensitive to this modification. We choose a power function here.

$$g(x) = \alpha_2 * x^{\alpha_1} \tag{5}$$

Where $0 < \alpha_1 < 1$, $\alpha_2 > 0$. The function makes SINR values more intensive by increasing lower SINR values and decreasing higher SINR values. The modified MMIB model is as follows.

$$ESINR = g^{-1}I(\frac{1}{N}\sum_{i=1}^{N}I(g(SINR_i)))$$
$$BLER = B_{AWGN}(ESINR) \tag{6}$$

Where I(.) is the mean mutual information per bit in one symbol. The parameters α_1, α_2 in function g(.) are searched in the link level simulation under the criterion for minimizing the logarithm mean square error [6]

$$\alpha = \arg_{\min} \{ \sum_{i=1}^{P} \log_{10}(BLER_i) - \log_{10}(BLER_{AWGN}(ESINR_i(\alpha))) \} \tag{7}$$

Where P is the number of simulated channel snapshots. $BLER_i$ is derived from link level simulation on the set of snapshots. $BLER_{AWGN}$ is the block error rate on AWGN channel. By using the logarithm mean square error the algorithm tries to get low error at high SINR, which is the region of interest [6].

4   Simulations for Verification

4.1   Simulation Condition

Simulation scenario is described in Section 2(A). LDPC encoder is chosen with code rate of 13/25 and 17/25. Modulation type is 16QAM. Four data streams are used. We take choosing antennas by transmitting power as our precoding scheme, which maps four data streams to eight transmitting antennas. Power control is not used. Ideal channel estimation is assumed and MMSE detector is used. SINR after detection is defined as [4]

$$SINR_k^i = \frac{\sigma_s^2 \| (R(k)H(k))_{ii} \|^2}{\sigma_s^2(((R(k)H(k))^H(R(k)H(k)))_{ii} - \| (R(k)H(k))_{ii} \|^2) + \sigma_n^2(R(k)^H R(k))_{ii}} \tag{8}$$

Where $SINR_k^i$ refers to SINR on k^{th} symbol and i^{th} data stream in a coded block. H is channel matrix. σ_s^2 is signal power. σ_n^2 is Gauss noise power. R is MMSE detection matrix. The noise on the denominator composes of interference from other data streams and Gauss noise.

The channel model uses six paths and each path contains twenty sub-paths. The power rate between direct path and sum of all other non-direct paths is 13.3721. The carrier frequency is 6GHz. The bandwidth is 100MHz. User speed is 2m/s. We build the model by modifying the SCME model [5].

We choose channel snapshots randomly at different positions and different moments. 10000 code blocks are simulated to get BLER on each channel snapshot.

4.2   Simulation Results

Fig. 7 shows results that code rate is 13/25. Fig. 8 shows results that rate is 17/25. Dots refer to mapping between ESINR and BLER in actual channel and solid line refer to AWGN reference curve. We can see that the deviations become large as ESINR is high (Fig. 7(a), Fig. 8(a)) , which is the region that is important to system level simulation and adaptive transmission. The modified MMIB algorithm is more close to AWGN reference curve at high ESINR (Fig 7(b), Fig 8(b)). The deviations are less than 0.1dB in most cases.

Table 1 shows the values of α_1, α_2 and MSE (mean square error) under different conditions. Results also show that the modified algorithm outperforms the original algorithm.

Table 1. Accuracies of the two models

Code rate	MMIB model	α_1	α_2	MSE
13/25	Original			0.0515
	Modified	1.000	0.910	0.0096
17/25	Original			0.0517
	Modified	0.999	0.940	0.0071

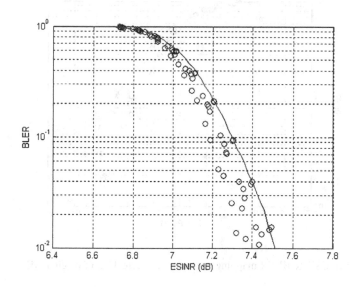

Fig. 7 (a). ESINR-BLER mapping curve for code rate-13/25 (original MMIB)

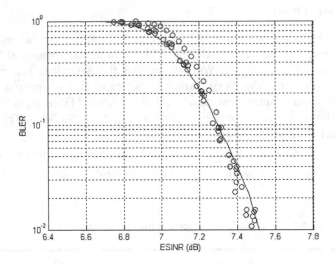

Fig. 7 (b). ESINR-BLER mapping curve for code rate-13/25 (modified MMIB)

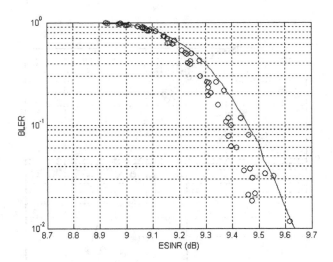

Fig. 8 (a). ESINR-BLER mapping curve for code rate-17/25 (original MMIB)

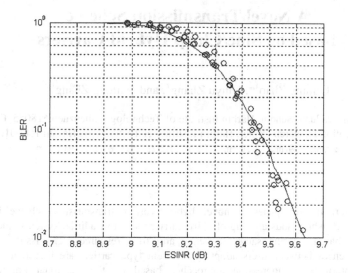

Fig. 8 (b). ESINR-BLER mapping curve for code rate-17/25 (modified MMIB)

5   Conclusion

MMIB algorithm is of high accuracy in SISO systems, but with considerable deviations in distributed MIMO systems. This paper proposes a modified method based on power function. The simulation shows that when applied to distributed MIMO systems, the modification can greatly improve the performance of MMIB algorithm. The enhanced algorithm can be applied to system level simulation and the adaptive transmission in practical systems.

References

1. Wachsmann, U., Pauli, M., Tsai, S.: Quality Determination for a Communications Link. U.S. Patent Office publication No. US 2004/02119883 A1 (2004)
2. Wan, L., Tsai, S., Almgren, M.: A Fading-Insensitive Performance Metric for a Unified Link Quality model. In: WCNC 2006, pp. 2110—2114 (2006)
3. IEEE 802.16 Broadband Wireless Access Working Group, Sayana, K., Zhuang, J., Stewart, K., Motorola Inc.: Link Performance Abstraction on Mean Mutual Information per Bit (MMIB) of the LLR Channel (2006)
4. IEEE 802.16 Broadband Wireless Access Working Group, Zhuang, J., Jalloul, L., Novak, R., Park, J.: IEEE 802.16m Evaluation Methodology Document (EMD) (2009)
5. Baum, D.S., Salo, J., Del Galdo, G., Milojevic, M., Kyösti, P., Hansen, J.: An Interim Channel Model for Beyond-3G System. In: Porc. IEEE VTC 2005, Stockholm, Sweden (2005)
6. Olmos, J., Ruiz, S., García-Lozano, M., Martín-Sacristán, D.: Link Abstraction Models Based on Mutual Information for LTE Downlink. COST 2100 TD(10)11052 (2010)
7. He, X., Niu, K., He, Z., Lin, J.: Layer Abstraction in MIMO-OFDM System. In: IEEE International Workshop on Gross Layer Design (2007)

A Novel Transmission Scheme
Based on Sine/Chirp Hybrid Carriers

Qiming Zhao[1,2], Qinyu Zhang[1], and Naitong Zhang[1,2]

[1] Shenzhen Graduate School, Harbin Institute of Technology, Shenzhen 518055, China
[2] Communication Research Center, Harbin Institute of Technology, Harbin 150001, China
zqmhit@gmail.com, {zqy,ntzhang}@hit.edu.cn

Abstract. In this paper, a novel hybrid carrier transmission scheme is presented, which adds a group of chirp-carrier users to tradition systems sine-carrier based, sharing same frequency and time resources. The issues of interferences between users adopting different type carriers are investigated, and interference suppression approaches based on the fractional Fourier transform (FRFT) are proposed.

Keywords: hybrid carriers, chirp signals, fractional Fourier transform, interference suppression.

1   Introduction

Traditional wireless communications systems sine-carrier based are challenged sometimes, such as applications in dense users [1] and some other emergency communications scenes. When frequency bands available are insufficient, it's difficult to increase capacities and data rates of the systems based on traditional schemes. In this work, we propose a novel scheme which adds a group of chirp-carrier users into a tradition system. Chirp signals are typical time-varying signals, which have large time-bandwidth product properties [2] and flexible time-frequency distribution. With signal processing methods such as matched filtering, finite length chirp signals can be compressed into a narrow pulse [3], so called pulse compression. Due to the properties of pulse compression, chirp signals can be employed as a type of spread spectrum waves. Transmission schemes based on the chirp spread spectrum (CSS) have been verified to be robust over multi-path propagation and fast fading channels [4, 5]. Besides, chirp signals have different fractional Fourier transform (FRFT) [6] properties from sine-type signals. Therefore, when chirp signals are regarded as carriers, it's possible to separate them from sine carriers by processing in the FRFT domain, and the interferences between users chirp and sine based users would be suppressed into an acceptable level.

In the remaining part of this paper, the principle of the hybrid carriers transmission scheme is discussed, and the interference between subsystems sine and chirp carriers based is the main issue concerned.

P. Ren et al. (Eds.): WICON 2011, LNICST 98, pp. 154–163, 2012.

2   System Modeling

2.1   System Structure

A system structure considered is shown in Figure 1, in which two group of users are modulated by sine-type and chirp carriers respectively. The subsystem sine-carrier based can be regarded as a traditional system adopting typical multiple access schemes. In our research, it is considered to be a primary a FDMA (or OFDMA) system for discussion. Two key problems remained are schemes of the chirp-carrier subsystem and issues of the interference between the subsystems.

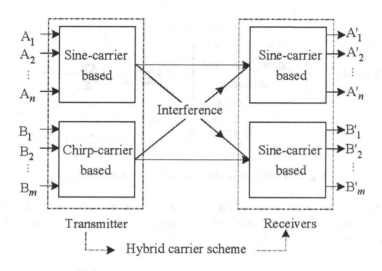

Fig. 1. A structure of hybrid carrier transmission scheme

2.2   Single-Link Transmission Based on Chirp Carriers

A modulated chirp-carrier signal can be represented as

$$s(t) = Eb(t)\exp\left[j\left(2\pi f_0 t + k\pi t^2 + \theta\right)\right] \tag{1}$$

where $b(t)$ is a base-band modulated signal, adopting a typical modulation scheme such as MPSK or MQAM, etc; parameters E, θ, f_0 and k are the amplitude, initial phase, central frequency at $t{=}0$ and chirp-rate respectively of the chirp carrier signal. Instantaneous frequency of a chirp signal is time-varying, the speed and direction of which decided by the chirp-rate parameter. The $s(t)$ can be regarded as a common modulation signal using chirp signal instead of the sine carrier. Since (1) can be also represented as

$$s(t) = Eb(t)\exp\left[j\left(2\pi f_{IF}t + k\pi t^2\right)\right]\exp\left[j\left(2\pi f_c t + \theta\right)\right] \qquad (2)$$

Modulation of a chirp carrier can be implemented with a structure shown in Figure 2, which is a conventional sine-carrier transmission scheme added a CCS block at the intermediate frequency (IF) part. The modulation of CSS by $b(t)$ is so-called the direction modulation (DM) method [7].

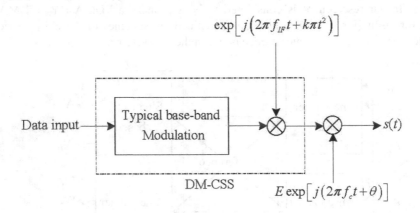

Fig. 2. A structure of chirp carrier modulation block

The demodulation of $s(t)$ is based on matched filtering. For each symbol, when the symbol duration is Ts and if $|k|T_s \gg 1$, the frequency spectrum of $s(t)$ at IF is represented as [8]

$$S_{IF}(f) \approx \frac{EB_i}{\sqrt{|k|}}\exp\left\{j\pi\left[-\frac{(f-f_{IF})^2}{k}+\frac{1}{4}\right]\right\}, \quad |f-f_{IF}| \leq \frac{|k|T_s}{2} \qquad (3)$$

where B_i is the bandwidth of base-band modulation. After chirp modulation, the transmission bandwidth of each symbol spreads into $B_i+|k|T_s$.

A matched filter of $S_{IF}(f)$ is

$$H(f) = \exp\left\{j\pi\left[\frac{(f-f_{IF})^2}{k}-\frac{1}{4}\right]\right\}, \quad |f-f_{IF}| \leq \frac{|k|T_s}{2} \qquad (4)$$

The output signal filtered by $H(f)$ represented in time domain is

$$s_o(t) = \mathrm{IFT}\left[S_{IF}(f)H(f)\right] = ET_s\sqrt{|k|}\,b_i(t)\exp\left(j2\pi f_{IF}t\right)\frac{\sin\left[\pi t|k|T_s\right]}{\pi t|k|T_s} \qquad (5)$$

When $s_o(t)$ is sampled at $t=0$ (central of the symbol duration), the primary symbol b_i is obtained with processing gain G_p

$$G_p = T_s \sqrt{|k|} \tag{6}$$

2.3   Multiple Access Scheme of the Chirp-Carrier Subsystem

In this subsection, we propose a multiple access scheme based on FRFT. According to definition [9], the FRFT of function $f(t)$ is represented as

$$F_p(u) = \int_{-\infty}^{\infty} f(t) K_p(u,t) dt \tag{7}$$

where p is the transform order. When $p=2n+1$ ($n \in Z$), the FRFT is just the Fourier transform, and when $p \notin Z$ the kernel $K_p(u, t)$ is defined as

$$K_p(u,t) = \sqrt{1 - j \cot \alpha_p} \exp\left[j\left(\cot \alpha_p u^2 + \cot \alpha_p t^2 - 2ut \csc \alpha_p \right) \right] \tag{8}$$

where $\alpha_p = \pi p/2$ is considered to be a rotational angle between time axis and the transform domain axis in the time-frequency plane [10].

Therefore, the FRFT of a finite chirp signal of T duration is

$$C_p(u) = E \sqrt{1 - j \cot \alpha_p} \exp(j\theta)$$
$$\cdot \int_{-T/2}^{T/2} \exp\left\{ j\pi \left[\left(k + \cot \alpha_p\right) t^2 + 2\left(f_0 - u \csc \alpha_p\right) + u^2 \cot \alpha_p \right] \right\} dt \tag{9}$$

For $p \in [-1, 1]$, only if $\cot \alpha_p = -k$, in other words $p = 2\text{arccot}(-k)/\pi$

$$C_p(u) = ET \sqrt{1 - j \cot \alpha_p} \exp\left[j\left(\pi \cot \alpha_p u^2 + \theta\right) \right] \frac{\sin\left[\pi \left(f_0 - u \csc \alpha_p\right) T \right]}{\pi \left(f_0 - u \csc \alpha_p\right) T} \tag{10}$$

The $|C_p(u)|$ in (10) has a Sinc function envelope whose peak appears at $u_0 = f_0 \sin \alpha_p$, and most of the energy is concentrated in interval $|u-u_0| < 2|\sin \alpha_p|/T$. It means that if two chirp signals have a same chirp-rate k and the central frequency interval Δf satisfying $\Delta f > 2/T$, they can be separated by filtering in the FRFT domain of $2\text{arccot}(-k)/\pi$ order. Besides, for $\Delta f = k\Delta t$, if the interval Δt between the beginning time of each chirp signal satisfies $\Delta t > 2/|k|T$, these chirp signals can also be separated.

The principle of chirp signals separation discussed above is regard as the multiple access scheme of the chirp-carrier subsystem, which is a generalization of FDMA or TDMA.

3   Analysis of the Interference between Subsystems

First, a hybrid system including a FDMA subsystem and only one chirp-carrier user is considered. The FDMA subsystem has N carriers and each carrier channel has B_0 transmission bandwidth. For the total transmission bandwidth available is limited, time-varying of the chirp-carrier's instantaneous frequency must be periodic. Assuming that chirp-rate and period of frequency time-varying of the chirp carrier are NB_0/T and T respectively, under this circumstance, each user in FDMA subsystem suffers from the interference from the chirp-carrier user periodically. Denoting T_s as the duration of symbols FDMA users transmitted, when T is much larger than T_s, the BER performances of the FDMA users would not be degraded seriously. In contrast, the chirp-carrier user suffers from the interference from the FDMA users all the time. In order to achieve an acceptable BER performance, extending the symbol durations to increase processing gain of matched filtering may be necessary, according to (6). The time-frequency relationship between FDMA and the chirp-carrier users is shown in Figure 3, which gives an explanation of the interference issue discussed above.

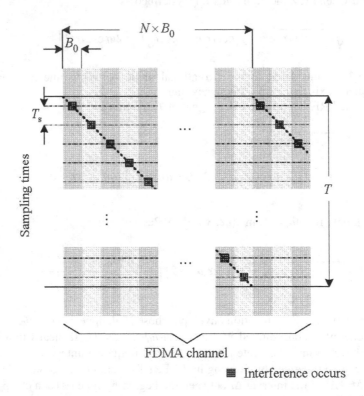

Fig. 3. Issue of interference explained by time-frequency relationship

BER performances of FDMA users and the chirp-carrier user are examined, as shown in Figure 4. The parameters in simulation are set as follows: for the FDMA subsystem, there are 10 carriers (denoted as $c_0 \sim c_9$) with interval 2 KHz and symbols are QPSK modulated, with 1ms duration; for the chirp carrier, the chirp-rate is 2 KHz/ms, frequency time-varying period is 10ms, and symbols are also QPSK modulated with 1Kbps or 0.5Kbps bit rate; powers of all carriers are same (SIR=0dB). (E_b: bit energy; n_0: noise power spectrum density)

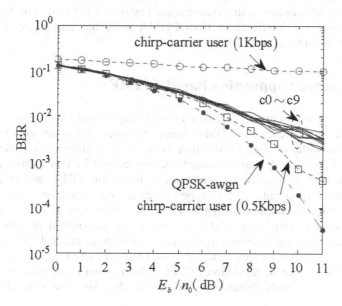

Fig. 4. BER performance of different users

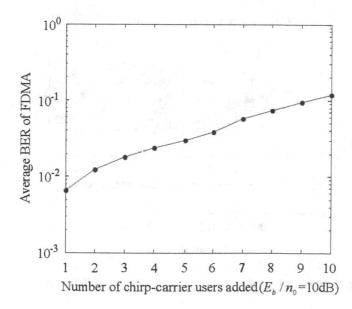

Fig. 5. BER performance of FDMA degrades as chirp-carrier users added

When more chirp-carrier users are added, interference to the FDMA users appears more frequently. Just keep the parameters in simulations above, the average BER performance of the FDMA users are examined according to different number of chirp-carrier users added, at E_b/n_0=10dB, as shown in Figure 5. It means that a traditional FDMA system would fail when too many chirp-carrier users are added without efficient approaches of interference suppression employed. For the chirp-carrier users, since the interferences from FDMA users are unchanged, the BER performances will not be degraded.

4   Interference Suppression Based on FRFT

For interference to users chirp-carrier based can be suppressed by matched filtering, suppressing the interference to FDMA users becomes the main problem. For transmission bandwidth of each FDMA user is covered by chirp signals. Band-pass filtering in the frequency domain is invalid. Considering FRFT properties of chirp signals, approaches of interference suppression based on FRFT are practicable. Comparing with chirp signals' FRFT properties discussed in Section 2, energy of a sine signal can not be concentrated by FRFT except at ± 1orders, as shown in Figure 6. Therefore, when a chirp signal and a sine signal are transmitted in a same band synchronously, employing a band-stop filtering (BSF) in an optimal FRFT domain can eliminate a chirp signal almost completely and remain part of the sine signal. The energy concentrated interval $\Delta u=2|\sin\alpha_p|/T_s'$ of a chirp signal is regarded as the stop band of BSF, where T_s' is the duration of symbols the chirp signal modulated.

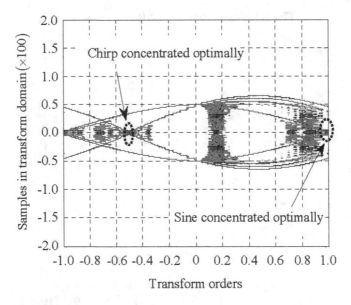

Fig. 6. An example of sine and chirp signals' different FRFT properties

Certainly, BSF in the FRFT domain causes energy loss of the sine signal concerned inevitable. In order to estimate the degree of energy loss, calculation of a modulated sine signal's general bandwidth in the FRFT domain, denoted as U, is required. Although an accurate value of U is non-available, a geometrical method can be used for approximate calculation, as shown in Figure 7, and U can be represented as

$$U = \sqrt{B^2 + \frac{1}{T_s^2}} \cos\left(\alpha_p' - \arctan\frac{B}{T_s}\right) \tag{11}$$

where α_p'=sgn(sinα_p)arccot($-k$), and B and T_s are the bandwidth and symbol duration of the modulated sine signal respectively. Therefore, the degree of energy loss can be estimated by the ratio

$$\eta \approx \frac{2\sin\alpha_p'}{T_s'\sqrt{B^2 + \frac{1}{T_s^2}}\cos\left(\alpha_p' - \arctan\frac{B}{T_s}\right)} \tag{12}$$

Performances of interference suppression by BSF in the FRFT domain are examined, as shown in Figure 8. The parameters of the FDMA users and chirp carriers are kept as ones in Section 3, and 10 chirp-carrier users are added this time. Assuming the bit rate of each chirp-carrier user is 1 or 0.5Kbps, denoted as interference type I or II respectively, performances of interference suppression via BSF in the FRFT domain are examined, with about 2.6 or 1.3 dB loss of E_b/n_0 accordingly.

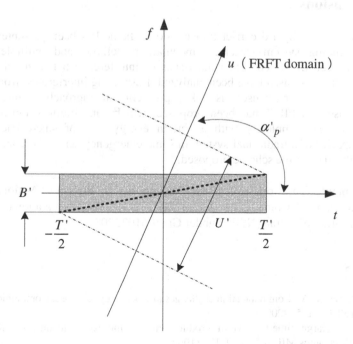

Fig. 7. Approximate calculation of a sine signal's general bandwidth in a FRFT domain

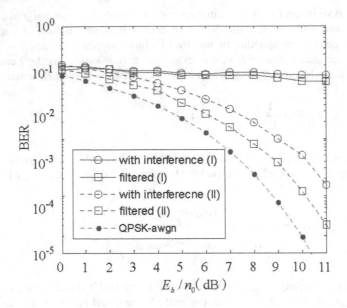

Fig. 8. Performances of interference suppression via BSF in the FRFT domain (the bit rate of chirp users in I and II are 1 and 0.5Kbps)

5   Conclusions

In this paper, a novel hybrid carrier transmission scheme has been presented. First, principles including system structure, modulation methods and multiple access schemes have been discussed. Then the issues of interference between subsystems sine and chirp carriers based have been analyzed. Respecting interference from chirp-carrier users to sine-carrier users is a key problem, an approach of interference suppression based on FRFT has been proposed, which can eliminate chirp signals interference almost completely with a certain energy loss of sine-carrier users. Increasing capacity of a traditional system in some emergency senses is regarded as a potential application of the scheme proposed.

Acknowledgments. The work in this paper is supported by Project of National Basic Research Program of China under Grant 2007CB310606, and National Natural Science Foundation of China (NSFC) under Grant 61032003.

References

1. Manoj, B., Baker, A.: Communication challenges in emergency response. Communications of the ACM 50(3), 51–53 (2007)
2. Thor, R.: A large time-bandwidth product pulse compression technique. IRE Tran. Military Electronics MIL-6(2), 169–173 (1962)

3. Wang, Y., Chen, R., Zhang, W.: Design and simulation of a Chirp Pulse Compression Ultra-Wideband Communication System. In: IEEE ICECT 2009 Conf., pp. 415–419. IEEE Press, New York (1962)
4. Tsai, Y., Chang, J.: The feasibility of combating multipath interference by chirp spread spectrum techniques over Rayleigh and Rician fading channels. In: 3rd IEEE ISSSTA Conf., pp. 282–286. IEEE Press, New York (1994)
5. Shen, H., Papandreou-Suppappola, A.: Diversity and channel estimation using time-varying signals and time-frequency techniques. IEEE Tran. Microwave Theory and Techniques 54(9), 3400–3413 (2006)
6. Qi, L., Tao, R., Zhou, S., Wang, Y.: Detection and parameter estimation of multi-component LFM signal based on the fractional Fourier transform. Sci China Inf Sci 47(2), 184–198 (2004)
7. Pinkney, J., Sesay, A., Nichols, S., Behin, R.: A robust high speed indoor wireless communications system using chirp spread spectrum. In: IEEE CCECE 1999 Conf., vol. 1, pp. 84–89. IEEE Press, New York (1999)
8. Pinkney, J.: Low complexity indoor wireless data links using chirp spread spectrum. PhD. Thesis, The University of Calgary (2003)
9. Almeida, L.: The Fractional Fourier Transform and Time-Frequency Representations. IEEE Tran. Signal Processing 42(11), 3084–3091 (1994)
10. Tao, R., Deng, B., Wang, Y.: Research progress of the fractional Fourier transform in signal processing. Sci China Inf. Sci 49(1), 1–25 (2006)

Dynamic Bayesian Spectrum Bargaining with Non-myopic Users

Yang Yan[1], Jianwei Huang[2], Ming Zhao[1], and Jing Wang[1]

[1] State Key Laboratory on Microwave and Digital Communications,
Tsinghua National Laboratory for Information Science and Technology,
Department of Electronic Engineering, Tsinghua University, Beijing 100084, China
[2] Department of Information Engineering, CUHK, Hong Kong, China
yanyang07@mails.tsinghua.edu.cn, jwhuang@ie.cuhk.edu.hk,
{zhaoming,wangj}@mail.tsinghua.edu.cn

Abstract. In this paper, we investigate a cooperative spectrum sharing mechanism realized by a *dynamic Bayesian spectrum bargaining* between a pair of *non-myopic* primary user and secondary user. The primary user has only incomplete information of the secondary user's energy cost. We model such a bargaining process as a dynamic Bayesian game, and discuss the equilibria under all possible system parameters. Furthermore, we discuss in details the *sequential equilibrium* where the *reputation effect* plays an important role. Our analysis shows that the secondary user with a low energy cost can exploit the primary user's lack of complete information for its own benefits.

Keywords: dynamic Bayesian spectrum bargaining, cooperative spectrum sharing, sequential equilibrium, incomplete information, game theory, reputation effect.

1 Introduction

Rapid growth of today's wireless data communications leads to spectrum resource scarcity and demands more efficient resource allocation schemes. *Cooperative spectrum sharing (CSS)* is one class of mechanisms that can greatly enhance the efficiency of spectrum utilization through user cooperations. One possible CSS mechanism is to allow a licensed primary user (PU) with a poor channel link between its transmitter and receiver to improve its data rate by using a secondary user (SU) as a relay. Such interaction can increase the PU's data rate through creating cooperation diversity [1]. In fact, the benefit of cooperative communication has been well studied in the literature [2,3], and cooperative communication has already been incorporated into various wireless communication standards (*e.g.*, IEEE 802.16J standard [4]).

Different from the traditional cooperative communication technology, CSS also considers the compensation to the SU for its relay effort to create a *win-win* situation. The key issue that we study in this paper is how to determine the proper compensation with incomplete network information. A brief illustration

P. Ren et al. (Eds.): WICON 2011, LNICST 98, pp. 164–179, 2012.

of the network topology and interaction scheme is shown in Fig. 1. Detailed notations will be introduced in Section 2.1.

CSS with complete network information has been considered in [5–7]. Reference [8] considered a contract-based CSS in a *static* network. Our prior work [9] analyzed the CSS with *incomplete* information in a *dynamic* network environment. The focus of [9] is to consider the multi-stage bargaining between one PU and one SU within a *single* time slot. Our recent work [10] considered the CSS between one PU and one SU over multiple time slots, where the reputation effect happens due to incomplete information of SU's energy cost. In [10], SU is non-myopic but PU is assumed to be myopic. Our current paper extends the analysis to a more realistic where the PU is also non-myopic and wants to maximize its benefit in the long run. The analysis turns out to be much more involved compared with the one in [10].

In this paper, we analyze a bargaining-based CSS between one PU and one SU over a finite number of time slots, where both users are non-myopic and want to maximize their long-term utilities. The main results and contributions of this paper are as follows:

- *Non-myopic players:* We assume both PU and SU are non-myopic rational players, who maximize their long-term utilities. This assumption better captures the reality in dynamic spectrum bargaining.
- *Incomplete information and sequential equilibrium:* We model the SUs energy cost as the incomplete information to PU, and characterize the sequential equilibrium of the bargaining game.
- *Reputation effect:* We show that a weaker SU can take advantage of the incomplete information by establishing a strong reputation to obtain a higher long-term utility by establishing a certain reputation.

The rest of the paper is organized as follows. We introduce the system model in Section 2. In Section 3, we analyze and summarize the equilibria of the multi-slot bargaining under different system parameters. In Section 4, we focus on discussing when and how the reputation effect will affect the equilibrium. In Section 5, we discuss about the equilibrium outcome by comparing with the model under complete information. Finally, we conclude in Section 6.

2   PU-SU Cooperation and Bargaining Model

2.1   Cooperative Communication

We consider a time-slotted system with the network model as shown in Fig. 1, where one PU bargains with one SU about the spectrum allocation scheme. Here, TP and RP represent PU's transmitter and receiver, and TS and RS represent SU's transmitter and receiver. Parameter h_p, h_s, h_{ps}, and h_{sp} denote the fixed channel gains of the link TP-RP, TS-RS, TP-TS, and TS-RP, respectively. We further assume that both PU and SU know the channel gains of all links through a proper feedback mechanism. The PU and SU transmit with fixed power P_t and P_s, respectively.

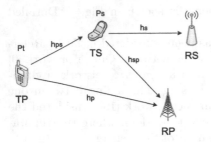

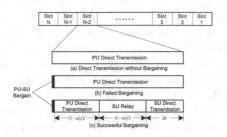

Fig. 1. PU-SU Cooperation Model

Fig. 2. The Slotted System Model with Three Possible Bargaining Results in a Single Time Slot

2.2   Dynamic Spectrum Bargaining

The bargaining process consists of N successive time slots as shown in Fig. 2. In order to facilitate later backward induction analysis, *we index time backwards, i.e., the bargaining starts with time slot N and ends in time slot 1*. Without loss of generality, we normalize each time slot length to 1. During each time slot, the PU can choose either *direct transmission only* or *bargaining with the SU*. There are three possibilities following PU's two options, which are illustrated in Fig. 2.

- Figure 2(a): If PU's direct channel gain h_p is good enough, then it will choose direct transmission only and achieves a data rate $R_{dir} = \log(1 + P_t h_p)$. In this case, The SU cannot transmit and achieves a zero utility.
- Figure 2(b): If PU believes that the SU's cooperation may be beneficial, it can offer α fraction of the time slot for SU's own transmission as remuneration for SU. If SU rejects the offer, PU proceeds with direct transmission for the remaining time.
- Figure 2(c): If SU accepts PU's offer α, then the PU and SU work in the amplified and forward (AF) relay mode. The PU achieves a data rate (per unit time) [1]

$$R_r = \log\left(1 + P_t h_p + \frac{P_t P_s h_{ps} h_{sp}}{P_t h_{ps} + P_s h_{sp} + 1}\right), \tag{1}$$

and the SU achieves a data rate (per unit time)

$$R_s = \log(1 + P_s h_s). \tag{2}$$

PU and SU will bargain over the value of α in each time slot after observing the bargaining history and anticipating the future, so as to maximize their own long-term utilities.

2.3   Incomplete Information of Energy Cost

We assume that the SU is an *energy-constrained* device (*e.g.*, wireless sensor or mobile device) with an energy cost C, which belongs to one of two types: High type C_h and Low type C_l with $(C_h > C_l)$. The SU knows its own type, but the PU does not. However, the PU has a *belief* on C's distribution in each time slot $(n = N, ..., 1)$, *i.e.*, $\Pr(C = C_h) = q_n$ and $\Pr(C = C_l) = 1 - q_n$. The belief will be updated based on the interactions between the PU and SU.

3   Multi-Slot Spectrum Bargaining Game with Non-myopic Players

In this section, we will explore how the PU and SU maximize their utilities in this dynamic Bayesian bargaining game. We assume that both PU and SU are the non-myopic players, who will maximize their total utilities in the N time slots. As the first step, we will study the single-slot bargaining game (*e.g.*, $N = 1$), which serves as a base for the study of the multi-slot case later on.

3.1   Utility Function in the Single-Slot Game

The SU's single-slot utility $U_s(\alpha)$ after accepting an offer α is

$$U_s(\alpha) = \alpha R_s - \frac{1+\alpha}{2} P_s C, \tag{3}$$

which is the difference between the SU's achievable data rate R_s (as in (2)) and energy cost. If we view C as the data rate per *watt* that the SU can get if it does not relay for PU, then $U_s(\alpha)$ is SU's *data rate increase* by accepting offer α. Note that the SU can always achieve a zero utility without participating in the cooperative communication. Given PU's offer α, it is *optimal* for SU to accept the offer if and only if $U_s(\alpha) > 0$.

The PU's single-slot utility $U_p(\alpha)$ is its *achievable data rate*. Without SU's relay, the PU can achieve a data rate R_{dir}. If PU's offer α is accepted by SU, then the PU's data rate is $\frac{1-\alpha}{2}R_r$, where R_r is given in (1). In each time slot, the PU aims to maximize its utility

$$U_p(\alpha) = \max\left\{ R_{dir}, \frac{1-\alpha}{2}R_r \right\}. \tag{4}$$

3.2   Sequential Equilibrium

In this subsection, we consider the multi-slot bargaining game. This bargaining process is a dynamic Bayesian game [11], which includes the PU's and SU's dynamic decision-making and belief updates. The commonly used equilibrium concept for this dynamic Bayesian game is the *sequential equilibrium* (SE), which satisfies the following three requirements [12]:

Requirement 1. *The player taking the action must have a belief (probability distribution) about the incomplete information, reflecting what that player believes has happened so far.*

Requirement 2. *The action taken by a player must be optimal given the player's belief and the other players' subsequent strategies.*

Requirement 3. *A player's belief is determined by the Bayes' rule whenever it applies and the players' hypothesized equilibrium strategies.*

The belief in Requirement 1 is the PU's probability assessment q_n about the High type SU in time slot n, with an initial value $q_N = \eta$ in the first time slot (*i.e.*, time slot indexed as N). As the bargaining proceeds, both the PU and SU can observe all prior history actions, which might enable the PU to *update* its belief about the SU's type so that PU can accordingly make new decisions. The SU knows its own type and there is no incomplete information in the PU, thus the SU's belief is deterministic during the game.

3.3 Equilibrium Characterization

Generally, the equilibrium outcome depends crucially on both players' parameter settings, *i.e.*, the PU and SU will both influence the game result. On the one hand, an SU will only choose to cooperate and serve as a relay for PU if it can get a positive *total* utility in N time slots. It implies that the equilibrium outcome not only depends on the SU's energy cost (either C_h or C_l), but also on SU's achievable average data rate per unit power, R_s/P_s. On the other hand, the equilibrium outcome also relies on whether and how the PU decides to cooperate with the SU. This indicates that the equilibrium outcome is related to the relationship between PU's direct transmission rate R_{dir} and relay rate $\frac{1-\alpha}{2}R_r$.[1]

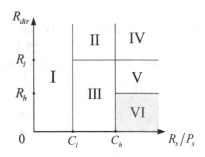

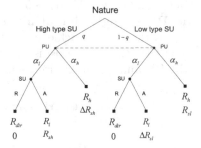

Fig. 3. Equilibrium Outcomes in Different Regions

Fig. 4. Game Tree of the Single-Slot Bargaining with $R_l > R_h > R_{dir}$ and $C_l < C_h < R_s/P_s$

Next we will discuss several equilibrium contingencies based on different parameter settings of both PU and SU. Figure 3 illustrates six different cases for equilibrium discussions. Due to the page limit, we summarize the equilibria in

---

[1] Specifically, the relay rate has two values, *i.e.*, R_l and R_h, which will be discussed later. See [13] for details.

Regions I-V in the following theorem. We will discuss the equilibrium outcome with *reputation effect* of Region VI in next section.

Let us define

$$\alpha_h = \frac{1}{\frac{2R_s}{C_h P_s} - 1} + \varepsilon, \ \alpha_l = \frac{1}{\frac{2R_s}{C_l P_s} - 1} + \varepsilon, \tag{5}$$

where ε is an arbitrarily small positive value. Here, α_h and α_l are the PUs respective optimal offer to the High and Low type SU under the AF relay mode. For ease of discussion later on, we further define

- $R_h = \frac{1-\alpha_h}{2} R_r$: the PU's single-slot data rate if SU accepts the offer α_h.
- $R_l = \frac{1-\alpha_l}{2} R_r$: the PU's single-slot data rate if SU accepts the offer α_l.

Obviously, we have $\alpha_h > \alpha_l$ and $R_h < R_l$.

Theorem 1. *Consider a multi-slot bargaining game where the PU and SU are non-myopic players. In Regions I, II, and IV, PU always chooses direct transmission only regardless of SU's type. In Regions III and V, PU always offers α_l to SU. A High type SU rejects the offer α_l, and a Low type SU accepts the offer α_l.*

The proof of Theorem 1 is given in our online technical report [13]. In Regions I-V, we can decompose the multi-slot bargaining game into N independent single-slot bargaining game. The PU's decisions in these regions do not rely on its belief about the SU's type.

The remaining region is Region VI, where we cannot simplify the analysis of the multi-slot bargaining into N single-slot ones. We will discuss the SE of this region in next section.

4 Dynamic Bargaining with Reputation Effect

In this section, we study the SE result in Region VI. In this case, R_{dir} is small, and PU will never choose direct transmission.

4.1 Basic Analysis of the Single-Slot Bargaining Game

To attract the help from SU, PU needs to provide an offer α that makes the SU's single-slot utility $U_s(\alpha)$ *slightly* larger than zero. The PU's optimal offer to the High and Low type SU can be given in (5). For ease of discussion later on, we define two more notations,

- $\Delta R_{sh} = \left(R_s - \frac{1}{2} P_s C_h\right) \varepsilon$: the High type SU's single-slot utility if accepting α_h.
- $\Delta R_{sl} = \left(R_s - \frac{1}{2} P_s C_l\right) \varepsilon$: the Low type SU's single-slot utility if accepting α_l.

In Region VI, an SU may reject or accept the PU's offer α_h or α_l. However, no matter what happenes, PU's *expected* utility will not be worse than R_{dir} since $R_l > R_h > R_{dir}$. Therefore, PU will never choose direct transmission only without bargaining (Figure 2(a)). Thus, PU has *two* options here: offer α_h or offer α_l, with the corresponding PU's utility R_h and R_l if SU accepts the offer.

Let us first consider the game tree of the *single-slot* game in Fig. 4, where *nature* moves first and determines SU's type. PU and SU make decisions alternatively at the *non-leaf* nodes (black solid dot); each possible game result is denoted by a *leaf* node (black solid square) together with the corresponding PU utility (upper value) and SU utility (lower value). PU's belief (about SU's type) is $\Pr(C = C_h) = q$. Here, we further define

- $R_{sh} = \alpha_l R_s - \frac{1+\alpha_l}{2} P_s C_h$: the High type SU's single-slot utility if it accepts the low offer α_l.
- $R_{sl} = \alpha_h R_s - \frac{1+\alpha_h}{2} P_s C_l$: the Low type SU's single-slot utility if it accepts the high offer α_h.

When ε approaches zero in (5), we have $R_{sh} < 0$ and $R_{sl} > 0$. Thus, a High type SU will not accept a low offer, while a Low type SU has the *incentive* to accept a high offer, which leads to the reputation effect in our later analysis.

In Fig. 4, PU first decides to offer α_h or α_l. Then, the SU selects the acceptance (**A**) or rejection (**R**). If PU offers α_h, the SU will always accept regardless of its type since $\Delta R_{sh} > 0$ and $R_{sl} > 0$. Hence there is only one leaf node following the offer α_h. If PU offers α_l, a High type SU will reject as $R_{sh} < 0$, and a Low type SU will accept since $\Delta R_{sl} > 0$.

Anticipating the SU's responses, PU's *expected* utility if offering α_l is

$$U_p^{\alpha_l} = q R_{dir} + (1 - q) R_l. \tag{6}$$

PU's utility is R_h if it offers α_h. Thus, PU will offer α_l if $U_p^{\alpha_l} > R_h$, *i.e.*, $q < (R_l - R_h)/(R_l - R_{dir})$. The relationship between (6) and R_h depends on the value of q.

4.2   Sequential Equilibrium of the Multi-slot Bargaining

Now we return to the multi-slot bargaining game ($N > 1$), where the PU's belief might change over time (*i.e.*, q_n for time slot n instead of a fixed value q as in (6)) based on the game history. The SU's strategy may also change depending on the game history and its anticipation of the PU's future response. In particular, a Low type user has an incentive to reject α_l in earlier time slots even though α_l brings a positive utility for each time slot. The purpose of the Low type SU's *predation* strategy is to establish a *reputation* of a High type SU and induce the PU to offer α_h in the future, which improves the SU's total utility in N time slots. We will find the SE result based on such a prediction.

The SE of the multi-slot bargaining includes the following components: (i) the update of PU's belief q_n (*i.e.*, the probability of a High type SU) in each time slot $n = N, ..., 1$, (ii) PU's strategy (offer α_l or α_h) in each time slot n, (iii) SU's strategy (accept or reject) in each time slot n.

Theorem 2. *The sequential equilibrium of the multi-slot bargaining game with non-myopic PU and SU is given in (a) to (l), where the parameter*

$$d = \frac{R_l - R_h}{R_l - R_{dir}} \in (0,1). \tag{7}$$

- **PU's Belief Updates:**[2]
  (a) *If* $q_{n+1} = 0$, *then* $q_n = 0$.
  (b) *If* $q_{n+1} > 0$ *and SU accepts the high offer* α_h *in time slot* $n + 1$, *then* $q_n = q_{n+1}$.
  (c) *If* $q_{n+1} > 0$ *and SU accepts the low offer* α_l *in time slot* $n + 1$, *then* $q_n = 0$.
  (d) *If* $q_{n+1} > 0$ *and SU rejects the low offer* α_l *in time slot* $n + 1$, *then* $q_n = max(d^n, q_{n+1})$.
- **PU's Strategy:**
  (e) *If* $q_n < d^n$ *in time slot* n, *offers* α_l.
  (f) *If* $q_n > d^n$ *in time slot* n, *offers* α_h.
  (g) *If* $q_n = d^n$ *in time slot* n, *offers* α_h *with probability* $\frac{\Delta R_{sl}}{R_{sl} - \Delta R_{sl}}$ *and offers* α_l *with probability* $1 - \frac{\Delta R_{sl}}{R_{sl} - \Delta R_{sl}}$.[3]
- **The High type SU's Strategy:**
  (h) *Always accepts* α_h *and rejects* α_l.
- **The Low type SU's Strategy:**
  (i) *Always accepts* α_h.
  (j) *If* $n = 1$ *(the last time slot), accepts* α_l.
  (k) *If* $n > 1$ *and* $q_n \geq d^{n-1}$, *rejects* α_l.
  (l) *If* $n > 1$ *and* $q_n < d^{n-1}$, *rejects* α_l *with probability* $y_n = \frac{(1-d^{n-1})q_n}{d^{n-1}(1-q_n)}$ *and accepts* α_l *with* $1 - y_n$.

Proof. First, let us look at the High type SU's strategy. In the multi-slot bargaining game, we can show that there is no incentive for the High type SU to accept α_l. This is because accepting α_l leads to negative SU's utility in the current time slot, and will make PU believe that the SU is a Low type. This means that all future offers will be α_l, and thus the SU's total utility will be negative.

Next, we verify the PU's strategy and its belief update scheme. Let us first discuss PU's *limiting belief* q_n^*, which can be interpreted as a decision threshold to determine which offer (α_l or α_h) the PU should provide. It can also be viewed as the SU's *limiting threshold reputation* as the High type, above which the PU will not offer α_l.[4] We should consider the PU's utility by summing its utilities from the current time slot n to the last time slot. Define $U_{\mathbb{P}_n}(q_n)$ to be the expected utility of PU in time slot n with the belief q_n.[5] Furthermore, we use

---

[2] Recall that we index time backwards, and thus we will compute q_n based on q_{n+1} as time slot n is after time slot $n + 1$. See Fig. 2.

[3] As ε is an arbitrary small positive, ΔR_{sl} is arbitrarily small. Therefore, the assumption $R_{sl} > 2\Delta R_{sl}$ holds.

[4] For the standard definition of "reputation", see Section 5.

[5] For clear illustrations, we interchangeably use different notations, *i.e.*, $\mathbb{P}_1$, $\mathbb{P}_2$, ..., $\mathbb{P}_N$ to mark the PU in different time slots. However, these notations all indicate the *unique* PU in the multi-slot bargaining game.

$U_{\mathbb{P}_n}(q_n|\alpha_l)$ and $U_{\mathbb{P}_n}(q_n|\alpha_h)$ to denote PU's expected utilities when offering α_l and α_h, respectively.

It is easy to analyze the last time slot ($n = 1$) since there is no other time slot following it. PU in the last time slot is indifferent between offering α_l and α_h if

$$q_1 R_{dir} + y_1(1 - q_1)R_{dir} + (1 - y_1)(1 - q_1)R_l = R_h. \qquad (8)$$

The LHS of (8) is PU's utility if offering α_l, and the RHS is the utility if offering α_h. y_n denotes the probability that the Low type SU rejects α_l in time slot n. Note that for the Low type SU, accepting α_l is optimal in the single-slot game (see Fig. 4). Obviously, such a strategy also applies in the last time slot. Thus, if PU offers α_l in the last time slot indexed by $n = 1$, the Low type SU will accept and hence $y_1 = 0$ holds. Given that $y_1 = 0$, we get the limiting belief q_1^* for the case of $n = 1$,

$$q_1^* = \frac{R_l - R_h}{R_l - R_{dir}} \triangleq d. \qquad (9)$$

The utility $U_{\mathbb{P}_1}(q_1|\alpha_l) = q_1 R_{dir} + (1 - q_1)R_l$ and $U_{\mathbb{P}_1}(q_1|\alpha_h) = R_h$. Further, if the actual belief $q_1 > q_1^*$, then $U_{\mathbb{P}_1}(q_1|\alpha_l) < U_{\mathbb{P}_1}(q_1|\alpha_h)$ and PU will choose to offer α_h. Otherwise PU will offer α_l. Therefore, we have $U_{\mathbb{P}_1}(q_1)$,

$$U_{\mathbb{P}_1}(q_1) = \begin{cases} q_1 R_{dir} + (1 - q_1)R_l, & \text{if } q_1 \leq q_1^* = d, \\ R_h, & \text{if } q_1 > q_1^* = d. \end{cases} \qquad (10)$$

Now consider the second to last time slot indexed by $n = 2$. Recall Requirement 3, which states that the belief should be consistent with strategies and satisfies the Bayes' rule whenever it applies. Such a requirement also holds when the actual belief is the limiting belief. Thus, q_1^* should satisfy the Bayes' rule and should be derived from q_2 and y_2, i.e.,

$$q_1^* = \text{Prob}(\text{SU is High type} \mid \text{SU rejects } \alpha_l). \qquad (11)$$

Note that the Bayesian process only applies if PU provides α_l and SU rejects it. Recall that accepting α_l is an evidence of indicating that the SU belongs to the Low type. Therefore, SU's accepting α_l in time slot $n = 2$ will result in $q_1 = 0$, which contradicts the fact $q_1^* = d$. If PU provides α_h and SU accepts it, from (b) we get $q_2 = q_1^* = d$ since there is no information provided to help update PU's belief. By the Bayes' rule, we can proceed the derivation with (11) to obtain y_2 as

$$y_2 = \begin{cases} \frac{q_2(1-d)}{(1-q_2)d}, & \text{if } q_2 \leq d, \\ 1, & \text{if } q_2 > d. \end{cases} \qquad (12)$$

When $q_2 \leq d$, $\mathbb{P}_2$'s expected utility $U_{\mathbb{P}_2}(q_2|\alpha_l)$ can be expressed as

$$q_2(R_{dir} + U_{\mathbb{P}_1}(d)) + (1 - q_2)y_2(R_{dir} + U_{\mathbb{P}_1}(d)) + (1 - q_2)(1 - y_2)(R_l + U_{\mathbb{P}_1}(0)), \quad (13)$$

if it offers α_l. When α_l is rejected by SU in the second to last period, we apply the Bayes' rule to get

$$q_1 = \frac{q_2}{q_2 + (1 - q_2) \times \left(\frac{(1-d)q_2}{d(1-q_2)} \right)} = d.$$

Therefore, the updated belief in the last time slot will be $q_1 = d$. If SU accepts α_l, then PU will update its belief as 0. Thus, we have the belief update results in (13). Substitute (12) into (13), then we have

$$U_{\mathbb{P}_2}(q_2|\alpha_l) = \frac{q_2}{d}[R_{dir} + U_{\mathbb{P}_1}(d)] + \left(1 - \frac{q_2}{d}\right)[R_l + U_{\mathbb{P}_1}(0)]. \quad (14)$$

When $q_2 > d$, $U_{\mathbb{P}_2}(q_2|\alpha_l)$ will be

$$U_{\mathbb{P}_2}(q_2|\alpha_l) = R_{dir} + U_{\mathbb{P}_1}(q_2). \quad (15)$$

Note that the updated belief in the last time slot keeps unchanged in (15). With the Bayes' rule, we have

$$q_1 = \frac{q_2}{q_2 + (1 - q_2) \times \text{Prob(SU rejects } \alpha_l \mid \text{Low type SU})} = q_2. \quad (16)$$

Hence, we obtain the result in (15). The expected utility of PU when offering α_h is

$$U_{\mathbb{P}_2}(q_2|\alpha_h) = R_h + U_{\mathbb{P}_1}(q_2). \quad (17)$$

If PU's belief is the limiting belief, then the balancing condition must hold, *i.e.,*

$$U_{\mathbb{P}_2}(q_2|\alpha_l) = U_{\mathbb{P}_2}(q_2|\alpha_h). \quad (18)$$

However, from (15) and (17) we can observe that the limiting belief q_2^* cannot be larger than d. Recall the expression of $U_{\mathbb{P}_1}(q_1)$ in (10), we have $U_{\mathbb{P}_1}(d) = R_h = dR_{dir} + (1 - d)R_l$ and $U_{\mathbb{P}_1}(0) = R_l$. Let (14) equal to (17), and we have

$$q_2^* = d \times \frac{R_l - R_h}{R_l - R_{dir}} = d^2. \quad (19)$$

Furthermore, it is easy to show that $U_{\mathbb{P}_2}(q_2|\alpha_h) > U_{\mathbb{P}_2}(q_2|\alpha_l)$ when $q_2 > q_2^*$. We thus have PU's expected utility in the second to last time slot as

$$U_{\mathbb{P}_2}(q_2) = \begin{cases} \frac{q_2}{d}[R_{dir} + U_{\mathbb{P}_1}(d)] + \left(1 - \frac{q_2}{d}\right)[R_l + U_{\mathbb{P}_1}(0)], & \text{if } q_2 \leq q_2^* = d^2, \\ R_h + U_{\mathbb{P}_1}(q_2), & \text{if } q_2 > q_2^* = d^2. \end{cases} \quad (20)$$

For $n \geq 3$, we first conjecture that the limiting belief in time slot n is

$$q_n^* = d^n. \quad (21)$$

Given the above assumption, we have PU's expected utility in time slot n as

$$U_{\mathbb{P}_n}(q_n) = \begin{cases} \frac{q_n}{d^{n-1}}[R_{dir} + U_{\mathbb{P}_{n-1}}(d^{n-1})] + \left(1 - \frac{q_n}{d^{n-1}}\right)[R_l + U_{\mathbb{P}_{n-1}}(0)], & \text{if } q_n \leq q_n^* = d^n, \\ R_h + U_{\mathbb{P}_{n-1}}(q_n), & \text{if } q_n > q_n^* = d^n. \end{cases} \quad (22)$$

where we define the *initial* conditions as $U_{\mathbb{P}_0}(0) = U_{\mathbb{P}_0}(1) = 0$. Obviously, (21) and (22) hold for the cases $n = 1$ and $n = 2$. Again, we apply the Bayes' rule to $q_{n-1}^* = d^{n-1}$ and get the restriction condition between q_n and y_n,

$$q_{n-1}^* = d^{n-1} = \frac{q_n}{q_n + y_n(1 - q_n)}. \quad (23)$$

From (23), we get

$$y_n = \frac{q_n(1 - d^{n-1})}{(1 - q_n)d^{n-1}}. \tag{24}$$

Besides, we get the *balancing strategy* y_n^* in time slot n by substituting $q_n^* = d^n$ into (24),

$$y_n^* = y_n(q_n^*) = \frac{d^n(1 - d^{n-1})}{(1 - d^n)d^{n-1}} = \frac{d - d^n}{1 - d^n}. \tag{25}$$

For the case of time slot $n + 1$, the Bayes' rule still applies to the limiting belief q_n^*, and thus we have

$$y_{n+1} = \begin{cases} \frac{q_{n+1}(1-d^n)}{(1-q_{n+1})d^n}, & \text{if } q_{n+1} \leq d^n, \\ 1, & \text{if } q_{n+1} > d^n. \end{cases} \tag{26}$$

By considering (26), PU's expected utility when offering α_l in time slot $n + 1$ is given

$$U_{\mathbb{P}_{n+1}}(q_{n+1}|\alpha_l) = \begin{cases} \frac{q_{n+1}}{d^n}\left[R_{dir} + U_{\mathbb{P}_n}(d^n)\right] + \left(1 - \frac{q_{n+1}}{d^n}\right)\left[R_l + U_{\mathbb{P}_n}(0)\right], & \text{if } q_{n+1} \leq d^n, \\ R_{dir} + U_{\mathbb{P}_n}(q_{n+1}), & \text{if } q_{n+1} > d^n. \end{cases} \tag{27}$$

PU's expected utility when offering α_h will be

$$U_{\mathbb{P}_{n+1}}(q_{n+1}|\alpha_h) = R_h + U_{\mathbb{P}_n}(q_{n+1}). \tag{28}$$

Similarly, from (27) and (28) we can see that if the balancing condition holds, then $q_{n+1} \leq d^n$ must be satisfied. According to the balancing condition, we have

$$\frac{q_{n+1}}{d^n}\left[R_{dir} + U_{\mathbb{P}_n}(d^n)\right] + \left(1 - \frac{q_{n+1}}{d^n}\right)\left[R_l + U_{\mathbb{P}_n}(0)\right] = R_h + U_{\mathbb{P}_n}(q_{n+1}). \tag{29}$$

where

$$\begin{cases} U_{\mathbb{P}_n}(d^n) = U_{\mathbb{P}_{n-1}}(d^n) + R_h, \\ U_{\mathbb{P}_n}(0) = R_l + U_{\mathbb{P}_{n-1}}(0), \\ U_{\mathbb{P}_n}(q_{n+1}) = \frac{q_{n+1}}{d^{n-1}}\left[R_{dir} + U_{\mathbb{P}_{n-1}}(d^{n-1})\right] + \left(1 - \frac{q_{n+1}}{d^{n-1}}\right)\left[R_l + U_{\mathbb{P}_{n-1}}(0)\right]. \end{cases} \tag{30}$$

Substitute (30) into (29), and we can simplify the equation to get

$$q_{n+1}^* = d^{n+1}. \tag{31}$$

Thus, the limiting belief in time slot $n + 1$ conforms to our prior assumption in (21). Besides, it is easy to see that PU will offer α_l if $q_{n+1} < q_{n+1}^* = d^{n+1}$ and offer α_h if $q_{n+1} > q_{n+1}^* = d^{n+1}$.

As of now, we have solved the PU's limiting belief and its corresponding strategy when the actual belief is not the limiting belief in each time slot. At the same time, we also verify the Low type SU's strategy (y_n) and the High type SU's strategy. Since $\Delta R_{sh} > 0$ and $R_{sl} > 0$, SU always accepts α_h regardless of its type.

Next let us verify the PU's belief update scheme. If there is an offer α_h in time slot $n+1$, an SU will definitely accept it. This does not help to update the PU's belief about the SU's type. Thus, we have $q_n = q_{n+1}$ as shown in (b). Then we will verify (a) and (c) from two aspects:

- If there is an offer α_l in time slot $n+1$ and the SU accepts it, then PU immediately knows that the SU is a Low type. Therefore, PU will update its belief as $q_n = 0$.
- If $q_{n+1} = 0$, then PU knows that the SU is a Low type for time slot $n+1$ and the whole later time slots. Therefore, PU will always set its belief as zero.

From the above discussions, we complete the proof of the PU's belief update scheme in (a) and (c).

When $q_{n+1} > 0$ and SU rejects the offer α_l in time slot $n+1$, (with the Bayes' rule) q_n is determined by

$$\frac{q_{n+1} \times 1}{q_{n+1} + (1 - q_{n+1}) \times \text{Prob(SU rejects } \alpha_l \mid \text{Low type SU)}}$$

According to the Low type SU's strategy, it could be further divided into two cases:

- When $q_{n+1} \geq d^n$ in time slot $n+1$, the Low type SU will always reject α_l. Thus, we have

$$q_n = \frac{q_{n+1} \times 1}{q_{n+1} + (1 - q_{n+1}) \times 1} = q_{n+1}. \tag{32}$$

- When $q_{n+1} < d^n$ in time slot $n+1$, the Low type SU will reject α_l with probability $\frac{(1-d^n)q_{n+1}}{d^n(1-q_{n+1})}$. We have

$$q_n = \frac{q_{n+1}}{q_{n+1} + (1 - q_{n+1}) \times \left(\frac{(1-d^n)q_{n+1}}{d^n(1-q_{n+1})}\right)} = d^n. \tag{33}$$

From (32) and (33), we have

$$q_n = \max(d^n, q_{n+1}) = \max(q_n^*, q_{n+1}). \tag{34}$$

Thus, we complete the verification of (d).

Finally, let us consider PU's *mixed* strategy in (g). Note that the utility in (22), denoted as $U_{\mathbb{P}_n}(q_n^*)$ when PU's actual belief is equal to the limiting belief, is constant if the *balancing strategy* y_n^* applies. It is also subject to the limiting belief q_n^*, and independent of whether $\mathbb{P}_n$ chooses α_l or α_h, or randomizes on both alternatives. Thus we have

$$U_{\mathbb{P}_n}(x_n, y_n^*/q_n^*) = \text{constant, for all } x_n \text{ in } X_n, \tag{35}$$

where X_n is the set of all possible $\mathbb{P}_n$'s strategies in time slot n. The mixed strategy $[x_n, 1 - x_n]$ denotes PU's choosing α_h with probability x_n and choosing

α_l with probability $1 - x_n$. When $q_n = q_n^*$, from (22) we can see that the utility on the limiting belief is $R_h + U_{\mathbb{P}_{n-1}}(d^n)$, which can be *iteratively* calculated by considering PU's expected utility in time slot $n - 1$, $n - 2$,..., and 1. Since PU's utility in each time slot is fixed, $R_h + U_{\mathbb{P}_{n-1}}(d^n)$ is a constant for a given n. Thus it implies that all x_n in X_n are the *best response* to y_n^*.

However, when $q_n = q_n^*$ the Low type SU will only be expected to choose *the balancing strategy* y_n^*, which is the requirement of the Bayesian consistency (Requirement 3), thus y_n^*, as an equilibrium strategy, *should* maximize the Low type SU's total utility. If we choose $[x^*, 1 - x^*]$ from the set X_n as $\mathbb{P}_n$'s optimal mixed strategy, then it implies that the balancing strategy y_n^* is the *best response* to x^* for the corresponding beliefs.

To solve it, we first *conjecture* that there exists a strategy for the PU in each time slot when the actual belief is equal to the limiting belief, given as follows,

$$\mathcal{X} = (x_N, ..., x_n, ..., x_1), \ x_N = \cdots = x_1 = x^* > 0 \qquad (36)$$

where x_n is the PU's mixed strategy, *i.e.*, the probability of offering α_h in time slot n when $q_n = q_n^*$ and making the Low type SU *indifferent* between rejecting and accepting α_l. Since accepting α_l will result in the utility $\Delta R_{sl} > 0$, the strategy profile $\mathcal{X}$ implies the Low type SU's utility is $n\Delta R_{sl}$, irrespective of what strategy the Low type SU will choose. Therefore, any strategy will maximize the Low type SU's utility, including the equilibrium strategy y_n^*. It means that y_n^* is the best response to x^*. If we can verify that the strategy in (36) does exist and further obtain the value of x^*, then we solve x^* in PU's strategy (g). In fact, we get $x^* = \frac{\Delta R_{sl}}{R_{sl} - \Delta R_{sl}}$. Due to the page limit, we omit the proof here. See [13] for details. Therefore, we completed the proof of Theorem 2. ∎

5   Reputation Effect Analysis

In noncooperative game theory, a player's "reputation" is its opponents' current beliefs about its type [11]. In the multi-slot bargaining game, the Low type SU's reputation can be viewed as the PU's belief about the SU's type in time slot n, *i.e.*, Pr(High type)=q_n. The "reputation effect" refers to the fact that a *non-myopic* Low type SU has incentive to reject α_l to sustain a reputation of the High type so as to get higher utility in the future (see (k), (l)). This is the most interesting part of our model, and we will discuss the intuitions behind it in more details and compare it to the complete information benchmark.

Intuitively, such incentive of doing so becomes higher when the bargaining process lasts longer, which means that the reputation effect is more likely to happen in long term relationships than in short ones [11]. Therefore, it is more interesting to discuss such an effect when N is sufficiently large.

Since $d \in (0, 1)$, d^N can be arbitrarily small when N is large enough, and thus condition $q_N = \eta > d^{N-1}$ can be easily satisfied, even if the initial belief η (in the first time slot N) is small. From (k), the Low type SU will reject α_l in the initial time slot. Anticipating this, the non-myopic PU will offer α_h according to (f). Thus, a Low type SU gets the high utility R_{sl} in the first time slot $n = N$.

Interestingly, such a set of strategies will last in the early several time slots. As the bargaining progresses and slot index n deceases, parameter d^n increases. If PU's belief q_n cannot increase accordingly and becomes 0 (*e.g.*, as in (c)), then PU begins to offer α_l. It indicates that the Low type SU's benefits from the reputation effect ends. To clarify the discussions, we define

$$k(\eta) = \inf \left(n : d^n < q_N = \eta \right), \tag{37}$$

Obviously, PU will offer α_h from time slot N to $k(\eta)$ according to (b), (f), (h), and (i). In time slot $k(\eta) - 1$, PU begins to offer α_l based on (e). Facing α_l, the Low type SU might reject or accept it based on (l). Since only the Low type SU might accept α_l based on (h), acceptance of α_l will reveal the Low type SU's true type to PU, after which the PU will offer α_l in each time slot till the game ends according to (a), (c), and (e).

For the purpose of comparison, let us consider the case with complete information, where the PU knows the SU's true type from the very beginning. To begin with, let us discuss the single-slot bargaining with complete information in SU's energy cost. There are two different optimal strategy profiles according to the SU's type. For the PU and Low type SU, if the PU offers α_l, the Low type SU chooses between utility 0 if it rejects and $\Delta R_{sl} > 0$ if it accepts, so definitely it will accept PU's offer. Anticipating this response, the PU chooses between R_h if it provides α_h (SU will accept it as we discussed above) and R_l if it provides α_l, and so it will offer α_l. This is the *unique* Nash equilibrium for this single-slot bargaining game with complete information.

Figure 5 (a) indicates the equilibrium discussed above. We mark the PU's and Low type SU's equilibrium decisions by the black bold line on the possible decision paths. Similarly, we can obtain the equilibrium in the case of PU and High type SU as shown in Figure 5 (b).

Next, let us consider the case that the two different single-slot games in Figure 5 are separately played a *finite* number times. The PU plays with the SU (High type or Low type) during a succession of N time slots. Take the PU and Low type SU game as an example. The analysis for the PU and High type SU case follows similarly and is omitted to due space constraint.

This is a *finitely-repeated* game with *complete* information. It allows both PU and Low type SU to perfectly observe all moves in earlier time slots. In the last time slot ($n = 1$), the SU will not reject PU's offer α_l since there are no later chances for PU to provide offers. Anticipating this, PU will definitely provide α_l in the last time slot. Backwardly, in the second to last time slot the SU will have no incentive to reject α_l because doing so is costly in the short run and will have no effect on the decisions in the last time slot. Realizing this, the PU will offer α_l to get a higher utility R_l for itself. This logic can be repeated till the first time slot ($n = N$): *in each time slot, PU offers α_l and SU always accepts.* Moreover, this is the unique *subgame perfect Nash equilibrium* (SPE) of the game.[6] We have

---

[6] SPE is a commonly used solution concept for dynamic game with complete information, which can effectively eliminate the *incredible threat* from the opponent. See [11] for more details.

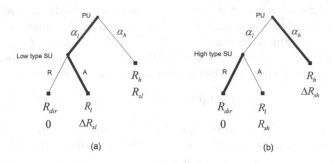

Fig. 5. Game Tree of the Single-Slot Bargaining with Complete Information: (a) PU and the Low type SU, (b) PU and the High type SU

the similar conclusion for the case of PU and High type SU, *i.e.*, PU's offering α_h and SU's rejection of α_l always occur in each time slot.

Based on the above analysis, we can see that the reputation effect does not emerge in a repeated game with complete information. The sequential equilibrium of the multi-slot (finite-repeated) bargaining game in Theorem 2 deviates from the equilibrium outcome discussed above because of *incomplete information* in SU's energy cost. In the dynamic Bayesian bargaining game, the Low type SU might convince PU that it is the High type by rejecting the offer α_l from PU and thus obtains a higher utility. This means that information incompleteness in SU's energy cost results in the reputation effect, with which the Low type SU can benefit more from the cooperative communication.

6   Conclusion

In this paper, we investigate a cooperative spectrum sharing mechanism achieved by a dynamic Bayesian spectrum bargaining between one PU and one SU. We model the bargaining as a dynamic Bayesian game, and characterize all possible equilibria under different system parameter settings. In particular, we focus on characterizing the sequential equilibrium, where the reputation effect brings higher utilities for the Low type SU. Analysis shows that the Low type SU could exploit the PUs lack of information for its own benefits, which will not happen with the complete information scenario.

Acknowledgement. This work has been supported by CSC Postgraduate Scholarship, NSF of China No.60832008, National S&T Major Project 2010ZX03003-002-02, TNList Cross-discipline Foundation, China's 973 Project 2007CB310608, PCSIRT, and National S&T Pillar Program 2008BAH30B09. This work is also supported by the General Research Funds (Project No. 412509 and 412710) established under the University Grant Committee of the Hong Kong Special Administrative Region, China.

References

1. Laneman, J., Tse, D., Wornell, G.: Cooperative Diversity in Wireless Networks: Efficient Protocols and Outrage Behavior. IEEE Transaction on Information Theory 50(12), 3062–3080 (2004)
2. Cover, T.M., El Gamaal, A.: Capacity Theorems for the relay channel. IEEE Transaction on Information Theory 25(5), 572–584 (1979)
3. Nosratinia, A., Hunter, T.E., Hedayat, A.: Cooperative communication in wireless networks. IEEE Communications Magazine 42, 74–80 (2004)
4. Genc, V., Murphy, S., Yang, Y., Murphy, J.: IEEE 802.16J Relay-Based Wireless Access Networks: An Overview. IEEE Wireless Communications Magazine 15, 56–63 (2008)
5. Wang, H., Gao, L., Gan, X., Wang, X., Hossain, E.: Cooperative Spectrum Sharing in Cognitive Radio Networks: A Game-Theoretic Approach. In: IEEE ICC, South Africa (2010)
6. Simeone, O., Stanojev, I., Savazzi, S., Bar-Ness, Y., Spagnolini, U., Pickholtz, R.: Spectrum leasing to cooperating secondary ad hoc networks. IEEE Journal on Selected Areas in Communications 26(1), 203–213 (2008)
7. Zhang, J., Zhang, Q.: Stackelberg Game for Utility-Based Cooperative Cognitive Radio Networks. In: ACM MobiHoc, New Orleans, USA (May 2009)
8. Duan, L., Gao, L., Huang, J.: Contract-Based Cooperative Spectrum Sharing. In: IEEE DySPAN, Aachen, Germany (May 2011)
9. Yan, Y., Huang, J., Zhong, X., Wang, J.: Dynamic Spectrum Negotiation with Asymmetric Information. In: GameNets, Shanghai, China (April 2011)
10. Yan, Y., Huang, J., Zhong, X., Zhao, M., Wang, J.: Sequential Bargaining in Cooperative Spectrum Sharing: Incomplete Information with Reputation Effect. Submitted to Globecom (2011)
11. Fudenberg, D., Tirole, J.: Game Theory. The MIT Press, Cambridge (1991)
12. Kreps, D.M., Wilson, R.: Sequential equilibria. Econometrica 50, 863–894 (1982)
13. Yan, Y., Huang, J., Zhong, X., Zhao, M., Wang, J.: Sequential Bargaining in Cooperative Spectrum Sharing: Incomplete Information with Reputation Effect. Technical Report, http://home.ie.cuhk.edu.hk/jwhuang/publication/BargainReputationTechReport.pdf
14. Kreps, D.M., Wilson, R.: Reputation and imperfect information. Journal of Economic Theory 27, 253–279 (1982)
15. Holler, M.J.: The Kreps-Wilson monopoly-entrant game and cautiously rationalizable sequential equilibria. Quality & Quantity 25, 69–83 (1991)

Study on Frequency Synchronization in 3GPP LTE System for FDD and TDD Modes[*]

Meilin Wang, Xin Qi, Limin Xiao, Min Huang, and Ming Zhao

Tsinghua National Laboratory for Information Science and Technology,
Tsinghua University, Beijing, P.R. China
meilinwang@126.com

Abstract. In this paper, we propose a novel frequency synchronization method in 3GPP long term evolution (LTE) system downlink for both frequency division duplex (FDD) and time division duplex (TDD) modes. The proposed method includes coarse frequency offset estimation (FOE) using primary synchronization signal (PSS) based correlation in time domain, and fine FOE using phase difference between PSS and secondary synchronization signal (SSS) in frequency domain. Traditionally, cyclic prefix (CP) based method is widely used for fine FOE which is however sensitive to the time synchronization error and multi-path fading channel environment. The proposed fine FOE shows an apparent advantage in both FDD and TDD modes compared with CP based method. In addition, both theoretical analysis and simulation results show that the proposed fine FOE in TDD mode outperforms that in FDD mode under the same system assumptions. The simulations are done under a dual-cell scenario where there is co-frequency interference from the adjacent cell.

Keywords: 3GPP LTE, cell search, dual-cell, frequency synchronization.

1   Introduction

The 3GPP long term evolution (LTE) is acknowledged as one of the dominant technologies for next-generation wireless cellular communication systems, which can provide wide bandwidth access and high data-rate throughput of exceeding 100Mbps in downlink and 50Mbps in uplink, as well as lower latency with round-trip-time of less than 10ms. LTE supports both frequency division duplex (FDD) mode and time division duplex (TDD) mode, as well as frequency flexibility with from 1.4MHz to 20MHz allocations.

The multiple access scheme in LTE downlink employs orthogonal frequency division multiple access (OFDMA) in downlink and single carrier frequency division multiple access (SC-FDMA) in uplink [1]. These solutions provide orthogonality between the users, reducing the interference and improving the network capacity.

---

[*] This work was supported by National Basic Research Program of China (2007CB310608), National Natural Science Foundation of China (60832008), China's 863 Project (2009AA011501), National S&T Major Project (2009ZX03002-002), NCET and PCSIRT.

P. Ren et al. (Eds.): WICON 2011, LNICST 98, pp. 180–191, 2012.
© Institute for Computer Sciences, Social Informatics and Telecommunications Engineering 2012

However, Carrier frequency offset (CFO) introduces interference among sub-carriers and deteriorate the system performance. To overcome the imperfection, tight frequency synchronization is required.

The frequency synchronization of LTE system usually requires two steps: coarse frequency offset estimation (FOE) and fine FOE. Coarse FOE is used to reduce the frequency error within a certain range, then fine FOE is applied to make a finer correction and track further frequency shifting after initial synchronization is done. Traditionally, primary synchronization signal (PSS) or secondary synchronization signal (SSS) based cross-correlation in frequency domain is widely used for coarse FOE to estimate the integer part of CFO, and cyclic prefix (CP) based autocorrelation is applied for fine FOE to estimate the fractional part [2][3]. However, in the multi-path channel environment, CP based method suffers from performance degradation, especially in the practical multi-cell scenario. Though the performance can be improved by increasing the number of OFDM symbols in the CP autocorrelation, the computational complexity is increased greatly as well. Moreover, in TDD mode, there is no signal in uplink subframes, so extra effort should be taken in the tracking loop, e.g. adding an uplink-downlink switch to stop tracking residual CFO during the uplink subframe duration [4].

In this paper, we propose a frequency synchronization method including coarse FOE based on PSS and fine FOE jointly based on PSS and SSS. The proposed fine FOE executed in frequency domain can combat the multi-path channel more effectively and obtain better performance compared with CP based method. In FDD and TDD modes, the gaps between the PSS and SSS have different lengths, which leads to that the proposed FOE using the phase difference has different detecting ranges and estimation accuracies. The simulation results show that the proposed fine FOE in TDD could estimate the CFO more accurately but may need higher computational complexity in coarse FOE than that in FDD.

2   LTE Synchronization Overview

LTE defines two radio frame structures, i.e. Type1 and Type2 which are applicable to FDD mode and TDD mode respectively [5]. One radio frame has 10 ms duration and consists of 10 subframes, each with two consecutive slots. Hierarchical synchronization signals including PSS and SSS are designed for the purpose of setting up downlink synchronization between the E-UTRAN NodeB (eNB) and the User Equipment (UE) in LTE system. There are 504 unique physical-layer cell identities. The physical-layer cell identities are grouped into 168 unique physical-layer cell-identity groups represented by $N_{\text{ID}}^{(1)}$ (from 0 to 167), each group containing three unique identities represented by $N_{\text{ID}}^{(2)}$ (from 0 to 2), thus the cell identity is uniquely determined by $N_{\text{ID}}^{\text{cell}} = 3N_{\text{ID}}^{(1)} + N_{\text{ID}}^{(2)}$. As shown in Fig. 1, in time domain, PSS and SSS are transmitted periodically, twice per 10ms. SSS is transmitted in the symbol immediately preceding PSS in FDD mode, while 3 OFDM symbols ahead of PSS in TDD mode. In both modes, PSS and SSS are transmitted in the central 6 resource blocks (RBs) in frequency domain, which is independent to the system bandwidth. More specifically, PSS and SSS are both 62-point sequences mapped to the central 62 resource elements (REs) with 5 REs guarded at each of the two sides of frequency domain.

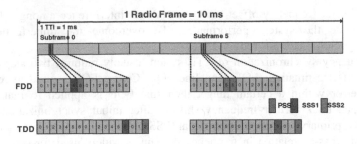

Fig. 1. PSS and SSS locations in FDD and TDD Frame structures

2.1   PSS Sequence

The sequence $d(n)$ used for the PSS is generated from a frequency-domain Zadoff-Chu sequence according to

$$d_u(n) = \begin{cases} e^{-j\frac{\pi u n(n+1)}{63}} & n = 0,1,...,30 \\ e^{-j\frac{\pi u(n+1)(n+2)}{63}} & n = 31,32,...,61 \end{cases}. \tag{1}$$

where the Zadoff-Chu root sequence index μ can be 25, 29, 34 corresponding to $N_{ID}^{(2)}$ equaling to 0, 1, 2 respectively.

2.2   SSS Sequence

SSS is a length-62 frequency-domain sequence $q(n)$ which is an interleaved concatenation of two 31-bit binary M-sequences $s_0(n)$ and $s_1(n)$ with cyclic shifts dependent on a pair of integers, m_0 and m_1, which are uniquely determined by $N_{ID}^{(1)}$. In order to distinguish between the cells within a cell group and reduce the peak to average power ratio (PAPR), both sequences are scrambled with one of two M-sequence $c_0(n)$ or $c_1(n)$, which are cyclic shift versions of $\tilde{c}(n)$ determined by $N_{ID}^{(2)}$. Moreover the even sequence is scrambled with one of another two scrambling sequences $z_1^{(m_0)}(n)$ and $z_1^{(m_1)}(n)$ which are defined by two cyclic shifts of the M-sequence $\tilde{z}(n)$. The combination of two length-31 sequences defining the SSS differs between subframe 0 and subframe 5 according to

$$q(2n) = \begin{cases} s_0^{(m_0)}(n)c_0(n) & \text{in subframe 0} \\ s_1^{(m_1)}(n)c_0(n) & \text{in subframe 5} \end{cases}.$$

$$q(2n+1) = \begin{cases} s_1^{(m_1)}(n)c_1(n)z_1^{(m_0)}(n) & \text{in subframe 0} \\ s_0^{(m_0)}(n)c_1(n)z_1^{(m_1)}(n) & \text{in subframe 5} \end{cases} \tag{2}$$

2.3 Overall Initial Cell Search Procedure

When a UE accesses to LTE cellular network, it needs to establish synchronous connection as fast as possible with the best serving eNB. According to synchronization signals and frame structure, the initial cell search procedure can be divided into 3 steps. Firstly, cross-correlation between the received signal and 3 local PSS replicas in time domain has to be done on different available carrier frequencies to identify the serving carrier frequency. Once it succeeds, symbol timing, half-frame timing, as well as PSS identity $N_{\text{ID}}^{(2)}$ are acquired. Secondly, SSS detection is executed to obtain the SSS identity $N_{\text{ID}}^{(1)}$ and the frame timing. Since CFO has severe impact on the performance of SSS searching, coarse FOE is needed before SSS detection. The last step is the fine FOE which estimates and compensates residual frequency error.

3 Frequency Synchronization

3.1 System Model

In LTE cellular network, we suppose all the cells operate at the same frequency carrier. Let eNB$_i$ denote the i-th eNB. In downlink, each eNB$_i$ generates a serial discrete baseband OFDM sample stream $s_i(n)$; Transmitting over multi-path fading channel under consideration of a carrier frequency misalignment Δf_i between transmitter and receiver as well as gaussian noise $w(n)$, the received signal $r(n)$ at UE will be

$$r(n) = \sum_i (s_i(n) \otimes h_i(n,l))e^{j2\pi\Delta f_i nT_s} + w(n) \ . \tag{3}$$

where $h(n,l)$ denotes the time-variant channel impulse response for the l-th OFDM symbol, T_s denotes the system sampling period, $\otimes$ stands for the linear convolution.

3.2 FOE Algorithm

In this paper, a two-step FOE method including coarse FOE done in time domain using PSS, and fine FOE done in frequency domain using both PSS and SSS is applied. Before fine FOE, coarse FOE is needed to compensate the initial CFO, so that the residual CFO is within the fine FOE detectable range.

The proposed coarse FOE is performed in time domain with local replica of PSS sequence based correlation. The sequence $p(l)$, i.e. IDFT of the sequence $d(n)$ defined in (1), is given by

$$p(l) = \sum_{n=1}^{31} d(n+30)e^{j\frac{2\pi nl}{N_s}} + \sum_{n=N_s-31}^{N_s-1} d(n-N_s+31)e^{-j\frac{2\pi nl}{N_s}}, 0 \leq l \leq N_s-1 \ . \tag{4}$$

where the IDFT size N_s is determined by the sampling rate of the received data, e.g. for 20MHz-bandwith system with normal CP, the sample rate is recommended to be 30.72MHz, and the IDFT size is 2048 accordingly.

A set of sequences is needed to be prepared firstly. Each sequence $q_m(l)$ is based on a distorted $p(l)$ sequence with a CFO f_m which is equally spaced in the searching range of $[-f_{coarse\_max}, +f_{coarse\_max}]$ with a certain granularity, and it is expressed by

$$q_m(l) = p(l) \cdot e^{j2\pi \cdot f_m l T_s} . \tag{5}$$

Then for each f_m, correlation can be done according to

$$R^{(m)} = \sum_{l=0}^{N_S-1} y(l) \cdot q_m^*(l) = \sum_{l=0}^{N_S-1} y(l) \cdot p^*(l) \cdot e^{-j2\pi \cdot f_m l T_s} . \tag{6}$$

where the notation $(\cdot)^*$ means the complex conjugate of its argument; $y(l)$ denotes the received samples of the OFDM symbol with PSS. The coarse frequency error can be estimated by the correlation values comparison according to

$$FOE_{coarse} = \arg \max_{f_m} |R^{(m)}|^2 . \tag{7}$$

So a grid searching of FOE_{coarse} is needed to perform this algorithm. The smaller the searching grid granularity is, the higher the FOE accuracy will be, and the more computational cost is needed. So the granularity can be chosen according to the fine FOE range. And the searching range could be calculated by the minimum requirement about the oscillator stability. For example, as described in [6], the carrier frequency of the BS and UE shall be accurate to within ±0.5ppm and ±2.0ppm observed over a period of one frame respectively, given the carrier frequency of 2.5GHz, the coarse FOE range f_{coarse_max} should be 6.25 KHz.

In fine FOE, the phase difference due to the certain gap between PSS symbol and SSS symbol is utilized to estimate the residual CFO. The algorithm runs in the frequency domain. We Let $PSS(k)$ denote the local PSS replica in frequency domain which is a re-ordered $d(n)$ according to

$$PSS(k) = \begin{cases} d(k+30) & k = 1, 2...31 \\ d(k-N_s+31) & k = N_s - 31,...N_s - 1 \\ 0 & others \end{cases} . \tag{8}$$

Denote channel frequency response (CFR) for frequency-time element (k, l_0) as $H(k, l_0)$, i.e. the DFT version of $h(n, l_0)$ defined in (3), the frequency misalignment as Δf, and the initial phase offset as φ_0. Then the received PSS sequence $y_{PSS}(n)$ in the l_0-th OFDM symbol can be represented by

$$y_{PSS}(n) = \frac{1}{N_s} \sum_{k=0}^{N_s-1} PSS(k) H(k, l_0) e^{j2\pi(\frac{nk}{N_s} + \Delta f T_s + \varphi_0)} + \eta_{PSS}(n) . \tag{9}$$

where $n \in [0, N_s -1]$, η_{PSS} denotes the noise plus interferences from other cells at the receiver. After applying N_s-point DFT, the sequence $Y_{PSS}(k)$ is expressed by

$$Y_{PSS}(k) = PSS(k)H(k,l_0)\frac{\sin(\pi N_s \Delta f T_s)}{N_s \sin(\pi \Delta f T_s)} e^{j\pi(N_s-1)\Delta f T_s + j\varphi_0} + \sum_{m \neq k} I_{k,m}^{PSS} + \eta_{PSS}'(k) \quad . \tag{10}$$

where η_{PSS}' denotes the DFT version of η_{PSS}; and $I_{k,m}^{PSS}$ represents the Inter-Carrier Interference (ICI) due to the CFO, which is given by

$$I_{k,m}^{PSS} = PSS(m)H(m,l_0) \cdot \frac{\sin(\pi(m-k-N_s \Delta f T_s))}{N_s \sin(\pi(m-k-N_s \Delta f T_s)/N_s)} e^{-j\pi(1-\frac{1}{N_s})(m-k-N_s \Delta f T_s)+j\varphi_0} \quad . \tag{11}$$

Thus, the product of $Y_{PSS}(k)$ multiplying by $PSS^*(k)$ is given by

$$Y(k) = Y_{PSS}(k)PSS^*(k) = \Theta(k,l_0)e^{j\pi(N_s-1)\Delta f T_s + j\varphi_0} + \eta_{PSS}''(k) \quad . \tag{12}$$

where $\Theta(k,l_0)$ equals to $\dfrac{\sin(\pi N_s \Delta f T_s)}{N_s \sin(\pi \Delta f T_s)} H(k,l_0)$. The first part of $Y(k)$ is the dominant item carrying the information of Δf, while η_{PSS} is considered to be an interfering part, composed of ICI, noise, and interference.

Similarly, we can also get the sequence $X(k)$ for SSS in the l_1-th OFDM symbol by

$$X(k) = \Theta(k,l_1)e^{j(\pi(N_s-1)\Delta f T_s + \varphi_0 - 2\pi N_{gap}\Delta f T_s)} + \eta_{SSS}'(k) \quad . \tag{13}$$

where N_{gap} denotes the delay from PSS to SSS measured in time samples. As it can be observed from (12) and (13), there is a phase difference proportional to N_{gap} and Δf between dominant part of $X(k)$ and $Y(k)$, so that we can calculate the sequence $Z(k)$ according to

$$Z(k) = Y(k)X^*(k) = \Theta(k,l_0)\Theta^*(k,l_1)e^{j2\pi N_{gap}\Delta f T_s} + \eta^{\sim} \quad . \tag{14}$$

where $k \in [1,31] \cup [N_s-31, N_s-1]$ according to the mapping in (8), and the interference $\eta^{\sim}$ is

$$\eta^{\sim} \approx \Theta(k,l_0)e^{j\pi(N_s-1)\Delta f T_s + j\varphi_0}(\sum_{m \neq k} I_{k,m}^{SSS} + \eta_{SSS}'(k))^* SSS(k) + $$
$$\Theta^*(k,l_1)e^{-j\pi(N_s-1)\Delta f T_s - j\varphi_0 + j2\pi N_{gap}\Delta f T_s}(\sum_{m \neq k} I_{k,m}^{PSS} + \eta_{PSS}'(k))PSS^*(k) \tag{15}$$

Then we can get the FOE_{fine} from the phase of the average of $Z(k)$ as

$$FOE_{fine} = \frac{1}{2\pi N_{gap}T_s} phase\{\frac{1}{N_d}\sum_k Z(k)\} \quad . \tag{16}$$

where N_d denotes the effective length of Z(k), i.e. 62.

From (14) and (15) it can be found that the estimation error comes from 3 factors: ICI ($\sum_{m \neq k} I_{k,m}$), noise and interference from other cells (η'_{PSS}, η'_{SSS}), time variance of the CFR ($H(k,l_0)H^*(k,l_1)$). As a result, the performance would have degradation if the residual frequency error remains still high after coarse FOE. And high vehicular speed, stronger interference and noise could degrade the performance as well. Nevertheless, to compare with conventional CP based method with the same correlation length and system assumptions, the proposed method can combat the multi-path fading effectively because it operates in frequency domain. Moreover, since there are other physical channels mapped to the subcarriers of PSS symbol and SSS symbol, the DFT computations for these symbols which are always required whether the proposed FOE is applied or not, should not be included when evaluating the computational complexity.

3.3   Comparisons between TDD and FDD for the Proposed Fine FOE

In order to compare the performance of the proposed fine FOE in FDD mode with that in TDD mode, the interference $\eta^\sim$ in (15) can be regarded as a phase interference $\Delta\theta$ to Z(k), as shown in Fig. 2. Obviously, $\Delta\theta$ is relevant to both magnitude and phase of $\eta^\sim$. Here we assume the residual CFO, channel state and carrier to interference plus noise ratio (CINR) are all the same for both modes. Then the only difference in $\eta^\sim$ between FDD and TDD is the phase offset of $e^{-j\pi(N_x-1)\Delta f T_s - j\varphi_0 + j2\pi N_{gap}\Delta f T_s}$ as shown in the second part of (15); however the phase of η'_{PSS} rotate randomly, thus the phase offset take little effect on the variance of $\Delta\theta$, and $|\Delta\theta|$ can be weighed mainly dependent on mean magnitude of $\eta^\sim$ as

$$mean(|\Delta\theta|) \propto \frac{mean(|\eta^\sim|)}{\Phi} \ . \tag{17}$$

where $\propto$ means a positive relationship; Φ denotes the average magnitude of dominant part of Z(k).

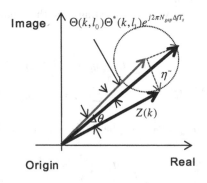

Fig. 2. Estimation error regarded as phase interference

Thus with the same assumptions, the average phase error $|\Delta\theta|$ can be considered almost the same in both FDD and TDD modes, and the fine FOE error Δf_{fine_error} is mainly determined by

$$\Delta f_{fine\_error} \propto \frac{mean(|\eta^-|)}{N_{gap}T_s\Phi}.$$ (18)

Due to that N_{gap} in TDD mode is longer than that in FDD mode; TDD mode can get higher estimation accuracy than FDD mode if the CFO is within both estimation ranges.

On the other hand, considering that the period of complex exponent equals to 2π, according to (14) the estimation range depends on the N_{gap} which differs in FDD and TDD modes, given by

$$\left|2\pi N_{gap}\Delta f T_s\right| < \pi$$

$$|\Delta f| < \frac{F_s}{2*N_{gap}}.$$ (19)

For FDD mode, the theoretical searching range is from -7.003 KHz to +7.003 KHz, while it declines to the region of [-2.33KHz, +2.33KHz] for TDD mode. Therefore, we should choose different granularities in coarse FOE for the two modes. For FDD mode, the grid granularity could be 3 KHz as recommended, while for TDD mode, a more accurate coarse FOE is required, e.g. 1 KHz is recommended, otherwise the desired performance cannot to be guaranteed. For low CINR or bad channel state in TDD mode, we need to do extra compensation based on CP [7] to attain the requirement. As a result, TDD mode could estimate the CFO more accurately but need higher computational complexity in coarse FOE.

4   Simulation Results

In order to evaluate the algorithms in a more practical scenario, a multi-cell environment setup is needed. In this paper we simplify the model to a dual-cell scenario to get a revelatory simulation result.

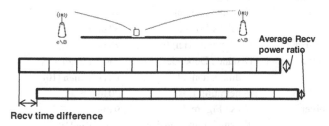

Fig. 3. Dual-cell system model

In the dual-cell scenario, it is assumed that the UE locates on the straight line of the two eNBs, as shown in Fig. 3. The inter-cell distance can be set as 1732 m as recommended in [8]. Besides, the two eNBs are supposed to be strictly synchronous and share the same transmitting carrier frequency. Thus the received time and power differences at UE mainly depend on its distances toward these two eNBs without taking shadowing deviation into account. System parameters are listed in Table I. And the parameters of the transmitter, Okumura-Hata propagation model [9], and the receiver are provided in Table II. One eNB can be selected as the target eNB from which the average received signal power is stronger, and the other is considered as the interfering one. Given the distances from UE to the two eNBs, the system bandwidth, and the RF carrier frequency, the power of the received signal from both eNBs, $P_{t\,\arg et}$ and $P_{\text{int}\,erf}$ can be simply calculated without considering the shadowing effect, and the noise power W of the receiver, thus the CINR can be calculated according to

$$CINR = \frac{P_{t\,\arg et}}{P_{\text{int}\,erf} + W} \quad . \tag{20}$$

And the performance is to be evaluated based on such a set of practical and reasonable CINR according to (20).

Table 1. System Parameters Description

Parameters	Explanations & Assumptions
Multi-cell Model	Dual-cell
Inter-cell distance	1732 m
Carrier frequency	2.5 GHz
Bandwidth	20 MHz
Antenna Configuration	SISO
Network synchronization	Synchronous

Table 2. Downlink Link Level Parameters

	Parameters	Explanations & Assumptions
eNB Transmitter	Tx Power	43 dBm
	Tx Antenna Gain	14 dBi
	Total Tx Power	57 dBm
Okumura-Hata	BS Antenna Height	15 m
Propagation Model	Distance Dependent Loss	$130.2 + 37.6 \lg(r_{km})$
	Fading Channel	ETU 70km/h [10]
	Penetration Loss	20dB
UE receiver	Noise Figure	9 dB
	Thermal noise density	-174 dBm/Hz
	Rx antenna Gain	0 dBi
	Rx noise Effected Power	-92.45 dBm

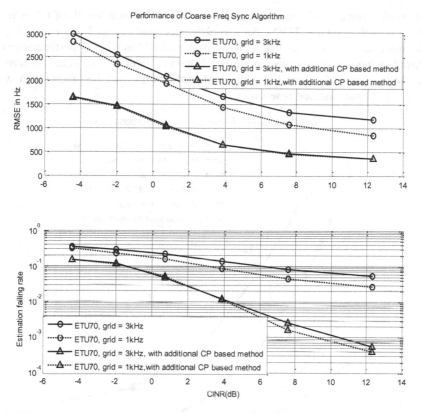

Fig. 4. RMSE and failing rate of coarse frequency synchronization vs. CINR, with grid granularity of 1KHz and 3KHz, searching range of [-9K, 9K], and frequency misalignment uniformly distributed in the searching range.

Fig. 4 shows the performance of coarse FOE in terms of root mean square errors (RMSE) in subplot(a), and failing rate with the threshold of 2 KHz residual frequency error illustrated in subplot(b) respectively. We can see that coarse FOE with 1 KHz grid granularity outperforms the case with 3 KHz granularity. Extra effort based on CP is taken to meet the requirement of fine FOE for TDD mode, whose performance is also illustrated in the figure. With additional CP based method, both the failing rate and RMSE reduce prominently.

In Fig. 5, the RMSE of fine FOE measured in Hz for both FDD and TDD against CINR is illustrated. We consider a frequency misalignment of 1.5K and 1K respectively. From the figure we can see that the residual RMSE of TDD is smaller than that of FDD, with a 4-5dB performance gap. Moreover, we can see that the performance of these two modes is sensitive to the CFO, the larger the original CFO is, the larger residual CFO would be after fine FOE.

The performance of CP based method with autocorrelation length of 62, which is identical in both FDD and TDD modes, is also illustrated in Fig. 5. By comparing the simulation results, we can see that the proposed method has a better performance than CP based method in both modes. In multi-cell environment, the advantage is foreseen to be more apparent because the equivalent multi-path effect becomes much worse which the CP based method is sensitive to.

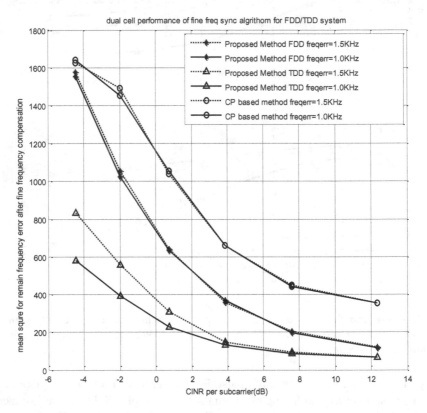

Fig. 5. RMSE of fine frequency synchronization vs. CINR, for both TDD and FDD modes together with CP based method, with assuming frequency errors of 1.5KHz and 1.0KHz.

5   Conclusion

In this paper, we propose a new frequency synchronization method based on synchronization signals including coarse FOE and fine FOE for both FDD and TDD modes. To compare with traditional CP based method, the proposed fine FOE can estimate the CFO more accurately, especially in the practical multi-cell environment. In addition, both the mathematical analysis and the comparison results show that the proposed fine FOE in TDD has higher estimation accuracy but needs more computational cost in coarse FOE than that in FDD.

References

1. Holma, H., Toskala, A.: LTE for UMTS- OFDMA and SC-FDMA Based Radio Acess, pp. 2–22. John Wiley & Sons (2009)
2. Manolakis, K., Gutierrez Estevez, D.M., Jungnickel, V., Wen, X., Drewes, C.: A Closed Concept for Synchronization and Cell Search in 3GPP LTE Systems. In: IEEE Wireless Communications and Networking Conference (2009)
3. Tsai, P.-Y., Chang, H.-W.: A new cell search scheme in 3GPP long term evolution downlink, OFDMA systems. IEEE Wireless Communications & Signal Processing (April 2009)
4. Shim, M.J., Han, J.S., Roh, H.J., Choi, H.J.: A frequency synchronization method for 3GPP LTE OFDMA system in TDD mode. IEEE Communications and Information Technology (2009)
5. 3GPP TS 36.211 V9.1.0, Physical channels and modulation (March 2010)
6. 3GPP TS 36.101 V9.1.0, User Equipment (UE) radio transmission and reception (September 2009)
7. Sandell, M., van de Beek, J.J., Börjesson, P.O.: Timing and Frequency Synchronization in OFDM Systems Using the Cyclic Prefix. In: Proc. IEEE Int. Symp. Synchronization, Essen, Germany (December 1995)
8. ITU Publications, Guidelines for evaluation of radio interface technologies for IMT-Advanced, ITU-R Reports M.2135 (2008)
9. Hata, M.: Empirical formula for propagation loss in land mobile radio services. IEEE Transactions on Vehicular Technology, 29(3) (1980)
10. 3GPP TS 36.141 V8.8.0, Base Station (BS) conformance testing (September 2010)

Optimal Power Allocation for OFDM-Based Wire-Tap Channels with Arbitrarily Distributed Inputs

Haohao Qin*, Yin Sun*, Xiang Chen, Ming Zhao, and Jing Wang

State Key Laboratory on Microwave and Digital Communications
Tsinghua National Laboratory for Information Science and Technology
Department of Electronic Engineering, Tsinghua University,
Beijing 100084, P.R. China
{haohaoqin07,sunyin02,chenxiang98,zhao.ming29}@gmail.com
wangj@mail.tsinghua.edu.cn

Abstract. In this paper, optimal power allocation is investigated for maximizing the secrecy rate of orthogonal frequency division multiplexing (OFDM) systems under arbitrarily distributed input signals. Considering the discrete inputs are used in practical systems rather than the commonly assumed Gaussian inputs, we focus on secrecy rate maximization under more practical finite discrete constellations in this paper. It is known that the secrecy rate achieved by Guassian distributed inputs is concave with respect to the transmission power. However, we prove that the secrecy rate of finite discrete constellations is non-concave, which makes traditional convex optimization methods not applicable to our problem. To address this non-concave power allocation problem, we propose an efficient power allocation algorithm. Its gap from optimality vanishes asymptotically at the rate $O(1/\sqrt{N})$, and its complexity grows in order of $O(N)$, where N is the number of sub-carriers. Numerical results are provided to illustrate the benefits and significance of the proposed algorithm.

Keywords: OFDM wire-tap channel, arbitrarily distributed inputs, duality theory, nonconvex problem, optimal power allocation.

1 Introduction

In recent years, many privacy sensitive wireless services have become more and more popular, such as pushmail, mobile wallet, Microblogging, etc. While it is convenient to access to these services through mobile phone, this also leads to more concerns of secrecy due to the easy wiretap of the subscribers' transmission signals in broadcast wireless channel. The security of wireless communications is previously guaranteed by cryptographic techniques on application layer, which recently face several challenges, such as the emergence of new cracking algorithms

---

* Contribute equally to this work.

P. Ren et al. (Eds.): WICON 2011, LNICST 98, pp. 192–203, 2012.

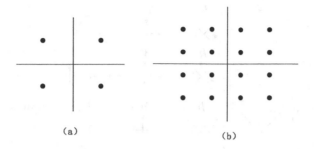

Fig. 1. (a). QPSK inputs. (b). 16QAM inputs.

and the increasing computational capability of eavesdroppers. Recently, physical layer security [1] has received considerable attentions in wireless communication communities as a complement to traditional cryptographic encryption to provide additional security mechanism.

Physical layer security was firstly studied from an information-theoretic perspective in [2], where secrecy rate was defined as the achievable data rate from a transmitter to its legitimate destination while keeping the eavesdropper completely ignorant of the secret massage. Later, the research in this field was extended to various scenes, such as Gaussian wire-tap channel [3]-[4], multiple input multiple output (MIMO) channel [5]-[7], orthogonal frequency division multiplexing (OFDM) channel [8]-[11], etc.

Recently, OFDM-based secure communications obtain much attention for its capability of countermining the dispersive of wideband wireless channels and enhance secrecy rate [8]-[9]. Optimal power allocation of secure OFDM system is investigated in [8] where the distribution of input signals is assumed to be Gaussian. However, Gaussian distributed input signals are unrealistic in practise for its infinite peak-to-average ratio. Discrete distributions, such as PSK, QAM (see Fig.1), are used in practical systems.

In this paper, we investigate optimal power allocation for OFDM-based wiretap channels with arbitrarily distributed channel inputs. While the secrecy rate achieved by Guassian distributed inputs is concave with respect to the transmission power, we show that the secrecy rate for finite discrete constellations is non-concave. Therefore, the optimal power allocation strategy for secure communications with Gaussian distributed inputs [8]-[10] is not optimal any more to the considered problem. Following the lead of [12]-[14], we propose a low complexity power allocation algorithm which achieves asymptotic optimal performance as the number of sub-carriers increases, and its complexity grows in order of sub-carrier number. Numerical results are provided to illustrate the efficiency of the proposed algorithm.

The remainder of this paper is organized as follows: section 2 provides the system model and problem formulation. Optimal power allocation for arbitrarily distributed channel inputs is presented in Section 3. Numerical results and conclusions are given in Section 4 and Section 5.

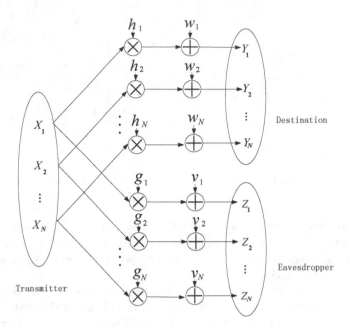

Fig. 2. System model

2 System Model and Problem Formulation

We consider wideband secure communications from a transmitter to its legitimate receiver, in the presence of an eavesdropper who intends to extract the transmitter's secret message. We assume that each node employs an OFDM air interface with N sub-carriers. The transmitter's signal in each sub-carrier follows an arbitrary but predetermined distribution, which can be either continuous constellations[1], such as Gaussian distribution, or finite discrete constellations, including PSK, QAM, etc.

The complex channel coefficients of the legitimate and eavesdropping channels for ith sub-carrier are denoted by h_i and g_i, respectively, as illustrated in Fig. 2. The transmitted signal over the ith sub-carrier is denoted as x_i, which is given by

$$x_i = \sqrt{p_i}s_i, i = 1, \ldots, N, \qquad (1)$$

where p_i is the ratio between transmitting power of x_i and the noise power, and s_i represents the normalized channel input with predetermined distribution and unit variance. The power constraint of the transmitter is given by

$$\frac{1}{N}\sum_{i=1}^{N} p_i \leq P. \qquad (2)$$

---

[1] The words "distribution" and "constellation" are used alternatively throughout the paper.

The received signals of the legitimate receiver and eavesdropper are given by

$$y_i = h_i\sqrt{p_i}s_i + w_i, i = 1, \cdots, N, \tag{3}$$

$$z_i = g_i\sqrt{p_i}s_i + v_i, i = 1, \cdots, N, \tag{4}$$

where the w_i and v_i are zero-mean complex Gasussian noises with unit-variance for ith sub-carrier. According to the information theoretical studies of [8], the secrecy rate from transmitter to its legitimate receiver is determined by

$$\sum_{i=1}^{N}[I(s_i; h_i\sqrt{p_i}s_i + w_i) - I(s_i; g_i\sqrt{p_i}s_i + v_i)]^+, \tag{5}$$

where $[x]^+ \triangleq \max\{x, 0\}$, and $I(x; y)$ denotes the mutual information between random variables x and y. The expression in (5) is quite illuminating: the secrecy rate of each sub-channel is non-negative; if it is positive, it is exactly the difference of the data rates of the legitimate and eavesdropping channels. The total secrecy rate is simply the sum secrecy rate of all the N sub-carriers.

For fixed constellations of $\{s_i\}_{i=1}^{N}$, we need to optimize the power allocation to obtain the maximal secrecy rate, which is described as the following optimization problem:

$$R^* = \max_{\mathbf{p}} \quad R_s(\mathbf{p}) \triangleq \frac{1}{N} \sum_{i=1}^{N}[I(s_i; h_i\sqrt{p_i}s_i + w_i) - I(s_i; g_i\sqrt{p_i}s_i + v_i)]^+$$
$$\text{s.t.} \quad \frac{1}{N}\sum_{i=1}^{N} p_i \leq P, \tag{6}$$
$$\mathbf{p} \geq 0$$

where $\mathbf{p} \in \mathcal{R}^N$ is the vector of transmission power of the N subcarriers, i.e., $\mathbf{p} = \{p_1, p_2, ..., p_N\}$; R^* denotes the optimal value.

3   Optimal Power Allocation for Arbitrarily Distributed Channel Inputs

3.1   Non-concavity of the Secrecy Rate $R_s(\mathbf{p})$

If s_i follows Gaussian distribution, the secrecy rate $R_s(\mathbf{p})$ in (6) has explicit expression [4], i.e.,

$$R_s^G(\mathbf{p}) = \frac{1}{N} \sum_{i=1}^{N}[\, \log_2(1 + |h_i|^2 p_i) - \log_2(1 + |g_i|^2 p_i) \,]^+. \tag{7}$$

It is worth while to mention that $R_s^G(\mathbf{p})$ is a concave function of $\mathbf{p}$. Thus, problem (6) is a convex optimization problem. Let us define

$$R_{s,i}(p_i) \triangleq [I(s_i; h_i\sqrt{p_i}s_i + w_i) - I(s_i; g_i\sqrt{p_i}s_i + v_i)]^+ \tag{8}$$

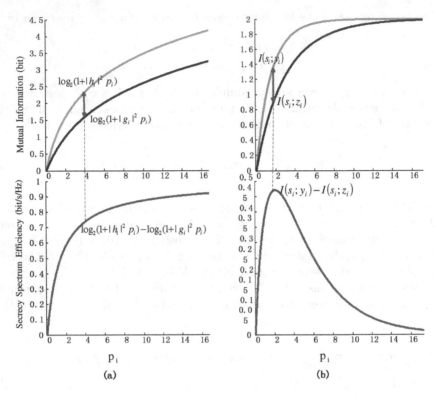

Fig. 3. (a). Secrecy rate achieved by Gaussian distributed inputs. (b). Secrecy rate achieved by discrete inputs (eg. QPSK). And p_i is the ratio of the signal power and noise power.

for the facility of latter expression. The secrecy rate for Gaussian distributed inputs is illustrated in the left part of Fig. 3. One can observe that the mutual information $\log_2(1 + |h_i|^2 p_i)$, $\log_2(1 + |g_i|^2 p_i)$ and the secrecy rate $\log_2(1 + |h_i|^2 p_i) - \log_2(1 + |g_i|^2 p_i)$ are all concave, provided that $|h_i|^2 > |g_i|^2$. In [8], [9] and [10], the authors utilized the concavity of $R_s^G(\mathbf{p})$ to obtain the optimal power allocation, i.e.,

$$p_i^* = \begin{cases} \dfrac{-(|h_i|^2+|g_i|^2)+\sqrt{(|h_i|^2+|g_i|^2)^2-4|h_i|^2|g_i|^2\frac{u+|g_i|^2-|h_i|^2}{u}}}{2|h_i|^2|g_i|^2} \\ \qquad\qquad\qquad\qquad , \text{if } |h_i|^2 - |g_i|^2 > u \\ 0 \qquad\qquad\qquad\quad , \text{others}, \end{cases} \tag{9}$$

where the Lagrange multiplier $u > 0$ is chosen to meet the power constraint:

$$\frac{1}{N}\sum_{i=1}^{N} p_i = P. \tag{10}$$

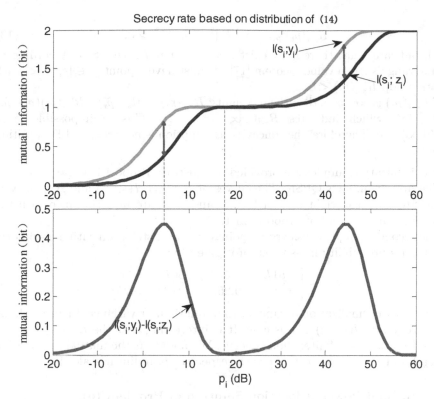

Fig. 4. Secrecy rate achieved by distribution of (14)

One may expect the concavity of $R_s(\mathbf{p})$ still holds for general input distributions. Unfortunately, our investigation shows that this is not true, which is formally described in the following proposition:

Proposition 1. *The secrecy rate function $R_s(\mathbf{p})$ for any discrete constellation with finite points is non-concave with respect to $\mathbf{p}$.*

Proof. When $p_i = 0$, one can derive $I(s_i; y_i) = I(s_i; z_i) = 0$; when $p_i = +\infty$, we have $I(s_i; y_i) = I(s_i; z_i) = H(s_i)$, where $H(x)$ is entropy of x. Therefore, $R_{s,i}(0) = R_{s,i}(+\infty) = 0$.

According to [15],

$$\frac{\partial I(s; \sqrt{p}s + n)}{\partial p} = \text{MMSE}(p), \qquad (11)$$

where $\text{MMSE}(p)$ is defined as:

$$\text{MMSE}(p) \triangleq \mathbb{E}[|s - \mathbb{E}(s|\sqrt{p}s + n)|^2], \qquad (12)$$

where $\mathbb{E}[x]$ is the expectation of random variable x; $\mathbb{E}[x|y]$ is the conditional expectation of x for given y, the derivative of $R_{s,i}(p_i)$ at $p_i = 0$ is given by[2]

---

[2] Only the sub-carriers that satisfy $|h_i|^2 > |g_i|^2$ are considered, as $R_{s,i}(p_i) \equiv 0$ for those sub-carriers with $|h_i|^2 \leq |g_i|^2$ which do not affect the concavity of $R_s(\mathbf{p})$.

$$R'_{s,i}(p_i)|_{p_i=0} = \left[|h_i|^2 - |g_i|^2\right]^+ > 0, \tag{13}$$

which indicates that there must exist a $\hat{p}_i > 0$ that $R_{s,i}(\hat{p}_i) > 0$. According to the Lagrange's mean value theorem [17], it must have a point $\tilde{p}_i \in [\hat{p}_i, +\infty]$ with negative slop $R'_{s,i}(\tilde{p}_i) < 0$.

If $R_{s,i}(p_i)$ is concave, then the inequality $R_{s,i}(p_i) \leq R_{s,i}(\tilde{p}_i) + R'_{s,i}(\tilde{p}_i)(p_i - \tilde{p}_i)$ holds [18], which indicates $R_{s,i}(+\infty) = -\infty$. This is impossible since $R_{s,i}(+\infty) = 0$. Therefore, the concavity assumption is not true, and Proposition 1 holds.

Two evidentiary examples are provided to illustrate Proposition 1:

The first example is QPSK. The curves of $I(s_i; y_i)$, $I(s_i; z_i)$ and $R_{s,i}(p_i)$ versus p_i are shown in right part of Fig. 3, and they are in accordance with the statements in the proof of Proposition 1.

The second example considers a 4 points PAM constellation with non-uniform spacing. Its probability mass function is given by:

$$P_{s_i} \sim \begin{bmatrix} -51L & -50L & 50L & 51L \\ 0.25 & 0.25 & 0.25 & 0.25 \end{bmatrix} \tag{14}$$

where L is a normalization parameter to maintain unit variance. Figure 4 shows the secrecy rate $R_{s,i}(p_i)$ of this case. It is interesting that the $R_{s,i}(p_i)$ has two peaks. Hence, it is definitely non-concave. We note that the mutual information $I(s_i; y_i)$ and $I(s_i; z_i)$ are concave with respect to p_i in linear scale [16].

3.2   Optimal Power Allocation Solution of Problem (6)

Although problem (6) is non-convex, there are still some efficient algorithms to solve it and obtain near-optimal solutions. One of them is the Lagrangian duality method [18]. Some recent studies [12]-[14] showed that asymptotic optimal performance can be achieved by this method.

The Lagrangian of problem (6) is given by

$$L(\mathbf{p}, u) = \frac{1}{N} \sum_{i=1}^{N} [I(s_i; h_i\sqrt{p_i}s_i + w_i) - I(s_i; g_i\sqrt{p_i}s_i + v_i)]^+ + u\left(P - \frac{1}{N}\sum_{i=1}^{N} p_i\right), \tag{15}$$

where u is Lagrangian dual variable. The corresponding dual function can then be written as

$$g(u) \triangleq \max_{\mathbf{p} \geq 0}\; L(\mathbf{p}, u). \tag{16}$$

Hence the dual optimization problem is expressed as

$$D^* = \min_{u \geq 0}\; g(u), \tag{17}$$

where D^* denotes the optimal dual value. Since the objective function of primal problem (6) is non-concave, there is a positive gap between R^* and D^*, i.e., $D^* - R^* > 0$. However, according to the recent studies of Luo and Zhang [12], [13], asymptotic strong duality holds for problem (6), i.e. the duality gap $D^* - R^*$ goes to zero as $N \to \infty$, as is expressed in the following proposition:

Table 1.

Algorithm : Lagrangian dual optimization method
Initialize u
repeat
for i=1 to N
find $p_i = \arg\max\limits_{p_i}\left[[I(s_i;y_i) - I(s_i;z_i)]^+ - up_i\right] + uP.$
end
update u using bisection method.
until u converges.

Proposition 2. *If the channel coefficients g_i and h_i are Lipschitz continuous and bounded in the sense*

$$|h_i - h_j| \leq L_h \frac{|i - j|}{N}, \forall\ i, j \in \{1, 2, ..., N\} \tag{18}$$

$$|g_i - g_j| \leq L_g \frac{|i - j|}{N}, \vee\ i, j \in \{1, 2, ..., N\} \tag{19}$$

where $L_h, L_g > 0$ is the Lipschitz constant. Then we have

$$0 \leq D^* - R^* \leq O\left(\frac{1}{\sqrt{N}}\right). \tag{20}$$

Proof. According to (11) and (12), we have [15]

$$0 \leq \frac{\partial I(s; \sqrt{p}s + n)}{\partial p} = \mathtt{MMSE}(p) \leq \mathbb{E}[|s|^2], \tag{21}$$

which implies that the derivative of $R_{s,i}(p_i)$ with respect to p_i is bounded. Then the derivative of $R_{s,i}(p_i)$ with respect to $|g_i|^2$ and $|h_i|^2$ are also bounded. Since g_i and h_i are Lipschitz continuous, according to chain rule, the secrecy rate $R_{s,i}(p_i)$ is also Lipschitz continuous. Hence according to Theorem 2 of [12], the duality gap between D^* and R^* is in the order of $1/\sqrt{N}$, which is expressed as

$$0 \leq D^* - R^* \leq O(\frac{1}{\sqrt{N}}), \tag{22}$$

and Proposition 2 holds.

The procedures to solve (16) and (17) are provided in the following.

For each fixed u, problem (16) can be decoupled into N independent sub-carrier problems

$$g(u) = \max\limits_{p_i \geq 0}\ L(p_i, u),$$
$$= \sum_{i=1}^{N} \max\limits_{p_i \geq 0}[[I(s_i; y_i) - I(s_i; z_i)]^+ - up_i] + uP. \tag{23}$$

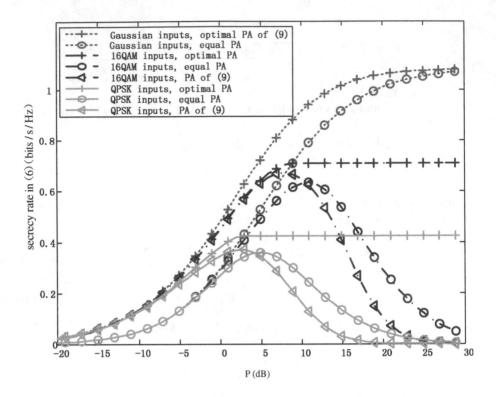

Fig. 5. The secrecy rate versus total power P

While the sub-carrier problem in (23) is still non-convex, it has only one variable p_i and can be solved by simple one dimension line search. As the dual function $g(u)$ is convex in u and its subgradient $g'(u) = P - \frac{1}{N} \sum_{i=1}^{N} p_i^*$, where p_i^* is optimal solution for problem (16) with fixed u, is an increasing function in u, bisection method can be used to solve dual problem (17), so that either $u = 0$, $P \geq \frac{1}{N} \sum_{i=1}^{N} p_i^*$ or $u > 0$, $P = \frac{1}{N} \sum_{i=1}^{N} p_i^*$ is satisfied. Table.1 summarizes the algorithm.

The complexity of this algorithm is $N \frac{1}{e_p} \log_2(\frac{1}{e_d})$, where e_p is the accuracy of one dimension exhausitive search to solve (16) and e_d is the accuracy of the bisection search to solve (17). Since its complexity is linear with respect to the number of sub-carriers N, it is quite convenient for practical large values of N, such as 64~4096. We note that the complexity of solve (6) directly is $\frac{1}{e_p^N}$, which is exponential in N and thus unrealistic.

4   Numerical Results

In this section, we provide some simulation results to illustrate the performance of our proposed power allocation algorithm and show how different channel input distributions affect the secrecy rate and power allocation results.

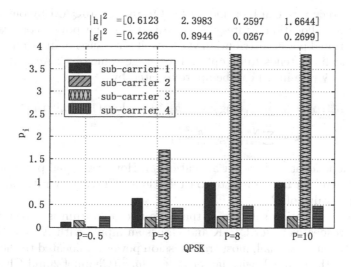

Fig. 6. Power allocation results versus P for QPSK inputs

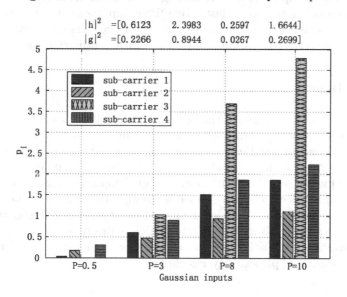

Fig. 7. Power allocation results versus P for Gaussian inputs

We first consider an OFDM-based secure system with $N = 128$ subcarriers. The secrecy rate versus total power constraint for different power allocation strategies and input distributions are illustrated in Fig. 5. Two reference strategies are considered to compare with our strategy: the optimal strategy for Gaussian inputs, i.e., (9), which is denoted by "PA of (9)" in Fig. 5; the equal power allocation strategy, which equally allocates total power among the subcarriers that satisfy $|h_i|^2 > |g_i|^2$ and is denoted by "equal PA".

Higher secrecy rate can be achieved for QPSK and 16QAM by our proposed optimal power allocation strategy, especially when the power constraint P is quite large. Equal power distribution works well for Gaussian distributed inputs. More specifically, it tends to be optimal for large value of P. Actually, when P is large, secrecy rate in (9) can be approximated by

$$R_s^G(\mathbf{p}) = \frac{1}{N} \sum_{i=1}^{N} [\, \log_2(1 + |h_i|^2 p_i) - \log_2(1 + |g_i|^2 p_i) \,]^+$$
$$\approx \frac{1}{N} \sum_{i=1}^{N} [\, \log_2(\frac{|h_i|^2}{|g_i|^2}) \,]^+, \tag{24}$$

which is independent with power allocation p_i. However, equal power allocation can be quite bad for finite discrete constellations. The secrecy rate can drops to zero for large value of P.

The power allocation solution of the proposed algorithm is shown in Fig. 6 and Fig. 7, respectively, for QPSK and Gaussian inputs with $N = 4$. When the power constraint P is small, most transmission power is allocated to the stronger sub-channels, the channels with larger $|h_i|^2 - |g_i|^2$ (Channel 2 and Channel 4 in our simulation example). However, as P grows, the transmission power of the weak sub-channels grows quite fast. For QPSK input signals, the transmission power allocated to every sub-channels will stop increasing as P grows. But the transmission power for Guassian input signals still continues to increase.

5   Conclusion

In this paper, we have obtained the optimal power allocation for OFDM-based wire-tap channels with arbitrarily distributed inputs. While the secrecy rate achieved by Gaussian distributed channel inputs is concave with respect to the transmission power, we have found and rigorously proved that the secrecy rate is non-concave for any practical finite discrete signal constellations. A power allocation algorithm has been proposed, which is asymptotic optimal as the number of sub-carrier increases. Our numerical results show that more transmitting power may results in a huge loss in secrecy rate, which is rarely seen in previous power allocation studies. This indicates that optimal power allocation is quite essential in practical studies of physical layer security.

Acknowledgement. The authors would like to thank Dr. Tsung-Hui Chang and Prof. Shidong Zhou for valuable suggestions in this paper.

This work is supported by National S&T Major Project (2009ZX03002-002), National Basic Research Program of China (2007CB310608), National S&T Pillar Program (2008BAH30B09), National Natural Science Foundation of China (60832008) and PCSIRT, Tsinghua Research Funding-No.2010THZ02-3. This work is also sponsored by Datang Mobile Communications Equipment Co., Ltd.

References

1. Liang, Y., Poor, H.V., Shamai, S.: Information theoretic security. Found. Trends Commun. Inf. Theory 5, 355–580 (2008)
2. Wyner, A.: The wire-tap channel. Bell. Syst. Tech. J. 54(8), 1355–1387 (1975)
3. Csiszar, I., Korner, J.: Broadcast channels with confidential messages. IEEE Trans. Inf. Theory 24(3), 339–348 (1978)
4. Cheong, S.L.Y., Hellman, M.: The Gaussian wire-tap channel. IEEE Trans. Inf. Theory 24(4), 451–456 (1978)
5. Oggier, F., Hassibi, B.: The secrecy capacity of the MIMO wiretap channel. In: Proc. 45th Annu. Allerton Conf. Communication, Control and Computing, Monticello, IL, pp. 848–855 (September 2007)
6. Liu, T., Shammai, S.: A note on the secrecy capacity of the multi-antenna wiretap channel. IEEE Trans. Inf. Theory 55(6), 2547–2553 (2009)
7. Ekrem, E., Ulukus, S.: Gaussian MIMO multi-receiver wiretap channel. In: Global Telecommunications Conference, Honolulu, HI (November 2009)
8. Li, Z., Yates, R., Trappe, W.: Securecy capacity of independent parrallel channels. In: Proc. IEEE int. Symp. Information Theory(ISIT), Seattle, WA, pp. 356–360 (July 2006)
9. Liang, Y., Poor, H.V., Shamai, S.: Secure communication over fading channels. IEEE Trans. Inf. Theory 54(6), 2470–2492 (2008)
10. Jorswieck, E., Wolf, A.: Resource allocation for the wire-tap multi-carrier broadcast channel. In: Proc. International Workshop on Multiple Access Communications (MACOM), St. Petersburg, Russia (June 2008)
11. Renna, F., Laurenti, N., Poor, H.V.: Physical layer security for OFDM systems. In: European Wireless Conference, Vienna, Austria (April 2011)
12. Luo, Z., Zhang, S.: Duality Gap Estimation and Polynomial Time Approximation for Optimal Spectrum Management. IEEE Trans. Signal Processing 57(7), 2675–2689 (2009)
13. Luo, Z., Zhang, S.: Dynamic spectrum management: Complexity and duality. IEEE J. Sel.Topics Signal Process., Special Issue on Signal Process., Netw. Dyn. Spectrum Access 2(1), 57–73 (2008)
14. Yu, W., Lui, R.: Dual methods for nonconvex spectrum optimization of multicarrier systems. IEEE Trans. Commun. 54, 1310–1322 (2006)
15. Guo, D., Shamai, S., Verdu, S.: Mutual information and minimum mean-square error in Gaussian channels. IEEE Trans. Inf. Theory 51(4), 1261–1283 (2005)
16. Guo, D., Wu, Y., Shamai, S., Verdu, S.: Estimation in Gaussian noise: Properties of the minimum mean-square error. IEEE Trans. Inf. Theory 57(4), 2371–2385 (2011)
17. Jeffreys, H., Jeffreys, B.S.: Methods of Mathematical Physics, 3rd edn. Cambridge University Press, Cambridge (1988)
18. Boyd, L., Vandenberghe, S.: Convex Optimization. Cambridge University Press (2004)

MASS: Multiple ASSociation Scheme in IEEE 802.11 Wireless Mesh Networks

Haidong Zhang, Pin Lv, Yingwen Chen, and Ming Xu

Department of Network Engineering,
School of Computer National University of Defense Technology
Changsha, China 410073
{zhanghaidong,lvpin08,chenyingwen,xuming}@nudt.edu.cn

Abstract. Traditional association mechanism in IEEE 802.11 is in the form of one-to-many. It indicates that an access point (AP) can associate with many clients at the same time, while one client is capable to be associated with only one AP at a time. Such policy is inefficient and inflexible in the context of wireless mesh network (WMN). In this paper, we propose a many-to-many association scheme called Multiple ASSociation (MASS) for IEEE 802.11 WMN. The MASS allows a Mesh Client (MC) to be associated with multiple Mesh APs (MAPs) simultaneously. The most appropriate MAP is selected adaptively from a group of MAPs to actually serve the MC based on its correspondence node. Consequently, when the MC communicates with different nodes, probably distinct MAPs are employed to forward its packets. The protocol is compatible with current IEEE 802.11 standards and does not need any modification on the MC. We conduct extensive experiments which demonstrate the effectiveness and flexibility of the proposed scheme.

Keywords: multiple association, MASS, IEEE 802.11, wireless mesh networks, WMN.

1 Introduction

As an emerging technology to provide last few miles connectivity, Wireless Mesh Network (WMN) [1] [2] has received considerable attention from both academic and industrial communities in recent years. In IEEE 802.11 based WMN, there usually exist two types of nodes: Mesh Routers (MRs) and Mesh Clients (MCs). The MRs are interconnected to form a multi-hop infrastructure to forward packets for the MCs. The MR who can provide access service for the MCs is referred to as Mesh Access Point (MAP). The MC (e.g. laptop, PDA, WiFi IP phone, etc.) can access the WMN after being associated with an MAP. With the assistance of the infrastructure, each MC can communicate with other MCs within the same WMN, as well as access the Internet through an Internet Gate-Way (IGW) of the WMN. Hence, both of these two traffic types should be considered.

The association procedure defined in IEEE 802.11 standards uses the Received Signal Strength Indication (RSSI) value as the sole metric. Namely, the MC scans

P. Ren et al. (Eds.): WICON 2011, LNICST 98, pp. 204–215, 2012.

all available channels and selects the MAP that has the strongest RSSI to be associated with and would not change its decision until the RSSI becomes below a certain threshold. However, this scheme is prone to severe traffic load imbalance as well as inefficient utility of network resources in WLAN environment [3] [4] since the RSSI-based metric cannot reflect the traffic load of access points. The problem is even more serious in the context of the WMN where association decision can affect routing selection in the backhaul and both access link and routing path should be taken into account [5] [6].

Previous works, such as [7] [8] [9], have proposed some new association metrics. G. Athanasiou et al. [10] argued that the backhaul latency should be considered for association in the WMN, and used the airtime cost defined in the IEEE 802.11s draft [11] to evaluate link quality. In [5], two different metrics for access link and backhaul are proposed. Recent research work [12] used end-to-end airtime cost to determine the MAP to be associated with. But all approaches mentioned above inevitably require a modification to the IEEE 802.11 standards or the wireless interface driver at both MAP and MC sides, which result in the infeasibility in practical applications.

Actually, traditional association mechanisms have a potential rule that a MC is capable to be associated with only one MAP at one time. But the fixed access point cannot always be optimal when correspondence nodes are changed. The paper [13] breaks the rule and proposes a network-leading association scheme which allows the MC to be associated with a group of MAPs. On one hand, the MAPs can adaptively elect the one having the optimal performance to cater for the MC. On the other hand, from the MC's point of view, there seems only one MAP around to serve it, and it cannot perceive the handoff even it moves across different MAPs' coverage. Furthermore, the scheme is compatible with current widely used IEEE 802.11 standards and do not need any modification at the MC side. This scheme is only designed for the traffic from/to the IGW, however, it does not take the internal peer-to-peer traffics into consideration.

When an enterprise or a community builds a WMN not only for Internet accessing but also for internal information sharing, the traffics among MCs within the same WMN are also dominating. Take the scenario shown in Fig.1 for example. A_1 to A_5 are five MAPs that constitute the backbone of the WMN while C_1 to C_3 are three MCs. According to the RSSI-based association scheme, the three MCs are associated with A_1, A_3 and A_5 respectively. Under such circumstances, a four-hop routing path C_1-A_1-A_2-A_3-C_2 is established to support communication between C_1 and C_2. But obviously the performance of the two-hop routing path C_1-A_2-C_2 may be better than the four-hop one and A_2 may be the optimal access point for C_1 to communicate with C_2 although it is not with the strongest RSSI for both C_1 and C_2. If C_1 wants to transmit data to C_3 at the same time, maybe A_1 is the best choice for C_1 this time. Therefore, the MC can benefit from being associated with multiple MAPs at the same time rather than with only one fixed MAP, especially when internal peer-to-peer traffic is dominating.

In this paper, we propose a novel association scheme called Multiple ASSociation or MASS for the WMN which supports both two traffic types. We configure

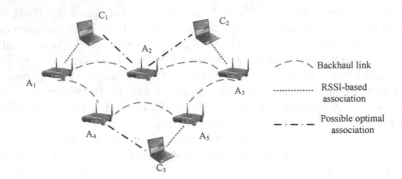

Fig. 1. A Sample Scenario of Association in WMN

the interfaces serving as access points of all MAPs in the WMN with same MAC address, same IP address, same ESSID and same channel. An MC will be associated with a group of MAPs rather than a specific one. The MAPs which associate with the MC will cooperate with each other to elect the most appropriate one to serve the MC on the basis of its correspondence node. Unlike prior works to select the optimal MAP for the MC (such as [14]), in our MASS scheme, an MC can be associated with multiple MAPs simultaneously. The MC does not need to trigger a handoff to the other optimal MAP when its correspondence node changes.

Our novel design mainly achieves the following three advantages:

(1) The multiple association scheme can adaptively assign an optimal MAP to the MC according to its correspondence targets respectively, which is able to improve the performance of the WMN.

(2) The multiple association scheme can help MCs to achieve seamless handoff in dynamic circumstances.

(3) The multiple association scheme is totally transparent to the traditional MC. The MC can be associated with our MAP as normal without any modification.

The rest of this paper is organized as follows. The next section will describe the system model. In Section 3, we will discuss the MASS scheme in detail. The performance evaluation based on simulations is given in Section 4. Finally, we summarize our work in Section 5.

2   System Model

In this paper, we mainly focus on the infrastructure/backbone WMN in which MCs must access the WMN by direct association with MAPs rather than by relays of other MCs through multi-hop paths. And only MAPs in the backhaul of the WMN are considered in our research. The MRs without access function work normally. We assume that each MAP has two radios. One radio works in Ad-Hoc mode to form the backbone of the WMN. The backbone uses AODV routing protocol to find destinations and forward data packets. The other radio operates in AP mode to provide access service for MCs. They are assigned non-overlapping channels from different frequency bands. Only end-to-end link is considered in this paper. The IGW will be treated as a special MC.

$$C_{ij} = \alpha AC_{ia} + (1 - \alpha)BC_{ab} + \alpha AC_{bj} \tag{1}$$

We employ the airtime cost introduced in the 802.11s draft [15] as the serving MAP election metric in MASS. Equation (1) is the end-to-end airtime cost used in our proposed association scheme. C_{ij} is the total airtime cost from MC_i to MC_j, which includes the access link airtime cost AC_{ia} between MC_i and MAP_a, the backhaul airtime cost BC_{ab} between MAP_a and MAP_b and the access link airtime cost AC_{bj} between MAP_b and MC_j. The alterable weighting coefficient $\alpha(0 \leq \alpha \leq 1)$ indicates the respective influence of AC and BC. The α value can be adjusted to improve the accuracy of the association scheme. Here we set 0.5 as its default value in our experiments. The equation contains two ACs. Although both of these two ACs indicate the access link airtime cost, there are still some differences between them. The first AC is the airtime cost from an MC to an MAP, i.e. "uplink" channel, and the second one is for the "downlink" channel.

2.1   Access Link Airtime Cost Calculation

$$AC_{ia} = [O_{ca} + O_p + \frac{B}{r_i}]\frac{1}{1 - e_{pt}^i} \tag{2}$$

In Equation (2), O_{ca} is the channel access time overhead and O_p is the time overhead caused by protocols. Both of them are constant values. B is the dominant size in bit of the test traffic. r_i is the available bandwidth that MC_i can acquire from MAP_a. e_{pt}^i is the frame error rate between MC_i and MAP_a.

Equation (2) is for the uplink channel. The downlink channel airtime cost is calculated similarly, but the e_{pt}^i is a little different for each downlink associated for every MC. In our MASS scheme, we do not want any modification on the MCs. It means that the airtime cost between MC and MAP cannot be calculated on the MCs. Thus it only should be operated on the MAPs. Since the difference of airtime costs between uplink and downlink cannot be too far, we can use the downlink airtime cost calculated on the MAP instead of which computed on the MC. In other words, we can calculate AC_{ia} on MAP_a instead of MC_i.

The calculation equation is same as Equation (2), but all the test traffics and calculations are operated on the MAP. The rate r_i depends on the local implementation of rate adaptation. The estimation of e_{pt}^i is also a local implementation choice.

2.2   Backhaul Airtime Cost Calculation

We use ETT [16] as the routing metric in the communication infrastructure. Therefore, the backhaul airtime cost calculation can use the ETT calculation.

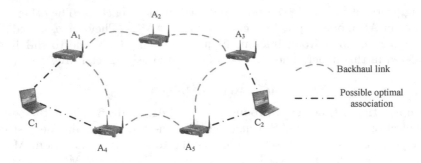

Fig. 2. A Sample Scenario For MASS

ETT is the expected time to successfully transmit a packet at the MAC layer. According to the ETT measured in link of a real network, the calculation equation is as follows:

$$BC = \frac{S}{B} \cdot \frac{1}{D_f \cdot D_r} \tag{3}$$

In Equation (3), S denotes the average size of packet and B represents current link bandwidth. We define that P_f is the packet loss probability in forward direction and P_r is the packet loss probability in the reverse direction. Then D_f is the forward delivery ratio (1-P_f) and D_r is the reverse delivery ratio (1-P_r). The delivery ratios D_f and D_r are measured by broadcasting dedicated link probe packets of a fixed size every average period from each MAP to its neighbors.

3   MASS: The Multiple Association Scheme

3.1   Basic Setting

Take Fig.2 for example. All the interfaces providing accessing function of all the MAPs are set to the same MAC address, the same IP address, the same ESSID and the same channel. When an MC scans channels, it will only find a single MAP around. After its association with the MAP in its view, in fact it is associated with a group of MAPs. All the data emitted by the MC will be received by all of these MAPs normally. But if all the MAPs reply with the ACKnowledgment frame (ACK) to MC normally, there will be conflict occurred at the receiver. In order to avoid such collision, the wireless driver on the MAP needs a little modification to control the ACK transmission. The MAP should be able to handle the ACK reply for every MC. When it replies the ACK to an MC, it acts as a normal MAP communicating with MC. When it doesn't reply ACK to an MC, it just works as a sniffer. In order to guarantee the normal communication between an MAP and an MC, there should be only one MAP replying ACK to a specific MC at one time.

S_MAC	T_MAC	Airtime_Cost	Nexthop	Flag	Seq

Fig. 3. Route Table Design

3.2   Protocol Specifications

The MAP should maintain a routing table to record both source and target MCs' MAC addresses, the airtime cost, next-hop node, serving flag, sequence number and so on.

The format of the entry in the routing table is depicted Fig.3. S_MAC is the MAC address of the source MC while T_MAC refers to which of the target MC. The item of Airtime_Cost is the airtime cost from this MAP to the MC. The value is calculated by the MAP itself. The field of Nexthop tells the MAP to whom the packets should be forwarded. The Flag item indicates whether the MAP replies ACK frame to the MC and the Seq item is used to avoid outdated messages. The routing table is maintained by the MAP for every MC being associated with it, and is updated periodically. According to this table, an MAP decides to calculate the airtime, update the route table, forward the packet or just keep silence. Thus, the MAP can have four states to a specific MC which are *idle*, *calculating*, *silence* and *serving*. The idle state means the MC is out of the MAP's range and there is no entry of the MC in the MAP's routing table. When an MC is associated with the MAP, the MAP turns into the calculating state. It calculates the airtime from the MC to the target MC or the IGW. The MAPs exchange their routing table information through broadcasting only in the backbone. Truly, it may incur some overhead, but the influence can be weakened by establishing high bandwidth backbone. The best MAP with lowest airtime cost will be selected to serve the MC. It will turn into serving state and the others will be in silence state. The unique MAP in serving state will forward the data to the next-hop node as a normal MAP. The other silent MAPs just drop the packet from the specific MC. The MAP can stay in distinct states to different MCs. The state transition diagram is illustrated in Fig.4.

Next we will describe the complete process when two MCs in MASS WMN communicate with each other.

Association. In the beginning, the MAPs are idle and broadcast beacons normally. Because of the special settings of the MAC address, ESSID and channel, an MC considers that there is only one MAP after scanning all available channels. When the MC find an available AP, it will send an association request frame to the MAP. All the MAPs that receive this request add a new entry into its routing table and set the S_MAC field with the MC's MAC address. The MAP will calculate the AC (access link airtime cost) by sending some testing packets to the MC and fill the Airtime_Cost field. All the MAPs exchange the information through broadcasting the routing table. The best one with lowest airtime cost will be selected to reply the association request, and its state turns into serving and the others keep in silence to this MC. At this time, the MC

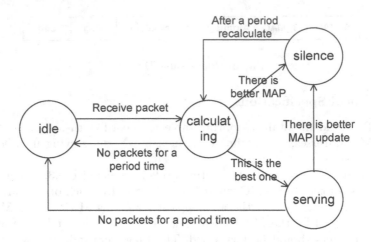

Fig. 4. State Transition Diagram

associates with the MAP successfully. Because there is only one MAP serving for the MC, the authentication and IP assignment can be operated as usual. The MC can either be pre-assigned a unique IP address or require the IP address through DHCP service.

Communication. When the MC wants to communicate with another MC or IGW, the MAP will check its route table firstly. If there is no route path to the target. The MAP will add a new entry for it and send airtime request packet to get the BC and the other AC value. Notice that all the MAPs hearing the MC's data will do it including the silent MAPs for the MC and then add them together and fill the Airtime_Cost field of the item. After calculation, it broadcasts its routing table to each other. To avoid the outdated message, the MAP pluses the route table entry's Seq value with 1 and then broadcasts it. When an MAP receives an updated table entry with lower Seq, it will be considered out of date and will be dropped directly. If the MAP receives an updated entry with a better routing path, it turns itself into silence state for the MC. If there is no better route received by the MAP before a timer expires, then it will be the best MAP for this data flow. And this MAP will enable its ACK function for the MC and serve to forward the data from the MC to its destination.

Recalculation. Owing to the MCs' mobility, the variable link quality and the unstable traffic load, the serving MAP cannot always be the best one. Therefore, recalculation will be operated when a timer expires or the serving MAP loses the connection with the MC. In the recalculation process, the MAPs in silence state turn into the calculating state and elect the best MAP serving for the MC again. If the MAP doesn't receive any data from the MC for a period of time, it will delete the route table entry of the MC and move back to the idle state because the MC may have been out of communication scope or powered off.

3.3   Further Discussion

In our proposed scheme MASS, an MC can be associated with a group of MAPs but it believes to connect to a single MAP because all MAPs are transparent to the MC. The MC will not be conscious of the alteration of the serving MAP when it communicates with other MCs. This means there is no handoff when the MC re-associates from an old MAP to a new MAP indeed. Hence, the MC can achieve seamless handoff within the whole coverage area of the WMN in this way.

It may inhibit concurrent transmission to configure all the access links into the same channel. Actually, our approach can be easily extended to multi-channel access links. When multi-channel configuration is applied, the MAPs with the same access link channel will operate as MASS. Hence the entire WMN will be viewed as several overlays.

Because of the broadcast updating scheme, MASS is just suite for the WMN with limited scale. But we will design an effective routing table exchange scheme next step. The new exchange process will only operate among the MAPs associating with the MC. MASS will be improved for large scale WMNs.

4   Performance Evaluation

In this section, we conduct simulations using the NS-3 network simulator [17] to evaluate the performance of MASS.

We generate a WMN of 16 MAPs and 5 MCs. The MAPs are placed in a 600m×600m rectangular area to form a 4×4 grid and their locations are fixed. The distance from any MAP to its nearest neighbor is 200m. Each MAP is equipped with two radios, one is connected with other MAPs to constitute the infrastructure and the other provides access function for MCs. The MCs are distributed uniformly and we consider the static scenario only, which is the same to the mobility scenario. The topology of the simulation test is illustrated in Fig.5.

To show the improvements of the multiple association scheme MASS, we compare it with the traditional RSSI-based mechanism. Our simulations include two independent parts. In the first part, we evaluate the performance of a single data flow. While in the second part, we evaluate the overall performance of multiple data flows. The following three metrics are considered. The throughput is the end-to-end traffic being successfully transmitted. The average delay is the packet transmission time in the access link and the mesh backhaul. And the packet loss rate is calculated as the lost packets number divides the total transmitted packets number.

4.1   Experiment 1: Single Flow Performance

In this subsection, we evaluate the end-to-end performance of one flow between two MCs.

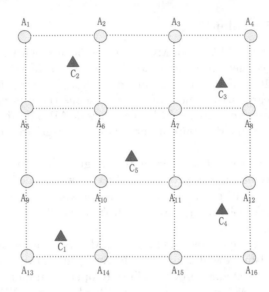

Fig. 5. WMN Topology of the Simulation

In simulation, a single flow from C_1 to C_2 is set up. The nearest MAPs to them are A_{13} and A_2 respectively. Suppose for an MC, the nearest MAP is just the one with the highest RSSI. In the light of RSSI-based scheme, C_1 will be associated with A_{13} and C_2 will be associated with A_2. But in our MASS scheme, C_1 will likely select A_{10} or A_9 to be associated with according to the airtime cost between C_1 and C_2.

Fig.6 shows the results of the comparisons between MASS and RSSI-based scheme on the above three metrics. We can see that, the throughput is improved by 30% and the average delay is reduced by 50%. The average packet loss rate is also reduced in MASS scheme by as much as 30%.

Obviously, the results reveal that, in the single flow situation, the proposed MASS achieves a significant higher performance than the RSSI-based scheme.

4.2   Experiment 2: Multiple Flows Performance

Consider the scenario in Fig.5 again. C_1 to C_5 are five independent MCs, and the nearest MAPs to them are A_{13}, A_2, A_8, A_{12} and A_{10} respectively. C_1, C_2, C_3 and C_4 all establish a data flow to C_5. According to the RSSI-based method, these five MCs will be associated with the respective nearest MAPs, and A_{10} is the unique MAP serving C_5. The link A_{10}-C_5 is prone to be the bottleneck of the entire WMN. In MASS however, C_1 to C_4 will select the MAP with the lowest airtime to C_5 to be associated with, which may be A_{10}, A_6, A_7 and A_{11} respectively. In addition, C_5 will get aid from four MAPs when communicating with different targets.

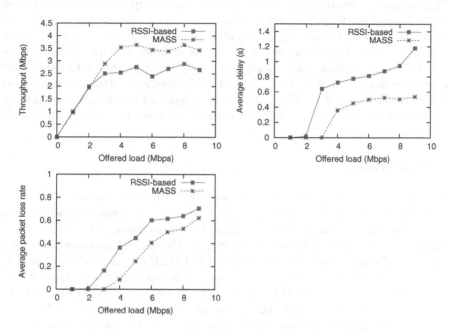

Fig. 6. Single Flow Performance Evaluation

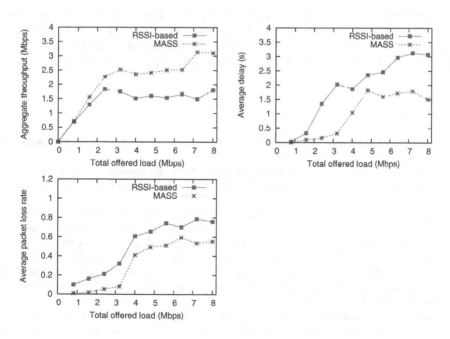

Fig. 7. Multiple Flows Performance Evaluation

Fig.7 demonstrates the results of the performance comparisons between MASS and RSSI-based strategy. Note that, in this experiment part, we measure the aggregate throughput, the average delay and the average packet loss rate, which represent the overall performance of the multiple flows. Compared with traditional 802.11 mechanism, the throughput of MASS is improved by 50% while the average delay is reduced by 45%. In MASS scheme, the average packet loss rate is also reduced by 35%. The results explains that the proposed MASS also performs better than the RSSI-based scheme when multiple flows exist in the WMN.

5   Conclusion

In this paper, we proposed Multiple ASSociation (MASS) scheme in IEEE 802.11 wireless mesh networks. The MASS scheme is a MAC layer protocol and does not need any modification on MCs and is completely transparent to the MCs. Different from the traditional methods, in MASS, an MC can set up association with multiple MAPs simultaneously, and the optimal MAP can be elected adaptively from these MAPs to serve the MC according to its correspondence node. Simulation results reveal that our MASS scheme performs significant better than the RSSI-based scheme on metrics such as throughput, delay and packet loss rate. Our extensive simulation-based experiments also demonstrate the effectiveness and flexibility of the proposed MASS scheme.

Acknowledgment. The work is partially supported by grant No. 60773017 and No. 61003304 from Natural Science Foundation of China, grant No. 09ZZ4034 from the Hunan Provincial Natural Science Foundation of China and grant No. SBK201021610 from the Jiangsu Provincial Natural Science Foundation of China.

References

1. Akyildiz, I.F., Wang, X., Wang, W.: Wireless mesh networks: a survey. Computer Networks 47(4), 445–487 (2005)
2. Pathak, P.H., Dutta, R.: A survey of network design problems and joint design approaches in wireless mesh networks. IEEE Communications Surveys and Tutorials 12(4), 1–33 (2010)
3. Mhatre, V., Papagiannaki, K.: Using smart triggers for improved user performance in 802.11 wireless networks. In: Proceedings of the 4th International Conference on Mobile Systems, Applications and Services, pp. 246–259. ACM (2006)
4. Lee, H., Kim, S., Lee, O., Choi, S., Lee, S.J.: Available bandwidth-based association in IEEE 802.11 wireless LANs. In: Proceedings of the 11th International Symposium on Modeling, Analysis and Simulation of Wireless and Mobile Systems, pp. 132–139. ACM (2008)
5. Luo, L., Raychaudhuri, D., Liu, H., Wu, M., Li, D.: Improving end-to-end performance of wireless mesh networks through smart association. In: Proceedings of the Wireless Communications and Networking Conference (WCNC 2008), pp. 2087–2092. IEEE (2008)

6. Lv, P., Chen, Y., Xiao, W., Xu, M.: A cross-layer scheme for access point selection in wireless mesh networks. In: Proceedings of the 6th IEEE International Conference on Wireless Communications, Network and Mobile Computing (WiCOM 2010), pp. 1–5. IEEE (2010)
7. Bejerano, Y., Han, S.J., Li, L.E.: Fairness and load balancing in wireless lans using association control. In: Proceedings of the 10th Annual International Conference on Mobile Computing and Networking, pp. 315–329. ACM (2004)
8. Vasudevan, S., Papagiannaki, K., Diot, C., Kurose, J., Towsley, D.: Facilitating access point selection in IEEE 802.11 wireless networks. In: Proceedings of the 5th ACM SIGCOMM Conference on Internet Measurement, pages 26. USENIX Association (2005)
9. Fujiwara, A., Sagara, Y., Nakamura, M.: Access point selection algorithms for maximizing throughputs in wireless LAN environment. In: 2007 International Conference on Parallel and Distributed Systems, vol. 2, pp. 1–8. IEEE (2007)
10. Athanasiou, G., Korakis, T., Ercetin, O., Tassiulas, L.: Dynamic cross-layer association in 802.11-based mesh networks. In: 26th IEEE International Conference on Computer Communications, INFOCOM 2007, pp. 2090–2098. IEEE (2007)
11. IEEE 802.11s: Wireless LAN Medium Access Control (MAC) and Physical Layer (PHY) Specifications: Simple Efficient Extensible Mesh (SEE-Mesh) Proposal
12. He, Y., Perkins, D., Velaga, S.: Design and Implementation of CLASS: a Cross-Layer ASSociation Scheme for Wireless Mesh Networks. In: INFOCOM IEEE Conference on Computer Communications Workshops, pp. 1–6. IEEE (2010)
13. Lv, P., Wang, X., Xu, M., Chen, Y.: Network-Leading Association Scheme in IEEE 802.11 Wireless Mesh Networks. In: Proceedings of International Conference on Communications (ICC 2011), pp. 1–5. IEEE (2011)
14. Tu, W., Sreenan, C.J., Chou, C.T., Misra, A., Jha, S.: Resource-aware video multicasting via access gateways in wireless mesh networks. In: IEEE International Conference on Network Protocols, ICNP 2008, pp. 43–52. IEEE (2008)
15. Aboul-Magd, O., Abraham, S., Agre, J., Aoki, H., Bahr, M., Siebert, M., Walke, B., Conner, W., Kruys, J., Kim, K.: Joint SEE-mesh/Wi-mesh proposal to 802.11 TGs. In: IEEE LMSC Meeting, p. 93. Citeseer (November 2006)
16. Draves, R., Padhye, J., Zill, B.: Routing in multi-radio, multi-hop wireless mesh networks. In: Proceedings of the 10th Annual International Conference on Mobile Computing and Networking, pp. 114–128. ACM (2004)
17. The ns-3 network simulator, http://www.nsnam.org/

A Weighted UWB Transmitted-Reference Receiver for Indoor Positioning Using MMSE Estimation[*]

Gang Yang, Hui Jiang, Zhiqiang Bao, and Jie Shan

School of Communications and Information Engineering
Xi'an University of Posts & Telecommunications
Xi'an, 710121 P.R. China
{yanggang,jianghui,baozhiqiang,shanjie}@xupt.edu.cn

Abstract. Many emerging wireless intelligent network applications have the requirement of ranging and localization services besides data transfer. The impulse ultra-wideband (UWB) technology has accurate positioning capability as well as low to medium rate communication, so it is especially suitable in above applications. Due to implementation complexity concerns, UWB transmitted-reference (TR) receiver has become a good choice for this case recently. In this paper, considering the multipath components segment distribution characteristic of UWB received signals, a novel weighted UWB averaged TR receiver based on minimize-mean-square-error (MMSE) estimation for indoor positioning is presented by using segmentation-weighting-combination idea. Those segments which hold the intensive multipath signals are given the bigger weight coefficients, so that more useful multipath energy are captured meanwhile the noise product term is highly suppressed, thus the bit-error-rate (BER) performance of the receiver is efficiently improved. The suitable weight coefficients are obtained by using MMSE estimation via training data sequence. This receiver was analyzed and simulated in IEEE CM3 indoor multipath channel. The results show that it has superior detect performance compared with a conventional averaged TR receiver. The receiver can be used for those wireless intelligent network applications with indoor positioning capability.

Keywords: ultra-wideband (UWB) communications, weighted transmitted-reference (TR) receiver, minimize-mean-square-error (MMSE) estimation, indoor positioning.

1   Introduction

In recent years, ultra-wideband (UWB) wireless communication technology has aroused wide attention for its pulse characteristics essentially different from traditional narrowband sine-wave carrier and particular advantage of coexistence with the current

---

[*] This work was supported by the Shaanxi Provincial Education Department Scientific Research Program Foundation Item (No. 2010JK830).

P. Ren et al. (Eds.): WICON 2011, LNICST 98, pp. 216–224, 2012.

communication system by its extremely low transmission power spectrum. Especially, an impulse UWB (IR-UWB) system adopts the nanosecond narrow pulse so that it has very accurate temporal and spatial information which can be used for precise time of arrival (TOA) estimation. The merit make it can not only realize robust low to high rate communications but also has accurate positioning capabilities. With the development of wireless communication and network technology, many new emerging applications can be generally classified as one kind of wireless intelligent network applications which often need ranging and positioning services besides medium data transfer [1][2], such as homeland security monitoring, remote patient healthcare, transportation object tracking, environment status monitoring, and assembling line automation, logistics package tracking, search and rescue (communications with fire fighters, or earthquake victims), and military team cooperative fighting, etc. UWB signaling is especially suitable in above application's requirements because it allows centimeter accuracy in ranging, as well as low-power and low-cost implementation of communication systems [3]. In these wireless intelligent networks, each node equipped with IR-UWB transceiver will be capable of a tremendous diversity of functionality such as sensing capabilities, signal processing, network protocol, short-range communication, and positioning capabilities. Some can be selected as beacon nodes, which are aware of their relative position, and others are peer nodes which can localize themselves by communicating with three or four beacon nodes, depending whether we are in presence of 2-dimensional or 3-dimensional positioning scenarios.

The types of IR-UWB receiver include the coherent RAKE receivers and the non-coherent transmitted-reference (TR) receivers. As the traditional RAKE receiver has high complexity in tap structure while serious multipath of UWB pulse at indoor situation, UWB TR receivers with simple structure & no channel estimation are more suitable for above wireless intelligent network applications and have been widely researched [4][5]. But a basic TR receiver has one major drawback of poor detection performance because the correlation template signal is formed by only one reference received waveform. In order to improve its performance, aiming at the approximate time-unvarying characteristic of UWB channel during a short period, reference [6] proposes an averaged transmitted-reference (ATR) receiver which transmits several repeated reference pulses before data signals and averages these reference received waveforms to decrease the noise level of correlation template, thereby improving the detection performance.

In this paper, by exploring and using the segments distribution characteristic of multipath components in UWB received signal, we proposed a further improved weighted ATR receiver base on minimize-mean-square-error (MMSE) estimation, which has better bit-error-rate (BER) performance. The idea of the proposed receiver is described in Section 2 and its structure is presented in Section 3. In Section 4, MMSE weight coefficient estimation is described and analyzed. Section 5 presents its performance simulation under multipath channel compare with a conventional ATR receiver and conclusions are drawn in Section 6.

2   Idea of Proposed Weighted ATR Receiver

The expression of bit-error-rate P_b of the ATR receiver [7] is derived as follows:

$$P_b = Q\left(\sqrt{\frac{N_s}{(\frac{N_r+1}{2N_r})(\frac{N_0}{E_p}) + \frac{2W\tau_{max}}{4N_r}(\frac{N_0}{E_p})^2}}\right)$$

(1)

Therefore, the detection performance of the ATR receiver mainly depends on the noise product term $(\frac{N_0}{E_p})^2$ when the signal-to-noise ratio (SNR) of received signals is low. Because in UWB multipath channel impulse response $h(t)$ multipath components arrive in cluster and distribute sparsely on the time axis [8], if the time axis is divided into several time segments, certain time segments definitely contain more multipath components, while certain time segments contain fewer multipath components. Taking IEEE 802.15.3a of UWB indoor CM3 multipath channel as example [9], if the first 100ns is taken to be divided into five time segments, the distribution of the multipath components amplitude (absolute values) of received signals through the CM3 channel is shown in Fig. 1. There is no noise shown for clarity, and each peak is absolute value waveform of one UWB received pulse.

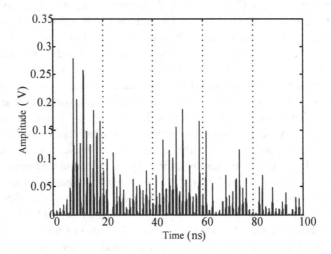

Fig. 1. Distribution of multipath components amplitude (absolute values) of received signals through CM3 channel in different time segments

In Fig.1, we can obviously see the distribution of signal energy of multipath components contained in different time segments: the first and the third time segments contain the most multipath signal energy, the second and the fourth time segments follows, and the fifth time segment contains the least multipath signal energy. Noise must exist in UWB received signals, especially when the SNR is low, so those time segments containing less multipath signal energy would contain stronger noise energy. Therefore, when we use the ATR receiver to carry out the correlation demodulation, these time segments contribute less for capturing useful signal energy but greatly increase noise signal energy in judgment item, and the noise product term $(\dfrac{N_0}{E_p})^2$ is increased resulting in obvious increase of the BER of the receiver.

In order to minimize the noise product term as much as possible to decrease the BER of the ATR receiver, aiming to above multipath components distribution characteristic of UWB received signal, we proposes a weighted ATR receiver by using segmentation-weighting-combination idea. It gives the segments different weights and gives the segment which holds the dense multipath components signal the bigger weight factor, thus the combined judgment item must include more useful multipath components energy and less noise energy ratio. Then the influence caused by noise-on-noise term in final judgment item is greatly reduced and according to equation (1), the receiver has better detection performance with lower $(\dfrac{N_0}{E_p})^2$ item.

Moreover, we try to use training data sequence and MMSE estimation theory [10] to find the suitable the weight coefficients of segments.

3   Structure of Weighted ATR Receiver

The structure of the proposed weighted ATR receiver is shown in Fig. 2. In this receiver, the time axis for received signals is divided into several time segments, according to the amount of multipath signal energy contained by the time segment, its delayed product item in a correlator is multiplied by a corresponding weighting function $w(t)$, that is to say, the time segments containing more signal energy have larger weighted values, and the time segments containing less signal energy have smaller weighted values. After combined signals are integrated, more useful multipath signal energy will be captured and the SNR of output decision signals is increased, then BER performance of the receiver will be improved.

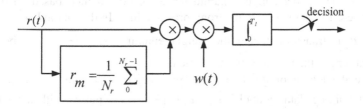

Fig. 2. Structure of weighted ATR receiver

In Fig. 2, suppose the time axis is $T_l = \tau_{\max}$ and T_l is divided into time segments with the number of Q, for the approximate time-unvarying channel characteristic during a short period, then time-varying weighting function $w(t)$ actually is a segmental constant function $w_q, 0 \leq q \leq Q$. For example, from multipath distributions of five time segments in Fig 1, we can see that the first and the third time segments obviously should be given the largest weights, the second and the fourth time segments smaller weights, and the fifth time segments smallest weight, so signal energy can be captured more efficiently.

In terms of the number of divided time segments, because the weight coefficient w_q of each time segment is an average weight based on all multipath components of the time segment, if the time axis is divided into more smaller time segments, then fewer multipath signals falls in each time segments, the selection of weight is more targeted, and the detection performance can be further improved. Theoretically, if the time axis is subdivided enough into the interval of a pulse width, each time segment only has one multipath component or no multipath component (weight is equal to zero), then there is no need to average weights, the weight can be determined only according to the amplitude of the multipath component, so it is more reasonable and efficient, and the receiver can obtain optimal performance. But if so, the time axis may need to be divided into hundreds of or thousands of time segments resulting in over complex structure and over high realization cost of the receiver. Therefore, an actual weighted ATR receiver generally divides the axis into limited several or dozens of time segments through balancing the BER performance and the complexity cost to obtain overall optimization.

4   MMSE Weight Coefficient Estimation

The detection performance of the weighted ATR receiver depends on appropriate selection of the weight coefficient w_q to a great extent. Theoretically, the weight which enables the correlator to output the largest instant SNR at sampling time is optimal, but it is extremely difficult to obtain above weight due to unpredictability of channel noise, so we can only use some suboptimal weight selecting method in practice [11]. The paper adopts a parameter estimation method based on minimize-mean-square-error estimation with strong practicability. In the method, a training data sequence c_n is transmitted, and the weight enabling $E|\hat{c}_n - c_n|^2$ to be smallest through training is the proper weight coefficient.

Suppose the length of the transmitted training data sequence is N , the n th modulated training data symbol is c_n , $c_n \in \{+1, -1\}$, pulses with the number of N_s represent a data symbol, and then it is derived that the n th data symbol $\hat{c}_n$ of weighted correlator output sampling is as follows:

$$\hat{c}_n = \sum_{q=0}^{Q-1} \left(\frac{1}{N_s} \sum_{0}^{Ns-1} \int_{\frac{q}{Q}T_l}^{\frac{(q+1)}{Q}T_l} w_q\, r_m(t) r_{c,n}(t) d(t) \right)$$

$$= \sum_{q=0}^{Q-1} w_q \left(\frac{1}{N_s} \sum_{0}^{Ns-1} \int_{\frac{q}{Q}T_l}^{\frac{(q+1)}{Q}T_l} r_m(t) r_{c,n}(t) d(t) \right) \qquad (2)$$

$$= \sum_{q=0}^{Q-1} w_q\, y_n(q)$$

Where w_q is the weight of the q th time segment, $c_n \in \{0, 1, \cdots, Q-1\}$, $y_n(q)$ is the mean value of unweighted correlator output sampling of pulses with the number of N_s of the n th data symbol in the q th time segment. According to MMSE parameter estimation, the weight of corresponding time segment is obtained when the following cost function is a minimum.

$$E\,|\,\hat{c}_n - c_n\,|^2 = \frac{1}{N} \sum_{n=0}^{N-1} \left| \sum_{q=0}^{Q-1} w_q\, y_n(q) - c_n \right|^2 \qquad (3)$$

By solve formula (2) to obtain weight coefficient as follows:

$$\begin{pmatrix} w_0 \\ \vdots \\ w_q \\ \vdots \\ w_{Q-1} \end{pmatrix} = (\mathbf{YY}^{\mathbf{T}})^{-1}(\mathbf{YC}^{\mathbf{T}}) \qquad (4)$$

Where $\mathbf{C}^{\mathbf{T}} = \begin{pmatrix} c_1 \\ \vdots \\ c_n \\ \vdots \\ c_{N-1} \end{pmatrix}$ is training data symbol vector, autocorrelation matrix is:

$$Y = \begin{pmatrix} y_0(0) & \cdots & y_n(0) & \cdots & y_{N-1}(0) \\ \vdots & & \vdots & & \vdots \\ y_0(q) & \cdots & y_n(q) & \cdots & y_{N-1}(q) \\ \vdots & & \vdots & & \vdots \\ y_0(Q-1) & \cdots & y_n(Q-1) & \cdots & y_{N-1}(Q-1) \end{pmatrix} \qquad (5)$$

In actual using of the weighted ATR receiver for positioning applications, reference data signals and weight training data sequence can be combined into a whole one, i.e., reference data signals with the number of N_r can be taken as the training data sequence of MMSE weight estimation, so certain transmission power can be saved, and the data transmission efficiency also can be improved.

5   Performance Simulation under Multipath Channel

Considering indoor positioning applications as a example in this paper, IEEE CM3 (4 ~ 10m, NLOS) of UWB indoor multipath channel is taken as a model, for single user, in the condition of ideal synchronization and additive-white-Gaussian-noise (AWGN) in channel, we simulated the BER performances of proposed weighted ATR receiver and compared it with a common ATR receiver. The inter-frame interference (IFI) and inter-symbol interference (ISI) are not included because many actual wireless positioning applications work at low to medium bit rates (up to 1 Mbps), so the pulse repetition interval (PRI) is large enough to ignore IFI & ISI influences.

For other simulation parameters, the number of reference pulses is $N_r = 100$, the numbers of divided time segments are respectively $Q = 5$ and $Q = 10$, MMSE weight estimation method is employed. An individual weight training data sequence (pseudo-random sequence with the length of 64) is adopted for simplify simulation, which is put at the head of each frame of ATR sending data, i.e., MMSE weight estimation by using training sequence is carried out firstly, and then averaging, weighting and correlation demodulation are performed. Performance simulation results obtained by this way are shown in Fig. 3. For comparison purpose, the performance curves of a common ATR receiver with $N_r = 100$ are given simultaneously. In Fig. 3, we simply denote the proposed weighted ATR receiver as WATR, so WATR-100, $Q = 5$ and $Q = 10$ represents the weighted ATR receivers of $N_r = 100$, $Q = 5$ and $Q = 10$ respectively.

In Fig. 3, we can see that compared with a common ATR receiver of $N_r = 100$, Both weighted ATR receivers of $N_r = 100$, $Q = 5$ and $Q = 10$ have improved performance in BER by inhibiting noise product term. When BER is equal to 10^{-4}, WATR of $Q = 5$ receiver has about 0.7dB of SNR gain than ATR receiver, and WATR of $Q = 10$ receiver has about 1.2dB of gain than ATR receiver, which shows that the more the number Q of divided time segments, the better BER performance. But along with the increase of Q, the increment of obtainable gain is smaller, while the complexity of MMSE weight estimation increases.

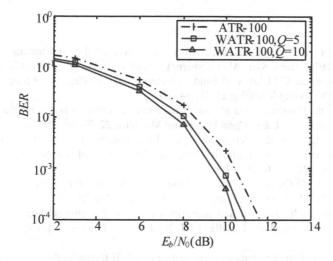

Fig. 3. Performance of weighted ATR receiver under CM3 multipath channel

In addition, in the lower SNR area of Fig. 3, WATR of $Q = 10$ is always better than WATR of $Q = 5$, and WATR of $Q = 5$ is also always better than ATR, which shows that this weighting method still can improve performance in the condition of low SNR but has smaller increment gain at this time. The case is partially because the error of weight coefficient estimated based on MMSE is larger when SNR is low, and when SNR increases, the weight coefficient estimated based on MMSE becomes more accurate, and the performance gain of the weighted ATR receiver gets larger.

6   Conclusion

In this paper, considering the multipath components segment distribution characteristic of ultra-wideband received signals, a novel weighted UWB averaged TR receiver for indoor positioning based on MMSE estimation is presented by using segmentation-weighting-combination idea. Each segment has different weight; larger weights are given to the segments with intensive distribution of multipath components; weight coefficients of segments are gotten by using MMSE estimate via training sequence; so the receiver has strong practicality and easy to realize. Because the noise product term is inhibited, the bit-error-rate performance of the receiver is efficiently improved compared with a common ATR receiver, and the conclusion is further proved correct by the performance simulation results under IEEE CM3 multipath channel. This receiver can be used for those wireless intelligent network applications with indoor positioning capability.

References

1. Liu, H., Darabi, H., Banerjee, P., Liu, J.: Survey of wireless indoor positioning techniques and systems. IEEE Trans. Syst., Man, Cybern. C, Appl. Rev. 37, 1067–1080 (2007)
2. Yang, L., Giannakis, G.: Ultra-Wideband communications: an idea whose time has come. IEEE Signal Processing Magazine 21, 26–54 (2004)
3. Gezici, S., et al.: Positioning via ultra-wideband radios: a look at positioning aspects for future sensor networks. IEEE Signal Processing Magazine 22, 70–84 (2005)
4. Choi, J.D., Stark, W.E.: Performance of Ultra-Wideband Communications With Suboptimal Receivers in Multipath Channels. IEEE Journal on Selected Areas in Communications 20, 1754–1766 (2002)
5. Franz, S., Mitra, U.: On optimal data detection for UWB transmitted reference system. In: Proc. GLOBECOM 2003 Conf., Francisco, USA, pp. 744–748 (2003)
6. Chao, Y., Scholtz, R.: Optimal and suboptimal receivers for ultra-wideband transmitted reference systems. In: Proc. GLOBECOM 2003 Conf., Francisco, USA, pp. 759–763 (2003)
7. Gang, Y., Jie, K., Ren, S.: Study of performance of UWB transmitted-reference receivers. Journal on Communications 26, 122–127 (2005)
8. Molisch, A., Foerster, J., Pendergrass, M.: Channel models for Ultra-wideband personal area networks. IEEE Wireless Communications Magazine 10, 14–21 (2003)
9. Foerster, J., et al.: Channel Modeling Sub-committee Report Final. P802.15-02/490r1-SG3a. IEEE P802.15 Wireless Personal Area Networks (2003)
10. Proakis, J.G.: Digital Communication, 4th edn. McGraw-Hill press, New York (2001)
11. Lahouti, F., Khandani, A.K.: Reconstruction of predictively encoded signals over noisy channels using a sequence MMSE decoder. IEEE Trans. Commun. 52, 1292–1301 (2004)

Multi-cell Joint Detection and Macrodiversity for TD-SCDMA Trunking System[*]

Xiaoxiang Shen[1], Hui Zhi[1], Shixiang Shao[1], and Meiling Ding[2]

[1] Wireless Communication Key Lab of Jiangsu Province
Nanjing University of Posts and Telecommunications
Nanjing, China
[2] ZTE Corporation
Shanghai, China
{sxx473623,zhihui.student}@163.com, shaosx@njupt.edu.cn,
ding.meiling@hotmail.com

Abstract. Broadcast transmission is used in the downlink for TD-SCDMA trunking systems in the same frequency and same time slot, so the MAI of multi-cell is very serious. In this paper, we discuss the classical joint detection algorithms used for interference suppression. Considering the characteristics of trunking system, we can consider multi-cell model as macro-diversity model, when users of target group are distributed in different cells. We simulate under three different channel models (described in section 2), and it is shown that joint detection and macro-diversity can significantly improve system performance. The impairing effect of error propagation on macro-diversity depends on the distribution of the target group.

Keywords: TD-SCDMA trunking system, multi-cell channel estimation, multi-cell joint detection, macro-diversity.

1   Introduction

Time Division-Synchronous Code Division Multiple Access (TD-SCDMA), which is an innovative mobile radio standard for the physical layer of a 3G air interface [1], is widely recognized in public communications because of its advanced technology and reasonable cost. Based on this, the digital trunking system with independent intellectual property rights is developed; it will help to expand the space of technology and industrial competitiveness for TD-SCDMA. In TD-SCDMA trunking system, since power control and downlink beamforming smart antenna technology can not be used and the scrambling of TD-SCDMA trunking system cell is short, the

---

[*] This paper is supported by Special Issues of Major National Science and Technology [2010ZX03001-002-02]; National 863 project [2009AA011302]; Special Issues of Major National Science and Technology [2009ZX03001-004-01].

P. Ren et al. (Eds.): WICON 2011, LNICST 98, pp. 225–233, 2012.

multiple access interference is very serious. So how to suppress MAI occupies a very important position in TD-SCDMA [2].

All along, the joint detection techniques are considered to be effective method for suppressing multiple access interference (MAI), and [3] showed that the Minimum Mean-Square-Error Block Linear Equalizer MMSE-BLE algorithm can effectively suppress MAI for CDMA system in the uplink. Considering the characteristics of trunking system, when there are users of target group in interference cells, signal of adjacent cells contains information of target groups, and so macrodiversity can improve the performance of system. This paper we propose a downlink multi-cell joint channel estimation method, two joint detection algorithms containing zero forcing block linear equalizer (ZF-BLE) and minimum mean square error block linear equalizer (MMSE-BLE), and maximum ratio combining for TD-SCDMA trunking system[4].

The rest of this paper is organized as follows. Section 2 introduces the system model as well as the channel estimation for TD-SCDMA trunking system multi-cell downlink. In section 3 the problem of classic joint detection algorithms in this system is analyzed. Section 4 described the performance of maximum ratio combining for this system. Simulations are carried out to evaluate the performance of the proposed scheme in section 5. In section 6 we analysis the results and describe the conclusions.

In the paper, vectors and matrices are in boldface. The symbols $(\bullet)^T, (\bullet)^H$ and $\|\bullet\|$ designate transposition, conjugate transposition, and the vector norm, respectively

2   System Model and Channel Estimation

In this section, the multi-cell models of TD-SCDMA trunking system downlink and channel estimation are introduced.

2.1   System Model

A block transmission TD-SCDMA system is considered in which k groups access the same channel at the same time and in the same frequency band. Each time slot consists of two data blocks, a midamble embedded between two data blocks for channel estimation, and a guard period, as shown in fig. 1.

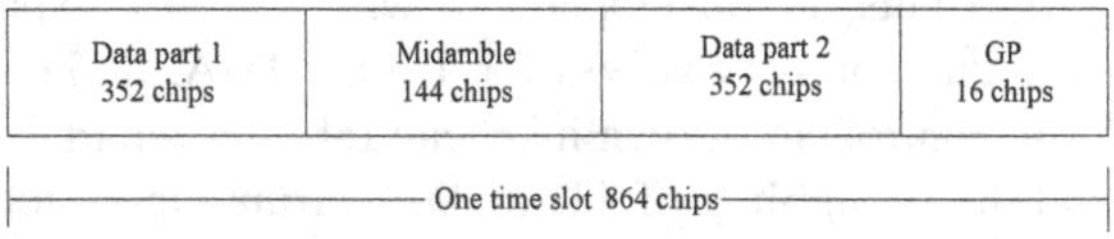

Data part 1 352 chips	Midamble 144 chips	Data part 2 352 chips	GP 16 chips

|————————— One time slot 864 chips —————————|

Fig. 1. Time slot structure in the TD-SCDMA system

In the following, only the first data part of each time slot is considered for simplicity. For the kth group, the transmitted data symbol can be represented as:

$$\mathbf{d}^{(k)} = \left(d_1^{(k)}, d_2^{(k)} \cdots d_N^{(k)} \right)^T \quad k = 1 \cdots K \tag{1}$$

Where, N is the number of data symbols in one data block. Each data symbol $d_n^{(k)}$ ($n = 1 \cdots N$), of group k is repeated 16 times and resulting 16-dimensional vector (OVSF) is multiplied element by the elements of the group-specific signature sequence;

$$\mathbf{c}^{(k)} = \left(c_1^{(k)}, c_2^{(k)}, \cdots c_{16}^{(k)} \right)^T \quad k = 1 \cdots K \tag{2}$$

In the downlink of single cell, a common midamble (eq.4) which is derived from a basic cell-specific midamble code (eq.3) is transmitted for all groups.

$$\mathbf{m}_{basic} = \left(m_1, m_2 \cdots m_P \right)^T \tag{3}$$

$$\mathbf{m} = \left(m_1, m_2 \cdots m_{P,} m_1 \cdots m_W \right)^T \tag{4}$$

Where, L is the number of path, which can be searched by terminal as strong-path. $W = 16$ is the maximum length of channel impulse responses and $P = L \times W$. Each of the L path channels is characterized by its impulse response

$$\mathbf{h}^{(l)} = \left(h_1^{(l)}, h_2^{(l)} \cdots h_W^{(l)} \right)^T \quad l = 1 \cdots L \tag{5}$$

In this paper, two interfering cells and one target cell are discussed, and assume that the transmit power of each base station is the equal.

In the downlink, each base station to the mobile terminal there is only one channel between a base station and the mobile terminal, so in our system model we just need estimate three channel paths, so $L = 3$.

2.2   Channel Estimation

The performance is very bad if Steiner algorithm employ in TD-SCDMA trunking system multi-cell, because signal for channel estimation of adjacent cells is processed as a white noise. In this paper, multi-cell joint channel estimation algorithm is discussed, which means that the transmission characteristics of strong-interference- cell (SIC) and target cell are estimated, and this can be divided into the following three steps:

2.2.1   Choose Strong-Interference-Cell (SIC)

As the mobile terminal is in constant, the SIC may change with time. We can select SIC by setting threshold: for example, assume the value which is 5 time of noise power is threshold. Whose power is greater than this value are considered as SIC. According to TD-SCDMA system, even if the mobile terminal moves in the speed of 120km/h, it can only move 1.6m in the time of one frame. Therefore we can confirm SIC once every many frames, in order to reduce computation. In this paper, assume that the number of SIC is fixed at two.

2.2.2   Multi-cell Joint Channel Estimation

When the channel impulse response is assumed to span with a maximum delay of W, the first $(W-1)$ chips of received midambles are contaminated by the data part preceding the midambles. Hence, the later P chips are selected for channel estimation, since they are completely determined by the midambles. The corresponding received part is expressed as:

$$\mathbf{e}_{mid} = \sum_{i=1}^{K_1} \mathbf{M}_1^{(i)} \mathbf{h}_1^{(i)} + \sum_{j=1}^{2} \sum_{i=1}^{K_2} \mathbf{M}_{j+1}^{(i)} \mathbf{h}_{j+1}^{i} + \mathbf{n}_{mid} \tag{6}$$

Where:

$$\mathbf{e}_{mid} = \left(\mathbf{e}_{W+1}, \mathbf{e}_{W+2} \cdots \mathbf{e}_{W+P} \right)^T \tag{7}$$

$$\mathbf{M}_i = \begin{Bmatrix} m_{W+1}^i & m_W^i & \cdots & m_2^i \\ m_{W+2}^i & m_{W+1}^i & \cdots & m_3^i \\ \vdots & \vdots & \ddots & \vdots \\ m_{W+P}^i & m_{W+P-1}^i & \cdots & m_{P+1}^i \end{Bmatrix} \tag{8}$$

$K_1 = 4$ is the number of active groups in target cell, and the number of SIC is $K_2 = 2$. The midambles and channel impulse response of all groups in a cell are the same.

Now, we define $\mathbf{G}$, which is made up of $\mathbf{M}$ of target cell and $\mathbf{M}$ of SIC:

$$\mathbf{G} = \left(\mathbf{M}_1, \mathbf{M}_2, \mathbf{M}_3 \right) \tag{9}$$

Eq.6 can be rewritten as:

$$\mathbf{e}_{mid} = \mathbf{G}\mathbf{h} + \mathbf{n}_{mid}$$

(10)

In the expression:

$$\mathbf{h} = \left[\left(\mathbf{h}^1 \right)^T , \left(\mathbf{h}^2 \right)^T , \left(\mathbf{h}^3 \right)^T \right]$$

(11)

Suppose the variance of noise n_{mid} is σ^2. By applying MMSE [5] criterion in the channel estimation, the channel impulse responses are estimated as eq. 12:

$$\hat{\mathbf{h}} = \left(\mathbf{G}^H \mathbf{G} + \sigma^2 \mathbf{I} \right)^{-1} \mathbf{G}^H \mathbf{e}_{mid}$$

(12)

2.3   Noise Reduction Processing

Noise reduction is introduced to remove unexpected noise taps. All the taps below the noise threshold are set to zero [6]. Here, assume that the threshold (χ) is changed with the channel transmission Characteristics. Three different channels are discussed in this paper, which are given Table 1 [7].

Table 1. Propagation Conditions for Multi-path Fading Environments

Case 1 speed 3km/h		Case 2 speed 3km/h		Case 3 speed 120km/h	
Relative Delay [ns]	Average power [db]	Relative Delay [ns]	Average power [db]	Relative Delay [ns]	Average power [db]
0	0	0	0	0	0
2928	-10	2928	0	781	-3
		12000	0	1563	-6
				2344	-9

In case 1, χ is the second biggest of the $\hat{\mathbf{h}}$, in case 2 is third and in case 3 is fourth. $\hat{\mathbf{h}}$ after noise reduction are denoted as $\hat{\mathbf{h}}_i$.

3   Data Estimation Techniques

As we can know from eq. 2 and eq. 12, MAI arises due to impaired orthogonality between OVSF codes under channel distortion. The combined channel impulse response with code spreading is defined by convolution:

$$\mathbf{b}_i^{(k)} = \mathbf{c}^{(k)} * \hat{\mathbf{h}}_i = \left(b_{1,i}^{(k)}, b_{2,i}^{(k)} \cdots b_{16+W-1,i}^{(k)} \right)^T \begin{cases} i=1,2,3 \\ k=1 \cdots K \end{cases}_i . \tag{13}$$

The received data signal e of mobile terminal can be written as:

$$\mathbf{e} = \mathbf{Ad} + \mathbf{n}$$

$$= \left(\mathbf{A}^1, \mathbf{A}^2, \mathbf{A}^3 \right) \begin{pmatrix} \mathbf{d}_1 \\ \mathbf{d}_2 \\ \mathbf{d}_3 \end{pmatrix} + \mathbf{n} \tag{14}$$

Where, system matrix $\mathbf{A}^i$ of i-th cell is defined in eq. 15, $\mathbf{d}_i$ is the summed data for all groups of i-cell , and $\mathbf{n}$ is the additive white Gaussian noise (AWGN) vector.

$$\mathbf{A}_{16(n-1)+t;n+16(k-1)}^i = \begin{cases} b_t^k & \begin{aligned} & k=1 \cdots K_i; n=1 \cdots N; \\ & t=1 \cdots (16+W-1) \end{aligned} \\ 0 & \text{others} \end{cases} \tag{15}$$

3.1   Whitening Matched Filter

Although the MF treats ISI and MAI as noise, it is introduced here, because all data estimation techniques presented in the following, which take into account both ISIand MAI can be interpreted as an extension of the MF. The continuous valued estimate of d_{MF} is given by:

$$\mathbf{d}_{MF} = \mathbf{A}^H \mathbf{e} \tag{16}$$

3.2   Zero-Forcing Block Linear Equalizer

Joint Detection is implemented in TD-SDMA as a key technique. The system model can be written as eq. 15, where matrix A consists of spreading codes, scrambling code and channel impulse responses obtained by channel estimator described in section 2. ZF-BLE algorithm presented in [3] lead can be expressed as:

$$\mathbf{d}_{ZF-BLE} = \left(\mathbf{A}^H \mathbf{A} \right)^{-1} \mathbf{A}^H \mathbf{e} \tag{17}$$

3.3   Minimum Mean-Square-Error Blocvk Linear Equalizer

Minimum mean square error criterion is to make $E(|\,d_{MMSE-BLE}-d\,|^2)$ tending to zero as much as possible, so $d_{c,MMSE-BLE}$ can be re-described as:

$$d_{c,MMSE-BLE} = (A^H A + \sigma^2 I)^{-1} A^H y \qquad (18)$$

4   Macrodiversity

In this method, we assume users of target group distributed in different cell, so base stations transmit the signal of target group simultaneously. Based on this, we can kwon signal that users of target group receive from neighbor cell is useful instead of interference, which can strengthen the useful signal and lower the interference.

We assume that receiver of target group can keep signals synchronization, so we can think maximum ratio combination can improve the performance of the system

$$d_{out} = \sum_{i=1}^{a} \lambda_i d_i \qquad .(19)$$

Where, a is the number of SIC which contains the users of target group, and λ_i is weighting coefficient of i-cell, and d_i is output of i-cell using an algorithm above-mentioned.

5   Simulation Results

In this section, the performance of three data estimation techniques introduced in section 3 and macro-diversity introduce in section 4 is analyzed by simulations for transmission over mobile radio channel mentioned in Table 1. We assume base stations transmit data to K_i active groups (K_i of target cell is 4, and SIC is 2), at the same time and QPSK modulation is used at transmitters.

As depicted in Fig. 2, since we assume that path loss of each base station to the terminal is equal, inter-cell MAI is very serious. We can see that joint detection (MMSE-BLE and ZF-BLE) can significantly improve system performance, and the performance of MMSE-BLE is slightly better than ZF-BLE in all three cases.

As we can see form Fig2-4, when macro-diversity exist, target groups is distributed more cells, the performance of system is better, and performance of MMSE-BLE is higher than ZF-BLE by about 0.5-1db.

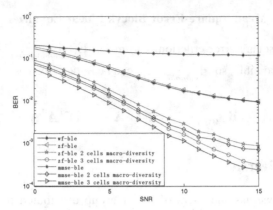

Fig. 2. The performance curves of system in case 1

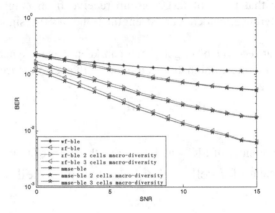

Fig. 3. The performance curves of system in case 2

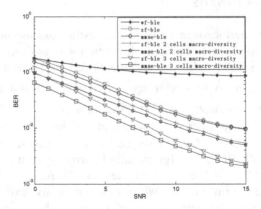

Fig. 4. The performance curves of system in case 3

6   Conclusion

In this paper, we first introduce a channel estimation method which is for downlink multi-cell model, and then two detection techniques have been presented performing channel equalization in TD-SCDMA trunking system, at last according to the characteristics of trunking system, we proposed that diversity combining technique is used for trunking system. Simulation results show that the macro-diversity further improves the system on the basis of joint detection.

References

1. Li, B., Xie, D., Chen, S., Zhang, P., Zhu, W., Li, B.: Recent Advances on TD-SCDMA in China. IEEE Communications Magazine 43(1), 30–37 (2005)
2. 3GPP TR 25.928 V4.0.1: 1.28 Mcps Functionality for UTRA TDD Physical Layer (March 2001)
3. Klein, A., Kaleh, G.K., Baier, P.W.: Zero Forcing and Minimum-Mean-Square Error Equalization for Multiuser Detection in Code-Division Multiple-Access Channels. IEEE Transactions on Vehicular Technology 45(5), 276–287 (1996)
4. Yue, L., Johnson, D.H.: Type-based detection in macro-diversity reception for mobile radio signals. In: IEEE International Conference on Acoustics, Speech, and Signal Processing (ICASSP 1997), vol. 5, pp. 4013–4016 (1997)
5. Dietrich, F.A., Utschick, W.: Pilot-assisted channel estimation based on second-order statistics. IEEE Trans. Signal Process. 53(3), 1178–1193 (2005)
6. Weber, T., Meurer, M.: Iterative multiuser detection for TD-SCDMA exploiting data estinate refinement techniques. In: Proc. IEEE 56th Vehicular Technology Conference (VTC 2002), Vancouver, vol. 3, pp. 1642–1646 (2002)
7. 3GPP TS 25.221 V.7.3.0-2007: Physical channels and mapping of transport channels onto physical channels (TDD)

New Half-Voting Cooperative Sensing Algorithms in Cognitive Radio

Haijun Wang, Yi Xu, Xin Su, Jie Zeng, and Jing Wang

Department of Electronic Engineering, Tsinghua University, Beijing, China
{wanghj02,yi-xu07}@mails.tsinghua.edu.cn,
{suxin,zengjie,wangj}@tsinghua.edu.cn

Abstract. In cognitive radio (CR) networks, hard fusion is widely applied for cooperative energy spectrum sensing, since it requires only one bit to transmit the decision results between sensing nodes and the sensing station. And half-voting is an effective algorithm in hard fusion. In this paper, two half-voting algorithms are proposed to enhance the sensing performance. In the first half-voting algorithm, we adopt linear data fusion with weights based on the SNR of each sensing node. In another algorithm, when the sensing station has no knowledge of each sensing node's SNR, the history decisions are utilized to estimate the weight factors. Analyses and numerical results show that the proposed new half-voting algorithms can significantly improve the sensing performance.

Keywords: cognitive radio, energy spectrum sensing, hard fusion, half-voting, linear data fusion.

1 Introduction

Recently, cognitive radio (CR) has emerged as a potential wireless communication technology to enhance spectrum usage efficienc by detecting and utilizing the spectrum holes [1]. And the first challenge of CR is spectrum sensing. Among the three main types of spectrum sensing: energy detection, matched filter detection and cyclostationary detection [2], energy detection has been widely applied since it doesn't require the priori knowledge of the primary users' signals..

However, the individual energy sensing performance suffers from the interference factors such as multi-path propagation and the shadow effect of the wireless channels. Therefor, many cooperative energy spectrum sensing algorithms have been proposed to tackle this problem. The cooperative sensing algorithms in CR networks can be mainly divided into soft fusion and hard fusion [3]. [4] studied the half-voting algorithm based twice cooperative spectrum sensing. [5] discussed the optimum number of sensing nodes in cooperative hard fusion spectrum sensing. [6] developed a partial spectrum sensing algorithm with decision result prediction and decision result modification techniques. [7] proposed a new decision combination scheme, in which the credibility of local spectrum sensing is taken into account to make the final decision. The linear cooperative algorithms with different weight factors were discussed in [8]~ [10]. These studies showed

P. Ren et al. (Eds.): WICON 2011, LNICST 98, pp. 234–242, 2012.
© Institute for Computer Sciences, Social Informatics and Telecommunications Engineering 2012

that although the soft fusion scheme could provide better sensing performance, the hard fusion scheme(requiring only one bit to transmit the decision result), especially the half-voting algorithm, is more practical with limited transmission resources.

In this paper, we propose two new half-voting algorithms for cooperative sensing which combine the advantages of linear soft fusion and traditional hard fusion algorithms. In the first algorithm, the SNR of each sensing node is used to obtain the weight factors for the linear fusion. When the sensing station has no knowledge of sensing nodes' SNRs, we propose another algorithm, which adopts the history decisions to estimate the weight factors.

The rest of this paper is organized as follows. In Section 2, the system model is introduced, then the cooperative sensing algorithms are discussed. In Section 3, we propose two half-voting algorithms for cooperative sensing and analyze their performance. Simulation results and analyses are given in Section 4. Conclusions are drawn in Section 5.

2 Energy Spectrum Sensing

2.1 Energy Sensing Model

In energy sensing, the sensing node detects M consecutive samples in the primary user's band each time:

$$Y[i] = \begin{cases} N[i], & H_0 \\ h * X[i] + N[i], & H_1 \end{cases} \tag{1}$$

where $N[i]$ is the noise of the i-th sample (here it is assumed that the noise is i.i.d. Gaussian white noise and $N[i] \sim \mathcal{N}(0, \sigma^2)$); $X[i]$ is the licensed user's signal at the i-th sample; $Y[i]$ is the signal detected by the cognitive sensing node; and h is the channel gain. Binary hypothesis is adopted here: H_0 indicates that there is no licensed user's signal, i.e. the band is idle; while H_1 indicates that the licensed user is using the band.

The objective of energy sensing is to decide whether H_0 or H_1 is true by sensing the energy of signal Y. The output of the energy detector is:

$$T = \frac{1}{M} \sum_{i=1}^{M} |Y[i]|^2 \tag{2}$$

According to the central limit theorem, when M is large enough, T is approximately Gaussian distributed. The mean and variance of T are given as [11]:

$$E(T) = \begin{cases} \sigma^2, & H_0 \\ \sigma^2 + P, & H_1 \end{cases} \tag{3}$$

$$Var(T) = \begin{cases} \frac{1}{M} 2\sigma^4, & H_0 \\ \frac{1}{M} 2\sigma^4 + \frac{1}{M} 4\sigma^2 P, & H_1 \end{cases} \tag{4}$$

where $P = \frac{1}{M}|h^2|\sum_{i=1}^{M}|X[i]|^2$ is the signal energy detected by the cognitive sensing node; $E(\cdot)$ and $Var(\cdot)$ denote mean and variance, respectively.

In energy sensing, a threshold η is predefined. If $T \geq \eta$, H_1 is true, which indicates the primary user is using the current band. On the contrary, if $T < \eta$, H_0 is true, which implies the band is currently idle. The detection probability (P_d) and false alarm probability (P_f) can be obtained by the following formulae:

$$P_d = P(T \geq \eta \mid H_1) = Q(\frac{\eta - E(T \mid H_1)}{\sqrt{Var(T \mid H_1)}}) \tag{5}$$

$$P_f = P(T \geq \eta \mid H_0) = Q(\frac{\eta - E(T \mid H_0)}{\sqrt{Var(T \mid H_0)}}) \tag{6}$$

where $Q(\eta) = \frac{1}{\sqrt{2\pi}}\int_{\eta}^{\infty}e^{-x^2/2}dx$ is the cumulative distribution function of Gaussian distribution. And $1 - P_d$, which stands for the collision probability between the licensed user and cognitive user, cannot exceed a given threshold in the interweave CR networks.

2.2   Cooperative Spectrum Sensing

Due to the interference factors such as multi-path propagation and shadow effect in wireless channels, energy sensing conducted by single cognitive sensing node with low SNR of the received signal may be unreliable [3]. This problem can be eased by cooperative sensing strategies. Fig.1 illustrates the shadow effect and the advantage of cooperative sensing. Apparently, sensing node 2 suffers from severe shadow effect and is not able to detect the licensed user's signal individually. But if combining the data collected by sensing node 1 and 2, sensing station is able to identify that the spectrum is currently occupied by the licensed user.

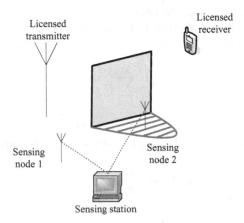

Fig. 1. The shadow effect and cooperative sensing [3]

In soft fusion algorithms, the sensing nodes send soft information (e.g. likelihood ratio or received signal power) to the sensing station. For hard fusion, the sensing nodes individually make binary decisions of whether the band is busy or idle by comparing the received power level to a threshold level. Then each binary decision will be transmitted to the sensing station with one bit. In both soft and hard schemes, the sensing station makes an overall decision based on the collected individual information under certain rules. In this paper we use half-voting rule [6] as our cooperative algorithm. That means the final decision is H_1 only when more than half of the total sensing nodes support H_1.

3   New Half-Voting Cooperative Sensing Algorithms

As discussed in Section 1, soft fusion cooperative algorithms can remarkably improve the sensing performance. In comparison, the hard fusion scheme requires only one bit to transmit the decision result between a sensing node and the sensing station. In this section, we propose two half-voting algorithms which contain the minimum transmission overhead and adopt the linear soft fusion scheme with weight factors to enhance the sensing performance.

3.1   Half-Voting Algorithm with Weights Based on SNRs

Denoting the individual decision of the i-th sensing node as d_i, where $d_i = 0$ (individual decision supports H_0) or 1 (individual decision supports H_1), the set of decision results received by the sensing station is $\{d_1, d_2, \cdots, d_N\}$ (N is the sensing nodes' number). The final cooperative decision result is denoted as $\bar{H}_1$ and $\bar{H}_0$. The traditional hard fusion scheme of half-voting can be written as:

$$D = \begin{cases} \sum_{i=1}^{N} d_i < \frac{N}{2}, & \bar{H}_0 \\ \sum_{i=1}^{N} d_i \geq \frac{N}{2}, & \bar{H}_1 \end{cases} \tag{7}$$

In fact, (7) can be regarded as a linear average weighted cooperative sensing algorithm since each weight factor of d_i is 1. It can be proved that that accounting for higher received SNRs and increasing weight factors accordingly can remarkably improve the cooperative sensing performance. Thereby, we propose a new half-voting algorithm whose weight factors are based on SNRs:

$$\bar{D} = \begin{cases} \sum_{i=1}^{N} \omega_i d_i < \frac{1}{2}, & \bar{H}_0 \\ \sum_{i=1}^{N} \omega_i d_i \geq \frac{1}{2}, & \bar{H}_1 \end{cases} \tag{8}$$

where $\omega_i = \frac{SNR_i}{\sum_{i=1}^{N} SNR_i}$. Here we assume the sensing station has full knowledge of the SNR information of the sensing nodes. The essence of (8) is that the sensing nodes with higher SNRs have greater impacts on the final decision.

Obviously $d_i, i = 1, 2, \ldots, N$, satisfies Bernoulli distribution and the probability is

$$P(d_i = 1) = \begin{cases} P_{f,i}, & H_0 \\ P_{d,i}, & H_1 \end{cases} \tag{9}$$

$$P(d_i = 0) = \begin{cases} 1 - P_{f,i}, & H_0 \\ 1 - P_{d,i}, & H_1 \end{cases} \tag{10}$$

where $P_{d,i}$ and $P_{f,i}$ are the detection probability and false alarm probability of the i-th sensing node. When N is large enough, $\bar{D}$ is approximately Gaussian distributed. The mean and variance of $\bar{D}$ are given as:

$$E(\bar{D}) = \begin{cases} \sum_{i=1}^{N} \omega_i P_{f,i}, & H_0 \\ \sum_{i=1}^{N} \omega_i P_{d,i}, & H_1 \end{cases} \tag{11}$$

$$Var(\bar{D}) = \begin{cases} \sum_{i=1}^{N} \omega_i^2 (P_{f,i} - P_{f,i}^2), & H_0 \\ \sum_{i=1}^{N} \omega_i^2 (P_{d,i} - P_{d,i}^2), & H_1 \end{cases} \tag{12}$$

So the cooperative detection probability $\bar{P}_d$ and false alarm probability $\bar{P}_f$ can be obtained in the same way as (5) and (6).

From (3) and (4), each T_i has the same mean and variance under H_0, so each node's false alarm probability $P_{f,i}$ determined by (6) is the same with the given threshold η. Here we denote $P_{f,i} = \alpha$ and (11) can be rewritten as

$$E(\bar{D}) = \begin{cases} \alpha, & H_0 \\ \sum_{i=1}^{N} \omega_i P_{d,i}, & H_1 \end{cases} \tag{13}$$

It's mathematically prohibitive to strictly prove that the proposed weighted half-voting algorithm (8) provides better performance than the traditional one (7). However, this advantage offered by (8) can be analyzed intuitively by (13). Under H_0, $E(\bar{D})$ is a constant despite of the choice of ω_i. Moreover, from (3), (4), (5), and the properties of $Q(\cdot)$, the sensing node with higher SNR will accordingly have higher $P_{d,i}$ with the fixed threshold η under H_1. Thereby, with sensing nodes of higher SNR allocated with greater weight factors, the $E(\bar{D})$ under H_1 could be greatly increased, which results in significant improvement of $\bar{P}_d$ but slightly increasing of $\bar{P}_f$.

3.2 Half-Voting Algorithm with Estimated Weights

(8) assumes that the sensing station accurately knows the SNR of each sensing node. However, this assumption may not be satisfied for two reasons: first, it's difficult to obtain the SNRs, since the sensing node has no priori information of the licensed user's signals and also there is not any cooperation between the sensing nodes and primary user; second, there may not be sufficient channels between the sensing nodes and sensing station for transmitting the information of SNRs in real-time. Therefore, we propose another half-voting algorithm whose weight factors are estimated by the history decision results.

To simplify the discussion, we suppose that the licensed user's state H has constant probability of busy (H_1) or idle (H_0). Denoting $P(H = H_1) = \varepsilon$, we obtain

$$P(\bar{H}_1) = P(\bar{H}_1 \mid H = H_1)P(H = H_1)$$
$$+P(\bar{H}_1 \mid H = H_0)P(H = H_0)$$
$$= \bar{P}_d\varepsilon + \bar{P}_f(1 - \varepsilon) \tag{14}$$

The bayesian posteriori probability of the licensed user's state $H = H_1$ under the final cooperative decision $\bar{H}_1$ is:

$$P(H = H_1 \mid \bar{H}_1) = \frac{P(\bar{H}_1 \mid H = H_1)P(H = H_1)}{P(\bar{H}_1)}$$

$$= \frac{\bar{P}_d\varepsilon}{\bar{P}_d\varepsilon + \bar{P}_f(1 - \varepsilon)} \tag{15}$$

Similarly,we have

$$P(H = H_0 \mid \bar{H}_1) = \frac{\bar{P}_f(1 - \varepsilon)}{\bar{P}_d\varepsilon + \bar{P}_f(1 - \varepsilon)} \tag{16}$$

Hence conditioned on the final cooperative decision $\bar{H}_1$, the i-th sensing node's probability of individual decision $d_i = 1$ is

$$P(d_i = 1 \mid \bar{H}_1) = \frac{\bar{P}_d\varepsilon}{\bar{P}_d\varepsilon + \bar{P}_f(1 - \varepsilon)}P_{d,i}$$

$$+ \frac{\bar{P}_f(1 - \varepsilon)}{\bar{P}_d\varepsilon + \bar{P}_f(1 - \varepsilon)}\alpha \tag{17}$$

For each sensing node, $\bar{P}_d$, $\bar{P}_f$, ε and α are the same. Since higher SNR_i corresponds to higher $P_{d,i}$, (17) indicates the probability of $d_i = 1$ will be larger if and only if the i-th sensing node has higher SNR compared with other sensing nodes. So this probability can be applied to estimate weight factors. Here we construct the weight factors of (8) as:

$$\omega_i = \frac{P(d_i = 1 \mid \bar{H}_1)}{\sum_{i=1}^{N} P(d_i = 1 \mid \bar{H}_1)} \tag{18}$$

Under the assumption that the received signal powers or SNRs do not change over a number of sensing slots (which is reasonable when the sensing slot is quite short or the channel between sensing nodes and primary user changes slowly), we can approximately calculate the probability of $d_i = 1$ under the final cooperative decision $\bar{H}_1$ by using history decision results. Set $S = \{s_1, s_2, ..., s_N\}$ to record history decision results. At the beginning $s_i = 1$ and when the final cooperative decision is $\bar{H}_1$, $s_i = s_i + d_i$. Then the weight factors in (18) can be approximately calculated as follow:

$$\omega_i = \frac{s_i}{\sum_{i=1}^{N} s_i} \tag{19}$$

4   Simulation Result and Analyses

To evaluate the proposed half-voting algorithms for cooperative sensing in CR networks, numerical simulations are conducted and the results are shown in Fig.2-Fig.3. In our simulation, $\sigma^2 = 1$, $M = 64$.

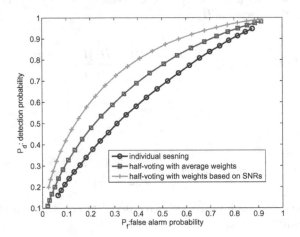

Fig. 2. P_d vs. P_f with different sensing algorithms, the number of the sensing nodes N is 10, and sensing nodes' received SNRs are set to be {-10.38, -14.77, -6.81, -16.89, -18.75, -13.80, -16.99, -14.16, -13.80, -12.22} in dB

Fig.2 depicts the relationship between P_d and P_f with different hard fusion schemes. This figure shows that compared with the individual sensing and the traditional half-voting algorithm, the proposed half-voting algorithm with weight factors based on SNRs provides better performance. Hence performance-wise, when the sensing station has the knowledge of each sensing node's SNR, the proposed half-voting algorithm would be the best choice for the cooperation. It is worth noting that the bigger the gaps of sensing nodes' SNRs are, more performance gains can be obtained since in the new algorithm the sensing node with higher SNR will have much greater impact on the final decision.

Fig.3 portrays the relationship between P_d and P_f of different half-voting algorithms. These curves illustrate that the proposed algorithm with estimated weights can evidently improve the cooperative sensing performance compared with the traditional half-voting algorithm with average weights. And the simulation result also indicates that there is an obvious performance gap between the algorithm with weights based on SNRs and the one with estimated weights. This gap can be explained by the difference between the $P(d_i = 1 \mid \bar{H}_1)$ and the received SNR_i, especially when $\bar{P}_f$ is high in (17). So the sensing performance with weight factors based on SNRs is always better than that based on estimation.

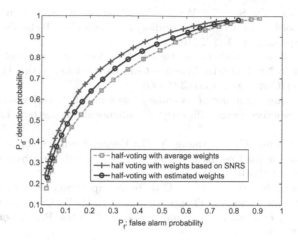

Fig. 3. P_d vs. P_f of different half-voting algorithms, the number of the sensing nodes N is 8, and sensing nodes' received SNRs are set to be {-12.73, -13.56, -7.78, -13.97, -17.44, -12.73, -10.96, -6.19} in dB

5   Conclusion

In this paper, we propose two half-voting algorithms for cooperative sensing in CR networks. In the first algorithm, the linear soft fusion scheme is adopt with weights based on the SNR of each sensing node. In another half-voting algorithm, when the sensing station has no knowledge of each sensing node's SNR, we calculate the weight factors with estimators which are consistent with the SNRs. These estimators can be obtained by the history decision results. We analyze and demonstrate the proposed half-voting algorithms can considerably improve sensing performances . Simulation results show that the performance of the algorithm with weights based on SNRs can offer significant performance gains compared with the traditional one. And when the sensing station has difficulty to obtain the information of the sensing nodes' SNRs, the half-voting algorithm with estimated weights can be adopted to improve the sensing performance.

Acknowledgement. This paper is supported by the China "863" project-No.2007AA01Z289, National Natural Science Foundation of China-No.60832008 and National Basic Research Program of China-No.2007CB310608.

References

1. Goldsmith, A., Jafar, S.A., Maric, I., Srinivasa, S.: Breaking Spectrum Gridlock With Cognitive Radios: An Information Theoretic Perspective. Proceedings of the IEEE 97(5), 894–914 (2009)
2. Haykin, S.: Cognitive radio: Brain-empowered wireless communications. IEEE Journal on Selected Areas in Communications 23(2), 201–220 (2005)

3. Wang, H., Xu, Y., Su, X., Wang, J.: Cooperative Spectrum Sensing with Wavelet Denoising in Cognitive Radio. In: Vehicular Technology Conference (VTC 2010-Spring), pp. 1–5 (2010)
4. Li, L., Lu, Y., Zhu, H.: Half-Voting Based Twice-Cooperative Spectrum Sensing in Cognitive Radio Networks. In: Wireless Communications, Networking and Mobile Computing, WiCom 2009, pp. 1–3 (2009)
5. Chen, Y.: Optimum number of secondary users in collaborative spectrum sensing considering resources usage efficiency. Communications Letters 12(12), 877–879 (2008)
6. Chien, W.-B., Yang, C.-K., Huang, Y.-H.: Energy-Saving Cooperative Spectrum Sensing Processor for Cognitive Radio System. Circuits and Systems I: Regular Papers PP(99), 1 (2010)
7. Peng, Q., Zeng, K., Wang, J.: A Distributed Spectrum Sensing Scheme based on Credibility and Evidence Theory in Cognitive Radio Context. In: IEEE 17th International Symposium on Personal, Indoor and Mobile Radio Communications, pp. 1–5 (September 2006)
8. Quan, Z., Cui, S., Sayed, A.H.: Optimal Linear Cooperation for Spectrum Sensing in Cognitive Radio Networks. IEEE Journal of Selected Topics in Signal Processing 2(1), 28–40 (2008)
9. Shen, B., Kwak, K., Bai, Z.: Optimal Linear Soft Fusion Schemes for Cooperative Sensing in Cognitive Radio Networks. In: Global Telecommunications Conference, pp. 1–6 (2009)
10. Shen, B., Huang, L., Zhao, C., Kwak, K., Zhou, Z.: Weighted Cooperative Spectrum Sensing in Cognitive Radio Networks. In: Convergence and Hybrid Information Technology, vol. 1, pp. 1074–1079 (2008)
11. Wang, H., Xu, Y., Su, X., Wang, J.: Cooperative Spectrum Sensing in Cognitive Radio under Noise Uncertainty. In: Vehicular Technology Conference (VTC 2010-Spring), pp. 1–5 (2010)

Fast Blind Spectrum Sensing Method Based on Multi-stage Wiener Filter

Zhiqiang Bao, Guangyue Lu, Gang Yang, and Huang Qingdong

School of Telecommunication and Information Engineering
Xi'an University of Posts and Telecommunications
Xi'an City, 710121, China
{baozhiqiang,gylu,yanggang,huangqingdong}@xupt.edu.cn

Abstract. Spectrum sensing is the key problem for cognitive radio systems. A fast blind sensing method on Multi-Stage Wiener Filter (MSWF) of the received signals is proposed to sense the available spectrum for the cognitive users with the help of the multiple antennas at the receiver of the cognitive users. The greatest advantage of the new method is that it requires no information of the noise power and without any eign-decomposition (or SVD). Both the simulation and the analytical results demonstrate that the proposed method is effective, and almost the same performance compare with the eigen-value based methods.

Keywords: Spectrum sensing, subspace projection, cognitive radio, random matrix theory.

1 Introduction

Cognitive radio (CR) [1] has recently emerged as a promising technology to increase the spectrum utilization in wireless communications. In a CR network, secondary users (SU) continuously sense the spectral environment, reliably detect weak primary signals over a targeted wide frequency band, and adapt transmission parameters (such as the transmitting power, modulation and coding scheme, carrier frequency, etc.) to opportunistically use the available spectrum. The typical sensing methods include the energy detector, the matched filter, the cyclostationarity feature detection, and so on.

The typical sensing methods required the knowledge of noise power, License Users' (LU) waveform or known patterns and signal cyclostationary feature. All the above methods need a subjectively pre-defined threshold, which affects the robustness of the methods.

Recently, some blind sensing algorithms are derived from the eigen-values of the covariance matrix. Among them, the detectors based on the sample covariance matrix, including the MME detector [2], MET detector [3], the information theoretic detector [4], [5], and DMM detector [6], have been recently proposed. All of them work well in the case of noise uncertainty, and can even perform better than the ideal ED (with perfect noise power estimate) when the detected signals are highly correlated.

P. Ren et al. (Eds.): WICON 2011, LNICST 98, pp. 243–253, 2012.

However, these methods suffer from the heavily computational load of the eigendecomposition, which may be unacceptable in real-time signal processing and large-dimension array system. To deal with this problem, a fast blind sensing method based on Multi-Stage Wiener Filter is proposed, which requires no information of the noise power and without any eigen-value decomposition (EVD). We also derive the threshold of our detector based on the random matrix theory.

2   Blind Spectrum Sensing Based on Multi-stage Wiener Filter

2.1   Array Model and Blind Sensing Algorithm Based on EVD

Multi-antenna is widely used in wireless communication due to its ability in improving the performance of the system. Here the multi-antenna is also served for sensing the LU signal.

Assume a uniform linear array is employed at the CR receiver side with M antennas. The array output data are

$$X(k) = A(\theta)S(k) + N(k) = \sum_{i=1}^{p} a(\theta_i)s_i(k) + N(k) \tag{1}$$

where $A(\theta) = [a(\theta_1) \, a(\theta_2) \cdots a(\theta_p)]$ is the steering vector of the array, $S(k) = [s_1(k) \, s_2(k) \cdots s_p(k)]^H$ is the signal-vector, and $N(k) = [n_1(k) \, n_2(K) \cdots n_M(k)]$ is the noise-vector. The covariance Matrix of output data is

$$R_{XX} = E[X(k)X^H(k)] = A(\theta)R_{SS}A(\theta)^H + R_{NN} \tag{2}$$

where $R_{SS} = E[S(k)S^H(k)]$ is the covariance of the signals, and H denotes the Hermitian Transpose. $R_{NN} = E[N(k)N^H(k)]$ is the noise covariance equal to $\sigma_n^2 I$ in Gaussian white noise. Here, we only consider the Gaussian white noise situation.

The EVD based methods are based on eigen-decomposition of the covariance matrix R, and the signal and noise subspace are obtained from the eigenvectors of eigen-values, $U_S = [u_1 \, u_2 \cdots u_p]$ and $U_N = [u_{P+1} \, u_{P+2} \cdots u_M]$, where $u_i \, (i = 1, \cdots, M)$ is the eigenvectors of R_{XX}. So R_{XX} can be expressed as

$$R_{XX} = U_S \Sigma_S U_S^H + U_N \Sigma_N U_N^H = \sum_{i=1}^{M} \lambda_i u_i u_i^H \tag{3}$$

where $\lambda_1 \geq \lambda_2 \geq \cdots \geq \lambda_p > \lambda_{P+1} = \lambda_{P+2} = \cdots = \lambda_M = \sigma_n^2$, if there are P LUs' signal impinging on the uniform linear array.

Once the eigen-values are obtained, some blind sensing algorithms can be derived[2], [3], [10].

A) MME detector: the ratio of largest eigen-value compared with the smallest eigen-value.

$$T_{MME} = \frac{\lambda_1}{\lambda_M} \overset{H_1}{\underset{H_0}{\overset{>}{<}}} \gamma_{MME} \tag{4}$$

B) MET detector: the ratio of largest eigen-value compared with the mean of all eigen-values.

$$T_{MME} = \frac{M\lambda_1}{Trace(R_{XX})} \overset{H_1}{\underset{H_0}{\overset{>}{<}}} \gamma_{MET} \tag{5}$$

C) DMM detector: the difference of largest eigen-value with the smallest eigen-value.

$$T_{DMM} = \lambda_1 - \lambda_M \overset{H_1}{\underset{H_0}{\overset{>}{<}}} \gamma_{DMM} \tag{6}$$

In noise only case, the covariance matrix R_{xx} is a Wishart random matrix. We can use the random matrix theory (RMT) to approximate the true CDF of detector based on largest and smallest eigen-values.

2.2   Fast Blind Sensing Algorithm Based on MSWF

The eigen-value based sensing methods for spectrum sensing has outstanding performance compared with other algorithms. However, these methods suffer from the heavily computational load of the eigen-decomposition. To deal with this problem, we use the Multi-Stage Wiener Filter technology to develop the fast and blind sensing algorithm. The multi-stage wiener filter (MSWF) technique is based on orthogonal projections, which was successfully used in adaptive beam-forming, adaptive reduced-rank interference suppression and space-time adaptive processing (STAP) . In our early work, it was adopted to develop the low complexity bearing estimation algorithms [11] successfully.

The MSWF was proposed by Goldstein et al [7] to find an approximate solution to the Wiener-Hopf equation which does not need the inverse of the covariance matrix. The MSWF algorithm is given by the following set of recursions:

Step1. Initialization: $d_0(k)$ and X0(k) = X(k)

Step2. Forward recursion: For $i = 1,2,\cdots,M$

$$h_i = E[d_{i-1}^*(k)X_{i-1}(k)] \Big/ \sqrt{\left|E[d_{i-1}^*(k)X_{i-1}(k)]\right|^2} \tag{7}$$

$$d_i(k) = h_i^H X_{i-1}(k) \tag{8}$$

$$B = null\{h_i\} = I_M - h_i h_i^H \tag{9}$$

$$X_i(k) = B_i^H X_{i-1}(k) \tag{10}$$

END FOR

Step3.Backward recursion: $e_M(k) = d_M(k)$

For $i = M, M-1, \cdots, 1$

$$w_i = E[d_{i-1}^*(k)e_i(k)] / E[|e_i(k)|^2] \tag{11}$$

$$e_{i-1}(k) = d_{i-1}(k) - w_i^* e_i(k) \tag{12}$$

END FOR

In this paper, we consider using the output data of an arbitrary array element as the reference signal which are easily obtained.

$$d_0(k) = x_i(k) = e_i^T A(\theta) S(k) + n_i(k) \tag{13}$$

where $e_i = [\underbrace{0\ 0 \cdots 1}_{i} 0 \cdots 0]^T$.

The covariance matrix can be tri-diagonalized by match filters. That is

$$R_d = H^H R_{X_0} H = \begin{bmatrix} \sigma_{d_1}^2 & \delta_2^* & 0 & \cdots & 0 \\ \delta_2 & \sigma_{d_2}^2 & \delta_3^* & \ddots & \vdots \\ 0 & \delta_3 & \sigma_{d_3}^2 & \ddots & 0 \\ \vdots & \ddots & \ddots & \ddots & \delta_M^* \\ 0 & \cdots & 0 & \delta_M & \sigma_{d_M}^2 \end{bmatrix} \tag{14}$$

where $H = [h_1\ h_2 \cdots h_M]$ is the matrix of match filters, $\sigma_{d_i}^2 = E[d_i(k)d_i^*(k)] = h_i^H R_{X_i} h_i$ represents the covariance of reference signal and $\delta_{i+1} = \sqrt{|E[X_i(k)d_i^*(k)]|^2} = \|r_{X_i d_i}\|_2$ is the module of ith cross-correlation vector. $\sigma_{d_i}^2$ is similar with the eigen-value λ_i . According to the $\sigma_{d_i}^2$, we can derived our blind sensing algorithm.

$$T_1 = \frac{\max\{\sigma_{d_i}^2 \mid i = 1,2,\cdots M\}}{\dfrac{1}{M-1}(\text{trace}(R_d) - \max\{\sigma_{d_i}^2 \mid i = 1,2,\cdots M\})} \underset{H_0}{\overset{H_1}{\gtrless}} \gamma \tag{15}$$

But in low SNR, the difference between $\sigma_{d_i}^2$ and the eigen-values λ_i is too large to be used for the detector. And also the detection threshold cannot be derived from the conclusion of random matrix theory. So get the estimation the largest eigen-value from tri-diagonal matrix R_d is the key problem. Using the conclusion in [8], we can find the bound of largest eigen-value of tri-diagonal matrix R_d , which has the same eigen-values of Rxx .

Theorem 1. Given a tri-diagonal matrix $A_{n \times n}$, the non-zero elements of A are all great than zero.

$$A = \begin{bmatrix} a_{11} & b_1 & 0 & \ddots & 0 \\ c_2 & a_{22} & b_2 & \ddots & \vdots \\ 0 & c_3 & \ddots & \ddots & 0 \\ \vdots & \ddots & \ddots & \ddots & b_{n-1} \\ 0 & \cdots & 0 & c_n & a_{nn} \end{bmatrix} \qquad (16)$$

Let $c_1 = b_n = 0$ and

(1) $a_i^{(m)} = c_i^{(m)} + a_{ii}^{(m)} + b_i^{(m)}, i = 1, 2, \cdots n$

(2) $r^{(m)} = \min_i a_i^{(m)}, R^{(m)} = \max_i a_i^{(m)}, m = 1, 2, \cdots$

(3) $D_m = diag\left(a_1^{(m)}, a_2^{(m)}, \cdots, a_n^{(m)}\right), m = 1, 2, \cdots$

(4) $A_{m+1} = D_m^{-1} A_m D_m, m = 1, 2, \cdots$ is the matrices sequence, which have the same eigen-values.

$$A_m = \begin{bmatrix} a_{11}^{(m)} & b_1^{(m)} & 0 & \ddots & 0 \\ c_2^{(m)} & a_{22}^{(m)} & b_2^{(m)} & \ddots & \vdots \\ 0 & c_3^{(m)} & \ddots & \ddots & 0 \\ \vdots & \ddots & \ddots & \ddots & b_{n-1}^{(m)} \\ 0 & \cdots & 0 & c_n^{(m)} & a_{nn}^{(m)} \end{bmatrix} \qquad (17)$$

If we set the stop condictions

$$\left| R^{(m)} - r^{(m)} \right| < \varepsilon \qquad (18)$$

So the largest eigen-value of Λ can be estimated iteratively [8].

$$\lambda_{\max}(A) = R^{(m)} \qquad (19)$$

The procedure of blind sensing based on MSWF is as followed:

Step1: Use the MSWF forward decomposition to compute the match filters $H = [h_1 \ h_2 \ \cdots h_M]$

Step2: Use equation (20) to get the tri-diagonal matrix R_d.

$$\begin{cases} \sigma_{d_i}^2 = E[d_i(k)d_i^*(k)], & i = 1, 2, \cdots M \\ \delta_{i+1} = \sqrt{E[X_i(k)d_i^*(k)]^2} = \|r_{x_i d_i}\|_2 \end{cases} \qquad (20)$$

Step3: According to Theorem 1, get the estimation of the largest eigen-value of tri-diagonal matrix $\boldsymbol{R}_d$.

Step4: Compute the detection statistics and compare with the threshold from equation (21).

$$T_2 = \frac{R^{(m)}}{\frac{1}{M-1}\left(\text{trace}\left(\boldsymbol{R}_{xx}\right) - R^{(m)}\right)} \overset{H_1}{\underset{H_0}{\gtrless}} \gamma \tag{21}$$

Remark 1. To estimate the largest eigen-value, our method merely requires $O(M^2N)$ complex products operations. However the EVD-based algorithms require $O(M^2N)$ complex products operations of estimating the covariance matrix and $O(M^3)$ decomposition operations. Thus the computation complexity of our method is significantly reduced.

2.3   Theoretic Analysis and the Threshold Determination

Practically, the statistical correlation matrix $\boldsymbol{R}_{xx}$ is estimated through a sample covariance matrix. Introduce N as the number of samples collected by each receiver during the sensing period. The $M \times M$ sample covariance matrix $\boldsymbol{R}_{xx}(N)$ is then defined as

$$\boldsymbol{R}_{xx}(N) = \frac{1}{N}\sum_{k=1}^{N} X(k)X^H(k) \tag{22}$$

Although $\boldsymbol{R}_{xx}(N)$ converges to $\boldsymbol{R}_{xx}$ as N tends to infinity, for finite N, its properties depart from those of the statistical covariance matrix, then the eigen-values of $\boldsymbol{R}_{xx}$ have the property that $\lambda_1 > \lambda_2 > \cdots > \lambda_p > \lambda_{P+1} > \lambda_{P+2} > \cdots > \lambda_M$. At low SNR, the performance of a sensing algorithm is very sensitive to the threshold. Since we have no information of the signal (actually we even do not know if there is signal or not) and noise, it is difficult to set the threshold based on the P_d. Hence, usually we choose the threshold based on the P_{fa}. We need to determine the behavior of eigen-values under null hypothesis, i.e., H_0.

In noise only case, the distribution of the largest eigen-value [9], [10] is described in the following Lemmas.

Lemma 1. Assume that the noise is complex.

Let $A(N) = \dfrac{N}{\sigma_n^2}R_{xx}(N)$, $\mu = \left(\sqrt{N} + \sqrt{M}\right)^2$ and $v = \left(\sqrt{N} + \sqrt{M}\right)\left(\dfrac{1}{\sqrt{M}} + \dfrac{1}{\sqrt{N}}\right)^{\frac{1}{3}}$.

Assume that $\lim\limits_{N\to\infty}\dfrac{M}{N} = \rho(0 < \rho < 1)$. Then $\dfrac{\lambda_{\max}(A(N)) - \mu}{v}$ converges (with probability one) to the Tracy-Widom distribution of order 2 (TW2) [9]. For the analytical formula of TW_2 refer to [9], and for the tables of its CDF refer to [10].

According to the lemmas, we can derive the threshold of our algorithm based on false alarm probability.

$$
\begin{aligned}
P_{fa} &= \Pr\left(\frac{\lambda_{max}(\boldsymbol{R}_{XX})}{\frac{1}{M-1}(\text{trace}(\boldsymbol{R}_{XX}) - \lambda_{max}(\boldsymbol{R}_{XX}))} > \gamma \right) \\
&= \Pr\left(\lambda_{max} > \frac{\gamma\,\text{trace}(\boldsymbol{R}_{XX})}{M-1+\gamma} \right) \\
&= \Pr\left(\frac{\sigma_n^2}{N}\lambda_{max}(A(N)) > \frac{\gamma\,\text{trace}(\boldsymbol{R}_{XX})}{M-1+\gamma} \right) \\
&= \Pr\left(\frac{\lambda_{max}(A(N)) - \mu}{v} > \frac{\gamma NM/(M-1+\gamma) - \mu}{v} \right) \\
&= 1 - F_2\left(\frac{\gamma NM/(M-1+\gamma) - \mu}{v} \right)
\end{aligned}
\tag{23}
$$

where $\text{trace}(\boldsymbol{R}_{XX}) = M\sigma_n^2$ is used.

So the threshold is

$$
\gamma = \frac{(M-1)\left(v F_2^{-1}(1-P_{fa}) + \mu \right)}{MN - v F_2^{-1}(1-P_{fa}) - \mu}
\tag{24}
$$

It can be seen that the threshold has nothing to do with the knowledge of noise power σ_n^2 and signal information, therefore our method is belong to blind sensing algorithm.

3   Simulation Results

To demonstrate the performance of the proposed methods, simulations are provided. A Uniform Linear Array (ULA) is used here with $M = 8$ sensors and half wavelength inter-element spacing. The QPSK signals are used in the simulations. The number of snapshots is 2048. In the following, all the results are averaged over 100000 Monte Carlo realizations.

Fig.1 shows our method, the T1 and T2 detectors' pdf of the received signal under H_1(SNR=-14dB) and H_0. From Fig.1 we can see that the pdf of T2 based on $R^{(m)}$ is more dispersed than $\sigma_{d_i}^2$ based T1 method, which demonstrates that our algorithm T2 works well at low SNR.

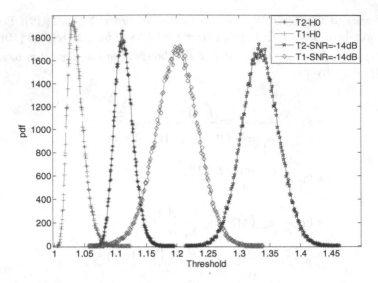

Fig. 1. Pdf of our method (T1 and T2 detectors)under H_0 and H_1

In fig.2, the ROC curves of of our method, MME [2] and DMM [6] method. are described at SNR=-16dB. It can be seen that our method (T2 detector) has outstanding performance compared with the eigen-value based algorithms.

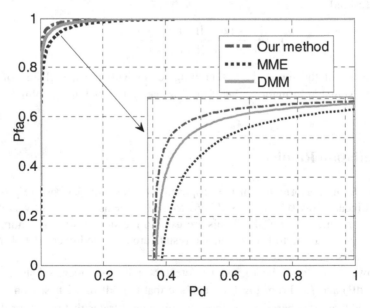

Fig. 2. ROC performance comparison (N=2048)

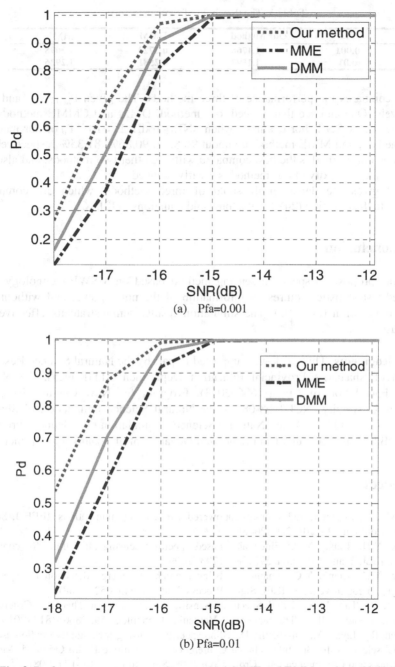

(a) Pfa=0.001

(b) Pfa=0.01

Fig. 3. Performance comparison of our method, MME and DMM method (*N*=2048)

Table 1. The threshold of three detectors

Pfa	Our Method	DMM	MME
0.001	1.1766	0.2723	1.3098
0.01	1.1597	0.2581	1.2936

Fig.3 compares the performance of three methods. The given P_{fa} is 10^{-3} and 10^{-2} respectively. One can see that, indeed, our method, DMM and CMME methods are well done at low SNR. For example, when SNR=-16dB, $P_{fa}=10^{-3}$, P_d of our method, DMM method, and MME method are about 96.83%, 90.86%, 81.35% respectively. It is clear that our method is the best compared with the other two methods, and also the computation complexity of our method is greatly reduced.

Table3 gives the detection threshold of three methods, which are computed according to the equation (24) and the threshold equations in [2], [6].

4   Conclusion

This paper proposes a spectrum sensing method based on MSWF technology. The employed test statistic requires no information of the noise power and without any eign-decomposition (or SVD). The simulation results demonstrate its effectiveness and robustness.

Acknowledgments. This work was supported in part by the Natural Science Research Program of Shaanxi's Provincial Education Department (11JK0925), the Nature Science Foundation of China (60602053), Program for New Century Excellent Talents in University (NCET-08-0891), the Natural Science Foundation of Shaanxi Province (2010JQ80241),the Natural Science Foundation of Hubei Province (2009CDB308) and the Fund from Education Department of Shaanxi Government.

References

1. Haykin, S.: Cognitive radio: brain-empowered wireless communications. IEEE J. Select. Areas Commun. 23, 201–220 (2005)
2. Zeng, Y.H., Liang, Y.C.: Eigenvalue based spectrum sensing algorithms for cognitive radio. IEEE Trans. Commun. 57, 1784–1793 (2009)
3. Zeng, Y.H., Liang, Y.C., Zhang, R.: Blindly combined energy detection for spectrum sensing in cognitive radio. IEEE Signal Process. Lett. 15, 649–652 (2008)
4. Wang, R., Tao, M.X.: Blind Spectrum Sensing by Information Theoretic Criteria for Cognitive Radios. IEEE Transactions on Vehicular Technology 59, 3806–3817 (2010)
5. Zayen, B., Hayar, A., Nussbaum, D.: Blind spectrum sensing for cognitive radio based on model selection. In: 3rd International Conference on Cognitive Radio Oriented Wireless Networks and Communications, CrownCom 2008, Singapore, pp. 15–17 (2008)
6. Wang, Y.X., Lu, G.Y.: DMM Based Spectrum Sensing Method for Cognitive Radio Systems. Journal of Electronics and Information Technology 32, 2571–2575 (2010)
7. Goldstein, J.S., Reed, I.S., Scharf, L.L.: A multistage representation of the Wiener filter based on orthogonal projections. IEEE Trans. Inf. Theory 44, 2943–2959 (1998)

8. Duan, F.J.: Bounds for the greatest eigenvalue of the three cornerwise matrix. Journal of Guilin Institute of Electronic Technology 21, 59–61 (2001)
9. Johnstone, I.: On the distribution of the largest eigenvalue in principal components analysis. Ann. Statist 29, 295–327 (2001)
10. Bejan, A.: Largest eigenvalues and sample covariance matrices, Tracy-Widom and Painleve II: computational aspects and realization in SPlus with applications (2005), http://www.vitrum.md/andrew/MScWrwck/TWinSplus.pdf
11. Bao, Z.Q., Wu, S.J., Zhang, L.R.: A Novel Algorithm for Joint Source-Number Detection and DOA Estimation. ACTA ELECTRONICA SINICA 34, 2170–2174 (2006)

A Distributed Resource Admission Control Mechanism Supporting Multicast and Heterogeneous Receivers for MANETs

Wei Wu[1,2], Jianli Guo[1,2], Xuan Zhu[3], Huixing Peng[3], Lianhe Luo[1,2], Changjiang Yan[1,2], and Yuebin Bai[3]

[1] Science and Technology on Information Transmission and Dissemination in Communication Networks Laboratory, Shijiazhuang, Hebei, 050081, China
[2] The 54th Research Institute of CETC, Shijiazhuang, Hebei, 050081, China
[3] School of Computer Science and Engineering, Beihang University, Beijing 100191, China
zhuxuan1989@gmail.com

Abstract. Resource admission control is widely introduced to control the network resources, schedule the resources and admit new services. Resource reservation protocol (RSVP) is a transport layer protocol designed to reserve resource across a network for an integrated services internet. RSVP makes an appointment for each flow and the information of status grows fast with the increase of flow number, it isn't suitable for Ad Hoc networks because the cost of connection maintenance is more expensive than establishment. In this paper, we introduce a distributed resource admission control mechanism for Ad Hoc networks (DRACM), which can adapt to dynamic changes in mobile Ad Hoc network by close to call or packet transmission time granularity. DRACM responses rapidly to re-routing, can re-build a resource reservation in minimal service degradation or least service interruption. Meanwhile, we adopt client-oriented control mechanism, can also support multicast and meet the heterogeneity of receivers.

Keywords: MANETs, resource admission control, multicast, heterogeneity.

1 Introduction

With the wide use of Internet technology, mobile communication technology and multimedia technology, mobile Ad Hoc network has great development recent years, and the requirements to transmit different types of services are increasing. Different types of services ranging from real-time multimedia services to data-transfer service to a fixed or mobile user are expected to be supported. For real-time applications, qualities of which are sensitive, it may cause instability while transmitting in mobile situation, one common idea to solve this problem is to use QoS guarantee mechanism.

Quality of service is the ability to provide different priorities to different applications, users, or data flows, or to guarantee a certain level of performance to a data flow. Quality of service guarantees are important if the network capacity is insufficient, especially for real-time streaming multimedia applications because they

P. Ren et al. (Eds.): WICON 2011, LNICST 98, pp. 254–264, 2012.

often require fixed bit rate and are delay sensitive. QoS guarantees are important in MANETs because the limitation of resource and dynamic changes of network topology.

Lajos Hanzo II. and Rahim Tafazolli propose that One of the most crucial components of a system for providing QoS assurances is admission control [1]. The purpose of admission control mechanism is to estimate the state of the network's resources and thereby to decide which application data sessions can be admitted without promising more resources than are available and thus violating previously made guarantees.

Mahmoud Pirhadi describes a resource and admission control architecture and QoS signaling scenarios in Next Generation Networks, he divided the QoS resource control process into three logical states [2]:

- Authorization: The QoS resource should be authorized for the new services first based on some rules.
- Reservation: The QoS resource should be reserved based on the authorized resource and resource availability.
- Commitment: The QoS resource is committed for the requested media flows when the admit decision is made.

Mobile Ad Hoc network has its own characteristics such as dynamic network topology, mobility and limited resource. So resource admission control for Ad Hoc networks should consider these factors, which can adapt to the network features.

In this paper, we proposed an INSIGNIA [3] protocol-based distributed resource admission control mechanism for Ad Hoc networks. INSIGNIA is an in-band signaling system for supporting quality of service in Ad Hoc networks. DRACM is based on INSIGNIA to send the resource admission control message in data packet header. We adopt the DiffServ approach to mark different types of services; only real-time services need resource reservation while best effort services don't. Meantime, we distribute the QoS calculation and resource control across multiple destination nodes; intermediate nodes only need simple operation and adjustments, so it can improve the efficiency of resource admission and not introduce too much cost in Ad Hoc networks.

The rest of this paper is organized as follows. Section 2 states related works about resource admission control recent years. Section 3 covers the design and trades off for our mechanism. Section 4 describes detail steps and multicast scenario of DRACM. Section 5 shows the analysis and discussion about DRACM. Section 6 shows the simulation results. And Finally, Section 7 concludes the whole paper as well as future work.

2   Related Works

The issue of QoS guarantee in MANETs has received a lot of attention lately due to its significance in terms of enabling the delivery of real-time services over these networks [4]. And various types of resource admission control mechanisms are proposed to achieve the issue.

Admission control mechanism is divided into stateless schemes and stateful ones. As a stateless scheme, SWAN [5] uses a probe packet to test a pre-discovered route when a new data session requires admission. P. A. Chaparro and J. Alcober [6] proposed a QoS framework supporting scalable video streaming in MANETs. They use a periodic probing process to measure the available bandwidth and the end-to-end delay on the path. The lack of state information storage at intermediate nodes means that they save memory and their operation can be less complex, but the lack of reservations at intermediate nodes reduces capabilities due to the lack of state information [1].

Stateful schemes mean intermediate nodes should store state information. INIGSIA [3] introduce a flexible in-band signaling system that supports fast reservation, restoration and adaptation. PDAC [7] builds upon the flow-state extensions of the latest version of DSR and each node only forwards the admission request if it has sufficient available capacity. Stateful schemes can store session state-related information in intermediate nodes so they can make admission decision which can improve the network response efficiency. But they may bring extra cost and methods of storing and refreshing service and nodes state.

In MANETs, the network topology and nodes state changes time to time, so we should trade off the resource admission control efficiency and network cost, as well as in multicast situation.

3   Design and Trades Off

3.1   Dynamic Resource Management in Ad Hoc Networks

The purpose of resource management is trying to improve resource utilization, and to the greatest degree of QoS to meet user expectations. In MANETs, it's better to adopt dynamic resource management mechanism to ensure efficient allocation of resource than static mechanism. The goal of dynamic resource allocation is to accept more services and ensure the traffic flow smoothly adapt to resource changes.

We allow resource reservation request to specify a range instead of a fixed value to deal with the problem that dynamic network characteristics cause. This QoS range is beneficial to the separation of routing and QoS maintenance, if the network needs to calculate a new routing due to the changes in network topology, the use of QoS range can increase the probability of routes maintenance within the scope of request rather than a fixed value. Dynamic resource management can only provide soft QoS guarantees that if route fails, re-routing is needed and QoSmin~QoSmax can dynamically adjusts to changes in network resources. A principle based on dynamic adaptive QoS management process is showed in Fig. 1.

When a new request for resource arrives, the network should consult whether it has enough resource to ensure the QoS that service requirements. If so, nodes reserve and allocate proper resource for the service; otherwise, the service would wait until there is enough available resource. After that, the service begins to transmit data in an appropriate flow rate. The whole network needs some schemes to monitor available resource to improve the efficiency of resource management.

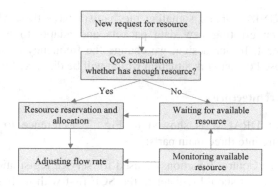

Fig. 1. Dynamic Adaptive QoS Management Based on Resource Admission Control

3.2   Distributed Resource Admission Control in DRACM

There are various QoS mechanisms so far to ensure service quality in networks. Early work used the "IntServ" philosophy of reserving network resource in which applications use the Resource Reservation Protocol (RSVP) to request and reserve resource through a network. But in this model, core routers would be required to accept, maintain, and tear down thousands or more reservations, so this approach would not scale with the growth of the Internet and the cost of network is huge.

The second and currently accepted approach is "DiffServ" or differentiated services. In this model, packets are marked according to the type of service they need. In response to these markings, routers and switches use various queuing strategies to tailor performance to requirements. The biggest advantage of DiffServ is scalability.

In order to distribute resource admission control cost in Ad Hoc networks, we adopt DiffServ approach. We distribute the QoS calculation and resource control across multiple destination nodes; intermediate nodes only need simple operation, so it can improve the efficiency of resource admission and not introduce too much cost in Ad Hoc networks.

3.3   Soft-State Adapting to Network Topology Changes

Another important factor is whether to choose soft-state or hard-state in our mechanism. Connection-oriented hard state isn't feasible in Ad Hoc network because it cannot adapt to dynamic changes of topology and resources. So we choose soft-state mechanism to adapt to the instability of wireless links, the random mobility of nodes and dynamic time that each session lasts.   Specially, we compare soft-state and hard-state as follows:

- Soft-state needs a timer while hard-state needn't;
- Soft-states can be automatically removed while hard-state can only be removed explicitly;
- When there is error or missing packets in the network, soft-state can adopt proper recovery action, while hard-state may stay in an unexpected state;
- Soft-state can adapt to the requirements of mobile networks but may introduce overhead because of periodic refreshment.

Soft-state in INSIGNIA in-band signaling mechanism have these characteristics, it refreshes only when creating new data packets and adapts to network topology changes at a low cost. In our design, we change the frequency of state refresh and resource request based on network situation which will be discussed in Section 5.

3.4   DRACM Architecture

The architecture of DRACM is showed in Fig. 2. Reference to [2], we divide DRACM architecture into three main parts:

- SCF (Service Control Functions) is used for service registration. When a new service arrives, it should register to the SCF first with its basic info, such as the needed bandwidth and other QoS requirements;
- RACF (Resource and Admission Control Functions) is the main function in this architecture. It consists of decision unit, QoS calculation unit, database and timer. Admission control decision unit is used to make decision that whether to admit the new service. QoS calculation unit is different between intermediate nodes and destination nodes, intermediate nodes only need to calculate bandwidth, but destination nodes need to calculate end-to-end QoS and compare them with user requirements. Database is used to store bandwidth information. Timer is important to calculate delay and control admission control status.
- TF (Transmit Function) is used to transmit data packets. Source node uses adaptive traffic controller to change data transition parameter as required. If route fails during transition, QoS routing unit would re-route immediately to adapt to dynamic changes in the network.

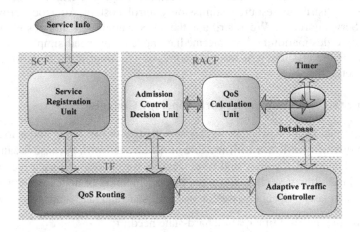

Fig. 2. DRACM Architecture

4   Resource Admission Control Mechanism and Scenarios

DRACM puts signaling message in the optional segment of IP header as an option. Table 1 shows the message format:

Table 1. DRACM Message Format

REQ/ RES	TOS	Max/ Min	Maxband	Minband	Metric		
					/	/	/

The REQ/RES segment indicates whether the message is a resource reservation request(REQ) message sent by the source node or a resource reservation response(RES) message sent by the destination node; TOS segment indicates the type of current service, BE(Best Effort) means the service doesn't need bandwidth authoritarian or reservation, RT(Real-Time) indicates that bandwidth calculation, authoritarian and reservation are required; Maxband and Minband are used to represent the bandwidth range that traffic flow needs, as we mentioned in Section III (A), we use a QoS range to adapt to dynamic resource changes inMANETs; Metric is used to record the ID of traffic and route information, such as bottleneck bandwidth, bottleneck node information and destination node information. Metric is an important segment for admission control along the whole multicast tree.

4.1 Source Node Sends a REQ Message

When a new service arrives, it should register to SCF of source node with its basic info, and then the source node will send a reservation request message along the multicast tree. For example, the reservation request message for a video service which requires a range of 50M~100M bandwidth is showed in Table 2, 1 presents the ID of video service, 12:00 presents the new service arrives at 12:00.

Table 2. Resource Reservation Request Message

REQ	RT	Max	100	50	Metric		
					1 12:00	/	/

4.2 Intermediate Node Receives the REQ Message

Intermediate node parses the first segment of REQ message as soon as receives it, REQ means it's a REQ message from the source node, RT means it's a real-time service so the node should calculate its bandwidth according to (1):

$$B_a = B_t - \sum_{i=1}^{n} B_{u_i} \tag{1}$$

B_t is the total bandwidth of the link, B_{u_i} represents the bandwidth that has been authorized or reserved, or has been occupied for data transmitting. All the bandwidth information should be stored in each node's database as Table 3 lists.

Table 3. Bandwidth Information Stored in Database

ID	Bandwidth	State	Info
2	20	Reserved	10.1.1.3
2	10	Reserved	10.1.1.5
3	10	Authorized	10.1.1.7
3	10	Authorized	10.1.1.9
4	30	Transmit	10.1.1.6

After calculating the available bandwidth, the intermediate node will do the following judgments:

If $B_a > 100M$, it will forward the message along the multicast tree without any change, then authorize 100M bandwidth to the appropriate service(service ID is 1) and insert a record in the database. Within a specified time (eg 10s), other service cannot occupy or reserve this part of bandwidth;

If $B_a < 50M$, which means the node cannot meet the minimum requirements of the service, so the node will prune and send a refuse message to the source, the refuse message should contain the node's info;

If $50M < B_a < 100M$, such as 80M, the node will check the "Min/Max" segment of REQ message. If the segment is "Max" which means it is the first bottleneck node, the node would replace "Max" by "Min", and add the node's information in the Point Info segment; Otherwise, the node would check the Metric segment of REQ message and compare its bandwidth with bottleneck bandwidth stored, it would update the REQ message by the smaller value and then authorize appropriate bandwidth to the service and insert a record in the database.

4.3   Destination Node Receives the REQ Message and Sends a RES Message

The REQ message information is continuously updated along the multicast tree until the destination node receives it. The whole link can meet the minimum require of the service if the destination node could receive the packet.

The destination node parses the REQ message to get the whole information of the route, including the bottleneck node, and the bottleneck bandwidth. The destination node calculates the end-to-end QoS(delay, jitter, packet loss rate etc),   then compares it with user's requirements, decides whether to accept or refuse   the service. If accept, the destination node would send a RES message to notify the source node to accept the service and inform the intermediate nodes to reserve proper bandwidth for the service. Otherwise, the destination node would prune and send a refuse message to the source with its information. A RES message is showed in Table 4. Both REQ and RES message obey the same format, but the destination node should add its node info in the Metric segment, which would be used for intermediate node in multicast situation.

Table 4. Resource Reservation Response Message

					Metric		
RES	RT	Min	100	50	1 12:00	80	DES: 10.1.1.1 Node: 10.1.1.5

4.4   Intermediate Node Receives the RES Message

Intermediate node parses the message and understands this is a RES message from destination node 10.1.1.1, and then the node resolves the Metric segment in the message, knows it should reserve 80M bandwidth for service 1. Next, the node queries the service ID 1 in its database and checks if the service has been authorized. If so, the node changes the status "Authorized" to "Reserved", sets the Bandwidth value to 80; otherwise, the node inserts a new record of reserving 80M bandwidth for flow 1.

4.5   Source Node Receives the RES Message

The RES message is forwarded from destination node to the source node along the multicast tree. Each node along the route reserves proper bandwidth for the service. When the source node receives the message, it will use the funnel and bucket mechanism to send the data along the multicast tree according to the bottleneck bandwidth, which is showed in Fig. 2 as Adaptive Traffic Controller.

4.6   DRACM Mechanism for Multicast Situation

As in multicast situation, an intermediate node may accept a REQ message but should forward to several nodes, or receive several RES messages from different destinations. In this case, the intermediate node should insert several records in the database as Table 3 shows for service 2 and 3. If the node forward a REQ message to two nodes, it should divide its bandwidth by two and insert two authorized records in database.

But for the source node, it should wait until receiving all messages from the destinations except those that have been pruned. if it receives several RES message from different destinations, it gives judgments that it should send the data along the multicast tree according to the smallest bandwidth and notice all the nodes along the multi tree then they can update the bandwidth info in the database.

5   Analysis and Discussion

5.1   Admission Control Adapting to Network Changes

All the REQ and RES messages are formatted in a certain format, and the frequency of REQ message should adapt to network changes based on the RES message source node receives, that means, if the source node receives a lot of RES messages, which indicates there is little pruning behavior and the status of network is stable so the frequency of RES message can be low, otherwise, if there is a lot of pruning behavior and little RES message is received which means the network is very unstable, the source should speed up the frequency of sending RES messages.

5.2   The States Transition Diagram of Nodes

Totally, each intermediate node has four states as shown in Fig. 3:

- Idle. If there is no traffic flow going through the node, we mark it as idle.
- Authorization. If the node receives an REQ message and can meet the minimum bandwidth of the service requirements, it will authorize proper bandwidth to the service and start the timer, the bandwidth authorized cannot be occupied by other service until timeout;
- Reservation. If the node receives a RES message and parses the bottleneck bandwidth along the route, it will change to reservation state; the band reserved cannot be occupied by other services unless being released by the service or timeout.
- Transition. This state indicates that a new service is accepted and new connection is built, the network begins to transmit data. When data transition is finished, the node returns to idle state.

5.3   DRACM Used for Heterogeneous Receivers

In our mechanism, the destination node receives RES message and makes decision for admission control according to the routing QoS calculated and its own demands. In multicast situation, different destinations have different requirements, so this client-oriented control mechanism can support multicast and meet the heterogeneity of receivers.

DRACM distributes the QoS calculation and resource control across multiple destination nodes; intermediate nodes only need simple operation and adjustments, so it can improve the efficiency of resource admission and would not introduce too much cost in Ad Hoc networks.

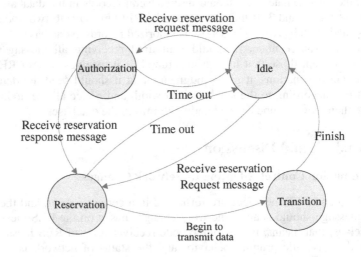

Fig. 3. States Transition Diagram of Intermediate Nodes

6   Simulation Results

We simulated DRACM on OPNET and the simulation parameters are showed in Table 5. We totally deployed 60 nodes in an area of 1000m * 1000m, where the source nodes and destination nodes are selected randomly. We both simulated none admission control scenario and DRACM scenario, collected four kinds of static including packets sent, packets received, end-to-end delay and jitter, and then calculated the results as Table 6 shows.

From the results, we can draw the conclusion that DRACM has brought good effects in network condition. As some of the services are refused by DRACM, the network can offer good QoS for the accepted services and stay in a good condition. As Table 6 shows, packet delay, jitter and packet drop ratio are reduced by 21.52%, 51.76% and 24.15%, and the network resources are utilized reasonably.

Table 5. Simulation Parameters

Simulation scenario	1000m * 1000m	Packets interval	0.1 s
Nodes number	60	Packets length	1000 bits
Type of service	Video Conference	Simulation time	200 s
Node speed	5m/s	Transport layer protocol	UDP

Table 6. Simulation Results

/	No Admission Control	DRACM	Reduction
Delay	0.0610332	0.0478973	21.52%
Jitter	0.0923473	0.0445499	51.76%
Packet Drop Ratio	10.4322%	7.9128%	24.15%

7   Conclusion

Resource admission control is widely used for resource utilization and can maintain good QoS for services as user expected. In this paper, we introduce DRACM, a distributed resource admission control, which can adapt efficiently to topology changes in MANETs. The mechanism distributes the QoS calculation and resource control across multiple destination nodes as well as the control decision. Meantime, intermediate nodes only need to do some simple actions with message and bandwidth management. As the first stage of our research, DRACM is a mechanism to support multicast and destination heterogeneity, the frequency of RES messages can adapt to the stability of network. It's also applicable in other types of wireless networks.

Our simulation results show that DRACM can bring great effects in network condition. In future, we will search for optimal methods to estimate and calculate bandwidth more accurately, to support DRACM.

Acknowledgments. This work is supported by the National Science Foundation of China under Grant No. 61073076, Science and Technology on Information Transmission and Dissemination in Communication Networks Laboratory under Grant No. ITD-U10001, and Beihang University Innovation & Practice Fund for Graduate. The authors would like to thank great support.

References

1. Hanzo II., L., Tafazolli, R.: Admission Control Schemes for 802.11-BasedMulti-Hop Mobile Ad hoc Networks: A Survey. IEEE Communications & Tutorials 11(4), 78–108 (2009)
2. Pirhadi, M., Hemami, S.M.S., Khademzadeh, A.: Resource and Admission Control Architecture and QoS Signaling Scenarios in Next Generation Networks. World Applied Sciences Journal 7(Special Issue of Computer & IT), 87–97 (2009)
3. Lee, S., Ahn, G., Zhang, X., Campbell, A.: INSIGNIA: An IP-Based Quality of Service Framework for Mobile ad Hoc Networks. J. Parallel and Distributed Computing 60(4), 374–406 (2000)
4. Calafate, C.T., Oliver, J., Cano, J.-C., Manzoni, P., Malumbres, M.P.: A distributed admission control system for MANET environments supporting multipath routing protocols. Microprocessors and Microsystems 31, 236–251 (2007)
5. Ahn, G.-S., Campbell, A.T., Veres, A., Sun, L.-H.: Supporting Service Differentiation for Real-Time and Best-Effort Traffic in Stateless Wireless Ad Hoc Networks (SWAN). IEEE Trans. Mobile Computing 1, 192–207 (2002)
6. Chaparro, P.A., Alcober, J., Monteiro, J., Calafate, C.T., Cano, J.-C., Manzoni, P.: Supporting scalable video transmission in MANETs through distributed admission control mechanisms. In: 18th Euromicro Conference on Parallel, Distributed and Network-based Processing (2010)
7. Pei, Y., Ambetkar, V.: Distributed Flow Admission Control for Mul-timedia Services Over Wireless Ad Hoc Networks. Wireless PersonalCommunications 42(1), 23–40 (2006)

Visual Cognitive Radio

Tian Liu, Daixiong Ye, Shihai Shao, Youxi Tang, and Juan Zhou

National Key Laboratory of Science and Technology on Communications,
University of Electronic Science and Technology of China, Chengdu, China
{liutian,yedaixiong,ssh,tangyx,zhoujuan06}@uestc.edu.cn

Abstract. Cognitive radio are always based on spectrum sensing to cognize the physical characteristics of the wireless channel and carry out wireless communication resource scheduling. This kind of method has limited predictive ability and cognitive content, which cause it is hard for cognitive radio to response to the change of radio environment in advance. This paper proposes a new system called visual cognitive radio, which use visual information to cognize radio environment. Visual observation has well predictive ability and abundant cognitive information, which enables the visual cognitive radio to deal with the change of radio environment in advance and make optimal configuration to the process of wireless communication. This paper presents a typical communication scene as an example to explain the advantage of visual cognitive radio, and also makes a preliminary analysis of the application and challenge of visual cognitive radio.

Keywords: cognitive radio, visual cognition.

1 Introduction

With the rapid development of radio communication technology, radio spectrum has become a precious resource. Therefore, how to improve spectrum utilization is an important research issue in wireless communication [1]. Over the past decade, the cognitive radio (CR) based on spectrum sensing (monitoring) captured significant interest in academic research. It has been proved that CR is an effective method to improve the spectrum efficiency of wireless communication [2].

1.1 The Features of Conventional Cognitive Radio

The conventional cognitive radio can exchange information intellectively with communication network by sense the spectrum hole of electromagnetic environment, use radio knowledge representation language (RKRL) [3] and combine with software radio technology to adjust the communication parameters, in order to maintain efficient spectrum utilization. Its main features include [4]:

P. Ren et al. (Eds.): WICON 2011, LNICST 98, pp. 265–275, 2012.
© Institute for Computer Sciences, Social Informatics and Telecommunications Engineering 2012

Cognitive Ability. It includes three processes [5]: spectrum sensing, spectrum analysis and spectrum decision. Spectrum sensing is to monitor and detect spectrum hole; spectrum analysis is to estimate the feature of the spectrum hole; and spectrum decision is to select appropriate frequency band to transmit data according to the feature of spectrum hole and user demand.

Reconstitution Ability. It can program the parameters of transmitter and receiver dynamically according to radio electromagnetic environment, and have different radio transmission technologies to send and receive data. This reconstitution ability can utilize the idle spectrum and provide a reliable communication service on condition that not disturb the authorized user.

1.2   The Shortages of Conventional Cognitive Radio

The conventional cognitive radio based on spectrum sensing (monitoring) to collect information, monitor radio channel environment passively, and learn an event (such as be shaded by a building) only after it has happened. It has no preventability, and the remedial measure is relatively laggard, which will cost extra consumption. Its main shortages include:

The Poorness of Predictive Ability. It always begins to allocate new frequency band to user and adjust the parameters of radio communication only after the user's geographical position changed (the available frequency band also changed). It can hardly do any prediction to response to the change of radio environment.

The Simpleness of Cognitive Content. It only focus on the feature of radio signal to cognize radio environment. The cognitive content is too simple for cognitive radio to obtain the panoramic and multidimensional radio environment, and make the optimal communication plan.

1.3   The Proposition of Visual Cognitive Radio

This paper will propose an innovative cognitive radio called visual cognitive radio, which uses the visual information to cognize radio environment. It can analyze user's wireless scenario in advance, enable the communication system to have strong adaptability and maintain high spectrum utilization.

2   Visual Cognitive Radio

Visual cognitive radio can "see" user's forthcoming radio environment by analyzing the real time image of user's environment, and do a series of parameter adjustment to deal with the real time change of user's radio environment, guarantee the robustness of communication link. As Fig. 1 shows, the structure of visual cognitive radio consists of the following four modules.

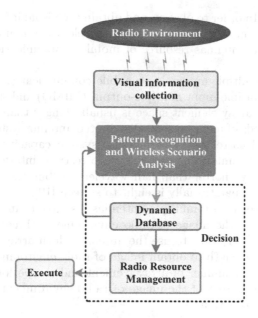

Fig. 1. The structure of visual cognitive radio

2.1   Visual Information Collection Module

This module is an essential step, its purpose is to obtain the real time visual information of the users radio environment by the use of multiple antennas resource of wireless mobile network. Therefore, the visual cognitive radio can "see" the radio environment, not like the conventional cognitive radio to "hear" . The multiple antennas of the next generation mobile wireless communication system provide the behavior of "see" with technical feasibility.

The use of multiple antennas to obtain visual information has been successfully applied to microwave and millimeter wave radar imaging [6] and medical imaging [7][8]. A typical technology of radar imaging is synthetic aperture radar (SAR)[9]. Its main idea is to add a number of antenna elements together (the array element space is usually shorter than half wavelength), to constitute a bigger antenna array, and radiate signal by electronic scanning, then obtain high resolution radar image by correlating processing of the received echo from different locations.

A typical technology of medical imaging is phased array ultrasonic imaging [10]. Its main idea is that it firstly processes acoustic beam scanning, and changes the phase relationship when the sound wave arrive at the body, by controlling the time delay of each array element of phased array transducer, in order to realize the change of focus point and acoustic beam, then finish the imaging of need checking organ.

In the above multiple antennas imaging technologies, the antenna array is contract designed, which is to eliminate grating lobe and provide the real image of observed object. In order to observe and obtain the visual information of radio environment in the next generation mobile wireless communication network, the help of multiple antennas resource of mobile communication equipment is needed.

At present, the multiple antennas of mobile communication equipment have two mechanisms: multiple-input multiple-output (MIMO) and smart antenna. In MIMO system, the array element space is usually longer than half wavelength (even can be hundreds of meter in some distributed antenna system)[11], in order to decrease channel correlation and increase system capacity. Smart antenna system uses digital beamforming technology to restrain interference, the array element space usually shorter than half wavelength, but the number of array element is relatively small, usually is eight to sixteen [12].

Therefore, in order to use multiple antennas resource of mobile communication system to obtain the image of radio environment, three aspects research work are still needed: (1) How to use the antenna which array element space is longer than half wavelength to obtain image of radio environment? (2) What is the relationship of the number of array element and the performance of visual cognition? (3) What extent of the image of radio environment visual cognitive radio system needs to obtain?

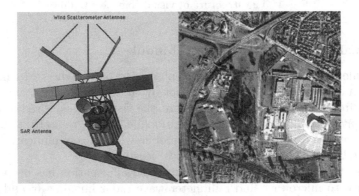

Fig. 2. Multiple antennas in radar imaging

2.2   Wireless Scenario Analysis Module

This module is to cognize the obtained image of radio environment and use the cognition results to analyze and output wireless communication scenario parameters. This kind of method uses visual information to cognize and analyze wireless scenario, and is different from the conventional cognitive radio which is focus on frequency spectrum. It via cognizing the image of wireless scenario to output wireless communication scenario parameters, and enable the cognitive radio equipment to obtain the real-time and panoramic information of radio environment. Specifically, it can obtain three kinds of information, which are shown in Fig. 3.

Users Location. Cognizing the users visual information obtained by visual information collection module, visual cognitive radio can obtain the precise geographic information of the user, base station and obstruction, and also the relative position information of user and base station between obstruction.

Users Mobile Trend. Analyzing the cognized image of user, visual cognitive radio can obtain the information of the users displacement. And considering the duration of a frame, visual cognitive radio also can know the users speed and direction.

Users Interference. Using the relative position information of user and base station between obstruction, visual cognitive radio can know users current interference. And using users mobile trend, visual cognitive radio can analyze the time when user will be interfered. Detect and cognize the image of obstruction, visual cognitive radio can know the feature of this obstruction, and then obtain the feature of interference.

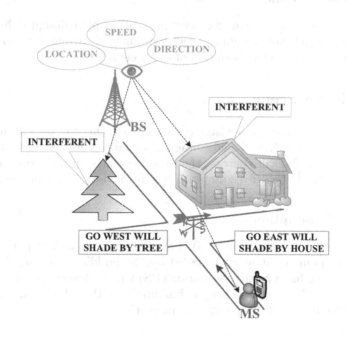

Fig. 3. Visual information

It is worth to mention that the users mobile trend cannot obtain by conventional cognitive radio, and the users interference obtained by visual cognitive radio gives more information of the radio signal feature of the users radio environment.

2.3 Decision Module

This module includes dynamic database and radio resource management module.

Dynamic database includes geographic feature database and radio feature database. Geographic feature database stores the feature of the user's communication environment. Radio feature database stores the radio signal feature of the user's radio environment. Dynamic database's prior information include basic communication model (modulator approach, encoding and decoding method, waveform of physical layer under all kinds of communication system), estimation algorithm (estimate attenuation, multi-path, Doppler shift and user's mobile trend), and initialized geometric data.

Radio resource management module inputs the wireless scenario parameters obtained by wireless scenario analysis module, combines with the prior information of dynamic database to analyze and select the communication mode which user needs and allocates radio resource to user, finally update dynamic database.

2.4 Execute Module

This module executes the concrete communication plan designed by decision module, adjusts relevant communication parameters, allocates radio resource, outputs the response to the cognition of radio environment.

3 Particular Scene

In order to describe the above visual cognitive idea, this section will introduce a particular scene, and show the advantage of visual cognitive radio in the aspect of power control. We will contrast the visual cognitive power control (VCPC) method and conventional fixed step power control (FSPC)[13] method.

3.1 Scene Description

As Fig. 4 shows, mobile station (MS) is moving from point A to point B. When MS comes to point C, it will be shaded by the building. And d_1 denotes the distance from the building to base station (BS) and d_2 denotes the distance from the building to MS, d_3 and d_4 are the building's width and length, respectively, d denotes the distance from point A to point C.

3.2 Method Analysis

Suppose the MS use the code division multiple access (CDMA) system with binary phase shift keyed (BPSK) signaling, the conventional fast closed-loop power control strategy is a fixed-step approach, which is defined by [13]. Due to the loop delay and limited maximum power adjustment in FSPC, the effects of deep shadow fading can hardly be accommodated.

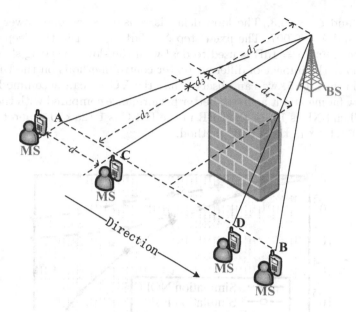

Fig. 4. Particular scene

By the visual cognitive way, according to visual information collection module, the VCPC can know the following visual information: (1) mobile trend and velocity v; (2) distance d from point A to point C; (3) the power loss ΔL at point C; (4) whether MS is shaded by the building or not.

Given the mobile velocity v, the number of power control group (PCG)[14] needed from point A to point C can be expressed as $N_v = \lfloor \frac{d/v}{T} \rfloor$, where $\lfloor \cdot \rfloor$ means the rounds to the nearest integers towards minus infinity and T represents the power control sampling period. Given the instantaneous fading loss ΔL and fixed step size δ, the number of PCG needed to increase enough power is given as $\Delta N = \lfloor \Delta L/\delta \rfloor$.

To accommodate the effects of the deep shadow fading, the transmit power of MS should be increased ahead of the fading. Let N_d denotes the loop delays in samples, then the command to increase power should be sent after N_s PCGs in the BS, which can be described as $N_s = N_v - \Delta N - N_d$.

When the VCPC "see" the MS will be shaded by the building, it begins to read the visual information to get v, d, ΔL, and compute ΔN and N_s, then adjust the power of BS to deal with the forthcoming deep shadow fading.

3.3   Simulation Result

The simulation result is shown in Fig. 5, in the simulation we assume that the visual information provides $v = 50$km/h, $d = 25$m, $\Delta L = 21$dB, and the values of d_1, d_2, d_3, and d_4 are 20m, 10m, 10m, and 25m, respectively. The autocorrelation of the slow shadow fading is $\sigma_A^2 \zeta_D^{(vT/D)|k|}$[14], where $\sigma_A = 4.3$dB, $T = 5$ms,

$D = 10$m, and $\zeta_D = 0.3$. The loop delay is considered as one power control interval T and $\lambda = 0.007$. The fixed step $\delta = 3$dB is used in the deep shadow fading process, and $\delta = 1$dB is used to deal with the slowly varying shadow.

Fig. 5 shows the impact of different power control methods on the BER performance. From Fig. 5, we can observe that the VCPC can accommodate the deep shadow fading and it achieves better performance compared with the FSPC method. When SNR is 10dB, the BER in the FSPC is 1.128×10^{-3} and the BER can be 1.501×10^{-5} in the VCPC method.

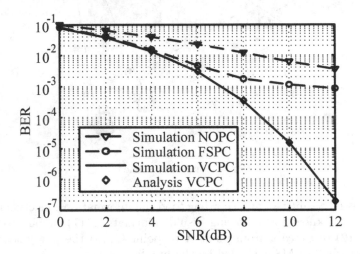

Fig. 5. BER performance comparison of different methods. NOPC, FSPC, and VCPC denote no power control, fixed step power control, and visual cognitive power control, respectively.

4   Application and Challenge

Visual cognitive radio not only has better performance, compared with conventional cognitive radio, in improving spectrum utilization, but also has some special applications and along with challenges as discussed in the following paragraphs.

4.1   Emergency Scenario

Visual cognitive radio can be applied to emergency scenario. In the case of emergency, for example, when a bus had an accident in some remote place, all the passengers need timely rescue. According to [15], the single-antenna mobiles in a multi-user environment can "share" their antennas in a manner that creates a virtual MIMO system. Therefore the single-antenna mobile phones of the passengers can constitute an antenna array, and with the technologies mentioned in visual information collection module, the virtual MIMO system can imaging the real time scene of the accident, which enables the rescue team to response timely and efficiently.

In order to apply visual cognitive radio in emergency scenario, the problems mentioned in the visual information collection module are need to be solved. How to use virtual MIMO technology to get the image of accident scene and what extent of the image of radio environment visual cognitive radio system needs to obtain are still need further research.

4.2 Visual Cooperation

Visual cognitive radio can be applied to cooperative communication [16]. The base station can cooperate with each other to provide the best communication service to mobile station. For example, in Fig. 6, MS is moving from point D to point G. At point D, BS A is serving MS, and "see" MS will come to point E, where the propagation of MS and BS A will be shaded by the house, so BS A asks BS B, which is near MS and have no obstruction, to serve MS. Similarly, when MS comes to point F, BS C begins to serve MS.

In order to apply visual cognitive idea in cooperative communication, there are two main issues need to be solved. One is the synchronization of the visual cooperation, the other is base station switching. The synchronization and switching of the cooperative communication system is a difficult problem, adding the visual cognition, these problems can be even harder.

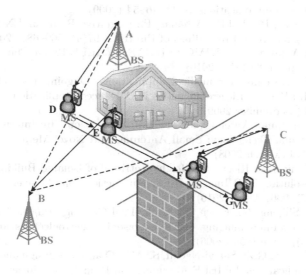

Fig. 6. Visual cognitive radio applied in cooperative communication

5 Conclusion

Analyzing the feature of conventional cognitive radio based on spectrum sensing, this paper summarizes its bottleneck problem in poor predictive ability and simple cognitive content. A new system called visual cognitive radio which use visual information to cognize radio environment is proposed. The visual cognitive information can be obtained by the multiple antennas of the next generation mobile wireless communication system. The visual cognitive radio can response to the change of radio environment in advance and guarantee the robustness of communication link. The process of visual cognitive power control is presented as an example to explain the advantage of visual cognition. In sum, the visual cognitive radio can be widely used in many fields and also the technical challenge coexist.

References

1. Mitola, J.: Cognitive radio architecture evolution. Proceedings of the IEEE 97(4), 626–641 (2009)
2. Matinmikko, M., Mustonen, M., Sarvanko, H., et al.: A Motivating Overview of Cognitive Radio: Foundations, Regulatory Issues and Key Concepts. VTT Technical Research Centre of Finland, Oulu (February 2008)
3. Yarkan, S., Arslan, H.: Exploiting Location Awareness toward Improved Wireless System Design in Cognitive Radio. IEEE Communications Magazine 46(1), 128–136 (2008)
4. Niyato, D., Hossain, E.: Cognitive radio for next-generation wireless networks: an approach to opportunistic channel selection in IEEE 802.11-based wireless mesh. IEEE Wireless Communications 16(1), 46–54 (2009)
5. MacKenzie, A.B., Reed, J.H., Athanas, P.: Cognitive Radio and Networking Research at Virginia Tech. Proceedings of the IEEE 97(4), 660–688 (2009)
6. Sharma, R.: Application of MIMO to IFSAR. In: IEEE Radar Conference, Washington, DC, pp. 81–84 (May 2010)
7. Topsakal, E.: Antennas for medical applications: Ongoing research and future challenges. In: ICEAA Electromagnetics in Advanced Applications, Torino, Italy, pp. 890–893 (September 2009)
8. Ito, K.: Recent Small Antennas for Medical Applications. In: International Workshop on Antenna Technology: Small Antennas and Novel Metamaterials, Chiba, Japan, pp. 1–4 (March 2008)
9. Guida, R., Iodice, A., Riccio, D.: Height Retrieval of Isolated Buildings From Single High-Resolution SAR Images. IEEE Transactions on Geoscience and Remote Sensing 48(7), 2967–2979 (2010)
10. Hungliu, J., Shijeng, G., Kewu, T., Chili, P.: ECG triggering and gating for ultrasonic small animal imaging. IEEE Ultrasonics, Ferroelectrics and Frequency Control 53(9), 1590–1596 (2006)
11. Mohajer, M., Rafi, G.Z., Safavi-Naeini, S.: MIMO antenna design and optimization for mobile applications. In: IEEE Antennas and Propagation Society International Symposium, Charleston, USA, pp. 1–4 (June 2009)
12. Das, S.: Smart antenna design for wireless communication using adaptive beam-forming approach. In: TENCON 2008-2008 IEEE Region 10 Conference, Hyderabad, India, pp. 1–5 (November 2008)

13. Ariyavisitakul, S.: SIR based power control in a CDMA system. In: Proc. IEEE GLOBECOM, Orlando, USA, pp. 868–873 (December 1992)

14. Song, L., Mandayam, N., Gajic, Z.: Analysis of an up/down power control algorithm for the CDMA reverse link under fading. IEEE Journal on Selected Areas in Communications 19(2), 277–286 (2001)

15. Jayaweera, S.K.: Energy efficient virtual MIMO-based cooperative communications for wireless sensor networks. In: International Conference on Intelligent Sensing and Information Processing, Bangalore, India, pp. 1–6 (January 2005)

16. Nosratinia, A., Hunter, T.E., Hedayat, A.: Cooperative Communication in Wireless Networks. IEEE Communications Magazine 42(10), 74–80 (2004)

A Full-Rate Cooperative Communication Strategy in Wireless Relay Networks

Lei Zhan[1], Fei Yang[1], Sihai Zhang[1,2], and Wuyang Zhou[1]

[1] Wireless Information Network Lab.,
Department of Electronic Engineering and Information Science,
University of Science and Technology of China, Hefei, Anhui, China, 230026
[2] Key Laboratory of Wireless Sensor Network & Communication,
Shanghai Institute of Microsystem and Information Technology,
Chinese Academy of Sciences865 Changning Road, Shanghai, China, 200050
{shzhang,wyzhou}@ustc.edu.cn, genyang@mail.ustc.edu.cn

Abstract. In this paper, we propose a new full-rate cooperative communication strategy in wireless relay networks without direct path between source and destination. This strategy coined full-rate amplify-and-forward (FRAF) utilizes multiple relay nodes to take turns to amplify and forward data package for the transmitter at different time slot. Thus the source node could continue sending without cessation. On the other hand, prevailing linear constellation precoding process is adopted at the source node to solve the problem caused by the imbalance of the error performance of the data sent at odd and even time slots. Furthermore, we analyze the outage probability and certificate that FRAF strategy can achieve the full diversity gain. The simulation results indicate that FRAF could improve the performance of the system effectively compared to the conventional amplify-and-forward (AF) and decode-and-forward (DF) strategy.

Keywords: Wireless relay networks, full-rate cooperative communication, precoding, wireless communication.

1 Introduction

In the wireless communication environment, the transmitting performance is impacted by the fading characteristic of the wireless channel seriously. By utilizing the independence of the different channels and broadcast trait of the wireless channel, cooperative communication makes the mobile nodes in the network help each other to transmit information and yield cooperative diversity gain. It is one of the most effective ways to mitigate the fading of the wireless channels in the networks. Among the cooperative schemes which have been proposed, amplify-and-forward and decode-and-forward are the most famous [1][2].

Because of the lack of the wireless frequency resource, wireless communication in high frequency band attracts considerable attention. Considering the characteristic of fast fading of the high-frequency transmission, the source node at the

P. Ren et al. (Eds.): WICON 2011, LNICST 98, pp. 276–286, 2012.

edge of the scenario can communicate with the destination node only with the help of the relays for guaranteeing the enough coverage of networks. That means there is no direct path between the source and destination. The performance of traditional AF strategy with best relay selection in this kind scene is analyzed, with the diversity gain order provided as well [3]. But the conventional cooperative communication strategies make the source transmit one data package in two time slot for obtaining the diversity gain, which means the data transmission rate between source and destination is halved. Some schemes have been proposed to solve this problem. Non-orthogonal AF (NAF) transmission strategy makes the source node send data continuously and the relay node only forwards the data sent by source node at the odd time slot [4]. It is proved that NAF strategy can obtain the optimal diversity-multiplex tradeoff [5], but it causes the imbalance of the error performance of the data sent at odd time slots and even time slots. Furthermore, a strategy which utilizes precoding and space-time coding to achieve full-rate transmission shows better performance [6]. However, all schemes mentioned above are applied in the scene where the direct path between source and destination exists, which is essential for full-rate transmission of them. So these full-rate transmission strategies are not applicable in the scenario without the direct path.

In this paper, a new cooperative communication strategy called FRAF which can achieve full-rate transmission in the scenario without direct path between source and destination is proposed. This strategy utilizes multiple relay nodes to take turns to help source node forward data at the odd and even time slots, which can guarantee the source node to send out continuously without cessation. Furthermore, precoding process avoids the imbalance of error performance of information transmitted at odd and even time slots. We analyze the performance of FRAF strategy and verify that it can achieve full diversity gain.

2   System Model

The system model is illustrated in Fig.1 where one source node S sends information to destination node D with the help of L relay nodes $R_i (i = 1, 2, \cdots, L)$. All of the nodes are equipped with only one antenna and work in the half-duplex mode. There is no direct path between source and destination which makes the help of relay nodes essential. All wireless channels are slow-fading and independent. Furthermore, the channel fading coefficient is modelled as zero-mean, independent, circularly symmetric complex Gaussian random variable. Considering slow fading, the fading coefficient remains constant over the transmission of one source data block and independent in different transmission. The additive channel noise is modelled as a complex Gaussian random variable with mean zero and variance N_0. To guarantee the full-rate transmission, we suppose the source node and relay node operating at different frequency band which causes no interference between them.

Fig.1 presents the process of FRAF strategy in which we set the i-th and $(i + 1)$-th time slots as a time slot pair. The data which will be sent in the time slot pair is precoded in the source node. At the i-th time slot, the source node S sends data to relay nodes, and then all of relay nodes receive the data except the one which is chosen to be the forward node at the $(i-1)$-th time slot (This node is sending data to destination at this time). Among the relay nodes receiving the data, the one with best channel condition is selected to be the forward node of the next time slot. At the $(i+1)$-th time slot, the relay node selected at i-th time slot forwards the data to the destination node and the others receive the data transmitted by source node. Duplicating this process, the full-rate transmission can be achieved.

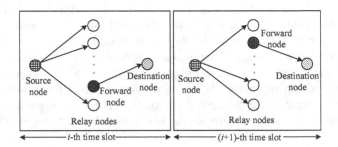

Fig. 1. System model of FRAF strategy

3   Mathematic Description and Performance Analysis

3.1   Precoding

At a time slot, the data transmitted by the source node is forwarded by the forward node selected from $(L-1)$ relay nodes according to the channel condition. If one relay node's channel situation is very good continuously, this relay node would be always selected as the forward node at the odd or even time slot which causes the imbalance of error performance of the data transmitted at odd and even time slot. To solve this problem and improve the stability of the whole system, precoding is adopted to process the data transmitted at a pair of time slots at the source node. The length of single data package is denoted as N and $\mathbf{s} = (s_1, s_2, \cdots, s_{2N})^T$ represents the source data which will be transmitted at a pair of time slots. Furthermore, $\mathbf{x} = (x_1, x_2, \cdots, x_{2N})^T$ denotes the data that have been precoded and $\mathbf{K}$ denotes the precoding matrix. Thus we obtain:

$$\mathbf{x} = \mathbf{K}_{2N \times 2N}\mathbf{s} \tag{1}$$

The source data is overlapped through precoding and can be decoded with maximum likelihood (ML) decoding algorithm. Linear constellation precoding (LCP) matrix is a common precoding matrix, which is a kind of unitary orthonormal matrix with excellent ability to overlap the source information effectively. Therefore, we select a LCP matrix mentioned in [10] to be the precoding matrix of FRAF strategy, as follow:

$$\mathbf{K} = \frac{1}{\sqrt{2N}} \begin{pmatrix} 1 & \beta_0 & \cdots & \beta_0^{2N-1} \\ 1 & \beta_1 & \cdots & \beta_1^{2N-1} \\ \vdots & \vdots & \ddots & \vdots \\ 1 & \beta_{2N-1} & \cdots & \beta_{2N-1}^{2N-1} \end{pmatrix} \tag{2}$$

where $\beta_k = e^{j\frac{k+1/4}{N}\pi}$ and $N = 2^{q-1}$, and q is an integer which is greater than one.

3.2 Mathematic Description and Performance of FRAF

The performance of FRAF strategy is analyzed with a pair of time slots as one unit. Assuming R_1, R_2 denote the relay nodes selected as the forward nodes at the first and the second time slot separately, P_S, P_{R_1}, P_{R_2} denote the sending power of the source node and relay nodes. The data received by the relay nodes can be described as follow:

$$y_{R_i} = \sqrt{P_S} h_{SR}^i x_i + n_i', i = \{1, 2, \cdots, 2N\} \tag{3}$$

$$h_{SR}^i = \begin{cases} h_{SR_1}, & 1 \le i \le N; \\ h_{SR_2}, & N < i \le 2N. \end{cases}$$

where h_{SR}^i is the channel fading coefficient of the channel between the source node and the relay node. Also we can get the mathematics description of the data received by the destination node:

$$y_i = \sqrt{P_R^i} h_{RD}^i s_{Ri} + n_i, i = \{1, 2, \cdots, 2N\} \tag{4}$$

where h_{RD}^i is the channel fading coefficient of the channel between the relay node and the destination node. On the other hand, $s_{Ri} = y_{Ri}/\theta_i$ is the data which is normalized at the relay node. We have:

$$h_{RD}^i = \begin{cases} h_{R_1D}, & 1 \le i \le N; \\ h_{R_2D}, & N < i \le 2N. \end{cases}$$

$$P_R^i = \begin{cases} \sqrt{P_S|h_{SR_1}|^2 + 1}, & 1 \le i \le N; \\ \sqrt{P_S|h_{SR_1}|^2 + 1}, & N < i \le 2N. \end{cases}$$

$$\theta_i = \begin{cases} h_{R_1D}, & 1 \le i \le N; \\ h_{R_2D}, & N < i \le 2N. \end{cases}$$

Considering the whole transmission procedure at a pair of time slots, the description with matrix form can be obtained as follow:

$$\mathbf{y} = \mathbf{HKs} + \mathbf{n} \tag{5}$$

where $\mathbf{s} = [s_1, s_2, \cdots, s_{2N}]^T$ and $\mathbf{y} = [y_1, y_2, \cdots, y_{2N}]^T$ denote the data sent by source and received by destination separately, and

$$\mathbf{H}_{2N \times 2N} = diag\{\sqrt{P_S P_R^1} h_{SR}^1 h_{RD}^1 / \theta_1, \cdots, \sqrt{P_S P_R^{2N}} h_{SR}^{2N} h_{RD}^{2N} / \theta_{2N}\}$$

$$\mathbf{n} = [n_1 + \sqrt{P_R^1} h_{RD}^1 n_1' / \theta_1, \cdots, n_{2N} + \sqrt{P_R^{2N}} h_{RD}^{2N} n_{2N}' / \theta_{2N}]^T$$

The sum-rate achieved by the proposed strategy can be written as:

$$I = \frac{1}{2N} \log_2 \det\{\mathbf{I}_{2N} + \mathbf{HKK}^H \mathbf{H}^H \mathbf{N}^{-1}\} \tag{6}$$

where

$$\mathbf{N} = diag\{1 + P_R^1 |h_{RD}^1|^2 / \theta_1^2, \cdots, 1 + P_R^{2N} |h_{RD}^{2N}|^2 / \theta_{2N}^2\}$$

For the simplicity to analyze the performance of FRAF strategy, we suppose all nodes have the same transmitting power as $P = P_S = P_{R_1} = P_{R_2}$ and the high signal-to-noise ratio (SNR) assumption is applied. Also, the SNR is denoted as ρ. Considering the matrix $\mathbf{K}$ is unitary orthonormal, the following result can be obtained:

$$\begin{aligned}
I &= \frac{1}{2N} \log_2 \left[\prod_{i=1}^{2N} \left(1 + \frac{\rho |h_{SR}^i|^2 |h_{RD}^i|^2}{1/\rho + |h_{SR}^i|^2 + |h_{RD}^i|^2} \right) \right] \\
&\approx \frac{1}{2} \log_2 \left[\left(1 + \frac{\rho |h_{SR_1}|^2 |h_{R_1D}|^2}{|h_{SR_1}|^2 + |h_{R_1D}|^2} \right) \times \right. \\
&\qquad \left. \left(1 + \frac{\rho |h_{SR_2}|^2 |h_{R_2D}|^2}{|h_{SR_2}|^2 + |h_{R_2D}|^2} \right) \right]
\end{aligned} \tag{7}$$

Define $\lambda = |h_{SR}^i|^2 |h_{RD}^i|^2 / (|h_{SR}^i|^2 + |h_{RD}^i|^2)$. As shown in (7), the performance of the whole system can be maximized if the relay node with maximal λ value is selected as the forward node. So λ is set as the criterion to select the forward node.

The desired data transmitting rate of the source node is denoted as R. The outage probability is selected as the indicator of the performance of the communication system. When the maximal transmitting rate provided by the system cannot satisfy the requirement of source node, the outage occurs. The outage probability denoted as P_{outage} can be written as:

$$P_{\text{outage}} = \Pr(I < R) \tag{8}$$

Utilizing formula (7), we obtain:

$$
\begin{aligned}
I = \frac{1}{2}\log_2 \Bigg(1 & + \frac{\rho|h_{SR_1}|^2|h_{R_1D}|^2}{|h_{SR_1}|^2 + |h_{R_1D}|^2} \\
& + \frac{\rho|h_{SR_2}|^2|h_{R_2D}|^2}{|h_{SR_2}|^2 + |h_{R_2D}|^2} \\
& + \frac{\rho|h_{SR_1}|^2|h_{R_1D}|^2}{|h_{SR_1}|^2 + |h_{R_1D}|^2} \times \frac{\rho|h_{SR_2}|^2|h_{R_2D}|^2}{|h_{SR_2}|^2 + |h_{R_2D}|^2} \Bigg) \\
> \frac{1}{2}\log_2 \Bigg(1 & + \frac{\rho|h_{SR_1}|^2|h_{R_1D}|^2}{|h_{SR_1}|^2 + |h_{R_1D}|^2} \\
& + \frac{\rho|h_{SR_2}|^2|h_{R_2D}|^2}{|h_{SR_2}|^2 + |h_{R_2D}|^2} \Bigg)
\end{aligned} \tag{9}
$$

Taking it into (8), the outage probability can be shown as:

$$
P_{\text{outage}} = \Pr(I < R) < \Pr\left(y_1 + y_2 < \frac{2^{2R} - 1}{\rho} \right) \tag{10}
$$

where $y_1 = \rho|h_{SR_1}|^2|h_{R_1D}|^2/(|h_{SR_1}|^2+|h_{R_1D}|^2)$, $y_2 = \rho|h_{SR_2}|^2|h_{R_2D}|^2/(|h_{SR_2}|^2+|h_{R_2D}|^2)$. Because the modulus square of channel fading coefficient is an exponentially distributed variable, we can get the probability distribution function of y_1, y_2 as follow [7]:

$$
\begin{aligned}
P(y) &= \int_y^{+\infty} e^{-z}\left(1 - e^{-\frac{yz}{z-y}} \right) dz + \int_0^y e^{-z} dz \\
&= 1 - 2ye^{-2y}K_1(2y)
\end{aligned} \tag{11}
$$

where $K_1(x)$ is the modified Bessel function of the second kind with first order. Defining $\alpha = (2^{2R} - 1)/\rho$, it is obvious that $\alpha \to 0$ for large SNR. The Bessel function can be approximated as $K_1(x) \approx 1/x$ with small value of x. Furthermore, considering the relay selection of FRAF strategy, the relay node with the largest value of selection criterion will be chosen as forward node. Therefore, the probability distribution function of y_1, y_2 changes. With (10) and (11), the following approximation can be obtained as:

$$
\begin{aligned}
\Pr(I < R) &< \int_0^\alpha P'(y)P(\alpha - y)^{L-1} dy \\
&\approx \int_0^\alpha 2^L(\alpha - y)^{L-1} dy \\
&\sim \alpha^L
\end{aligned} \tag{12}
$$

The diversity gain order of FRAF strategy is denoted as d, we can have:

$$
d = \lim_{\rho \to +\infty} \left(-\frac{\log P_{\text{outage}}}{\log \rho} \right) = L \tag{13}
$$

Considering that L is the number of the relay nodes, it is demonstrated that FRAF strategy achieves the full diversity gain with (13) which is also achieved by many existing cooperative communication strategy. But FRAF is a full-rate transmission strategy with full diversity gain at the scenario without direct path between source node and destination node.

4   Simulation Results

In this section, we give some simulation result to validate our theoretical analysis and the performance of FRAF strategy. Assuming $R = 2.5\text{bits/s/Hz}$ and the channels between the transmitters and receivers have the identical SNR ρ. The conventional AF and DF cooperative communication strategies which select the relay node with best channel condition as the forward node are chosen as the comparison scheme.

Fig.2 shows the outage probability of three strategies when $L = 2$. Considering there are only two relay nodes, no selection of relay nodes is required and two relay nodes serve as the forward node at the odd and even time slot separately for FRAF strategy. Because the FRAF strategy achieves the full-rate transmission and the source node can send out data continuously without cessation, it is not necessary to guarantee transmission at each sending time slot to achieve the transmission rate of $2R$. Therefore, it is definite to see that FRAF strategy manifests better performance and the outage probability of it is much less compared to the other two cooperative communication strategies. On the other hand, three strategies' curves show the similar decreasing slope as the SNR goes down, which indicates that the three strategies have the same diversity gain and verifies the accuracy of our theory analysis. Furthermore, the transmission rates of three strategies are illustrated in Fig.3. It is obvious that the transmission rate achieved by FRAF strategy is much higher than the other two strategies and the advantage of full-rate transmission is manifested clearly.

The outage probabilities of three strategies are compared in Fig.4 when $L = 4$. It is obvious that the performance of each strategy is improved effectively and the slope of the curve of outage probability is much higher compared to the one in Fig.2. The reason is that the diversity gain order increases as the growth of the number of the relay nodes. Furthermore, FRAF strategy still displays much better performance than the conventional AF and DF cooperative transmission strategies.

The effect of precoding is measured by BER (the bit error ratio) of data sent at odd and even time slot separately. Assuming $L = 2$ and QPSK is adopted as the modulation mode. The SNR of the channel between relay node which is selected to forward the data sent by source node at even time slot and destination node is $(\rho - 5)\text{dB}$ as the others are ρdB. It means this relay node has worse channel condition to communication with destination node than the other one. The simulation results are shown in Fig.5 and Fig.6. It is obvious that the BER of the data sent by source node at even time slot is much higher than the one sent at odd time slot when the precoding is not adopted as illustrated in Fig.5. On the

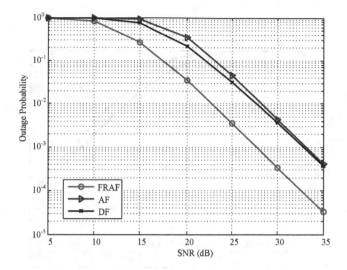

Fig. 2. Outage probability of different strategies, $L = 2$

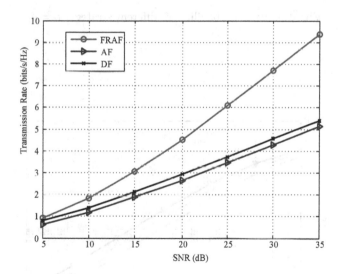

Fig. 3. Transmission rate of different strategies, $L = 2$

other hand, the imbalance of BER at odd and even time slot does not exist after the source data is operated with the precodingin the Fig.6. So the precoding is effective enough to solve the imbalance problem. Furthermore, we can find out that the total average BER of FRAF strategy decreases as the precoding is adopted through comparing the curves in Fig.5 and Fig.6. The reason is that the data is overlapped effectively by precoding and some errors can be rectified through ML decoding. It makes the ability of system to consist fading improved.

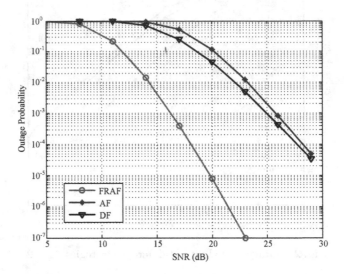

Fig. 4. Outage probability of different strategy, $L = 4$

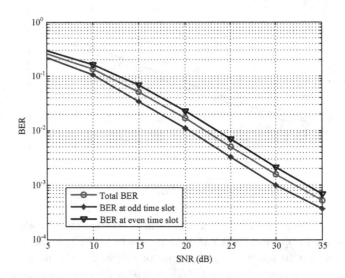

Fig. 5. The BER of FRAF without precoding

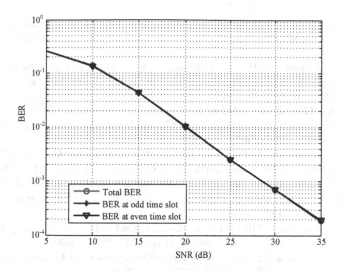

Fig. 6. The BER of FRAF with precoding

5   Conclusion

A new full-rate cooperative communication strategy called FRAF in wireless relay networks scenario without direct path between source and destination is proposed in this paper. This strategy utilizes multiple relay nodes to cooperate with one source node. At the odd and even time slot, the forward node is acted by the different relay node. Hence the source node can transmit data continuously without cessation and full-rate transmission is achieved. In addition, the precoding process at the source node avoids the imbalance of error performance of data sent at odd and even time slot. The theoretical analysis and computer simulation indicate that FRAF strategy can achieve both full-rate transmission and full diversity gain, which can improve the performance of system effectively. Furthermore, designing a specific protocol and measuring the additional expense of FRAF strategy are the next work of us.

Acknowledgment. This work was supported by the China High-Tech 863 Plan under Grant 2009AA011506, the National Major Special Projects in Science and Technology of China under Grant 2009ZX03003-009, 2010ZX03003-001, 2010ZX03005-003, and 2011ZX03003-003-04, National Key Technology R&D Program under Grant 2008BAH30B12, and National Basic Research Program of China under Grant 2007CB310602.

References

1. Sendonaris, A., Erkip, E., Aazhang, B.: User Cooperation Diversity-part I: System Description. IEEE Trans.on Commu. 51(11), 1927–1938 (2003)
2. Laneman, J.N., Tse, D.N.C., Wornell, G.W.: Cooperative diversity in wireless networks: efficient protocols and outage behavior. IEEE Trans. on Information Theory 50, 3062–3080 (2004)

3. Jing, Y., Jafarkhani, H.: Single and Multiple Relay Selection Schemes and their Achievable Diversity Orders. IEEE Trans. on Wireless Commu. 8(3), 1414–1423 (2009)
4. Nabar, R.U., Bolcskei, H., Kneubuhler, F.W.: Fading Relays Channels: Performance Limitsand Space-Time Signal Design. IEEE Journalon Selected Areas in Commu. 22(6), 1099–1109 (2004)
5. Azarian, K., Gamal, H.E., Schniter, P.: On the Achievable Diversity-Muplexing Tradeoff in Half-Duplex Cooperative Channels. IEEE Trans. on Inform. Theory 51(12), 4152–4172 (2005)
6. Zhang, W., Letaief, K.B.: Full-Rate Distributed Space-Time Codesfor Cooperative Communications. IEEE Trans. onWireless Commu. 7(7), 2446–2451 (2008)
7. Ding, Z., Ratnarajah, T., Leung, K.K.: On the study of network coded AF transmission protocol for wireless multiple access channels. IEEE Trans. on Wireless Commu. 8(1), 118–123 (2009)
8. Ding, Z., Leung, K.K., Goeckel, D.L.: On the study of network coding with diversity. IEEE Trans. on Wireless Commu. 8(3), 1247–1259 (2009)
9. Yang, S., Belfiore, J.C.: On Slotted Amplify-and-Forward Cooperative Diversity Schemes. In: IEEE ISIT, pp. 2446–2450 (July 2006)
10. Kwon, U.K., Choi, C.H., Im, G.H.: Full-Rate Cooperative Communications with Spatial Diversity for Half-Duplex Uplink Relay Channels. IEEE Trans. on Wireless Commu. 8(11), 5449–5454 (2009)

A Semi-distributed Network Selection Scheme in Heterogeneous Wireless Networks

Juan Fan[1], Sihai Zhang[1,2], and Wuyang Zhou[1]

[1] Wireless Information Network Lab.,
Department of Electronic Engineering and Information Science,
University of Science and Technology of China, Hefei, Anhui, China, 230026
[2] Key Laboratory of Wireless Sensor Network & Communication,
Shanghai Institute of Microsystem and Information Technology,
Chinese Academy of Sciences865 Changning Road, Shanghai, China, 200050
rosa144@mail.ustc.edu.cn, {shzhang,wyzhou}@ustc.edu.cn

Abstract. Joint radio resource management (JRRM) mechanism helps to optimize the radio resource usage of heterogeneous wireless networks but the introduction of central new entity which manages the information of all networks in JRRM may require unbearable change to current network architecture. Aiming at easily integrating with existing and forthcoming heterogeneous wireless networks, this paper proposes a semi-distributed scheme without centralized entity, in which user terminal make decision on network selection through fuzzy neural network method based on local information and the selected network finishes the admission control to user terminal according to its actual resource condition. Our scheme is verified by the simulation in the UMTS/WLAN scenario and can effectively balance the load between the UMTS/WLAN networks while maintaining the level of blocking probability compared to traditional distributed WLAN-prefer algorithm.

Keywords: heterogeneous wireless networks, semi-distributed, access network selection, fuzzy neural network.

1 Introduction

In the last decade, wireless mobile communication system has a significant development, leading to the deployment of a series of radio access technologies (RATs). At present, global system for mobile communications (GSM) technology co-exist with general packet radio service (GPRS) and universal mobile telecommunications system (UMTS) technologies. In addition, there are many other interface technologies: high-speed downlink packet access (HSDPA), IEEE 802.11 standards, long-term evolution (LTE) system, etc. Therefore, these different wireless technologies constitute heterogeneous wireless access environment.

With the availability of multi-mode user terminals capable of accessing different technologies, the introduction of heterogeneous wireless access environment raises a new challenge for the study of radio resource management. In heterogeneous scenarios, the joint radio resource management (JRRM) is considered a

P. Ren et al. (Eds.): WICON 2011, LNICST 98, pp. 287–297, 2012.

appropriate method to manage dynamically allocation and deallocation of radio resources among different radio access networks, and has been widely studied (e.g.[1] -[4]). In particular, selecting a radio access network for users, while improving the whole heterogeneous networks radio resource utilization, has become a hot topic in radio resource management of heterogeneous networks.

Considering the problem of access network selection, the concept of ABC (always best connected) allows a user terminal connectivity to applications and access technologies that best suit the user's needs[5]. However, how to define "the best" is not much accurate because it depends on many different aspects, such as user preferences, terminal capabilities, service QoS, network coverage, network load, price and many other factors. The decision making of access network has been considered[3][4][6] -[9]. However, most schemes published are based on JRRM mechanism, and need a new entity above all of radio access technologies (RATs). The entity has to acquire global information to make a centralized decision. So that, because of requiring unbearable change, these schemes are difficult to implement in current network structure.

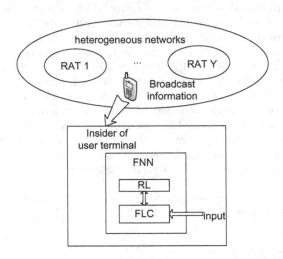

Fig. 1. This figure shows the architecture of the semi-distributed access network selection scheme we proposed. It is user-based and network-assisted. After collecting all the information for decision, user terminal intelligently selects the access network based on fuzzy neural network which consists of FLC and RL. The selected network just does the admission control.

In this paper, we present a semi-distributed access network selection scheme in which the user terminal decides which network to access. This scheme can be implemented in current networks because of no need of central entity. After collecting the information for decision, user terminal intelligently selects the access network based on fuzzy neural network, and then sends an access request message to the selected network. The selected network may refuse this request, because the information at the user terminal may not be exactly up-to-date which is cased by the delay of broadcast message. If being refused, the user terminal should do the selection process again based on the latest information, and then apply for access until receiving the reply. Otherwise, the user terminal should realize that the coverage of the current location is not good enough, and then change its own location. The architecture of the scheme we proposed is shown in Fig.1.

The innovation of this paper can be summarized as follows: first of all, the scheme we proposed is semi-distributed, and the user terminal selects the access network, while the selected network just do the admission control. Secondly, the decision made by user terminal adopts fuzzy neural mechanism with load balance reinforcement learning techniques to achieve the intelligent access network selection.

The rest of this paper is organized as follows. In Section 2, the system model of radio resource management (RRM) is described. The details of the proposed semi-distributed scheme are described in Section 3. Section 4 gives simulation results of the UMTS/WLAN scenario and related discussions, and the conclusion is made in Section 5.

2   System Model

We define the heterogeneous wireless networks system as: $y = \{1, 2, ...Y\}$, and each subsystem has its own cellular structure and access points, such as, BSs in UMTS subsystem, APs in WLAN system and ground stations in satellite system.

We define the set of service as: $s = \{1, 2, ...S\}$, and each type of service demands different QoS: date rate, bandwidth, delay and so on. For the simplicity, we only consider date rate here. Let $N_s = \{N_1, N_2, ...N_S\}$, $R_s = \{R_1, R_2, ...R_S\}$ represent the number of users of each service and the average date rate of each service respectively. R denotes the total heterogeneous networks system capacity constraints.

We define $U_s(R_s)$ as the utility function on behalf of the service. In general, the utility function of user i is expressed as $U_i(R_i)$.

Therefore, radio resource management (RRM) comes down to the optimization problem of the overall heterogeneous networks utility, as follows:

$$\max_{R_s} \sum_{s=1}^{S} N_s U_s(R_s),$$

$$s.t. \sum_{s=1}^{S} N_s R_s \leq R$$

(1)

Because the utility functions are assumed to be strictly concave, there must exist a unique optimal solution Rs^*. However, it is a essentially global optimization and NP-hard problem. So that the optimal solution is so hard to compute. In this paper, taking into account the feasibility with the existing network architecture, we propose a semi-distributed network selection scheme that will be described in part 3.

3   The Semi-distributed Scheme

3.1   The Access Selection-Admission Process

The semi-distributed scheme we proposed is user-based and network-assisted. The user terminal does the access selection process, and after that the selected network does the admission control. The flowchart is shown in Fig.2.

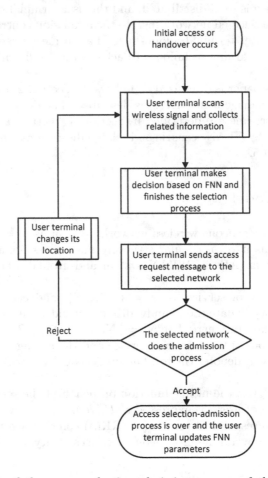

Fig. 2. Flowchart of the access selection-admission process of the semi-distributed scheme we proposed

When initial access or handover occurs, the access selection process in user terminal is triggered.

As access selection is triggered, the user terminal can detect the set of available networks by scanning the wireless signals. At the same time, the user can also acquires the load indicator of each available network which is assumed to broadcast periodically.

Then, after network coverage indicator, load indicator and terminal mobility rate have been collected, the user terminal input these parameters to the fuzzy neural network to get an output of the most suitable network to access. At this point, the user terminal completes the selection process.

The user terminal sends an access request message to the selected network, along with the user's QoS requirement (service type, rate requirements, etc). The selected network starts the process of admission. If the user's QoS could be satisfied, this request will be accepted. Otherwise, the network will reply a reject message. And then, the process of admission is over.

When the user terminal receives the accept message from the selected network, it means that the whole access selection-admission process is over, and the user terminal should use the updated load indicator to adjust the parameters of fuzzy neural network. Otherwise, the user terminal should change the location and start the access selection-admission process again.

3.2 Decision-Making Based on FNN

The fuzzy neural network (FNN) method we takes presented in literatures[10]. FNN is a type of neural network, and takes the advantage of fuzzy logic and neural network methods together.

The reason that we use fuzzy neural network (FNN) is twofold. On the one hand, we can take advantage of the ability of fuzzy logic controller (FLC) to make effective decisions in situations where the available sources of information are qualitatively interpreted and heterogeneous in nature. On the other hand, by using of neural networks to enhance the learning ability of fuzzy logic controller (FLC), which called reinforcement learning (RL) techniques, the scheme we proposed has the ability to interact with the surrounding environment and accordingly, self-tuning and acting.

The FNN used in this paper consists of fuzzy logic control (FLC) and reinforcement learning (RL). Fuzzy logic control (FLC) implements the fuzzifier, the inference engine, and the defuzzifier. The FNN works in two phases. The first one is the decision-making process, through which the FLC based on the selected input linguistic variables, generates the corresponding output linguistic variables, and then access selection decision is made. The second phase is the parameters-tuning process, during which the reinforcement signal is propagated to adjust the FNN parameters.

For the simplify, we take two RATs for example, and the structure of FNN is shown in Fig.3.

Fuzzy Logic Controller. The FNN can be represented by the five-layered structure described in Fig.3.

The first layer nodes are input nodes. We consider five input linguistic variables here: receive signal strength (SS), resource available (RA) with both of the considered RATs and user mobile speed.

The second layer nodes execute the fuzzification operation. They calculate the degree of membership for the input received by the input nodes to the particular

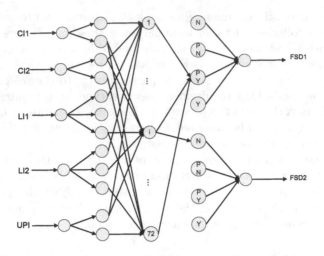

Fig. 3. The five-layer structure of fuzzy neural network

fuzzy set associated with the second layer node, which is defined by a membership function. The term sets defined for each input linguistic variable are as follows.

- $T(SS_n) = T\{low, high\}$,
- $T(RA_n) = T\{low, medium, high\}$,
- $T(UPI) = T\{low, high\}$,

where $n = 1, 2$. So that the second layer consists of 12 nodes. In case of Gaussian membership functions, the degree of membership μ_{ij} for the input variable i, the fuzzy set j is calculated by

$$\mu_{ij}(x_i) = \exp(-\frac{(x_i - m_{ij})^2}{2\sigma_{ij}^2}), \tag{2}$$

where x_i ($i = 1, 2, ...5$) is one of the input linguistic variables, m_{ij} and σ_{ij} ($i = 1, 2, ...5$; $j = 1, 2$ or $j = 1, 2, 3$) are mean and variance of the related Gaussian membership function at the second layer.

The third layer nodes calculate the degree of membership of the precondition of the fuzzy logic rule corresponding to the specific node by means of the AND operator, so that the rule node takes the minimum among the received inputs from the second layer. Considering the term sets defined in the second layer, the number of the third layer nodes is $2 \times 2 \times 3 \times 3 \times 2 = 72$. Therefore, the degree of the third layer node is calculated by

$$a_{j_1 j_2 j_3 j_4 j_5} = \min(\mu_{1j_1}, \mu_{2j_2}, \mu_{3j_3}, \mu_{4j_4}, \mu_{5j_5}), \tag{3}$$

where $a_{j_1 j_2 j_3 j_4 j_5}$ ($j_i \in [1, 72]$, $i = 1, 2, 3, 4, 5$).

The fourth layer nodes calculate the degree of membership of the consequence of the fuzzy logic rule. The number of this layer nodes depends on the output linguistic variable of the fifth layer. The term sets defined for each output linguistic variable are as follows.

- $T(FSD_j) = T\{N(not), PN(probabily\ not), PY(probabily\ yes), Y(yes)\}$,

where $j = 1, 2$. FSD denotes fuzzy selection decision. So that, the fourth layer consists of 8 nodes.

The fourth layer nodes sum the degree of membership of the third layer nodes, which related to the specific fourth layer node as a consequence of the fuzzy logic rule. So,

$$b_i = \min(\sum a_{j_1 j_2 j_3 j_4 j_5}, 1), \tag{4}$$

where $a_{j_1 j_2 j_3 j_4 j_5}$ denote the third layer nodes that related to specific node i in fourth layer.

The fifth layer nodes finally perform the defuzzication process, and compute the output of fuzzy selection decision (FSD) by the center of area method.

$$FSD_i = \frac{\sum_{j \in T_i} m_j \sigma_j b_j}{\sum_{j \in T_i} \sigma_j b_j}, i = 1, 2 \tag{5}$$

m_j and σ_j ($j = 1, 2$) are mean and variance of the related Gaussian membership function at the fourth layar. T_i is the set of the fourth layer nodes that related to node i of the fifth layer.

Reinforcement Learning. The reinforcement learning procedure is executed after the access selection-admission process is over, and then activate an error backpropagation learning algorithm that minimizes a quadratic error function. The quadratic error function for minimization is defined as

$$E_t = \frac{1}{2}(y_t - y^*)^2, \tag{6}$$

where y_t denotes the current networks load balance indicator, which we use the difference between the highest network and the lowest network. Meantime, y^* denotes the expected value of load balance indicator, which we choose as 0.

Parameters of fuzzy neural network modified by the method of negative gradient descent. The parameter x_t according to E gradient in the opposite direction to adjust. Formula is as follows, where γ is the learning speed.

$$x_{t+1} = x_t + \gamma(-\frac{E_t - E_{t-1}}{x_t - x_{t-1}}), \tag{7}$$

According to the error propagation, fuzzy neural network updates the mean m and standard deviation σ of the fuzzification and defuzzification membership function.

In our proposed scheme, the adjustment of parameters divides into two phases. The first phase is initial offline training. We can use software simulation to adjust the parameters until E_t less than the predetermined threshold. The second phase is online training. By using the FNN already trained offline, the scheme we proposed can adjust the parameters after the each access selection-admission process. Therefore, our scheme can dynamically adapt to the heterogeneous networks condition.

Making Decision. In accordance with the fuzzy neural network output parameters FSD_i, $(i = 1, 2)$, the user terminal selects the network with greater FSD value. However, if FSD_1 and FSD_2 are both lower than 0.5, which means the available networks both are not suitable for access. Then the user terminal should change the location, and start a new access selection process.

4   Numerical Result and Discussion

In this paper, we choose wireless local area network (WLAN) as a high-bandwidth, low coverage wireless access technology, as well as universal mobile telecommunications system (UMTS) as a low-bandwidth, high coverage access technology. So that, simulation scenario of heterogeneous wireless networks HWN = {UMTS, WLAN}.

According to Part 3, the input of FNN are SS, RA and UPI that described in detail as follow.

– SS(dbm): Signal strength received by the user terminals from UMTS and WLAN.
– RA: Resource available that the user terminals can get from broadcast message. For UMTS, $RA_{UMTS}(100\%) = 1 - \mu$, where μ denotes the uplink load factor. For WLAN, $RA_{WLAN}(units)$ = Maximum number of users (28 in simulation) − number of users allocated in the WLAN cell.
– UPI(m/s): User preference indicator, and we use the speed of the user terminals here.

4.1   Single-User Performance

Fig.4 show when the SS received from UMTS and WLAN are equal, as well as RA of WLAN is enough, how the RA of UMTS effects the output of FNN. We can get that if user terminal moving high speed, FSD_{WLAN} will be always

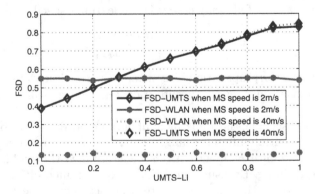

Fig. 4. Load of UMTS effects on decision when the speed of MS is $2m/s$ and $40m/s$, while $SS_{UMTS} = SS_{WLAN} = -84dbm$, $RA_{WLAN} = 10$

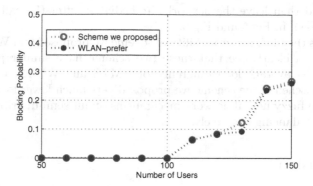

Fig. 5. This figure shows blocking probability when maximum number of users UMTS can accept is 50, and maximum number of users WLAN can accept is 28. The users initiate the call according the poisson process with arrival rate of 10 calls per hour, and the average call duration is 180 seconds.

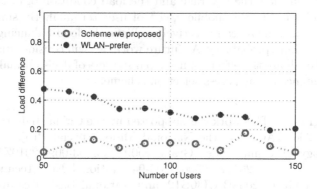

Fig. 6. This figure shows load difference when maximum number of users UMTS can accept is 50, and maximum number of users WLAN can accept is 28. The users initiate the call according the poisson process with arrival rate of 10 calls per hour, and the average call duration is 180 seconds.

below 0.5, which assistant with the fact that WLAN would be an inappropriate choice for high-speed users. However, with the condition of moving lowly, When RA of UMTS is less than 0.3, user terminal would choose WLAN, and when RA of UMTS is more than 0.3, the user terminal would attempt to choose UMTS instead. It means that, at the cross point, the load condition of both network are almost equal.

4.2   Multi-user Performance

In order to get the multi-user performance of semi-distributed scheme we proposed, we compares it with the traditional WLAN-prefer scheme. In simulation process, the users initiate the call according the poisson process with arrival rate of 10 calls per hour, and the average call duration is 180 seconds. Each user calls only once, and then leave the networks immediately after the call. Simulation results are shown in Fig.5 and Fig.6.

Fig.5 shows the blocking probability of scheme we proposed and WLAN-prefer scheme. We can clearly see that these two scheme have similar performance. Fig.6 shows the average load difference of UMTS and WLAN. Compared to WLAN-prefer scheme, the scheme we proposed gets much lower load difference. Therefore, the fuzzy neural network mechanisms of our semi-distributed scheme achieves load balancing effectively.

5   Conclusion

The heterogeneous wireless networks compose of multiple radio access technologies, and the selection of the appropriate access network for user terminal is a crucial issue for overall system performance. In this paper, we propose a semi-distributed network selection scheme based on fuzzy neural network. The proposed scheme considers the coverage and the load condition of of the available networks in addition to the mobile speed of user terminal. By simulation, we point out that our scheme can effectively achieve the load balancing and maintain the low blocking probability. As future work, we will consider more complex scenarios and evaluate the effects of more parameters of decision-making process on the performance of the access selection scheme.

Acknowledgment. This work was supported by the China High-Tech 863 Plan under Grant 2009AA011506, the National Major Special Projects in Science and Technology of China under Grant 2009ZX03003-009, 2010ZX03003-001, 2010ZX03005-003, and 2011ZX03003-003-04, National Key Technology R&D Program under Grant 2008BAH30B12, and National Basic Research Program of China under Grant 2007CB310602.

References

1. Prez-Romero, J., Sallent, O., Agust, R., Daz-Guerra, M.A.: Radio Resource Management Strategies in UMTS, Ed. John Wiley & Sons (2005)
2. Luo, J., Mohyeldin, E., Dillinger, M., Demestichas, P., Tsagkaris, K., Dimitrakopoulos, G., Schulz, E.: Performance Analysis of Joint Radio Resource Management for Reconfigurable Terminals with Multiclass Circuit-switched Services. In: WWRF 12th Meeting, WG6, Toronto, Canada (November 2004)
3. Agusti, R., Sallent, O., Prez-Romero, J., Giupponi, L.: A fuzzy- neural based approach for joint radio resource management in a beyond 3G framework. In: 1st International Conference on Quality of Service in Heterogeneous Wired/Wireless Networks, Qshine 2004, Dallas, USA (October 2004)
4. Giupponi, L., Agust, R., Prez-Romero, J., Sallent, O.: A novel joint radio resource management approach with reinforcement learning mechanisms. In: Proc. 1st IEEE Int. Workshop Radio Resource Manage. Wireless Cellular Netw., Phoenix, AZ, pp. 621–626 (April 2005)

5. Gustafsson, E., Jonsson, A.: Always best connected. IEEE Wireless Commun. Mag. 10(1), 49–55 (2003)
6. Giupponi, L., Agust, R., Prez-Romero, J., Sallent, O.: Fuzzy neural control for economic-driven radio resource management in beyond 3G networks. IEEE Trans. Syst., Man, Cybern. C: Appl. Rev. 39(2), 170–189 (2009)
7. Yilmaz, O., et al.: Access Selection in WCDMA and WLAN Multi-access Networks. In: Proc. of IEEE VTC Spring, pp. 2240–2244 (2005)
8. Hasib, A., Fapojuwo, A.O.: Cross-Layer Radio Resource Management in Integrated WWAN and WLAN Networks. Computer Networks 54, 341–356 (2010)
9. Kalliokulju, J., Meche, P., Rinne, M.J., Vallstrom, J., Varshney, P., Haggman, S.-G.: Radio access selection for multistandard terminals. IEEE Commun. Mag. 39(10), 116–124 (2001)
10. Lin, C.T., Lee, C.S.G.: Neural-network-based fuzzy logic control and Decision System. IEEE Trans. Comput. 40, 1320–1336 (1991)

A Practical Performance Analysis
of CRS-Aided Channel Estimation Algorithms
for LTE Downlink System

Yannan Yuan, Lianfen Huang[*], Ruogui Xiao, Xin Qi, and Min Huang

Department of Communication Engineering, Xiamen University, P.R. China
lfhuang@xmu.edu.cn

Abstract. Channel estimation algorithms are employed in 3GPP Long Term Evolution (LTE) downlink system to help with coherent demodulation. Several CRS-aided channel estimation algorithms over multipath Rayleigh fading channel have been investigated in this paper. Based on theoretical analysis and simulation, Wiener interpolation channel estimator is proposed for LTE downlink system. In consideration of practical implementation and universality for different channels, we propose that CRSs in Wiener interpolation should be contained in the time window of $10e^{-3}$ second as well as in the frequency window of two adjacent resource blocks, which symmetrically distribute around the current estimated resource block in frequency domain.

Keywords: 3GPP LTE, channel estimation, CRS-aided channel estimation, Wiener interpolation.

1   Introduction

The third generation partnership project (3GPP) long term evolution (LTE), which is favored by most telecommunication operators all over the world, has been generally recognized as the internationally powerful mobile communication system [1].The LTE targets at significantly increased instantaneous peak data rates, higher average spectrum efficiency and the cell-edge user throughput efficiency [2]. Some advanced technologies which are new to cellular applications are employed by 3GPP LTE physical layer, e.g. multiple Input Multiple Output (MIMO) and Orthogonal Frequency Division Multiplexing (OFDM) are adopted.

MIMO technology as well as adaptive technology is used in LTE to enhance the data rate and system performance, which makes the peak data rate reach over 100Mbit/s in the downlink (DL). Multiple antennas provide with an additional degree of freedom to the channel scheduler. Depending on user's selection over individual resource blocks (RBs) in the spatial domain, different MIMO schemes could be used in the 3GPP standards.

---

[*] This work was supported by National Basic Research Program of China (2007CB310608), National Natural Science Foundation of China (60832008), China's 863 Project (2009AA011501), National S&T Major Project (2009ZX03002-002), NCET and PCSIRT.

P. Ren et al. (Eds.): WICON 2011, LNICST 98, pp. 298–311, 2012.

In the physical layer of 3GPP LTE DL system, OFDM has been used due to its high bandwidth efficiency and the capability to mitigate the inner symbol interference (ISI) in a severe multi-path fading channel. 3GPP LTE uses orthogonal frequency division multiplexing access (OFDMA) scheme for transmission in DL and single carrier frequency division multiple access (SCFDMA) for uplink. A dynamic channel estimation algorithm tracking of fading channel at the receiver is necessary before demodulation of OFDM symbols, because the radio channel is mostly frequency-selective and time-varying for wideband mobile communication systems [3]. In OFDM symbols, cell-specific reference signals (CRS) are used to do help with channel estimation. The receiver could estimate the whole channel response of each OFDM symbol by processing the received signals at predefined positions of CRS. Such kind of CRS-aided channel estimation has been proven as a feasible method for OFDM systems. CRS-aided channel estimation algorithms can be based on Least Square (LS) or Minimum Mean Square Error (MMSE) [4]. LS is relatively simple, which dose not need relevant channel information and is easily affected by noise. As for MMSE, channel response is estimated with the help of channel statistic information and relevance between subcarriers.

Although many papers about channel estimation have been published, to the best of our knowledge, there are few methods based on numerous practical elements. Moreover, there is no detailed performance evaluation on how to select CRS. In this paper, Wiener filter interpolation with different configurations and linear interpolation have been investigated for 3GPP LTE DL. Analysis of channel estimation performance has been done on all the antenna ports. Based on statistic property of different channels and performance v.s. complexity ratio, an appropriate channel estimation algorithm has been selected.

The rest of the paper is organized as follows: 3GPP DL system model is introduced in Section 2, and some channel estimation algorithms are presented in Section 3. Scenario, parameters description and the analysis of channel estimation performance are shown in Section 4, followed by Section 5 which concludes this paper.

2   System Model in LTE DL

2.1   CRS Structure

In LTE DL, CRS sequence $r_{l,n_s}(m)$ shall be mapped to complex-valued modulation symbols $a_{k,l}^{(p)}$ used as reference symbols for antenna port p in slot n_s, where $r_{l,n_s}(m)$, $a_{k,l}^{(p)}$ and the mapping function between them are defined in Section 6.10.1 in [5]. As shown in figure 1, the white grid represents resource elements (REs) for data transmission, and the colored grid means REs for CRSs. The shaded grid denotes unused RE, because REs used for reference signal transmission on any of the antenna ports in a slot shall not be used for any transmission on any other antenna port in the same slot and set to zero. Based on the definition in [5], the m of CRS is decided by the length of cyclic prefix, cell ID and antenna port. And the density of CRS on antenna port 2 (or 3) is half as much as it on antenna port 0 (or 1).

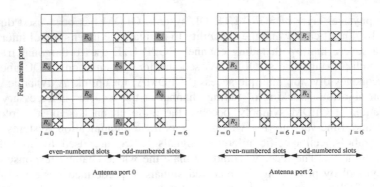

Fig. 1. Mapping of DL reference signals (normal cyclic prefix) [5]

2.2   OFDM in LTE

As shown in figure 2, $x(k)$ is the input data at the transmitter and $y(k)$ is the output data at the receiver. $w(i)$ is complex additive white Gaussian noise(AWGN). At the transmitter, a modulated sequence $x(k)$ is transformed into a N-point sequence $x(n)$, where N is the length of IFFT. A cyclic prefix for avoiding Inter-symbol interference is added before transmitting. It is an inverse process at the receiver, and channel estimation is done after FFT in receiver.

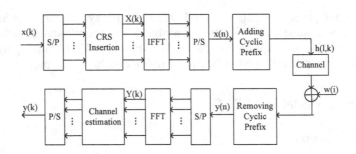

Fig. 2. The block diagram of OFDM transmitter and receiver

2.3   Frame Structure

There are two radio frame structures supported in 3GPP LTE. One is applicable to both full duplex and half duplex FDD, which is shown in figure 3. The other is applicable to TDD. In [5], seven kinds of uplink-downlink configurations for TDD frames are also presented.

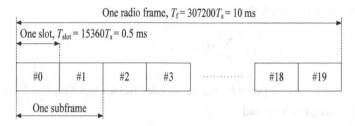

Fig. 3. FDD frame structure [5]

3   Channel Estimation Algorithms

A number of channel estimation techniques have been proposed to estimate channel response in LTE DL, such as LS, MMSE and maximum likelihood (ML). In all the CRS-aided techniques, channel response on CRS is estimated first based on the above principles. And two-dimension Wiener interpolation [6] or linear interpolation is performed to estimated channel response on data REs based on the known channel response on CRSs.

3.1   Two-Dimension Wiener Interpolation

The time-variable channel impulse response could be written as:

$$h(t,\tau) = \sum_{l=0}^{L-1} \alpha_l(t)\delta(\tau-\tau_l) \; . \tag{1}$$

Then, the frequency response of the channel at time t is written as:

$$H(t,f) = \int_{-\infty}^{\infty} h(t,\tau)e^{-j2\pi f\tau}d\tau = \sum_{l=0}^{L-1} \alpha_l(t)e^{-j2\pi f\tau_l} \; . \tag{2}$$

Assume that $\alpha_l(t)$ has the following correlation function in time domain:

$$r_{\alpha_l}(t+\Delta t,t) = E\left\{\alpha_l(t+\Delta t)\cdot\alpha_l^*(t)\right\} = \sigma_l^2 r_t(\Delta t) \; . \tag{3}$$

Assume that different paths are independent, and then the correlation function in frequency domain written as:

$$
\begin{aligned}
r_H(\Delta t,\Delta f) &= E\left\{H(t+\Delta t, f+\Delta f)\cdot H^*(t,f)\right\} \\
&= \sum_{l=0}^{L-1} r_{\alpha_l}(\Delta t)e^{-j2\pi\Delta f\tau_l} = r_t(\Delta t)\sum_{l=0}^{L-1}\sigma_l^2 e^{-j2\pi\Delta f\tau_l}
\end{aligned} \; . \tag{4}
$$

If the channel is normalized, that is

$$\sum_{l=0}^{L-1} \sigma_l^2 = 1 \ . \tag{5}$$

And $r_t(\Delta t)$ could be computed by the zero-order Bessel function of 1st kind [7], f_d is the Doppler frequency spread.

$$r_t(\Delta t) = J_0(2\pi f_d \Delta t). \tag{6}$$

Assume that the propagation channel do not vary during the duration of one OFDM symbol. After sampling, channel response in frequency domain could be written as:

$$H(n,k) = H\left(nT, k\frac{1}{NT_s}\right) = \sum_{l=0}^{L-1} \alpha_l(nT)e^{-j2\pi\frac{d_l \cdot k}{N}} \ . \tag{7}$$

$$r_H(n,k) = r_H\left(nT, k\frac{1}{NT_s}\right) = r_t(nT)\sum_{l=0}^{L-1} \sigma_l^2 e^{-j2\pi\frac{d_l \cdot k}{N}} \ . \tag{8}$$

where $d_l = \tau_l / T_s$, T_s is the sampling time, and T is the duration of an OFDM symbol (including cyclic prefix). What's more, n means the interval of two REs in time domain; k means the interval of two REs in frequency domain.

$$T = (N_{CP} + N) \cdot T_s \ . \tag{9}$$

where N_{CP} is the length of cyclic prefix, N is the length of IFFT/FFT.

Assume that the duration of cyclic prefix is larger than impulse response of channel and there is no inter-symbol interference. After the CRSs are faded by the channel, the corresponding received signal could be written as:

$$\vec{Y} = \vec{H} + \vec{W} = \begin{pmatrix} H(n_1,k_1) \\ H(n_2,k_2) \\ \vdots \\ H(n_P,k_P) \end{pmatrix} + \vec{W} \ . \tag{10}$$

All the vectors in (10) are $P \times 1$ vectors, $\vec{Y}$ could correspond to any combination of CRSs. n_p and k_p are the indices of CRSs in time and frequency domain, respectively, where $p = 0, 1, \cdots, P$. $\vec{W}$ is the vector of additive white Gaussian noise, the variance of each of which is σ_w^2.

Based on the time-frequency two-dimensional Wiener, channel response in frequency of any RE could be written as:

$$\hat{H}(n,k) = \bar{C}(n,k)\bar{Y} .$$ (11)

where,

$$\bar{C}(n,k) = \bar{r}_{H(n,k)\bar{Y}} \cdot \bar{r}_{\bar{Y}\bar{Y}}^{-1} .$$ (12)

$$\bar{r}_{H(k,n)\bar{Y}} = E\{H(k,n) \cdot \bar{Y}^H\}$$
$$= E\{H(k,n) \cdot (H^*(n_1,k_1), \quad H^*(n_2,k_2), \quad \cdots \quad H^*(n_p,k_p))\}$$ (13)
$$= (r_H(n-n_1,k-k_1), \quad r_H(n-n_2,k-k_2), \quad \cdots \quad r_H(n-n_p,k-k_p))$$

$$\bar{r}_{\bar{Y}\bar{Y}} = E\{\bar{Y}\bar{Y}^H\} = E\{\bar{H}\bar{H}^H\} + \sigma_n^2 \bar{I}$$
$$= \begin{bmatrix} r_H(0,0) & r_H(n_1-n_2,k_1-k_2) & \cdots & r_H(n_1-n_p,k_1-k_p) \\ r_H^*(n_1-n_2,k_1-k_2) & r_H(0,0) & \cdots & \vdots \\ \vdots & \vdots & \ddots & \vdots \\ r_H^*(n_1-n_p,k_1-k_p) & \cdots & \cdots & r_H(0,0) \end{bmatrix} + \sigma_n^2 \bar{I}$$ (14)

3.2   Linear Interpolation

The basic assumption of linear interpolation is that the relationship of channel response between estimated REs and known REs is linear. Then, channel response of RE could be calculated base on the slope. Assume that there are two known REs, which can be denoted as (x_1, y_1), (x_2, y_2), and the unknown RE can be denoted as (x, y) accordingly. Then the estimated channel response of RE can be written as:

$$y = \frac{x - x_1}{x_2 - x_1}y_2 + \frac{x_2 - x}{x_2 - x_1}y_1 .$$ (15)

Two-dimension linear interpolation can be divided into two one-dimension linear interpolation. Generally, one-dimension linear interpolation in time (or frequency) domain is done firstly, and then the other one-dimension linear interpolation in frequency (or time) domain is done. One-dimensional interpolation in time domain can be done as follows:

$$\hat{H}(n+m,k) = (1-\frac{m}{\Delta})H(n,k) + \frac{m}{\Delta}H(n+\Delta,k) .$$ (16)

where $0 \le m \le \Delta$ and Δ is the duration between two known REs.

4   Performance and Complexity Analysis with Different Configuration

A cellular OFDM downlink system over multipath Rayleigh fading environment is considered to compare the performance of the above estimators. In simulation, channel types are pedestrian A 3km/hour, vehicular A 30km/hour and vehicular A120km/hour are selected, which are defined in Rec. ITU-R M.1225 [8] and denoted as PedA, VehA30 and VehA120 in the following context, respectively.

4.1   Parameters Description

The performance of channel estimators is evaluated at bandwidth of 5MHz, 10MHz and 20MHz. The performance of channel estimators at 20MHz is shown and analyzed. The performance at 5MHz and 10MHz is similar with it at 20MHz.

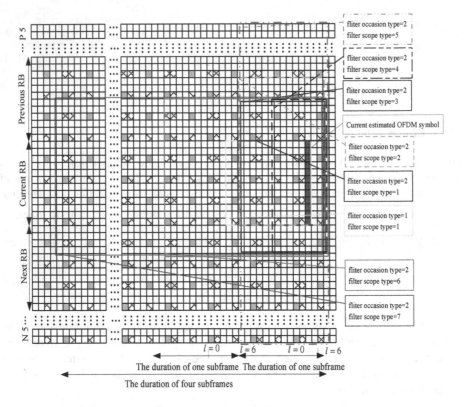

Fig. 4. Various types of configurations in Wiener interpolation on port 0

As shown in (11), the performance of 2D Wiener interpolation is determined by $\bar{C}(n,k)$, which is determined by selected CRSs. Thus the performance and complexity of 2D Wiener interpolation are fully decided by pattern of the selected CRSs. In order to choose a better interpolation method with appropriate configuration, antenna port 0 is taken as an example, and figure 4 shows different CRSs pattern in 2D Wiener interpolation.

Wherein "filter occasion type" indicates when channel estimation is done in time domain. It is used in both linear and Wiener interpolation. "filter occasion type = 1" represents that channel estimation (CE) for an OFDM symbol is done as soon as it is received. And "2" represents that CE is done for the previous 2 or 3 OFDM symbols in the time domain on Port 0 when a new OFDM symbol with CRS is received. If it is Port 2, "2" represents that CE is done for the previous 6 OFDM symbols in the time domain when a new OFDM symbol with CRS is received. "filter scope type" is only used in Wiener interpolation, which indicates CRS used in CE. Moreover, "the previous (or next) XX RBs" means the previous (or next) XX RBs in frequency domain. "filter scope type = 1" represents that CRSs in current RB in 10^{-3} second are used, which is equal to the duration of one subframe. "2" represents that CRSs in previous and current RB in 10^{-3} second are used for CE. "3" represents that CRSs in half of previous and next RBs, as well as the current RB in 10^{-3} second are used. "4" represents that CRSs which are closer to current OFDM symbol from CRSs in "3" are chosen to be used. "5" represents that CRSs in previous five and next five RBs in 10^{-3} second are used, as well as current RB. "6" represents that CRSs in half of previous and next RBs, as well as the current RB in 2×10^{-3} second are used, which is equal to the duration of two subframes. "7" represents that CRSs in half of previous and next RBs, as well as the current RB in 4×10^{-3} second are used. And for VehA120, 4×10^{-3} second is approximate to its coherence time.

4.2   Channel Statistic Information

The coherence time of the three channel types are different from each other, which is shown in table 1.

Table 1. Coherence Time over Three Types of Channel

	PedA	VehA30	VehA120
Coherence time (s)	0.1714	0.0171	0.0043

4.3   Performance of Channel Estimation on Port 0

As shown in figure 5, the performance of Wiener channel estimator becomes better as the growth of CRSs, which is used in Wiener interpolation. When MSE is 10^{-1}, the required SNR can be decreased about 10 dB from "filter scope type=1" to "filter scope type=7" over PedA. Meanwhile, figure 6 and 7 show the similar tendency. Yet, the required SNR is decreased about 5 dB when MSE is 10^{-1} over VehA120, because part of selected CRSs in Wiener interpolation with "filter scope=7" approach to the limit of channel coherence time.

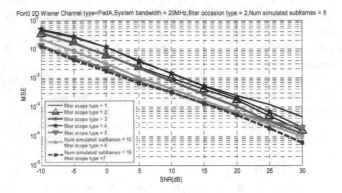

Fig. 5. The performance of Wiener channel estimator over PedA on port 0

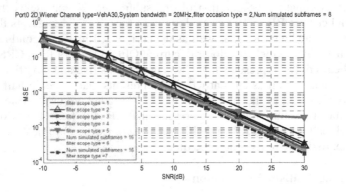

Fig. 6. The performance of Wiener channel estimator over VehA30 on port 0

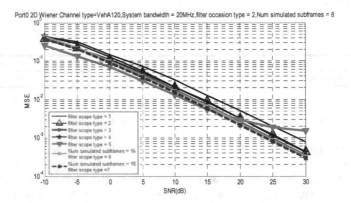

Fig. 7. The performance of Wiener channel estimator over VehA120 on port 0

As for figure 6 and figure 7, the performance of Wiener channel estimator does not become better when filter scope is 5 over VehA30 and VehA120, because the selected CRSs in "filter scope=5" are from more than ten RBs in frequency domain, which exceeds the coherence bandwidth. Based on statistic properties of channel, the coherence bandwidth is only about 398kHz over VehA30 and VehA120, which is approximate to two RBs in frequency domain. Nevertheless, Wiener estimator with "filter scope=5" uses much uncorrelated CRSs, the effect of which is equal to noise. Thus there is a MSE bound when SNR is high. When the duration of CRS is 10^{-3} second, the performance of Wiener channel estimator with "filter scope=3" is better than others over VehA30 and VehA120.

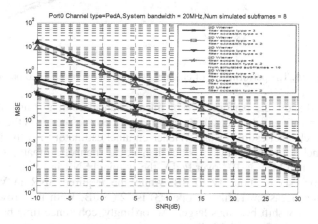

Fig. 8. The performance of channel estimation over PedA on port 0

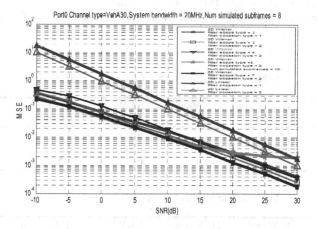

Fig. 9. The performance of channel estimation over VehA30 on port 0

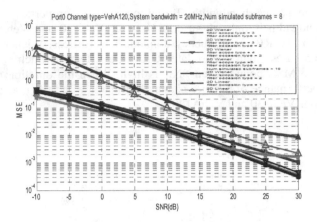

Fig. 10. The performance of channel estimation over VehA120 on port 0

Figure 8-10 show the performance of linear channel estimator and Wiener channel estimator over different channels. The performance becomes better as the growth of SNR in both linear channel estimator and Wiener channel estimator. Yet the performance of Wiener channel estimator is always better than linear channel estimator, especially when SNR is low. When MSE is 10^{-1} over PedA, the required SNR in linear channel estimator (filter occasion =1) is about 12.30 dB, while the required SNR in Wiener channel estimator (filter occasion=1, filter scope =3) is -2.65 dB. With the growth of velocity, Doppler frequency shift becomes larger. Accordingly, coherence time becomes smaller. Coinciding with this, Figure 8-10 above show that the performance of channel estimation becomes worse as the velocity grows. Moreover, the performance of Wiener estimator with "filter occasion=2" is much better than that of Wiener estimator with "filter occasion=1", especially when users' velocity is high. Table 2 shows the value of SNR over different channels when MSE is 10^{-1}, and table 3 shows the value of SNR over different channels when MSE is 10^{-2}. Wherein, the parameters of Wiener estimator consist of filter scope type and filter occasion type, respectively. And the parameter of linear estimator is filter occasion type.

Table 2. The Value of SNR (dB) When MSE is 10^{-1}

Channel Type	2D-Wiener (s=3,o=1)	2D-Wiener (s=3,o=2)	2D-Wiener (s=7,o=2)	2D-Linear (o=1)	2D-Linear (o=2)
PedA	-2.65	-2.45	-8.90	12.30	9.75
VehA30	-1.65	-1.75	-4.00	12.20	9.78
VehA120	2.35	-0.15	-0.62	12.63	9.83

Table 3. The Value of SNR (dB) When MSE is 10^{-2}

Channel Type	2D-Wiener (s=3,o=1)	2D-Wiener (s=3,o=2)	2D-Wiener (s=7,o=2)	2D-Linear (o=1)	2D-Linear (o=2)
PedA	8.55	8.90	2.80	22.20	19.90
VehA30	12.82	11.30	9.20	22.20	19.87
VehA120	16.1	13.10	12.17	27.20	20.30

4.4   Performance of Channel Estimation on Port 2

As it is defined in [5], the density of CRS on port 0 is twice of CRS on port2. Thus the performance of CRS-aided channel estimation on port 0 is better than it on port 2, although the same channel estimator is used.

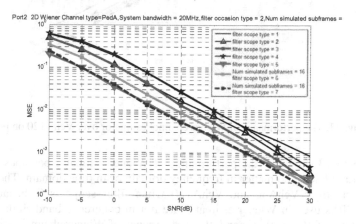

Fig. 11. The performance of Wiener channel estimator over PedA on port 2

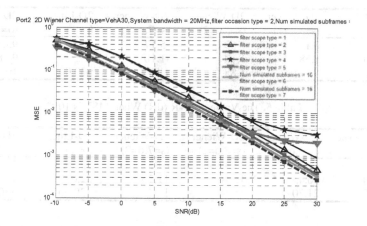

Fig. 12. The performance of Wiener channel estimator over VehA30 on port 2

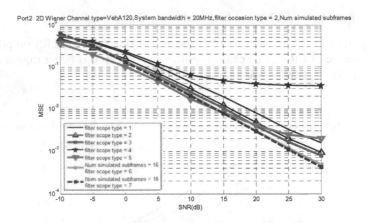

Fig. 13. The performance of Wiener channel estimator over VehA120 on port 2

Figure 11-13 show that the performance of Wiener estimator becomes better with the growth of CRSs, no matter in frequency domain or in time domain. There is also a MSE bound over VehA30 and VehA120 when filter scope is 5, because part of selected CRSs used in Wiener estimator are not in coherence bandwidth. And when the duration of CRS is 10^{-3} second, the performance of Wiener channel estimator with "filter scope=3" is better than others over VehA30 and VehA120.

Table 4. The Value of SNR (dB) When MSE is 10^{-1}

Channel Type	2D-Wiener (s=3,o=1)	2D-Wiener (s=3,o=2)	2D-Wiener (s=7,o=2)	2D-Linear (o=1)	2D-Linear (o=2)
PedA	0.15	0.60	-5.17	12.53	9.85
VehA30	1.58	1.10	-1.10	12.55	9.78
VehA120	5.77	1.85	1.50	>30.00	10.40

Table 5. The Value of SNR (dB) When MSE is 10^{-2}

Channel Type	2D-Wiener (s=3,o=1)	2D-Wiener (s=3,o=2)	2D-Wiener (s=7,o=2)	2D-Linear (o=1)	2D-Linear (o=2)
PedA	11.65	11.40	6.45	22.55	19.70
VehA30	16.45	13.40	11.25	22.65	19.70
VehA120	21.70	15.17	13.70	>30.00	>30.00

The contrast between linear estimator and Wiener estimator is shown in table 4, when MSE is 10^{-1}. The required SNR in linear channel estimator (filter occasion =1) is about 12.53 dB, while the require SNR in Wiener channel estimator (filter occasion=1, filter scope =3) is 0.15 dB, when MSE is 10^{-1} over PedA. Yet the performance of channel estimator is worse than it on port 0, no matter linear estimator or Wiener estimator. And when MSE is 10^{-2}, the contrast is shown in table 5. Wherein, the parameters of Wiener estimator consist of filter scope type and filter occasion type, respectively. And the parameter of linear estimator is filter occasion type.

5   Conclusion

In this paper, two-dimension linear interpolation and two-dimension Wiener interpolation channel estimation methods for LTE DL have been investigated over multipath Rayleigh fading environment. Based on theoretical analysis and simulation, we propose that channel estimation should be done for the previous 2 or 3 OFDM symbols in the time domain on port 0 when a new OFDM symbol with CRS is received. If it is on port 2, channel estimation should be done for the previous 6 OFDM symbols in the time domain when a new OFDM symbol with CRS is received. In view of performance, computational complexity and universality for different channels, we propose that Wiener interpolation channel estimator should be used, which uses CRSs in half of previous and next RB, as well as the current RB in 10^{-3} second (one subframe). Wherein, "the previous and next RB" means the previous and next RB in frequency domain. In time domain, the CRSs in the time window of 10^{-3} second should be used.

References

1. Hou, J., Liu, J.: A novel channel estimation algorithm for 3GPP LTE downlink system using joint time-frequency two-dimensional iterative Wiener filter. In: IEEE International Conference on Communication Technology (November 2010)
2. 3GPP TR 36.814 V0.4.1, Further Advancements for E-UTRA Physical Layer Aspects (Release 9) (February 2009)
3. Bahai, A.R.S., Saltzberg, B.R.: Multi-Carrier Digital Communication: Theory and Applications of OFDM. Kluwer Academic/Plenum (1999)
4. van de Beek, J.-J., Edfors, O., Sandell, M., Wilson, S.K., Borjesson, P.O.: On channel estimation in OFDM systems. In: IEEE 45th Vehicular Technology Conference, pp. 815–819 (1995)
5. 3GPP TS 36.211 V9.1.0, Technical Specification Group Radio Access Network for E-UTRA Physical channels and Modulation (Release 9) (March 2010)
6. Qin, Y., Hui, B., Chang, K.H.: Performance evaluation of pilot-based channel estimation and equalization techniques in 3GPP LTE downlink. In: Proc. Of KICS Summer Conference (November 2009)
7. Zhou, W., Lam, W.H., A novel method of Doppler shift estimation for OFDM systems. In: IEEE Military Communication Conference (November 2008)
8. Recommendation ITU-R M.1225, Guidelines for Evaluation of Radio Transmission Technologies for IMT-2000(Question ITU-R 39/8) (1997)

A Joint Optimal Algorithm Based on Relay Nodes Selection and Power Allocation

Zhao Shen[1,2,*], Daiyu Fu[2], and Yu Jin[2]

[1] Coll. Elect. Engn., Naval Univ. Engn.
Wuhan, China
[2] Department of Elect. & Informat. Engn., Huazhong Univ. of Sci. & Technol.,
Wuhan, China
{clingerlisa,fudaiyu}@gmail.com, shenzhao_0@163.com

Abstract. In this paper, we proposed a joint optimal algorithm based on relay nodes selection and power allocation, which utilizes the theory utility maximization modeling system by adopting convex optimization, and obtains the optimal power allocation between source node and relay nodes by applying the Karush-Kuhn-Tucker (KKT) condition. In addition, the relay nodes allocated with power unequal to zero are the selected relay nodes, therefore, the selection of relay nodes is realized. Moreover, the optimal number of relay nodes is discussed. Simulation results show that the proposed algorithm achieves a better performance than the traditional equal power allocation algorithm.

Keywords: Relay, convex optimization, nodes selection, power allocation.

1 Introduction

In the wireless communication network, forwarding by the assistance of relay can reduce the transmission path loss and improve overall system throughput, which makes the overall system performance significantly enhanced[1-2]. Therefore, the researches on relay-assisted transmission make a significant contribution to the study of the future wireless communication system.

At present, the research about relay communication is not mature. The correlative research focuses on the multi-user two-hop relay-assisted network with one source, one destination and signal or multiple relay. The two main problems that need to be solved are the selection of relay nodes and the power allocation[3-4]. So far, there are a variety of relay transmission strategies, such as Amplify-Forward (AF), Decode-Forward (DF), partial DF, etc[5-7]. In this paper, we utilize AF for the system modeling. While the system power is limited, the power allocation among the relay nodes transmitting simultaneity is a very important problem

* This work is supported by the National High-Tech. R&D Program of China (863 Program) under Grant No. 2009AA01Z205, and by the National Science Key Special Project of China under Grants No. 2010ZX03003-001,2008ZX03003-004 and 2009ZX03003-007.

P. Ren et al. (Eds.): WICON 2011, LNICST 98, pp. 312–322, 2012.

that affects the system performance greatly. Nowadays, the studies about the problem are mainly on the power allocation between relay node and source in signal relay network, and the power allocation among relay nodes in multiple relay networks. In the previous studies, while selecting signal relay node among multiple relay nodes, the power allocation between source and relay nodes are considered at the same time. However, while multiple relay nodes selected, the power allocation among relays nodes transmitting simultaneity is not considered. In order to reduce the complexity, the equal power allocation among relay nodes is taken into account in most of the existing researches.

By utilizing the Network Utility Maximization (NUM) idea and applying the convex optimization theory, a joint optimal algorithm based on relay nodes selection and power allocation is proposed in this paper. NUM is the method that utilizing the description of consumer income during accepting service in economics, defining the service satisfaction provided by the wireless communication network for the node (user) as network utility, making the utility maximization model for transmission and allocation problem in the wireless network, and applying the optimization tool for optimal system resource allocation. After applying NUM thinking to obtain the optimization modeling, we can utilize convex optimization to solve complicated optimization problem. Simulation results show that the proposed algorithm can acquire greater performance gain than the traditional equal power allocation algorithm.

The rest of this paper is organized as follows. Section 2 provides the system model. Section 3 presents the details of the Optimization algorithm based on relay nodes selection and power allocation. In section 4 the simulation results are provides. Finally, Section 5 concludes the paper.

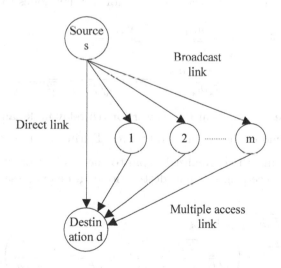

Fig. 1. System model

2   System Model

We consider a two-hop multi-relay assisted system as depicted in (Fig. 1), which consists of $m+2$ nodes: a source (s), $a destination$(d), and m relay $(1, 2, \ldots, m)$. The source communicates with the destination by the assistance of relay. The transmission channel is orthogonal by time division. Therefore, the communication between the source and the destination consists of $m+1$ time slots. Let the time slot is equal to unit length. In addition, full channel state information is assumed. We suppose that all channels are Gaussian White noise the mean is zero, variance is $N0$. The power gain of the node i to node j is denoted by $|h_{i,j}|^2$. During the first time slot, the source transmits signal to destination and m relays. The signal at destination and m relays are given:

$$y_{s,d} = \sqrt{E_s}h_{s,d} + n_{s,d}$$

$$y_{s,i} = \sqrt{E_s}h_{s,i} + n_{s,i}, i = 1, 2, \ldots, m \qquad (1)$$

Where E_s denotes transmitting power, $n_{s,d}$, $n_{s,i}$ are the noise.

3   Optimization Algorithm Based on Relay Nodes Selection and Power Allocation

For AF, m relay nodes receive the signal transmitted by source, normalize the receiving signal, and transmit a new signal $tildey_{s,i} = \gamma y_{s,i}$ to the destination, the normalization coefficient γ satisfies $\gamma = 1/\sqrt{E|y_{s,i}|^2}$.

After normalization, the receiving signal for m relay nodes turns into:

$$\tilde{y}_{s,i} = \frac{\sqrt{E_s}h_{s,i}}{\sqrt{E|y_{s,i}|^2}}s + \frac{n_{s,i}}{\sqrt{E|y_{s,i}|^2}}$$

$$= \frac{\sqrt{E_s}h_{s,i}}{\sqrt{E_s|h_{s,i}|^2 + N_0}}s + \frac{n_{s,i}}{\sqrt{E_s|h_{s,i}|^2 + N_0}} \qquad (2)$$

Where E_i denotes the transmitting power for ith relay node, and satisfies $E_s + \sum_{i=1}^{m} E_i \leq E$, E denotes the system total power. During the next m time slots, m relay nodes transmit the normalized signal to the destination with power E_i. in turn. Hence, the receiving signal at destination can be expressed as follows:

$$y_{i,d} = \sqrt{E_i}h_{i,d}\tilde{y}_{s,i} + n_{i,d}$$

$$= \sqrt{E_i}h_{i,d}\left(\frac{\sqrt{E_s}h_{s,i}}{\sqrt{E_s|h_{s,i}|^2 + N_0}}s + \frac{n_{s,i}}{\sqrt{E_s|h_{s,i}|^2 + N_0}}\right) + n_{i,d}$$

$$= \sqrt{\frac{E_sE_i}{E_s|h_{s,i}|^2 + N_0}}h_{i,d}h_{s,i}s + \sqrt{\frac{E_sE_i}{E_s|h_{s,i}|^2 + N_0}}h_{i,d}n_{s,i} + n_{i,d} \qquad (3)$$

The signal that forwarded by m relay nodes at the destination can be normalized as follows:

$$\tilde{y}_{i,d} = \frac{y_{i,d}}{\sqrt{\frac{E_i|h_{i,d}|^2}{E_s|h_{s,i}|^2+N_0}+1}} \tag{4}$$

Adopting maximal ratio combining for the $m+1$ signals at the destination, the total SNR is given:

$$SNR = \frac{E_s|h_{s,d}|^2}{N_0} + \sum_{i=1}^{m} \frac{E_s E_i \frac{|h_{s,i}|^2}{N_0} \cdot \frac{|h_{i,d}|^2}{N_0}}{E_s \frac{|h_{s,i}|^2}{N_0} + E_i \frac{|h_{i,d}|^2}{N_0} + 1} \tag{5}$$

Let $a_0 = \frac{|h_{s,d}|^2}{N_0}, a_i = \frac{|h_{s,i}|^2}{N_0}, b_i = \frac{|h_{i,d}|^2}{N_0}$, we get:

$$SNR = E_s a_0 + \sum_{i=1}^{m} \frac{E_s E_i a_i b_i}{E_s a_i + E_i b_i + 1} \tag{6}$$

For the system as above, in order to minimize the outage probability, the simplest solution is maximizing the total SNR. Here we consider the total SNR as the system utility. Utilizing NUM to model the system, the problem becomes how to allocate power between the source and relay nodes for maximizing the total SNR when the total system power satisfied $E_s + \sum_{i=1}^{m} E_i \leq E$. Mathematically, this constrained optimization problem can be formulated as:

$$\text{maximize} \quad E_s a_0 + \sum_{i=1}^{m} \frac{E_s E_i a_i b_i}{E_s a_i + E_i b_i + 1}$$

$$\text{subject to} \quad E_s + \sum_{i=1}^{m} E_i \leq E$$

$$0 \leq E_s \leq E_{s\,max}$$

$$0 \leq E_i \leq E_{i\,max} \tag{7}$$

The above optimization problem can be distributed into two parts: the first part is object function, namely the total SNR, the object is to maximize the total SNR; the second part is constrained conditions including three parts: the first condition is the total system power constrain, the second condition is the power constrain at source, the third condition is the power constrain at each relay node. The variables of the above optimization problem (7) are E_s, E_i where $i = 1, \ldots, m$. From (7), we can know that there are coupling relationship among the variables of object function Es and Ei ,for $i = 1, \ldots, m$. Therefore, the solution process of the problem will be very complex. Then we will consider the problem from another point of view, because:

$$SNR = E_s a_0 + \sum_{i=1}^{m} \frac{E_s E_i a_i b_i}{E_s a_i + E_i b_i + 1} = E_s \sum_{i=0}^{m} a_i - \sum_{i=1}^{m} \frac{E_s^2 a_i^2 + E_s a_i}{E_s a_i + E_i b_i + 1}$$

Therefore, the optimization problem (7) can be expressed as:

$$\text{maximize} \quad E_s \sum_{i=0}^{m} a_i - \sum_{i=1}^{m} \frac{E_s^2 a_i^2 + E_s a_i}{E_s a_i + E_i b_i + 1}$$

$$\text{subject to} \quad E_s + \sum_{i=1}^{m} E_i \leq E$$

$$0 \leq E_s \leq E_{s\,max}$$

$$0 \leq E_i \leq E_{i\,max}$$

If E_s is fixed, the first part of the object function will transmit into a constant. Hence, the above problem is equivalent to:

$$\text{minimize} \quad \sum_{i=1}^{m} \frac{E_s^2 a_i^2 + E_s a_i}{E_s a_i + E_i b_i + 1}$$

$$\text{subject to} \quad \sum_{i=1}^{m} E_i \leq E - E_s$$

$$0 \leq E_i \leq E_{i\,max} \tag{8}$$

The transformed problem (8) is equivalent to transmit signal with a fixed power at source, and allocate power among relay nodes. The optimal value must be satisfied $\sum_{i=1}^{m} E_i = E - E_s$, therefore, the variable of the optimization problem are E_i, for $i = 1, \ldots, m$. The optimal value must be satisfied $\sum_{i=1}^{m} E_i = E - E_s$, therefore, the variable of the optimization problem are Ei, for $i = 1, \ldots, m$. By utilizing convex theory, it is easy to verify that the object function is satisfied to the second order condition of convex function. In addition, the equality and inequality constrain conditions are affine. Therefore, the problem is a convex optimization problem. Moreover, the constrain conditions are linear, the problem can be transformed into a convex optimization problem in standard form as follows:

$$\text{minimize} \quad f_0(x) = \sum_{i=1}^{m} \frac{E_s^2 a_i^2 + E_s a_i}{E_s a_i + E_i b_i + 1}$$

$$\text{subject to} \quad g(x) = 1^T x - (E - E_s) = 0$$

$$h_i(x) = -x_i \leq 0$$

$$p_i(x) = x_i - E_{i\,max} \leq 0 \text{for} \quad i = 1, \ldots, m \tag{9}$$

Hence, the solution process for the problem (9), is just the process of allocation power among the relay nodes. In addition, since $x_i = 0$ is satisfied to the constrain condition. For any relay node, if the transmitting power is 0, the relay node will not forward the signal. We can select the relay nodes that will forward signal when allocation the power. The convex optimization problem can be solved by utilizing Lagrange duality. Then we will introduce the solution process. The Lagrange function corresponding to problem (9) is:

$$L(x, \lambda, \mu, \nu) = f_0(x) + \sum_{i=1}^{m} \lambda_i h_i(x) + \sum_{i=1}^{m} \mu_i p_i(x) + \nu g(x)$$

Because the object function and constrain condition of problem (9) are differentiable, and the constrain condition is satisfied to Slater condition, therefore, we can utilize the KKT condition to obtain the optimal value. The KKT condition for the problem is as follows.

$$h_i(x^*) = -x_i^* \leq 0$$
$$\lambda_i^* \geq 0$$
$$p_i(x^*) = x_i^* - E_{i\,max} \leq 0$$
$$\mu_i^* \geq 0$$
$$g(x^*) = 1^T x^* - (E - E_s) = 0 \tag{a}$$
$$\lambda_i^* h_i(x^*) = 0 \tag{b}$$
$$\mu_i^* p_i(x^*) = 0 \tag{c}$$
$$\nabla f_0(x^*) + \sum_{i=1}^{m} \lambda_i^* \nabla h_i(x^*) + \sum_{i=1}^{m} \mu_i^* \nabla p_i(x^*) + \nu^* \nabla g(x^*) = 0$$

That is $\quad -\dfrac{(E_s^2 a_i^2 + E_s a_i) b_i}{(E_s a_i + x_i^* b_i + 1)^2} - \lambda_i^* + \mu_i^* + \nu^* = 0 \tag{d}$

From (d), we can get $\mu_i^* = \frac{(E_s^2 a_i^2 + E_s a_i) b_i}{(E_s a_i + x_i^* b_i + 1)^2} + \lambda_i^* - \nu^*$. Take it into (c), we can obtain:

$$\left[\frac{(E_s^2 a_i^2 + E_s a_i) b_i}{(E_s a_i + x_i^* b_i + 1)^2} + \lambda_i^* - \nu^* \right] \cdot (x_i^* - E_{i\,max}) = 0 \tag{10}$$

In order to simplify the problem, from $\lambda_i^* x_i^* = 0$, we can tighten the constrain condition $x_i^* \geq 0$ to $x_i^* \geq 0$, then λ_i^* for $i = 1, \ldots, m$, and (10) can be simplified as:

$$\left[\frac{(E_s^2 a_i^2 + E_s a_i) b_i}{(E_s a_i + x_i^* b_i + 1)^2} - \nu^* \right] \cdot (x_i^* - E_{i\,max}) = 0 \tag{11}$$

$$\nu^* \leq \frac{(E_s^2 a_i^2 + E_s a_i) b_i}{(E_s a_i + x_i^* b_i + 1)^2} \tag{12}$$

Formula (11) can be discussed in three parts as following:

$$x_i^* = \begin{cases} 0 & , \quad \nu^* \geq \frac{E_s a_i b_i}{E_s a_i + 1} \\ \sqrt{\frac{E_s^2 a_i^2 + E_s a_i}{\nu^* b_i}} - \frac{E_s a_i + 1}{b_i} & , \quad \frac{(E_s^2 a_i^2 + E_s a_i) b_i}{(E_s a_i + E_{i\,max} b_i + 1)^2} \leq \nu^* \leq \frac{E_s a_i b_i}{E_s a_i + 1} \\ E_{i\,max} & , \quad \nu^* \leq \frac{(E_s^2 a_i^2 + E_s a_i) b_i}{(E_s a_i + E_{i\,max} b_i + 1)^2} \end{cases}$$

x_i^* can be written as:$x_i^* = min\{max\{0, \sqrt{\frac{E_s^2 a_i^2 + E_s a_i}{\nu^* b_i}} - \frac{E_s a_i + 1}{b_i}\}, E_{i\,max}\}$,from $\sum\limits_{i=1}^{m} E_i = E - E_s$, that is $\sum\limits_{i=1}^{m} x_i = E - E_s$ the optimal solution must satisfy:

$$\sum_{i=1}^{m} min\left\{ max\left\{ 0, \sqrt{\frac{E_s^2 a_i^2 + E_s a_i}{\nu^* b_i}} - \frac{E_s a_i + 1}{b_i} \right\}, E_{i\,max} \right\} = E - E_s \quad (13)$$

The left part of (13) is the piecewise monotone function of ν^*,which has two inflection points $\nu^* = \frac{(E_s^2 a_i^2 + E_s a_i) b_i}{(E_s a_i + E_{i\,max} b_i + 1)^2}$ and $\nu^* = \frac{E_s a_i b_i}{E_s a_i + 1}$, so we can get the only solution of the formula (13) easily using water filling.

4   Simulation Results

In the section, we compare the proposed algorithm with traditional equal power allocation algorithm, and the modulation is 16QAM. Figure 2 shows the bit error rate (BER) when $m = 10$ and $Es = 0.75E$. The result shows the proposed algorithm outperforms the equal power algorithm with $2\,dB$ gain.

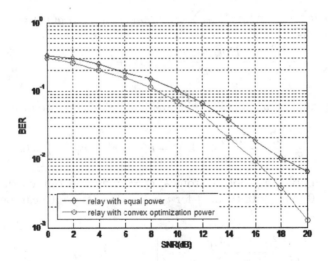

Fig. 2. Comparison of the proposed and equal power algorithm

The proposed algorithm fixes E_s, actually E_s/E with different values will affect the system performance.Fig.3 and Fig.4 show the BER when E_s/E has different values and $SN = 15dB$.

Figure 3 shows that when Es/E has small values, the performance will decrease sharply. When $SNR = 15dB$, $Es/E = 0.7$ is optimal. From figure 3 to figure 7, we can see the number of relay node should be 3.

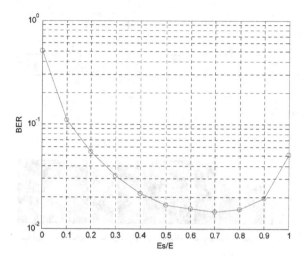

Fig. 3. Comparison of the proposed and equal power algorithm

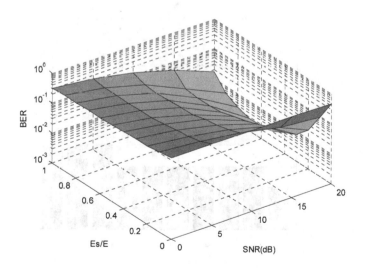

Fig. 4. The BER of the system with different E_s/E

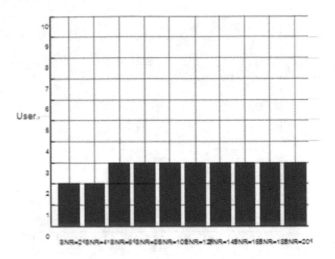

Fig. 5. The number of relay nodes when $E_s/E = 0.5$

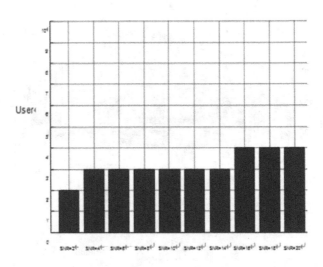

Fig. 6. The number of relay nodes when $E_s/E = 0.3$

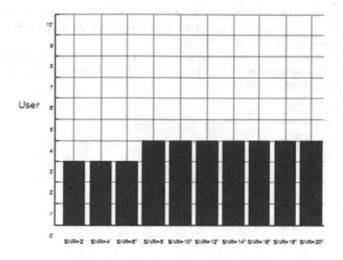

Fig. 7. The number of relay nodes when $E_s/E = 0.1$

5   Conclusion

In this paper, we propose a joint optimal algorithm based on relay nodes selection and power allocation, which utilizes the theory utility maximization modeling system by adopting convex optimization, and obtains the optimal power allocation between source node and relay nodes by applying KKT condition. Moreover, the relay nodes allocated with power unequal to zero are the selected relay nodes, therefore, the selection of relay nodes is realized. Simulation results show the proposed algorithm outperforms the traditional equal power allocation algorithm, and the number of the relay nodes should be 3, which is the optimal.

References

1. Chiang, M.: Geometric programming for communication systems. Foundations and Trends in Communications and Information Theory 2(12), 1–154 (2005)
2. Mung, C., Low Steve, H., Calderbank, A.R.: Laying as optimization decomposition: A mathematical theory of network architectures. Proceedings of the IEEE 95(1), 255–312 (2007)
3. Rossi, M., Sorrentino, S., Spagnolini, U., Moretti, L.: Convex Optimization Strategies for Precoding of Broadcast Channels. In: Internationalitg Workshop on Smart Antennas, IEEE, pp. 42–47 (2008)
4. Dua, A., Medepalli, K., Paulraj, A.J.: Receive Antenna Selection in MIMO System using Convex Optimization. IEEE Tranctions on Wireless Communications 5(9), 2355–2357 (2006)
5. Lo, C.K., Vishwanath, S., Heath, R.W.: Relay Subset Selection in Wireless Networks Using Partial Decode- and-Forward Transmission. IEEE Transactions on Vehicular Technology 58(2), 692–704 (2009)

6. Yi, Z., Kim, I.M.: Joint optimization of relay-precoders and decoders with partial channel side information in cooperative networks. IEEE Journal on Selected Areas in Communications 25(2), 447–458 (2007)
7. Tam, W.P., Lok, T.M., Wong, T.F.: Flow Optimization in Parallel Relay Networks with Cooperative Relaying. IEEE Journal on Selected Areas in Communications 8(1), 278–287 (2009)

A Novel Simple User Scheduling Algorithm
for MIMO Downlink System

Haitao lin[1,*], Zhao Shen[1,2], and Desheng Wang[2]

[1] Coll. Elect. Engn., Naval Univ. Engn.,
Wuhan, China
[2] Department of Elect. & Informat. Engn., Huazhong Univ. of Sci. & Technol.,
Wuhan, China
figue2000@sina.com, {clingerlisa,fudaiyu}@gmail.com

Abstract. In this paper, we propose a user scheduling algorithm based on the codebook for multiuser MIMO system. Users can feedback the CDI information based on the codebook in the multiuser MIMO system. Based on the CDI information, the base station can effectively schedule the users semi-orthogonally. Simulation results show that substantial system throughput gains are achievable by the proposed joint optimal algorithm with appropriate correlation threshold factor.

Keywords: multiuser MIMO, CDI, user scheduling.

1 Introduction

Since a multiuser multiple-input multiple-output(MIMO) system has higher achievable throughput than a single user MIMO system, next generation cellular systems such as Long Term Evolution(LTE) include the multiuser MIMO techniques to achieve the high data rate[1]. For multiuser MIMO system, it's known that dirty paper coding(DPC) can achieve the information theoretical capacity, but the implementation of DPC is difficult in practice[2]. Several sub-optimal algorithms such as channel inversion[3], vector perturbation[4], and multiuser eigenmode transmission[5] have been studied for practical systems. However, the precoding technique requires the perfect channel state information(CSI) at the base station, which means huge feedback overhead. So in the practical system, the precoding matrix is selected based on the codebook, and partial CSI is achieved.

In the multiuser MIMO system, the number of active users which is the number of simultaneously supported users, is restricted by the number of transmit antennas at the base station and the rank of the channels. Therefore, the base

---

* This work is supported by the National High-Tech. R&D Program of China (863 Program) under Grant No. 2009AA01Z205, and by the National Science Key Special Project of China under Grants No. 2010ZX03003-001,2008ZX03003-004 and 2009ZX03003-007.

P. Ren et al. (Eds.): WICON 2011, LNICST 98, pp. 323–330, 2012.

station must consider user scheduling to maximize the system capacity. The exhaust algorithm is the optimal user scheduling algorithm[6], but because of its complexity, the implementation is difficult. [7] proposed a greedy user scheduling algorithm with low complexity, where block diagonalization can maximize the system sum-capacity. The scheduling algorithm based on the channel norm had been proposed in[8], a scheduling algorithm based on the channel correlation was proposed in [9]. All the algorithms require the perfect CSI at the base station, but in the practical system, the base station just knows partial CSI considering the feedback overhead. Especially the LTE system is a limited feedback system based on the codebook, and the base station knows limited CSI[10]. A user scheduling algorithm base on the PMI(Precoding Matrix Index) was proposed in [11]. In the algorithm, the users first select the PMIs from the codebook based on the SINR(Signal Interference Noise Ratio) and feedback the PMIs to the base station, the base station selects the first user with the maximum SINR, then selects the users with maximum SINR in the users whose precoding matrix is orthogonal to the codewords of the pre-selected users. Since the codewords in the codebook are not pairwise orthogonal, the number of scheduled users is restricted.

In this paper, we focus on the user scheduling based on the codebook in the multiuser MIMO downlink system. We propose a semi-orthogonal user scheduling algorithm based on the CDI(Channel Direction Index) information, the base station schedules the users using the CDI information, and makes the zero-forcing precoding for the selected users. The simulation results show that the algorithm improves the system sum-capacity and guarantees the low complexity.

The rest of the paper is organized as follows: In Section 2,we briefly describe the multiuser MIMO system and summarize the feedback procedures for the user scheduling. In the Section 3, we presents the details of the proposed scheduling algorithm. Section 4 provides the simulation results. Finally, Section 5 concludes the paper.

In the paper, $(\bullet)^T, (\bullet)^H, |\bullet|, \|\bullet\|$ denote the transpose, conjugate and transpose operation(Hermitian), inner product and Frobenius norm. I means the identity matrix.

2   System Model

We consider the multiuser MIMO downlink system with M_T transmit antennas at the base station and N_k receive antennas at the kth user as shown in Fig.1. $H_k \in \mathbb{C}^{N_k \times M_T}$ expresses the channel matrix of the kth user. We assume the channel is flat rayleigh fading and independent for different users. Let $S_k \in \mathbb{C}^{r_k \times 1}$ is the kth user's transmit data, $W_k \in \mathbb{C}^{M_T \times r_k}$ is the precoding matrix, the received signal of the kth user, y_k is given by:

$$y_k = H_k \sum_{j=1}^{K} W_j s_j + n_k \tag{1}$$

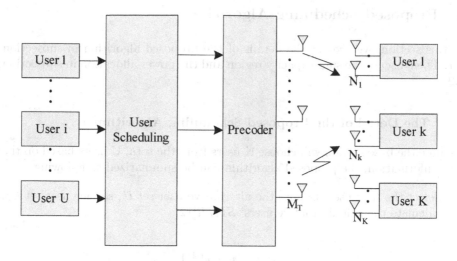

Fig. 1. MU-MIMO Downlink System Modem

Where $n_k \in \mathbb{C}^{N_k \times 1}$ denotes the additive Gaussian noise of the kth user whose elements have zero mean and unit variance. After the linear processing, the formula(1) can be expressed as:

$$\hat{y}_k = R_k^H(H_k \sum_{j=1}^{K} W_j s_j + n_k) \tag{2}$$

In order to eliminate the interference, the precoding matrix W_k of the kth user should be orthogonal with the channels of other users, that is:

$$H_k W_j = 0, k \neq j, 1 \leq k, j \leq k \tag{3}$$

The users will feedback the CDI information, first the users estimate their channel matrixes, then calculate their principal right singular vectors, which are their CDI information, finally, the users choose appropriate codeword and feedback the index to the base station. Assume F denotes the system codebook, in this paper, the LTE rel.8 codebook is used. The kth user chooses its codeword ν_k following the criterion as:

$$\nu_k = \arg \min_{\nu \in F} d(\nu, \bar{H}_k) = \arg \min_{\nu \in F} e_k \tag{4}$$

$\bar{H}_k = H_k / \|H_k\|$ is the kth user's normalized channel, $e_k = d(\nu, \bar{H}_k)$ presents the quantization error:

$$d(\nu, \bar{H}_k) = 1 - |\nu^H \bar{H}_k| \tag{5}$$

3   Proposed Scheduling Algorithm

In this section, we present the details of the proposed algorithm in subsection 3.1. Then discuss the sum-capacity region and the power allocation in subsection 3.2.

3.1   The Detail of the Proposed Scheduling Algorithm

Assume the base station will choose K users from the total U users based on the CDI information, the proposed algorithm can be summarized as following:

1. Select the first user: Denote the alternative user set U, service user set U_s, calculate the kth alternative users' $SINR$[12]:

$$SINR_k = \frac{p\|H_k\|^2(1 - e_k)}{1 + p\|H_k\|^2 e_k} \tag{6}$$

p is the transmit power, we assume the equal power allocation here, when the appropriate users are chosen , the power will be allocated by the water-filling. Then choose the first user μ_1 as following:

$$\mu_1 = \arg \max_{k \in U} SINR_k \tag{7}$$

Then update the sets: $U_1 = U_s/\{u_1\}, U_s = U_s \cup \{u_1\}$.
2. Select the ith user: if $|U_s| \leq K$, then

$$U_i = \left\{ k \in U_{i-1}, k \notin U_s \| \nu_k^H \nu_j | \leq \alpha, j \in U_s \right\} \tag{8}$$

α expresses the correlation threshold, which is constant number, in Section 4, we will discuss the value of α. If $|U_i|$, stop choosing users, else, choose the ith user:

$$\mu_i = \arg \max_{k \in U_i} SINR_k \tag{9}$$

3. Repeat step 2, until enough users are chosen.

3.2   The Sum-Capacity of the System and the Precoding

Assume we have selected K(or less than K) users, making zero-forcing(ZF) precoding to the selected servicing users. Denote the accumulated channels of the service users as: $W = [w_1, \ldots, w_i, \ldots, w_k]$, the accumulated precoding matrixes of the service users are $\hat{H} = [\nu_1^T, \ldots, \nu_i^T, \ldots, \nu_K^T]^T$, wi expresses the precoding matrix of the ith user. Calculate the pseudoinverse of $\hat{H}$:

$$W = \hat{H}^+ = \hat{H}^H(\hat{H}\hat{H}^H)^{-1} \tag{10}$$

According to formula (1), we can get the system sum-capacity:

$$R = \max_{w_k} \sum_{k=1}^{K} \log \left\{ 1 + \frac{p_j |h_k w_k|^2}{1 + \sum_{j=1, j \neq k}^{K} p_j |h_k w_j|^2} \right\}, \text{s.t} \sum_{k=1}^{K} p_k \|w_k\|^2 \leq P_T \quad (11)$$

p_j expresses the power efficient of jth user,P_T expresses the total transmit power.

After the ZF precoding, if the quantization error is small, we can assume the formula (3) is valid, then the sum-capacity of the system can be expressed as:

$$R^{ZF} \approx \max_{w_k} \sum_{k=1}^{K} \log\{1 + p_k\}, \text{s.t} \sum_{k=1}^{K} p_k \|w_k\|^2 \leq P_T \quad (12)$$

The optimal power allocation can be achieved by water-filling.

After normalization, the receiving signal for m relay nodes turns into:

$$\tilde{y}_{s,i} = \frac{\sqrt{E_s} h_{s,i}}{\sqrt{E|y_{s,i}|^2}} s + \frac{n_{s,i}}{\sqrt{E|y_{s,i}|^2}}$$

$$= \frac{\sqrt{E_s} h_{s,i}}{\sqrt{E_s |h_{s,i}|^2 + N_0}} s + \frac{n_{s,i}}{\sqrt{E_s |h_{s,i}|^2 + N_0}} \quad (13)$$

4   Simulation Results

In the Section, we compare our proposed algorithm with the algorithm in [11](we denote it as PMI algorithm) from the sum-capacity of the system and discuss the value of the correlation threshold . The simulation parameter is listed in TABLE 1.

Table 1. The simulation parameter of Mu-MIMO downlik system

Channel	Flat fading Rayleigh channel
Data stream	2
The number of BS antenna	4
The number of MS antenna	1
The number of total users	10
The number of service users	2

In the Fig. 2-4, PMI capacity expresses the system sum-capacity using the PMI algorithm, ZF capacity expresses the optimal ZF capacity following the formula (12), Proposed Algorithm capacity expresses the real system sum-capacity using the proposed algorithm. When the quantization error is small, the curves of ZF capacity and Proposed Algorithm nearly coincide.

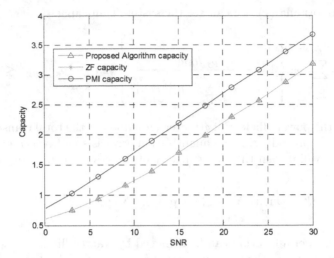

Fig. 2. $\alpha = 0.1$, Comparison of sum-capacity of different algorithms

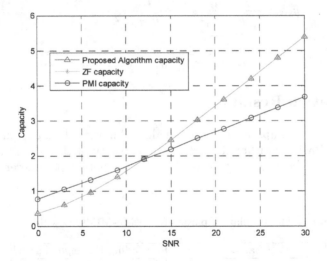

Fig. 3. $\alpha = 0.5$, Comparison of sum-capacity of different algorithms

In the Fig. 2, because the value of the correction threshold is small, the number of the scheduled users is restricted. The base station can not select enough service users, so the sum-capacity of the system loses.

In the Fig.3, the value of the correction threshold is moderate, then the base station can select enough service users. In the low SNR region, the performance of the proposed algorithm is slightly worse than PMI algorithm, because all the users' channel state are bad, the proposed algorithm based on the $SINR$ can not select users with good performance. As the SNR increasing, the performance of the proposed algorithm outperforms the PMI algorithm, because when the

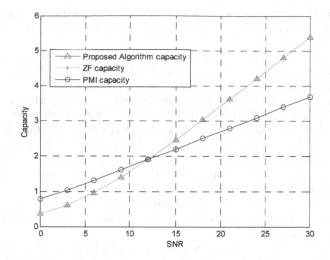

Fig. 4. $\alpha = 0.9$,Comparison of sum-capacity of different algorithms

channel state is good, the proposed algorithm can select good users and the paired users are semi-orthogonal, the interference of the service users is small.

In the Fig.4, the value of the correction threshold is large, the base station can schedule more users, but the orthogonality of the paired users is worse, meanwhile, the scheduling complexity increases. Comparing the Fig.3 and the Fig.4, increasing the value of the correction threshold contributes little to the system performance and increases the scheduling complexity. So correlation factor of about 0.5 is the best.

5   Conclusion

In this paper, we propose a semi-orthogonal user scheduling algorithm based on the CDI(Channel Direction Index) information in the multiuser MIMO system. By setting a reasonable correlation factor in ensuring the low complexity, the proposed algorithm can schedule semi-orthogonal users with good channel quality, thus ensuring little interference between service users. Simulation conclusions show that the proposed algorithm has improved the sum-capacity of the system significantly in high SNR region.

References

1. Caire, G., Shamai, S.: On the achievable throughput of a multi-antenna Gussian broadcast channel. IEEE Trans. Inf. Theory 43(7), 1691–1760 (2003)
2. Costa, M.: Writing on dirty paper. IEEE Trans. Inf. Theory 29(5), 439 (2003)
3. Hochwald, B.M., Peel, C.B., Swindlehurst, A.L.: A vector perturbation technique for near-capacity multiantenna multiuser communication part I:Channel Inversion and regularization. IEEE Trans. Commun. 53(7), 195–202 (2005)

4. Viswanath, H., Venkatesan, S., Huang, H.: Downlink capacity evaluation of cellular networks with kown-interference cancellation. IEEE J. Sel. Areas Commun. 21(6), 802–811 (2003)
5. Boccardi, F., Huang, H.: A Near-Optimum Technique Using Linear Precoding for the MIMO Broadcast Channel. In: Proc. IEEE ICASSP 2007, vol. 34(2), pp. 464–481 (2007)
6. Caire, G., Shamai, S.: On the achievable throughput of a multi-antenna Gussian broadcast channel. IEEE Trans. Inf. Theory. 43(7), 1691–1760 (2003)
7. Shen, Z., Chen, R., Andrews, J.G.: Low Complexity User Selection Algorithm for Multiuser MIMO Sysem. IEEE Trans. Signal Process 54(9), 3658–3663 (2006)
8. Shen, Z., Chen, R., Andrews, J.G.: Sum Capacity of Multiuser MIMO Broadcast Channels with Block Diagonalization. In: IEEE International Symposium, vol. 54(9), pp. 886–890 (2006)
9. Yoo, T., Goldsmith, A.: On the Optimality of Multiantenna Broadcast Scheduling Using Zero-Forcing Beamforming. IEEE Journal on Selected Areas in Communications 24(3), 528–541 (2006)
10. 3GPP TS 36.211. Technical Specification Group Radio Access Network
11. 3GPP TSG RAN WG1 Meeting #59 R1-095019. TI. Downlink MU-MIMO and Related Feedback Support
12. Lim, B.-M., Ahn, K., Kim, H.: Improved User Scheduling Algorithms for Codebook Based MIMO Precoding Schems. In: 2010 IEEE 71st Vehicular Technology Conference (VTC 2010-Spring), vol. 14(3), pp. 658–663 (2010)

Frequency Saving OFDMA Resource Allocation with QoS Provision*

Guanying Ru[1,2], Hongxiang Li[1,2], Yanhui Lu[3], Yong Cheng[4], and Weiyao Lin[5]

[1] Electrical and Computer Engineering Department,
North Dakota State University, Fargo, USA
[2] Electrical and Computer Engineering Department,
University of Louisville, Louisville, USA
[3] Zhengzhou University, Zhengzhou, China and University of California, Davis, USA
[4] Communication Systems Group, Institute of Telecommunications,
Darmstadt University of Technology, Darmstadt, Germany
[5] Institute of Image Communication and Information Processing,
Shanghai Jiao Tong University, Shanghai, China
{guanying.ru,hongxiangli}@gmail.com

Abstract. With the increasing wireless communication demands, frequency spectrum has become more and more limited and expensive. This paper proposes a novel optimization objective: minimizing the required frequency resource, on the premise that both the power constraints and users' quality of service (QoS) demands can be met. With the frequency saving objective, the primary system can release the unnecessary frequencies for other applications, such as subordinate or cognitive networks. In this paper, we formulate the number of subcarriers minimization problem for both uplink and downlink OFDMA-based networks, which is a mixed NP-hard problem. For the downlink case, we propose an efficient near-optimal algorithm to solve the problem. For the uplink case, we derive low complexity greedy algorithms to obtain tight lower bound and upper bound. Simulation results show that our algorithms can significantly save the system's frequency resource.

Keywords: Frequency adapting, OFDMA, QoS, resource allocation.

1 Introduction

Due to the increasing communication demands, multiple wireless network (multi-radio) coexistence [1] has become an inevitable trend. Meanwhile, how to improve the resource (frequency and power) utilization efficiency has always been a hot research topic. Under the context of multi-network co-existence, the existing resource allocation methods can be classified into three categories:

---

* This work was supported in part by the National Science Foundation of USA (#1032567) and in part by the National Science Foundation of China (#61001146) and (#60702020).

P. Ren et al. (Eds.): WICON 2011, LNICST 98, pp. 331–344, 2012.

1) Single network dynamic resource allocation. It assumes each network independently allocates its resource without considering the other co-existed networks. The resource allocation within this category mainly consists of margin adaptive (MA) and rate adaptive (RA) approaches [2] [3]. The objective of MA is to minimize the total transmit power with the constraints of bandwidth and individual user's QoS requirement, and the objective of RA is to maximize the system throughput under the available power and bandwidth constraints.

2) Spectrum sharing in cognitive radio (CR) [1]. It allows the secondary users to share the spectrum in an opportunistic way when the primary users are silent. The success of CR requires fast and sufficient spectrum sensing.

3) Joint resource allocation with inter-network cooperation. In this approach multiple networks jointly allocate the shared resources to achieve mutual benefits. For example, our recent work [4] proposed a collaborative hybrid network that supports both TV broadcasting and cellular data access on a single-frequency platform that can greatly enhance the aggregate capacity.

Intuitively, we expect the combination of the above three approaches can further improve the resource utilization efficiency. However, under the context of multi-network co-existence, most existing optimization objectives are either too selfish or unrealistic. For example, let's consider a cellular (primary) and ad-hoc (cognitive) coexisting networks. With dynamic resource allocation, the primary cellular users tend to use all the frequency resource to maximize their performance according to MA or RA optimization objective. As a result, the performance of the CR network can be jeopardized due to an insufficient amount of available frequencies. Meanwhile, these two coexisting networks can't be cast into the collaborative hybrid structure in [5] because they don't share the same transmitter. In this case, if the primary network is aware of the existence of the cognitive network and the latter agreed to somehow share the cost, at least some limited coordination can be done between the two networks. As is well known, the scarcest resource in wireless communications is the radio spectrum. A fundamental question in multi-radio coexistence is: how to minimize the required frequency resource of any single network without sacrificing its performance (i.e., guaranteed QoS to its users)?

On the other hand, the orthogonal frequency division multiple access (OFDMA) has been widely used as the prime multiple access scheme in many wireless standards (IEEE 802.16, IEEE 802.22, LTE, etc.). One prominent advantage of OFDMA is that it can exploit the multi-user diversity embedded in diverse frequency-selective channels through intelligent resource allocation. To date, most existing research on OFDMA resource allocation focuses on either cellular networks (see [3-6] and references therein) or on CR systems [1] [7] [8], without inter-network coordination. In this paper, we *propose a new resource allocation objective that minimizes the required number of subcarriers in an OFDMA based network, on the premise that both the power constraints and the users' QoS requirements can be met*. The motivation of such a frequency saving objective can be found in many applications. In addition to the aforementioned CR application where the subcarriers saved by the primary network can be used by the secondary users, the cellular system itself can also benefit from the frequency savings (For example, the saved frequencies can be used by other cellular applications such as mobile TV broadcasting).

The main contributions of this paper are summarized as follows:

1) In contrast to the existing RA and MA optimization objectives, we formulate a new frequency saving optimization problem for both uplink and downlink cellular systems.

2) In downlink case, we propose the decoupled bisection search and feasibility test algorithm for multi-user frequency adaptive optimization" (BF-MUFA), which has near optimal performance.

3) For uplink, we derive low complexity greedy methods to obtain very tight upper bound and lower bound for multi-user frequency adaptive optimization. The proposed greedy methods can also be easily adapted to downlink case to eliminate the bisection searching scope.

2   System Model and Problem Formulation

Consider an OFDMA cellular network with K users, and N subcarriers. The subcarrier bandwidth is W. Assume this network has some other co-existing subordinate network(s), which can be a cognitive radio network or a network that shares the same frequency with a lower priority. In such a configuration, the frequency saving scheme in the primary network can benefit others without affecting its own users. Let $P_{k,n}$ denote the power allocated to the k-th user. Then the maximum achievable data rate of the k-th user on channel n is:

$$C_{k,n} = W \cdot log_2\left(1 + P_{k,n} \cdot \frac{|H_{k,n}|^2}{\sigma_{k,n}^2}\right) \qquad (1)$$

where $H_{k,n}$ is the instantaneous frequency response of user k on subcarrier n and is assumed to be known at both the transmitter and receiver; and $\sigma_{k,n}^2$ is the corresponding noise power which is assumed the same for all users on all subcarriers. Define channel signal to noise ratio (SNR) $|H_{k,n}|^2/\sigma_{k,n}^2$ as $e_{k,n}$. Denote matrix $\mathbf{X}$ as the subcarrier allocation schedule, i.e. the (k, n)-th element of $\mathbf{X}$ is:

$$X_{k,n} = \begin{cases} 1 & \text{subcarrier} n \text{ is assigned to user } k \\ 0 & \text{otherwise} \end{cases} \qquad (2)$$

Hence, the overall maximum rate for user k in this system is:

$$C_k = \sum_{n=1}^{N} X_{k,n} C_{k,n} \qquad (3)$$

Correspondingly, the total power allocated to user k in this system is: $\sum_{n=1}^{N} X_{k,n} P_{k,n}$.

Since the transmission delay is small in the cellular system, we assume user k's QoS requirement is specified by its transmission rate R_k. Thus, the frequency minimization problem can be formulated as follows:

$$P0: \quad f = \min \sum_{k=1}^{K} \sum_{n=1}^{N} X_{k,n} \tag{4}$$

$$\text{Subject to:} \sum_{k=1}^{K} X_{k,n} \leq 1, \ \forall n; X_{k,n} = 0 \text{ or } 1, \ \forall n,k \tag{4a}$$

$$C_k \geq R_k, \forall k \tag{4b}$$

$$P_{k,n} \geq 0, \forall n,k \tag{4c}$$

$$\text{Downlink:} \sum_{k=1}^{K} \sum_{n=1}^{N} X_{k,n} P_{k,n} \leq P_T \tag{4d}$$

$$\text{Uplink:} \quad \sum_{n=1}^{N} X_{k,n} P_{k,n} \leq P_k, \ \forall k \tag{4e}$$

where (4) is our optimization objective. The OFDMA constraints (4a) indicate each subcarrier can be used by no more than one user at any time slot to avoid multi-user interference. Inequalities (4b) make sure each user's QoS demand is met; inequalities (4c) restrict the power cannot be negative. For downlink, the total transmission power constraint is shown in (4d); for uplink, each user is subject to an individual power constraint as shown in (4e).

P0 is a mixed integer and continuous optimization problem, because the optimization variables contain both the discrete variables $\{X_{k,n}\}$ and continuous variables $\{P_{k,n}\}$. Also, P0 is a NP-hard question [9]; to find its optimal solution needs a brutal search which has $\sum_{i=1}^{N} \binom{N}{i} K^i$ possible combinations.

Notice that for downlink optimization, the base station's sensitivity towards the transmission power is less than the cellular users' sensitivity towards the battery life in uplink optimization. However, for uplink optimization, this model is still useful when the cellular users are less sensitive to their battery life. Moreover, when the operator charges users according to their data rates, users will prefer MA algorithm which, however, affects the operators' benefits by taking too much radio frequency. One way to solve this problem is to prioritize users. For high priority users, the system carries out MA resource allocation to save users' transmission power; for low priority users, the system applies subcarrier minimization algorithm to save the frequency resource. In the next section, the optimization algorithms for both downlink and uplink are introduced.

3   Frequency Saving Algorithms

In this section, we propose near optimal algorithms for downlink and uplink OFDMA, respectively. In the downlink case, the bisection and feasibility test combined algorithm for multi-user frequency adapting optimization (BF-MUFA) has been proposed, and the original problem is decomposed into two sub-problems. In the uplink, we propose low complexity greedy algorithms to obtain both a tight lower bound and a tight upper bound.

3.1   The Optimal Solution for Single User System

If the OFDM system has only one user, then problem P0 is trivial. Obviously, with the given power, user rate is a mono increasing function of the number of subcarriers. Hence, the optimal solution can be easily obtained by the bisection method combined with the traditional single user waterfilling algorithm [10]. We first introduce a single user frequency adapting algorithm (SUFA) as follows (Table 1). Let $\mathbf{e}$ be the channel SNR matrix with $(1, n)$-th element as $e_{1,n}$, other parameters are defined in Section 2. Note that in Step 3, the waterfilling algorithm we use was proposed in [10] which can easily obtain the global optimal for single user resource allocation.

Table 1. Single user frequency adapting algorithm (SUFA)

Input: $P_T, R, \mathbf{e}$; Output $f, \mathbf{X}$
Step 1: Initialize $f_{\min}=1$ and $f_{\max}=N$. $E \leftarrow$ sort subcarriers according to their SNR $\mathbf{e}$ in the descending order.
Step 2: $f = \mathrm{int}\left(\left(f_{\min} + f_{\max}\right)/2\right)$;
Step 3: $[C, \mathbf{X}] \leftarrow waterfill(P_T, E(1:f))$;
Step 4: If $C > R$, then set $f_{\max} = f$;
else set $f_{\min} = f$;
Step 5: If $f_{\min} = f_{\max}$, stop; otherwise $\downarrow$ step 2.

3.2   Downlink OFDMA Frequency Optimization (Multi-User System)

From Section 3.1, we can see that the bisection method can be used to derive the optimal solution for the single user OFDM system. However, in the multi-user case, the optimization problem of P0 is NP-hard [9], to solve this problem optimally we need a brutal forth search. Hence, we need a low complexity optimization algorithm. Inspired by the single user case, we now consider can a similar method be used for the multi-user case? Can this similar method obtain the optimal solution? To answer these questions, we first introduce Lemma 1.

Lemma 1: In a given OFDMA system with K users and N possible subcarriers, the minimum total power required to satisfy all users' QoS requirements is the mono decreasing function of f, where f is the number of subcarriers allowed to use.

Proof: Firstly, in the single user case, this lemma was proved in the Appendix A of literature [11]. In a multi-user system, it's safe to assume two cases with $f = f_1$ and $f = f_2$, while $f_2 = f_1 + 1$. Denote the total minimum power required when $f = f_1$ and $f = f_2$ as P_{T1} and P_{T2}, respectively. By the contradiction method, suppose the Lemma 1 is not true, which means $P_{T2} > P_{T1}$. For $f = f_2$, assume all users maintain their subcarrier schedule as when $f = f_1$, except for user k who has one more subcarrier to use. Therefore, to meet all users' QoS, user k's power requirement decreases, while other users' power requirements remain the same; hence, $P_{T2} \leq P_{T1}$ which results in a contradiction of this assumption. Above all, Lemma 1 is proved.   ∎

Note that the number of subcarriers f is in one-dimensional space, and the total power constraint is obviously in one dimensional space. Supported by Lemma 1, we propose the following bisection feasibility test combined method to solve the optimization problem P0 (Table 2). The BF-MUFA contains mainly an outer loop and inner loop. The outer loop adjusts the number of subcarriers by bisection method, and chooses the best subcarriers from the subcarrier pool (Step 2 and Step 3); the inner loop tests the feasibility of meeting users' QoS with the given power constraint for the chosen subcarrier group of outer loop by comparing the minimum power required to meet QoS demands with the available total power (Step 4 and Step 5). Let $\mathbf{R}$ be the set that contains all users' rate requirements, and f_{opt} be the optimal number of subcarriers.

Table 2. Bisection and feasibility test combined algorithm for multi-user frequency adapting Optimization (BF-MUFA)

Input: $P_T, \mathbf{R}, \mathbf{e}$; Output $f, \mathbf{X}$
Step 1: Initialize $f_{min} = 0$ and $f_{max} = N$,
Step 2: $f = \text{int}\big((f_{min} + f_{max})/2\big)$
Step 3: Find best f number of subcarriers E_f, such that
if $f \geq f_{opt}, E_f \supseteq E_{opt}$.
Step 4: $[P_{min}, \mathbf{X}] \leftarrow \min power(\mathbf{R}, E_f)$;
Step 5: If $P_{min} \leq P_T$, then set $f_{max} = f$;
else set $f_{min} = f$
Step 6: If $f_{min} = f_{max}$, stop; otherwise ↓ Step 2

The above procedure contains two sub-problems (S1 and S2) which take up most of the computational complexity.

S1: Find best f number of subcarriers set E_f, such that if $f \geq f_{opt}$, $E_f \supseteq E_{opt}$, where E_{opt} represents the optimal set of subcarriers.

To meet S1's requirement, an exhaustive search is required. So we propose a suboptimal method. Among all possible N subcarriers, we select f number of subcarriers with the highest weight. We weigh each subcarrier s by $\sum_{k=1}^{K} \alpha_{k,s} e_{k,s}$. The parameter $\alpha_{k,s}$ is determined by possibility that it will be used by user k. In this paper, we assume $\alpha_{k,s} = R_k / |\mathbf{R}|$, where $|\mathbf{R}|$ is the norm-1 of the vector $\mathbf{R}$.

S2: Total power minimization:

$$\min \sum_{k=1}^{K} \sum_{n=1}^{N} P_{k,n} \tag{5}$$

$$\text{Subject to} : \sum_{n=1}^{N} X_{k,n} \cdot W \cdot \log_2 \left(1 + P_{k,n} e_{k,n}\right) \geq R_k, \forall k \tag{5a}$$

$$P_{k,n} \geq 0, \forall k, n \tag{5b}$$

$$\sum_{k=1}^{K} X_{k,n} \leq 1, \forall n, \text{ where } X_{k,n} = 1 \text{ or } 0 \tag{5c}$$

Sub-problem S2 is the traditional MA optimization. Among all the existing algorithms for MA optimization, the dynamic programming based resource allocation (DPRA) [11] is a recent method with low complexity and good performance. However, the DPRA method is a single loop method, and we cannot refine it simply by repeating it. Inspired by [11] and [12], we propose a new algorithm based on the Lagrangian dual decomposition method, which uses the DPRA's result as the initial solution and achieves better performance with low complexity.

The Lagrangian expression of (5) is as follows:

$$L(\mathbf{P}, \lambda) = \sum_{k=1}^{K} \sum_{n=1}^{N} P_{k,n} + \sum_{k=1}^{K} \lambda_k \left(R_k - \sum_{n=1}^{N} W \log_2 \left(1 + P_{k,n} e_{k,n}\right) \right)$$

$$\text{Subject to} : P_{k,n} \geq 0, \forall k, n \tag{6}$$

$$\sum_{k=1}^{K} X_{k,n} \leq 1, \forall n, \text{ where } X_{k,n} = 1 \text{ or } 0.$$

Then the Lagrangian dual function is:

$$g(\lambda) = \min_{P,X}\{L(P,X,\lambda)\} = \sum_{n=1}^{N} g_n(\lambda) + \sum_{k=1}^{K} \lambda_k R_k \qquad (7)$$

In the OFDMA system, each subcarrier can be only used by at most one user; hence,

$$g_n(\lambda) = \min_{k}\{P_{k,n} - \lambda_k W \log_2(1 + P_{k,n} e_{k,n})\} \qquad (8)$$

The subcarrier n is allocated only to user k^* such that:

$$k^* = \arg\min_{k}\{P_{k,n} - \lambda_k W \log_2(1 + P_{k,n} e_{k,n})\} \qquad (9)$$

With fixed λ, the problem (8) is a convex function of $P_{k,n}$. So we let the derivation of (8) over $P_{k,n}$ equal to 0, and obtain:

$$P_{k,n}^* = \left(\lambda_k W \ln 2 - \frac{1}{e_{k,n}}\right)^+ \qquad (10)$$

Finally, the Lagrangian dual variable λ_k can be obtained from:

$$\sum_{n \in S_k} W \log_2\left(1 + \left(\lambda_k W \ln 2 - \frac{1}{e_{k,n}}\right)^+ e_{k,n}\right) = R_k \qquad (11)$$

in which S_k represents the set of subcarriers given to user k with $P_{k,n} > 0$. Hence:

$$\lambda_k = 2^{t/(W|S_k|)}/(W \ln 2), \text{ where } t = \left(R_k - \sum_{n \in S_k} W \log_2 e_{k,n}\right) \qquad (12)$$

To optimally update this dual variable is nontrivial. Because of the discontinuity in the power allocation by (8), the existing methods, e.g. the ellipsoid method and subgradient based method, will result in slow convergence or even no convergence. Hence, by observing the above equations' structures, we propose an efficient algorithm as is shown in Table 3.

Table 3. Lagrangian dual decomposition based margin adaptive optimization (LDD-MA)

Input: **R, e** ; Output $P_{\min}, \mathbf{X}$

Step 1: Initialization. Assume iteration $i=0$, assign
  subcarriers according to the DPRA solution.

Step 2: For $n=1$ to N

Step 3: Let $X_{k,n} = 1, \ \forall k$;

Step 4: Apply (12) and derive λ_k ;

  then plug λ_k in (10), and obtain $P^*_{k,n}, \ \forall k$.

Step 5: $k^* \leftarrow \arg\min_{k} \left\{ P^*_{k,n} - \lambda_k W \log_2 \left(1 + P^*_{k,n} e_{k,n} \right) \right\}$

Step 6: Let $X_{k,n} = 0$, and update λ_k and $P_{k,n}, \ \forall k \neq k^*$

Step 7: $i = i+1$; $P^{(i)}_{\min} \leftarrow sum\left(P_{k,n} \right)$

Step 8: If $P^{(i)}_{\min} - P^{(i-1)}_{\min} \geq \xi$, then $\downarrow$ step 2; otherwise, stop.

3.3   Uplink OFDMA Frequency Optimization (Multi-User System)

In uplink OFDMA system, each user has an individual power constraint; hence, the former BF-MUFA with the total power constraint for the feasibility test is not applicable to the uplink case. However, we propose low complexity greedy algorithms to find the upper bound and lower bound of the minimum number of required subcarriers for uplink cases. The general idea of the greedy algorithm is: rank users in the descending order according to their QoS requirements, and then minimize the number occupied subcarriers for each subscriber using SUFA from the first user to the last one, until all users' QoS demands have been met. To obtain the upper bound, each subcarrier can only be used by one user at most; on the other hand, we allow subcarrier sharing among multiple users to get the lower bound. The detail to attain the upper bound is presented in Table 4.

Table 4. Upper bound for multi-user frequency adapting optimization (UB-MUFA)

Input: **P, R, e** ; Output $f_{UB}, \mathbf{X}_{UB}$

Step 1: $\{k^*\} \leftarrow sort\,(QoS)$;

Step 2: For $k^* = 1$: K

  $\mathbf{X}_{k*} \leftarrow$ SUFA (P_{k*}, R_{k*}, e_{k*}),

  if $X_{k*,n} = 1$, rule out subcarrier n; $\forall k \neq k^*, \forall n$

Step 3: $f_{UB} \leftarrow count\left(X_{k,n} = 1 \right)$

Step 4: If all users' QoS requirements are satisfied,
  output $f_{UB}, \mathbf{X}_{UB}$; otherwise, perform multi-user access control.

Note that in this greedy algorithm, whenever multiple users contend for the same subcarrier, the user with the highest QoS requirement is selected. What's more important, the selected subcarriers is a sufficient subcarriers set E_f for the optimal solution, i.e. $E_f \supseteq E_{opt}$. The reason is that: if no subcarrier has been ruled out in Step 2, which means all users need distinct subcarriers to minimize the required frequency, then the greedy solution is the optimal solution; however, if some subcarriers are ruled out in Step 2, these subcarriers actually have already been given to the current user which means they are already included as candidates for optimal solution.

Similar as the UB-MUFA, we propose a greedy algorithm in Table 5 to obtain the lower bound. LB-MUFA differs from UB-MUFA in the following manner: we give all frequency resource to each user, and no subcarrier is ruled out even if multiple users occupy the same subcarrier; what's more, multi-user interference is not considered. Owing to the way to choose subcarriers for each user, the subcarriers selected from this approach are the necessary subcarriers to meet the users' requirements.

In the simulation section, we can see the lower bound and the upper bound of uplink OFDMA are very close which indicates their tightness.

Furthermore, for the uplink and downlink case, we can also apply the UB-MUFA and LB-MUFA to eliminate the searching scope. For simplicity, we assume each user has the equal power constraint as P_T/K in UB-MUFA algorithm to obtain the upper bound; also, we assume each user has P_T in LB-MUFA as the power constraint to obtain a rough lower bound of minimum number of subcarriers. With the lower bound and upper bound being considered, the searching scope of bisection in BF-MUFA searching scope can be reduced greatly.

Table 5. Lower bound for multi-user frequency adapting (LB-MUFA)

Input: $\mathbf{P}, \mathbf{R}, \mathbf{e}$; Output $f_{LB}, \mathbf{X}_{LB}$

Step 1: For $k = 1 : K$
$\qquad \mathbf{X}_k \leftarrow \text{SUFA}(P_k, R_k, e_k),$
Step 2: $f_{LB} \leftarrow \text{count}(X_{k,n} = 1)$
Step 3: If all users' QoS requirements are satisfied, output

$\qquad f_{LB}, \mathbf{X}_{LB}$; otherwise, perform multi-user access control.

---

4   Experimental Results

This section provides simulation results to validate the proposed algorithms in Section 3. For an OFDMA system with 20 users and 128 subcarriers, Fig. 1 compares our new LDD-MA algorithm and the DPRA algorithm proposed by [11]. After extensive simulations, we observe that whenever the system has more users, higher QoS requirements, or less subcarriers, the performance gap between LDD-MA and DPRA algorithm increases.

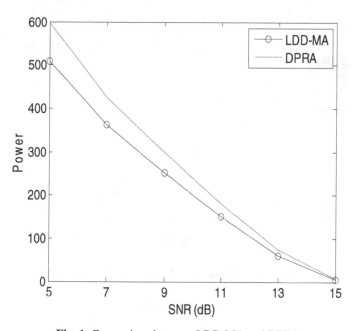

Fig. 1. Comparison between LDD-MA and DPRA

Fig. 2 and 3 are the typical numerical results of downlink OFDMA, which show the number of required subcarriers as a function of SNR and K respectively. In Fig. 2 and 3, "Random" represents the results obtained by first predefining each user has equal total available power and then randomly assign subcarriers to users till their QoS demands are met; "BF-MUFA" is our aforementioned algorithm using bisection search and feasibility test. In Fig. 2, we assume the 128 subcarriers are shared between 20 users, and each user has a random rate requirement. In Fig. 3, we assume each user has the same rate requirement, and SNR=10.

For uplink, extensive simulations have shown that the upper bound and lower bound are extremely close so that our algorithm for upper bound is almost always optimal, as shown by Fig. 4 and 5. Fig. 4 and 5 show the relationship between SNR and the number of required subcarriers, as well as number of users vs. the number of required subcarriers, respectively. In all cases, our proposed algorithms can significantly save the number of required subcarriers.

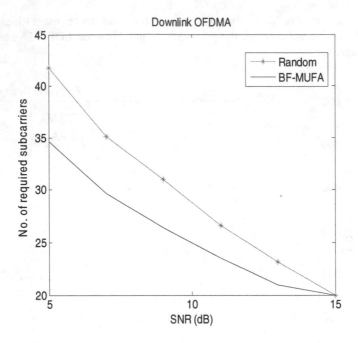

Fig. 2. SNR vs. No. of required subcarriers in downlink OFDMA

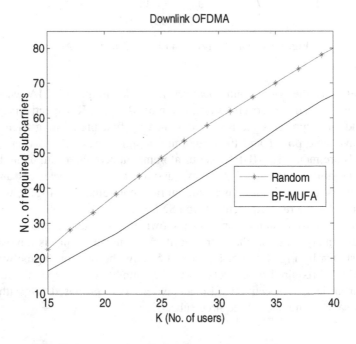

Fig. 3. K vs. No. of required subcarriers in downlink OFDMA

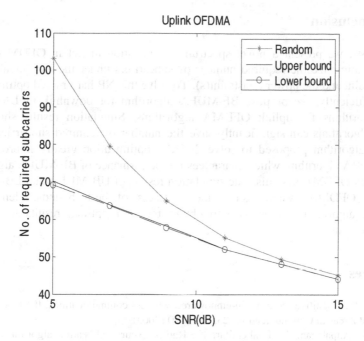

Fig. 4. SNR vs. No. of required subcarriers in uplink OFDMA

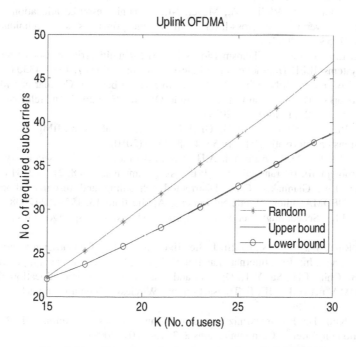

Fig. 5. K vs. No. of required subcarriers in uplink OFDMA

5   Conclusion

In this paper, we present a novel spectrum optimization model in OFDMA-based systems to minimize the required number of subcarriers under the individual user's QoS constraint and the power constraint(s). To solve this NP-hard mixed optimization problem efficiently, we propose BF-MUFA algorithm for downlink OFDMA and greedy algorithms for uplink OFDMA algorithms. Simulation results show our proposed algorithms can significantly save the number of required subcarriers. The LDD-MA algorithm proposed to solve the MA optimization greatly improves the existing DPRA algorithm, which guarantees the performance of BF-MUFA algorithm for downlink OFDMA systems. The simulation results of UB-MUFA and LB-MUFA for uplink OFDMA systems show the tightness of both bounds. Hence, the UB-MUFA algorithm can be used to obtain the near optimal results for uplink OFDMA systems.

References

1. Haykin, S.: Cognitive radio: brain-empowered wireless communications. IEEE Journal on Selected Areas in Communications 23, 201–220 (2005)
2. Sadr, S., Anpalagan, A., Raahemifar, K.: Radio resource allocation algorithms for the downlink of multiuser OFDM Communication Systems. IEEE Communications Survey & Tutorials 11, 92–105 (2009)
3. Bohge, M., Gross, J., Wolisz, A., Meyer, M.: Dynamic resource allocation in OFDM systems: an overview of cross-layer optimization principles and techniques. IEEE Network 21, 53–59 (2007)
4. Li, H.X., Liu, B., Liu, H.: Transmission schemes for multicarrier broadcast and unicast hybrid systems. IEEE Transaction on Wireless Communications 7, 4321–4330 (2008)
5. Huang, K.B., Lau, V.K.N., Chen, Y.: Spectrum Sharing between Cellular and Mobile Ad Hoc Networks: Transmission-Capacity Trade-Off. IEEE Journal on Selected Areas in Communications 27, 1256–1267 (2009)
6. Li, H.X., Ru, G.Y., Kim, Y., Liu, H.: OFDMA capacity analysis in MIMO channels. IEEE Transactions on Information Theory 56, 4438–4446 (2010)
7. Attar, A., Nakhai, M.R., Aghvami, A.H.: Cognitive radio game for secondary spectrum access problem. IEEE Transactions on Wireless Communications 8, 2121–2131 (2009)
8. Bazerque, J.A., Giannakis, G.B.: Distributed scheduling and resource allocation for cognitive OFDMA radios. Mobile Networks & Applications 13, 452–462 (2008)
9. Pinedo, M.L.: Scheduling: theory, algorithms, and systems. Springer Press, NewYork (2008)
10. Yu, W., Rhee, W., Boyd, S., Cioffi, J.: Iterative water-filling for Gaussian vector multiple access channels. In: IEEE International Symposium on Information Theory, p. 322 (2001)
11. Lin, Y.B., Chiu, T.H., Su, Y.T.: Optimal and near-optimal resource allocation algorithms for OFDMA networks. IEEE Transaction on Wireless Communications 8, 4066–4077 (2009)
12. Ma, Y., Kim, D.: Rate-maximization scheduling schemes for uplink OFDMA. IEEE Transaction on Wireless Communications 8, 3193–3204 (2009)

Distributed Fast Convergent Power Allocation Algorithm in Underlay Cognitive Radio Networks

Yanan Mei[1], Yanhui Lu[1,2,*], Xiaomin Mu[1], and Xin Liu[2]

[1] School of Information Engineering, Zhengzhou University, Zhengzhou, Henan, China
[2] Department of Computer Science, University of California, Davis, CA, USA
ieyhlu@zzu.edu.cn, luyanhui710@gmail.com

Abstract. In underlay cognitive radio networks, secondary users can share the same frequency band with primary users under the condition of meeting interference temperature constraint. In order to improve their spectrum efficiency, we consider a market competitive equilibrium (CE) model to formulate the multi-channel power allocation problem. In this paper, we prove the existence and uniqueness of CE. We simplify the CE to Nash equilibrium (NE) first, which exists and is unique under weak-interference conditions, for the fixed price; we then prove that the prices converge to the equilibrium price and present the sufficient condition of unique CE solution. Furthermore, we propose a distributed fast convergent power allocation algorithm (FCPAA) with round robin rules. The simulation results show that FCPAA can satisfy the interference temperature constraint perfectly and converge faster than the one in literature [9].

Keywords: Cognitive Radio, power allocation, competitive equilibrium, Nash equilibrium, distributed algorithm.

1   Introduction

With the development of wireless communication technology, the conflict is increasing between the fast growing demand for wireless spectrum resources and the scarcity of spectrum resources can be allocated. However, the actual measuring results show that a lot of the allocated spectrum resources are unutilized or underutilized [1]. Cognitive radio [2] which is considered as a promising technology to solve the current spectrum plight is being extensively studied. Typically, cognitive radio systems based on spectrum reuse approach is divided into three categories: underlay, overlay and interweave. In the underlay cognitive radio system [3], the primary users (authorized users) share the spectrum resources with the secondary users (non-authorized users), and the interference caused by secondary users must be lower than the interference temperature threshold, so secondary users' transmit powers need to be effectively controlled.

---

* This work was funded by the National Natural Science Foundation of China (NSFC No 60702020).

P. Ren et al. (Eds.): WICON 2011, LNICST 98, pp. 345–358, 2012.

In the underlay cognitive radio, power allocation is an important issue due to the interference temperature regulation of the primary system. This multichannel power allocation problem has been formulated as a non-cooperative game [4-6] and the Nash equilibrium is considered as the corresponding solution. However, the power allocation in a NE may be inefficient or not socially optimal [12]. Some literatures [7, 8] use Stackelberg game mechanism for power allocation. They maximize the primary user's benefits, but do not consider that the interference caused by secondary users to the primary users must be lower than interference threshold. Therefore we propose to use the competitive market model presented by literatures [9, 10] to solve this problem. In the competitive market model, a primary user sets a set of prices for channels to leverage the power allocation, which can satisfy its interference temperature constraint. The competitive equilibrium (CE) of this game is a set of prices and power allocations of all secondary users, which is a two-variable optimization problem and it is difficult to prove the existence and uniqueness of the solution. Moreover, wasting opportunity [15] may be caused when secondary user adjust their strategies, which is affecting the convergent speed.

So, this paper focuses on solving these problems. We first prove the existence and the uniqueness of CE, by predigesting the two-variable optimization problem to a simple one, when the price is fixed. Second, we derive the convergence of price and sufficient conditions of unique CE solution. Lastly, a distributed fast convergent power allocation algorithm (FCPAA) with round robin rules is proposed through which all the secondary users' power allocation can quickly converge to the unique CE while the interference temperature constraints of primary system are satisfied.

The rest of the paper is organized as follows. The competitive market model is formulated in Section 2. Section 3 investigates the existence and uniqueness of CE for this model. The distributed FCPAA with round robin rules is described in Section 4. Section 5 presents the simulation results to show that the proposed FCPAA meets the interference temperature constraint and converges fast.

2   System Model and Problem Formulation

2.1   System Model

We consider a cognitive radio system that consists of one primary user, a set of $N=\{1,2,\ldots,n\}$ secondary users, and a set of $M=\{1,2,\ldots,m\}$ channels, as shown in Fig. 1. All the users coexist in each channel and may access multiple channels at the same time. As in [11], the primary user sets a spectrum mask c_j for the jth ($j \in M$) channel, and requires the interferences caused by secondary users to be less than this level. Supposed that the power allocated by user i ($i \in N$) to channel j is $x_{ij}>0$, the interference constraint implemented by primary user in the jth channel is:

$$\sum_{i=1}^{n} b_{ij} x_{ij} < c_j .\tag{1}$$

where b_{ij} is the interference coefficients of the ith secondary user on the jth channel, that experienced by the primary user. To achieve an efficient allocation of spectrum, we associate a price $p_j>0$ with each channel j.

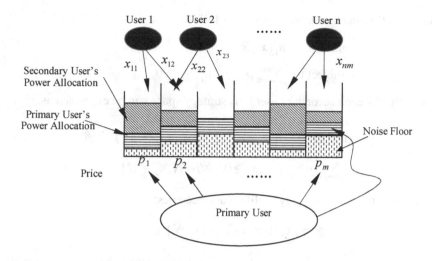

Fig. 1. Competitive spectrum market model

For a given vector of prices, $p=[p_1, \ldots, p_m]^T$, each user i chooses the power allocation $x_i=[x_{i1}, \ldots, x_{im}]^T$ that maximizes its utility function subject to its budget w_i. The ith secondary user has its utility (i.e., sum data rate) as:

$$u_i(x_i, \bar{x}_i) = \sum_{j=1}^{m} \log(1 + \frac{x_{ij}h_{ii}^j}{\sigma_{ij} + \sum_{k \neq i} h_{ik}^j x_{kj}}) \ . \tag{2}$$

In (2), $\bar{x}_i = \{x_1, \cdots, x_k \mid k \in N, k \neq i\}$ are other n-1 users' power allocations. The interference experienced by the secondary users, are characterized by coefficients $h_{ik}^j > 0$, on channel j from user $k \neq i$ to user i. $\{h_{ii}^j\}_{j=1}^m$ is the channel gain of the direct link for each secondary pair i, here we define $\{h_{ii}^j\}_{j=1}^m = 1$. The noise level and interference caused by primary user to i^{th} secondary users in the jth channel is σ_{ij}.

Meanwhile, the power allocation of each secondary user is limited by its own budget, that is, the total payment of "purchased" power spectral density does not exceed its endowed budget w_i. Here we describe as:

$$\sum_{j=1}^{m} p_j x_{ij} \leq w_i \ . \tag{3}$$

2.2 Problem Formulation

As stated above, the optimization problem of power allocation is formulated as a competitive equilibrium problem: Each secondary user aims at maximizing its own utility $u_i(x_i, \bar{x}_i)$ under the local budget constraints in (3) and the interference constraints in (1).

So, this CE problem can be expressed as follows:

$$\text{maximize} \quad u_i(\boldsymbol{x}_i, \overline{\boldsymbol{x}}_i)$$

$$\text{subject to:} \quad \sum_{j=1}^{m} p_j x_{ij} \le w_i, \, x_{ij} \ge 0 \quad .$$

(4)

Specifically, for each secondary user i, its strategy space can be expressed as:

$$\chi_i = \{ \boldsymbol{x}_i \in \Omega_i, \sum_{i=1}^{n} b_{ij} x_{ij} < c_j \, | \, \Omega_i = (x_{i1}, x_{i2}, \cdots, x_{im})^T \in \Re^m,$$

$$\sum_{j=1}^{m} p_j x_{ij} \le w_i, x_{ij} \ge 0, \quad \forall i \in N, \forall j \in M \}$$

Consequently the entire strategy profile space becomes:

$$\chi = \{ \boldsymbol{x}_i \in \chi_{i \in N} \Omega_i, \forall i \in N \} \quad .$$

(5)

The secondary users are ignorant of the spectrum mask of the primary user when making their power allocations. So to keep the interference level low, the primary user adjusts its price p_j until (1) holds.

The competitive equilibrium (CE) [12] of this model is the vector of prices $\boldsymbol{p}^*$ and the corresponding optimal power allocations of the secondary users $\boldsymbol{x}_i^*$. The optimal power allocation of spectrum is when the total interference level from secondary users reaches the spectrum mask, thus all spectrum opportunities have been utilized. Our goal is to find such a competitive equilibrium.

3   Existence and Uniqueness of Equilibrium Point

In this section we prove the existence and the uniqueness of CE for the proposed competitive market model. Competitive equilibrium (CE) is a set of prices and corresponding power allocations of secondary users. When the price $\boldsymbol{p}$ is fixed, CE can be simplified to NE which is a optimization problem easily to solve. So the existence and uniqueness of NE is proved when the price is fixed. The existence of NE follows Lemma 1.

Lemma 1. There exists an equilibrium point over the strategy profile space χ for the competitive market mode if the price is fixed and the weak-interference condition ($h_j^i < 1$) is satisfied.

Proof: We use Theorem 4.4 in [13] to prove the existence of the equilibrium point. First, the strategy profile space χ in (5) is a closed and bounded set. Meanwhile it is convex which is derived as follows. Now we consider the complete necessary and sufficient conditions that characterize the optimal problem (4), they can be summarized as:

$$w_i \cdot \nabla_{x_i} u_i(x_i, \bar{x}_i) \leq (\nabla_{x_i} u_i(x_i, \bar{x}_i)^T x_i) \cdot p, \quad \forall i$$

$$\sum_{j=1}^{m} p_j x_{ij} = w_i, \quad \forall i$$

$$\sum_{i=1}^{n} b_{ij} x_{ij} = c_j, \quad \forall j \tag{6}$$

$$x_{ij} \geq 0, \quad \forall i, j.$$

where $\nabla_{x_i} u_i(x_i, \bar{x}_i) \in \mathfrak{R}^n$ denotes any sub-gradient vector of $u_i(x_i, \bar{x}_i)$ with respect to x_i. The inequalities and equalities in (6) are all linear, except the first:

$$w_i \cdot \nabla_{x_i} u(x_i, \bar{x}_i) \leq (\nabla_{x_i} u(x_i, \bar{x}_i)^T x_i) \cdot p. \tag{7}$$

Now we use $\sum_i x_i = x_{tot}$ (x_{tot} is total power provided by primary user) to prove that (7) is actually a convex inequality. Let $h_j^i = h_i^{j^T} = \{h_{i1}^j, h_{i2}^j, \cdots, h_{ik}^j \mid k \in N, k \neq i\}^T$, the partial derivative of $u_i(x_i, \bar{x}_i)$ to x_{ij} is:

$$(\nabla_{x_i} u_i(x_i, \bar{x}_i))_j = \frac{1}{\sigma_{ij} + h_j^i(\sum_{k \neq i} x_{kj}) + x_{ij}}, \quad \forall j. \tag{8}$$

So that: $\nabla_{x_i} u_i(x_i, \bar{x}_i)^T x_i = \sum_{j=1}^{m} \dfrac{x_{ij}}{\sigma_{ij} + h_j^i(\sum_{k \neq i} x_{kj}) + x_{ij}}$ and $\sum_{k \neq i} x_{kj} = (x_{tot} - x_i)_j$.

Thus:

$$(\nabla_{x_i} u_i(x_i, \bar{x}_i))_j = \frac{1}{\sigma_{ij} + h_j^i x_{tot} + (1 - h_j^i) x_i}, \quad \forall j$$

$$\nabla_{x_i} u_i(x_i, \bar{x}_i)^T x_i = \sum_{j=1}^{m} \frac{x_{ij}}{\sigma_{ij} + h_j^i x_{tot} + (1 - h_j^i) x_i}.$$

Then, using the logarithmic transformation, we can rewrite the nonlinear inequality (7) as:

$$\log(\sigma_{ij} + h_j^i x_{tot} + (1 - h_j^i) x_i) + \log(p_j) + \log(\sum_{j=1}^{m} \frac{x_{ij}}{\sigma_{ij} + h_j^i x_{tot} + (1 - h_j^i) x_i}). \tag{9}$$

$$\geq \log(w_i), \quad \forall ij$$

We know the price p is fixed, so (9) is actually a convex inequality for $1 - h_j^i \geq 0$ constantly. Therefore, under the weak-interference and fixed price condition, the strategy profile space χ is convex.

Second, the utility function u_i is continuous on the strategy profile space χ. Meanwhile, given a fixed $\bar{x}_i$, u_i is strictly concave in x_i, because $\nabla_{x_i x_i}^2 u_i(x_i, \bar{x}_i)$ is negative definite:

$$\nabla_{x_i x_i}^2 u_i(x_i, \bar{x}_i) = diag\{-\frac{1}{(\sigma_{ij} + h_j^i(\sum_{k \neq i} x_{kj}) + x_{ij})^2} \forall j\}.$$

Therefore, according to Theorem 4.4 in [13] there exists a equilibrium point NE. ∎

To investigate the uniqueness of NE, we use the similar method in [14] and the uniqueness follows Lemma 2.

Lemma 2. The equilibrium point is unique over the strategy profile space χ for the competitive market mode if the price is fixed and the weak-interference condition is satisfied.

Proof: we know if $x_{ij} > 0$, for all i and j:

$$(\nabla_{x_i^*} u(x_i^*, \bar{x}_i^*)^T x_i^*) \cdot p - w_i \cdot \nabla_{x_i^*} u(x_i^*, \bar{x}_i^*) = 0 . \tag{10}$$

(i.e., every user only purchases most valuable power). Now we use (9) and (10) to derive:

$$\log(\sigma_{ij} + h_j^i x_{tot} + (1 - h_j^i)x_i^*) + \log(p_j) + \log(\sum_{j=1}^m \frac{x_{ij}^*}{\sigma_{ij} + h_j^i x_{tot} + (1 - h_j^i)x_i^*}) = \log(w_i), \forall ij, x_{ij}^* > 0$$

Assume there are two different NEs denoted by points $A = \{a_i\}_{i=1}^n$ and $B = \{b_i\}_{i=1}^n$, so that:

$$\Gamma(A) = \log(\sigma_{ij} + h_j^i x_{tot} + (1 - h_j^i)a_i) + \log(p_j) + \log(\sum_{j=1}^m \frac{a_{ij}}{\sigma_{ij} + h_j^i x_{tot} + (1 - h_j^i)a_i}) - \log(w_i), \forall ij$$

$$\Gamma(B) = \log(\sigma_{ij} + h_j^i x_{tot} + (1 - h_j^i)b_i) + \log(p_j) + \log(\sum_{j=1}^m \frac{b_{ij}}{\sigma_{ij} + h_j^i x_{tot} + (1 - h_j^i)b_i}) - \log(w_i), \forall ij .$$

We have both $\Gamma(A) = 0$ and $\Gamma(B) = 0$, it follows that $\Gamma(A) - \Gamma(B) = 0$. So we define $\Gamma(A) - \Gamma(B)$ as formula (11).

$$\Gamma(A) - \Gamma(B) = \log(\sigma_{ij} + h_j^i x_{tot} + (1 - h_j^i)a_i) + \log(\sum_{j=1}^m \frac{a_{ij}}{\sigma_{ij} + h_j^i x_{tot} + (1 - h_j^i)a_i})$$

$$- \log(\sigma_{ij} + h_j^i x_{tot} - (1 - h_j^i)b_i) - \log(\sum_{j=1}^m \frac{b_{ij}}{\sigma_{ij} + h_j^i x_{tot} + (1 - h_j^i)b_i}), \forall i, j \tag{11}$$

When $h^i_j < 1$, (7) is a convex inequality, so the left of (9) is a monotonous function, that is: for distinct equilibrium points A and B, we have $\Gamma(A) - \Gamma(B) \neq 0$, so (11) is not equal to 0. Therefore, the previous assumption is invalid.

Therefore, under the weak-interference and the fixed price condition, there exists a unique equilibrium point over the strategy profile space χ. ■

Lemma 3. Under the weak-interference condition, the price p can converge to the optimal p^*, so there exists a unique equilibrium point CE over the strategy profile space χ for the competitive market mode.

Proof. Now we prove the only optimal p^* which can satisfy (4) and (1). To meet the formula (1), we have the complementary condition:

$$0 \leq \{ p^* \perp (c_j - \sum_{i=1}^{n} b_{ij} x_{ij})^m_{j=1} \} \geq 0 .$$

where the compact notation $0 \leq a \perp b \geq 0$ meas $ab=0$, $a \geq 0$, and $b \geq 0$. We have:

$$\Phi(p^*) = \sum_{j=1}^{m} p^*_j (c_j - \sum_{i=1}^{n} b_{ij} x_{ij}) . \tag{12}$$

The strategy profile of p can be seen as a closed convex set and Φ is continuous, so price equilibrium p^* exists.

Supposed that p_a^* and p_b^* are two distinct equilibrium points, we can get $\Phi(p_a^*) = \Phi(p_b^*) = 0$. Let:

$$\Phi(p_a^*) - \Phi(p_b^*) = \sum_{j=1}^{m} p^*_{aj}(c_j - \sum_{i=1}^{n} b_{ij} x_{ij}(p^*_{aj})) - \sum_{j=1}^{m} p^*_{bj}(c_j - \sum_{i=1}^{n} b_{ij} x_{ij}(p^*_{bj}))$$

$$= \sum_{j=1}^{m} (p^*_{aj} - p^*_{bj}) c_j - \sum_{j=1}^{m} \sum_{i=1}^{n} b_{ij} [p^*_{aj} x_{ij}(p^*_{aj}) - p^*_{bj} x_{ij}(p^*_{bj})] \tag{13}$$

$$= \sum_{j=1}^{m} (p^*_{aj} - p^*_{bj}) c_j - \sum_{j=1}^{m} \sum_{i=1}^{n} b_{ij} [w_i - w_i] = \sum_{j=1}^{m} (p^*_{aj} - p^*_{bj}) c_j .$$

We know formula (13) is not equal to 0 constantly for different p_a^* and p_b^*. It is contradicts with $\Phi(p_a^*) = \Phi(p_b^*)$. Therefore our hypothesis does not hold. There exists the only price equilibrium p^*. ■

In the condition of $h^i_j \leq 1$, the price p can converge to the optimal p^*, so there exists a unique equilibrium point CE over the strategy profile space χ for the competitive market mode.

4   Distributed Power Allocation Algorithm

In this section we design a distributed algorithm (FCPAA) with round robin rules through which all the secondary users' power allocation can converge to the unique CE proved in the previous section, while the interference temperature constraints of the primary system are still satisfied. At the same time, round robin rules are used to prevent secondary users from wasting opportunity, so FCPAA has a higher convergent speed.

From the previous section, it is obtained that when the price p is fixed, a CE problem can be predigested to a NE problem which can be found by water filling. Specifically, $\bar{x}_i$ are the power allocations of other users, we derive water filling solution for the power allocation problem (4) according to literature [6] as follows:

$$x_{ij}^* = WF_{ij}(\bar{x}_i; p_j) = (\frac{v_i}{p_j} - \sigma_{ij} - \sum_{k \neq i} h_{ik}^j x_{kj})^+ . \tag{14}$$

That is, x_{ij}^* is the NE solution.

Secondly, we adjust the price p and have the optimal p^* to make the process converges to a CE. Here we use *Tâtonnement* process [12], which is described as: if the total demand $\sum_i x_{ij}$ exceeds the supply c_j on channel j, then increase the price p_j, if the demand falls short of supply, then decrease it.

Finally, we use the round robin rules proposed in [15] for a distributed network to accelerate the convergence speed. The round robin rules are as follow: we assume the number of secondary users involved in the game is n, at the beginning each user in the game adjusts its strategy with probability of $1/n$; After a stage game if the utility of ith user is $u_i^t = u_i^{t-1}$ at the stage t, then the user i exits the game, and update the number $n=n-1$.Therefore the rules will let the user who can not increase its utility exit the game in time, which avoid wasting opportunity and increase the convergent speed.

Here is the FCPAA to all secondary users for getting the unique CE, which is as follow:

Step 1: Set $p^{(0)} \geq 0$, initialize iterations: $t_2=0$.

Step 2: Set $x^0(p^{(t_2)}) \geq 0$, initialize iterations: $t_1=0$.

Step 3: If $x_i^{(t_1)}(p^{(t_2)})$ meets the stop condition, stop, and the output is: $x_i^*(p^{(t_2)}) = x_i^{(t_1)}(p^{(t_2)})$.

Step 4: According to (13), all users ($i=1,..,n$) update in phase $x_i^{(t_1+1)}(p^{(t_2)})$ as follows:

$$x_i^{(t_1+1)}(p^{(t_2)}) = WF_i(\overline{x}_i^{(t_1+1)}; p^{(t_2)}) \quad \forall i = 1,\ldots,n$$

Step 5: Determine if utility $u_i^{t_1+1}$ of the user i is equal to $u_i^{t_1}$, if it is, update $n=n-1$; otherwise, return to Step 4.

Step 6: Increase t_1 to t_1+1, return step 3.

Step 7: If $p^{(t_2)}$ meet the stop condition, stop, then output: $p^* = p^{(t_2)}$, $x^* = x^*(p^{(t_2)})$.

Step 8: Primary user gets power allocation of all secondary users, and updates the price:

$$p_j^{t_2+1} = p_j^{t_2} + f_j(y_j(p^{t_2})) .$$

(15)

Where $f_j(y_j(p^{t_2}))$ is the marginal pricing function: $f_j(y_j(p^t)) = \dfrac{\partial p_j(t)}{\partial t}$.

Step 9: Increase t_2 to t_2+1, return step 3.

5   Simulation Results

5.1   Parameter Setting

The simulation results are presented to validate our proposed algorithm (FCPAA). Let us consider a cognitive radio environment with one primary and six secondary users coexist in ten channels (i.e. $n=6$ and $m=10$). In order to meet weak interference condition, we let the interference coefficients h_{ik}^j are randomly generated from $[1, 1/(n-1)]$. Furthermore, the noise levels are symmetric, σ_j in each channel is independent and identically distributed with uniform distribution [0, 1]. For all secondary users, their budgets are $w=[w_1,\ldots,w_n]=1$, the spectrum mask is $c=[c_1,\ldots,c_m]=1$. The Nash equilibrium is solved by iterative water filling with $p=1$. The number of iteration is 100.

5.2   Convergence of FCPAA

Figure 2 shows the convergence of FCPAA with 6 users' utilities. We can see that their utility functions approach the steady state after 40 iterations. Figure 3 demonstrates the price variations of 10 channels are all less than 10^{-2} after 40 iterations. That is said that they converge to the optimal solution when reach to 40 iterations.

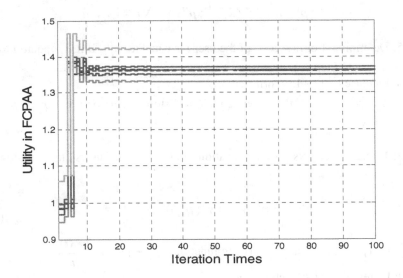

Fig. 2. Utility VS Iterations

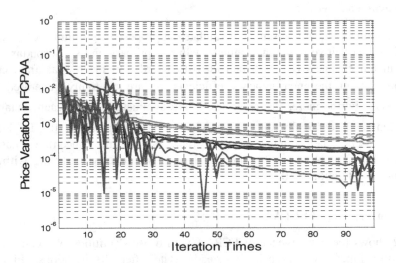

Fig. 3. Price VS Iterations

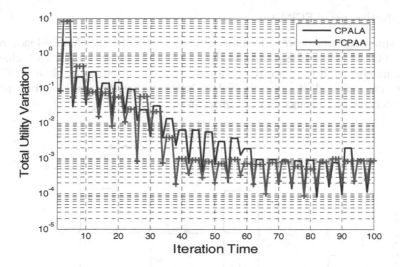

Fig. 4. Comparison of total utility of FCPAA and CPALA

Figure 4 compares the convergent speed of the proposed FCPAA and CPALA (competitive power allocation algorithm as LCP, proposed in literature [9]), we can see that FCPAA has reached convergence when the iteration time is 40. However, the total utility of CPALA converges after 60 iterations. That is said FCPAA converge faster than CPALA.

Figure 5 shows the relationship between noise levels with equilibrium prices. From the *Tâtonnement* processes, we know that it is necessary to reduce prices when noise level of each channel is higher than the spectrum mask. This simulation shows roughly in each channel (channel number is from 1 to 10) when the channel noise level is lower, the channel equilibrium price is higher as we expected.

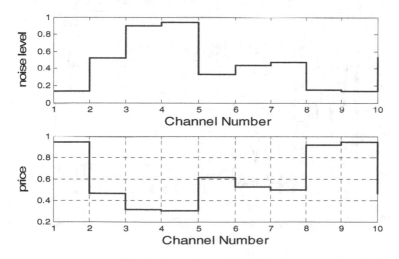

Fig. 5. Channel noise level VS price

5.3   Effectiveness of FCPAA

Figure 6 shows the total power allocation for each channel (or the channel load) in the proposed FCPAA and NE respectively. Here we know channel load of each channel (channel number is from 1 to 10) is lower than the spectrum mask in FCPAA. However, channel load of some channel in NE is higher than the spectrum mask, which affects the performance of the primary user.

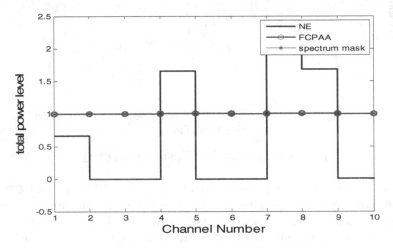

Fig. 6. Spectrum mask VS FCPAA VS NE

Figure 7 shows the convergence process of the system utility based on the proposed algorithm under different interfere threshold. From this figure we can see when interference threshold $c=1$, the system utility converges after 40 iterations; When $c=3$

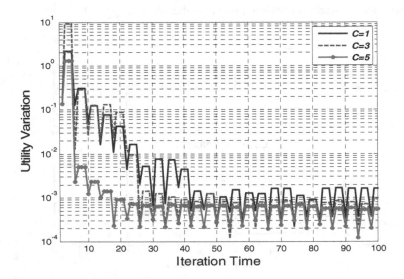

Fig. 7. System utility under different interfere thresholds VS Iterations

and $c=5$, it converges after 25 and 15 iterations, respectively. That is said that the convergent speed of the proposed algorithm will be accelerated when the interference threshold increases. As shown in Table 1, when the interference threshold increases to a certain level, such as $c=5$, here comes $p=0$ due to the interference temperature constraint redundancy, then the algorithm is close to the performance of the algorithm based on the global optimal solution which don't consider the interference constraint.

Table 1. Comparison of system utility under different interfere thresholds and the global optimal solution

	Interfere thresholds			Global optimal solution
	$c=1$	$c=3$	$c=5$	
Total utility	8.181727	14.620557	19.030864	19.255959

6   Conclusion

In this paper, the multichannel power allocation problem in underlay cognitive radio networks is investigated. As in the literatures [9] and [10], we formulate this problem as a competitive market model and design a distributed fast convergent power allocation algorithm (FCPAA) with round robin rules. We prove the existence and the uniqueness of CE for the proposed FCPAA. Simulation results demonstrate that FCPAA is close to the global optimal solutions when the interference threshold increases and can converge to the CE solution more quickly than the algorithm in [9].

References

1. Haykin, S.: Cognitive radio: Brain-empowered wireless communication. IEEE Journal on Selected Areas in Communication 23(2), 201–220 (2005)
2. Le, B., Rondeau, T.W., Bostian, C.W.: Cognitive radio reslities. In: Wireless Communication and Mobile Computing, pp. 1037–1048. Wiley Interscience (2007)
3. Yao, H.-P., Zhou, Z.: An Efficient Power Allocation Scheme in Joint Spectrum Overlay and Underlay Cognitive Radio Networks. In: ISCIT 2009 Proceedings of the 9th International Conference on Communication and Information Technologies, 28-30, pp. 102–105 (2009)
4. Wu, Y., Tsang, D.H.K.: Distributed Multichannel Power Allocation Algorithm for Spectrum Sharing Cognitive Radio Networks. In: IEEE Wireless Communications and Networking Conference, pp. 1436–1441 (2008)
5. Luo, Z.-Q., Zhang, S.: Spectrum management: Complexity and duality. IEEE Journal of Selected Topics in Signal Processing 2(1), 55–73 (2008)
6. Pang, J.-S., Scutari, G., Palomar, D.P., Facchinei, F.: Design of Cognitive Radio Systems Under Temperature-Interference Constraints: A Variational Inequality Approach. IEEE Transactions on Signal Processing 58(6), 3251–3271 (2010)
7. Daoud, A.A., Alpcan, T., Agarwal, S., Alanyali, M.: A stacklberg game for pricing uplink power in wide-band cognitive radio network. In: IEEE Conference on Decision and Control, Cancun, Mexico, pp. 1422-1427 (2008)

8. Goldsmith, A., Jafar, S.A., Maric, I., Srinivasa, S.: Breaking spectrum gridlock with cognitive radios: An information theoretic perspective. Proceedings of the IEEE 97(5), 894–914 (2009)
9. Xie, Y., Armbruster, B., Ye, Y.: Dynamic spectrum management with the competitive market model. IEEE Transactions Signal Processing, 2442–2444 (2010)
10. Ling, M., Tsai, J., Ye, Y.: Budget allocation in a competitive communication spectrum economy. EURASIP Journal on Advances in Signal Processing, 1155–1166 (2009)
11. Niyato, D., Hossain, E.: Microeconomic Models for Dynamic Spectrum Management in Cognitive Radio Networks. ser. Cognitive Wireless Communication Networks, ch. 14. Springer, US (2008)
12. Samuelson, P.: Foundations of economic analysis. Harvard University Press (1983)
13. Basar, T., Olsder, G.T.: Dynamic noncooperative game theory, 2nd edn. SIAM series classics in applied mathematics. SIAM, Philadelphia
14. Rosen, J.B.: Existence and Uniqueness of Equilibrium Point for Concave n-person Games. Econometrica 33(3), 520–548 (1965)
15. Nie, N., Comaniciu, C.: Adaptive channel allocation spectrum etiquette for cognitive radio network. Mobile Network and Application 11, 779–797 (2006)

An Adaptive Anti-narrowband Jamming Receiver for CI/OFDM System

Xiaohu Chen, Jun Wang, Pei Gao, and ShaoQian Li

National Key Laboratory of Science and Technology on Communications,
University of Electronic Science and Technology of China, Chengdu, 611731, P.R. China
cxh4389@163.com, {junwang,gaopei,lsq}@uestc.edu.cn

Abstract. To overcome the inherent shortcomings of orthogonal frequency division multiplexing (OFDM) system, a so-called carrier interferometry OFDM (CI/OFDM) system has been proposed. In CI/OFDM system, data symbols are spreading over all OFDM subcarriers through CI coding so that better frequency diversity gain and lower peak to average power ratio (PAPR) can be obtained. In this paper, we investigated the anti-narrowband jamming performance of CI/OFDM system. We analyzed the post-detection signal-to-jamming plus noise ratio (SJNR) of two kinds of CI/OFDM receiver schemes, which are differentiated each other based on whether the jamming subcarriers are discarded. By comparing their performance in different jamming scenarios, we concluded that each scheme can only work well under specified suitable jamming scenario, in which the one outperforms the other. According to this observation, we further propose an adaptive anti-narrowband jamming CI/OFDM receiver, which adjusts the detection scheme according to the jamming power and bandwidth, to match the corresponding jamming scenarios. Simulation results are provided to validate our scheme.

Keywords: Carrier interferometry, narrowband jamming, orthogonal frequency division multiplexing (OFDM).

1   Introduction

In orthogonal frequency division multiplexing (OFDM)[1] based wideband wireless communication systems, high speed data streams are converted to parallel sub-streams, which are simultaneously transmitted over different narrow-band subcarriers with flat fading, so that , inter-symbols interference (ISI) can be effectively avoided and then better utilization of spectrum resources can be obtained. Therefore, OFDM has been widely applied in wideband wireless systems [2]-[4]. However, OFDM also suffers from some deficiencies, such as high peak and average power ratio (PAPR) and symbol loss due to subcarrier deep fading. To overcome these drawbacks, Wiegandt introduced carrier interferometry (CI) spreading codes into traditional OFDM system, which is referred to as carrier interferometry OFDM (CI/OFDM) [5]-[6]. In CI/OFDM system, each data symbol is spreading to all OFDM subcarriers by using CI codes [7]-[8]. Then, frequency diversity gain can be fully

P. Ren et al. (Eds.): WICON 2011, LNICST 98, pp. 359–370, 2012.
© Institute for Computer Sciences, Social Informatics and Telecommunications Engineering 2012

utilized to improve system bit-error-rate (BER) performance [5]-[6]. Moreover, as CI/OFDM is essentially equivalent to single carrier system, there is not significant PAPR problem compared to traditional OFDM system [9].

Besides channel fading, wireless communication system may face hostile jamming in practical application environments. Therefore, anti-jamming performance is an important system metric, especially for security and military application. As each data symbol is transmitted over a unique OFDM subcarrier, one or more information symbols are likely to be lost when the corresponding subcarriers experiencing jamming, i.e., narrowband jamming. Therefore, OFDM is sensitive to jamming. On the other hand, as CI/OFDM can make better use of frequency diversity gain than traditional OFDM, it can be expected that CI/OFDM can has better anti-narrowband jamming performance than that of traditional OFDM system. For this purpose, [10] has studied the performance of CI/OFDM system under narrowband jamming via simulation, and shows that CI/OFDM system is very robust to narrowband jamming. However, our analysis shows that CI/OFDM system only has better performance than that of OFDM under some specified conditions. According to our simulation results, the CI/OFDM is only superior to OFDM when the power of the jamming is relatively small as the narrowband jamming is spreading to all subcarriers due to the CI codes dispreading at the receiver. So, a scheme, in which the subcarriers experiencing jamming are discarded at the CI/OFDM receiver, is proposed in [10]. In this paper, we call this receiver scheme as zero setting CI/OFDM (ZS-CI/OFDM) receiver, in which those subcarriers experiencing jamming are set to be zero at the receiver. Unfortunately, our preliminary research reveals that this ZS-CI/OFDM can just works well under specific narrowband jamming scenarios as significant signal power loss introduced by discarding subcarriers. Therefore, an important problem is how to make a good tradeoff between jamming spreading and signal power loss for CI/OFDM system under narrowband jamming environments.

To address the above problem, we investigated the anti-narrowband jamming performance in terms of post-detection signal-to-jamming plus noise ratio (SJNR) of CI/OFDM and ZS-CI/OFDM receiver with minimum mean square error (MMSE) equalization in this paper. By comparing SJNR of these two kinds of CI/OFDM receiver under narrowband jamming scenarios, we concluded that each scheme has its suitable jamming scenario, in which one of the receivers outperforms the other. Then, we further investigated the threshold in terms of jamming bandwidth and power to determine the suitable receiver scheme.. Based the obtained threshold, we further propose an adaptive anti-narrowband jamming receiver scheme for CI/OFDM system, which self-adaptively selects suitable receiver scheme based on jamming detection. Simulation results are also provided to validate our adaptive receiver scheme.

The rest of this paper is organized as follows. Section 2 describes the system model for CI/OFDM with and without ZS-CI/OFDM receiver under narrowband jamming. Section 3 presents the analysis and comparison of SJNR between CI/OFDM and ZS-CI/OFDM receivers with MMSE equalization under narrowband jamming. Then, the suitable narrowband jamming scenario for each receiver schemes and the selection threshold is investigated. Section 4 proposes the adaptive anti-narrowband jamming receiver for CI/OFDM system. Simulation results are presented in Section 5 to verify the analysis. Finally, this paper is concluded in Section 6.

2 System Model under Narrowband Jamming

The transmitter and receiver model of CI/OFDM system with and without ZS-CI/OFDM receivers is shown in Fig.1, where ZS means that the subcarriers experiencing jamming are set to be zero based on the results of jamming detection. At the receiver, MMSE equalization is performed to combat with the impact of channel fading and noise. Meanwhile, and represent the jamming and Additional White Gaussian Noise (AWGN) in time domain, respectively. The process of ZS is described in Fig.2, where we assume that the subcarriers suffer from jamming is located at the last part of the band without loss of generality.

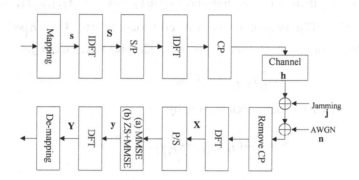

Fig. 1. System model under narrowband jamming

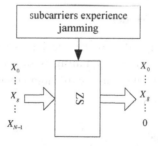

Fig. 2. The process of Zero Setting

2.1 Transmitting Signal Model

As it is depicted in [8], considering there are N data symbols to be transmitted during a OFDM symbol, the corresponding complexity baseband signal model of the transmitting signal in CI/OFDM is given by

$$S(t) = A \sum_{k=0}^{N-1} \sum_{i=1}^{N-1} s(k) e^{j2\pi i \Delta ft} e^{j\frac{2\pi}{N}ki} g(t), \qquad (1)$$

where A is a constant that normalizes symbol energy to be one, $s(k)$ is the kth

data symbol, $e^{j\frac{2\pi}{N}ki}$ is the CI code associate with the ith data symbol element, $\Delta f = 1/T_s$ is the subcarrier bandwidth, and $g(t)$ is a rectangular pulse of duration T_s. (1) can be further rewritten as discrete form with Nyquist sampling, i.e. ,

$$S(t) = A\sum_{k=0}^{N-1}\sum_{i=1}^{N-1} s(k) e^{j\frac{2\pi}{N}ni} e^{j\frac{2\pi}{N}ki} \qquad n = 0,\cdots,N-1 \tag{2}$$

As it is illustrated in Fig. 1, CI codes spreading is implemented by N points weighted inverse discrete Fourier transform (IDFT). Let $\mathbf{s} = \left[s(1),s(2),\cdots,s(N)\right]^T$ denote one CI/OFDM symbol vector with co-variance matrix $\mathbf{C}_s = E\left[\mathbf{ss}^H\right] = E_s\mathbf{I}_N$. Here, $\mathbf{I}_N$ denotes a N by N identity matrix. After CI spreading, we can get

$$\mathbf{S} = \left[S(l)\right]_{N\times 1} = \mathbf{F}^H\mathbf{s}, \tag{3}$$

where $\mathbf{F}$ is the DFT matrix which is given by

$$\mathbf{F} = \frac{1}{\sqrt{N}}\left(f_{kl}\right)_{N\times N} = \frac{1}{\sqrt{N}}\left(e^{-j\frac{2\pi}{N}(k-1)(l-1)}\right)_{N\times N} \tag{4}$$

and the notation $(\cdot)^H$ denotes complex conjugate transposition. Meanwhile, the second IDFT operation in Fig. 1 performs the typical OFDM modulation.

2.2   Narrowband Jamming Model

The narrowband jamming is added into the received signals. For the simplicity of modeling, we assume the narrowband jamming is zero mean independent identical distributed (I.I.D.) Gaussian white noise with auto-covariance matrix $\mathbf{C}_J = \sigma_J^2\mathbf{I}_N$, where σ_J^2 is the variance of jamming .

2.3   Receiving Signal Model

Based on Fig. 1, the received signal is distorted by there factors, which are the channel fading, the narrowband jamming, and the noise. To mitigate these influences, MMSE equalization is firstly applied. Two DFT operations are used to demodulate and de-spread the signals, respectively.

According to [11], the received OFDM signal can be expressed as

$$\mathbf{X} = \mathbf{HS} + \mathbf{J} + \mathbf{W}, \tag{5}$$

where the $N\times N$ fading channel matrix $\mathbf{H}$ is given by

$$\mathbf{H} = diag\left(H_0,H_1,\cdots,H_{N-1}\right) \tag{6}$$

Let $\tilde{\mathbf{H}} = \left(H_p \right)_{N \times 1} = \mathbf{Fh}$ be the $N \times 1$ frequency response vector of the fading channel. Here, $\mathbf{h} = \left[h(0), \cdots, h(L-1), 0, \cdots, 0 \right]_{1 \times N}^{T}$ is the time domain channel impulse response of length L. $\mathbf{J} = \mathbf{Fj}$ and $\mathbf{W} = \mathbf{Fn}$ are the jamming and AWGN in frequency domain, respectively. Here, the auto-covariance matrix of $\mathbf{W}$ is $\mathbf{C}_W = \sigma_n^2 \mathbf{I}_N$. Note that there is only $D(D < N)$ nonzero elements in $\mathbf{J}$, i.e., the number of subcarriers which is subject to the jamming is D.

3   SJNR Analysis under Narrowband Jamming

In this section, we analyze the performance of CI/OFDM and ZS-CI/OFDM under narrowband jamming. Since it is very hard to analyze BER performance associated with CI/OFDM and ZS-CI/OFDM receivers under MMSE equalization, we focus the analysis on post-detection SJNR. It is well-known that the BER is a monotonically decreasing function of SJNR.

3.1   SJNR Analysis of CI/OFDM

For CI/OFDM receiver, the jamming is simply ignored. As it is illustrated in Fig.1, MMSE equalization is performed to compensate the impact of channel fading and noise. According to [12], the MMSE equalizer Λ is a $N \times N$ matrix which can be expressed by

$$\Lambda = diag \left(\frac{H_0^*}{|H_0|^2 + \sigma_n^2 / E_s}, \cdots, \frac{H_{N-1}^*}{|H_{N-1}|^2 + \sigma_n^2 / E_s} \right) \quad (7)$$

By applying DFT transformation to de-spread the CI code, the signal before de-mapping can be expressed by

$$\mathbf{Y} = \mathbf{F} \cdot \mathbf{y} = \mathbf{F\Lambda H} \cdot \mathbf{F}^H \mathbf{S} + \mathbf{F\Lambda J} + \mathbf{F\Lambda W} \quad (8)$$

So, the g th entry of $\mathbf{Y}$ can be expressed as

$$
\begin{aligned}
Y(g) = & \frac{1}{\sqrt{N}} \sum_{n=0}^{N-1} \frac{|H_n|^2}{|H_n|^2 + \sigma_n^2 / E_s} S(n) \exp\left(-j2\pi \frac{ng}{N} \right) \\
& + \frac{1}{\sqrt{N}} \sum_{n=0}^{N-1} \frac{H_n^*}{|H_n|^2 + \sigma_n^2 / E_s} J(n) \exp\left(-j2\pi \frac{gn}{N} \right) \\
& + \frac{1}{\sqrt{N}} \sum_{n=0}^{N-1} \frac{H_n^*}{|H_n|^2 + \sigma_n^2 / E_s} W(n) \exp\left(-j2\pi \frac{gn}{N} \right)
\end{aligned}
\quad (9)
$$

Without loss of generality, we assume that the subcarriers influenced by the jamming are the last parts of the band, i.e. ,

$$J(n) = \begin{cases} 0 & n < N-D \\ J\big(n-(N-D)\big) & N-D \le n \le N-1 \end{cases} \tag{10}$$

Then, it follows (3) that (9)can be expressed as

$$
\begin{aligned}
Y(g) = & \frac{1}{N}\sum_{n=0}^{N-1}\frac{|H_n|^2}{|H_n|^2+\sigma_n^2/E_s}s(g) + \\
& \frac{1}{N}\sum_{n=0}^{N-1}\sum_{\substack{i=0\\i\ne g}}^{N-1}\frac{|H_n|^2}{|H_n|^2+\sigma_n^2/E_s}s(i)\exp\left(j2\pi\frac{n(i-g)}{N}\right) + \\
& \frac{1}{\sqrt{N}}\sum_{n=0}^{N-1}\frac{H_n^*}{|H_n|^2+\sigma_n^2/E_s}J(n)\exp\left(-j2\pi\frac{gn}{N}\right) + \\
& \frac{1}{\sqrt{N}}\sum_{n=0}^{N-1}\frac{H_n^*}{|H_n|^2+\sigma_n^2/E_s}W(n)\exp\left(-j2\pi\frac{gn}{N}\right)
\end{aligned} \tag{11}
$$

where the first item represents the desired signal, the second item denotes the inter-carrier interference (ICI) caused by MMSE equalization, the third item is due to the contribution of jamming, and the fourth item represents the contribution of AWGN.

According to(9), we can have the overall power except jamming as

$$P_{\text{jamming-except}} = \alpha E_s, \tag{12}$$

where $\alpha = \dfrac{1}{N}\sum_{n=0}^{N-1}\dfrac{|H_n|^2}{|H_n|^2+\sigma_n^2/E_s}$. Meanwhile, the power introduced by jamming can be expressed as

$$P_{\text{jamming}} = \frac{\sigma_J^2}{N}\sum_{n=N-D}^{N-1}\frac{|H_n|^2}{\left(|H_n|^2+\sigma_n^2/E_s\right)} = \sigma_J^2\eta \tag{13}$$

where $\eta = \dfrac{1}{N}\sum_{n=N-D}^{N-1}\dfrac{|H_n|^2}{\left(|H_n|^2+\sigma_n^2/E_s\right)^2}$ .Then, we can have the SJNR of CI/OFDM as

$$\gamma_{\text{CI-OFDM}} = \frac{\alpha^2 E_s}{\left(\alpha-\alpha^2\right)E_s+\sigma_J^2\eta} \tag{14}$$

3.2   SJNR of ZS-CI/OFDM

In order to eliminate the impact of jamming, we set the received signal to be zeros on the subcarriers influenced by the jamming at the ZS-CI/OFDM receiver. Because each of the N low-rate symbol streams is spreading across all the N subcarriers, CI/OFDM can still have the capacity to recover all the data symbols based on the remainder subcarriers in this case. It is just similar to the analysis of CI/OFDM receiver, the operations of ZS and MMSE can be expressed by

$$y = \Lambda X = \Lambda MHS + \Lambda MW, \tag{15}$$

where $M = diag\left(\underbrace{1,\cdots,1}_{N-D},\underbrace{0,\cdots,0}_{D}\right)$. After de-spreading the CI codes, we can have

$$Y = Fy = F\Lambda MHS + F\Lambda MW \tag{16}$$

then, the gth entry of Y can be expressed as

$$
\begin{aligned}
Y(g) = & \frac{1}{\sqrt{N}} \sum_{n=0}^{N-D-1} \frac{|H_n|^2}{|H_n|^2 + \sigma_n^2/E_s} S(n) \exp\left(-j2\pi\frac{ng}{N}\right) \\
& + \frac{1}{\sqrt{N}} \sum_{n=0}^{N-D-1} \frac{H_n^{*}}{|H_n|^2 + \sigma_n^2/E_s} W(n) \exp\left(-j2\pi\frac{gn}{N}\right)
\end{aligned}
\tag{17}
$$

It follows (3) that (17) can be expressed as

$$
\begin{aligned}
Y(g) = & \frac{1}{N} \sum_{n=0}^{N-D-1} \frac{|H_n|^2}{|H_n|^2 + \sigma_n^2/E_s} s(g) \exp\left(-j2\pi\frac{ng}{N}\right) \\
& + \frac{1}{N} \sum_{n=0}^{N-D-1} \sum_{\substack{i=0 \\ i \neq g}}^{N-1} \frac{|H_n|^2}{|H_n|^2 + \sigma_n^2/E_s} s(i) \exp\left(j2\pi\frac{n(i-g)}{N}\right) \\
& + \frac{1}{\sqrt{N}} \sum_{n=0}^{N-D-1} \frac{H_n^{*}}{|H_n|^2 + \sigma_n^2/E_s} W(n) \exp\left(-j2\pi\frac{gn}{N}\right)
\end{aligned}
\tag{18}
$$

where the first item represents the desired signal, the second item is the inter-carrier interference (ICI) caused by MMSE equalization and ZS, and the third item denotes the contribution due to AWGN. According to(17), we have

$$E\left(|Y(g)|^2\right) = \left(\alpha*\right)^2 E_s, \tag{19}$$

where $\alpha* = \dfrac{1}{N} \sum_{n=0}^{N-D-1} \dfrac{|H_n|^2}{|H_n|^2 + \sigma_n^2/E_s}$. Then, based on the methods used in [14], we can obtain the SJNR of ZS-CI/OFDM as

$$\gamma_{\text{ZS-CI/OFDM}} = \frac{\alpha*}{1-\alpha*} \tag{20}$$

3.3   SJNR Comparison

According to the analysis in the previous subsections, there exist two factors associate with the jamming needed to be considered, which are the ratio of jamming bandwidth versus total bandwidth, i.e., $\beta = \dfrac{D}{N}$, and the power of jamming, i.e., σ_j^2. In this paper, we assumed that these two factors can be detected by the jamming detection perfectly.

According to (14) and(20), we presents the numerically SJNR comparison between CI/OFDM and ZS-CI/OFDM receiver in Fig. 3, where JSR= E_s / σ_j^2 is Jamming-to-Signal Ratio. In this figure, the blue plane corresponds to the plane that $\gamma_{ZS-CI/OFDM} / \gamma_{CI/OFDM} = 1$.

From Fig. 3, it can then be seen that the curved surface which is above the blue plane illustrates that the SJNR performance of ZS-CI/OFDM receiver is better than that of CI/OFDM receiver. In this case, the influence of power loss at ZS-CI/OFDM receiver due to discarding subcarriers experiencing jamming is less than that of CI/OFDM receiver, at which jamming is spreading over all subcarriers. So, it is evidently that we should choose ZS-CI/OFDM receiver in this case. Otherwise, CI/OFDM receiver is a better choice.

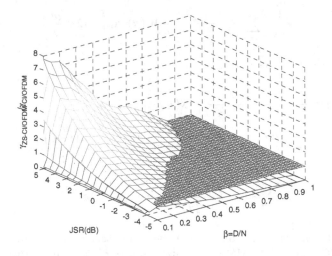

Fig. 3. Comparison of the SJNR between CI/OFDM and ZS-CI/OFDM receivers

4   Adaptive Anti-narrowband Jamming Receiver

According to the results obtained in the above Section, we can find that CI/OFDM and ZS-CI/OFDM receivers can only work well under specified jamming scenarios, respectively. Based on this observation, we propose an adaptive anti-narrowband jamming receiver which can be adjusted to match the narrowband jamming scenarios. In other words, the proposed receiver can make a good tradeoff between the jamming spreading introduced by CI de-spreading in CI/OFDM receiver and power loss due to subcarriers discarding in ZS-CI/OFDM receiver.

The proposed adaptive receiver is presented in Fig. 7. It is the combination of CI/FODM and ZS-CI/OFDM receivers. The key point is that we introduce an adaptive selection between CI/OFDM receiver and ZS-CI/OFDM receiver based on jamming detection.

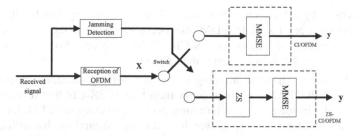

Fig. 4. The adaptive anti-Narrowband jamming receiver

The corresponding selection criterion includes two factors mentioned in the previous section, i.e., the jamming bandwidth ratio β and the jamming power σ_J^2. All of them can be obtained by jamming detection. Obviously, the optimal threshold of β and σ_J^2 should be determined based on Fig. 3. According to Fig.3, we choose ZS-CI/OFDM receiver if (β, σ_J^2) lies in the region that corresponding to $\gamma_{ZS\text{-}CI/OFDM}/\gamma_{CI/OFDM} > 1$. Otherwise, we choose CI/OFDM receiver.

5   Simulation Results

In this section, we further perform simulations to compare the BER performance of CI/OFDM, ZS-CI/OFDM and adaptive receivers under different jamming scenarios to validate the proposed receiver scheme. The channel models of "COST207TUx6" [15] are adopted in our simulations. In the simulation, Quadrature Phase Shift Keying (QPSK) is used. Signal-to-Noise Radio (SNR= E_s/σ_n^2) is set to be 20dB. The other simulation parameters used are given in Table 1. For the sake of comparison, we also provide the BER performance of OFDM system.

Table 1. Simulation Parameters in "COST207TUX6"

Subcarrier number	1024
Bandwidth	10MHz
Maximum delay	5 us
Guard interval	6.4us
Subcarrier interval	9.8kHz

In Fig. 5, we present the BER versus JSR when β =4% and 8%. It can be seen that the performance of ZS-CI/OFDM receiver is much better than that of CI/OFDM receiver and OFDM if the jamming power is large and the ratio of bandwidth of jamming β is small, i.e. , $\beta = 4\%$. This is because the jamming power is spreading across all N subcarriers due to CI de-spreading and the resulted SJNR is too small to recover the data symbols. Meanwhile, the performance of ZS-CI/OFDM receiver is not relevant to the power of jamming as all the subcarriers experiencing jamming are discarded. The recovery of data can be done by the information spreading over the other subcarriers by CI coding. However, when the jamming bandwidth becomes large, the performance of ZS-CI/OFDM also becomes worse as the power loss due to subcarriers discarding increases at ZS-CI/OFDM receiver. So, the performance corresponding to $\beta = 4\%$ is much better than $\beta = 8\%$.

On the other hand, when the jamming power is relatively small, i.e., JSR<0dB, the performance of CI/OFDM receiver is better than that of ZS-CI/OFDM receiver. This is because that the influence due to jamming power spreading for CI/OFDM receiver is less than the influence due to power loss due to subcarriers discarding for ZS-CI/OFDM receiver. So, by making an adaptive receiver selection, the proposed adaptive receiver achieves the best performance between these two receivers.

Moreover, we find that the performance of OFDM is better than that of CI/OFDM without ZS-CI/OFDM receiver when JSR is relatively large. This because the influence due to jamming power spreading for CI/OFDM receiver is larger than the influence data symbols loss for OFDM in high JSR region. So, CI/OFDM is not always superior to OFDM under narrowband jamming. But the proposed adaptive CI/OFDM receiver can always obtain the best performance.

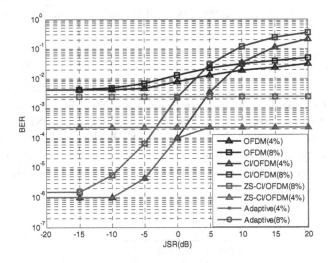

Fig. 5. BER performance comparison under different JSR (β =4% and 8%)

In Fig. 6, we further provide the performance comparison when β =20% and 40%. It can be seen that the advantage of ZS-CI/OFDM does not exist any more due to the loss of signal power and ICI interference caused by the process of ZS, especially when β is relatively large, the data can't be recovered again in the ZS-CI/OFDM system. So, CI/OFDM can not well under the environment with large jamming bandwidth. Even though, the proposed adaptive receiver can still achieve the best performance.

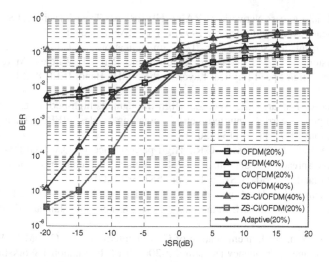

Fig. 6. BER performance comparison under different JSR (β =20% and 40%)

6   Conclusion

In this paper, we investigated the performance of CI/OFDM system with and without ZS-CI/OFDM receiver with MMSE equalization under narrowband jamming. We derived the expression of SJNR and compared the performance of two kinds of CI/OFDM receiver under different jamming scenarios. We find that each scheme can only work well in some specified jamming scenario. Then, we proposed an adaptive anti-narrowband jamming receiver for CI/OFDM system to combine these two receiver schemes so that better performance can be obtained under practical environments. Simulation results validate our proposed receiver scheme.

Acknowlegement. This paper is supported in part by the Foundation Project of National Key Laboratory of Science and Technology on Communications under grant No. 9140C0202061004, the Fundamental Research Funds for the Central Universities under grant No. ZYGX2009X002, National Natural Science Foundation of China under Grant No. 61071102, High-Tech Research and Development Program (863 Program) of China under Grant No. 2009AA011801 and 2009AA012002, National Basic Research Program (973 Program) of China under Grant No. 2009CB320405, National Science and Technology Major Project of China under Grant No.2009ZX03007-004, 2009ZX03005-002, 2009ZX03004-001, 2009ZX03005-004, 2010ZX03006-002-02.

References

1. Weinstein, S., Ebert, P.: Data Transmission by Frequency-Division Multiplexing Using the Discrete Fourier Transform. IEEE Transactions on Communications 19(5), 624–628 (1971)
2. Rohling, H., May, T., Bruninghaus, K., Grunheid, R.: Broad-band OFDM radio transmission for multimedia applications. Proceedings of the IEEE 87, 1778–1789 (1999)

3. Broadband Radio Access Networks (BRAN); HIPERLAN Type 2 Technical Specification-Part I: Physical Layer, ETSI (October 1999) DTS/BRAN030003-1
4. Draft Supplement to Standard for Telecommunications and Information Exchange Between Systems-LAN/MSN Specific Requirements-Part I I: Wireless MAC and PHY Specifications: High Speed Physical Layer in the 5 GHz Band, IEEE 802.11 (May 1999) P802.llaJD6.0
5. Wiegandt, D.A., Nassar, C.R., Wu, Z.: High-throughput, high-performance OFDM via pseudo-orthogonal carrier interferometry spreading codes. IEEE Transactions on Communications 51(7), 1123–1134 (2003)
6. Wu, Z., Wiegandt, D.A., Nassar, C.R.: High-performance 64-QAM OFDM via carrier interferometry spreading codes. In: IEEE 58th Vehicular Technology Conference (VTC 2003 Fall), Orlando, Florida, USA, vol. 4, pp. 557–561 (2003)
7. Anwar, K., Yamamoto, H.: A new design of carrier interferometry OFDM with FFT as spreading codes. In: 2006 IEEE Radio and Wireless Symposium, January 17-19, pp. 543–546 (2006)
8. Xu, F., Xu, R., Sun, H.: Implementation of Carrier Interferometry OFDM by Using Pulse Shaping Technique in Frequency Domain. In: 2007 IEEE International Workshop on Anti-counterfeiting, Security, Identification, April 16-18, pp. 319–323 (2007)
9. Wiegandt, D.A., Nassar, C.R., Wu, Z.: Overcoming peak-to-average-power ratio issues in OFDM via carrier-interferometry codes. In: IEEE Vehicular Technology Conference (VTC), vol. 2, pp. 660–663 (2001)
10. Wu, Z., Nassar, C.R.: Narrowband Interference Rejection in OFDM via Carrier Interferometry Spreading Codes. IEEE Transactions on Wireless Communications 4(4), 1491–1505 (2005)
11. Wang, Z., Giannakis, G.B.: Wireless multicarrier communications., IEEE Signal Processing Mag., pp. 29–48 (May 2000)
12. Kim, N., Park, H.: Bit Error Performance of Convolutional Coded MIMO System with Linear MMSE Receiver. IEEE Transactions on Wireless Communications 8(7) (July 2009)
13. Banelli, P.: Theoretical Analysis and Performance of OFDM Signals in Nonlinear Fading Channels. IEEE Trans. Communications 2(2), 284–293 (2000)
14. Gao, P., Wang, J., Li, S.: Performance comparison between CI/OFDM and OFDM systems. In: IEEE International Conference on Communications, Circuits and Systems (ICCCAS), pp. 23–27 (2010)
15. Goldsmith, A.J., Varaiya, P.: Capacity of fading channels with channel side information. IEEE Trans. Inform. Theory 43, 1986–1992 (1997)

Cooperative Coarse Timing Synchronization for OFDM-Based Distributed Antenna Systems

Chaojin Qing[1,2], Shihai Shao[2], Mintao Zhang[1], and Youxi Tang[2]

[1] School of Electrical and Information Engineering,
Xihua University, Chengdu, 610039, China
qingchj@uestc.edu.cn
[2] National Key Lab. of Communications,
University of Electronic Science and Technology of China,
Chengdu 610054, China

Abstract. In this paper, a cooperative coarse timing synchronization method for OFDM-based distributed antenna systems is proposed. Without increasing the false alarm probability at each remote antenna, we exploit the cooperation of the multiple remote antennas, and a new detection threshold is formulated to avoid the missed detection that occurs according to the independent timing synchronization. The analytical and simulation results confirm the effectiveness of the proposed method.

Keywords: coarse timing synchronization, cooperative processing, distributed antenna systems, OFDM.

1 Introduction

Coarse timing synchronization for orthogonal frequency-division multiplexing (OFDM) systems is needed to indicate the beginning of the fast Fourier transform (FFT) window. Many proposed approaches, which estimate timing offset by using the autocorrelation of the training sequence consisting of two or more identical parts, have been summarized in [1]. However, these autocorrelation methods are not robust in wideband fading scenarios [2], [3]. Therefore, the cross-correlation method with threshold-based detection for timing synchronization are proposed in [2] and [3].

Timing synchronization for OFDM-based distributed antenna systems (DAS) has been investigated in [4]–[6]. These synchronization methods estimate the timing offset at each remote antenna (RA) independently, without any cooperation among the RAs. To exploit the advantages of cooperation, a cooperative coarse timing synchronization (CCTS) method is proposed in this paper. With the helping from two or more RAs that have achieved coarse timing synchronization according to the pre-defined detection threshold, a new detection threshold can be formulated for some missed RAs to avoid a miss without increasing the false alarm probability at each RA. The analytical and simulation results show that the failure of coarse timing synchronization can be improved by employing the CCTS method.

P. Ren et al. (Eds.): WICON 2011, LNICST 98, pp. 371–380, 2012.

The rest of this paper is organized as follows. In the next section, we describe the system model. In Section 3, we present the coarse timing synchronization method. Some numerical results are given in Section 4. Finally, Section 5 concludes this paper.

2   System Model

In this paper, we assume $M_r(M_r > 2)$ RAs are connected to the central processor of the receiver for receiving the signal transmitted from the transmitter with a single antenna. The OFDM baseband signal at the transmitter is generated by the IFFT transform

$$x(n) = \frac{1}{\sqrt{N}} \sum_{k=0}^{N-1} s_k e^{j2\pi kn/N}, \quad -G \leq n \leq N-1, \tag{1}$$

where N is the FFT size, s_k represents the data sequence modulated on the kth subcarrier, which is independently and identically distributed with zero mean and variance $E\left\{|s_k|^2\right\} = \sigma_s^2$. G is the length of cyclic prefix (guard time). The received signal samples at RA_i, $i = 1, \cdots, M_r$ can be expressed as

$$r_i(n) = \sum_{m=0}^{L_i-1} \sqrt{\xi_i} h_i(m) x(n - m - \tau_i) e^{j2\pi\varepsilon_i n/N} + w_i(n), \tag{2}$$

where L_i $(L_i \leq G)$ is the memory length of the multipath fading channel, $\sqrt{\xi_i}$ denotes the large-scale fading that captures the effects of mean path loss and log-normal shadow fading, $h_i(m)$ represents the channel impulse response of mth path for small-scale fading, τ_i stands for the timing offset, ε_i is the normalized carrier frequency offset, and w_i denotes the samples of a zero-mean complex white Gaussian noise random process with variance $E\left\{|w_i(n)|^2\right\} = \sigma_w^2$ and is assumed independent with respect to $x(n)$.

3   Coarse Timing Synchronization

In this section, we recall the cross-correlation based synchronization method with pre-defined detection threshold, and we will base on this scheme to describe our proposed algorithm. Note that the proposed method can also apply to the autocorrelation method to obtain similar conclusion. However, for a pre-defined false alarm probability, the closed-form expression of the detection threshold in autocorrelation method cannot be obtained [7] (resorted to numerical calculations, see subsection A of section IV in [7]). For convenience, the cross-correlation method for coarse timing synchronization is considered in this paper.

Similar to [8], the constant envelop preamble is considered in this paper. We describe the preamble structure as

$$\mathbf{S} = \tilde{\mathbf{S}} \odot \mathbf{S}_{PN}, \tag{3}$$

where $\mathbf{S} = [s(0), \cdots, s(N-1)]$ is $1 \times N$ preamble sequence, $\tilde{\mathbf{S}}$ is the repetitive sequences of the form $\tilde{\mathbf{S}} = [\mathbf{A}_{N/2} \ \mathbf{A}_{N/2}]$, $\mathbf{A}_{N/2}$ is a random complex vector of length $N/2$ [1], the operator "$\odot$" indicates the Hadamard product, and the pseudo-noise (PN) sequence weighted factors are introduced by the $1 \times N$ vector $\mathbf{S}_{PN}$ [8]. In (3), we reserve the repetitive form $\tilde{\mathbf{S}}$ in [1] for the fine synchronization and fractional frequency offset estimation after coarse timing sychronization, and the PN sequence is adopted to avoid the multiple peaks appear in [2] and [3].

Using the cross-correlation detection method [2], [3], we compute the cross-correlation between the received signal and the known preamble sequence, i.e.,

$$P_i(d_i) = \sum_{k=0}^{N-1} r_i(d_i + k)s^*(k), \quad i = 1, 2, \cdots, M_r, \tag{4}$$

where "$*$" denotes the complex conjugate. From [2] and [3], $|P_i(d_i)|$ at all other timing instants apart from those corresponding to the channel paths, denoted as $|P_i(\beta_{NC,i})|$, can be regarded as a Rayleigh distributed random variable. Hence, the detection threshold for each RA can be given by [3]

$$T_{c,i} = \sqrt{-2\sigma_i^2 \ln(P_{FA})}, \quad i = 1, \cdots, M_r, \tag{5}$$

where P_{FA} is the pre-defined false alarm probability for each RA. According to [3], the σ_i in equation (5) can be estimated by $\hat{\sigma}_i = \sqrt{2/\pi} \cdot E\{|P_i(\beta_{NC,i})|\}$.

3.1   Independent Coarse Timing Synchronization

For DAS, the M_r RAs are deployed at different locations, and the transmitted signal is experienced different paths to reach the M_r RAs. Thus, $\tau_i, i = 1, \cdots, M_r$ are generally different. If the coarse timing synchronization is done at each RA independently, we call it as *independent coarse timing synchronization* (**ICTS**) in this paper. Thus, the timing offset for each RA$_i$ ($i = 1, \cdots, M_r$) can be estimated as

$$\hat{d}_i = \arg\max_{d_i} \{|P_i(d_i)| \geq T_{c,i}\}, \ d_i \in [0, U - N], \tag{6}$$

where U is the observation vector length, which is assumed to be long enough to incorporate the whole preamble sequence.

In multi-path channels, the trajectory peak of $|P_i(d_i)|$ would be delayed due to the channel dispersion [9]. Hence, the coarse-timing estimate should be pre-advanced by some samples to guarantee that the estimate of τ_i, i.e., $\hat{\tau}_i$, satisfies $|\hat{\tau}_i - \tau_i| \leq G/2$ (i.e., pre-advanced towards the middle of the cyclic prefix zone [3], [9]). We express $\hat{\tau}_i$ as

$$\hat{\tau}_i = \hat{d}_i - \frac{G}{2}, \ i = 1, 2, \cdots, M_r. \tag{7}$$

Since the ICTS method do not need the cooperation among the receive antennas, the existing coarse timing synchronization methods, e.g., [1]–[9], can also be adopted by ICTS method. In DAS, the signal-to-noise ratios (SNR) at different RAs are imbalance. Hence, the ICTS method performs very bad at some RAs with relatively low received SNRs. To improve the ICTS method, we propose a *cooperative coarse timing synchronization* (**CCTS**) in the following subsection.

3.2   Cooperative Coarse Timing Synchronization

When the transmitted signal experiences deep fading and cannot be synchronized by RA_k according to the detection threshold $T_{c,k}$ (see Equation (5)), a missed detection happens at RA_k in ICTS method. In fact, as two or more RAs have reached the detection threshold given in (5), the false alarm probability at the central processor is generally more lower than the given P_{FA} according to the "data fusion rule" in [10]. Thus, the false alarm probability at the central processor can guarantee that the false alarm probability at RA_k is not higher than the pre-defined P_{FA}. Then, a lower detection threshold $\tilde{T}_{c,k}$, i.e., $\tilde{T}_{c,k} < T_{c,k}$ can be exploited for RA_k without increasing the false alarm probability at RA_k.

3.2.1   Initial Estimation

The CCTS method searches the number of RAs that $|P_i(d_i)|$ can reach $T_{c,i}$ according to (6) firstly. We denote the indexes of the M_u RAs that $|P_i(d_i)|$ can reach $T_{c,i}$ as set $\mathbf{M}_u$, and the indexes of the $M_r - M_u$ RAs that $|P_i(d_i)|$ cannot reach $T_{c,i}$ are denoted as $\mathbf{M}_n$, i.e.,

$$\begin{cases} \mathbf{M}_u = \left\{ i \,\middle|\, \max_{d_i} \{|P_i(d_i)|\} \geq T_{c,i} \right\}, \\ \mathbf{M}_n = \left\{ i \,\middle|\, \max_{d_i} \{|P_i(d_i)|\} < T_{c,i} \right\}. \end{cases} \tag{8}$$

In (8), $\mathbf{M}_n$ can be viewed as the complement of $\mathbf{M}_u$. Then, at least M_u RAs can detect the signal from transmitter with the detection threshold $T_{c,i}$. The estimate for timing offset τ_i, $i \in \mathbf{M}_u$ can be obtained according to (6) and (7).

3.2.2   Detection Threshold $T_{c,i}^{(1)}$

When $1 < M_u < M_r$, a detection threshold $T_{c,i}^{(1)}$ based on the false alarm probability $\tilde{P}_{FA}$ for RA_i is considered. Since there are M_u RAs can reach the detection threshold $T_{c,i}$, then at least M_u RAs can reach the $T_{c,k}^{(1)}$ as $T_{c,k}^{(1)} < T_{c,k}$ is considered.

Denoting B_j as the event that there are M_u RAs have synchronized the signal from the transmitter according to the detection threshold $T_{c,i}^{(1)}$, then we have

$$N_{combi} = \frac{M_r!}{M_u! (M_r - M_u)!}, \tag{9}$$

where N_{combi} is the combinations from M_r RAs for the event B_j. According to the "data fusion rule" in [10], the false alarm probability that M_u RAs have detected the signal from the transmitter at the central processor according to the detection threshold $T_{c,i}^{(1)}$ is

$$P_{false} \{B_j\} = \left(\tilde{P}_{FA}\right)^{M_u}, \tag{10}$$

where $P_{false}\{B_j\}$ is the false alarm probability that event B_j occurs, and $\tilde{P}_{FA}$ is the false alarm probability that each RA independently detects the signal according to detection threshold $T_{c,i}^{(1)}$.

Considering any M_u RAs among the M_r RAs have detected the signal, then the false alarm probability at central processor can be expressed as

$$\begin{aligned}
\tilde{P}_{FA}^C &= Pr_{false} \{B_1 \cup B_2 \cup \cdots \cup B_{N_{combi}}\} \\
&\le Pr_{false} \{B_1\} + \cdots + Pr_{false} \{B_{C_{combi}}\} \\
&= N_{combi} \cdot \left(\tilde{P}_{FA}\right)^{M_u}.
\end{aligned} \tag{11}$$

To guarantee the false alarm probability will be not higher than pre-defined false alarm probability P_{FA} for each RA, we can choose $\tilde{P}_{FA}^C \le N_{combi} \cdot \left(\tilde{P}_{FA}\right)^{M_u} \le P_{FA}$. Then we have

$$\tilde{P}_{FA} \le \left(\frac{P_{FA}}{N_{combi}}\right)^{1/M_u}. \tag{12}$$

Replacing P_{FA} in (5) by the maximum of $\tilde{P}_{FA}$, the new detection threshold $T_{c,i}^{(1)}$ for RA_i, $i \in \mathbf{M}_n$ is given by

$$T_{c,i}^{(1)} = \sqrt{\frac{-2\sigma_i^2}{M_u} \cdot \ln\left(\frac{P_{FA}}{N_{combi}}\right)}. \tag{13}$$

To achieve $T_{c,i}^{(1)} < T_{c,i}$, a constraint can be formulated according to (5) and (13), i.e.,

$$N_{combi} < (P_{FA})^{-M_u+1}. \tag{14}$$

As $N_{combi} = M_r$, $M_u = 1$ and (14) cannot be satisfied. Meanwhile, all RAs have detected the signal with the detection threshold $T_{c,i}$ when $M_u = M_r$. Therefore, the detection threshold $T_{c,i}^{(1)}$ in (13) can be employed for the scenarios that $1 < M_u < M_r$.

3.2.3 Detection Threshold $T_{c,i}^{(2)}$

Although the detection threshold $T_{c,i}^{(1)} < T_{c,i}$ can be obtained without increasing the false alarm probability for each RA when $1 < M_u < M_r$, too low detection threshold cannot ensure the effectiveness of the synchronized RAs. Hence, a desired correct detection probability $\bar{P}_D$ should be considered.

Setting $X = \max |P_i(\beta_{NC,i})|$ for $|\beta_{NC,i} - \tau_i| > G/2$, then $|P_i(\beta_{NC,i})|$ is a Rayleigh distributed random variable, the cumulative distribution function (CDF) of X is

$$F_X(x) = \left(1 - \exp\left(-\frac{x^2}{2\sigma_i^2}\right)\right)^{\bar{U}}, \tag{15}$$

where $\bar{U} = U - N - G$. Considering a detection threshold $T_{c,i}^{(2)}$, then we have

$$\Pr\left(X < T_{c,i}^{(2)}\right) = \left(1 - \exp\left(-\frac{\left(T_{c,i}^{(2)}\right)^2}{2\sigma_i^2}\right)\right)^{\bar{U}}. \tag{16}$$

According to the desired correct detection probability $\bar{P}_D$, we choose

$\Pr\left(X < T_{c,i}^{(2)}\right) \geq \bar{P}_D$. Then $T_{c,i}^{(2)}$ should satisfy $T_{c,i}^{(2)} \geq \sqrt{-2\sigma_i^2 \ln\left(1 - (\bar{P}_D)^{1/\bar{U}}\right)}$. That is, the $T_{c,i}^{(2)}$ can be set as

$$T_{c,i}^{(2)} = \sqrt{-2\sigma_i^2 \ln\left(1 - (\bar{P}_D)^{1/\bar{U}}\right)}. \tag{17}$$

In (17), the $\bar{P}_D$ should be chosen according to $T_{c,i}^{(2)} < T_{c,i}$. From (5) and (17), we have

$$\bar{P}_D < (1 - P_{FA})^{\bar{U}}. \tag{18}$$

3.2.4 Additional Remote Antennas

To guarantee the effectiveness of the synchronized RAs, a new detection threshold $\tilde{T}_{c,i}$ should be chosen according to (13) and (17) for each RA, i.e.,

$$\tilde{T}_{c,i} = \max\left\{T_{c,i}^{(1)}, T_{c,i}^{(2)}\right\}. \tag{19}$$

For $1 < M_u < M_r$, we employ the new detection threshold $\tilde{T}_{c,i}$ (given in (19)) to estimate the timing offset τ_i, $i \in \mathbf{M}_n$, i.e.,

$$\hat{\tau}_i = \arg\max_{d_i}\left\{|P_i(d_i)| \geq \tilde{T}_{c,i}\right\} - \frac{G}{2}, \tag{20}$$

where $d_i \in [0, U - N]$, the missed detection at RA_i, $i \in \mathbf{M}_n$ can be avoided as the $P_i(d_i)$ reaches to the new detection threshold $\tilde{T}_{c,i}$.

From (13) and (17), $T_{c,i}^{(1)} = T_{c,i}^{(2)}$ is equivalent to $(P_{FA}/N_{cb})^{1/M_u} = 1 - (\bar{P}_W)^{1/\bar{U}}$. If the parameters P_{FA}, M_r, $\bar{P}_W$, and $\bar{U}$ are given, the $\tilde{T}_{c,i}$ is decided by M_u. For example, given $P_{FA} = 10^{-6}$, $M_r = 6$, $\bar{P}_W = 90\%$, and $\bar{U} = 112$ (assuming $N = 128$, $U = 2N$, $G = N/8$, and $\bar{U} = U - N - G$), $\tilde{T}_{c,i}$ is equal to $T_{c,i}^{(1)}$ for $M_u = 2$ and $T_{c,i}^{(2)}$ for M_u is 3, 4, and 5. In general, P_{FA}, M_r, $\bar{P}_W$, and $\bar{U}$ are known before the starting of a synchronization process. Thus, according to M_u, we select $T_{c,i}^{(1)}$ or $T_{c,i}^{(2)}$ to compute $\tilde{T}_{c,i}$, rather than to compute both $T_{c,i}^{(1)}$ and $T_{c,i}^{(2)}$ to formulate $\tilde{T}_{c,i}$. Then, the operation of CCTS method is simplified.

3.2.5 Summary for CCTS Method

We briefly summarize the proposed coarse timing synchronization method as follows.

1) Take an initial estimation, including computing $P_i(d_i)$ according to (4), detecting the presence of the transmitted signal according to (6), and returning M_u, $\mathbf{M}_u$, and $\mathbf{M}_n$.
2) If $\mathbf{M}_u$ is not null, we estimate $\tau_i, i \in \mathbf{M}_u$, according to (7). Else, we return to step 1), i.e., we wait for the timing synchronization of the next time.
3) If $2 \leq M_u < M_r$ is not satisfied, jump to step 8). Else, we do the next step.
4) If equation (14) is not satisfied, jump to step 8). Else, we compute $T_{c,i}^{(1)}$ according to (13).
5) If equation (18) is not satisfied, jump to step 8). Else, we compute $T_{c,i}^{(2)}$ according to (17).
6) Compute $\tilde{T}_{c,i}$ according to (19) and estimate the timing offset $\tau_i, i \in \mathbf{M}_n$ with the detection threshold $\tilde{T}_{c,i}$ according to (20).
7) Add the index of the detected DRXs according to (20) into the set $\mathbf{M}_u$.
8) Go to the fine synchronization for DRX_i, $i \in \mathbf{M}_u$.

4 Numerical and Simulation Results

Computer simulation results are presented in this section. We set $N = 128$, $G = 16$, $M_r = 6$, $P_{FA} = 10^{-6}$, $U = 256$, the sample period is $1/1.5\mu s$. Two cases for $\bar{P}_D$ are considered, i.e., $\bar{P}_D = 90\%$ and $\bar{P}_D = 99\%$.

The channel model for computer simulation follows the power delay profile of the Vehicular-A channel in [11]. From the transmitter to the M_r RAs, the channels are independent of each other (the different paths from the transmitter to a given RA are also mutually independent). The carrier frequency and the speed of relative movement between the RAs and the transmitter are set to 2GHz and 120km/h, respectively, then the maximum Doppler frequency is given by

$$\frac{120\text{km/h} \times 2 \times 10^9 \text{Hz}}{3 \times 10^8 \text{m/s}} \approx 222.2\text{Hz}. \tag{21}$$

To confirm the effectiveness of the proposed CCTS method, the **failure probability** of coarse timing synchronization is plotted in Fig. 1 and Fig. 2, where the **failure of coarse timing synchronization** is an event either a missed detection or $|\hat{\tau}_i - \tau_i| > G/2$ (without a miss) occurs. The $T_{c,i}^{(1)}$ (see (13)) is employed to improve the missed detection probability, and $T_{c,i}^{(2)}$ (see (17)) is employed to guarantee the desired probability $\bar{P}_D$. Thus, the **failure probability** is reasonable consideration to measure the improvement of the coarse timing synchronization, rather than making a single evaluation on missed detection.

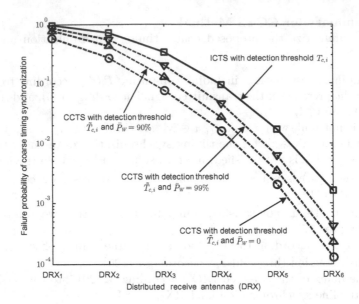

Fig. 1. Failure probability of coarse timing synchronization, where the SNRs from DRX$_1$ to DRX$_6$ are respectively set to be $\{-10\text{dB} \ -6\text{dB} \ -2\text{dB} \ 2\text{dB} \ 6\text{dB} \ 10\text{dB}\}$

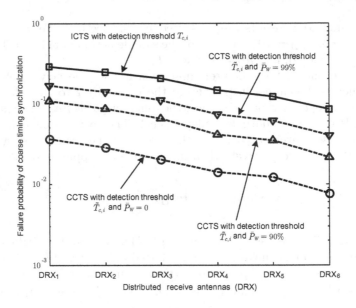

Fig. 2. Failure probability of coarse timing synchronization, where the SNRs form DRX$_1$ to DRX$_6$ are set to be $\{0\text{dB} \ 0.5\text{dB} \ 1\text{dB} \ 2\text{dB} \ 3\text{dB} \ 4\text{dB}\}$, respectively

In Fig. 1, the SNRs from DRX$_1$ to DRX$_6$ are set to be $\{-10\text{dB} \ -6\text{dB} \ -2\text{dB}$ $2\text{dB} \ 6\text{dB} \ 10\text{dB}\}$, respectively. This scenario can be viewed as the attenuation of the transmitted signal for one of the DRXs (i.e., DRX$_6$) is evidently less than the other DRXs, the transmitter may be close to the DRX_6 while it is relatively far from the other DRXs. In Fig. 2, the SNRs form DRX_1 to DRX_6 are set to be {0dB 0.5dB 1dB 2dB 3dB 4dB}, respectively. The attenuation differences of the transmitted signal among the 6 DRXs are not significant, e.g., similar distances from the transmitter to each DRX are considered.

From Fig. 1 and Fig. 2, the failure probability of each DRX in CCTS method is lower than ICTS method when the detection threshold $T_{c,i}^{(1)}$ (see (13), i.e., $\tilde{T}_{c,i} = T_{c,i}^{(1)}$ without considering $T_{c,i}^{(2)}$ in (17)) or $\tilde{T}_{c,i}$ (see (19)) is employed.

In Fig. 1 and Fig. 2, with detection threshold $\tilde{T}_{c,i} = T_{c,i}^{(1)}$, the failure probability of each DRX in the CCTS method is much lower than the others, i.e., the CCTS method with detection threshold $\tilde{T}_{c,i}$ (including $\bar{P}_W = 90\%$ and $\bar{P}_W = 99\%$) and the ICTS method with threshold $T_{c,i}$. We discard some DRXs to guarantee the desired correct detection probability $\bar{P}_D$. Thus, the detection threshold $\tilde{T}_{c,i}$ in (19) is a tradeoff between the presence of a new frame, i.e., keeping the pre-defined false alarm probability not be exceeded, and the desired probability $\bar{P}_D$ can be obtained.

Both in Fig. 1 and Fig. 2, $\bar{P}_W = 90\%$ and $\bar{P}_W = 99\%$ are considered. As can be seen in the two figures, the failure probability for $\bar{P}_W = 90\%$ is lower than the case of $\bar{P}_W = 99\%$. From the discussion for $\tilde{T}_{c,i}$ in subsection (3.2.4), $\tilde{T}_{c,i} - T_{c,i}^{(1)}$ for $M_u = 2$ and $\tilde{T}_{c,i} = T_{c,i}^{(2)}$ for M_u is 3, 4, and 5. In general, $M_u \geq 3$ is obtained for the SNRs configuration in Fig. 1 and Fig. 2 (note that $M_u = 2$ is also occurred). Thus, $\bar{P}_W$ is main reason to effect the failure probability according to (17), and the lower desired probability $\bar{P}_W$ yields lower failure probability can be obtained. The lowest failure probability is obtained as $\bar{P}_W = 0$, i.e., $\tilde{T}_{c,i} = T_{c,i}^{(1)}$ in (19), and can also be derived from (17) and (19).

5   Conclusion

In this paper, the CCTS for OFDM-based DAS has been investigated. By cooperating among the RAs, the detection threshold can be reduced without increasing the false alarm probability at each RA. Relative to the ICTS method, the analytical and simulation results have been shown that the failure of coarse timing synchronization can be improved by employing the CCTS method.

Acknowledgment. This work is supported in part by the National Natural Science Foundation under Grant number 60832007, 60901018, 60902027, U1035002/L05, 61001087, 863 Project under Grant number 2009AA01Z236, the National major projects under Grant number 2010ZX03003–002, 2011ZX03001–006–01, and the Fundamental Research Funds for the Central Universities under Grant number ZYGX2009J008, ZYGX2009J010 of China.

References

1. Morelli, M., Jay Kuo, C.-C., Pun, M.-O.: Synchronization techniques for orthogonal frequency division multiple access (OFDMA): A tutorial review. Proc. IEEE 95(7), 1394–1427 (2007)
2. Awoseyila, A.B., Kasparis, C., Evans, B.G.: Improved preamble-aided timing estimation for OFDM systems. IEEE Commun. Lett. 12(11), 825–827 (2008)
3. Awoseyila, A.B., Kasparis, C., Evans, B.G.: Robust time-domain timing and frequency synchronization for OFDM systems. IEEE Trans. Consumer Electron. 55(2), 391–399 (2009)
4. Zhang, Y.Y., Zhang, J.H., Sun, F.F., Feng, C., Zhang, P., Xia, M.H.: A Novel Timing Synchronization Method for Distributed MIMO-OFDM Systems in Multi-path Rayleigh Fading Channels. In: Proc. IEEE Vehicular Technol. Conf, Singapore, pp. 1443–1447 (May 2008)
5. Feng, G., Li, D., Yang, H.W., Cai, L.Y.: A novel timing Synchronization method for distributed MIMO-OFDM system. In: Proc. IEEE Vehicular Technol. Conf, Melbourne, Vic, pp. 1933–1936 (May 2006)
6. Liu, G., Ge, J.H., Guo, Y.: Time and frequency offset estimation for distributed multiple-input multiple-output orthogonal frequency division multiplexing systems. IET Commun. 4(6), 708–715 (2010)
7. Shi, K., Serpedin, E.: Coarse frame and carrier synchronization of OFDM systems: a new metric and comparison. IEEE Trans. Wireless Commun. 3(4), 1271–1284 (2004)
8. Ren, G., Chang, Y., Zhang, H., Zhang, H.: Synchronization methods based on a new constant envelope preamble for OFDM systems. IEEE Trans. Broadcast. 51(1), 139–143 (2005)
9. Minn, H., Bhargava, V.K., Letaief, K.B.: A robust timing and frequency synchronization for OFDM systems. IEEE Trans. Wireless Commun. 2(4), 822–839 (2003)
10. Elias-Fust, A.R., et al.: CFAR Data Fusion Center with Inhomogeneous Receivers. IEEE Trans. Aerospace and Electron. Syst. AES-28(1), 276–285 (1992)
11. ITU-R M.1225, Guidelines for evaluation of radio transmission technologies for IMT-2000, Recommendation ITU-R M 1225 (1997)

Pilot Design Based on Distributed Transmit Antennas in V-BLAST for Full Frequency Reuse

Zhigang Li, Tian Liu, Shihai Shao, and Youxi Tang

National Key Laboratory of Science and Technology on Communications,
University of Electronic Science and Technology of China, 611731 Chengdu, China
{lizhigang,liutian,ssh,tangyx}@uestc.edu.cn

Abstract. Spectrum resources are very valuable. This paper presents a pilot design for full frequency reuse system in the vertical Bell Labs layered space-time with distributed transmit antennas. In this system, the transmit antennas are placed distributed and the pilot symbols of adjacent 9 antennas are placed at different times or on different subcarriers. A simulation is carried out under the condition of three transmit and three received antennas, multipath Rayleigh fading channel, and antenna spacing of 500 meters. The simulation results show that, at the area averaged mean square error of 5×10^{-2}, the propose method is superior by about 2dB to the traditional method in bit signal-to-noise ratio.

Keywords: full frequency reuse, distributed transmit antennas, V-BLAST.

1 Introduction

In order to fully utilize the scarce spectrum resources, future cellular networks are expected to be full frequency reuse (FFR). For achieving FFR, distributed antenna systems (DAS) are attractive technique over traditional co-located antenna systems (CAS) due to its power and capacity advantages [1]. The power saving and capacity increase of DAS are significantly influenced by antenna placement and channel estimation, which is typically achieved by pilot symbols placed at different times or on different subcarriers [2].

There are challenges for pilot-assisted channel estimation in the traditional co-located antenna systems (CAS): (a). severe co-channel interference (CCI) in the cell boundary may be produced if simply applying FFR; (b). the predicted gains can not be achieved due to spatial correlation in CAS; (c). the effective data transfer rate is reduced in vehicle environments with fast pilot insertion.

Studies on pilot design generally focus on orthogonal pilot design in either time domain or frequency domain [3], without utilizing the antenna placement of DAS. Recently, the work in [4] investigates a four-antenna based structure in DAS with directional antennas for capacity improvement. And the work in [5] the work in proposes pilot coordination in DAS to combat CCI, combined with interference cancellation on the terminal side. Yet, the advantages of distributed transmit antennas

P. Ren et al. (Eds.): WICON 2011, LNICST 98, pp. 381–387, 2012.

need to be further exploited. In this paper, we investigate on how to achieve FFR for pilot-assisted channel estimation in DAS, where V-BLAST and OFDM are employed.

2   System Setup

2.1   Transmitter

The system model is presented in Fig. 1. In traditional regular hexagonal cell, the topology of placement for base station (BS) is equilateral triangle [6]. To maintain such topology in the distributed MIMO model we investigated, only a single transmit antenna are located at the vertex of the triangle. In a large region, these transmit antennas are connected to a single BS by fiber optic or coax cables, where the processing/control functions are realized at the BS. Each antenna transmits signals using the same carrier frequency. In addition, assume a mobile station (MS) is uniformly distributed over a triangle cell. The MS with M_r received antennas is served by M_t transmit antennas nearby.

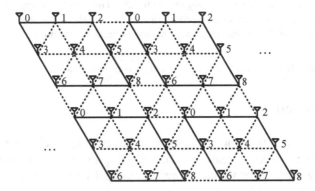

Fig. 1. System model of distributed transmit antennas. Solid lines present that the placements of the adjacent 9 antennas constitute a regular shape.

In CAS, 3 transmit antennas are located at BS centrally, and assume that the pilots of 9 transmit antennas for adjacent 3 cells at least are orthogonal. To maintain this pilot overhead in DAS, assume the pilot symbols of adjacent 9 antennas are orthogonal, i.e. they are placed at different times or on different subcarriers. The placements of these antennas constitute a regular shape, which can cover the entire region without overlap or gap.

We consider a downlink single frequency reuse V-BLAST OFDM with M_t transmit antennas and M_r receive antennas. System bandwidth B is divided into N subcarriers. A cyclic prefix (CP) with N_{cp} subcarriers is added in front of the OFDM symbol. Note that in the scenario with DAS, the CP length must equal to or greater than the sum of the maximum multipath delay and the maximum relative propagation delay caused by the different distances between the receiver and transmit antennas.

2.2 Receiver

The received signal for k-th subcarrier and t-th time of j-th received antenna $R_j(k,t)$ can be expressed as [6]

$$R_j(k,t) = \sum_{i=0}^{M_t-1} H_{ji}(k,t) X_i(k,t) + W_j(k,t) + V_j(k,t) \tag{1}$$

where $H_{ji}(k,t)$ denotes the fading channel coefficient from the i-th transmit antenna to the j-th received antenna $X_i(k,t)$ is the transmitted symbol for the i-th transmit antenna, $W_j(k,t) = \sum_{i=0}^{M_I-1} \sum_{m=0}^{M_I-1} H_{ji}^{(m)}(k,t) X_i^{(m)}(k,t)$ denotes the received M_I signals of co-channel interference (CCI), $V_j(k,t)$ is assumed to be independent and identically distributed complex Gaussian with zero-mean and variance σ_V^2.

2.3 Channel

Consider the effect of path loss and time-variant multipath Rayleigh fading. $H_{ji}(k,t)$ can be expressed as [6]

$$H_{ji}(k,t) = \sqrt{\xi_{ji}} \sum_{n=0}^{L-1} h_{ji}(n,t) e^{j\pi f_{D_n}T} \frac{\sin(\pi f_{D_n}T)}{\pi f_{D_n}T} W_N^{k\tau_n} \tag{2}$$

where ξ_{ji} is path loss, L is the total number of propagation paths, $h_{ji}(n,t)$ is the complex impulse response of the n-th path $(n = 0,1,\cdots,L-1)$, f_{D_n} is the n-th path Doppler shift which causes intercarrier interference (ICI), and τ_n is the n-th path delay time, $W_N = e^{-j2\pi/N}$, $j = \sqrt{-1}$. Channel Energy is normalized, namely $\sum_{n=0}^{L-1} E\{|h_{ji}(n,t)|^2\} = \sum_{n=0}^{L-1} \sigma_{h,n}^2 = 1$.

The path loss ξ_{ji} can be simplified to ξ_i, since the receive antennas are centrally located. We model ξ_i as [6]

$$\xi_i = \begin{cases} \left(\dfrac{\lambda}{4\pi}\right)^2 d_i^{-2}, & d_i \leq \Upsilon \\ (h_b h_s)^2 d_i^{-4}, & d_i > \Upsilon \end{cases} \tag{3}$$

where λ is the wavelength, h_b is the transmit antenna height, h_s is the mobile station (MS) antenna height, d_i is the distance between the i-th transmit antenna and the j-th received antenna of MS, and $\Upsilon = 4\pi h_s h_b / \lambda$ is the break point.

3   Channel Estimation

To estimate the channel frequency response, N_p pilot tones are inserted into the useful subcarriers. Let D_f and D_t present the pilot spacing in time domain and frequency domain, respectively. Then, the pilot spacing D_f satisfy $D_f = N/N_p$. The pilot tone labels for the i-th transmit antenna is $k' = i, D_f + i, \cdots, N - D_f + i$, where $i = \mathrm{mod}(m, D_f)$, after modulo operation, $m = 0, \cdots, M_p - 1$. Hence, the received signal at pilot tones (k', t') for the j-th received antenna is

$$R_j(k', t') = H_{ji}(k', t') X_i(k', t') + W_j(k', t') + V_j(k', t') \tag{4}$$

The DFT-based channel estimation can be in the following steps [7]: Firstly, the channel coefficient $\hat{H}_{ji}(k', t')$ at the pilot tones obtained by using LS channel estimation are given by

$$\hat{H}_{ji}(k', t') = \frac{R_j(k', t')}{X_i(k', t')} \tag{5}$$

Secondly, by the N_p-point IDFT operation, we transform $\hat{H}_{ji}(k', t')$ into the time domain, that is

$$\hat{h}_{ji}(n, t') = \frac{1}{N_p} \sum_{m=0}^{N_p - 1} \hat{H}_{ji}(i + mD_f, t') W_{N_p}^{-mn} \tag{6}$$

Lastly, the time domain signal is in zero-padding operation as following

$$\tilde{h}_{ji}(n, t') = \begin{cases} \hat{h}_{ji}(n, t'), & n = 0, 1, \cdots, N_p - 1 \\ 0, & n = N_p, N_p + 1, N - 1 \end{cases} \tag{7}$$

By the N-point DFT operation for $\tilde{h}_{ji}(n, t')$, the channel frequency response $\tilde{H}_{ji}(k, t')$ is

$$\tilde{H}_{ji}(k, t') = \sum_{n=0}^{N-1} \tilde{h}_{ji}(n, t') W_N^{nk}, \quad k = 0, 1, \cdots N - 1 \tag{8}$$

Lastly, after linear difference between $\tilde{H}_{ji}(k,t')$ and $\tilde{H}_{ji}(k,t'+D_t)$, the channel frequency response is given by

$$\tilde{H}_{ji}(k,t)=\left(1-\frac{t-t'}{D_t}\right)\tilde{H}_{ji}(k,t')+\frac{t-t'}{D_t}\tilde{H}_{ji}(k,t'+D_t) \tag{9}$$

where $t'<t<t'+D_t$.

The channel estimation mean square error (MSE) is

$$\text{MSE}=\sum_{j=0}^{M_r-1}\sum_{i=0}^{M_t-1}\sum_{t=0}^{T-1}\sum_{k=0}^{N-1}\frac{E\left\{\left|\tilde{H}_{ji}(k,t)-H_{ji}(k,t)\right|^2\right\}}{\xi_i} \tag{10}$$

where $E\{\cdot\}$ represents expectation.

4   Simulation Results

We demonstrate the performance of the proposed scheme through computer simulation. According to 3GPP TS 36.101 [8], the simulation parameters are assumed as follows: $M_t=3$, $M_r=3$; $B=30\text{MHz}$, $N=2048$, $N_{cp}=160$; quadrature phase shift keying (QPSK) modulation; LTE Extended Typical Urban (ETU) channel model; vehicle speed of 350km/h and carrier frequency of 1GHz, which result in $f_{D\max}=324\text{Hz}$. From parameters above, we can choose $D_f=4$, $D_t=6$. Assume the transmit correlation factor $\rho=0$ in DAS due to the large antenna spacing, and $\rho=0.1$, 0.5 and 0.9 in CAS according to 3GPP TR 25.996 [9]. Regardless of the effect of the receive correlation. The CCI from last layer antennas are considered in both methods. Finally, Eb/N0 is defined as a ratio of received bit energy to the power spectral density of noise, i.e. Eb/N0= $\sigma_p^2\sum_{i=0}^{M_t-1}\xi_i/M_t\sigma_v^2$.

Simulation results of the proposed DAS method and the traditional CAS method are compared based on the area averaged mean square error (AAMSE) and the area averaged bit error probability (AABEP), respectively. The AAMSE and AABEP are derived by averaging the mean square error (MSE) and the bit error probability (BEP) over the cell, respectively.

Fig. 2 shows the AAMSE performance for V-BLAST OFDM systems. From Fig. 2 we can see that, at AAMSE of 5×10^{-2}, the proposed method is 2dB to the traditional method in Eb/N0. With the increase of Eb/N0, the two methods tend to different error platforms of channel estimation. Since the proposed method utilizes the advantages of DAS, the error platform in DAS is lower than that in CAS.

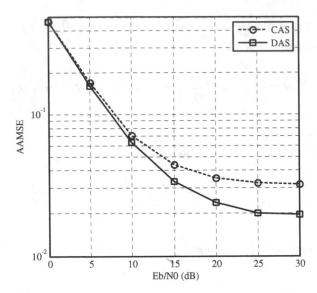

Fig. 2. AAMSE performance for V-BLAST OFDM systems. (M_t=3, M_r=3, f_{Dmax}=324Hz, ρ=0, antenna spacing of 500m).

Fig. 3 shows the AABEP performance for V-BLAST OFDM systems with a variable correlation of transmit antennas ρ. From Fig. 3 we can see that, at AABEP of 4×10^{-2}, relative to the case with ρ=0.1 and 0.5 in CAS, the performance is getting better by 0.7dB and 2dB, respectively. For the case with ρ=0.9 in CAS, the performance is getting deterioration.

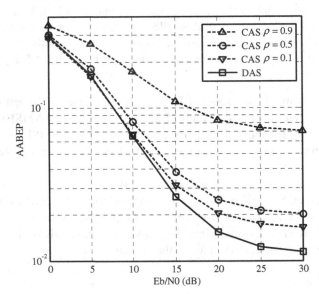

Fig. 3. Example of a figure caption. (M_t=3, M_r=3, QPSK modulation f_{Dmax}=324Hz, antenna spacing of 500m).

5   Conclusions

This letter presents a method of pilot arrangement for distributed V-BLAST OFDM with FFR. The pilot symbols of any antenna and its adjacent antennas are placed at different times or on different subcarriers. Simulation results show that the impact of CCI and transmit correlation in proposed DAS is lower than that in CAS for achieving FFR. Furthermore, the pilot overhead of proposed method will not increase in vehicle environments.

Acknowledgments. This work was supported by the National 863 High Technology Development Project (2009AA01Z236), National Natural Science Foundation of China (60902027, 60832007 and 60901018), the Funds (9140A21030209DZ02), and the Fundamental Research Funds for the Central Universities (ZYGX2009J008 and ZYGX2009J010).

References

1. Castanheira, D., Gameiro, A.: Distributed Antenna System Capacity Scaling. IEEE Wireless Commun. 17, 68–75 (2010)
2. Barhumi, I., Leus, G., Moonen, M.: Optimal Training Design for MIMO-OFDM Systems in Mobile in Mobile Wireless Channels. IEEE Transactions on Signal Processing 51, 1615–1624 (2003)
3. Vithanage, C., Cepeda, R., Coon, J., McGeehan, J.: MIMO-OFDM Pilot Placement Algorithms for Wideband Indoor Communications. IEEE Trans. on Commun. 59, 466–475 (2011)
4. Wang, W., Cai, J., Guo, Z., et al.: Four-antenna Based Structure for Cellular Networks with Frequency Reuse Factor of One. In: IEEE ICC 2009, pp. 1–5. IEEE Press, Dresden (2009)
5. Kamoun, M., Yang, S., De Courville, M.: Multi-RAU Pilotas for ROF Enabled Distributed Antenna Systems. In: IEEE Wireless VITAE 2009, pp. 177–181. IEEE Press, Aalborg (2009)
6. Andrews, J.G., Ghosh, A., Muhamed, R.: Fundamentals of WiMAX: Understanding Broadband Wireless Networking. Prentice Hall, Upper Saddle River (2007)
7. Zhao, Y., Huang, A.: A Novel Channel Estimation Method for OFDM Mobile Communication Systems Based on Pilot Signals and Transform-domain Processing. In: Proc. IEEE 47th Vehicular Technology Conference, pp. 2089–2093. IEEE Press, Phoenix (1997)
8. 3GPP: User Equipment (UE) Radio Transmission and Reception for Evolved UTRA. 3GPP TS 36.101 (v9.3.0) (2010)
9. 3GPP: Spatial Channel Model for Multiple Input Multiple Output (MIMO) Simulations. 3GPP TR 25.996 (v9.0.0) (2009)

Energy-Efficient Distributed Relay Selection Based on Statistical Channel State Information

Haifang Jiang[1], Sihai Zhang[1,2], and Wuyang Zhou[1]

[1] Wireless Information Network Lab.,
Department of Electronic Engineering and Information Science,
University of Science and Technology of China, Hefei, Anhui, China, 230026
[2] Key Laboratory of Wireless Sensor Network & Communication,
Shanghai Institute of Microsystem and Information Technology,
Chinese Academy of Sciences865 Changning Road, Shanghai, China, 200050
jhf@mail.ustc.edu.cn, {shzhang,wyzhou}@ustc.edu.cn

Abstract. In this paper, distributed relay selection algorithms based on statistical Channel State Information (CSI) in amplify-and-forward mode are proposed, aiming to maximize energy efficiency. With the limited CSI, a tradeoff is made between the total power consumption and the target outage probability at the source. A forwarding threshold is obtained by minimizing the average transmission power. Each relay individually decides whether to participate in forwarding the source signals according to the forwarding threshold. Firstly, a Distributed Multiple Relay Selection (DMRS) algorithm is proposed, in which all candidate relays have the possibility of transmitting the source signals and the threshold is obtained by numerical search. Then a Distributed Single Relay Selection (DSRS) algorithm with low complexity is investigated under the assumption that only one relay forwards the signals. Simulation results indicate that the proposed algorithms provide significant performance gain in terms of energy efficiency over the existing AF-mode relay selection algorithms.

Keywords: Amplify-and-Forward(AF), statistical CSI, energy efficiency, distributed relay selection.

1 Introduction

Cooperative communication has drawn increasing research attention due to its ability to resist the impact of wireless fading channels. Compared to direct communication, cooperative communication has the potential of providing benefits of space diversity [1]. It has been widely accepted as an effective way to improving the energy efficiency in the energy-limited network, such as wireless sensor network and ad hoc network. Various cooperative schemes have been studied in the literature. Distributed Space-Time Coding (DSTC) for cooperative network is developed in [2]. "All Participate Forwarding" (APF) scheme is also proposed, where all relay nodes transmit the source signals to the destination. Several

P. Ren et al. (Eds.): WICON 2011, LNICST 98, pp. 388–399, 2012.
© Institute for Computer Sciences, Social Informatics and Telecommunications Engineering 2012

cooperative protocols are presented in [3], including fixed relaying, selection relaying and incremental relaying. These protocols allow relay nodes to operate in AF mode or Decode-and-Forward (DF) mode. Then their outage behaviors and diversity gains are also analyzed.

The performance of a wireless relay-assisted network can be improved by selecting relay nodes appropriately. Opportunistic Relay Selection (ORS) algorithm is proposed using a timer that is set inversely proportional to the channel gain [4,5]. It has been proved that the ORS algorithm is optimal in terms of outage behavior among all single-relay-forward algorithms. Y. Jing presents suboptimal multi-relay-forward algorithm with low complexity and full diversity obtained [6]. A new transmission protocol by combining AF mode and DF mode has even better outage behavior [7]. In this protocol, AF mode is adopted instead of direct link when the relay can't decode the source signals. These algorithms above all use equal power allocation, however, effective utilization of power can further improve the performance of the network. Power allocation about the APF algorithm and the ORS algorithm is analyzed to obtain lower outage probability [8,9].

Most of researches on relay selection focus on the outage behavior or symbol error rate analysis, however, energy efficiency is of great practical significance for the energy-limited network [10,11,12,13]. Distributed power allocation strategies are investigated in [10], attempting to minimizing the power consumption while providing a target outage probability. Energy-efficient single-relay selection cooperative scheme is discussed for wireless sensor networks in [11,12], which jointly considers the MAC design and the physical layer power control. Based on a simple selective relay cooperative scheme, the tradeoff is analyzed between decreasing the energy cost of data transmission by using more relays and decreasing overhead for CSI acquisition by using less relays [13]. Nevertheless, the results are all obtained under the DF mode and the feedback overhead is often overwhelmed when the number of relay nodes becomes larger since the instantaneous CSI of the relay-destination links is needed.

In this paper, we propose distributed relay selection algorithms in AF mode, aiming to minimize the average total power consumption. Given the limited CSI, the source makes a tradeoff between the power consumption and the outage probability. Furthermore, the forwarding threshold and its own transmission power are obtained. The threshold decision mechanism is adopted and each relay individually decides on whether to forward the source signals according to the threshold. We first develop the upper bound of minimal power consumption (MPC-UB) with the assumption of perfect CSI. Then we propose the Distributed Multi-relay Mode (DMRM) algorithm based on statistical CSI. Finally, the Distributed Single-relay Mode (DSRM) algorithm with low computational complexity is studied. Our main contribution is developing distributed algorithms of high energy efficiency in AF mode by employing the threshold relaying criterion and the statistical CSI. These schemes reduce the amount of feedback overhead.

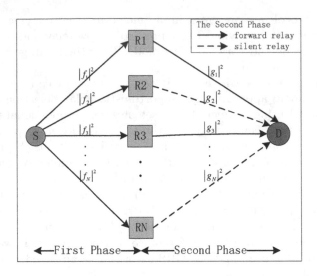

Fig. 1. Scheme Description

2   System Model

The system model of the relay-assisted network is illustrated in Fig. 1, including one source S, one destination D and N relay nodes $R_i(i = 1, 2, ...N)$. It is assumed that the source communicates with the destination only through AF-mode relay nodes because of deep fading in the direct link. All the nodes are equipped with one antenna and operate in half-duplex mode. The channels of source-relay links and relay-destination links all experience flat rayleigh fading and are independent of each other.

In the first phase, S broadcasts signal x, the signal received at relay $R_i(i = 1, 2, ...N)$ is :

$$y_{ri} = \sqrt{P_s} f_i x + n_{ri} \tag{1}$$

where P_s denotes the transmission power of the source. f_i and n_{ri} are respectively the channel coefficient and zero-mean Additive White Gaussian Noise (AWGN) with variance N_0 of the source-relay link for the ith relay node, $f_i \sim CN(0, \eta_i^2)$.

In the second phase, each relay individually checks the relaying criterion according to local CSI. If satisfy, the relay forwards the signal to the destination using orthogonal channel. Otherwise the relay keeps silence. The signal received from the ith relay at the destination is:

$$y_{di} = \sqrt{\frac{P_i}{P_s |f_i|^2 + N_0}} g_i x + n_{di} \tag{2}$$

where P_i denotes the transmission power of R_i. g_i is zero-mean complex Gaussian random variable, denoting the channel coefficient of the relay-destination link for the ith relay node, $g_i \sim CN(0, \sigma_i^2)$. n_{di} is zero-mean AWGN of the relay-destination link with variance N_0. Maximal Ratio Combining (MRC) is applied on the signals. Thus the Signal-to-Noise Ratio (SNR) at the destination is:

$$SNR_D = \sum_{i \in A_R} \frac{P_s |f_i|^2 \cdot P_i |g_i|^2}{P_s |f_i|^2 + P_i |g_i|^2 + N_0} \cdot \frac{1}{N_0} \tag{3}$$

where A_R is the set of forwarding relays.

3 Distributed Relay Selection Algorithm

3.1 Minimal Power Consumption with Perfect CSI

We assume that the source have completely instantaneous CSI, $f_i, g_i (i = 1, 2, ...N)$. Relay selection is made at the source. The source obtains its own transmission power, and then notices the relays in A_R. The problem can be expressed as:

$$\min_{P_s, A_R} \quad P_s + \sum_{i=1}^{N} P_i \tag{4}$$

$$s.t. \quad SNR_D \geq \Gamma$$

where Γ is defined as the target SNR. SNR_D can be approximated under high SNR range as follows:

$$SNR_D \approx \frac{P_s |f_i|^2 \cdot P_i |g_i|^2}{P_s |f_i|^2 + P_i |g_i|^2} \cdot \frac{1}{N_0} \tag{5}$$

The problem (4) is an multi-variable optimization problem and it is difficult to represent the solution with complete expressions. We assume that only one relay node participates in forwarding the signal, meanwhile others keep silence to save energy. It reduces the complexity of receiving at the destination. The problem (4) is simplified to a two-variable optimization problem which can be solved easily. The result of (4) with (5) is determined as:

$$A_R = \{i | \arg\min_{i} \frac{1}{|f_i|} + \frac{1}{|g_i|}\} \tag{6}$$

$$P_s = \frac{\Gamma N_0}{|f_i|^2} (1 + \frac{|f_i|}{|g_i|}) \tag{7}$$

$$P_i = \frac{\Gamma N_0}{|g_i|^2} (1 + \frac{|g_i|}{|f_i|}) \tag{8}$$

Obviously (6) (7) and (8) are the upper bound of minimal power consumption (MPC-UB) and it guarantees no outage in the network. However it is usually assumed that there is a centralized control entity gathering all instantaneous CSI in the network, which needs enormous feedback because of the time-varying characteristic of wireless channels. Thus it is impractical in implementation. In the follow, we devise effect distributed relay selection algorithms.

3.2 Distributed Multi-relay Model (DMRM) Algorithm

Relaying Criterion and Problem Description. In practice, the source generally acquire the instantaneous CSI of source-relay links easily, while only statistical CSI of relay-destination links, that is $f_i, \sigma_i^2 (i = 1, 2...N)$. The relay R_i knows the local CSI relevant to itself, that is f_i, g_i. The channel capacity in AF mode is associated with both source-relay link and relay-destination link, thus the channel quality of both links should be taken into account in the relaying criterion. Based on a distributed mechanism with a forwarding threshold, each relay individually makes its decision on whether to forward the source signal. Therefore the relaying criterion is as follows: if $R_i (i = 1, 2...N)$ satisfies $\frac{1}{|f_i|^2} + \frac{1}{|g_i|^2} \leq \gamma$ where γ is the forwarding threshold, R_i forwards the signal using the transmission power as (8) at the second phase. Here we define the set of candidate relays from which the forwarding relays are selected as follows:

$$A_s = \{i | 1/|f_i|^2 < \gamma\} \tag{9}$$

Maybe the outage event occurs when all relays keep silence because of the low threshold. So the target outage probability ρ is introduced into the network. The research problem is that given Γ and ρ, the source obtains the forwarding threshold γ and its own transmission power by mean of minimizing the average total power consumption of the source and the candidate relays. The problem is described as:

$$\min_{\gamma} \quad E[P_s] + \sum_{i \in A_s} E[P_i]$$

$$s.t. \ Pr\{SNR_D \leq \Gamma\} \leq \rho \tag{10}$$

Forwarding Threshold γ. For the sake of brevity, we set the result of arraying $|f_i|^2 (i = 1, 2...N)$ in ascending order as $|f_1|^2 \geq |f_2|^2 \geq ... \geq |f_N|^2$. Set $|A_s| = M$, and γ_M is supposed to satisfy:

$$\begin{cases} \frac{1}{|f_M|^2} < \gamma_M < \frac{1}{|f_{M+1}|^2}, M = 1, 2...N - 1 \\ \frac{1}{|f_N|^2} < \gamma_M, M = N \end{cases} \tag{11}$$

From the constraint condition in the problem (10) we obtain:

$$Pr\{SNR_D \leq \Gamma\} = \prod_{i \in A_s} Pr\{\frac{1}{|f_i|^2} + \frac{1}{|g_i|^2} > \gamma_M\}$$

$$= \prod_{i \in A_s} [1 - \exp(-\frac{1}{\sigma_i^2} \cdot \frac{1}{\gamma_M - 1/|f_i|^2})] \tag{12}$$

It can be seen from (12) that the outage probability decreases with increment of σ_i^2 or $|f_i|^2$. Thus the inequality can be derived by calculation as follows:

$$Pr_l < Pr\{SNR_D \leq \Gamma\} < Pr_r \tag{13}$$

$$Pr_l = [1 - \exp(-\frac{1}{\max\limits_{i \in A_s} \sigma_i^2} \cdot \frac{1}{\gamma_M - 1/|f_i|^2})]^M \tag{14}$$

$$Pr_r = [1 - \exp(-\frac{1}{\min\limits_{i \in A_s} \sigma_i^2} \cdot \frac{1}{\gamma_M - 1/|f_M|^2})]^M \tag{15}$$

An appropriate threshold is of the utmost importance. When γ increases, the number of relays satisfying the relaying criterion grows. It causes that the outage probability decreases at the destination, whereas the total power consumption increases, and vice versa. We need not only to ensure the target outage probability but also to consume the average total power as little as possible. The threshold decides the tradeoff between the power consumption and the outage behavior. Therefore we let (12) equal the target outage probability ρ. Considering the constraint condition (11), we obtain the range of γ:

$$\gamma_{\min M} < \gamma_M < \gamma_{\max M} \tag{16}$$

$$\gamma_{\min M} = \max(\frac{1}{|f_i|^2} - \frac{1}{\max\limits_{i \in A_s} \sigma_i^2 \cdot \ln(1 - \rho^{1/M})}, \frac{1}{|f_M|^2}) \tag{17}$$

$$\gamma_{\max M} = \begin{cases} \min(\frac{1}{|f_M|^2} - \frac{1}{\min\limits_{i \in A_s} \sigma_i^2 \cdot \ln(1 - \rho^{1/M})}, \frac{1}{|f_{M+1}|^2}), \\ \qquad\qquad\qquad\qquad M = 1, 2...N - 1 \\ \frac{1}{|f_M|^2} - \frac{1}{\min\limits_{i \in A_s} \sigma_i^2 \cdot \ln(1 - \rho^{1/M})}, M = N \end{cases} \tag{18}$$

γ_M can be obtained by way of numerical search in the interval $[\gamma_{\min M}, \gamma_{\max M}]$. It deserves to be specially noted that if $\frac{1}{|f_1|^2} - \frac{1}{\max\limits_{i \in A_s} \sigma_i^2 \cdot \ln(1 - \rho^{1/M})} > \frac{1}{|f_M|^2}$ and $\frac{1}{|f_M|^2} - \frac{1}{\min\limits_{i \in A_s} \sigma_i^2 \cdot \ln(1 - \rho^{1/M})} < \frac{1}{|f_{M+1}|^2}$, it is certain that γ_M has solution when $|A_s| = M$, or else γ may have no solution. In the worst situation, γ_M is unsolvable for all the cases $M = 1, 2, ...N$. Then γ_M takes the value of $\gamma_{\max M}$ in order to increase the possibility of relay forwarding signals to avoid interrupt event.

Transmission Power of Source. When $|A_s| = M(M = 1, 2...N)$ and γ_M has solution, we can obtain the average total power $E[P_{total}(M)]$. Set $Z = |g_i|^2$ and $X = |g_i|$, then the Probability Density Functions (PDF) of Z and X are respectively defined as:

$$f_Z(z) = \frac{1}{\sigma_i^2} \exp(-\frac{1}{\sigma_i^2} z) \tag{19}$$

$$f_X(x) = \frac{2x}{\sigma_i^2} \exp(-\frac{1}{\sigma_i^2} x^2) \tag{20}$$

For some relay R_i in the A_s which is selected as the reference in the transmission power of the source (7) , the average total power of the source and all the candidate relays is given as:

$$E[P_{total}(M)] = E[P_s] + \sum_{j \in A_s} E[P_j]$$

$$= \Gamma N_0 \cdot (\frac{1}{|f_i|^2} + 2\sqrt{\frac{\pi}{|f_i|^2 \sigma_i^2}} Q(\sqrt{\frac{2\gamma_i'}{\sigma_i^2}})) + C(\gamma_M) \tag{21}$$

where $Q(x) = \frac{1}{\sqrt{2\pi}} \int_x^{+\infty} \exp(-\frac{t^2}{2}) dt$ is complementary error function. $\gamma_i' = \frac{1}{\gamma - 1/|f_i|^2}$. $C(\gamma_M)$ is a constant:

$$C(\gamma) = \Gamma N_0 \cdot \sum_{j \in A_s} [-\frac{1}{\sigma_j^2} Ei(-\frac{\sqrt{\gamma_j'}}{\sigma_j^2})$$
$$+ 2\sqrt{\frac{\pi}{|f_j|^2 \sigma_j^2}} Q(\sqrt{\frac{2\gamma_j'}{\sigma_j^2}})] \tag{22}$$

where $Ei(x) = -\int_{-x}^{\infty} e^{-t}/t dt$ is the exponential integral function. Therefore we obtain with $|A_s| = M$:

$$i = \arg \min_i \frac{1}{|f_i|^2} + 2\sqrt{\frac{\pi}{|f_i|^2 \sigma_i^2}} Q(\sqrt{\frac{2\gamma_i'}{\sigma_i^2}})$$

$$E[P_{total}(M)] = \Gamma N_0 \cdot [\frac{1}{|f_i|^2} + 2\sqrt{\frac{\pi}{|f_i|^2 \sigma_i^2}} Q(\sqrt{\frac{2\gamma_i'}{\sigma_i^2}})] + C(\gamma_M) \tag{23}$$

Taking the minimum value among the $E[P_{total}(M)](M = 1, 2...N)$, we develop the solution to the problem (10) as follows:

$$M^* = \arg \min_M E[P_{total}(M)]$$
$$\gamma^* = \gamma_{M^*} \tag{24}$$

As a consequence of the above, there is a tradeoff between the outage probability and the power consumption, which depends on the threshold γ. Besides, from the analysis above we can see that there is an interdependent relationship between A_s and γ: on the one hand, obtaining γ depends on A_s ; on the other hand, γ determines A_s conversely. It leads to the difficulty in solving the problem. We first assume $|A_s| = M$, and then γ can be obtained according to the constraint of ρ. Based on γ, the average total power values are developed. Finally we select the minimal value and further identify the transmission power of the source. The overview flowchart of DMRM algorithm is as Fig. 2.

3.3   Distributed Single-Relay Model (DSRM) Algorithm

The DMRM algorithm proposed to this point generally results in certain calculation in the threshold-solving procedure. In this section, we investigate the

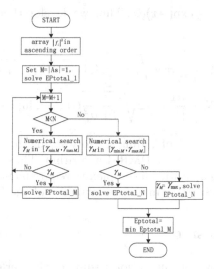

Fig. 2. DMRM algorithm flowchart

case where only one relay node is assumed to transmit, that is the average total power of the source and just this relay is considered by the source. The DSRM algorithm is motivated by limitations on the available CSI as well as ease of implementation. It is re-emphasized that the same channel information assumption in DMRM algorithm is adopted here. The problem is described as:

$$\min_i \quad E[P_s] + E[P_i]$$
$$s.t. \ Pr\{SNR_D \leq \Gamma\} \leq \rho \tag{25}$$

where SNR_D is as (5). According to the constraint condition about outage probability in (25), when the relay i is selected we have:

$$Pr\{SNR_D \leq \Gamma\} = Pr\{\frac{1}{|f_i|^2} + \frac{1}{|g_i|^2} \geq \gamma_i\}$$
$$= 1 - \exp(-\frac{1}{\sigma_i^2} \cdot \frac{1}{\gamma_i - 1/|f_i|^2}) = \rho \tag{26}$$

Thus the threshold γ_i should satisfy:

$$\gamma_i = \frac{1}{|f_i|^2} - \frac{1}{\sigma_i^2 \cdot \ln(1-\rho)} \tag{27}$$

Further we get $\gamma_i' = \dfrac{1}{\gamma_i - \frac{1}{|f_i|^2}} = \sigma_i^2 \cdot \ln(1-\rho)$. The average total power is:

$$E[P_{total}] = \Gamma N_0 \cdot [\frac{1}{|f_i|^2} + 4\sqrt{\frac{\pi}{|f_i|^2\sigma_i^2}} Q(\sqrt{-2\ln(1-\rho)} + \frac{C(\rho)}{\sigma_i^2})] \tag{28}$$

where $C(\rho) = \int_{-\ln(1-\rho)}^{+\infty} \frac{1}{x} \exp(-x)dx$. Thus we develop the solution to the problem (25) :

$$i = \arg \min_{i} \frac{1}{|f_i|^2} + 4\sqrt{\frac{\pi}{|f_i|^2\sigma_i^2}} Q(\sqrt{-2\ln(1-\rho)}) + \frac{C(\rho)}{\sigma_i^2}$$
$$E[P_s] = \Gamma N_0 \cdot [\frac{1}{|f_i|^2} + 2\sqrt{\frac{\pi}{|f_i|^2\sigma_i^2}} Q(\sqrt{-2\ln(1-\rho)})]$$

(29)

Observe that in (27), the task of finding the forwarding threshold can be substantially simplified compared to the DMRM algorithm. Thus the DSRM algorithm has significantly less computational complexity requirement. However we will see that there is a modest sacrifice in the performance of the DSRM algorithm.

4   Simulation Result

In this section, we show the simulation results of the performance of the algorithms proposed in this paper as well as other existing algorithms. The simulation scene is depicted as Fig. 1, where the coordinates of the source and the destination is (0, 0) and (0, 100) respectively. The relay nodes are normally distributed in vertical linearity. Set $\Gamma = 10dB$ as the target SNR. We adopt the channel model in [2] and the detail channel parameters are illustrated in Table 1.

Table 1. Channel Parameters

Parameters	Value
Antenna gain G_t/G_r	1
Wavelength λ	1/3m
System loss factor L	1
Constant C	$G_tG_r\lambda^2/(4\pi)^2L$
Path loss factor α	3
Channel gain of source-relay	$\eta_i^2 = C/d_{Si}^\alpha$
Channel gain of relay-destination	$\sigma_i^2 = C/d_{iD}^\alpha$
Variance of noise N_0	10^{-10}

At first we make a comparison between the proposed algorithms and the existing algorithms to demonstrate the performance. In particular, we plot the average total power $E[P_{total}]$ versus the target outage probability ρ in Fig. 3. Set $N = 4$ relay nodes in the network. The upper bound of the minimal power consumption (MPC-UB) is also given. Note that there is no outage in MPC-UB, because the source and the relay can satisfy the target SNR requirement by adjusting their transmission power. For a fair comparison, the definition of outage event for MPC-UB in [10] is introduced, that is an outage occurs when the total power is higher than a given power value. We observe that at the same outage probability, the average total power consumption of the DMRM algorithm is the least. The APF algorithm [2] has the most power consumption caused by additional relays. In the ORS algorithm [5], the relay with the minimal value $\frac{1}{|f_i|^2} + \frac{1}{|g_i|^2}$ is considered to decide the transmission power by the source. It is observed that the ORS algorithm is not optimal for energy efficiency problem. The DSRM algorithm makes sacrifices in performance for low computational complexity. However the DMRM algorithm has an additional power expenditure as the penalty of lack of complete CSI. The additional power expenditure decreases as ρ increases, which reflects the tradeoff between the power consumption and the outage probability as discussed in Section III. As expected, the curve of DMRM approaches to, or even drops bellow the curve of MPC-UB in high ρ range.

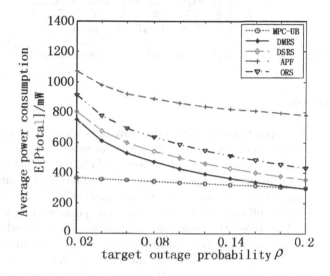

Fig. 3. $E[P_{total}]$ vs ρ for different algorithms (N=4)

Then we investigate the effect of the number of relay nodes in performance in Fig. 4. Set $\rho = 0.1$ as the target outage probability. It is observed that as the number of relay nodes increases, the additional power expenditure of APF algorithm increases due to the fact that more relays which are supposed unnecessarily to forward signals waste power. It is suggested that more relay nodes may not be more energy-efficient. However, for other algorithms, the increment of relays means that the high space diversity order can be obtained. In other words, the possibility of good channel increases for each channel realization. Thus the average total power consumption decreases. Fig. 4 also remarks that the more relays there are in the relay-assistant network, the more power savings is obtained in DMRM algorithms compared to others.

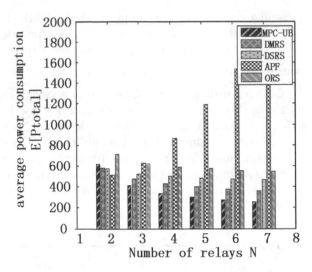

Fig. 4. $E[P_{total}]$ vs N_{relay} for different algorithms ($\rho=0.1$)

5   Conclusion

In this paper, we propose two distributed algorithms for relay selection under statistical CSI in AF mode. The relay decision mechanism is adopted. In order to meet the target SNR and the target outage probability, the source makes a tradeoff between the power consumption and the outage probability. Furthermore, the forwarding threshold and its own transmission power are obtained. In the DMRM algorithm, all candidate relays have the possibility of transmitting the source signals. We obtain the threshold by numerical search and the average total power consumption of the DMRM algorithm is the least. In contrast, the low-complexity DSRM algorithm assumes that only one relay forwards the signals and consequently, has a modest sacrifice in performance. Simulation results indicate that compared to the APF and the ORS relay selection algorithms, the proposed algorithms have better performance in energy efficiency, which are more suitable for the energy-limited network.

Acknowledgment. This work was supported by the China High-Tech 863 Plan under Grant 2009AA011506, the National Major Special Projects in Science and Technology of China under grant 2009ZX03003-009, 2010ZX03003-001, 2010ZX03005-003, and 2011ZX03003-003-04, National key technology R&D program under Grant 2008BAH30B12, and National Basic Research Program of China under Grant 2007CB310602.

References

1. Sendonaris, A., Erkip, E., Aazhang, B.: User Cooperation Diversity-part I: System Description. IEEE Transactions on Communication 51(11), 1927–1938 (2003)
2. Laneman, J.N., Womell, G.W.: Distributed space-time-coded protocols for exploiting cooperative diversity in wireless networks. IEEE Transcations on Information Theory 49(10), 2415–2425 (2003)
3. Laneman, J.N., Tse, D.C.N., Womell, G.W.: Cooperative diversity in wireless networks: Efficient protocols and outage behavior. IEEE Transaction On Information Theory 50(12), 3062–3082 (2004)
4. Bletsas, A., Khisti, A., Reed, D., Lippman, A.: A simple cooperative diversity method based on network path selection. IEEE J. Select. Areas Communications 24, 659–672 (2006)
5. Bletsas, A., Shin, H., Win, M.Z.: Cooperative Communications with Outage-Optimal Opportunistic Relaying. IEEE Transactions on Wireless Communications 7, 3450–3460 (2007)
6. Jing, Y., Jafarkhani, H.: Single and multiple relay selection schemes and their achievable diversity orders. IEEE Transactions on Wireless Communications 8, 1414–1423 (2009)
7. Su, W., Liu, X.: On optimum selection relaying protocols in cooperative wireless networks. IEEE Transcations on Wireless Communications 58, 52–57 (2010)
8. Zhao, Y., Adve, R.S., Lim, T.J.: Improving amplify-and-forward relay networks: Optimal power allocation versus selection. IEEE Trans. Wireless Communications 6, 3114–3123 (2007)
9. Beres, E., Adve, R.: Selection cooperation in multi-source cooperative networks. IIEEE Transactions on Wireless Communications 7(1), 118–127 (2008)
10. Chen, M., Serbetli, S., Yener, A.: Distributed power allocation strategies for parallel relay networks. IEEE Transactions on Wireless Communications 7, 552–561 (2008)
11. Zhou, Z., Zhou, S., Cui, S., Cui, J.: Energy-efficient cooperative communication in clustered wireless sensor networks. In: Proc. IEEE Military Communications Conference, pp. 1–7 (October 2006)
12. Zhou, Z., Zhou, S., Cui, J., Cui, S.: Energy-Efficient Cooperative Communication Based on Power Control and Selective Single-Relay in Wireless Sensor Networks. IEEE Transactions on Wireless Communications 7, 3066–3078 (2008)
13. Madan, R., Mehta, N., Molisch, A., Zhang, J.: Energy-Efficient Cooperative Relaying over Fading Channels with Simple Relay Selection". IEEE Transactions on Wireless Communications 7, 3013–3025 (2008)

Secondary User Selection in Cooperative Sensing Scheduling: A Spectrum Opportunity-Energy Tradeoff View

Xiangxia Sun, Tengyi Zhang, and Danny H.K. Tsang

Department of Electronic and Computer Engineering
The Hong Kong University of Science and Technology
{sunie,zhangty,eetsang}@ust.hk

Abstract. Cognitive Radio (CR) is regarded to be suitable for improving energy efficiency in wireless communications. In this paper we focus on the critical mechanism for practical implementation of the Cognitive Radio Networks (CRNs), i.e. cooperative sensing. Under the context of cooperative sensing, selecting more Secondary Users (SUs) for spectrum sensing can bring higher expected throughput, but more energy will be consumed on the sensing process, which is the major energy consumption in the CRNs. After selecting the SUs for sensing, how to properly assign them to sense the Primary User (PU) channels to strike the balance between sensing accuracy and spectrum opportunities is another essential problem. We formulate this two-dimensional Spectrum Opportunity-Energy Tradeoff (SOET) problem as a combinatorial optimization problem, and analytically exploit its inherent structures. Efficient algorithm is proposed to obtain the optimal solutions based on the properties found. Numerical results are also provided to validate our analysis.

Keywords: cognitive radio, cooperative sensing scheduling, opportunity-energy tradeoff, energy efficiency.

1 Introduction

The next generation wireless networks are expected to meet people's ever-growing demand of high speed access. However, it has been reported that three percent of the world-wide energy is consumed by the ICT (Information & Communications Technology) infrastructure that causes about two percent of the world-wide CO_2 emissions [1]. Therefore, now it is time for the ICT society to include the objective of energy saving in the evolution path of the next generation wireless networks, i.e. to investigate *green communications*.

With its inherent intelligence, Secondary Users (SUs) in a Cognitive Radio Network (CRN) are able to interact and learn from their radio environment, adaptively change their working parameters (power, bandwidth, frequency, etc.) to dynamically utilize the unused spectrum of Primary Users (PUs). Due to its powerful cognitive capabilities, Cognitive Radio (CR) opens up a new direction and possibility for green communications [2]. New functionalities introduced in

P. Ren et al. (Eds.): WICON 2011, LNICST 98, pp. 400–410, 2012.

CRN bring unparalleled agility, but at the same time introduce additional power consumption. One of the major overheads is the spectrum sensing procedure, which is required before SUs could access the PU channels.

In this paper, we study the energy consumption in CRNs due to the spectrum sensing. Specifically, we focus on the cooperative sensing technology, which is considered to be a promising spectrum sensing technology for practical implementation [3]. The scheduling problem is the most critical issue in cooperative sensing. Basically, for a CRN applying cooperative sensing, two questions should be answered:

(1) How to select the set of SUs for spectrum sensing?
(2) Given this set of SUs, how to assign them to sense different PU channels?

For the first question, selecting more SUs for sensing implies higher expected throughput; but on the other hand, the energy consumed in the sensing will also increase. Therefore, this question reveals the tradeoff between throughput and energy. For the second question, assigning more SUs to sense one channel can improve sensing accuracy, but in return will lose some spectrum opportunity since less channels are exploited. This question gives rise to the tradeoff between opportunity and accuracy, which is referred as the Cooperative Sensing Scheduling (CSS) problem in our previous works [4]. The two questions lead to two dimensional tradeoffs, which should be jointly optimized. In this paper, we thoroughly analyze this Spectrum Opportunity Energy Tradeoff (SOET) problem. We exploit the solution structure and show some interesting properties. Based on the analytical results, we develop an efficient algorithm to obtain the optimal solutions. Our algorithm and results apply for arbitrary number of SUs and PU channels.

The rest of the paper is organized as follows. The system model is presented in Section 2. We formulate the SOET problem in Section 3. In Section 4, the inherent structure of the problem is studied and the algorithm for finding the optimal solutions is provided. Numerical results are given in Section 5 and we conclude this paper in Section 6.

2   System Model

Suppose there are N PU channels denoted by $\mathcal{N} \triangleq \{1, ..., N\}$ which can be opportunistically accessed by SUs. Let $s_n = 0$ and $s_n = 1$ denote that the occupancy state of channel $n \in \mathcal{N}$ being idle and busy, respectively. The CRN of our interest consists of M SUs and a Base Station (BS), which is responsible for scheduling and assigning SUs to sense PU channels, collecting individual sensing results and making the final decision on the occupancy state of PU channels.

Assume that the CRN works in a slotted frame structure as mentioned in [5] and the length of each frame is fixed to T. Each frame consists of three durations: a fixed sensing duration τ, a fixed scheduling and results fusing duration η, and a data transmission duration $T - \tau - \eta$. In the sensing duration, each SU selected for sensing will sense PU channels using energy detection [5] and each SU can only sense one channel due to physical limitations. Suppose the PU signals are complex-valued PSK signals while the noise is the Circular Symmetric Complex Gaussian (CSCG) [5] [6]. Let the sensing performance of each SU, i.e. detection probability and false alarm probability, be denoted by p_d and p_f respectively, then the relationship between them is given by [5]

$$p_f = Q(\sqrt{2\gamma + 1}Q^{-1}(p_d) + \sqrt{\tau f_s}\gamma), \tag{1}$$

where γ denotes the signal-to-noise ratio (SNR) of the PU signals received at SU and f_s represents the sampling rate[1], $Q(\cdot)$ denotes tail probability of the standard Gaussian distribution and $Q^{-1}(\cdot)$ is the inverse of $Q(\cdot)$.

Under the context of cooperative sensing, each SU will report its one bit sensing result (idle or busy) to the BS after sensing its assigned PU channel. Then the BS will perform results fusion to generate final decision on the occupancy state of PU channels using "OR" rule [7]. Suppose channel $n \in \mathcal{N}$ is cooperatively sensed by m SUs. Similar to [6] [8], we assume the received SNR at each SU is identical and denoted as γ. The discussion on heterogeneous SNR will be left as our future work. In this case, the sensing performance of channel n at the BS can be described as

$$P_d^n(m) = 1 - [1 - p_d^n(m)]^m, \quad P_f^n(m) = 1 - [1 - p_f^n(m)]^m, \tag{2}$$

where $p_d^n(m)$ and $p_f^n(m)$ denote the detection probability and false alarm probability of individual SU that senses channel n, respectively.

3   Problem Formulation

As aforementioned, two tradeoffs need to be tackled in this paper. The first one is between expected throughput and sensing energy consumption, i.e. if we let more SUs participate in sensing, the CRN can get higher expected throughput whereas the energy consumption also increases. This tradeoff could be tackled by finding a proper set of SUs to participate in the sensing process. Because of the homogeneous assumption of SUs, this problem becomes selecting an appropriate number of SUs to sense PU channels. The other tradeoff is between the exploration of spectrum opportunity and sensing accuracy, namely, if more SUs are assigned to sense one channel, the sensing accuracy can be improved while the spectrum opportunity may not be fully explored. To tackle this tradeoff is to find a proper assignment of SUs to sense PU channels such that a good balance between spectrum opportunity exploration and sensing accuracy is achieved.

Denote κ as the total number of SUs participated in sensing and $\mathbf{a}(\kappa) \triangleq \{a_n \mid \sum_{n=1}^{N} a_n = \kappa, n \in \mathcal{N}\}$ as the assignment of SUs, where a_n is the number of SUs assigned to sense channel $n \in \mathcal{N}$. Then the objective of the BS is to select an optimal number of SUs to participate in sensing and to find an optimal assignment of selected SUs so that a good balance between expected throughput and energy consumption is achieved. The expected throughput of the CRN is expressed as

---

[1] Note that τ and f_s are decided by the BS, and are the same for all SUs.

$$\tilde{R}(\mathbf{a}(\kappa)) = \frac{T - \tau - \eta}{T} \sum_{n:a_n > 0} \left\{ C_0 [1 - P_f^n(a_n)] \Pr(s_n = 0) + C_1 [1 - P_d^n(a_n)] \Pr(s_n = 1) \right\}, \tag{3}$$

where C_0 and C_1 denote the throughput of CRN when it operates in the absence and presence of PUs, respectively. Let $\Pr(s_n = 0)$ and $\Pr(s_n = 1)$ denote the stationary probability that channel n is idle and busy, respectively. Without loss of generality, we assume $\Pr(s_n = 0)$ and $\Pr(s_n = 1)$ are the same for all channels. The case that channels with different stationary probabilities will be left as our future work. According to [5], $C_0 >> C_1$ and the throughput of the CRN when PUs are absent dominates. As a result, the expected throughput can be rewritten as

$$R(\mathbf{a}(\kappa)) = \frac{T - \tau - \eta}{T} \sum_{n:a_n > 0} \left\{ C_0 [1 - P_f^n(a_n)] \Pr(s_n = 0) \right\}. \tag{4}$$

The energy consumption of the CRN during the sensing process is given by $E(\kappa) = \tau \phi \kappa$, where ϕ is the power spent for sensing. After taking both expected throughput and energy consumption into consideration, the utility function of the OE tradeoff problem can be defined as

$$U(\mathbf{a}(\kappa), \kappa) = w_t R(\mathbf{a}(\kappa)) - w_e E(\kappa), \tag{5}$$

where w_e and w_t are the weighting factors for throughput and energy consumption, respectively. These two weighting factors reflect how the CRN evaluates the importance of the two conflicting objectives mentioned above.

In order to protect the priority of PUs, SUs are required to achieve a specific probability of detection, $\bar{P}_d^n$, for each PU channel n they sense. Without loss of generality, we assume $\bar{P}_d^n = \bar{P}_d, \forall n \in \mathcal{N}$. Therefore, the SOET problem can be formulated as

$$(\mathbf{P1}) : \max_{\mathbf{a}(\kappa), \kappa} U(\mathbf{a}(\kappa), \kappa) \tag{6}$$

$$s.t. \ \kappa \le M \tag{7}$$

$$\sum_{n=1}^{N} a_n = \kappa, \ a_n \in \{0, 1, ..., \kappa\} \tag{8}$$

$$P_d^n(a_n) \ge \bar{P}_d, \ \forall n \in \mathcal{N}. \tag{9}$$

According to [5] [6], the optimal solution of problem (**P1**) is achieved with equality constraint in (9). Problem (**P1**) is a combinatorial optimization problem which is generally difficult to deal with. In the following sections, we will show some nice properties of this problem and propose efficient methods to solve it.

4   Analytical Analysis

To find the optimal solution of problem (**P1**), we decompose it into the following two subproblems:

Subproblem 1: Find the optimal assignment of SUs to sense the PU channels for a given number of SUs participated in sensing.

Subproblem 2: Find an appropriate number of SUs to participate in sensing so that a desirable balance between sensing energy consumption and expected throughput can be achieved.

In the remainder of this section, we will discuss these two subproblems one by one.

4.1   Subproblem 1: How to Assign SUs to Sense the PU Channels

In this subsection, we will propose an optimal assigning mechanism for SUs to sense PU channels for given number of SUs participated in sensing (i.e., κ). According to our previous work [4], we have the following Lemma 1, Proposition 1 and Theorem 1. Here we simply present existing results, please refer to [4] for detailed proof. To facilitate our analysis, we first present the following definition.

Definition: Let the combinations (i.e., the assigning methods for SUs to sense PU channels) in which exactly i PU channels are sensed form a *group G_i*, $i = 1, ..., I$, where $I = \min\{\kappa, N\}$. Also, denote the number of combinations in group G_i as $|G_i|$. The l-th ($l = 1, ..., |G_i|$) combination in group G_i is denoted as $C_{i,l} = \{a_{i,l}^j\}$ ($j = 1, ..., i$), where $a_{i,l}^j$ represents the number of SUs assigned to sense channel j.

We will omit all the superscripts n which indicates different channels in the rest of this paper, since all channels are homogeneous in terms of stationary probabilities and the SNR of the PU signals received at SUs are identical. Define $\nabla f(x)$ as the derivative of function $f(x)$ with respect to x, and we have the following Lemma 1.

Lemma 1. *Let m be a continuous variable representing the number of SUs assigned to sense a channel with domain $[1, +\infty)$. Then $P_f(m)$ is decreasing and convex, where m is the number of SUs assigned, if the following condition holds*

$$\left[\ln(1 - p_f(m)) - \frac{m}{1 - p_f(m)}\nabla p_f(m)\right]^2 < \frac{2\nabla p_f(m) - m\nabla^2 p_f(m)}{1 - p_f(m)} - \left[\frac{\sqrt{m}\nabla p_f(m)}{1 - p_f(m)}\right]^2. \tag{10}$$

In fact, condition (10) holds for most of practical systems. Hence, without loss of generality, we assume this condition (10) always holds in this paper. Under this assumption, we have the following Proposition 1, which shows how to optimally assign SUs to sense PU channels.

Proposition 1. *For $i = 1, ..., I$, let $C_{i,\max}$ denote the combination that produces the largest value of the objective function (6) in group G_i, where*

$$a_{i,\max}^j = \lceil \frac{\kappa}{i} \rceil \text{ or } a_{i,\max}^j = \lfloor \frac{\kappa}{i} \rfloor, \; j = 1, ..., i \tag{11}$$

and $\sum_j a_{i,\max}^j = \kappa$, then $C_{i,\max}$ ($i = 1, ..., I$) has the following property:

$$\sum_j P_f(a^j_{i,\max}) \leq \sum_j P_f(a^j_{i,l}), \ l = 1, ..., |G_i|. \tag{12}$$

According to Proposition 1, the optimal number of SUs assigned to each channel is either $\lceil \frac{\kappa}{i} \rceil$ or $\lfloor \frac{\kappa}{i} \rfloor$, where i is the number of sensed PU channels. That is to say, SUs are spread out to all the channels that the CRN determined to sense as evenly as possible. Here another problem arises: how many channels the CRN should sense in order to produce the largest value of objective function (6). The following Theorem 1 will answer it.

Theorem 1. *The optimal solution of Subproblem1 is $C_{I,\max}$, i.e. to assign each SU to sense one different channel respectively, if the condition*

$$2P_f(1) - P_f(2) - 1 < 0 \tag{13}$$

holds, which is a necessary and sufficient condition.

Theorem 1 shows that if condition (13) holds, the CRN will reach its capacity in terms of the number of sensed PU channels (i.e., sense I PU channels). According to [4] and extensive simulations, condition (13) always holds in practical systems, for example, under the parameters used in [5] as well as in section 5 of this paper. In this paper, we only focus on practical systems and assume that condition (13) holds throughout this paper.

4.2 Subproblem 2: How to Select the Number of SUs for Sensing

Our objective in this subsection is to find an appropriate number of SUs to participate in sensing such that a desirable balance between sensing energy consumption and expected throughput can be obtained. To find the optimal solution, we need to first figure out the structure of the utility function (6), i.e. how the utility function varies with respect to different κ. The following Proposition 2 can answer this question.

Proposition 2. *Denote $U(\mathbf{a}^*(\kappa), \kappa)$ as the utility function (6) under the optimal SU assigning mechanism for given κ SUs (i.e., the given κ SUs are assigned according to the optimal assigning method provided in Proposition 1). Also, let N' denote the number of PU channels selected for sensing. Define $\Delta U(\mathbf{a}^*(\kappa), \kappa) \triangleq U(\mathbf{a}^*(\kappa + 1), \kappa + 1) - U(\mathbf{a}^*(\kappa), \kappa)$ as the first difference of function $U(\mathbf{a}^*(\kappa), \kappa)$ with respect to κ. Then $\Delta U(\mathbf{a}^*(\kappa), \kappa)$ is piecewise constant.*

Proof. The first difference of $U(\mathbf{a}^*(\kappa), \kappa)$ with respect to κ can be given by

$$\Delta U(\mathbf{a}^*(\kappa), \kappa) = \alpha \Delta P(\mathbf{a}^*(\kappa), \kappa) - \beta, \tag{14}$$

where $\alpha = w_t \frac{T-\tau-\eta}{T} C_0 Pr(s_n = 0)$, $\beta = w_e \tau \phi$, $P(\mathbf{a}^*(\kappa), \kappa) = \sum_{n:a_n>0}[1 - P^n_f(a_n)]$, and $\Delta P(\mathbf{a}^*(\kappa), \kappa)$ is the first difference of $P(\mathbf{a}^*(\kappa), \kappa)$, which is similarly defined as $\Delta U(\mathbf{a}^*(\kappa), \kappa)$. Since the second term in (14) is constant, we only need to delve into the first term.

Denote J as the quotient and K as the remainder of the division $\frac{\kappa}{N'}$, i.e. $\kappa = JN' + K$. Since κ SUs, in total, engage in sensing, K channels are sensed by $\lceil \frac{\kappa}{N'} \rceil$ SUs and $(N' - K)$ channels are sensed by $\lfloor \frac{\kappa}{N'} \rfloor$ SUs. Suppose one more SU participates in sensing, then it will be assigned to one of these $(N' - K)$ channels which are sensed by $\lfloor \frac{\kappa}{N'} \rfloor$ SUs. According to Proposition 1, now the optimal assignment $a^*(\kappa + 1)$ is that $(K + 1)$ channels are sensed by $\lceil \frac{\kappa}{N'} \rceil$ SUs and $(N' - K - 1)$ channels are sensed by $\lfloor \frac{\kappa}{N'} \rfloor$ SUs. Therefore, the improvement of $P(\mathbf{a}^*(\kappa), \kappa)$ after adding one additional SU is given by

$$\Delta P(\mathbf{a}^*(\kappa), \kappa) \triangleq P(\mathbf{a}^*(\kappa+1), \kappa+1) - P(\mathbf{a}^*(\kappa), \kappa) = P_f(\lfloor \frac{\kappa}{N'} \rfloor) - P_f(\lceil \frac{\kappa}{N'} \rceil). \quad (15)$$

From (15), we can conclude that $\Delta P(\mathbf{a}^*(\kappa), \kappa)$ is identical within each interval, where $\kappa \in [(j - 1)N', jN' - 1]$, $j = 1, ..., J$. This completes the proof.

It is worth mentioning that the analysis above reveals that the value of $\Delta P(\mathbf{a}^*(\kappa), \kappa)$ only changes when κ increases from jN' to $(jN' + 1)$, where $j = 1, ..., J$. We are interested in further exploring how $\Delta P(\mathbf{a}^*(\kappa), \kappa)$ changes with respect to κ, hoping that more insights can be found. Here we use N' to denote the number of PU channels selected to sense. According to Theorem 1, we have $N' = \min\{M, N\}$. Here we have two scenarios: (1) when $M \leq N$, κ PU channels will be sensed, and each channel is sensed only by one SU; (2) when $M > N$, all the PU channels will be sensed and some channels will be cooperatively sensed by more than one SU. For the rest of the paper, we only study the second scenario and assume $M > N$ (i.e., $N' = N$) since the first scenario is a special case of the second one. Define $\delta_j \triangleq \Delta P(\mathbf{a}^*(\kappa), \kappa)_{\kappa=jN-1} - \Delta P(\mathbf{a}^*(\kappa), \kappa)_{\kappa=jN}$ as the change for the value of $\Delta P(\mathbf{a}^*(\kappa), \kappa)$ when κ increases from $(jN - 1)$ to jN, where $j = 1, ..., J$. The following Proposition 3 summarizes the properties of δ_j.

Proposition 3. δ_j *is positive and monotonically decreasing with respect to* j, *where* $j = 1, ..., J$.

Proof. From (15) and Lemma 1, we have

$$\begin{aligned}\delta_j &= \Delta P(\mathbf{a}^*(\kappa), \kappa)_{\kappa=jN-1} - \Delta P(\mathbf{a}^*(\kappa), \kappa)_{\kappa=jN} \quad (16)\\ &= [P_f(J - 1) - P_f(J)] - [P_f(J) - P_f(J + 1)] > 0,\end{aligned}$$

and

$$\begin{aligned}&\delta_j - \delta_{j+1}\\ &= \left\{ \Delta P(\mathbf{a}^*(\kappa), \kappa)_{\kappa=jN-1} - \Delta P(\mathbf{a}^*(\kappa), \kappa)_{\kappa=jN} \right\}\\ &\quad -\left\{ \Delta P(\mathbf{a}^*(\kappa), \kappa)_{\kappa=(j+1)N-1} - \Delta P(\mathbf{a}^*(\kappa), \kappa)_{\kappa=(j+1)N} \right\}\\ &= \left\{ [P_f(J - 1) - P_f(J)] - [P_f(J) - P_f(J + 1)] \right\}\\ &\quad -\left\{ [P_f(J) - P_f(J + 1)] - [P_f(J + 1) - P_f(J + 2)] \right\} > 0.\end{aligned}$$

Hence δ_j is positive and monotonically decreases with respect to j. The proof is completed.

Physical explanation of Proposition 3 is as follows. When $\kappa \leq N$, the improvement of $P(\mathbf{a}^*(\kappa), \kappa)$ by adding more SUs results from sensing more channels, while when $\kappa > N$, the improvement is due to improved sensing accuracy caused by cooperative spectrum sensing. Sensing more channels will result in larger improvement on expected throughput than merely improving the sensing accuracy of existing channels. Also, the marginal improvement of expected throughput caused by improved sensing accuracy decreases as κ increases. Based on Proposition 2 and Proposition 3, the optimal solution of problem (**P1**) is given by the following Theorem 2.

Theorem 2. *Denote κ^* as the optimal solution of problem (**P1**). The optimal solution κ^* has the following properties.*
(i) Multiple optimal solutions, $\kappa^* = jN, jN + 1, ..., (j+1)N - 1$, exist when the following condition holds

$$\Delta P(\mathbf{a}^*(\kappa), \kappa)_{\kappa=jN} = \frac{\beta}{\alpha}. \tag{17}$$

(ii) Single optimal solution, $\kappa^* = jN$, exists when both of the following two conditions hold

$$\Delta P(\mathbf{a}^*(\kappa), \kappa)_{\kappa=jN-1} > \frac{\beta}{\alpha}, \quad \Delta P(\mathbf{a}^*(\kappa), \kappa)_{\kappa=jN} < \frac{\beta}{\alpha}. \tag{18}$$

Proof. Since $U(\mathbf{a}^*(\kappa), \kappa) = \alpha \Delta P(\mathbf{a}^*(\kappa), \kappa) - \beta$ is a linear transformation of $P(\mathbf{a}^*(\kappa), \kappa)$, it shares the same property of $P(\mathbf{a}^*(\kappa), \kappa)$ as mentioned in Proposition 2 and Proposition 3. Therefore, the optimal value of problem (**P1**) occurs at the point when $\Delta U(\mathbf{a}^*(\kappa), \kappa) = 0$ or at the jumping point when $U(\mathbf{a}^*(\kappa), \kappa)$ changes from positive to negative. When condition (17) holds, $U(\mathbf{a}^*(\kappa), \kappa) = 0$ at points $\kappa = jN, ..., (j+1)N - 1$. In this case, the improvement of expected throughput by assigning more SUs to sense PU channels just offsets the punishment for extra energy consumption caused by inserting additional SUs. In other words, the improvement in objective function (6) remains zeros for $\kappa = jN, jN+1, ..., (j+1)N-1$. When condition (18) holds, there is only one optimal solution for problem (**P1**). According to (18) and (14), we have

$$U(\mathbf{a}^*(\kappa), \kappa)_{\kappa=jN} - U(\mathbf{a}^*(\kappa), \kappa)_{\kappa=jN-1} > 0, \tag{19}$$

$$U(\mathbf{a}^*(\kappa), \kappa)_{\kappa=jN+1} - U(\mathbf{a}^*(\kappa), \kappa)_{\kappa=jN} < 0. \tag{20}$$

Inequality (19) means that by adding one additional SU to the CRN where $\kappa = jN - 1$, the improvement of objective function (6) is still positive. Inequality (20) indicates that the improvement of objective function (6) becomes negative when one more SU is added to the CRN where $\kappa = jN$. Therefore, the optimal solution for problem (**P1**) is $\kappa^* = jN$ in the CRN where condition (18) holds.

4.3   Algorithm to Find the Optimal Solution of Problem (P1)

Based on the theoretical analysis in subsection 4.1 and 4.2, we propose the following algorithm (**A1**) to find the optimal solution of problem (**P1**). It is worth emphasizing that the efficiency of algorithm **(A1)** results from using the solution structure given by Theorem 2. In step 3, m is the number of SUs assigned for each channel, and the loop is executed at most $\lceil \frac{M}{N} \rceil$ times. The optimal solution is found by searching the point when $\Delta P < \lambda$ (i.e., $\Delta U(\mathbf{a}^*(\kappa), \kappa) < 0$).

Algorithm (A1)

1: Given the objective function U, the total number of SUs M and the total number of PU channels N.

2: **Initialization:** Set $m = 1$, $J = 0$, $J' = 0$, $\Delta P = 0$ and $\lambda = \frac{w_e \tau \phi T}{w_t (T - \tau - \eta) C_0 Pr(s_n = 0)}$

3: **Repeat** $\Delta P = P_f(m) - P_f(m+1)$, $m = m + 1$
    Until $\Delta P < \lambda$ or $m = \lceil \frac{M}{N} \rceil$

4: $J = m$

5: **if** $\Delta P < \lambda$ **then**

6:     **if** $P_f(J - 1) - P_f(J) = \lambda$ **then**

7:         $\kappa^* = (J - 1)N, (J - 1)N + 1, ..., JN - 1$ and
            $J' = J - 1$

8:     **else** $\kappa^* = JN$ and $J' = J$

9: **else** $\kappa^* = M$ and $J' = J - 1$

10: $\mathbf{a}^*(\kappa^*) = \{J', ..., J', (J' + 1), ..., (J' + 1)\}$, where the number of J' is $(N - K)$ and the number of $(J' + 1)$ is K, K is the remainder of the division $\frac{\kappa^*}{N}$, then stop.

---

5   Numerical Results

In this section, we provide several numerical examples to illustrate and validate our analysis. The system parameters are selected similar to [5] and given as follows: the frame length is $T = 100ms$, while $\eta = 0.1T$ and $\tau = 5ms$. There are $N = 15$ PU channels, the required detection probability of each is $\bar{P}_d = 0.9$, and $Pr(s_n = 0) = 0.7$, $\forall n$. The SNR of the received PU signal is $\gamma = -25dB$, sampling rate $f_s = 2MHz$ and $C_0 = 6.6582$ [5]. For simplicity, we normalize $\alpha = w_t \frac{T - \tau - \eta}{T} C_0 Pr(s_n = 0)$ to 1.

Figure 1 shows the values of $\Delta P(\mathbf{a}^*(\kappa), \kappa)$ with respect to the number of SUs engaged in sensing, κ. It can be seen that the values of $\Delta P(\mathbf{a}^*(\kappa), \kappa)$ are piecewise constant, as we proved in Proposition 2. The jumping point occurs when the number of SUs engaged in sensing changes from $\kappa = JN$ to $\kappa = JN + 1$, and the improvement of $\Delta P(\mathbf{a}^*(\kappa), \kappa)$ at the jumping point, i.e. δ_j, monotonically decreases as κ increases. The horizontal lines in both sub-figures denote different values of $\beta = w_e \tau \phi$. In the upper sub-figure, single optimal solution exists, i.e. to select 15 SUs to sense all 15 PU channels, as described in Theorem 2. In the lower sub-figure, the β value is identical to the improvement of adding one more SU for sensing, within the range of $\kappa = 16$ to $\kappa = 30$. In this case, as long as the number of SUs are selected within this range, it makes no difference to the objective value of problem **(P1)**.

In Figure 2, we plot the objective value of $U(\mathbf{a}(\kappa), \kappa)$ versus the number of SUs engaged in sensing, κ. Both sub-figures show that the objective function is unimodal and possesses single optimal solution if (18) holds. It can also be observed that if the total number of PU channels available increases, the optimal objective value increases as well. The reason is under practical system parameters, condition (13) always holds, and the CRN will exploit as many channels as possible to fully make use of the under-utilized spectrum.

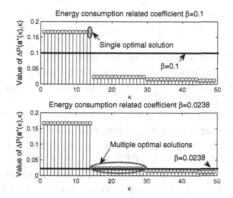

Fig. 1. Illustration of the value of $\Delta P(\mathbf{a}^*(\kappa), \kappa)$

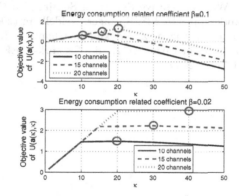

Fig. 2. Value of the objective function $U(\mathbf{a}(\kappa), \kappa)$ with respect to different number of PU channels

6   Conclusions

In this paper, the SU selection and assignment issues of the CRN are studied under the context of cooperative spectrum sensing. These two issues can be formulated as a two dimensional SOET problem. In order to find the optimal solution, we decompose the SOET problem into two subproblems. By solving these two subproblems, we find the optimal number of SUs participated in sensing and the optimal assignment of these SUs to sense PU channels. Finally, the optimal solution structure of the SOET problem is presented and some useful properties are shown. Based on these properties, we propose an efficient algorithm to obtain the optimal value of the SOET problem under practical system parameters. Numerical results are also presented to verify the theoretical analysis. In the future, we will deal with the case where SUs have heterogenous sensing capability and PU channels have heterogenous requirements in terms of detection probability.

References

1. Call for papers of 1st International Workshop on Green Wireless 2008 (W-GREEN) (September 2008), http://www.cwc.oulu.fi/workshops/W-Green2008.pdf
2. Gur, G., Alagoz, F.: Green Wireless Communications via Cognitive Dimension: An Overview. IEEE Network 25(2), 50–56 (2011)
3. Ofcom Consultation, Digital Dividend: Cognitive Access, (February 16, 2009), http://www.ofcom.org.uk/consult/condocs/cognitive/summary
4. Zhang, T., Tsang, D.H.K.: Cooperative Sensing Scheduling for Energy-Awear Cognitive Radio Networks. To appear in IEEE ICC 2011 (2011)
5. Liang, Y.C., Zeng, Y., Peh, E.C.Y., Hoang, A.T.: Sensing-Throughput Tradeoff for Cognitive Radio Networks. IEEE Trans. Wireless Commun. 7(4), 1326–1337 (2008)
6. Peh, E.C.Y., Liang, Y.C., Guan, Y.L., Zeng, Y.: Optimization of Cooperative Sensing in Cognitive Radio Networks: A Sensing-Throughput Tradeoff View. IEEE Trans. Vehicular Technology 58(9), 5294–5299 (2009)
7. Letaief, K.B., Zhang, W.: Cooperative Spectrum Sensing. In: Cognitive Wireless Communication Networks, pp. 115–138. Springer, Heidelberg (2007)
8. Shen, J., Jiang, T., Liu, S., Zhang, Z.: Maximum Channel Throughput via Cooperative Spectrum Sensing in Cognitive Radio Networks. IEEE Trans. Wireless Commun. 8(10), 5166–5175 (2009)

Performance Analysis of Opportunistic Spectrum Sharing System

Wanbin Tang, Yanfeng Han, Hua Jin, and ShaoQian Li

National Key Laboratory of Science and Technology on Communications,
University of Electronic Science and Technology of China,
Chengdu, Sichan, China
wbtang@uestc.edu.cn

Abstract. Frequency spectrum is a limited resource for wireless communications. Cognitive radio provides an approach to efficient utilization of spectrum. Spectrum handoff is an indispensable component in cognitive radio networks to provide resilient service for the secondary users. In this paper, we analyze the handoff performance of an opportunistic spectrum sharing systems over a coverage area. In the OSS systems, If an active secondary user detects the arrival of a primary user on a given channel, it releases the channel and switches to another idle channel. If no channel is available, the call waits in a buffer until either one channel becomes available or a maximum waiting time is reached. We examine the performances in terms of the link maintenance probability and mean handoff numbers of the secondary user's. In the last, we prove the simulation result in session V.

Keywords: Opportunistic spectrum sharing, Markov process, Handoff.

1   Introduction

Frequency spectrum is a limited resource for wireless communications. Cognitive radio provides an approach to efficient utilization of spectrum and become a important research issue [1].

According to Federal Communications Commission (FCC), temporal and geographical variations in the utilization of the assigned spectrum range from 15% to 85% [2]. Then, frequency agile radios (FARs) have attracted more interest in the research community. In a scenario of opportunistic spectrum sharing (OSS), the FARs is called secondary users (SUs) and the owners of the allocated spectrum are the primary users (PUs).

In the OSS system, SU opportunistically use channels that are not occupied by PU. In order not to cause harmful interference to the PU, if an active SU detects that a PU will accesses the channel, then it moves to another idle channel, or moves to a waiting buffer. In the latter case, the SU waits in a buffer until either a new channel becomes available or a timeout occurs after a predefined maximum waiting time. So spectrum handoff is a major difficulty and also an inherent capability to support reliable service. On detecting a PU appearance, the SU has to vacate the channel for the PU. After the channel release, the SU will re-construct the communications. During this

P. Ren et al. (Eds.): WICON 2011, LNICST 98, pp. 411–423, 2012.

procedure, the SU may search the idle channel and transfer its communications to this channel. This procedure is referred as spectrum handoff.

In this paper, we model an opportunistic spectrum sharing system and evaluate its handoff performance. The rest of the paper is organized as follows. Section 2 describes the system model and assumptions. Section 3 develops a Markov model of the system, while Section 4 derives the performance metrics. In section 5, We present the numerical results to illustrate the performance of the OSS system. Finally, the paper is concluded in Section 6.

2   Model and Assumptions

In this paper, we shall assume an SU can perfectly detect the arrival of a new PU, and an arriving SU also can detect that the given channel is idle. We also assume that there are a total of N channels in the OSS systems. Each channel is assumed to be of equal bandwidth. We further assume that each user occupy one channel for simplicity. This is explained with the help of Fig. 1[7]. There are a total five channels of which two are occupied by PUs and one by an SU. When a new SU arrives as shown in Fig. 1a, it chooses a random free channel. A PU can choose any random channels and as shown in Fig. 1b, if it chooses a secondary occupied channel, the SU jumps to a different free channel. If there is no other channel available, the SU will be queued in the buffer in Fig. 1c.

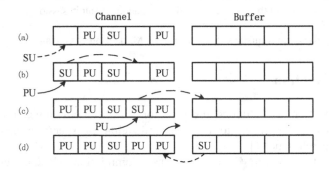

Fig. 1. The model of channel occupy in OSS system (N=5)

In Fig. 1d, the queued SUs are served in first-come first-served (FCFS) order. The head-of-line SU will reconnect to the system when a channel becomes idle before the maximum waiting time expires. We set the maximum waiting time of a SU equal to its residence time in the cell.

3   Performance Analysis

In this section, we analyze the OSS system performance in a given service area. Arrivals of the PU and SU are assumed to form independent Poisson processes with rates λ_1 and λ_2, respectively. The holding times of the PU and SU are assumed to be exponentially distributed with means h_1^{-1} and h_2^{-1}, respectively. The residence times for the PU and SU in the service area are also assumed to be exponentially distributed with means r_1^{-1} and r_2^{-2}, respectively. Hence, the channel holding times for the PU and SU are exponentially distributed with means $\mu_1^{-1} = (r_1 + h_1)^{-1}$ and $\mu_2^{-1} = (r_2 + h_2)^{-1}$, respectively.

Let $X_1(t)$ denote the number of PUs in the OSS system at time t .Similarly, let $X_2(t)$ be the number of SUs in the system at time t, including the SUs being served and those waiting in the buffer. The process $(X_1(t), X_2(t))$ is a two-dimensional Markov process with state space $S = \{(n_1, n_2) | 0 \le n_1 \le N, 0 \le n_2 \le N\}$.

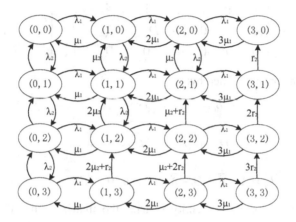

Fig. 2. State diagram of OSS system

We take $N = 3$ for example to analyze the State diagram of OSS system, the state transition diagrams of the OSS system can be presented in Fig.2 [8].

The transition rate from state (n_1, n_2) to (n_1^*, n_2^*) denote by $T_{n_1, n_2}^{n_1^*, n_2^*}$ is given by:

$$T_{n_1, n_2}^{n_1+1, n_2} = \lambda_1 1_{\{0 \le n_1 < N, 0 \le n_2 \le N\}} \tag{1}$$

$$T_{n_1, n_2}^{n_1-1, n_2} = n_1 \mu_1 1_{\{1 \le n_1 \le N, 0 \le n_2 \le N\}} \tag{2}$$

$$T_{n_1, n_2}^{n_1, n_2+1} = \lambda_2 1_{\{0 \le n_1 \le N-1, 0 \le n_2 < N-n_1\}} \tag{3}$$

$$T_{n_1, n_2}^{n_1, n_2-1} = [(n_2 - N + n_1)r_2 + (N - n_1)\mu_2] 1_{\{1 \le n_1 \le N, N-n_1 < n_2 \le N\}}$$
$$+ n_2 \mu_2 1_{\{0 \le n_1 \le N-1, 1 \le n_2 \le N-n_1\}} \tag{4}$$

where $1_{\{x\}}$ is an indicator function defined as 1 if x is true and 0 otherwise.

Let $\pi(n_1, n_2)$ denote the steady-state probability. The steady-state system probability vector can be represented as $\pi = (\pi_0, \pi_1, ..., \pi_N)$, where

$$\pi_n = (\pi(n,0), \pi(n,1), ...\pi(n,N)), 0 \leq n \leq N. \tag{5}$$

The vector π is the solution of the following equations:

$$\pi Q = 0 \bigcup \pi e = 1$$

where e and 0 are column vectors of all ones and zeros, respectively. The infinitesimal generator, Q, of the two dimensional Markov process is given by:

$$Q = \begin{bmatrix} E_0 & B_0 & 0 & \cdots & 0 & 0 & 0 \\ D_1 & E_1 & B_1 & \cdots & 0 & 0 & 0 \\ \vdots & \vdots & \vdots & \vdots & \vdots & \vdots & \vdots \\ 0 & 0 & 0 & \cdots & D_{N-1} & E_{N-1} & B_{N-1} \\ 0 & 0 & 0 & \cdots & 0 & D_N & E_N \end{bmatrix} \tag{6}$$

where each sub matrix is defined by:

$$B_i = \lambda_1 I_{N+1}, 0 \leq i < N \tag{7}$$

$$D_i = i\mu_1 I_{N+1}, 1 \leq i \leq N \tag{8}$$

$$E_i = A_i - \bar{\delta}(i)D_i - \bar{\delta}(N-i)B_i, 0 \leq i \leq N \tag{9}$$

where I_n denotes an n-by-n identity matrix, the matrix A_i has the same size as E_i. The (j,k) element of the matrix A_i is given by:

$$A_i(j,k) = \begin{cases} (1-p_f - \bar{\delta}(i)p_m)\lambda_2 & 0 \leq i \leq N-1, 0 \leq j < N-i, k=j+1, \\ \lambda_2 & 0 \leq i \leq N, N-i \leq j < N, k=j+1, \\ j\mu_2 & 0 \leq i \leq N-1, 1 \leq j \leq N-i, k=j-1, \\ (N-i)\mu_2 + (j-N+i)r_2, & 1 \leq i \leq N, N-i < j \leq N, k=j-1, \\ -[A_i(j,j-1) + A_i(j,j+1)] & 0 \leq i \leq N, 0 \leq j \leq N, k=j, \\ 0 & \text{otherwise,} \end{cases} \tag{10}$$

4   Performance Metrics

Next, we obtain various performance measures of interest.

A.   Blocking Probabilities

According to preference [4], we can obtain the blocking probability of PUs and SUs.

$$P_1 = \sum_{n_2=0}^{N} \pi(N, n_2) = \pi_0 \prod_{i=1}^{N} [B_{i-1}(-C_i)^{-1}]e \qquad (11)$$

$$P_2 = \sum_{n_1=0}^{N} \sum_{n_2=N-n_1}^{N} \pi(n_1, N) \qquad (12)$$

B. Mean Reconnection Probability

According to preference [4], we can obtain the mean reconnection probability.

$$\gamma = \frac{\sum_{n_1=1}^{N} \sum_{j=0}^{n_1-1} \pi(n_1, N-n_1+j+1)\beta(j)}{\sum_{n_1=1}^{N} \sum_{j=0}^{n_1-1} \pi(n_1, N-n_1+j+1)} \qquad (13)$$

and $\beta(j)$ is defined as following:

$$\beta(j) = \frac{n_1\mu_1 + (N-n_1)\mu_2}{n_1\mu_1 + (N-n_1)\mu_2 + (j+1)r_2} \qquad (14)$$

C. The Number of Spectrum Handoff

When a PU appears there are four consequences on SU's behaviour: (a) the SU need not to release its channel; (b) the SU releases the channel and comes into another idle channel; (c) the SU releases the channel and comes into the buffer, and in the last, returns a channel within the maximum waiting time; and (d) the SU in the buffer leaves the system. Because of behaviour (b) and behaviour (c), there are two patterns of spectrum handoff, Let P_V [6]denote the probability that an SU leaves its channel when a PU appears. This probability is equal to the probability that a particular channel is reclaimed by a PU. When the number of PU is i, the probability that a particular channel is reclaimed by the PU is given by $1/(N-i)$. Then, we have

$$P_V = \frac{\sum_{i=0}^{N-1} \sum_{j=0}^{N} \frac{1}{N-i} P_r(i, j)}{1-P_1} \qquad (15)$$

here, the item $(1-P_1)$ shows the probability that the PU can insert the channel. Let P_{NV} denote the probability that an SU need not vacate its channel. So we can conclude:

$$P_{NV} = \frac{\sum_{i=0}^{N-1} \sum_{j=0}^{N} (1 - \frac{1}{N-i})P_r(i, j)}{1-P_1} \qquad (16)$$

Because there are two patterns of spectrum handoff, we let q_{s1} denote the link maintenance probability of spectrum handoff which is caused by behaviour (b). So the probability q_{f1} that the SU fails to return the channel is 0. Let q_{s2} denote the link maintenance probability of spectrum handoff which is caused by behaviour (c), and let q_{f2} denote the probability of the spectrum handoff is failed. Link maintenance probability refers to the probability that link is successfully maintained when the SU vacates the channel. So we can conclude:

$$q_{s1} = P_V[P_r(i, j)\delta(i + j < N)] \tag{17}$$

$$q_{f1} = 0 \tag{18}$$

$$q_{s2} = P_V[P_r(i, j)\delta(i + j \geq N)]\gamma \tag{19}$$

$$q_{f2} = P_V[P_r(i, j)\delta(i + j \geq N)](1 - \gamma) \tag{20}$$

Let H denote the number of spectrum handoff for an SU from its beginning of service to the end of the service. In this section, we will develop the probability mass function of the discrete random variable H. Let t_{cs} denote the SU call holding time with the average $1/\mu_2$, pdf $f_{t_{cs}}(t)$, CDF $F_{t_{cs}}(t)$, and Laplace Transform of pdf is $f_{t_{cs}}^*(s)$. Let $\overline{F_{t_{cs}}}(t)$ denote the complementary cumulative distribution function (CCDF), $\overline{F_{t_{cs}}}(t) = 1 - F_{t_{cs}}(t)$. Let $t_{pu,j}$ denote the PU inter-arrival time between $(j-1)th$ and jth PU with the generic form t_{pu}. Here, the first PU refers to the immediate next PU after SU admission in the system. Denote $\tau_k = \sum_{j=1}^k t_{pu,j}$. For poisson process, τ_k follows Erlang distribution with pdf

$$f_{\tau_k}(t) = \frac{\lambda_1(\lambda_1 t)^{k-1}}{(k-1)!} e^{-\lambda_1 t} \tag{21}$$

1)   Zero Spectrum Handoff

For an accepted SU, there are two situations leading to zero spectrum handoff. If the SU call holding time is smaller than the PU inter-arrival time, the SU can complete its service before a PU appears. On the other hand, there are several PU arrivals when the

SU using the channel, but these PUs use different channels from the one used by the SU. In this case, the SU need not to vacate the channel to perform spectrum handoff. Considering these two conditions leading to zero spectrum handoff, we have:

$$P(H = 0) = P(t_{cs} < t_{pu}) + \sum_{j=1}^{\infty} P(\tau_j < t_{cs} < \tau_{j+1}) P_{NV}^j \tag{22}$$

We first compute the first item in the right-side of (22).

$$P(t_{cs} < t_{pu})$$
$$= \int_0^{\infty} f_{t_{cs}}(x) \int_x^{\infty} f_{t_{pu}}(y) dy dx$$
$$= f_{t_{cs}}^*(\lambda_1) \tag{23}$$

Before computing the second item, we develop an identity which will be used frequently in the following.

$$P(\tau_j < t_{cs} < \tau_{j+1})$$
$$= \int_0^{\infty} f_{t_{cs}}(t) P(\tau_j < t < \tau_{j+1}) dt$$
$$= \int_0^{\infty} f_{t_{cs}}(t) \int_0^{\infty} f_{\tau_j}(x) \int_{t-x}^{\infty} f_{t_{pu}}(y) dy dx dt$$
$$= \int_0^{\infty} f_{t_{cs}}(t) \frac{\lambda_1^j t^j e^{-\lambda_1 t}}{j!} dt$$
$$= \frac{(-\lambda_1)^j}{j!} f_{t_{cs}}^{*(j)}(\lambda_1) \tag{24}$$

where $f_{t_{cs}}^{*(j)}(s)$ denotes the derivative of jth order. We continue the second item in the right-side of (22).

$$\sum_{j=1}^{\infty} P(\tau_j < t_{cs} < \tau_{j+1}) P_{NV}^j$$
$$= \sum_{j=1}^{\infty} \int_0^{\infty} f_{t_{cs}}(t) \frac{(\lambda_1 t)^j e^{-\lambda_1 t}}{j!} dt P_{NV}^j$$
$$= \int_0^{\infty} f_{t_{cs}}(t) e^{-\lambda_1 t} [\sum_{j=1}^{\infty} \frac{(\lambda_1 t P_{NV})^j}{j!}] dt$$
$$= \int_0^{\infty} f_{t_{cs}}(t) e^{-\lambda_1 t} (e^{\lambda_1 t P_{NV}} - 1) dt$$
$$= f_{t_{cs}}^*(\lambda_1 (1 - P_{NV})) - f_{t_{cs}}^*(\lambda_1) \tag{25}$$

Substituting (23) (25) into (22), we obtain:

$$P(H = 0) = f_{t_{cs}}^{*}(\lambda_1(1 - P_{NV}))$$ (26)

2)   k (k ⩾ 1) Spectrum Handoff

During the SU call holding time t_{cs}, there are k spectrum handoffs. And these k spectrum handoff are caused by SU behavior (b) and (c). In this section, we consider two conditions, after k spectrum handoff, the SU successfully completed connection or fail to complete connection. Let $succ_k$ and $fail_k$ denote the successful and failful events, respectively. Then, the probability for k spectrum handoff is expressed by:

$$P(H = k) = P(succ_k) + P(fail_k)$$ (27)

The successful events include the following possibilities. During the SU service, there are $k + j$ PU arrivals. Among these PU arrivals, k PU requests the same channel used by the SU and in this k spectrum handoff, there are two patterns of spectrum handoff, and the other j PU arrivals requests different channels. Hence, the SU has to perform k number of spectrum handoff and all these spectrum handoff are successful. Consider all possibilities on the variable j, we obtain the probability for the event $succ_k$.

$$
\begin{aligned}
&P(succ_k)\\
&= \sum_{j=0}^{\infty} P(\tau_{k+j} < t_{cs} < \tau_{k+j+1})\binom{k+j}{j}P_{NV}^{j}(\sum_{i=0}^{k}\binom{k}{i}q_{s1}^{i}q_{s2}^{k-i})\\
&= \sum_{j=0}^{\infty}[\int_{0}^{\infty} f_{t_{cs}}(t)\frac{(\lambda_1 t)^{k+j}e^{-\lambda_1 t}}{(k+j)!}dt]\frac{(k+j)!}{j!k!}P_{NV}^{j}(q_{s1}+q_{s2})^{k}\\
&= \int_{0}^{\infty} f_{t_{cs}}(t)\frac{(\lambda_1 t)^{k}e^{-\lambda_1 t}}{k!}][\sum_{j=0}^{\infty}\frac{(\lambda_1 t)^{j}}{j!}P_{NV}^{j}]dt(q_{s1}+q_{s2})^{k}\\
&= \int_{0}^{\infty} t^{k} f_{t_{cs}}(t)e^{-\lambda_1(1-P_{NV})t}dt\frac{\lambda_1^{k}}{k!}(q_{s1}+q_{s2})^{k}\\
&= \frac{(-\lambda_1(q_{s1}+q_{s2}))^{k}}{k!}f_{t_{cs}}^{*(k)}(\lambda P_V)
\end{aligned}
$$ (28)

The failure events include the following possibilities. During the SU service, there are $k + j(k \geq 1, j \geq 0)$ PU arrivals. Compare with the successful events, the kth spectrum handoff is failed. Considering all possibilities on the variable j, we obtain the probability.

$P(fail_k)$

$$= \sum_{j=0}^{\infty} P_r(\tau_{k+j} < t_{cs}) \binom{k+j-1}{j} P_{NV}^j [\sum_{i=0}^{k-1} \binom{k-1}{i} q_{s1}^i q_{s2}^{k-i-1}] q_{f2}$$

$$= \sum_{j=0}^{\infty} \int_0^{\infty} f_{\tau_{k+j}}(t)(1-F_{t_{cs}}(t))dt \binom{k+j-1}{j} P_{NV}^j (q_{s1}+q_{s2})^{k-1} q_{f2}$$

$$= \sum_{j=0}^{\infty} \int_0^{\infty} \frac{\lambda_1(\lambda_1 t)^{k+j-1} e^{-\lambda_1 t}}{(k+j-1)!} \overline{F}_{t_{cs}}(t)dt \frac{(k+j-1)!}{j!(k-1)!} P_{NV}^j (q_{s1}+q_{s2})^{k-1} q_{f2}$$

$$= \frac{\lambda_1^k}{(k-1)!} \int_0^{\infty} t^{k-1} \overline{F}_{t_{cs}}(t) e^{-\lambda_1 P_V t} dt (q_{s1}+q_{s2})^{k-1} q_{f2}$$

$$= \frac{[-\lambda_1(q_{s1}+q_{s2})]^{k-1} \lambda_1 q_{f2}}{(k-1)!} \overline{F}_{t_{cs}}^{*(k-1)}(\lambda_1 P_V) \tag{29}$$

Substituting the two expressions into (26), we can obtain:

$$P(H=k) = \frac{[-\lambda_1(q_{s1}+q_{s2})]^k}{k!} f_{t_{cs}}^{*(k)}(\lambda_1 P_V)$$

$$+ \frac{[-\lambda_1(q_{s1}+q_{s2})]^{k-1} \lambda_1 q_{f2}}{(k-1)!} \overline{F}_{t_{cs}}^{*(k-1)}(\lambda_1 P_V) \tag{30}$$

3)   Average Spectrum Handoff

In this section, we may conclude the expectation of the number of spectrum handoff H. Following the definition of expectation, we have:

$$E(H)$$

$$= \sum_{k=0}^{\infty} k P(H=k)$$

$$= \sum_{k=0}^{\infty} k P(succ_k) + \sum_{k=0}^{\infty} k P(term_k) \tag{31}$$

where $E(*)$ represents the expectation of a non-negative random variable.

$$\sum_{k=0}^{\infty} k P(succ_k)$$

$$= \int_0^{\infty} f_{t_{cs}}(t) e^{-\lambda_1 P_V t} \sum_{k=1}^{\infty} \frac{[\lambda_1(q_{s1}+q_{s2})t]^k}{(k-1)!} dt$$

$$= \lambda_1(q_{s1}+q_{s2}) \int_0^{\infty} t f_{t_{cs}}(t) e^{-\lambda_1 q_{f2} t} dt$$

$$= -\lambda_1(q_{s1}+q_{s2}) f_{t_{cs}}^{*(1)}(\lambda_1 q_{f2}) \tag{32}$$

$$\sum_{k=1}^{\infty} kP(term_k)$$

$$= \lambda_1 \int_0^\infty \overline{F}_{t_{cs}}(t) e^{-\lambda_1 P_t t} \left[\sum_{k=1}^{\infty} \frac{k(\lambda_1 q_s t)^{k-1}}{(k-1)!} \right] dt q_f$$

$$= \lambda_1 \int_0^\infty \overline{F}_{t_{cs}}(t) e^{-\lambda_1 P_t t} \left[(1 + \lambda_1 q_s t) e^{\lambda_1 q_s t} \right] dt q_f$$

$$= \lambda_1 q_f \left[\overline{F}_{t_{cs}}^*(\lambda_1 q_f) - \lambda_1 q_s \overline{F}_{t_{cs}}^{*(1)}(\lambda_1 q_f) \right]$$

$$= \frac{(q_s + q_f)(1 - f_{t_{cs}}^*(\lambda_1 q_f))}{q_f} + \lambda_1 q_s f_{t_{cs}}^{*(1)}(\lambda_1 q_f) \tag{33}$$

Substituting the two expressions into (30), we can obtain the theorem for the average number of spectrum handoff.

$$E(H) = \frac{(q_{s1} + q_{s2} + q_{f2})(1 - f_{t_{cs}}^*(\lambda_1 q_{f2}))}{q_{f2}} \tag{34}$$

5   Numerical Results

In this section, we present numerical results for the OSS system model under the following parameter settings: $N = 16, \mu_1 = 10, \mu_2 = 10, r_2 = 5$.

Fig. 3 shows the PU blocking probability P_1. We observe that P_1 increases with the PU intensity ρ_1, but don't depend on the SU intensity ρ_2. Fig. 4 shows the ST call blocking probability P_2. We observe that P_2 increases with ρ_1 or ρ_2.

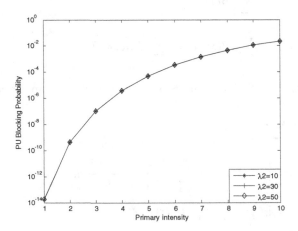

Fig. 3. PU blocking probability

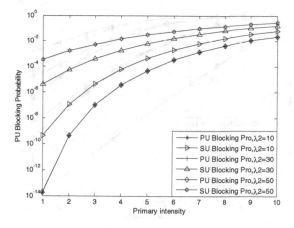

Fig. 4. SU blocking probability

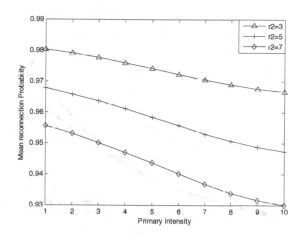

Fig. 5. Mean reconnection probability of the queued SUs

Fig. 5 shows the mean reconnection probability. We observe that γ decreases as ρ_1 increases and increases as the mean value $E[\tau]$ increases. The reason is as follows: the increase of ρ_1 results in the lower probability of the reconnection to system. While a longer maximum queueing time leads to a higher chance of reconnection.

Fig. 6 shows the function for the number of spectrum handoff in terms of λ_1 / μ_1. We observe that H increases as ρ_1 increases, compare with literature [6] , the probability and the mean number of spectrum handoff are higher than literature [6], the reason is as follows: after vacate the channel, the SU can come into the buffer, if a channel idle, the SU will reconnect the channel, this procedure is also spectrum handoff.

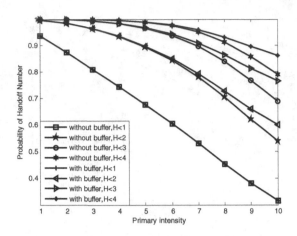

Fig. 6. The function for the number of spectrum handoff

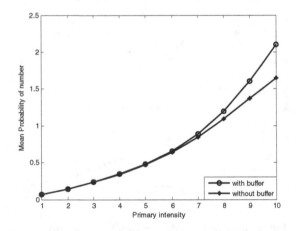

Fig. 7. Mean number of spectrum handoff

6   Conclusion

We analyze the spectrum handoff performance of OSS system. In the OSS system, spectrum handoff is an inherent operation to support resilient and continuous communications. In this paper, the spectrum handoff procedure is characterized, and because of the buffer, the number of spectrum handoff is higher, but the blocking probability is lower, so these is a trade-off between blocking probability and handoff number.

Acknowledgments. This work is supported in part by High-Tech Research and Development Program (863 Program) of China under Grant No. 2009AA011801 and 2009AA012002, National Fundamental Research Program of China under Grant A1420080150, and National Basic Research Program (973 Program) of China under Grant No. 2009CB320405, Nation Grand Special Science and Technology Project of China under Grant No. 2008ZX03005-001, 2009ZX03007-004, 2009ZX03005-002, 2009ZX03005-004, 2010ZX03006-002, 2009ZX03004-001, 2010ZX03002-008-03.

References

1. Akyildiz, I.F., Lee, W.Y., Vuran, M.C., et al.: NeXt generation/dynamic spectrum access/cognitive radio wireless networks: a survey. Computer Networks (50), 2127–2159 (September 2006)
2. McHenry, M.: Frequency agile spectrum access technologies. In: Proc. FCC Workshop (May 2003)
3. Tang, S., Mark, B.L.: Performance analysis of a wireless network with opportunistic spectrum sharing. In: Proc. IEEE Globecom 2007, Washington, D.C., USA (November 2007)
4. Tang, S., Mark, B.L.: Modeling and analysis of opportunistic spectrum sharing with unreliable spectrum sensing. IEEE Trans. Wireless Commun. (2009) (to appear)
5. Tang, S., Mark, B.L.: Analysis of opportunistic spectrum sharing with Markovian arrivals and phase-type service, Dept. of Electrical and Computer Eng., George Mason University, Tech. Rep.GMU-NAPL-Y08-N2 (December 2008)
6. Zhang, Y.: Spectrum Handoff in Cognitive Radio Networks: Opportunistic and Negotiated Situations. In: IEEE ICC 2009 (2009)
7. Kondareddy, Y.R., Andrews, N., Agrawal, P.: On the Capacity of Secondary Users in a Cognitive Radio Network. IEEE Xplore (December 9, 2009)
8. Capar, F., et al.: Comparison of bandwidth utilization for controlled and uncontrolled channel assignment in a spectrum pooling system. In: Proc. VTC Spring 2002 (2002)

A Cellular-Assisted Mobile UE Cluster Head Selection Algorithm for Wireless Sensor Networks

Lianhai Shan[1], Yuling Ouyang[1], Zhi Yuan[1], Honglin Hu[1], and Zhenhong Li[2]

[1] Shanghai Research Center for Wireless Communications, Shanghai, P.R. China
Shanghai Institute of Microsystem and Information Technology,
Key Laboratory of Wireless Sensor Network & Communication,
Chinese Academy of Sciences, P.R. China
[2] Renesas Mobile Corporation, Shanghai, P.R. China
{lianhai.shan,yuling.ouyang,zhi.yuan,honglin.hu}@shrcwc.org,
zhenhong.li@renesasmobile.com

Abstract. Wireless sensor networks (WSN) have been applied in different areas, which consist of numerous autonomous sensor nodes with limited energy. Therefore, energy efficient algorithms and protocols have been one of the most challenging issues for WSNs. Many researchers have focused on developing energy efficient clustering algorithms for WSNs, but less research has concerned about the mobile user equipment (UE) acting as a cluster head (CH) for data transmission between cellular networks and WSNs. In this paper, we present a cellular-assisted mobile UE CH selection algorithm and describe particular procedure for the WSN system. Simulation results show that better system performance, in terms of system energy cost and WSNs life time, can be achieved in WSNs by using interactive optimization with cellular networks.

Keywords: WSN, cluster head, gateway_CH level, energy cost.

1 Introduction

With the continued requirement of information society development, wireless sensor networks (WSNs) generated an increasing interest from industrial and research perspectives. WSNs have played a vital role in our daily lives, i.e. e-Health care, environment monitoring, industrial metering, surveillance systems etc. WSN can be generally described as a network of intelligent sensing nodes, and can provide the detected results of the surrounding environment [1]. One great challenge is to create an organizational structure amongst these nodes. Since the fundamental advantage of WSNs can be deployed in Ad-Hoc manner, a typical deployment of large number sensor nodes is necessitated energy-awareness for the WSN network structures algorithms, as WSN are limited by the sensor nodes battery lifetime. There has been a large amount of research in creating WSN network structures (i.e. Flat or Hierarchical) [2]. In the hierarchical architecture, grouping sensor nodes into cluster has been widely pursued by the research community in order to achieve the network scalability objective. In each cluster, a sensor node is selected, termed as the cluster

P. Ren et al. (Eds.): WICON 2011, LNICST 98, pp. 424–437, 2012.

head (CH). Then, these cluster heads collect sensor data from other nodes in the vicinity and transmit the aggregated data to the gateway. The CH is responsible for not only the general request but also receiving the sensed data of other sensor nodes in the same cluster and routing (transmitting) these data to the gateway. Thus, the CHs have higher energy cost because all of the transmitting data packet will pass through them and be sent to the gateway [3]. And so, the cluster head selection is an important part for WSN network structures.

In the traditional selection methods, the random selection method is famous. Heinzelman [4] introduced a hierarchical clustering algorithm for sensor networks called Low Energy Adaptive Clustering Hierarchy (LEACH), which handles the distributed information from the clusters. LEACH randomly selects a few nodes and designates them as CH, and periodically rotates this function among the nodes to equally distribute the extra energy consumption. In paper [5], another system has improved upon LEACH: hierarchical Power-Efficient Gathering in Sensor Information Systems (PEGASIS) protocols in which the nodes form chains and the multi-hop method is used for transmission. In PEGASIS, each node communicates only with a close neighbor and takes turns transmitting to the gateway, thus reducing the amount of energy spending. In paper [6], Manjeshwar proposed a hierarchy protocols: TEEN (Threshold-sensitive Energy Efficient sensor Network protocol). In TEEN, the sensors constantly take readings from the environment, but the data are transmitted using a lower frequency. The cluster head will send two values including the triggering value and the minimum threshold value, to the cluster members indicating the value of the measured attribute and the granularity of the reports. In paper [7], it presented a protocol, HEED (Hybrid Energy-Efficient Distributed clustering), that periodically selects cluster heads according to a hybrid of the node residual energy and a secondary parameter, such as node proximity to its neighbors or node degree. HEED incurs low message overload, and achieves fairly uniform cluster head distribution across the network. The concept of dividing the geographical region to be covered into small zones has been presented implicitly as clustering in literature [8]. Any node can become a cluster head if it has the necessary functionality, such as processing and transmission power. In [9], the proposed weight-based distributed clustering algorithm takes into consideration the transmission power, mobility, and battery power of mobile nodes.

About the above clustering algorithms, the cluster formations and cluster heads selection algorithms partially focus on energy consumption for CH selection fairness, which is caused by data aggregation and data fusion. In current research, a controllably mobile infrastructure for low energy WSN is proposed in paper [10] and [11]. The WSN node will use the contention scheme to access the gateway. The mobile terminals are used as a cluster head to collect the data and transmit to the BS, which greatly decrease the traditional cluster head energy cost [12]. However, when the serving mobile user equipment (UE) gateway CH is leaving its responsible area, it won't tell each WSN node about its leaving. This will cause WSN nodes of this area contend transmission channel to access the other UE gateway CH again, which will bring out overload of the signaling between mobile gateway CH and WSN nodes. In this paper, we propose a weight level based distributed clustering algorithm for mobile UE gateway as a cluster head. In our algorithm, the UE gateway CH selection procedure is choosing the optimal UE under the help of BS in order to reduce the WSN system energy cost.

The major contributions of the paper lie in the following folds:

1.   Proposed detailed parameters for calculating the proposed GW-CH level to choose a suitable UE gateway as the CH for sensor nodes.
2.   Decrease the traditional cluster head and each sensor node energy cost and its energy cost imbalance during data transmission process.

The remainder of paper is organized as follows. Section 2 presents the system description and mobile UE gateway CH selection algorithm under the cellular help is detailed. Section 3 describes an energy cost analytical model. Section 4 demonstrates the simulation results. Conclusions are finally offered in Section 5.

2   Proposed Scheme

2.1   System Architecture

In the convergence scenario for wireless sensor network (WSN) and cellular network is as follows. In the cellular system, the mobile UEs are under the control of a base station (BS). In the coverage area of a cellular network, there also exists a group of wireless sensor nodes constructing WSN. In the convergence scenario, the cellular UEs can act as the mobile gateways and cluster head for the WSN. The gateway CHs can provide access for the WSN nodes, i.e., gateway UEs are dual-mode and have both WSN and cellular interfaces [12]. In a WSN networks, the mobile UE gateway moves into the coverage area of the low energy sensor nodes, then they broadcast beacon packets to these nodes, and provide the backhaul access to these WSN nodes. Then, the detected data from WSN nodes can be forwarded to the BS via cellular system by the UE gateways CH as illustrated in Figure 1.

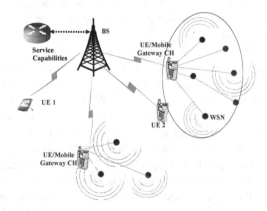

Fig. 1. System architecture of convergent WSN and cellular network

In the convergent network infrastructure, there may be a lot of UE gateway CH candidates in the WSN area, how a UE gateway CH is selected to be a WSN CH with less signaling overload is one of the key problems to be solved. There are two basic use cases:

1. One is that a new capable UE gateway enters into the WSN area;
2. The other is that the serving UE gateway leaves the coverage area of WSN.

In conventional WSN-cellular networks, the mobile UE gateway moves into the coverage area of the low energy nodes, they broadcast POLL packets to the low energy nodes, and provide the access to these WSN nodes. The WSN node will use the contention scheme to access the UE gateway. In the traditional algorithms, when the serving gateway is leaving its responsible area, it won't tell each WSN node about its leaving. This will cause WSN nodes of this area back-off and contend transmission channel, which will bring out overload of the signaling between mobile UEs and WSN nodes. Our proposed algorithm starts at the serving UE gateway leaving the WSN coverage area, and this will cause the UE gateway CH selection. The WSN topology in this paper mainly includes star and tree topology.

2.2 UE Cluster Head Selection Protocol Design

About mobile UE gateway CH selection procedure for the cellular and WSN system, the main define points include:

Define 1: Mobile UE gateway CH level is defined as the capability level that a mobile UE can serve as a gateway CH for the WSN. If the mobile UE is willing to act as a mobile gateway CH, it will calculate the gateway CH level (GW-CH_level).

Define 2: Some new signaling in cellular interface to realize the UE gateway CH replacement, i.e. leaving_REQ, GW-CH_ACK, replacement _REQ, replacement _RSP et al.

Define 3: GW-CH_level information table message field are shown in Table I.

Table 1. GW-CH_level Message Table

Dwelling time (D_t)	Coverage capability (C_r)	Capacity availability (C_a)	Channel quality (C_g)	Channel quality (C_s)

The procedure of a UE gateway CH selection, when the current mobile UE is going to leave the WSN area or disqualified to continue acting as a gateway CH, is illustrated in Figure 2 and Figure 3.

step 1. Once the current serving mobile UE gateway finds that it cannot serve the WSN cluster/group, then it sends the gateway CH leaving request (leaving_REQ) to the BS.

step 2. BS broadcasts the serving gateway CH information to the neighbor mobile UEs who have entered this WSN area after BS receives the leaving_request from the serving UE gateway CH, and BS chooses one neighbor UE gateway as mobile UE CH candidate. The broadcasting information will include at least the GW-CH_ID, GW-CH_level etc.

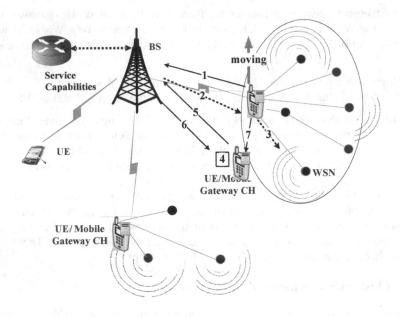

Fig. 2. Mobile gateway CH selection scenario

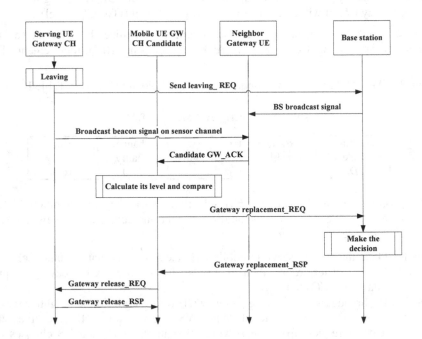

Fig. 3. Mobile gateway CH selection procedures

step 3.   The serving mobile UE gateway CH broadcasts a beacon signal through WSN channel for its leaving.

step 4.   The mobile UE CH candidate and neighbor UEs listen to the beacon signal from the serving mobile gateway CH, and neighbor UE gateways detect its ID and report itself GW-CH_level in the GW-CH_ACK to the candidate. The current mobile gateway UE candidates compare the neighbor GW-CH_level with its own and will be instead by the neighbor UE if its level is lower than the neighbor UE gateway level.

step 5.   The mobile UE gateway CH candidate signals the gateway replacement request (replacement_REQ) and GW-CH_level to BS via cellular uplink, only if its own level is higher than that of current serving gateway.

step 6.   BS will select the optimal candidate based on GW-CH_level. Then BS informs the best candidate to replace the current gateway CH (replacement_RSP) and the current serving gateway to prepare for releasing its role.

step 7.   The serving UE gateway and the selected mobile gateway CH candidate start the replacement process, which the gateway CH candidate will send gateway CH release request (release_REQ) to the current serving gateway CH. The current serving gateway CH will make a response (release_RSP) with the WSN information exchange including the sensor_ID, sensor remainder energy et al.

2.3   Optimal UE CH Selection Algorithm

In the proposed scheme, we have defined a new parameter named mobile UE gateway CH level (GW-CH_level), which defines the capability level of a UE acting as a gateway for a WSN. The detailed parameter for calculating the proposed mobile UE gateway CH level includes but not limited to below elements:

a)   Dwelling time D_t, which means the persistent time of mobile UE for the sensor node acting as a gateway.

b)   Coverage capability C_r, which means the number of sensor nodes of the UE covering.

c)   Capacity availability C_a, which means load capacity for the UE to serve sensor nodes.

d)   Channel quality C_g between the UE gateway candidates and the current serving gateway (assuming closer to the serving gateway, higher qualification to replace the old gateway).

e)   Channel quality C_s, which means the average SNR between the UE gateway candidates and sensor nodes.

Note: The above parameters could be included into taken into account for calculating the mobile UE gateway CH level whenever those parameters are feasible to obtain and meaningful.   If one or some elements are not available, then the weighting factor for that element(s) could be set to zero. The mobile UE gateway CH level could be defined as

$$\text{GW-CH\_level} = a \cdot D_t + b \cdot C_r + c \cdot C_a + d \cdot C_g + e \cdot C_s \qquad (1)$$

where a, b, c, d, e are pre-defined weighting factors in the system parameter table. Note that these weighing factors are chosen such that $a+b+c+d+e = 1$. The weighing factors of individual components can be adjusted during the WSN communication process.

In our proposed scheme, we define the GW-CH_level synthesis value including all the necessary and meaningful information enables the control unit (e.g., BS) to make the proper decision among the mobile UE gateway CH candidates. Moreover, there is no need for all the mobile UE CH candidates send each element to the control unit. This will save a lot of signaling overload. Further by introducing the configurable weighting factor to each element, the priority of the each element can be reflected easily in the system.

3   Performance Analysis

In this section we will analyze the energy cost of data transmission from a sensor node to the next node or gateway. And our analysis mainly focuses on system energy cost of transmitting packets from each sensor node using the traditional CH selection algorithm, normal UE gateway CH selection algorithm (just use the UE replacing CH) and optimal UE gateway CH selection algorithm, where the traditional CH selection algorithm is just using a low energy adaptive clustering hierarchy algorithm.

3.1   Network Model

In this paper we assume a sensor network model with following properties:

• The UE gateway locates at the center of clustered sensor nodes and has enough memory and computing capability.
• All sensor nodes are immobile and have a limited initiated energy.
• All nodes are equipped with power control capabilities to adjust their transmitted power.

3.2   WSN Radio Model

Currently, there have some researches in the low-energy WSN radios. Different assumptions about the WSN scenario characteristics make diversity in energy cost in the transmitting and receiving modes based on different protocols. In our work, we assume a simple model where the power cost E_{elec}=50nJ/bit to run the transmitter or receiver circuitry, and use ξ_{amp} =100nJ/bit/m^2 or 0.0013Pj/bit/m^4 according to the referenced distance for the transmit amplifier to achieve an acceptable E_b/N_o [13][14]. These parameters are slightly better than the current state in radio design, which is shown in table 2. Both the free space (d^2 power loss) and the multi-path fading (d^4 power loss) channel models were used, depending on the distance between the transmitter and receiver.

Table 2. Radio characteristics

Operation	Energy Cost
Transmitter Electronics (E_{Tx_elec}) Receiver Electronics (E_{Rx_elec}) ($E_{Tx\_elec} = E_{Rx\_elec} = E_{elec}$)	50 nJ/bit
Transmit Amplifier (ξ_{amp})	$\xi_{amp1} = 100$ pJ/bit/m^2 ($d < d_0$) $\xi_{amp2} = 0.0013$Pj/bit/m^4 ($d \geq d_0$)

Simple power control can be used to invert this loss by appropriately setting the power amplifier—if the distance is less than a threshold d_0, the free space model is used; otherwise, the multi-path model is used. Thus, to transmit a k-bit message a distance d using our radio model, the radio expends:

$$E_{Tx}(k,d) = E_{Tx\_elec}(k) + E_{Tx\_amp}(k,d) \tag{2}$$

$$E_{Tx}(k,d) = \begin{cases} E_{elec} \cdot k + \xi_{amp1} \cdot k \cdot d^2 & d < d_0 \\ E_{elec} \cdot k + \xi_{amp2} \cdot k \cdot d^4 & d \geq d_0 \end{cases} \tag{3}$$

and to receive this message, the radio expends:

$$E_{Rx}(k) = E_{Rx\_elec}(k) = E_{elec} \cdot k \tag{4}$$

For these parameter values, receiving a message is not a low cost operation; the protocols should thus try to minimize not only the transmit distances but also the number of transmit and receive operations for each message. We make the assumption that the radio channel is symmetric such that the energy required to transmit a message from node A to node B is the same as the energy required to transmit a message from node B to node A for a given SNR.

3.3   Energy Cost of Intermediate Nodes

In all proposed scheme, energy cost is analyzed using WSN radio models. In the proposed algorithm, WSN nodes will transmit data to the UE through intermediate nodes. In this case, the intermediate nodes are chosen such that the transmit amplifier energy (e.g., $E_{Tx\_amp}(k,d)$) is used and maybe some of them are not necessary, which will increase energy cost. But when to use the intermediate nodes transmit and when to use the direct communication with the next node if the previous node can communicate with the two next nodes, we use the following algorithm: previous node A would transmit to next node C through intermediate node B if and only if:

$$E_{Tx\_amp}(k, d = d_{AB}) + E_{Tx\_amp}(k, d = d_{BC}) + E_{Rx}(k)$$
$$< E_{Tx\_amp}(k, d = d_{AC}) \tag{5}$$

3.4   WSN Nodes Energy Cost Analysis

For our experiments, we assume that all sensors are sensing the environment at a fixed rate and thus always have k-bit data to send to the CH or UE gateway. For future versions of our protocol, we will implement event-driven simulation, where sensors only transmit data if some event occurs in the environment. WSN nodes energy cost is mainly composed of two parts: the end nodes energy cost $E_{Tx}(k, d)$, the intermediate nodes energy cost $E_{Tx\_amp}(k, d) + E_{Rx}(k)$. Node i transmits k-bit data energy cost from j hop to $j+1$ hop,

$$E_{cost}(i, j) = E_{tran} + E_{rec} = (E_{elec} * k + k * \xi_{amp1} * d^2_{(V(j),V(j+1))})$$
$$+ E_{elec} * k = k * \xi_{amp1} * d^2_{(V(j),V(j+1))}) + 2k * E_{elec} \qquad d<d_0 \tag{6}$$

$$E_{cost}(i, j) = E_{tran} + E_{rec} = (E_{elec} * k + k * \xi_{amp2} * d^4_{(V(j),V(j+1))})$$
$$+ E_{elec} * k = k * \xi_{amp2} * d^4_{(V(j),V(j+1))}) + 2k * E_{elec} \qquad d \geq d_0 \tag{7}$$

where $0 \leq j \leq m-1$, $d_{(V(j),V(j+1))}$ denotes distance between the j node and the $j+1$ node in transfer process.

Node i transmits k-bit data packet to UE gateway and total transferring energy cost for one round is

$$E_{cost}(i) = \sum_{j=1}^{m-1} E_{cost}(i, j) \tag{8}$$

where one round data transferring includes m hops.

So for N nodes data packets in the WSN, and the total energy cost for one round is

$$E_{total}(i) = \sum_{i=1}^{N} E_{cost}(i) \tag{9}$$

4   Numerical Results and Discussion

4.1   Simulation Scenario Description

The simulation environment is to distribute 150 and 200 sensor nodes to 200m*200m square randomly. The initial energy of each node is 0.25J. In each round, the sensor node will deliver a random size data packet between 10 and 100 Bytes. Firstly, we assume that the position of the CH is located at a fixed coordinate at the beginning. After the former CH is power off, it will choose a new CH by using a low energy adaptive clustering hierarchy algorithm, which we have used this as a traditional algorithm. The radio model and the transmission method of each round (simulation time) have been presented in Section 3. Moreover, in each round, each sensor has generated data to transmit. The sensor nodes random distribution scenario is shown in figure 4. This WSN area is composed by 200*200 meters square, where sensor nodes are distributed for environment monitoring.

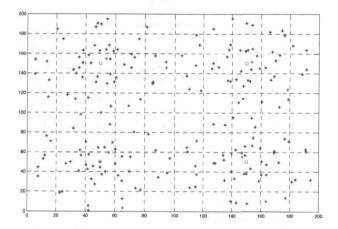

Fig. 4. WSN nodes distribution graph

4.2   Analysis of Simulation Results

The system energy cost with simulation time (rounds) can be described as follows. The nodes at the cluster have different distances to the next node. The energy cost of each transmission is based on the transmission distance, which the energy cost is exponentially incremental according to the transmission distance. In additional, the transmission hops is another important factor and more energy will cost for the extra hops. From figure 5 (a) and (b), we can see that the proposed algorithm greatly reduced the system energy cost because we use the UE gateway as the CH in the proposed optimal UE gateway CH selection algorithm.

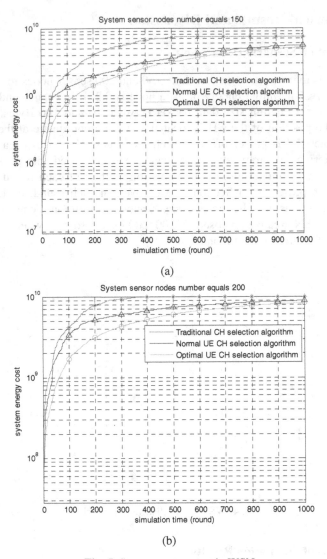

Fig. 5. System energy cost in WSN

The number of alive nodes with simulation time (rounds) is shown as Figure 6 (a) and (b) for 150 and 200 sensor nodes. After 400 rounds, the remain nodes of using traditional CH selection algorithm, normal UE gateway CH selection algorithm and optimal UE gateway CH selection algorithm are respectively 135, 120, and 55 for 150 system sensor nodes. And the remained nodes respectively are 150, 110, and 5 for 200 system sensor nodes after 400 rounds. The reason is mainly that the remaining energy of normal nodes is more than the CH nodes. Therefore, this random selection cannot have a better balance of the remained energy among sensors. In our proposed algorithm, it can select the optimal UE gateway CH to provide the access for the other sensor nodes, which not only reduced the system energy cost but also balanced the other sensor nodes energy cost with a long time rounds. The death nodes of using traditional CH selection algorithm, normal UE gateway CH selection algorithm and optimal UE gateway CH selection algorithm are respectively shown in figure 7 (a) and (b). All of the above results reveal our proposed method present better performance than the other two algorithms. Therefore, optimal UE CH selection method is efficient to be used in the sensor network because it selects a CH from several candidates by using the integrative level among these clusters. And this method can extend the death time of a cluster and the death time of the last sensor nodes are extended.

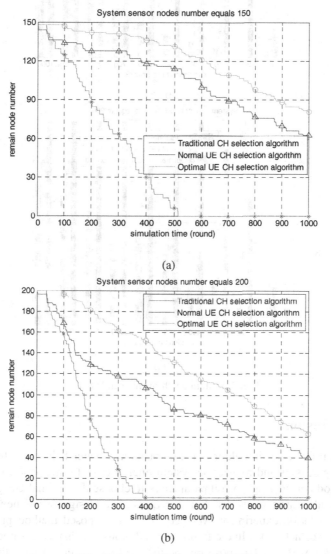

(a)

(b)

Fig. 6. System alive nodes in WSN

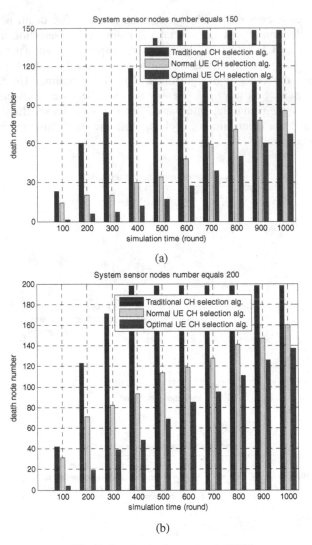

Fig. 7. System death number in WSN

5   Conclusions

The traditional CH selection algorithm cannot have a better balance of the remained energy among sensors and reduce the system energy cost. In this paper, we proposed a novel method considering several parameters to choose the optimal UE gateway CH for hierarchical sensor networks. For a request, we design some new additional signaling. Simulation experiments verified that our proposed method prolonged the lifetime of sensor networks. In the future, we will consider that sensor nodes have the capability to know themselves position and this will moreover optimize the WSN CH selection and decrease the energy consumption.

Acknowledgments. This work was supported by the National Science and Technology Major Projects of China under Grant No. 2011ZX03005-003-02, 2011ZX03001-007-03, 2010ZX03005-001-03 and Renesas Mobile Corporation Projects.

References

1. Verdone, R., Dardari, D., Mazzini, G.: Wireless Sensor and Actuator Networks. Elsevier Press, London (2008)
2. Ye, W., Heidemann, J., Estrin, D.: Medium access control with coordinated adaptive sleeping for wireless sensor networks. IEEE/ACM Transactions on Networking 12(3), 493–506 (2004)
3. Akyildiz, I.F., Su, W., Sankarasubramaniam, Y., Cayirci, E.: A survey on sensor networks. IEEE Communications Magazine 40(8), 102–114 (2002)
4. Heinzelman, W.R., Chandrakasan, A., Balakrishnan, H.: Energy-efficient communication protocol for wireless microsensor networks. In: Proceedings of the 33rd Annual Hawaii International Conference on System Sciences, pp. 4–7 (2002)
5. Lindsey, S., Raghavendra, C.S.: PEGASIS: Power-Efficient Gathering in Sensor Information Systems. In: Proceedings of IEEE Aerospace Applications Conference, pp. 1125–1130 (2002)
6. Manjeshwar, A., Agrawal, D.P.: TEEN: A routing protocol for enhanced efficiency in wireless sensor networks. In: Proceedings of the 15th International Parallel and Distributed Processing Symposium, pp. 2009–2015 (2002)
7. Younis, O., Fahmy, S.: HEED: A Hybrid, Energy-Efficient, Distributed Clustering Approach for Ad Hoc Sensor Networks. IEEE Transactions on Mobile Computing 3(4), 366–379 (2004)
8. Xu, Y., Heidemann, J., Estrin, D.: Geography-Informed energy conservation for ad hoc routing. In: Proceedings of the 7th Annual ACM/IEEE Int'l Conf. on Mobile Computing and Networking, pp. 70–84 (2001)
9. Chatterjee, M., Das, S.K., Turgut, D.: WCA: A Weighted Clustering Algorithm for Mobile ad Hoc Networks. Cluster Computing 2(2), 193–204 (2004)
10. Somasundara, A., Kansal, A., Jea, D., Estrin, D., Srivastava, M.: Controllably Mobile Infrastructure for Low Energy Embedded Networks. IEEE Transactions on Mobile Computing 5(8) (2006)
11. Al-Omari, S.A.K., Sumari, P.: An Overview of Mobile Ad Hoc Networks For the Existing Protocols and Applications. International Journals on Applications of Graph Theory in Wireless and Ad Hoc Networks and Sensor Networks 2(1), 87–110 (2010)
12. Singh, J., Singh, B., Chaudhary, A.: Ubiquity of Mobile Computing in Wireless Networks. International Journal of Technology And Engineering System 1(1), 1–4 (2009)
13. Puccinelli, D., Haenggi, M.: Wireless sensor networks:applications and challenges of ubiquitous sensing. IEEE Circuits and Systems Magazine 5(3), 19–31 (2005)
14. Gatzianas, M., Georgiadis, L.: A Distributed Algorithm for Maximum Lifetime Routing in Sensor Networks with Mobile Sink. IEEE Trans. on Wireless Communications 7(3), 984–994 (2008)

Interference Mitigation
Based on Enhanced Interference PMI Notification[*]

Jiqing Ni, Bingquan Li, Zesong Fei, and Jingming Kuang

School of Information and Electronics,
Beijing Institute of Technology,
Beijing, China
{njq,lbq,feizesong}@bit.edu.cn

Abstract. This paper considers interference mitigation in multicell scenarios where transmitters and receivers are both equipped with multiple antennas. In multicell system, both the local Pre-coding Matrix Index (PMI) and the interference PMI can be utilized by Interference Reject Combing (IRC) algorithm, and more interference information can be obtained from the enhanced interference PMI notification. The IRC interference mitigation algorithm can deal with both noise and interference. The specific formulas of calculating receiver weight vector (matrix) based on different criterions are given. And the IRC-adaptive algorithm is proposed, which can have a compromise effect between the complexity and interference mitigation. It is shown in the simulation results that the receiver algorithms can improve the system performance effectively.

Keywords: multi-cell scenarios, interference mitigation, weight vector, interference reject combine (IRC).

1 Introduction

Multicell multiple user Multi-input and Multi-output (MIMO) technology can achieve a very high sum capacity and spectral efficiency. The multicell coordinated beamforming is very helpful to exploit the multiuser diversity gain in the Multiuser MIMO (MU-MIMO) system [1]. However, the same subcarrier of the different users will cause co-channel interference (CCI). [2] indicates that user throughput will reach a performance limit with SNR increasing in multicell coordination scheme. This is because that the limited number of the feedback bit will cause channel information imprecise, and the multiuser interference can not be completely eliminated. In the high SNR, multiuser interference will become the main factor that affects the user performance. So how to eliminate the CCI is critical for the system performance.

In terms of how to eliminate interference, much previous work has been done [3]. There are several ways to eliminate interference: such as interference averaging techniques and interference avoidance techniques. The former averaged the interference

---

[*] This work was supported in part by the Sino-Swedish IMT-Advanced and Beyond Cooperative Program under grant No2008DFA11780, and ZTE Company.

P. Ren et al. (Eds.): WICON 2011, LNICST 98, pp. 438–446, 2012.

over all users, to reduce the interference experienced by individual users. The latter is to avoid interference, e.g. by setting restrictions on how the radio resources are used. [4] discussed about how to utilize zero forcing (ZF) algorithm and minimum mean square error (MMSE) algorithm to eliminate the interference between users in TD-CDMA system. [5] proposed a method which is called Hybrid Inter-cell Interference Mitigation scheme that utilized multiple sub-bands coordination scheme and soft frequency reuse scheme to achieve robust performance. [6] proposed a two-stage interference mitigation technique for coded Multiband Orthogonal Frequency Division Multiplexing (MB-OFDM), and showed that it was very effective for the WIMAX interference.

Interference Reject Combine (IRC) algorithm can distinguish the serving cell signal and interference cell signal by distinguishing space channel discrepancy from different base stations (BS) to mobile terminal. IRC algorithm deal with both interference and noise at the receiver by utilizing receive diversity, realizing the inhibition to the colored noise (interference and noise). And IRC algorithm is a receiver technology without requiring additional standardization work. Compared to IRC, both the traditional Maximum Ratio Combination (MRC) algorithm and MMSE algorithm ignore the impact of interference between users. It is why that the IRC algorithm could suppress the interference more effectively. [7] indicates that the IRC algorithm has greatly improved the system performance, in an ideal situation with one flat-fading timeslot synchronized. It could bring more than 15dB performance improvement than the MRC receiver in GSM system.

In this paper, an IRC interference eliminating method by utilizing the enhanced interference Pre-coding Matrix Index (PMI) notification from the BS is proposed. In this scheme, the signaling from BS to users not only includes the local PMI but also the interference PMI. Therefore, the users can get accurate interference information, and directly calculate the correlation matrix of interference and noise, which is used to eliminate multi-user interference. On this basis, an adaptive IRC receiver based on interference condition is future proposed. When the interference is larger relative to the noise, the IRC algorithm is adapted; If not, the traditional MRC algorithm can be directly used, which can greatly reduce the complexity without significant performance decrease.

The remainder of this paper is organized as follows. Section 2 presents system model. And Section 3 describes several IRC algorithms based on different criterions. Section 4 presents simulation results and conclusions are drawn in section 5 finally.

2   System Model

In this paper we consider a multicell MIMO system shown in fig.1 for an array of linearly arranged cells, which is based on the Wyner model [8]. Assumed that there are K base stations totally in the system, where K goes to infinity for the Wyner model. Each user could receive the data signal from its corresponding base station and the inter-cell interference signal from adjacent base stations. It is supposed that all the base stations are equipped with N antennas, and each user is equipped with M antennas.

With the assumption of linear precoding, the transmitted signal intended for the kth $k \in \{1, 2...K\}$ UE could be given by:

$$\mathbf{x}_k = \mathbf{w}_k \mathbf{s}_k \tag{1}$$

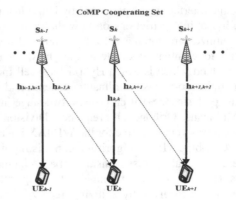

Fig. 1. System Model

where $s_k \in CN(0,1)$ denotes the data symbol intended for the kth user and $\mathbf{w}_k$ is denoted as the quantized precoding vector. Under above assumption, the signal received at the kth UE can be described as:

$$\mathbf{y}_k = \underbrace{\mathbf{H}_{k,k}\mathbf{w}_k s_k}_{data} + \underbrace{\mathbf{H}_{k-1,k}\mathbf{w}_{k-1}s_{k-1}}_{interference} + \mathbf{n}_k \tag{2}$$

where $\mathbf{H}_{k,k}$ denotes the local channel state information from the kth base station to the kth user, $\mathbf{H}_{k-1,k}$ denotes the interference channel, and $\mathbf{n}_k \in CN(0,\sigma^2)$ is the noise with zero mean and variance σ^2. Assumed that the users know the local and interference channel state information, and ZF-BF scheme is applied in this scheme. The pre-coding vector (matrix) is computed based on the quantized channel information. Since there are quantization errors existing, the interference item can not be eliminated completely.

Herein, the effective channel is defined as $\mathbf{h}_{ek} = \mathbf{H}_{k,k}\mathbf{w}_k$ $(k = 1, 2...K)$, and the effective interference channel is defined as $\mathbf{f}_{e(k-1)} = \mathbf{H}_{k-1,k}\mathbf{w}_{k-1}$. Then the formula (2) can be simplified as:

$$\mathbf{y}_k = \underbrace{\mathbf{h}_{ek}s_k}_{data} + \underbrace{\mathbf{f}_{e(k-1)}s_{k-1}}_{interference} + \mathbf{n}_k \tag{3}$$

Supposed that the receiver takes the linear detection with weight vector $\mathbf{g}$, then the detected signal $\mathbf{r}_k$ can be depicted as:

$$\mathbf{r}_k = \mathbf{g}_k^H \left(\underbrace{\mathbf{h}_{ek}s_k}_{data} + \underbrace{\mathbf{f}_{e(k-1)}s_{k-1}}_{interference} + \mathbf{n}_k \right) \tag{4}$$

The SINR of the received signal of the kth UE is given by:

$$SINR_k = \frac{\left| \mathbf{g}_k^H \mathbf{h}_{ek} \right|^2}{\left| \mathbf{g}_k^H \mathbf{f}_{e(k-1)} \right|^2 + \sigma^2} \tag{5}$$

The key problem is how to construct the linear weight vector (matrix) $\mathbf{g}$ to maximize (5). We study the long-term average throughput, and could get the rate at the kth UE as follows:

$$C_k = E\{\log_2(1 + SINR_k)\} \tag{6}$$

And the system sum rate can be given by:

$$C = \sum_{k=1}^{K} E\{\log_2(1 + SINR_k)\} \tag{7}$$

3   IRC Interference Mitigation Algorithm

In this section, several IRC algorithms based on different criteria are discussed. IRC algorithm is an effective receiver algorithm which can suppress the interference. Its basic idea is to construct a weight vector (matrix) $\mathbf{g}$ which can eliminate or reduce the interference, in the case of known interference PMI. The specific expressions of the weight vector (matrix) $\mathbf{g}$ of different IRC algorithms are given in the following parts.

A.   IRC-ZF Algorithm

The basic idea of IRC-ZF algorithm is to make the interference item zero. It can be described as follows:

$$\mathbf{r}_k = \left(null(\mathbf{f}_{e(k-1)})\mathbf{h}_{ek}\right)^H \left(null(\mathbf{f}_{e(k-1)})\mathbf{h}_{ek}s_k + null(\mathbf{f}_{e(k-1)})\mathbf{n}_k\right) \tag{8}$$

Equivalent weight vector (matrix) can be expressed as:

$$\mathbf{g}_{IRC-ZF}^H = \mathbf{h}_{ek}^H \mathbf{R}_{\pi}^{-1} \tag{9}$$

where $\mathbf{R}_{ff}$ is the autocorrelation matrix of the effective interference channel.

When using the above formula as a weighted vector, multi-user interference can be completely suppressed. Hence, in high SNR scenarios (interference limited), system performance will be greatly improved. But it doesn't consider the impact of noise, especially for the low SNR scenarios (noise limited).

B.   IRC-SINR Algorithm

Compared to IRC-ZF algorithm, IRC-SINR algorithm takes the noise into account, which makes up the shortage of the IRC-ZF algorithm in the low SNR scenarios. The goal of IRC-SINR algorithm is to maximize the SINR of the detected signals. For convenience, (3) is rewritten as:

$$\mathbf{y}_k = \underbrace{\mathbf{h}_{ek}s_k}_{data} + \underbrace{\mathbf{u}_k}_{interference} \tag{10}$$

where $\mathbf{u}_k$ is the sum of the interference and the noise. Then, the following objective function can be given by:

$$\max_{g} SINR = \frac{E\left\{\left|g^{H}h_{ek}s_{k}\right|^{2}\right\}}{E\left\{\left|g^{H}u_{k}\right|^{2}\right\}} = \frac{g^{H}h_{ek}h_{ek}^{H}g}{g^{H}R_{uu}g} \tag{11}$$

where R_{uu} is the autocorrelation matrix of matrix u_k.

According to the theory of generalized Rayleigh quotient, the optimal receive combining vector was given by [9]:

$$g_{IRC-SINR}^{H} = h_{ek}^{H}R_{uu}^{-1} \tag{12}$$

C.   IRC-MMSE Algorithm

IRC-MMSE algorithm also considers the noise. The goal of this method is to minimize the mean square error of the detected signal:

$$\min_{g} J = E\left\{\left|g^{H}y - s\right|^{2}\right\} = g^{H}R_{yy}g + I - g^{H}R_{ys} - R_{ys}^{H}g \tag{13}$$

where R_{yy} is the autocorrelation matrix of the received vector; R_{ys} is the correlation matrix of the received vector y and detected vector s. The optimal receive combining vector was given by:

$$g_{IRC\text{-}MMSE}^{H} = (I + h_{ek}^{H}R_{uu}^{-1}h_{ek})^{-1}h_{ek}^{H}R_{uu}^{-1} \tag{14}$$

D.   IRC-Adaptive Algorithm

To reduce the complexity of calculating receiver weight vector, the IRC-adaptive algorithm is proposed in this subsection. When the interference is relatively large, IRC-SINR algorithm is adapted to suppress the interference. And if the interference is relatively small, MRC algorithm is directly chosen to reduce the complexity. The key is to set a threshold for selecting the receiver algorithm. Here, the interference term is defined as $Z = \left\|f_{e(k-1)}\right\|^{2}$. Then, if $Z/\sigma^{2} \leq \alpha$, MRC algorithm is directly used. And if $Z/\sigma^{2} \leq \alpha$, the IRC-SINR algorithm is adapted. Hence, the weight vector (matrix) can be formulated as :

$$g_{IRC\text{-}adaptive}^{H} = \begin{cases} h_{ek}^{H} & Z/\sigma^{2} \leq \alpha \\ h_{ek}^{H}R_{uu}^{-1} & Z/\sigma^{2} \leq \alpha \end{cases} \tag{15}$$

How to set the threshold α is critical. It hopes to reduce the complexity of the receiver as much as possible without significant decline in performance. If the threshold α is too small, the IRC algorithm may be chosen at the low interference. IRC-adaptive algorithm will not reduce the complexity relative to the IRC-SINR algorithm. If α is set too large, the MRC algorithm may be used in the high interference situation. The system performance will decrease correspondingly. In the next section, the comparison curves of the system performance with different α will be presented.

It should be noted that the key of IRC algorithm is to calculate the covariance matrix R_{uu} of the interference and noise. In this scheme, UE can easily obtain the precise interference information f by the interference PMI. Hence, it is easy to get the interference correlation matrix $\mathbf{R_{ff}}=E\{\mathbf{ff}^H\}$, and the covariance matrix of the interference and noise $\mathbf{R_{uu}}=E\{\mathbf{uu}^H\}$. Suppose noise is the Gaussian white noise. It is irrelevant with the interference. It is easy to get the following formula:

Thus it can easily get $\mathbf{R_{uu}}$ and weight vector corresponding to IRC receiver algorithm. All kinds of the receiver algorithm are listed in Table 1.

Table 1. Different Receiver Algorithm In The Multi-antenna Scenarios

Receiver algorithm	Weight Vector(matrix)	Features	Performance
MRC	$\mathbf{g}_{opt}^{H}=\mathbf{h}_{ek}^{H}$	no considering interference	Performance limited at high SNR
MMSE	$\mathbf{g}_{opt}^{H}=\mathbf{h}_{ek}^{H}\left(\mathbf{h}_{ek}\mathbf{h}_{ek}^{H}+\sigma^{2}\mathbf{I}\right)^{-1}$	no considering interference	Performance limited at high SNR
IRC-ZF	$\mathbf{g}_{opt}^{H}=\mathbf{h}_{ek}^{H}\mathbf{R}_{ff}^{-1}$	no considering noise	Performance increase at high SNR
IRC-SINR	$\mathbf{g}_{opt}^{H}=\mathbf{h}_{ek}^{H}\mathbf{R}_{uu}^{-1}$	considering interference and noise	Performance increase at high SNR
IRC-MMSE	$\mathbf{g}_{opt}^{H}=(\mathbf{I}+\mathbf{h}_{ek}^{H}\mathbf{R}_{uu}^{-1}\mathbf{h}_{ek})^{-1}\mathbf{h}_{ek}^{H}\mathbf{R}_{uu}^{-1}$	considering interference and noise	Equivalent with IRC-SINR
IRC-adaptive	$\mathbf{g}_{opt}^{H}=\begin{cases}\mathbf{h}_{ek}^{H}& Z/\sigma^{2}\leq\alpha\\ \mathbf{h}_{ek}^{H}\mathbf{R}_{uu}^{-1}& Z/\sigma^{2}\leq\alpha\end{cases}$	Choose MRC or IRC adaptively	IRC-adaptive

$$\mathbf{g}_{\text{IRC-adaptive}}^{H}=\begin{cases}\mathbf{h}_{ek}^{H}& Z/\sigma^{2}\leq\alpha\\ \mathbf{h}_{ek}^{H}\mathbf{R}_{uu}^{-1}& Z/\sigma^{2}\leq\alpha\end{cases} \tag{16}$$

4   Simulations

In this section, numerical results of the proposed scheme are presented. It is assumed that the BS is equipped with four antennas and each user is equipped with two antennas. All the simulations are based on flat fading Rayleigh channel and Random Vector Quantization (RVQ).

Fig. 2 and 3 show the sum-rate and BER performance for different receiver algorithms. It can be seen that IRC algorithm have a great improvement in system performance at high SNR. With SNR increasing, the performance of IRC-ZF comes close to IRC-SINR. But at low SNR, the performance incensement of IRC algorithms is not obvious compared to traditional MRC. Besides, the performance of IRC-ZF decreases obviously. This is because that IRC-ZF reduces the received signal energy when the interference is not the key factor of affecting system performance.

Fig. 4 and 5 show the throughput and BER performance of IRC-adaptive algorithm for different α values. It can be seen that the IRC-adaptive algorithm can reduce the complexity while ensuring the system performance. When interference and noise are in the same order of magnitude, IRC-adaptive performance has a small little decline relative to IRC-SINR. And the greater α is, the larger performance loss is. When $\alpha = 1$, there is no obvious performance loss; When $\alpha = 5$, the performance loss is about 1dB. In practical application, α can be set to meet the system requirement.

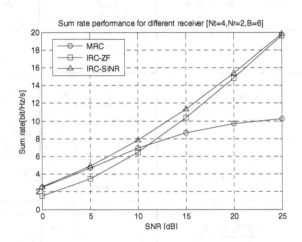

Fig. 2. Sum rate performances for different receiver

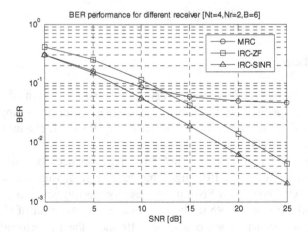

Fig. 3. BER performances for different receiver

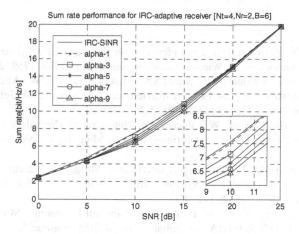

Fig. 4. Sum rate performance for IRC-adaptive receiver [Nt=4, Nr=2, B=6]

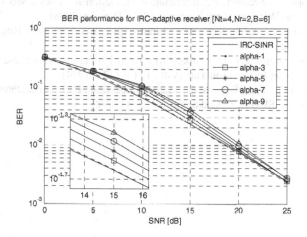

Fig. 5. BER performance for IRC-adaptive receiver [Nt=4, Nr=2, B=6]

5   Conclusions

This paper propose some kinds of IRC receiver algorithm based on enhanced interference PMI notification in multiuser system, to eliminate interference among users. Simulation results show that IRC algorithm performance comes close to MRC at low SNR (noise limited). And at high SNR, it has a great improvement for system performance. A new algorithm —IRC-ZF is also proposed, by utilizing which the interference can be completely eliminated in theory. However, IRC-ZF algorithm only considers the interference without noise, and there is some performance loss at low SNR. Because the complexity of IRC algorithm is relatively high comparing to traditional receiver algorithm, the IRC-adaptive algorithm based on interference situation is proposed. Adaptive receiver can balance the system performance and receiver algorithm complexity.

References

[1] Dahrouj, H., Yu, W.: Coordinated beamforming for the multicell multi-Antenna wireless system. IEEE Transactions on Wireless Communications 9(5), 1748–1759 (2010)

[2] Gesbert, D., Hanly, S., Huang, H., Shitz, S.S., Simeone, O., Yu, W.: Multi-Cell MIMO Cooperative Networks: A New Look at Interference. IEEE Journal on Selected Areas in Communications 28(9), 1380–1407 (2010)

[3] Aboutorab, N., Hardjawana, W., Vucetic, B.: Interference Cancellation in Multi-user MIMO Relay Networks Using Beamforming and Precoding. In: WCNC 2010 Proceedings (2010)

[4] Castoldi, P., Kobayashi, H.: Co-Channel Interference Mitigation Detectors for Multi-rate Transmission in TD-CDMA Sytems. IEEE Journal on Selected Areas in Communications 20(2), 273–286 (2002)

[5] Zhu, J., Liu, G., Wang, Y., Zhang, P.: A Hybrid Inter-cell Interference Mitigation Scheme for OFDMA based E-UTRA Downlink. In: IEEE Asia-Pacific Conference on Communications (August. 2006)

[6] Snow, C., Lampe, L., Schober, R.: Interference Mitigation for Coded MB-OFDM UWB. In: IEEE Radio and Wireless Symposium, pp.17–20 (January 2008)

[7] Dahlqvist, M.: Interference Rejection Combining System Performance. Royal Institute of Technology, Sweden (2000)

[8] Wyner, A.D.: Shannon-theoretic approach to a Gaussian cellular multiple-access channel. IEEE Transactions on Information Theory 40, 1713–1727 (1994)

[9] Borga, M.: Learning multidimensional signal processing. Ph.D. dissertation, Linkoping University, Sweden, SE-581 83 Linkoping, Sweden (1998)

Machine Learning Based Autonomous Network Flow Identifying Method

Hongbo Shi[1,3], Tomoki Hamagami[1,3], and Haoyuan Xu[2,3]

[1] Division of Physics, Electrical and Computer Engineering,
Graduate School of Engineering, Yokohama National University
[2] Information Technology Service Center, Yokohama National University
[3] 79-1 Tokiwadai, Hodogaya-ku, Yokohama 240-8501 Japan
{shi,hamagami,haoyuan}@ynu.ac.jp

Abstract. Recently, various applications and services start to be used in the Internet. Load balancing the increasing network traffic in real time can affect the network quality. The flow control technologies become much more important than before. Our research project proposes an intelligent network flow identifying method, smart flow, which is based on the learning algorithm. In this paper, we suggest to utilize the SOM for learning the properties of packets, such as timestamp, source and destination. Based on our proposed normalization, IP network flows can be formed autonomously during the learning process. Furthermore, the combination use of the new normalization with the GHSOM can classify the sub-IP flows belongs to the same flow. This paper indicates that a flow shall consist of several sub-IP flows, and sub-IP flow shall consist of several IP packets.

Keywords: IPv6, SIP, IP flow, SOM, GHSOM, classification.

1 Introduction

Now days, the principal technology of the Next Generation Network (NGN), IP telephony, is used widely in the world. It also causes the network traffic to be increased much faster than before. Until now, the packet is used as the network traffic unit for routing control. Meanwhile, these years, a new unit called IP flow is started to be used for describing a stream of packets in the Internet. The network packets grouped in the same IP flow usually means the packets belong to the same source and destination. Thus, a large amount of packets generated by the web and P2P applications can be routed as a single IP flow. This kind of new flow routing can save much more transmission cost than the traditional packet routing. Because the new flow routers do not need to route every packet, but the first packet of a flow. Utilizing the IP flows for the network load balancing and network analysis becomes more important.[1] Meanwhile, these products and standards group the packets to a flow not just only based on the source, destination and ports, but also a very principle parameter, time interval, which can be configured to different values by the administrators or affected by the memory size of a router.

P. Ren et al. (Eds.): WICON 2011, LNICST 98, pp. 447–457, 2012.
© Institute for Computer Sciences, Social Informatics and Telecommunications Engineering 2012

There are several network management products, such as sFlow[2], NetFlow[3], Openflow[4] used popularly in the world. There is also an international standard called IPFIX (IP Flow Information Export) in the Internet Engineering Task Force (IETF). [5][6] Due to using these new technologies, the network management can watch much larger network scale and analysis network condition in more detail than the IP packet based tools. Furthermore, network intrusion caused by the DDoS and worm can be detected quickly by using the flow collectors.

However, these flow technologies are based on the packet sampling and filtering algorithms. These existing algorithms may limit the watching scale of a target network and affect the characteristics of the original IP flows generated in the network. Moreover, the time interval for the packet sampling or filtering is configured by the network operations individually. In other words, network management is based on the administrator's experiment. Different managements used in a network may generate different flows. It causes that IP flow modeling difficultly.

This paper suggests a new solution for generating IP flow autonomously by using the machine learning, Self-Organizing Maps (SOM).[7] We suggest to group the packets with similar characteristics in a flow based on learning the packet information included in the packet headers. The new suggestion can generate IP flows autonomously without using the time interval and without being affected by any kinds of network managements.

2   Self-Organizing Maps, SOM

Self-Organizing Maps[7] suggested by T. Kohonen, is a kind of neural network algorithms. It is known as a data visualization technology for those high-dimension data during the competitive learning of Euclidean distance. Furthermore, it is mainly used for unsupervised learning, clustering, classification and data mining. The SOM algorithm in detail is shown as follows.

1. Initialize the weights of the nodes in the map, m_i, with random numbers
2. Use Euclidean distance to find similarity between the input vector and the weight vector of a node in the map. Winning unit m_c is most similar one, also called Best Matching Unit (BMU).

$$m_c(t) = min_i||x(t) - m_i(t)|| \tag{1}$$

3. Update the neighborhood of BMU to be closer to the input vector through the SOM learning. h_{ci} is the neighborhood function.

$$m_i(t+1) = \begin{cases} m_i(t) + \alpha(t) \cdot h_{ci}(t) \cdot [x(t) - m_i(t)], \\ \qquad\qquad\qquad\qquad\qquad (i \in N_c) \\ m_i(t), \ (i \notin N_c) \end{cases} \tag{2}$$

4. The learning rate $(0 \le \alpha(t) \le 1)$ and the neighborhood $(N_c = N_c(t))$ decrease with time. T means the number of learning times.

$$\alpha(t) = \alpha_0(1 - t/T) \tag{3}$$

$$N_c = N_c(0)(1 - t/T) \tag{4}$$

3 Growing Hierarchical Self-Organizing Map

The map size of SOM is required to be defined properly due to the users' experiment. Moreover, SOM uses the input data for learning and training the map. SOM doesn't have neither recursive mechanism for the coming data input in real time nor evolution mechanism for growing map. Thus, amount of data input may cause the difficult decision for the map size. The Growing Hierarchical Self-Organizing Map proposed by A. Rauber provides dynamic architecture for maps to grow in both hierarchical way and horizontal way. Thus, GHSOM can treat amounts of input data during an unsupervised training process due to its dynamically growing hierarchical map architecture. Fig. 1 shows that, Layer 0 only includes one unit and Layer 1 includes 2x3 units. There are 6 SOMs in the Layer 2. One for each unit in the Layer 1 map. Layer 3 has 2 SOMs which are expanded from the units in Layer 2.

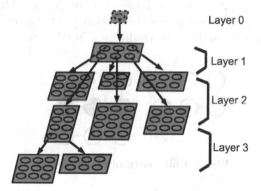

Fig. 1. Growing Hierarchical Mechanism of GHSOM

GHSOM growing process is started at a virtual Layer 0, which consists of only one single unit. Layer 0 is used for controlling the hierarchical growing process. The weight vector of this unit is initialized as the average of the entire input data. The unit is assigned a weight vector,

$$m_0 = [\mu_{01}, \mu_{02}, ..., \mu_{0n}]^T \tag{5}$$

The expression,

$$mqe_0 = \frac{1}{d} \cdot ||m_0 - x|| \tag{6}$$

shows the deviation of the input data, the mean quantization error of the single unit. d means the number of the input data x.

Training of the GHSOM is started at Layer 1 which is initialized with a grid of 2x2 units. Each unit is initialized with an n-dimensional weight vector,

$$m_i = [\mu_{i1}, \mu_{i2}, ..., \mu_{in}]^T, m_i \in \mathcal{R}^n \tag{7}$$

GHSOM uses the learning policy,

$$m_i(t) + \alpha(t) \cdot h_{ci}(t) \cdot [x(t) - m_i(t)] \tag{8}$$

The expression,

$$MQE_m = \frac{1}{u} \cdot \sum_i mqe_i \tag{9}$$

shows the mean quantization error of a map. u means the number of unit i in SOM m.

There are two parameters, τ_m and τ_u, used for controlling the growth of GHSOM. τ_m is used to manage the growth of each map, and τ_u is used to control the hierarchical growth. If $MQE_m \geq \tau_m \cdot mqe_0$, then a new row of units or a new column of units is inserted between the error unit, e and the dissimilar unit, d. (Fig. 2) The error unit means the highest mqe_e unit, after λ training iterations. The dissimilar unit means the neighbor of error unit with the most dissimilar weight vector. The weight vectors of the new units are initialized simply with the averages of the weight vectors of the existing neighbors. After the insertion, the learning rate (α) and neighborhood function (h_{ci}) are reset to their initial values and the training based on the traditional SOM process.

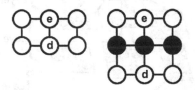

Fig. 2. Unit Insertion of GHSOM

After the growth of Layer 1 ($MQE_m < \tau_m \cdot mqe_0$), hierarchical control process in Layer 2 is started. The selection of unit depends on the mqe of Layer 0. Each unit, i begins the hierarchical expansion while the criterion, $mqe_i > \tau_u \cdot mqe_0$, is fulfilled.

4   New Proposal: Autonomous IP Flow Identifying

This paper focuses on the classification feature of SOM. We suggest to learn the characteristics included in the IP packet for identifying IP flow autonomously. The new proposal normalizes the timestamp , source and destination information included in IP packet as the input vector for the SOM learning.

4.1   Input Vector Normalization

In the Internet, hop or cost is used to express the distance between two nodes. The timestamp of a captured IP packet is usually affected by the distance between nodes, packet size, upper layer application and the network congestion. Therefore, this paper suggests to utilize the timestamp for estimating the network distance.

This paper also suggests to map the network peer communication to a vector. When there are j nodes in a network, then the communication peers can be mapped to a $2j$-dimension vector space. (Fig. 3) In other words, $2j$-dimension vector space is correspondent to a mesh network in this paper. *Packet_Header* means the set of IP addresses included in an IP packet. In our proposal, *Packet_Header*(t) shows the source and destination IP addresses due to the time window $(0 \leq t \leq T, t \in \mathcal{N})$.

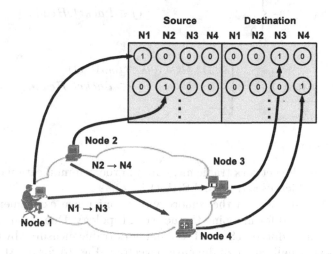

Fig. 3. Map Communication Peer to High Dimension Vector

$$Source_{init}(t)(j) = \begin{cases} 1, & (j \in Packet\_Header(t)) \\ 0 \end{cases} \qquad (10)$$

$$Destination_{init}(t)(j) = \begin{cases} 1, & (j \in Packet\_Header(t)) \\ 0 \end{cases} \qquad (11)$$

According to the timestamp, following formulas are used for normalization.

$$TIME(t) = \frac{(Timestamp(t) - Timestamp_{start})}{Counter(t)} \qquad (12)$$

$Timestamp(t)$ means the record time of the current captured packet. $Timestamp_{start}$ is the start of the time window. $Counter(t)$ shows the order number of captured IP packets. This paper uses

$$\alpha(t) = \sum_{t} \frac{TIME(t)}{Counter(t)} \qquad (13)$$

to normalize the timestamp, source and destination information included in IP packet as follows.

$$Source(t)(j) = \begin{cases} \alpha(j) \cdot Source_{init}(t)(j), & \\ & (j \in Packet\_Header) \\ 0 & \end{cases} \qquad (14)$$

$$Destination(t)(j) = \begin{cases} \alpha(j) \cdot Destination_{init}(t)(j), & \\ & (j \in Packet\_Header) \\ 0 & \end{cases} \qquad (15)$$

4.2   Experiment

This proposal uses the network traffic measured in the communication of remote video conference which uses IPv6 and SIP. (Fig. 4).

There are 11 hosts used in the remote video conference experiment. Thus, 22 dimensions are used for mapping the network topology. Due to our proposed normalization as introduced in Sec. 4.1, the network traffic measured by tcpdump (Fig. 5) can be normalized to 23-dimension vectors (Fig. 6) for SOM learning. This paper uses 150 normalized IP packets which are captured in above network. The 23 dimensions show the timestamp, source and destination of an IP packet.

4.3   Autonomous IP Flow Identifying

Fig. 9 shows the result of the SOM map training on the normalized characteristics of IP packet. The labels shown in the map consist of the captured order and parts of the source, destination IP addresses of an IP packet. For example, the label, 46.105.da8, means the 46th captured IP packet, the source is 2001:2f8:37::241:105 (omitted as 105) and the destination is 2001:da8:8005:1191:892:8385:1c85:5201 (omitted as da8).

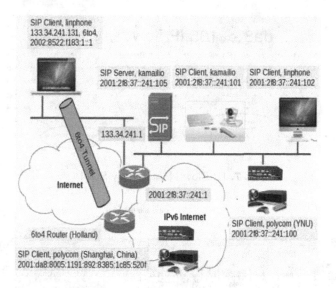

Fig. 4. SIP on IPv6 Testbed

```
12:41:56.289728 IP6 (hlim 128, next-header: ICMPv6 (58), length: 16) 2001:2f8:37::241:108 > 2001:2f8:37::241:102:
[icmp6 sum ok] ICMP6, echo reply, length 16, seq 1
12:41:59.669286 IP6 (hlim 64, next-header: UDP (17), length: 12) 2001:2f8:37::241:102.sip > 2001:2f8:37::241:105.sip:
[udp sum ok] SIP, length: 4
12:42:00.410380 IP6 (hlim 255, next-header: ICMPv6 (58), length: 32) 2001:2f8:37::241:102 > 2001:2f8:37::241:108:
[icmp6 sum ok] ICMP6, neighbor solicitation, length 32, who has 2001:2f8:37::241:108
12:42:00.410495 IP6 (hlim 255, next-header: ICMPv6 (58), length: 32) 2001:2f8:37::241:108 > 2001:2f8:37::241:102:
[icmp6 sum ok] ICMP6, neighbor advertisement, length 32, tgt is 2001:2f8:37::241:108, Flags [solicited, override]
12:42:01.638506 IP6 (hlim 255, next-header: ICMPv6 (58), length: 32) 2001:2f8:37::241:1 > 2001:2f8:37::241:105:
[icmp6 sum ok] ICMP6, neighbor solicitation, length 32, who has 2001:2f8:37::241:105
```

Fig. 5. tcpdump of SIP with IPv6

```
23
#time n1 n2 n3 n4 n5 n6 n7 n8 n9 n10 n11 n1 n2 n3 n4 n5 n6 n7 n8 n9 n10 n11
0041800001054 0 0 0 0 0 0.090096826667359 0 0 0 0 0 0.090096826667359 0 0 0 0 0 0 0 0 0 5.108.102
0.729961166666423 0.19674088333387 0 0 0 0 0 0 0 0 0 0 0.19674088333387 0 0 0 0 0 0 0 0 0 6.102.105
0.731551571429009 0.273142410204604 0 0 0 0 0 0 0 0 0 0 0 0.273142410204604 0 0 0 0 0 0 7.102.108
0.640121999999792 0 0 0 0 0 0.319014858929002 0 0 0 0 0 0.319014858929002 0 0 0 0 0 0 0 0 0 8.108.102
0.705443000000539 0 0 0 0 0 0 0.361951319048062 0 0 0 0 0 0.361951319048062 0 0 0 0 0 0 0 0 9.1.105
```

Fig. 6. Normalized Input Data for SOM and GHSOM Training

As snown in Fig. 9, the IP packets sent by node da8 to node 105 are grouped in a flow autonomously. As the same, the network communication between the nodes (labelled with 102.105, 105.102, 100.105 and 105.100) in 2001:2f8:37::241::/112 network are identified to several IP flows properly. The IP packets (labelled with 2002.105) sent by using IPv6 over IPv4 tunneling technology are also grouped in a flow properly. Because of the incomplete normalization for the start of input data, some of the IP flow classification is treated correctly.

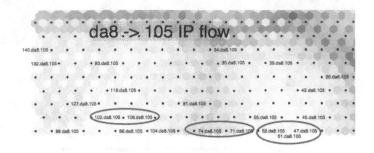

Fig. 7. IP Flow identified by SOM

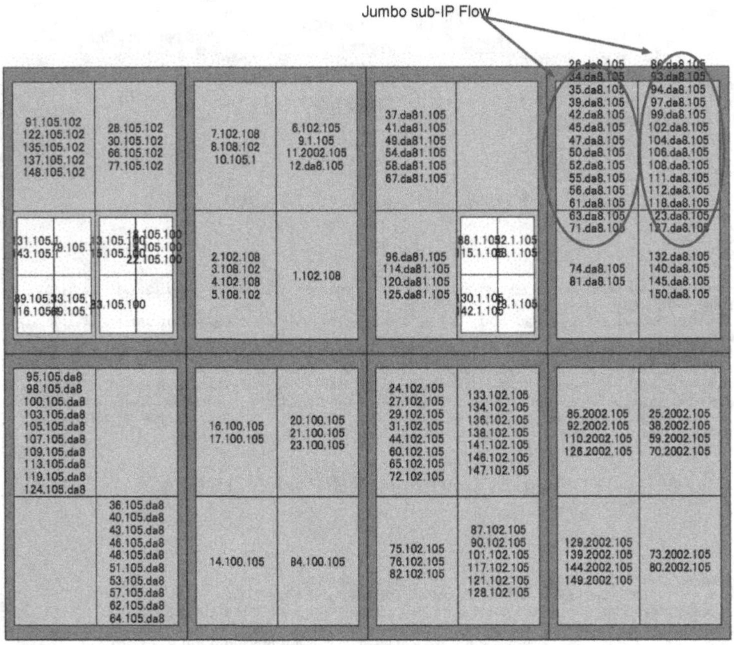

Fig. 8. IP Flow and sub-IP Flow generated by GHSOM Hierarchical Architecture

4.4 IP Flow in Hierarchical Classification with GHSOM

Usually, the network communications in the Internet may generated randomly. Communication between two nodes may consist of multiple IP flows. In other words, an IP flow may consist of multiple sub-IP flows in real Internet. Due to the growth of GHSOM map size, GHSOM shows the flow classification result more clearly than SOM. Because of the hierarchical architecture, there is more training on the characteristic, timestamp, in GHSOM than in SOM. These reasons cause that sub-IP flow and flow hierarchical architecture become visible in GHSOM map.

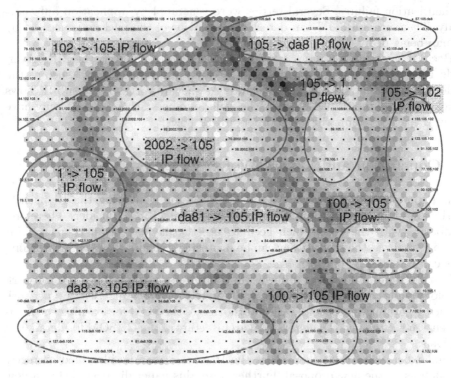

Fig. 9. Autonomous IP Flow Identifying

In this paper, we use GHSOM to learn the same normalized traffic data which is also used by SOM. Fig. 8 shows that IP packets can be grouped in different sub-IP flows (shown as different sizes of squares in the figure), according to the source and destination IP addresses. IP packets with the same direction are grouped to the same flow as well as the SOM. Moreover, the IP packets captured within a short interval time are classified to the same sub-IP flows correctly by GHSOM. In this experiment, there is only one session running between two nodes. Therefore, the packets grouped in the same flow or sub-IP flows shown in Fig. 9, are listed in order. Obviously, as shown in Fig. 8, IP packets sent from node da8 to node 105 can be identified to several sub-IP flows by GHSOM. Comparing with Fig. 7, it is clear that the original SOM learning can not identify the sub-IP flows as well as GHSOM. Affected by the incorrect normalization occurred at the start of the time window, there are still a few packets cannot be classified to flows or sub-IP flows correctly in GHSOM either. Thus, our proposal can classify IP packets to IP sub-IP flows correctly at a rate of 92%.

On the other hand, the classification of flows is affected by the applications, network congestion and users. As shown in Fig. 8, the IP sub-IP flow from node da8 to node 105 consist of much more IP packets than other IP sub-IP flows belong to different nodes. These large sub-IP flows are caused by the SIP authentication failures. Several retries were generated by application automatically. Therefore, GHSOM can detect the behavior of the packets generated by human being or by the programs properly.

Because of the retries caused by the authentication failures, the SIP server, node 105, becomes busy. Thus, the sub-IP flows from other clients, such as the node 2002 and the node 102 are affected. As shown in Fig. 8, the sub-IP flows which consist of the IP packets with the order numbers, from 74 to 82, only have a few IP packets comparing with other sub-IP flows.

5   Conclusion and Future Work

This paper suggests to use SOM and GHSOM for identifying the IP packets to IP flows by using the limited information included in IP header. Therefore, comparing with the tools which need to use the payload of an IP packet for network analysis, the user privacy can be protected well and the machine learning cost can be saved by our proposal.

In this paper, the vector dimension is utilized for describing the network topology and a new normalization is suggested for changing the raw network traffic to learning input vectors. The authors uses the SOM for learning the high-dimension vectors and the hierarchical architecture of the GHSOM for detail flow analysis.

Our experiment result shows that the IP packets can be identified correctly through using the new proposal. Furthermore, this paper discovered that a flow can consist of several sub-IP flows. According to the classified flows and sub-IP flows, we can detect abnormal behaviors during analyzing a few captured IP packets. As the future work, the proposal should be evaluated in a large scale network which has more network nodes and more network traffic. Also treating coming input data and classifying IP flows and sub-IP flows in real time are also remaining issues. Using AS number as the characteristic of network topology is also necessary in the normalization. Because of high-dimension vector space, our new suggestion is also supposed for being used to classify the packets used in multicast or multihoming environment. The evaluation test is required.

References

1. Mori, T., Takine, T., Pan, J., Kawahara, R., Uchida, M., Goto, S.: Identifying Heavy-Hitter Flows from Sampled Flow Statistics. IEICE Transaction 90-B(11), 3061–3072 (2007)
2. sFlow, http://www.sflow.org/
3. NetFlow, http://www.cisco.com
4. Openflow, http://www.openflowswitch.org/
5. Claise, B.: Specification of the IP Flow Information Export (IPFIX) Protocol for the Exchange of IP Traffic Flow Information, RFC 5401 (January 2008)
6. Sadasivan, G., Brownlee, N., Clasise, B., Quittek, J.: Architecture for IP Flow Information Export, RFC 5470 (March 2009)

7. Kohonen, T.: Self-Organizing Maps. Springer (2000)
8. SOM_PAK, http://www.cis.hut.fi/research/som_lvq_pak.shtml
9. IPv6 Specification, Internet Engineering Task Force, RFC 2460 (December 1998)
10. Rauber, A., Merkl, D., Dittenbach, M.: The growing hierarchical self-organizing map: exploratory analysis of high-dimensional data. IEEE Transactions on Neural Networks 13(6), 1331–1341 (2002)
11. Dittenbach, M., Merki, D., Rauber, A.: The Growing Hierarchical Self-Organizing Map. In: Proc. of the International Joint Conference on Neural Networks (IEEE IJCNN 2000) (July 2000)
12. Palomo, E.J., Domínguez, E., Luque, R.M., Muñoz, J.: A New GHSOM Model Applied to Network Security. In: Kůrková, V., Neruda, R., Koutník, J. (eds.) ICANN 2008, Part I. LNCS, vol. 5163, pp. 680–689. Springer, Heidelberg (2008)

Leasing and Pricing Strategies for Wireless Service Providers in Dynamic Spectrum Sharing

Peipei Chen, Qinyu Zhang, and Yazhen Ren

Harbin Institute of Technology,
Shenzhen Graduate School
Shenzhen, China
rickychen98@126.com, zqy@hit.edu.cn, renyazhen26@163.com

Abstract. In dynamic spectrum sharing, Wireless Service Providers (WSPs) can dynamically acquire spectrum by leasing from spectrum broker and sell spectrum to users. In this paper, we model the interactions between secondary WSPs and users as a three-stage game with objective of maximizing WSPs' profits. The competitive WSPs make leasing strategies in stage I and pricing strategies in stage II. Users follow Wardrop's principle and choose WSP with respect to price and quality of service (QoS) in stage III. We analyze the static game by means of backward induction. Given the users' equilibrium, the pricing sub-game and leasing full game for competitive WSPs both have a unique Nash equilibrium. The situation without complete information is also studied by dynamic game. The short term pricing dynamic game converges to the Nash equilibrium of the pricing sub-game, while the long term leasing dynamic game converges to the Nash equilibrium of the full game.

Keywords: Dynamic spectrum leasing, Leasing and pricing, Nash equilibrium, Three-stage game.

1 Introduction

Spectrum is an indispensable resource in wireless communications. Spectrum has been statically allocated by regulatory agency (e.g., FCC in USA, Ofcom in UK) to prevent the signals from interfering with each other. As wireless services increase dramatically these years, spectrum seems to be scarce. However, recent researches [1], [2] show that most of spectrum bands are underutilized because demand changes with time and location. Dynamic spectrum access can improve the spectrum utilization by allowing primary Wireless Service Providers (WSPs)/users to share the spectrum with secondary WSPs/users. With cognitive radio technology, dynamic spectrum access comes true. Devices with cognitive capability can reconfigure themselves according to the circumstances they sensed. Based on the manners of spectrum acquisition, we divide dynamic spectrum access mechanisms into opportunistic spectrum access and hierarchical spectrum access [3]. In opportunistic spectrum access, secondary WSPs /users acquire spectrum by spectrum sensing. In hierarchical spectrum access, secondary WSPs/users acquire spectrum by leasing.

P. Ren et al. (Eds.): WICON 2011, LNICST 98, pp. 458–471, 2012.

Recently, increasing researches focus on dynamic spectrum leasing. Literatures [4]-[6] have studied the secondary WSPs' strategies of obtaining spectrum from spectrum owners. Concerning secondary WSPs' competitive service providing, most existent works (e.g., [7], [8]) focus on pricing interaction between competitive WSPs. However, secondary WSPs' leasing strategies are tightly related with service pricing strategies. Only a few works (e.g., [9], [10]) jointly considered WSPs' strategies for spectrum acquiring and service pricing. In [9], the demand function of users is derived directly from economics area, which can not reflect the users' quality of service (QoS) requirements in communication. A concrete wireless spectrum sharing model is used in [10], which causes that the result is not general.

The key difference here is that we give an analytical study of leasing and pricing game for non-cooperative secondary WSPs with objectives of maximizing their own profit. Profit is the difference between the revenue earned by selling services and cost of leasing spectrum. The secondary users follow the Wardrop's principle [11] and choose WSP based on price and QoS. We use a three-stage (leader-follower) game to model the interactions between the WSPs and users as well as the WSPs' leasing and pricing decisions. Nash equilibrium of the game is solution to our problem. In the first stage, the WSPs lease bandwidth from spectrum broker. In the second stage, the WSPs make decision on service pricing to attract users. In the third stage, users decide which WSP to access.

The structure of this paper is as follows. In section 2, system model is described. In section 3, we give the static game formulation, and solve the game by backward induction. In section 4, we model WSPs' interactions as dynamic game with incomplete information, and analyze the convergence of the dynamic game. In section 5, through simulation results, some insights of static and dynamic game of non-cooperative WSPs are discussed. In section 6, conclusion is given.

2   System Model

As shown in Fig.1, we consider a duopoly case in which two secondary WSPs deploy their infrastructures in the same geography area. Secondary WSPs and users are equipped with cognitive capabilities. Primary WSPs put their temporarily unused spectrum into spectrum broker, gain extra revenue from leasing the spectrum to secondary WSPs and draw back spectrum after a specific period of time. Secondary WSPs can lease spectrum from spectrum broker and configure their infrastructures. Secondary users no longer have long term contract with specific WSPs and have the ability to choose WSP according to QoS and price. The WSPs can dynamically adjust their bandwidth leasing and service pricing decisions to attract users for maximizing their individual profit. We would like to study the behaviors of competitive secondary WSPs in making decisions of leasing spectrum and pricing service with the consideration of users' behavior. If not special specified, we refer WSP as secondary WSP and users as secondary users in remnant paper. As in [9] and [12], we consider the case where users pay for the capacity (resources) that they use instead of the services they receive.

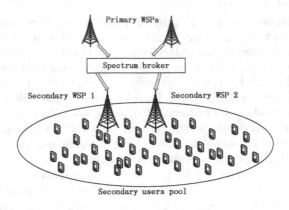

Fig. 1. System model

To acquire spectrum, the WSPs have to decide the amount of leasing bandwidth b_i ($i \in \{1, 2\}$). The spectrum broker charges WSPs according to the unit price function $F(b_1 + b_2)$ [13], in which $F(b)$ is strictly positive, non-decreasing and convex for $b > 0$. The WSPs are charged at the same unit price. The price function describe the characteristic of primary WSPs' cost of spectrum providing, since the more bandwidth leased to secondary WSPs the more influence introduced into their own services. In our paper, we use the following format for $F(b)$,

$$F(b) = C(b_1 + b_2) \tag{1}$$

in which C is a positive constant. We can see from (1) that spectrum cost for each WSP not only depends on its own leasing bandwidth but also depends on the other WSP's. To maximize its own profit, WSP i should consider its opponent's leasing strategy.

The system capacity s_i provided by WSP i is determined by the leasing spectrum,

$$s_i = k_i b_i \tag{2}$$

where k_i is WSP i's spectrum efficiency. Here, capacity is simply interpreted as the maximum amount of throughput a WSP can support. With adaptive modulation, the transmission rate can be dynamically adjusted based on the channel quality. Spectral efficiency can be obtained from [14],

$$k_i = \log_2 (1 + K_i \gamma_i), \tag{3}$$

where $K_i = 1.5 / (\ln 0.2 / BER_i^{tar})$, γ_i denotes the signal to noise ratio, and   denotes the target bit error rate BER_i^{tar}.

We model the interaction between WSPs and end users as a three-stage game ($i \in \{1, 2\}$).

Stage I (Leader): WSP   decides the leasing bandwidth (b_i).

Stage II (follower): WSP   decides the service pricing (p_i).

Stage III (follower): Users make decision on which WSP to access, and give the demand distribution (d_i).

3   Backward Induction of the Three-Stage Game

When the complete information is available for WSPs, we analyze the static game by means of backward induction.

3.1   User Sub-game in Stage III

(1) Definition of Effective Price

We assume d_i is WSP i's demand ($i \in \{1,2\}$). If $d_i \le s_i$, all packets are served. If $d_i > s_i$, demand exceeds WSP i's system capacity, then the packets in excess are lost which are uniformly chosen among the sent ones. Hence, a packet is correctly sent with probability $q_i = \min(1, s_i/d_i)$. Here we use congestion pricing as in [15].   In congestion period, the users are charged higher to prevent the situation from deteriorating.

Definition   1.   we   define   the   effective   price   of   WSP i as $\overline{p}_i = p_i/q_i = p_i \max(1, d_i/s_i)$.

Note that p_i is the price that WSP i decided for each packet sent in its network. As a consequence, the effective price $\overline{p}_i$ denotes average price to pay for successfully sending a packet. The effective price works just like the congestion price.

(2) Users' Behavior

We assumed that users are infinitesimal, and their behavior follows Wardrop's principle [12]: users always choose the WSP with lowest effective price. If $\overline{p}_1 > \overline{p}_2$, then $d_1 = 0$, and Vice versa.   All users perceive the same effective price is $\overline{p} = \min(\overline{p}_1, \overline{p}_2)$.

We defined total demand as the total number of packets for which the willingness to pay is larger than or equal to the effective price $\overline{p}$. Hence, total demand can be represented by a function $D(\cdot)$ of the effective price, and it is assumed to be continuous and strictly decreasing,

$$D(\overline{p}) = [\alpha - \beta \overline{p}]^+, \alpha > 0, \beta > 0, \tag{4}$$

which means that the users would rather not to transmit any data when the effective price is larger than α/β .

$$d_1 + d_2 = D(\overline{p}) \tag{5}$$

(3) Users Distribution Equilibrium

In Fig.2, we show the users equilibrium characterization for specific p_1 and p_2. Here we discuss the situation when $p_1 < p_2$. Meanwhile, we give some demand functions in 4 different cases. We can get the users' distribution according to the intersection of demand function and effective price curves.

If $D \leq s_1$, the effective price that all users perceive is p_1, and all users choose WSP 1 ($d_1 = D$, $d_2 = 0$), and the case d represents this situation.

If $s_1 < D \leq s_1 p_2 / p_1$, the effective price is $p_1 d_1 / s_1$. Although the needed capacity is larger than WSP 1's system capacity, all users still access to WSP 1 ($d_1 = D$, $d_2 = 0$), since $\overline{p} < p_2$. Case c corresponds to this situation.

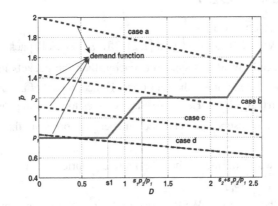

Fig. 2. Users' equilibrium demand with effective price

If $D > s_1 p_2 / p_1$, WSP 2 begins to get some demand. In case b, $s_1 p_2 / p_1 < D \leq s_1 p_2 / p_1 + s_2$, the effective price all users perceive equals to p_2, and $d_1 = s_1 p_2 / p_1$, then $d_2 = D - s_1 p_2 / p_1$. In case a, $D > s_1 p_2 / p_1 + s_2$, all WSPs are saturated. The effective price the users perceived is

$$\overline{p} = p_1 d_1 / s_1 = p_2 d_2 / s_2 \ . \tag{6}$$

The situation when $p_1 > p_2$ can be analyzed as the same as above. In special situation $p_1 = p_2$, we supposed that the demand distribution is proportioned to the system capacity, which means that

$$d_1 / s_1 = d_2 / s_2 \ . \tag{7}$$

3.2   WSP's Pricing Sub-game in Stage II

In this stage, the pricing strategies of non-cooperative WSPs are investigated. The WSPs have the information of the demand distribution as described in preceding section.

(1) Pricing Sub-game Model

The WSPs gain revenue by providing service to users, and the revenue is defined as

$$R_i(p_i, p_j) = p_i d_i \quad \text{for } i, j \in \{1, 2\}, \ i \neq j. \tag{8}$$

The pricing sub-game between WSPs is modeled as below.

Players: two WSPs.

Strategy space: WSP i can choose price p_i from the feasible set $P_i = [0, +\infty)$, $i \in \{1, 2\}$.

Payoff function: $R_i(p_i, p_j) = p_i d_i$, for $i, j \in \{1, 2\}$, $i \neq j$.

For pricing game, Nash equilibrium is a point of price strategies (p_1^*, p_2^*), each WSP maximizes its revenue assuming that the other WSP chooses the equilibrium price, and no WSP can increase its revenue by unilaterally changing its price [16], $\forall i, j \in \{1, 2\}, i \neq j$,

$$R_i(p_i^*, p_j^*) \geq R_i(p_i, p_j^*). \tag{9}$$

According to the analysis about demand distribution, we find that the payoff functions in (8) are not derivable. To determine the existence and uniqueness of Nash equilibrium is difficult for this model, therefore we analyze it numerically as [15]. The parameters are $s_1 = 1$, $s_2 = 2$, and $\alpha = 10$, $\beta = 3$.

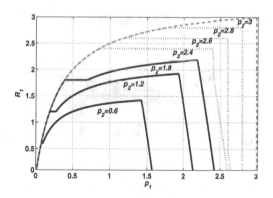

Fig. 3. Revenue of WSP 1 as a function of p_1

For given parameters as above and fixed values of p_2, we show the revenue of WSP 1 with changing p_1 in Fig.3. All the curves are the same when $p_1 > p_2 s_1 / D(p_2)$ is low enough, which means that all users choose WSP 1 as case d in Fig. 2. When $p_1 > p_2 s_1 / D(p_2)$, the curves have different characteristics.

For $p_2 \le (\alpha - s_2 - s_1)/\beta$, both WSPs are saturated at the user equilibrium as case a in Fig. 2. The revenue of WSP 1 would reach the maximum when $p_1 = (10 - s_1)/(s_2/p_2 + 3)$ as the blue curves in Fig.3.

For $(\alpha - s_2 - s_1)/\beta < p_2 \le (\alpha - s_1)/\beta$, only WSP 1 is saturated at the user equilibrium as case b in Fig. 2. The WSP 1's best price strategy p_1 is not unique, but an interval in $\left[s_1 p_2/D(p_2), s_1 p_2/(D(p_2) - s_2) \right]$ as the red curves in Fig.3.

For $(\alpha - s_1)/\beta < p_2 \le \alpha/\beta$, all users choose WSP 1 and $d_2 = 0$ at the user equilibrium as case c and d in Fig.2. The revenue of WSP 1 reaches the maximum when $p_1 = (10 - s_1)/\beta$ as the green curve in Fig. 3.

(2)   Nash Equilibrium of Pricing Sub-game

The best reply function of WSP i 's revenue is

$$BR_i(p_j) = \arg\max_{p_i \ge 0} R_i(p_i, p_j), \text{ for } i, j \in \{1, 2\}, i \ne j \quad (10)$$

The best reply is the price value which maximizes the revenue of the WSP i while the other WSP's price is fixed. Nash equilibrium can be represented by the set of points (p_1^*, p_2^*) , in which $p_1^* \in BR_1(p_2^*)$ and $p_2^* \in BR_2(p_1^*)$.

Fig.4 gives an example of best replies for non-cooperative WSPs, the model parameters we used are the same as in Fig.3. When $(\alpha - s_2 - s_1)/\beta \le p_2 \le (\alpha - s_1)/\beta$, best replies are not unique which is easy to understand from the analysis in Fig. 3. The   intersection   zones   of   best   replies   are   (0,0)   and   the   range $p_1 = p_2 \in \left[(\alpha - s_1 - s_2)/\beta, \min((\alpha - s_2)/\beta, (\alpha - s_1)/\beta) \right]$.

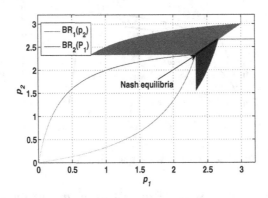

Fig. 4. Best reply curves of both WSPs

(3)   Nash Equilibrium Discussion

(0,0) is a trivial Nash equilibrium, because no WSP would set its price to be 0.

There exist infinite pricing best reply intersection points in the range $p_1 = p_2 \in \left[(\alpha - s_1 - s_2)/\beta, \min\left((\alpha - s_2)/\beta, (\alpha - s_1)/\beta\right)\right]$. In Fig.4, the solid black line represents this set of infinitely pricing intersection points. However, the intersection points $p_1 = p_2 \in ((\alpha - s_1 - s_2)/\beta, \min\left((\alpha - s_2)/\beta, (\alpha - s_1)/\beta\right)]$ correspond to the case that only one WSP is saturated while the other is not.   The unsaturated WSP i ($i \in \{1,2\}$) would like to decrease its price p_i unilaterally by a small amount to attract more users and gain more revenue. Obviously, there is no Nash equilibrium in that zone.   Both   WSPs   are   exactly   saturated   at   the   point $p_1 = p_2 = ((\alpha - s_1 - s_2)/\beta, (\alpha - s_1 - s_2)/\beta)$ and neither WSP would like to change its price unilaterally. As a result, $(p_1^*, p_2^*) = ((\alpha - s_1 - s_2)/\beta, (\alpha - s_1 - s_2)/\beta)$ is the unique Nash equilibrium of pricing sub-game that we are looking for.

Since both WSPs are saturated, then according to (4) (5) (6) (8), we get

$$R_i = \frac{\alpha p_i p_j s_i}{s_i p_j + p_i s_j + \beta p_i p_j} . \tag{11}$$

We can get that $\partial R_i / \partial p_i > 0$, R_i increases monotonously when both WSPs are in saturated range.   As the analysis of the blue curves in Fig.3 and $BR_i(p_j) = \arg\max_{p_i}(R_i)$, the best response function can be described as following. For $i, j = \{1,2\}, i \neq j$,

$$p_i^B(p_j) = \frac{\alpha - s_i}{s_j / p_j + \beta} . \tag{12}$$

Take the Nash equilibrium (p_1^*, p_2^*) into (11), the demand distribution can be presented as

$$d_i^* = \frac{\alpha p_j^* s_i}{\beta p_i^* p_j^* + p_i^* s_j + p_j^* s_i} . \tag{13}$$

From above, we can get $d_i^* = s_i$. If WSPs decide the prices according to the Nash equilibrium (p_1^*, p_2^*), leasing bandwidth can exactly satisfy the demand which means that the dynamic spectrum market reaches the market equilibrium [14].

3.3   WSP's Leasing Full Game in Stage I

(1) Leasing Full Game Model
In the first stage (full game leader), WSPs have to decide the leasing amount of the spectrum. Taking the demand distribution (d_1^*, d_2^*) in stage III and pricing strategy (p_1^*, p_2^*) in stage II into consideration, we give the leasing bandwidth decision (b_1, b_2) to maximize the WSPs' profits.

The WSP i's profit is defined as: $\forall i,j \in \{1,2\}, i \neq j$,

$$\pi_i(b_i, b_j) = R_i(k_i b_i, k_j b_j) - b_i C(b_i + b_j). \tag{14}$$

The leasing game can be modeled as follows.

Players: two WSPs.

Strategy space: WSP i can choose bandwidth amount b_i from the feasible set $b_i = [0, +\infty)$, $i \in \{1,2\}$. We assume that the bandwidth provided by spectrum broker is enough.

Payoff function: $\pi_i(p_i, p_j)$, for $i,j \in \{1,2\}$, $i \neq j$.

(2) Nash equilibrium of leasing full game

As the payoff function is derivable, Nash equilibrium of the leasing game exists and can be acquired through solving the function $\partial \pi_i / \partial b_i = 0$, for $i \in \{1,2\}$, $i \neq j$,

$$\pi_i = R_i(k_1 b_1, k_2 b_2) - b_i C(b_1 + b_2),$$

$$\frac{\partial \pi_i}{\partial b_i} = \left(\alpha k_i - 2k_i^2 b_i - k_i k_j b_j\right)\big/\beta - 2Cb_i - Cb_j = 0.$$

The best response function can be written as

$$b_i^B(b_j) = \frac{\alpha k_i - k_i k_j b_j - \beta C b_j}{2k_i^2 + 2\beta C} \tag{15}$$

Set $m = k_1 k_2 + \beta C$, $n = 2k_1^2 + 2\beta C$, $l = 2k_2^2 + 2\beta C$, we can get the unique Nash equilibrium as $\left(b_1^*, b_2^*\right)$.

$$b_1^* = \frac{\alpha l k_1 - \alpha m k_2}{nl - m^2} \tag{16}$$

$$b_2^* = \frac{\alpha n k_2 - \alpha m k_1}{nl - m^2} \tag{17}$$

4   Dynamic Game of WSPs

In section 3, WSPs are assumed to have the complete information about the strategies and payoff functions for both WSPs. Hence WSPs can make simultaneous decisions, and the three-stage game is static. However, the situation is different in reality. The strategies and payoff functions of the other WSP are not fully available. WSP can only observe each other's history of strategies, and we present dynamic game model for the competitive WSPs. We investigate how WSPs interact in such a dynamic game, and give an iterative algorithm to achieve its dynamic equilibrium. As in [9], we assume that the pricing sub-game at the users' side is a short term dynamic game, while leasing game at the spectrum broker's side is a long term dynamic game. This is because that these two competitions are done separately. We assume the following discussions are in the condition where users' market is stable.

4.1   Short Term Pricing Dynamic Game

With incomplete information, current decision of the opponent's pricing strategy is not available. We use the history record of the WSP j to decide the price of WSP i based on the best response function in (12). We give the pricing dynamic game as

$$p_i(t) = p_i^B\left(p_j(t-1)\right) \text{ for } i, j \in \{1, 2\}, i \neq j. \tag{18}$$

We describe the iterative algorithm of the pricing dynamic game as below.

Step 1. Initially $t = 0$, WSPs set prices as $p_i(0)$, $p_j(0)$.

Step 2. In each iteration $t > 0$, WSPs update their prices according to (18).

Step 3. Stop until the criteria is met. The criteria can be the maximum number of iteration or the difference between the WSP i's prices of two consecutive iterations is less than a predefined threshold.

Theorem 1: Given leasing bandwidth, pricing dynamic game converges to the Nash equilibrium point and it is stable.

Proof: It is obvious that the best response function in (12) is monotonous and bounded, so the pricing dynamic game is convergent. For the stable point, it satisfies $p_i = p_i^B(p_j)$, which is just the Nash equilibrium of pricing sub-game.

4.2   Long Term Leasing Dynamic Game

Leasing dynamic game is relative long term with respect to pricing dynamic game. We assume that leasing strategy only updates after pricing dynamic game finished.

According to (18), we give the leasing dynamic game as

$$b_i(T) = \frac{\alpha k_i - \left(k_i k_j + \beta C\right) b_j(T-1)}{2k_i^2 + 2\beta C}. \tag{19}$$

Equation (15) has the same characteristic as equation (12), so the long term leasing dynamic game also converges to the Nash equilibrium which has the same reason as short term pricing dynamic game. We can describe the leasing dynamic game's iterative algorithm as below.

Step 1. Initially $T = 0$, WSPs set leasing bandwidth $b_i(0), i \in \{1, 2\}$. Adjust the prices according to the short term pricing dynamic game and acquire the prices $p_i(0)$ ($i \in \{1, 2\}$) which meet the criteria.

Step 2. In each iteration $T > 0$, WSPs update their leasing bandwidth according to (19). $p_i(T)$ ($i \in \{1, 2\}$) can be obtained by short term pricing dynamic game.

Step 3. Stop until the criteria are met. The definition of stopping criteria is similar to previous part.

5   Simulation Results

(1) Static Game of Non-cooperative WSPs

The model parameters are $C = 1$, $\alpha = 10$, $\beta = 3$. Nash equilibrium of pricing sub-game is only influenced by the total leasing bandwidth given the particular spectrum efficiency of the WSPs. In Fig.5, it shows that the pricing sub-game's Nash equilibrium decreases with the total leasing bandwidth in linear relation. Fig.6 shows that spectrum efficiency influences the WSP's leasing strategy. We can see that WSP with bigger spectrum efficiency gets more bandwidth. Fig.7 shows that for given k_1, WSPs' leasing bandwidth and profits change as k_2 increases. The WSP 2's leasing bandwidth firstly increases as k_2 grows because the WSP with bigger spectrum efficiency gets more bandwidth, and then it decreases because as spectrum efficiency increase the WSP needs less bandwidth to fulfill the demand. The profit of WSP 2 increases as k_2 grows, while the profit of WSP 1 decreases. Hence with the same objective to maximize the profit, every WSP will have the incentive to promote its own spectrum efficiency.

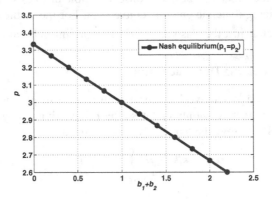

Fig. 5. Nash equilibrium of pricing with different leasing bandwidth

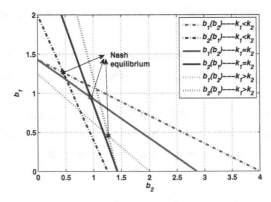

Fig. 6. Nash equilibrium of leasing with different spectrum efficiency

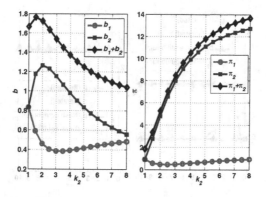

Fig. 7. With given $k_1 = 1$, the leasing bandwidth and profit varies with k_2

(2) Dynamic Game of Non-cooperative WSPs

We present some numerical results for the performance in dynamic spectrum market, and study the characteristic of the dynamic game. We set $s_1 = 1$, $s_2 = 2$, $\alpha = 10$, $\beta = 3$ in Fig.8 and $C = 1$, $k_1 = 1$, $k_2 = 2$, $\alpha = 10$, $\beta = 3$ in Fig.9.

For short term price adjustment in Fig.8, given the initial small value of prices, we can see that the iterative algorithm converges to the pricing Nash equilibrium very quickly. We also simulate the long term bandwidth adjustment in Fig.9, the convergence of leasing dynamic game is rather quick and it converges to the full game Nash equilibrium. Fig.9 also shows the corresponding prices at each stable point. The simulations show that the dynamic games converge to Nash equilibria.

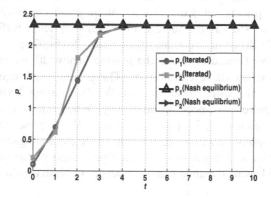

Fig. 8. Short term pricing dynamic game

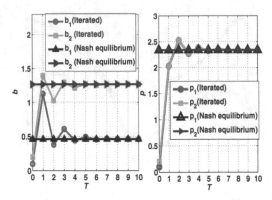

Fig. 9. Long term leasing dynamic game

6   Conclusion

In this paper, we use a three-stage game to model the interactions between competitive WSPs and users in dynamic spectrum leasing. The users choose WSP by taking price and QoS into considerations. The pricing sub-game has a unique Nash equilibrium. The pricing Nash equilibrium of WSPs is the same even when they lease different amount of bandwidth and have different spectrum efficiencies. Interestingly, with the pricing Nash equilibrium, the demand equals to the leasing bandwidth which means that the game reaches the market stable equilibrium. The pricing Nash equilibrium is only dependent on the total leasing bandwidth of WSPs. Leasing Nash equilibrium is unique and dependent on the spectrum efficiency. When information is incomplete, WSPs interact with each other in a dynamic game. We use the iterative algorithm based on the best response function as a solution to In this paper, we use a three-stage game to model the interactions between competitive WSPs and users in dynamic spectrum leasing. The users choose WSP by taking price and QoS into considerations. The pricing sub-game has a unique Nash equilibrium. The pricing Nash equilibrium of WSPs is the same even when they lease different amount of bandwidth and have different spectrum efficiencies. Interestingly, with the pricing Nash equilibrium, the demand equals to the leasing bandwidth which means that the game reaches the market stable equilibrium. The pricing Nash equilibrium is only dependent on the total leasing bandwidth of WSPs. Leasing Nash equilibrium is unique and dependent on the spectrum efficiency. When information is incomplete, WSPs interact with each other in a dynamic game. We use the iterative algorithm based on the best response function as a solution to the dynamic game. The short term pricing dynamic game converges to the Nash equilibrium of the pricing sub-game, while the long term leasing dynamic game converges to Nash equilibrium of the static full game.

There are many aspects to extend our results in this paper. For example, we can introduce the heterogeneous into WSPs for providing different services or into users with different QoS requirements in future works.

Acknowledgments. This work was supported by the National Basic Research Program under Grant No. 2009CB320402.

References

1. FCC Spectrum Policy Task Force: Report of the Spectrum Efficiency Working Group (2002), http://www.fcc.gov/sptf/reports.html
2. McHenry, M.A., McCloskey, D., Roberson, D.A., MacDonald, J.T.: Spectrum Occupancy Measurements: Chicago, Illinois, Shared Spectrum Company, Technology Report, November 16-18 (2005)
3. Chapin, J.M., Lehr, W.H.: The Path to Market Success for Dynamic Spectrum Access Technology. IEEE Communications Magazine 45(5), 96–103 (2007)
4. Zhu, J., Liu, K.J.R.: Cognitive Radios for Dynamic Spectrum Access-Dynamic Spectrum Sharing: A Game Theoretical Overview. IEEE Communications Magazine 45(5), 88–94 (2007)
5. Jayaweera, S.K., Li, T.: Dynamic Spectrum Leasing in Cognitive Radio Networks via Primary-Secondary User Power Control Games. IEEE Trans. on Wireless Communications 8(6), 3300–3310 (2009)
6. Chapin, J.M., Lehr, W.H.L.: Time-Limited Leases in Radio Systems. IEEE Communications Magazine 45(6), 76–78 (2007)
7. Xing, Y., Chandramouli, R., Cordeiro, C.M.: Price Dynamics in Competitive Agile Spectrum Access Markets. IEEE JSAC 25(3), 613–621 (2007)
8. Niyato, D., Hossain, E.: Competitive Pricing in Heterogeneous Wireless Access Networks: Issues and Approaches. IEEE Network 22(6), 4–11 (2008)
9. Jia, J., Zhang, Q.: Competitions and Dynamics of Duopoly Wireless Service Providers in Dynamic Spectrum Market. In: ACM MobiHoc 2008, pp. 313–322. ACM, New York (2008)
10. Duan, L.J., Huang, J.W., Shou, B.Y.: Competition with Dynamic Spectrum Leasing. In: IEEE Symposium on New Frontiers in Dynamic Spectrum, pp. 1–11. IEEE Press, New York (2010)
11. Chen, S., Mulgrew, B., Grant, P.M.: A Clustering Technique for Digital Communications Channel Equalization Using Radial Basis Function Networks. IEEE Trans. Neural Networks 4, 570–578 (1993)
12. Wardrop, J.: Some Theoretical Aspects of Road Traffic Research. Proceedings of the Institute of Civil Engineers 1, 325–378 (1957)
13. Xue, Y., Li, B., Nahrstedt, K.: Optimal Resource Allocation in Wireless Ad Hoc Networks: A Price based Approach. IEEE Trans. Mobile Computing 5(4), 347–364 (2006)
14. Niyato, D., Hossain, E.: A Game-theoretic Approach to Competitive Spectrum Sharing in Cognitive Radio Networks,". In: IEEE WCNC 2007, pp. 16–20. IEEE Press, New York (2007)
15. Maille, P., Tuffin, B.: Price War with Partial Spectrum Sharing for Competitive Wireless Service Providers. In: IEEE GLOBECOM 2009, pp. 1–6. IEEE Press, New York (2009)
16. Osborne, Rubenstein A.: A Course on Game Theory. MIT Press (1994)

LRD Traffic Predicting Based on ARMA

Bo Gao[1], Qinyu Zhang[1], and Naitong Zhang[2]

[1] Shenzhen Graduate School, Harbin Institute of Technology.
Shenzhen 518055, China
[2] School of Electronics and Information Engineering,
Harbin Institute of Technology. Harbin 150001, China
gaobo@hitsz.edu.cn, {zqy,ntzhang}@hit.edu.cn

Abstract. The prediction of long range dependence (LRD) is the critical problem in network traffic. The traditional algorithms, such as Markov model and ON/OFF model, may provide high computation cost and low precision. In this study, a novel method based on empirical mode decomposition (EMD) and ARMA model was proposed. The results show that EMD could offer the function of canceling the LRD in traffic data. After transforming LRD to SRD (short range dependence) by EMD processing, the LRD traffic data could be predicted with high accuracy and low complexity by ARMA model. Meanwhile, the results indicate the usefulness of EMD in the applications of network traffic prediction.

Keywords: LRD, EMD, ARMA, Predicting.

1   Introduction

The amount of network traffic increases day and day with the rapid development of the Internet. The LRD (long range dependence) characteristic of network traffic leads to larger packet loss rate and queuing delay in practice than theoretic analysis according to traditional queuing theory. Obviously, LRD property of network traffic should be studied deeply in order to insure the QoS of network. Unfortunately, the SRD (short range dependence) model can not capture the LRD characteristic which is one trait in network traffic. In order to predict the network traffic accurately, researchers studied mainly in two aspects: the first one was using SRD model to fit LRD traffic, but the results were not ideal; the second was trying to discover some LRD model to capture the network traffic LRD characteristics, but the time and space complexity of related algorithm was high.

The SRD models that are mainly related to Markov and regress model, have been already confirmed that they fit the LRD network traffic badly [1-4]. The LRD model included FARIMA (fractal ARIMA) and FBM model (Fractal Brownian Motion), etc. FARIMA model in [5] was used to structure LRD sequence and proved that this kind of model could fit the LRD network traffic efficiently by analyzing the autocorrelation function of sequence generated by model itself. Some scholars adopted other complex models, such as multi-fractal wavelet, wavelet neural network

P. Ren et al. (Eds.): WICON 2011, LNICST 98, pp. 472–479, 2012.

[6-8] and chaos model [9]. Although all of these models had good precision, the algorithm complexity was high. Besides those statistical model mentioned, ON/OFF model [4] that is one kind of physical model can be applied to predict LRD sequence and has specific physical meaning, nevertheless the precision and flexibility of the physical model is worse than statistical one. Researchers proposed methods that could transfer LRD sequence into SRD. Reference [6] figured that the multi-fractal model could obtain SRD traffic from LRD. It means that we can adopt SRD model to predict LRD which is hardly analyzed directly with SRD linear model. Furthermore, reference [7] and [8] found the wavelet transform coefficients of FBM and FGN had SRD property in the same scales, instead of LRD.

This paper presents a method base on EMD and ARMA which can transfer the LRD sequences into SRD sequences, then model and predict the LRD traffic. We proved the theory in our former paper [10] and presented the simulation results. In this paper we continued studying the prediction about those IMF components decomposed by EMD. The paper is organized as follows. In Section 2, we summarize the basic definition of LRD, EMD and ARMA model. Then the simulation results are given in Section 3, but we find IMF1 prediction results are not accurate. Then Section 4 presents a method to promote IMF1 prediction accuracy. Section 5 concludes the paper.

2   EMD and ARMA

2.1   LRD and Empirical Mode Decomposition

Firstly, let us have a look at the definition of LRD. Assume that there exists a stationary stochastic process $\{X(t), t > 0\}$ with the autocorrelation function expressed as $r(\tau)$. If $\int r(\tau)d\tau = \infty$, that means, the autocorrelation function is non-integrable, then $\{X(t), t > 0\}$ is an LRD process. Thus we can know the present data are related to all of historical data against SRD process which satisfies $\int r(\tau)d\tau < \infty$.

Then we talk about the definition and characteristic of EMD. EMD is used to decompose the original signal to a number of intrinsic mode functions (IMF) in Hilbert-Huang transform (HHT) [11]. The EMD method is a necessary pre-processing before signals are transformed by the Hilbert transform. It will separate the data into a collection of IMFs defined as the functions satisfying the following conditions: (a) in the whole data set, the number of extrema and the number of zero-crossing must either equal or differ at most by one, and (b) at any point, the mean value of the envelope defined by the local maxima and the envelope defined by the local minima is zero.

With above definition, we can decompose any function, for example $x(t)$, as follows: Identify all of the local extrema, and then connect all the local maxima by a cubic spline line as the upper envelope. Repeat the procedure for the local minima to produce the lower envelope. The upper and lower envelopes should cover all the data between them. The mean of the upper and lower envelopes is designated as $m(t)$, and the difference between the data and $m(t)$ is $h(t) = x(t) - m(t)$. If $h(t)$ satisfies IMF condition, we obtain the first IMF (named IMF1), or we see $h(t)$ as $x(t)$ and repeat the process above until:

$$\left\{\sum_{t=0}^{T}\frac{\left[h_{1,k-1}(t)-h_{1,k}(t)\right]^{2}}{h_{1,k-1}(t)^{2}}\right\}^{\frac{1}{2}}<0.1 \tag{1}$$

In (1), $h_{1,k}(t)$ means the difference value between $x(t)$ and the mean of envelops after k times iterations.

Then, we separate the first IMF designated as $C_{1}(t)$ from the rest of the signal by

$$l(t)=x(t)-C_{1}(t) \tag{2}$$

Treat $l(t)$ as the new data and subjected to the same sifting process as described above. The procedure can be repeated to obtain all the subsequent and finally we have

$$x(t)=\sum_{i=1}^{n}C_{i}(t)+r(t) \tag{3}$$

In [10], we proved that the LRD data did not possess LRD property after EMD and the computer simulation results also showed that every IMF component was SRD. Therefore, the LRD model can be replaced by some SRD model which is relatively simple, such as ARMA.

2.2   ARMA Model

ARMA is a famous SRD model which is widely applied in the field of data modeling and predicting. Its whole name is autoregressive moving average and the definition is as follows: assume that $\{X(n), n = 0, \pm1, \pm2, \dots\}$ is one stationary process with mean zero and $\xi(n)$ is a white noise process with variance σ, then for any n, if

$$X(n)-\phi_{1}X(n-1)-\cdots-\phi_{p}X(n-p)=\xi(n)-\theta_{1}\xi(n-1)-\cdots-\theta_{q}\xi(n-q) \tag{4}$$

then we call that $X(n)$ is a ARMA process or ARMA(p, q). In (4), the parameters ϕ, θ and σ need to be estimated according to some known data. To identify the value of p and q, we apply the AIC criterion which was proposed by H. Akaike [13] in 1974. The AIC function is

$$\text{AIC}=\ln\hat{\sigma}+\frac{2\cdot(p+q+1)}{N} \tag{5}$$

where $\hat{\sigma}$ is the estimation of $\xi(n)$'s variance σ and N is the number of observation data samples. Choose p and q from some certain range (p and q are both integer), such as the interval $(0, \ln N)$, to make AIC minimum, thus we can obtain the order of ARMA model. Then use the inverse function method [14] to estimate other parameters.

3   Prediction by Using ARMA

According to our research results in [10], we could apply ARMA to predict the LRD data which may be transformed to a series of SRD data. The simulation environment we adopt is Intel Pentium 4 CPU 2.8G Hz, two pieces of 512M memory, Matlab 7.0 and Microsoft Windows XP Professional SP2.

The LRD data are selected from Bellcore in 1989 named BC-pOct89 [12] which are the same with [10]. In [10] we decomposed the data to 8 IMFs every of which has 450 data. Now use ARMA to model and predict these 8 IMFs one by one in this paper. For each IMF component, select first 300 data as the training data to estimate parameters and establish the model, and the other 150 data are used to prediction process for detecting the difference between the forecast value and the actual one. The MSE (mean squared error) is applied to evaluate the result of predictions. Assume the value of MSE is M, then we have:

$$M = \frac{1}{n} \sum_{i=1}^{n} \left[\hat{x}(i) - x(i) \right]^2 \tag{6}$$

In (6), n is the number of traffic data, $\hat{x}(i)$ is the ith prediction value and $x(i)$ is the ith actual traffic data value. After the research we found that each forecast error from IMF2 to IMF8 is much lower than the error of IMF1 and with the IMF order increasing all of the MSEs decay nearly at an exponential speed. Fig. 1 shows the prediction results.

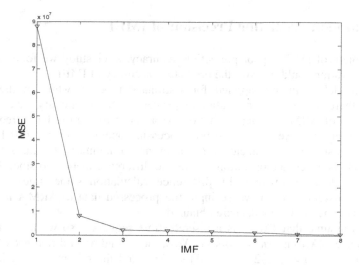

Fig. 1. The MSE of each IMF component after ARMA

We add the IMF components from IMF2 to IMF8 as a whole body to predict because of their higher accuracy, as a result, not only the number of our models is reduced, but also the prediction efficiency is raised. Fig. 2 is the prediction result of IMF1 and Fig. 3 is the prediction result of the sum of IMF2 to IMF8.

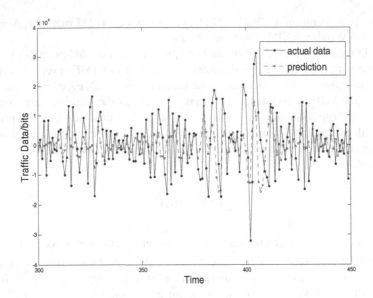

Fig. 2. IMF1 and its prediction

4   Promotion Predicting Precision of IMF1

For the problem of IMF1's poor prediction accuracy, after study we found that the difference operation could improve the prediction accuracy of IMF1.

ARMA model is mainly applied for stationary process, while in the actual engineering there are so many non-stationary processes. Non-stationary data will lead to the increase of ARMA model prediction error. Therefore, in order to reduce the IMF1 prediction error, we should add pre-processing operation on the IMF1 data to reduce its non-stationary characteristic. There are a number of data smoothing methods, such as difference operation, so we use difference method to smooth IMF1. Firstly, IMF1 data are operated by difference calculation some times, until the precision is satisfying. Secondly, we input the processed data to ARMA model for prediction, then the predicting data are obtained.

We could assume that $\{X(n)\}$ is a discrete time sequence, so we know the first order difference of $X(n)$ is $Y(n) = X(n+1) - X(n)$, the second order difference of $X(n)$ is $Z(n) = Y(n+1) - Y(n) = X(n+2) - 2X(n+1) + X(n)$, and the rest may be deduced by analogy. After the difference calculation, the new sequence's non-stationary characteristic can be inhibited. However, the amplitude of the new sequence has been changed, as a result, MSE can not be able to measure the prediction performance. Therefore, we select NMSE (Normalized Mean Squared Error) to measure the prediction performance for IMF1 components.

If the value of NMSE is N, then

$$N = \frac{1}{\hat{\sigma}n} \sum_{i=1}^{n} \left[\hat{x}(i) - x(i) \right]^2 \tag{7}$$

where $\hat{\sigma}$ is expressed to variance of prediction data, n is the number of traffic data, $\hat{x}(i)$ is the ith prediction value and $x(i)$ is the ith actual traffic data value. NMSE is the normalized MSE, so it can eliminate the impact of forecast errors with amplitude changing.

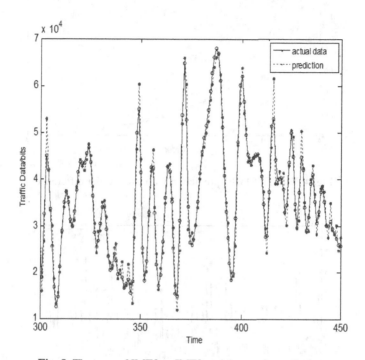

Fig. 3. The sum of IMF2 to IMF8 and the sum's prediction

Fig. 4 is the NMSEs of ARMA predicting by using 0-5th order difference operation. We can know that with the increase of difference order, the value of NMSE decreases at a fast speed, like exponential function. This means that difference plays a great role in promotion the IMF1 prediction accuracy and the effect is obvious. But the complexity of this method increases system overhead. In practice, by considering the time cost of model building and requirement of prediction accuracy, people should select the proper difference order to make the prediction system overall optimal. To illustrate feasibility of our proposal method, we choose 5th-order difference operation to process the traffic data. The prediction results obtained is shown in Fig. 5, from which we can see that the difference of the prediction results and the true value is very small. Table 1 is NMSE value of 0-5th order difference data prediction.

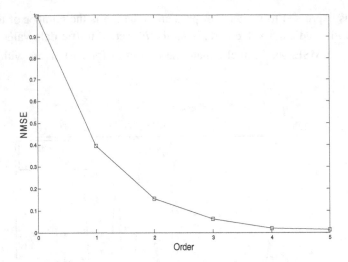

Fig. 4. NMSE of IMF1 prediction with every order difference

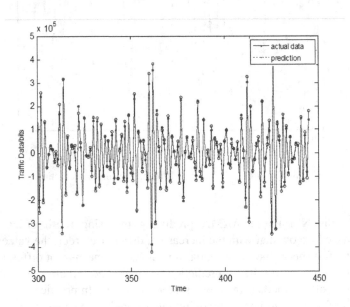

Fig. 5. IMF1 5th order difference and its prediction

Table 1. NMSE of IMF1 after 0-5th order difference

Order	0	1	2	3	4	5
NMSE	0.9958	0.3951	0.1543	0.0612	0.0191	0.0136

5   Conclusion

In this study, for the problem of the high complexity and the poor prediction accuracy of LRD traffic prediction, we research and propose one method which could be used in predicting LRD traffic data. The theoretical results indicate that LRD process decomposed by the EMD performs a SRD characteristic in each IMF component. Thus, some LRD model can be replaced by the simple models, such as ARMA, which could reduces the complexity of the model. The simulation results showed that IMF2~IMF8 components prediction had higher accuracy than IMF1 component and choosing the appropriate difference order could eliminate the non-stationary characteristic of IMF1 component. Then the accuracy of IMF1 component prediction was significantly improved.

Acknowledgments. This research was supported in part by the National Nature Science Foundation of China (NFSC) under grant No. 60672150 and 60702034.

References

1. Ji, Q.J.: Can Multifractal Traffic Burstiness be Approximated by Markov Modulated Poisson Processes? In: Proceedings 12th IEEE International Conference on Networks, pp. 26–30 (2004)
2. Shahram, S.H., Tho, L.N.: MMPP Modeling of Aggregated ATM Traffic. Electrical and Computer Engineering. In: IEEE Canadian Conference, Canada, pp. 129–132 (1998)
3. Zhou, B.X., Yao, Z.Q.: A Method to Stabilize Network Traffic. Journal on Communications 25(8), 14–23 (2004)
4. Rosario, G.G., Stefano, G., Marco, I., Michele, P.: On the Implications of the OFF Periods Distribution in Two-State Traffic Models. IEEE Communications Letters 3, 220–222 (1999)
5. Liu, J.K., Shu, Y.T., Zhang, L.F., et al.: Traffic Modeling Based on FARIMA Models. Electrical and Computer Engineering. In: IEEE Canadian Conference, Canada, pp. 162–167 (1999)
6. Rudolf, H.R., Matthew, S.C., Vinay, J.R., Richard, G.B.: A Multifractal Wavelet Model with Application to Network Traffic. IEEE Transactions on Information Theory 45, 992–1018 (1999)
7. Qigang, Z., Xuming, F., Qunzhan, L., Zhengyou, H.: WNN-Based NGN Traffic Prediction. In: Proceedings Autonomous Decentralized Systems, pp. 230–234 (2005)
8. Ahmad, B., Mohammad, F.A.: Generalized Wavelet Neuro-Fuzzy Model and its Application in Time Series Forecasting. In: International Symposium on Evolving Fuzzy Systems, pp. 253–258 (2006)
9. Mikio, H., Gang, W., Mitsuhiko, M.: Applications of Nonlinear Prediction Methods to the Internet Traffic. In: Proceedings IEEE International Symposium on Circuits and Systems, pp. 169–172 (2001)
10. Bo, G., Qinyu, Z., Yongsheng, L., Naitong, Z.: One Method from LRD to SRD. In: IEEE Wireless Communications, Networking and Mobile Computing (WiCOM 2009), Beijing, China, pp. 1–4 (2009)
11. Huang, N.E., Shen, Z., Long, S.R.: The Empirical Mode Decomposition and the Hilbert Spectrum for Nonlinear and Non-Stationary Time Series Analysis. Proc. Royal. Soc. London A 454, 903–995 (1998)
12. Bellcore Lab, http://ita.ee.lbl.gov/html/traces.html
13. Akaike, H.: A New Look at the Statistical Identification Model. IEEE Trans. on Automatic Control 19(6), 716–723 (1974)
14. Liu, J.K., Wang, G.S.: Applied Stochastic Processes. Science Press, Beijing (2004)

The Master-Slave Stochastic Knapsack Modelling for Fully Dynamic Spectrum Allocation

Sihai Zhang[1,2], Fei Yang[1], and Wuyang Zhou[1]

[1] Wireless Information Network Lab.,
Department of Electronic Engineering and Information Science,
University of Science and Technology of China, Hefei, Anhui, China, 230026
[2] Key Laboratory of Wireless Sensor Network & Communication,
Shanghai Institute of Microsystem and Information Technology,
Chinese Academy of Sciences865 Changning Road, Shanghai, China, 200050
{shzhang,wyzhou}@ustc.edu.cn, genyang@mail.ustc.edu.cn

Abstract. Scarcity problem of radio spectrum resource stimulates the research on cognitive radio technology, in which dynamic spectrum allocation attracts lots of attention. For higher access efficiency in cognitive radio context, we suggest a fully dynamic resource allocation scheme for primary and secondary users, which is modelled by a master-slave stochastic knapsack process. Equilibrium behavior is analyzed, and expressions of blocking probability of both slave and master classes are derived as performance criterion and verified by numeric simulation, as well as forced termination probability of the secondary users. Compared to traditional opportunistic spectrum access (OSA), which can be regarded as half dynamic, our scheme leads to less termination events for the slaves while keeping the same behavior for the master class, promoting the system access performance.

Keywords: Blocking, forced termination probability, master-slave stochastic knapsack, full dynamic spectrum allocation, cognitive radio.

1 Introduction

Modern technology of wireless communications faces a severe problem of spectrum scarcity. New technique such as cognitive radio (CR) is involved to make the spectrum management more flexible [1], compared to traditional allocation scheme which leads to inefficient utilization [2]. In a CR system, there are two classes of users, called primary user (PU) and secondary user (SU). The former are licensed users who have preemption over the latter who are not. With the admission of SUs when PUs do not make full use of the spectrum, more customers may be served with the same bandwidth, and allocation becomes more efficient. In [3][4], brief overviews on CR were introduced, where some major challenges were proposed as well, among which is the forced termination of SU when PU seizes its channel.

P. Ren et al. (Eds.): WICON 2011, LNICST 98, pp. 480–489, 2012.

Generally speaking there are two kinds of processing for the SU's forced termination. Some literatures [5][6] consider a handoff (or called handover) method, in which terminated SU is transferred to another idle channel and continues its transmission. It may be a little ideal as the transferring operation is not specified, handoff duration are ignored, and transferring is regarded surely successful. It has no doubt that handoff scheme needs complicated implementation for SU terminals. In a handoff-free manner [5][6][7], terminated SUs are just dropped. It may be suitable for the best-effort services, and asks for no additional modification to original devices. The two methods have the same termination probability, since newcome PU have not attempted to evade the channels occupied by SUs. This may be not reasonable, as there are still idle channels PU can access to, termination should have been evitable.

In the above schemes, PUs' privileges emerge in two types: when the spectrum is not all-occupied, a new PU may seize a channel from a SU if it just chooses that SU's channel; or when the spectrum is exhausted, the new PU drives away a SU if there is SU in the system. However, in this paper, we propose a novel "fully" dynamic scheme for the CR access process, which allows PUs only the second privilege. PUs monitor channels and prevent to interrupt SUs as long as the channels are not exhausted. Thus, it can be expected to have advantages over the half dynamic scheme, for it avoids unnecessary terminations of SUs. We modelled the access procedure as a stochastic knapsack of masters and slaves, where master represents for PU, and slave for SU. Major analysis includes:

- An elaborate transition diagram for the master-slave knapsack process is proposed, as well as equilibrium analysis. Blocking probability is directly derived from equilibrium distribution for both master and slave classes.
- Probability of forced termination of SUs is also derived analytically, which is not as obvious as the blocking case. It is validated by the simulation results.

Our analysis is especially important to the termination behavior of SUs, which reveals some characteristic of fully dynamic spectrum allocation, and may help to develop effective access policy for cognitive radio system.

The rest of this paper is organized as follows. In Section 2 some related works are reviewed in Section 2. We model the full dynamic spectrum allocation problem with a master-slave stochastic knapsack process, and the equilibrium state transition is given in Section 3. Analytic result of blocking and termination probability is derived in Section 4. Section 4 gives numerical results and related discussions, and the conclusion is made in Section 5.

2   Related Work

Spectrum sensing is the basis and precondition for cognitive radio and much work have been done, from sensing architecture [8], distributed sensing scheme [9] and capacity limits of cognitive radio [10]. Although there is no efficient and viable solution to this problem up to now, we may expect such spectrum sensing will in the future work efficiently.

Loss model is first studied systematically by the Denmark mathematician and engineer A.K. Erlang during 1909-1920 who published a series of papers to solve basic problems in this telephone communication field using probabilistic theory [11]. The Erlang loss model is the simplest of all loss systems, consisting of a collection of resources, for example, C circuits, to which calls, each with an associated *holdingtime* and *class*, arrive at random instances. An arriving call can either be admitted into the system or blocked and lost [12].

As a mathematical model to such problem in dynamic spectrum allocation for wireless communication, the dynamic and random *knapsack* model has been well-studied [13,14,15]: "Dynamic" requests for the resources arrive in time according to a stochastic process, while "Random" means the demands for the resource and their associated rewards are random and unknown until their arrival.

As for the performance analysis in the coexistence of primary and secondary communication networks, Watanabe considers the cognitive radio performance when coexisting with primary communication system and shows that cognitive radio technology can not avoid the interference to primary system [16]. J. Neel proposes techniques to model and analyze the interactions of cognitive radio whose purpose is to improve the design of cognitive radio and distributed radio resource management algorithms[17].

Recently, performance analysis on the secondary user's behavior includes the cognitive research in spectrum access with optimal channel reservation[18], cognitive Ad Hoc networks[7], and cognitive radio network[19,20]. The contribution of this paper is to propose a novel fully dynamic spectrum access patter and derive the solutions using Markov chain state transition equations, which differs from current work.

3   System Model

Consider a CR system model in which there are N parallel channels shared by primary and secondary users. We use terms "master" and "slave" to denote primary user and secondary user. A user (either master or slave) asks for a channel if it tries to access the system spectrum. Poisson processes with rates λ_m λ_s are assumed for traffic generation of master and slave class, and their service durations distribute exponentially with expectation $1/\mu_m$ and $1/\mu_s$, respectively. μ_m, μ_s are means of service rate for master and slave.

The access manner is illustrated in Fig.1. It is modelled as a knapsack of masters and slaves. Masters have higher priority over slaves. That is, when the channels are all busy, an arrival of slave is just rejected; only if all channels are occupied by masters, new master is excluded from the spectrum; otherwise it seizes a channel from a slave (which may be picked out randomly or based on some rules, making no difference to our analysis). Masters do not seize channels from slaves as long as idle channels exist, which avoids some unnecessary termination events of the slave class. This assumption does not impair masters' performance of access at all (it is verified later), and intuitively reduces slaves' blocking probability.

System state is defined as (n_m, n_s), in which n_m denotes current number of masters, and n_s slaves. The feasible state set is:

$$S = \{(n_m, n_s) | n_m \geq 0, n_s \geq 0, n_m + n_s \leq N\}, \tag{1}$$

and $p(n_m, n_s)$ is used to denote the probability of state (n_m, n_s).

The set of full states (blocking) is

$$S_b = \{(n_m, n_s) | n_m + n_s = N\}, \tag{2}$$

as well as the set of states that slave termination may happen:

$$S_t = \{(n_m, n_s) | n_s > 0, n_m + n_s = N\}. \tag{3}$$

These sets are useful when discussing blocking and termination probabilities.

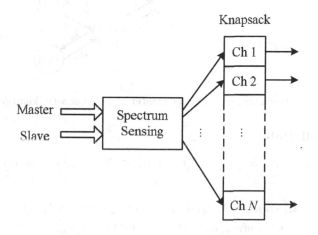

Fig. 1. System model for master and slave knapsack

4   Equilibrium State Transition Analysis

The knapsack manner leads to a 2-Dimension state transition diagram as shown in Fig. 2. Transitions marked by red dash lines are the differences from original stochastic knapsack without master-slave priority [12]. The red dotted arrow lines indicate the system behaviors when a master comes and knapsack is in its full state. Due to these transitions, the entire problem is no longer a reversible Markov process, and simple detailed balance conditions never stand. Hence solution to equilibrium distribution becomes complex to calculate the flow conservation equations for each state:

$$\sum_{v \in S} [p(v) \cdot t_{v,u}] - p(u) \cdot \sum_{v \in S} t_{u,v} = 0, \quad \forall u \in S, \tag{4}$$

where $t_{u,v}$ is the transition rate from state u to v .

The linear equations form a system of linear equations, with respect to $(N + 1)(N + 2)/2$ variables of equilibrium distribution. For details, these equations are categorized as following:

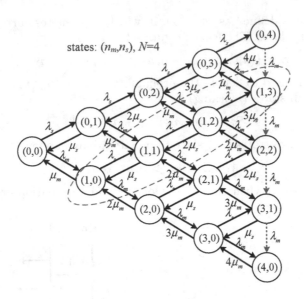

Fig. 2. States transition diagram for master-slave stochastic knapsack model

4.1   Non-full State

The states are $S \setminus S_b = \{(n_m, n_s) | n_m + n_s < N\}$. The corresponding balance equations are:

$$\lambda_m \cdot p(n_m - 1, n_s) + (n_m + 1)\mu_m \cdot p(n_m + 1, n_s)$$
$$+\lambda_s \cdot p(n_m, n_s - 1) + (n_s + 1)\mu_s \cdot p(n_m, n_s + 1)$$
$$-(\lambda_m + \lambda_s + n_m\mu_m + n_s\mu_s) \cdot p(n_m, n_s) = 0$$

4.2   Full State

The states are $S_b = \{(n_m, n_s) | n_m + n_s = N\}$. The corresponding balance equations are:

$$\lambda_m \cdot p(n_m - 1, n_s) + \lambda_m \cdot p(n_m - 1, n_s + 1) + \lambda_s \cdot p(n_m, n_s - 1)$$
$$-(\lambda_m + \lambda_s + n_m\mu_m + n_s\mu_s) \cdot p(n_m, n_s) = 0$$

5   Performance Analysis

5.1   Blocking Probability

Blocking probability of the master class is the probability that all N channels are occupied by master, which is:

$$P_b^m = \Pr(n_m = N) = p(N, 0). \tag{5}$$

Slaves' blocking events correspond to situations that channels are full, either with masters or slaves. So the blocking behavior of slave class is:

$$P_b^s = \Pr\{S_b\} = \sum_{i=0}^{N} p(i, N - i). \tag{6}$$

5.2   Forced Termination Probability

If all N channels are full, a new arrival of master will drive away a slave and grab its channel, which indicates a forced termination event of the slave class. The probability is calculated by:

$$P_t = c \Pr\{S_t\} = \frac{\lambda_m}{\lambda_s} \sum_{i=0}^{N-1} p(i, N - i), \tag{7}$$

This formula of forced termination probability (7) is a modification to that in [7]. It has a practical meaning: within the duration between two arrivals of slaves, there are $c = \lambda_m/\lambda_s$ master arrivals on average, inducing c termination events in condition that the knapsack is full and there is at least one slave in it.

Probability of forced termination is related to system parameters N, λ_m, μ_m, λ_s and μ_s, but not a simply monotonic function, like the blocking probability. An intuitive demonstration is, terminations of slaves may happen more frequent as masters get more; but when the master load $\rho_m = \frac{\lambda_m}{\mu_m}$ goes sufficient large, the channels are all occupied by masters with high probability. As a result, slaves are hardly let into the resource poll (which corresponds to a high blocking probability), to say nothing of terminations.

6   Numerical Result and Discussion

Parameters of system load are listed in Table.1. Linear system obtained in Section 4 with N equations has a rank of $(N - 1)$, so the solution is unique, considering the feature of probability distribution. MATLAB is used to directly calculate the linear equations. The simulations are executed by C program: channel amount is $N = 10$; arrival time and holding time are independently generated exponential random variables. A total number of 2×10^8 is set as the upper bound of iteration, both master and slave classes are counted in. A window is used to detect the standard deviation of blocking times, when the normalized deviation (i.e., deviation divided by mean value) gets below a certain threshold, the system is believed to have reached equilibrium. The window size is set 100, threshold 0.05, and the deviation is calculated from the amount of blocked cases out of 2000 arrivals. 100 realizations are averaged to obtain the final results. Fig.3, 4 and 5 are based on the results of case 1, 2, 3 in Table.1, respectively.

Table 1. Simulation parameter setting for three cases

	C	λ_m/μ_m	λ_s/μ_s
Case1	10	a	a
Case2	10	$2a$	a
Case3	10	a	$2a$

6.1   Comparison of Analytic and Numeric Results

The analytic results of blocking and termination performance with our scheme match the simulation results excellently in all cases illustrated by Fig.3, 4 and 5, affirming the analysis to be rational and correct. As far as we know, this is a pioneer study on the fully dynamic spectrum allocation, which extends the our understanding on OSA. Our mathematical analysis inducts a guideline for this new direction and provides basis for further research. Following our work, performance criterion can be evaluated for network design.

6.2   Discussions on Termination Probability

It is necessary to clarify the curves of the forced termination probability of slaves, as the red solid lines shown in all the Fig.3, 4, 5. Within the first ascending of traffic load, approximately in the region $0 < a < 10$, the probability goes up, because heavier load leads to more termination. However, as the value a continues to increase, corresponding to greater arrival rate of both masters and slaves, the system is overloaded. There are more masters occupying the spectrum and less slaves, and as a result few termination events happen. That's why the termination probability decreases when a gets very large.

6.3   Comparison with OSA

We also give the simulation performance of OSA as a comparison. Master performance exhibits no difference whether OSA or our scheme is adopted, which guarantees the masters' priority as expected. Considerable reduction of slaves' termination probability is exhibited by the fully dynamic scheme, and this is the main contribution of our innovation. However, the slave blocking probability with our scheme is a little higher than that with OSA, which is revealed by the figures, and can be explained in this way: in OSA, masters drive away slaves more frequently, leaving more idle channels, which allows easier access of new slaves. But this phenomenon is obvious only in light system load (a is small), because in heavy load the knapsack is almost exhausted by the masters.

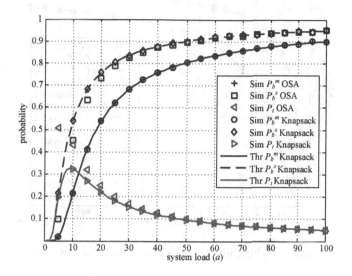

Fig. 3. Blocking and termination probability in Case1

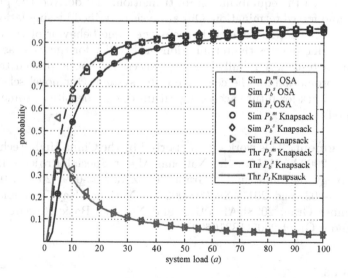

Fig. 4. Blocking and termination probability in Case2

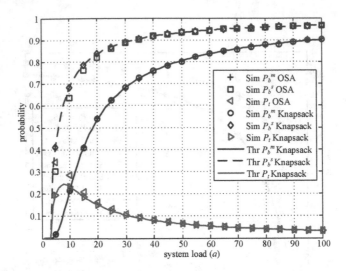

Fig. 5. Blocking and termination probability in Case3

7   Conclusion

In this paper, a fully dynamic spectrum allocation scheme for cognitive radio access is introduced and modelled by a master-slave stochastic knapsack process. We analyzed the equilibrium state transition, and derived the probability of blocking and forced termination. Our analysis is verified by simulation results. As a more flexible access manner, it keeps the same behavior of PUs as traditional OSA, while reduces the termination probability for the SUs, as shown in our simulation results. The fully dynamic access scheme is proved to have an encouraging promotion for the cognitive radio system. Our novel scheme introduces a framework for future access algorithm design, despite of some practical issues ignored.

Acknowledgment. This work was supported by the China High-Tech 863 Plan under Grant 2009AA011506, the National Major Special Projects in Science and Technology of China under Grant 2009ZX03003-009, 2010ZX03003-001, 2010ZX03005-003, and 2011ZX03003-003-04, National Key Technology R&D Program under Grant 2008BAH30B12, and National Basic Research Program of China under Grant 2007CB310602.

References

1. Mitola, J.: Cognitive Radio: An Integrated Agent Atchitecture for Software Defined Radio, Ph.D. dissertation, KTH, Stockholm, Sweden (December 2000)
2. Webb, W.: Wireless Communications: The Future. John Wiley & Sons (2007)

3. Haykin, S.: Cognitive Radio: Brain-Empowered Wireless Communications. IEEE Journal on Selected Areas in Communications, 23(2) (February 2005)
4. Akyildiz, I.F., Lee, W.-Y., et al.: NeXt generation dynamic spectrum access cognitive radio wireless networks: A survey. Computer Networks 50(2006), 2127–2159 (2006)
5. Diego Pacheco-Paramo, V.P., Martinez-Bauset, J.: Optimal Admission Control in Cognitive Radio Networks. In: Proc. 4th Int. Conf. on Cognitive Radio Oriented Wireless Networks and Commun. (June 2009)
6. Zhu, X., Shen, L., Yum, T.-S.P.: Analysis of Cognitive Radio Spectrum Access with Optimal Channel Reservation. IEEE Commun. Lett. 11(4), 304–306 (2007)
7. Kalil, M.A., Al-Mahdi, H., Mitschele-Thiel, A.: Analysis of Opportunistic Spectrum Access in Cognitive Ad Hoc Networks. In: Al-Begain, K., Fiems, D., Horváth, G. (eds.) ASMTA 2009. LNCS, vol. 5513, pp. 16–28. Springer, Heidelberg (2009)
8. Luu, L., Daneshrad, B.: An Adaptive Weave Architecture Radio With Spectrum Sensing Capabilities to Relax RF Component Requirements. IEEE Journal on Selected Areas in Communications 25(3), 538–545 (2007)
9. Gandetto, M., Regazzoni, C.: Spectrum Sensing: A Distributed Approach for Cognitive Terminals. IEEE Journal on Selected Areas in Communications 25(3), 546–557 (2007)
10. Jafar, S.A., et al.: Capacity Limits of Cognitive Radio With Distributed and Dynamic Spectral Activity. IEEE Journal on Selected Areas in Communications 25(3) (April 2007)
11. Brockmeyer, E., Halstrom, H.L., Jensen, A.: The life and Works of A.K. Erlang, The Copenhagen Telephone Co., Copenhagen (1948)
12. Ross, K.W., Hancock, P.J.: Multiservice Loss Models for Broadband Telecommunication Networks. Springer-Verlag New York, Inc., Secaucus (1995)
13. Papastavrou, J.D., Rajagopalan, S., Kleywegt, A.J.: The dynamic and stochastic knapsack problem with deadlines. Management Sci. 42, 1706–1718 (1996)
14. Puri, P.S.: A Linear Birth and Death Process under the Influence of Another Process. Journal of Applied Probability 12(1), 1–17 (1975)
15. Becker, N.G.: A Stochastic Model for Two Interacting Populations. Journal of Applied Probability 7(3), 544–564 (1970)
16. Watanabe, K., Ishibashi, K., Kohno, R.: Performance of Cognitive Radio Technologies in The Presence of Primary Radio Systems. In: The 18th Annual IEEE International Symposium on Personal, Indoor and Mobile Radio Communications (PIMRC 2007), Athens, Greece (September 2007)
17. Neel, J.: Analysis and Design of Cognitive Radio Networks and Distributed Radio Resource Management Algorithms, Ph.D. dissertation, Virginia Polytechnic Institute and State University, Stockholm, Virginia, USA (2006)
18. Martinez-Bauset, J., Pla, V., Pacheco-Paramo, D.: Comments on Analysis of Cognitive Radio Spectrum Access with Optimal Channel Reservation. IEEE Communications Letters 13(10), 739 (2009)
19. Ahmed, W., Gao, J., Faulkner, M.: Performance Evaluation of a Cognitive Radio Network with Exponential and Truncated Usage Models. In: 4th International Symposium on Wireless Pervasive Computing, pp. 1–5 (2009)
20. Heo, J., Shin, J., Nam, J., Lee, Y., Park, J.G., Cho, H.-S.: Mathematical Analysis of Secondary User Traffic in Cognitive Radio System. In: IEEE Vehicular Technology Conference (September 2008)

Evaluation and Enhancement of TCP with Network Coding in Wireless Multihop Networks

Yanli Xu[1,2], Xiaolin Bai[1], Ping Wu[1], and Lianghui Ding[1]

[1] Signals and Systems, Dept. of Engineering Sciences,
Uppsala University, Uppsala, Sweden
yanli.xu@angstrom.uu.se
[2] National Mobile Communications Research Laboratory,
Southeast University, Nanjing, China

Abstract. In this paper, we, based on NS-2 simulator, evaluate the performances of different TCP protocols with network coding in wireless multihop networks, and then propose two schemes to enhance the performances of TCPs with network coding. In particular the network coding scheme considered and used here is COPE, which is one of the well-known practical network coding schemes, the TCP protocols evaluated are TCP-NewReno, TCP-FeW and TCP-AP, and the TCP protocols with COPE are implemented in NS-2. The simulation results show that COPE performs very differently in improving the performances of the TCP's in different wireless network topologies. In some topologies COPE performs well, resulting in significant performance improvement; while in other ones it performs worse than the same cases without network coding. To overcome this problem, we propose two schemes to improve the performance of TCP with network coding. One is called Encode Once, which ensures the packet being encoded at most one time. The other is called Network Coding Aware TCP, in which the transmitting rate of TCP is made adaptive to the status of the node's output queue. The evaluation results indicate that the proposed two schemes can significantly improve the goodputs of TCP's with network coding, and the latter scheme performs better.

Keywords: TCP, COPE, NS-2, network coding, wireless multihop networks.

1 Introduction

In multihop wireless networks, it is challenging to provide high goodput service due to the scarce bandwidth resources and harsh radio propagation environments. Network coding is a promising techniques that can improve wireless goodghput essentially. Network coding was originally proposed for wired networks by Ahlswede *et.al.* [1], and then it was shown to be able to offer benefits for wireless networks [2,3,4]. The basic idea of network coding is to ask an intermediate node to mix the messages it received and forward the mixture to several

P. Ren et al. (Eds.): WICON 2011, LNICST 98, pp. 490–500, 2012.

destinations simultaneously. Compared to time sharing based schemes where destinations are served in turn, the use of network coding can increase the overall goodput dramatically. COPE is one of the practical network coding schemes for wireless networks. It was proposed by S. Katti *et.al.* in [5]. In COPE, each node opportunistically overhears those packets transmitted by its neighbors, which are not addressed to itself, and notices what packets the neighbors currently possess (by adding piggyback reception reports on the data packets the node transmits). Each node can intelligently XOR multiple packets destined to nodes in next hop such that multiple packets can be forwarded in a single transmission, resulting in a significant improvement in node transmission efficiency. Results obtained from the first test bed deployment of wireless network coding showed that COPE can substantially improve the goodput of multihop wireless networks.

However, extending coding technologies to the network setting in a practical way has been a challenging task. In the Internet, flow control and congestion control are predominantly based on transmission control protocol (TCP), i.e., controlling transmission rate according to sliding transmission window of packets, whose size is controlled based on feedback from destination nodes [6,7]. Most wireless applications rely on legacy TCP to communicate with TCP-dominant wired hosts, and it is likely that TCP will remain as the major transport protocol for the clients of 802.11 networks [8]. But it was shown in [9] that the performance gain of TCP with COPE in a 802.11 network can be neglected. A lot of research has been done on jointing implementation of TCP and network coding such as [10,11,12]. However, as we know, no attention has been paid to the performance degradation of TCP caused by the rate control mechanism of TCP itself and the routing protocol [8,13,14] has not been noted.

To find the reasons that cause the performance degradation of TCP in wireless multihop networks, especially with focus on the rate control mechanism of TCP, we will evaluate the performances of three TCP protocols: TCP-NewReno [15] for wired communication, TCP-FeW (Fractional Window Increment) [8] and TCP-AP (TCP with Adaptive Pacing) [14] for wireless communication using network simulator NS-2, and then compare the performances of the protocols with COPE to those without COPE in order to observe the improvement of performance due to use of COPE. Finally, we provide two new schemes which joint TCP and network coding better in wireless multihop networks.

The rest of the paper is organized as follows: we first introduce the three TCP protocols and the model for implementation of tcp with cope in NS-2 in Section 2. Then, we present simulation results in Section 3. Afterwards, we provide two novel schemes in Section 4 and conclude the whole paper in Section 5.

2 Implementation TCP with COPE on NS-2

2.1 COPE-Coding Opportunistically

COPE is the first practical network coding-based packet forwarding architecture that substantially improves the goodput of wireless networks. It inserts a coding shim between the IP and MAC layers, which identifies coding opportunities and benefits from them by forwarding multiple packets in a single transmission. COPE incorporates three main techniques: Opportunistic Listening: COPE sets the nodes in promiscuous mode, makes them snoop on all communications over the wireless medium and store the overheard packets for a limited period; Opportunistic Coding: the node aims to maximize the number of native packets delivered in a single transmission, while ensuring that each intended next hop has enough information to decode its native packet; Learning Neighbor State: each node announces to its neighbors the packets it stores in reception reports. When reception reports get lost in collisions, a node can not rely solely on reception reports to make code decisions, then it will leverage the routing computation to guess whether a neighbor has a particular packet. Occasionally, a node may make an incorrect guess, which causes the coded packet to be undecodable at some next hop. In this case, the relevant native packet is retransmitted, potentially encoded with a new set of native packets.

2.2   TCP Protocols

TCP is one of the core protocols of the Internet Protocol Suite, which is a connection oriented protocol, provides end-to-end, reliable and ordered delivery of a stream of bytes between computers. In this work, we consider the following three TCP protocols: TCP-NewReno, TCP-FeW and TCP-AP.

TCP-NewReno. TCP-NewReno is a slight modification over TCP Reno. When receiving three duplicate ACKs, TCP Reno assumes there is packet loss happening on the link, and then starts up the 'Fast Retransmit' and 'Fast Recovery' processes, which will immediately retransmit the lost packet. TCP Reno doesn't perform well under the condition of high packet loss. To overcome this problem, TCP-NewReno improves retransmission during the 'Fast Recovery' stage of TCP Reno. For every lost packet, TCP-NewReno retransmits it and waits for the acknowledgment before exiting from 'Fast Recovery' process. TCP-NewReno successfully prevents TCP from going back to 'Slow Start' when there are multiple packet drops. TCP-NewReno keeps the same performance at low packet loss ratio, and substantially outperforms TCP Reno at high packet loss ratio.

TCP-FeW. In the TCP-FeW scheme, it prevents the over-reaction of the on-demand routing protocol by limiting TCP's aggressiveness. TCP-FeW allows the TCP congestion window to grow by a fractional rate $\alpha \leq 1$ (packets) in each RTT (Round-Trip-Time). That means adding one packet into the congestion window at every $1/\alpha$ RTT. Assuming the size of the current congestion window is $W^{current}$, the source node transmits $W^{current}$ packets to destination node and receives the same number of ACKs from the destination node during each RTT. When receiving an ACK, the source node updates the current congestion window size through the following formula 1:

$$W^{new} = W^{current} + \frac{\alpha}{W^{current}} \tag{1}$$

where $0 < \alpha \leq 1$. When $\alpha = 1$, the pattern of increase of the formula above is the same as the traditional style, i.e., increasing the window size by 1 when receiving an ACK. So TCP-FeW keeps the original mechanism of TCP congestion window growth. In addition to that, TCP-FeW can monitor the network traffic without any other additional information and provide quick reactions.

TCP-AP. TCP-AP is a rate-based scheduling of transmissions within the TCP congestion window. The source node adapts its transmission rate according to the estimation of the current 4-hop propagation delay and coefficient of variation of recently measured RTTs. Unlike the previous solutions, TCP-AP keeps the end-to-end semantics of TCP, does not need to modify the routing or link layer, and does not rely on the cross-layer information from intermediate nodes along the path. Moreover, TCP-AP achieves excellent fairness and quick reaction to control network traffic conditions.

2.3   NS-2 and Simulation of TCP with COPE

Network Simulator NS-2. The network simulator, is a discrete event simulator targeted at networking research. NS-2 provides substantial support for simulation of TCP, routing, and multicast protocols over wired and wireless (local and satellite) networks [16]. NS-2 includes almost all the main parts of network, and it is a free and open-source platform for network simulation. That's why NS-2 is used widely in academic fields, and chosen here in this work for the simulation of TCP with network coding and the evaluation of its performance.

Implementation of TCP with COPE on NS-2. The core of the wireless module in NS-2 is mobile node, which was originally ported as CMU's (Carnegie Mellon University) Monarch group's mobility extension to NS [16]. It is a basic node object equipped with wireless functionalities, and the mobile node can move within the given topology, receive and send radio signals through wireless channel. The characteristics of mobility like node movement, periodic location update, topology maintenance, etc., are implemented by C++, while the internal network components (like classifier, Link Layer (LL), Media Access Control (MAC), Channel, etc.) are assembled using OTcl, which is an object oriented extension of the scripting language Tcl (Tool Command Language).

We implement three key parts of COPE as well as complementary parts for IEEE 802.11 network, pseudo-broadcast, asynchronous acknowledgment and retransmission. We modify IEEE 802.11 MAC and the Interface Queue (IFq) protocol stacks on NS-2 to adapt to the present application. Furthermore, the original structure of the mobile node in NS-2 are modified for COPE (refer to our work [17] for detail). For opportunistic listening, the up-target of MAC is no longer LL, because the COPE is implemented on IFq layer and all the incoming packets should pass through COPE. If the destination or next hop of incoming packet is this node, then the packet is passed to LL, which now is the up-target of IFq. Otherwise, COPE saves it in the packet pool or drops it depending on whether the packet can be decoded or not. The new structure of the mobile node with COPE looks like that shown in fig. 1.

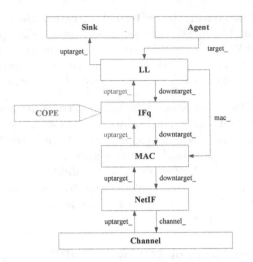

Fig. 1. Structure of mobile node with COPE in NS-2

3   Simulation Results and Performance Analysis

In this section, the performances of three different TCP protocols: TCP-Newreno, TCP-FeW and TCP-AP, are evaluated using NS-2 simulator. Three topologies, namely, chain topology, classic X topology (named as X-I topology) and an extended scenario of X-I topology (called X-II topology), are considered. For the MAC layer, IEEE 802.11 with RTS/CTS (Request to Send/Clear to Send) are adopted. For TCP traffic, FTP (File Transfer Protocol) traffic is used. In all the topologies, TCP flows start randomly between first $2sec$ and $3sec$. The evaluated metrics are listed as follows:

- *Network goodput:* the measured total end-to-end goodput of all flows. The average goodput T of each flow in the network is computed according to

$$T = \frac{received\_packets\_size \times 8}{simulation\_time}(kbps) \tag{2}$$

- *Goodput Gain:* the ratio between the measured network goodput with COPE to the traditional TCP[5], i.e.,

$$Goodput\_Gain = \frac{G_{cope}}{G_{nocope}} \tag{3}$$

where G_{cope} and G_{nocope} are the average goodputs of TCP with and without COPE, respectively.

The chain topology shown in fig. 2 is the first one considered in the present work. In this topology, the distance of the contiguous nodes is 200 meters and the transmission range of each node is 250 meters. The simulation results are shown in fig. 3, in which the network goodputs of TCP with COPE for TCP-NewReno and TCP-FeW are significantly higher than those without COPE, which proves the benefits of network coding. The results also show that TCP-NewReno is the worst choice for network coding, and TCP-AP with COPE performs better than TCP-FeW with COPE when the number of hops is less than and afterwards the former becomes worse than the latter.

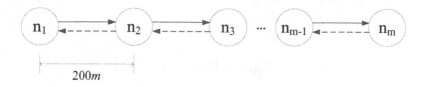

Fig. 2. Chain Topology

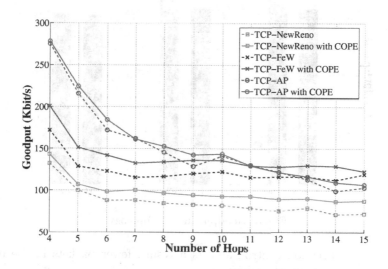

Fig. 3. Goodput in Chain Topology

More realistic topologies are X-shaped. The first X topology considered is shown in fig. 4 , and called X-I topology to distinguish from an extended X topology to be dealt with below. In this topology there are two flows: one from $n0$ to $n2$ via $n1$ and the other from $n3$ to $n4$ via $n1$. The simulation results for this topology are illustrated in fig. 5. From the figure we can observe that COPE brings marginal improvement of performances for both TCP-NewReno and TCP-FeW (with about and respectively); and the worst case is TCP-AP with COPE, where network coding has no contribution. One reason is that TCP-AP is based on the estimation of the current 4-hop propagation delay and coefficient of variation of recently measured RTTs. However, there are only 2 hops, which restricts the performance of TCP-AP. The other reason is that TCP-AP is too

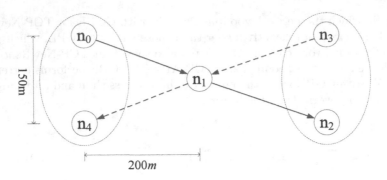

Fig. 4. X-I Topology

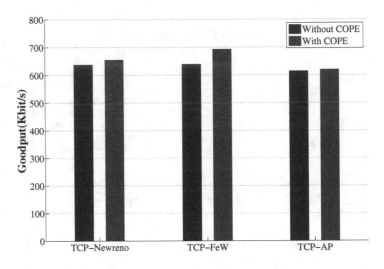

Fig. 5. Goodput in X-I Topology

proactive for congestion control, and as a result, fewer packets in the output queue are used for network coding.

To evaluate the performance of COPE and find out the reason that leads to no gain for TCP-AP, we extend the X-I topology to another X topology as shown in fig. 6, which is called as X-II topology. X-II topology is similar to X-I topology except it has four more nodes, so each of the two TCP flows traversing from $n0$ to $n4$ and from $n5$ to $n8$, respectively, has 4 hops, which satisfies the prerequisite of TCP-AP.

As described in fig. 7, both TCP-NewReno and TCP-FeW with COPE get worse results compared to TCP-NewReno and TCP-FeW without COPE. That's because of TCP-NewReno's bursty behavior and due to the fact that TCP is agnostic to the underlying network coding. While TCP-FeW alleviates this bursty situation, but still not so suitable for network coding. Similar to the X-I topology, TCP-AP with COPE still has no contribution to the TCP Performance. We believe that this is caused by the rate control mechanism of TCP-AP.

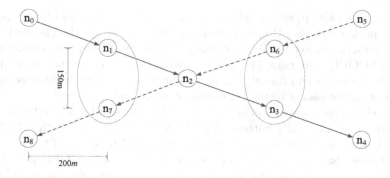

Fig. 6. X-II Topology

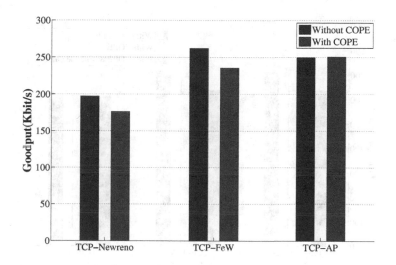

Fig. 7. Goodput in X-II Topology

4 Proposed Schemes

As shown above, COPE does not make performance improvement for X-II topology. In this section, we propose two schemes to improve the goodput of TCP with COPE. Improvement of the performance is made from two aspects: COPE mechanism and TCP protocols, respectively.

4.1 Encode Once

From simulation, we find that retransmission can not significantly improve the probability to decode a packet if the packet can not be decoded at the first time. For example, in the X-I topology, node n_1 encodes packet p_1 of node $n0$ and p_2 of node $n3$, then $n1$ broadcasts the encoded packet $p_1 \bigoplus p_2$. Node n_0 decodes the encoded packet correctly but node n_3 dose not. Therefore n_3 informs node n_1 that it has not yet obtained packet p_2. Then, node n_1 starts retransmission process, and encodes packets p_2 and p_3 which is a native packet of $n0$ and broadcasts the encoded packet $p_2 \oplus p_3$. However, node n_3 can not decode the encoded packet packet to obtain packet p_2. To solve this problem, we modify the retransmission scheme of COPE. The main idea is that each packet only can be encoded once, which, therefore, we call Encode Once. As a special case, a node directly retransmits a lost native packet instead of encode it again and then send.

Fig. 8 shows the comparison of the goodputs of three TCP's (TCP-NewReno, TCP-FeW and TCP-AP) without COPE, with COPE and with COPE and Encode Once scheme, respectively, in the case of X-I topology. The comparison demonstrates that the goodputs of the three TCP's with COPE and Encode Once scheme are improved by 5%, 4% and 2%, respectively, compared to the TCP's with COPE.

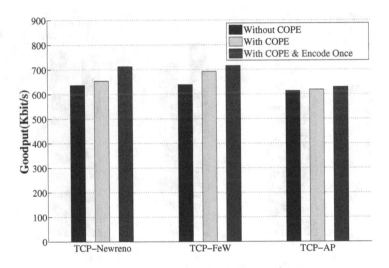

Fig. 8. Goodput of X-I topology with Encode Once

4.2   Network Coding Aware TCP

COPE carries out network coding on the packets within the output queue. So the performance of this scheme depends on the number of packets in the output queue. If the output queue is empty or holds only one packet there is no chance to do network coding, leading to no improvement made by network coding, e.g. TCP-AP with COPE in the X-I topology. If there are too many packets in the output queue, then severe congestion happens, giving rise to bad goodput, e.g., TCP-NewReno and TCP-FeW with COPE in the X-II topology.

To solve this problem, we let the TCP rate be adaptive to the length of the output queue to increase the opportunity of network coding. For example when the output queue does not contain enough packets for encoding for TCP-AP with X-I topology, we increase the number of the packets in the output queue by adapting the rate interval, which is the duration between successive packets to generate an appropriate number of packets. To let the number of packets change in a reasonable range, i.e., be large enough to implement network coding but not too large to cause the overflowing in the output queue, we introduce a factor λ to adjust the rate interval so that the new rate interval becomes

$$r_{new} = \lambda r_{old} \tag{4}$$

where r_{old} is the original rate interval of TCP-AP and r_{new} is the new one that is adaptive to improve the performance of TCP-AP with COPE. Through various simulations and analyses, we have found an empirical value for λ, namely $\lambda = 0.2$ at which TCP-AP achieves the highest goodput.

Using the TCP protocol with COPE proposed above, we calculate the goodput. The result is illustrated in fig. 9 together with TCP's in other three cases. The compassion of the goodputs in four cases in the figure shows that the proposed new TCP scheme with COPE yields about 12% increase of network goodput compared to TCP-AP with COPE, and performs even better than TCP with Encode Once.

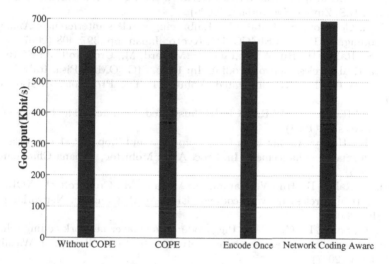

Fig. 9. Goodputs of TCP-AP without COPE, with COPE, with Encode Once and with Network Coding Aware, respectively

5 Conclusions

In this paper, we have presented three TCP protocols (i.e., TCP-NewReno, TCP-FeW and TCP-AP) with COPE and the implementation of them in network simulator NS-2. Then we have evaluated their performances in chain, classic X-I and X-II topologies, respectively. The simulation results demonstrate that in the chain topology both TCP-FeW and TCP-AP with COPE could greatly improve the performances of the TCP protocols without network coding; in the X-I topology COPE results in significant performance improvement for TCP- NewReno and TCP-FeW but not for TCP-AP; and in the X-II topology COPE only improves TCP-AP's performance. After evaluating TCP's with

COPE, we have proposed two schemes to improve the performances (in terms of goodputs) of the TCP protocols with network coding. The first scheme is called Encode Once that ensures the packet being encoded at most one time and the second is called Network Coding Aware TCP in which the transmitting rate of TCP is made adaptive to the status of the node's output queue. The NS-2 simulation results for TCP-AP demonstrate that the proposed two schemes provide significant improvement on the goodputs of TCP's with network coding, and the network coding aware TCP scheme yields even better improvement.

References

1. Ahlswede, R., Cai, N., Li, S.-Y.R., Yeung, R.W.: Network information flow, vol. IEEE Trans. on Information Theory 46(4), 1204–1216 (2000)
2. Wu, Y., Chou, P.A., Kung, S.Y.: Minimum-energy multicast in mobile ad hoc networks using network coding. IEEE Trans. on Comm. 53(11), 1906–1918 (2005)
3. Lun, D.S., Médard, M., Koetter, R.: Network coding for efficient wireless unicast. In: Proc. IZS, Zurich, Switzerland (2006)
4. Katti, S., Gollakota, S., Katabi, D.: Embracing wireless interference: Analog network coding. In: Proc. of SIGCOMM, Kyoto, Japan, pp. 397–408 (2007)
5. Katti, S., Rahul, H., Hu, W., Katabi, D., Médard, M., Crowcroft, J.: XORs in the air: Practical wireless network coding. In: Proc. SIGCOMM, Pisa, Italy (2006)
6. Stevens, W.R.: TCP/IP Illustrated: Volume 1: The Protocols. Addison-Wesley (1994)
7. Wright, G.R., Stevens, W.R.: TCP/IP Illustrated, Volume 2: The Implementation. Addison-Wesley (1994)
8. Nahm, K., Helmy, A., Jay Kuo, C.C.: Tcp over multihop 802.11 networks: Issues and performance enhancement. In: Proc. ACM MobiHoc, Urbana-Champaign, IL, USA (2005)
9. Katti, S., Rahul, H., Hu, W., Katabi, D.; Medard, M., Crowcroft, J.: XORs in the air: Practical wireless network coding. IEEE/ACM Trans. on Networking 16(3), 497–510 (2008)
10. Scalia, L., Soldo, F., Gerla, M.: Piggycode: a mac layer network coding scheme to improve tcp performance over wireless networks. In: Proc. GlobeCom, Washington, D.C., USA (2007)
11. Samuel David, P., Kumar, A.: Network coding for tcp throughput enhancement over a multi-hop wireless network. In: Proc. COMSWARE, Bangalore (2008)
12. Kumar Sundararajan, J., Shah, D., Médard, M., et al.: Network coding meets TCP. In: Proc. INFOCOM, Janeiro, Brazil (2009)
13. Ding, L., Wang, X., Xu, Y., Zhang, W., Liu, Y.: Vegas-W: An enhanced TCP-Vegas for wireless ad hoc networks. In: Proc. ICC, Beijing, China (2008)
14. ElRakabawy, S.M., Klemm, A., Lindemann, C.: TCP with adaptive pacing for multihop wireless networks. In: Proc. IEEE MobiHoc, Urbana-Champaign, IL, USA (2005)
15. Floyd, S., Henderson, T.: RFC 2582: The NewReno Modification to TCP's Fast Recovery Algorithm (1999), http://www.ietf.org/rfc/rfc2582.txt
16. Ns-2, http://nsnam.isi.edu/nsnam/index.php/MainPage
17. Bai, X.L., Wu, P., Ding, L.H.: Evaluation and enhancement of tcp with network coding in wireless multihop networks, Master's thesis, Uppsala University (2011)

Fine-Grained Metrics for Quantifying Admission Control Performance in Mobile Ad Hoc Networks

Jianli Guo[1,2], Wei Wu[1,2], Xiaoxia Liu[3], Lianhe Luo[1,2],
Changjiang Yan[1,2], and Yuebin Bai[3]

[1] Science and Technology on Information Transmission and Dissemination
in Communication Networks Laboratory, Shijiazhuang, Hebei, 050081, China
[2] The 54th Research Institute of CETC, Shijiazhuang, Hebei, 050081, China
[3] School of Computer Science and Engineering, Beihang University, Beijing 100191, China

Abstract. The admission control (AC) is one of the crucial components of in QoS-providing mobile ad hoc networks (MANET). The responsibility of AC is to estimate the state of the network resources and decide whether application data can be admitted without promising more resources. AC should achieve a right balance between admission accuracy and network resource waste. It aims to admit as many sessions as possible, while utilizing the network's resources fully and efficiently. Conversely, any inaccuracy in the admission decisions can result in the pledging of more resources than are available, leading to false admissions. However, the existing metrics are only network resource or performance related, thus, it is preferred to have a metric that can measure the effective AC protocols as it influences in achieving QoS demands of the sessions. Therefore, in this work we present observation-based admission control performance metrics quantifying the satisfaction of both single session and the entire network. Also we predict the possibilities of false admission and successful completion of a session and give discuss about the metrics. Finally, we proposed a design of feedback-based admission control using the metrics we presented for feedback parameters, the verification and implementation of our design and the effectiveness of the metrics is mentioned in the future works.

Keywords: admission control, evaluating metrics, mobile ad hoc networks, MANET, predict probability of false admission.

1 Introduction

As the progress in mobile ad hoc networks (MANETs), the desire to run real-time applications over MANETs increases. Real-time applications have strict requirements on the quality of service (QoS) provided by the network. These requirements have delivery rates of data packet, end-to-end delay, bandwidth or throughput-related constraints, etc. It is important that network resource should be adequate for the applications, otherwise the application will be inconvenient to use and user will suffer from bad experience.

P. Ren et al. (Eds.): WICON 2011, LNICST 98, pp. 501–510, 2012.

Providing QoS assurances to MANETs applications is difficult due to the lack of centralized control, node mobility, unreliable wireless channel and channel contention. Up to now, Admission control (AC) is one of the crucial components for providing QoS assurances. Additionally, a range of related mechanisms are required to make admission decisions.

The responsibility of AC is to estimate the state of the network resources and decide whether application data can be admitted without promising more resources. The key aspect of this problem is the collection of information about the available network resources and the performance of AC in MANET. Then according to the information collect, AC makes a decision whether the session should be admitted.

On the one hand, AC aims to admit as many sessions as possible, while utilizing the network's resources fully and efficiently. On the other hand, any inaccuracy in the admission decisions can result in the pledging of more resources than available, leading to false admissions. False admission usually results bad QoS and poor user experiences. In contrast, conservative decision causes the waste of network resources. AC should achieve a right balance between admission accuracy and network resource waste.

However, it is hard to get accurate information about the status of network and sessions' satisfaction. Existing metrics for admission control protocols are either QoS-related or admission decision related, like false rejection ratio, session admission ratio, false admission ratio, session completion and dropping ratios, etc. The existing metrics are surveyed in detail in Section 2 which has been highlighted in recent surveys [1], [2]. They were insufficient to evaluate the performance and the balance of AC, particularly with regard to evaluating the satisfaction of the session requirement and the network status offered.

We need new metrics to reflect the inherent balance of AC and the possible trade-off between the probabilities of false admissions and false rejections.

For the reasons mentioned above, this paper aims to address this issue while proposing fine-grained metrics for quantifying the balance of AC protocol.

The rest of this paper is organized as follows. Section 2 reviews the related works and covers the topic of some relevant background. Section 3 describes our design of new metrics for quantifying AC protocol performance and discusses the advantage and signification of these metrics. Section 4 represents a scheme to verify the design ideas. And finally, Section 5 concludes the whole paper and arranges the future work.

2   Related Works

Section 2.1 provides a brief list of the most prevalence QoS specification metrics, while metrics for AC performances are given and discussed in Section 2.2.

2.1   Metric for QoS Requirements Specification and Network Performance

Many metrics for specifying and measuring QoS were explained in [2], we give a recap of these metrics and also discuss the benefits and drawbacks. These QoS metrics can be used to define the MANET application requirements and evaluate the effect of AC in the system.

The requirements and AC performance are generally expressed by one or more of the following metrics:

- Minimum average throughput (bps) [3], [4], [5], [6].

- Propagation delay [4], [5], [7]. It is the *maximum* time difference between transmitting a packet by node and receiving this packet at the node, generally it is short.

- Maximum delay jitter bound[4], [7]. It can be defined as time gap difference between the maximum and minimum possible propagation delays across one link (including queuing delay) and the absolute minimum delay, which is determined simply by the cumulative propagation and packet transmission times A common alternative definition is the variance of the absolute packet delay[8].

- Maximum packet loss ratio (PLR) bound [4], [5. The maximum tolerable fraction of the generated data packets lost per route. The packet losses because of buffer overflow when congestion occurs, or in poor channel quality or after a node moves, the retransmission limit being exceeded, or due to a timeout while waiting for a new route to be discovered for the next hop.

In additions, other metrics of network resources (for example average processing time, consumed energy [9]) used to qualify AC performance.

Although these metrics can be use to reflect the AC performance ,they are subjective metrics and thus cannot be used to compare results from different networks, only for comparing results for different protocols operating in the same network with the same parameters and traffic load.

2.2   AC Protocol Performance Metrics

Admission control protocols in MANET is try to balance of the network resource abuse and pledging of too much resources. So metrics for AC should show this balance. On the one hand, metrics reflect the status of resource usage, such like the metric capacity utilization mentioned below; If AC admits as many sessions as possible, the network must be exploited fully; meanwhile, the usage of the network's resources should also be efficiently. On the other hand, any incorrect or not accurate admission control decision can lead to the pledging of more resources than are available.

If the network is under-utilized, and resources are sufficient, it will be easy to provide QoS assurance to admit sessions as the risk of congestion becomes impossible. The network is in low efficiency in terms of energy consumption and overhead and wastage of network resources. Rejecting a session which could have been served without degrading the QoS of previously admitted sessions may be termed a false rejection.

It is important of AC to hold an appropriate attitude. A positive attitude may lead to false admission and a too strict attitude would result in false rejection.

Thus, metrics can be categorized according to whether they measure the protocol's ability to utilize resources or its ability to satisfy applications' requirements. Although most AC protocol designers tend to demonstrate their protocols effectiveness by showing traces of QoS metrics, however this only shows the partial performance of the protocol. Some other metrics are as follows [1]:

Normalized Protocol Overhead (NPO): The average fraction of bytes of routing and AC packets and protocol headers, which are transmitted, normalized by the number of data bytes received at the destination. AC should achieve a balance between accuracy with overhead, which NPO can reflect [10].

Capacity Utilization (CU): The average fraction (over time) of the network's capacity that is utilized by data traffic. A large number of false rejections lead to a low capacity utilization. However, the capacity of wireless networks with random topologies can be difficult to quantify. Therefore, researchers often use the aggregate network throughput to reflect the level of capacity utilization, e.g. [6].

Session Admission Ratio (SAR): The fraction of requesting sessions that were admitted; this metric can be used as it is difficult to estimating capacity utilization efficiency. This metric reflects the number of data sessions admitted. It exposes the ability of the AC mechanism to estimate available resources and utilize them. For different protocols in the given traffic configurations and the same network, the AC protocol achieving a higher SAR, while not degrading the experienced QoS of data sessions, can be regarded a better one.

The weakness of this metric is that it depends on the offered traffic load and the absolute network capacity. It cannot be used to compare AC from different networks.

False Admission Ratio (FAR): The number of false admissions normalized by the number of admitted sessions or admission requests. Akin to the FRR, this metric is difficult to quantify. But some other methods are available for calculating the level FAR. One could measure the average proportion of packets [1]. In [6], the authors propose a method that FAR is quantified by an "actual network throughput minus the total throughput promised to admitted sessions" metric. However, both the FAR and FRR metrics are also affected by conditions outside of the AC protocol's control, such as node mobility and wireless channel confliction.

False Rejection Ratio (FRR): The fraction of false rejections normalized by the number of rejected sessions or admission requests. In a real system, the FRR is difficult to quantify, since whether a rejection is deemed false or not depends on the instantaneous states of resources and a session's requirements. FRR cannot be calculated accurately in a real system as to collect global admission information. It can only be used in simulation.

Session Completion and Dropping Ratios (SCR/SDR): The ratio of the number of data sessions completed to the application's satisfaction, or dropped before finished, to the number of sessions admitted into the network.

Session Completion Ratio (SCR): A fraction of the number of admitted sessions.

Intuitively, SDR = 1−SCR. the SCR and SDR can then easily be monitored and can partially reflect the accuracy of admission decisions and be used to monitor how well the protocol copes with these and can be used as a feedback of the AC[11]. However, these metrics are affected by factors outside of the protocol's control.

Also, there are subjective metrics like, numbers of admitted, flows rejection and blocking probability which can only for comparing results for different AC protocols performing in the same scheme and traffic load.

As stated above, some metrics are difficult to quantify, especially those related to resource utilization efficiency, some are not precise enough, for example, FAR, FFR, some are subjective and related with network and traffic load. Also, metrics for evaluating AC protocols should reflect this inherent balance, and possible trade-off between the probabilities of false admissions and false rejections.

3   New Metrics for Evaluating AC Performance

In this section, 3.1 not only describes the metrics briefly but also suggests the process of obtaining the metrics. Section 3.2 gives definitions of the metrics covering the session-level, local-level and system-level, also introduce two metrics deduced from the original metrics. Section 3.3 explains the meaning and benefits of these metric and describes the relationships between existing metrics in Section3.2.

3.1   Method to Obtain the Metrics

Our conclusions in Section 2 provided the motivation for us to design more exact and accurate metric to keep track of the effect of AC decision. The basic of our design is to monitor the data transfer stage and check whether the transfer state met the QoS requirements of the sessions in each time interval t_c during the transfer process. As illustrated in Fig.1.

When new sessions are admitted, they start the data transfer phrases.

Firstly, subdivide the data transfer stage into equal time intervals, a constant time interval is set as t_c which depends on how long it take to get the current QoS states.

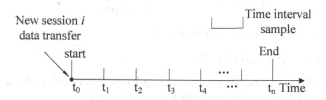

Fig. 1. Process of getting a metric

Secondly, collect the transfer status of the sessions in each time interval to see if the network performance reaches the demanded QoS.

The QoS requirements and experienced QoS during t_c time interval can be used to define the interval successful and failed conditions, for example, the specific QoS goal of the session is pre-defined by means of a set $\{Br, Dr, Jr, Priority\}$, the variables Br, Dr, Jr and $Priority$ represent the bandwidth, delay, jitter and priority of the session requirements respectively. After observing the transfer state of t_c, for instance, from t_0 to t_1, we count and statistic QoS parameters and then examine each in turn, check if each requirement is fitted. If the entire QoS goal is served, all the requirements are satisfied during the time interval $[t_0, t_1]$, it is regarded as a successful interval, otherwise as a failed interval.

Note that the length of t_c must depend on how much time need to collect the experienced network QoS status.

At the end of the sessions, we add up the number of the success and failed intervals.

3.2 Session and System Satisfaction Metrics

After the observation, all time intervals are categorized into two (2) types: success, during the intervals, the transfer status met the session's QoS requirements; fail, during the interval, the transfer status cannot fulfill with the requirements due to lack of resources. The type of the interval type can be autonomously classified by observing the QoS status of the time interval.

The number of time interval in each category are represented as $f_{success}$ and f_{fail}. As a summation, for session i, $F_i = f_{success\ i} + f_{fail\ i}$, F_i represents the number of all the time intervals during data transfer phrase of the session i.

Assume that session i is admitted, if session i transfers the data very fluently and successfully, then $F_i = f_{success\ i}$, $f_{fail\ i} = 0$; else longer the values of f_{fail}, the worse the session transfer status. In other words, we can use the fraction of f_{fail} and F_i to quantify the extent of session i's QoS.

Session Satisfaction Ratio (SeSR)

In developing our metric, we first define the total number of unsatisfied intervals session S1 during the course of data transfer phrase T1:

We define ρ_i as the measure of session satisfaction rate:

$$\rho_i = \frac{f_{success\ i}}{F_i} = \frac{f_{success\ i}}{f_{success\ i} + f_{fail\ i}} \tag{1}$$

Then, the session's disappointment ratio is $1 - \rho_i$.

System Satisfaction Ratio(SySR)

Grouping all the number of success and fail time intervals in all the sessions. We get the combined metric for system satisfaction ratio as:

$$\rho_{system} = \frac{\sum_{i=1}^{n} f_{success\ i}}{\sum_{i=1}^{n} F_i} \tag{2}$$

Then, the system disappointment ratio is $1 - \rho_{system}$.

Local Satisfaction Ratio (LSR)

As the topology structure in MANETs may be in irregularity and the satisfaction of the session may be different from area to area. We propose metric for local satisfaction ratio (LSR), for each session in the local session set L,

$$\rho_{local} = \frac{\sum_{j:j\in L} f_{success\,j}}{\sum_{j:j\in L} F_j} \qquad (3)$$

Then the local disappointment ratio is $1 - \rho_{local}$.

The following describes two new probabilities related metrics deduced from the satisfaction metrics. They can be predicted using a simple linear model.

Probabilities of False Admission (PFA)

FA can be an average value of system disappointment ratio in the long run. Probabilities of false admission can be predicted by satisfaction ratios as there is a connection between PFA and SeSR:

$$P_{FA} = \sum_{i=1}^{n} \frac{f(\rho_i)}{n} \qquad (4)$$

In formula (4), we have an assumption that n sessions are admitted by AC from start to end, besides f is a piecewise function:

$$f(x) = \begin{cases} 1, & x = 1 \\ 0, & else \end{cases} \qquad (5)$$

When a new session comes, the possibility of false admission is can be predicted by analyzing the previous period of T length behavior of AC. We can use the black box modeling approach to establish a linear model, then to derive the linear equation that models the relationship between the time and the PFA,

$$\hat{P}_{predict} = \beta \hat{t} + \hat{\varepsilon} \qquad (6)$$

The variable t represents the time and P represents predict value of the possibilities of false admission.

After creating this simple linear regression model, it is given a data set $\{t_m, P_m\}_{m=0}^{k}$ of k statistical units. For each pair of $\{t_m, P_m\}$, P_m is calculated for the prediction of PFA at the time of t_m.

In the model (6), we assume that the relationship between the dependent variable P_i and t_i is linear.

If an additional value of new time t_{i+1} is then given, using this model we are be able to get a prediction of the value of P_{i+1} very soon.

Probabilities of Completed Session (PCS)

Likewise, CS can be an average value of system satisfaction ratio in the long run. Probabilities of successful completed session can be predicted by satisfaction ratios as there is a connection between CS and SeSR:

$$P_{PCS} = 1 - P_{FA} = 1 - \sum_{i=1}^{n} \frac{f(\rho_i)}{n} \qquad (7)$$

The function f is defined in formula (5). In the same manner, we can have a prediction of probabilities of successful completed session.

3.3   Discuss about the Metrics

The effect of the satisfaction ratio metrics for AC performance is relevant to the density and extent of congestion of the network.

The satisfaction ratio is related to several factors as following:

- Conservative or aggressive of the AC protocol attitude.

- Sufficient network resources or not.

- The number of the data sessions, that is, traffic load.

- Node mobility and interferences caused by changing of topology or new sessions.

These metrics have the following benefits:

- SeSR reflects the quality of transmission for one session. In comparison with FAR, the influence of node mobility and interference from neighbors can be analyzed quantitatively.

- If new admitted session causes harmful interference to the existing sessions. SeSR declines with the interference, which is beyond the reach old metrics FAR and FRR.

- SySR can quantify the entire state of the network; it is also related to the total number of data sessions and available network resources. It indicates the imbalance between supply and the demand of network resources.

- If the value of satisfaction ratio is very close to 100 percent, it indicates that there is either sufficient network resource or a too much strict AC decision.

- If the value of satisfaction ratio is at a low level, it suggests that AC decision is made over optimistically.

PFA can be used as a feedback for AC control to improve the trueness and precision of AC decision.

4   Feedback-Based Admission Control Design

This section suggests a feedback-based admission control design to enhance the accuracy of admission decision, also the combining with combination of existing AC protocols.

As mentioned in section 3.2, the satisfaction series of metrics can be the used for feedback of admission control mechanism as our fine-grained metrics can be obtained be observing and calculated.

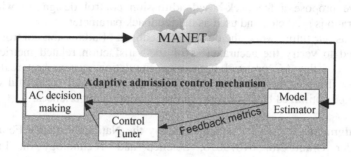

Fig. 2. Closed loop with feedback-based admission control

Model Estimator monitors the transmission state, and calculates the satisfaction ratio and possibility of false admission for each session or the entire MANET AC system. For a distributed AC protocol, session-level metrics are more suitable to be feedback parameter, for centralized one, system-level or local-level is more suitable. Control Tuner keeps automatically fine turns the received satisfaction ratios from Model Estimator and makes adjustments for AC decision making. Fine adjustments to precise the AC decision. Thus, the admission control mechanism can obtain better QoS and avoid congestion in MANET.

The feedback-based AC algorithm will consist of three stages: In the first one is the identification stage, the network identifies the quality, criteria of users that have not specified their requirements and, translates them into QoS metrics; The second stage is the probing stage or resource estimating stage, AC protocol estimates the current status of the network resources and calculates the value of PFA; Finally, in the decision stage, the AC searches and makes the decision according to both the state of the network resources and the value of PFA.

As this feedback-based design is independent with the routing protocols in MANETs, although there are the various behavior of existing AC, AC coupled with routing and without routing protocols, stateless and stateful admission control, distributed and centralized admission control, if the appropriate metrics is chosen as the feedback parameters. Our design can combine with these existing AC smoothly.

The above scheme can be implemented by a cross-layer approach, including an adaptive feedback scheme and admission scheme to provide information about the network status and the possibilities of false admission.

5   Conclusion and Future Work

This paper presents metrics for quantifying the satisfaction ratio of both the data sessions and the MANET with AC protocol, by monitoring the data transfer stage closely to get the number of time interval fail to meet the requirement, then by using existing metrics and values, returns a value along a linear trend, that is the pre-estimate of probabilities of false admission and successful completed transfer. Analysis shows that these new metrics are fine-gained and have a close relation with the existing AC performance metrics.

Also, we propose a feedback-based admission control design, in which, false admission ratio is predicted and used as the feedback parameter.

Further, as our future work, the design of feedback of admission control should be implemented to verify the accurateness of the satisfaction related metrics and the performance of the AC protocol both in a simulation system and real MANET environment. Beside, the predictions for false admission and successful completed session can be optimized by learning from the simulation experiences.

Acknowledgments. This work is supported by the National Science Foundation of China under Grant No. 61073076, Science and Technology on Information Transmission and Dissemination in Communication Networks Laboratory under Grant No. ITD-U10001, and Beihang University Innovation & Practice Fund for Graduate. The authors would like to thank great support.

References

1. Hanzo, L., Tafazolli, R.: Admission control schemes for 802.11-based multi-hop mobile ad hoc networks: a survey. IEEE Communications Surveys & Tutorials (2009)
2. Hanzo-II, L., Tafazolli, R.: A Survey of QoS routing solutions for Mobile Ad hoc Networks. IEEE Communications Surveys & Tutorials 9(2), 50–70 (2007)
3. Haitao, Z., et al.: A Soft Admission Control methodology for wireless Ad-Hoc networks: Evaluating the impact on existing flows before admission. In: 7th International Symposium on Communication Systems Networks and Digital Signal Processing, CSNDSP 2010 (2010)
4. Statovci-Halimi, B.: Adaptive admission control for supporting class-based QoS. In: 6th EURO-NF Conference on Next Generation Internet, NGI 2010 (2010)
5. Zhang, S., Yu, F.R., Leung, V.C.M.: Joint connection admission control and routing in IEEE 802.16-based mesh networks. IEEE Transactions on Wireless Communications 9(4), 1370–1379 (2010)
6. Yang, Y., Kravets, R.: Contention-Aware Admission control for ad-hoc networks. IEEE Transactions on Mobile Computing 4(4) (2005)
7. Hanzo II, L., Tafazolli, R.: QoS-Aware Routing and Admission Control in Shadow-Fading Environments for Multirate MANETs. IEEE Transactions on Mobile Computing 10(5), 622–637 (2011)
8. Bashandy, A.R., Chong, E.K.P., Ghafoor, A.: Generalized quality-of-service routing with resource allocation. IEEE Journal on Selected Areas in Communications 23(2), 450–463 (2005)
9. Saxena, N., Tsudik, G., Jeong, H.Y.: Efficient Node Admission and Certificateless Secure Communication in Short-Lived MANETs. IEEE Transactions on Parallel and Distributed Systems 20(2), 158–170 (2009)
10. Kone, V., Nandi, S.: QoS Constrained Adaptive Routing Protocol For Mobile Adhoc Networks. In: 9th International Conference on Information Technology, ICIT 2006 (2006)
11. Hongwei, L., Xinbing, W., Hsiao-Hwa, C.: Adaptive Call Admission Control for Multi-Class Services in Wireless Networks. In: IEEE International Conference on Communications, ICC 2008 (2008)

WiEyeTNB: A Wireless Sensor Based Drowning Detection System for Enhanced Parental Care

Balaji Hariharan, Riji N. Das, and Arjun S.

Amrita Center for Wireless Networks and Applications
AMRITA Vishwa Vidyapeetham, Amrita University
Kollam, Kerala, India
balajih@amrita.edu,
{rijindas,aarjun.amrita.uni}@gmail.com

Abstract. Drowning is considered as the third leading cause of unintentional injury death globally. In many low and middle income countries drowning is one of the leading causes of death, especially for children under 12 years old. According to the World Health Organization (WHO) report 388000 people died in 2004 as a result of drowning around the world. The overall global rate of drowning among children is 7.8 deaths per 10000 populations. Advances in sensing devices and integrated circuit technology pave the way for many smart sensing products. WiEyeTNB, Wireless Eye That Never Blinks, discusses the novel notion of designing a smart sensor product for detecting drowning in advance, especially among the children under the age of 5. Smart sensor devices consist of a microprocessor, RF transceiver, one or more sensors and powering devices. The proposed system issues an alarm through a wireless network so that immediate attention can be given to the casualty. Simulation of the system is performed using QualNet 5.0.2 Network Simulator and evaluated the performance of the proposed system architecture.

Keywords: Drowning, Wireless Sensor, Unintentional Death, WiEyeTNB, QualNet Simulator.

1 Introduction

This work started in view of the ever increasing death due to drowning especially in low and middle income countries. Children under 5 years of age have the highest drowning mortality rates worldwide [1]. In 2004, drowning took the life of approximately 175 000 children and youth under the age of 20 years around the world. Out of which 98.1% of these deaths registered in low-income and middle-income countries. The lack of direct adult supervision, even for very short periods of time, is the main cause in most of the drowning deaths of children under the age of 5. Causes may vary for other age group children. In general males are more prone to drowning than females. This may be due to increased exposure to water and riskier behavior of males. This paper concentrates on the unintentional drowning death of children especially under the age of 5.

P. Ren et al. (Eds.): WICON 2011, LNICST 98, pp. 511–520, 2012.

The proposed system, WiEyeTNB, uses a wireless sensor unit that collects process and transmits data. The sensor unit contains of a microprocessor, RF transceiver, one or more sensors and powering devices. The sensor unit is designed as a light weight wearable ear-ring so that it comes in the same level as the mouth of a human being. Water level crossing the mouth level can be dangerous and causes respiratory impairment that even leads to death. Therefore identifying an event, in which water reaches the mouth level, in advance through the sensors equipped along with the ear-ring helps to provide an early alarm to avoid unintentional drowning.

The sensor unit in the form of an ear ring detects the presence of water when the water-detecting sensor senses the presence of water. A high probability of drowning event is detected if the sensor unit detects the presence of water above a predefined threshold level. Data collected by the sensors are analyzed and issue an early alarm to avoid the child from drowning. The sensor periodically monitors the presence of water beyond a predefined threshold limit, and issues an alarm if the water level crosses the limit.

2   Related Works

2.1   POSEIDON Computer Aided Drowning Detection System

The Poseidon system is an intelligent system that uses proprietary computer vision technology to help provide constant surveillance [2] of the water pools and monitor the trajectories [3] of the swimmers. Cameras are mounted under the water in the walls of the pool for deep water or overhead to monitor shallower areas. All these cameras give a complete and overlapping view of the swimming pool. The network of all the cameras monitors swimmers in the pool in real-time. The images captured by the cameras are analyzed by the central processing system of Poseidon system. When the system detects a swimmer in difficulty, it issues an alarm so that the life-guards can attend the casualty. The system alerts lifeguards via a LED display or mobile phone or a pager and a supervision workstation within 10 seconds of the occurrence of the drowning activity. The workstation provides a way to provide and visualize the operation of the system. The user interface associated with the workstation allows operators to view and see the alerts when they happen. Real-time video images of the incident and its location are displayed and recorded immediately on a supervision workstation.

The Poseidon system is intended to complement lifeguards, not to replace them or reduce their responsibilities or vigilance. Under no circumstances should the presence or use of Poseidon result in the reduction or modification of lifeguard staffing or duties as required by regulation or normal practice.

2.2   SACUNDA Pool Security System

SACUNDA is a swimming pool safety vigilance system for preventing children from drowning. It's a unique state-of-the-art technology designed to alert parents and caregivers of potential drowning by creating an invisible ever present underwater passive "acoustic net" [4] below the surface of the water. When a child falls into the pool, acoustic net is broken immediately and send distinct signal to alert parents or guardians. SACUNDA system can send a response in less than 1 second in case of event detection. SACUNDA is not a system to replace parental care but to assist them to save lives in case of accidental drowning. In SACUNDA, sensors placed underwater act as invisible acoustic net. These sensors are capable of detecting intrusions in the form of drowning children.

The main components of SACUNDA are underwater sensor, command station, control panel and a remote control. The underwater sensor is used to detect acoustic energy in the water. The sensor is also capable of taking pictures of underwater acoustic energy. Analysis of the acoustic energy is done by a dedicated digital system equipped with specific DSP software. SACUNDA's central processing unit analyses the acoustic pictures received from all the sensors inside the pool in real-time. When SACUNDA detects an intrusion similar to a six year old baby, it sends a wireless alarm to the control panel. The control panel controls the main operations of the system.

A simple user interface associated with the control panel helps the parents to view the system status and alerts when it happens. A remote control, a hand-held wireless transmitter, is used for shutting down the siren from a distance, if needed.

3   System Design

Fig.1 shows the overall system architecture of WiEyeTNB. The architecture is based on the assumption that drowning happens in the premises of home or school due to the lack of attention from the adult, may be teachers or caregivers. WiEyeTNB is not an alternative to parental care; rather it assists parents or caregivers to understand drowning in advance and thereby avoids causality due to drowning.

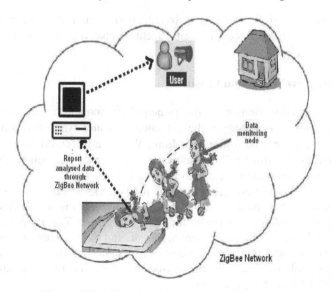

Fig. 1. WiEyeTNB Overall System Architecture

WiEyeTNB concentrates on the unintentional drowning death of children especially under the age of 5. The child to be monitored has to be equipped with a sensor unit in the form of an ear-ring. The sensor unit is designed as a compact one, so that it can be easily wearable even for a small child.

A ZigBee network monitors the area where the home or school is situated. The water-detecting sensor fixed in the form of an ear-ring detects a drowning event when it happens and sent the message to the processing unit through the wireless network. Then an alarm is issued so that immediate attention can be given to avoid drowning.

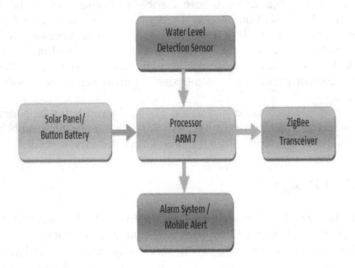

Fig. 2. WiEyeTNB System Design

The architecture of WiEyeTNB is based on five main components: water-level detection sensor, central processing unit, ZigBee transceiver, powering unit and alarm unit as shown in Fig 2.

3.1   Water-Level Detection Sensor

Water-level Detection Sensor is the principal component in the sensing unit of WiEyeTNB. This sensor detects the presence of water when the sensor comes in contact with water beyond a threshold limit, W_T. The threshold water limit is set in order to avoid false alarming. Fig. 3 shows how the sensor unit detects the presence of water, in case of a drowning event, and issues an alarm.

The water-level detection sensor continuously checks whether the sensor comes in contact with water beyond a threshold water level, W_T. If the sensor finds the current water-level is beyond W_T then the system issues an alarm. The alarm helps parents or caregivers to know about the potential threat and take necessary steps to avoid drowning. The sensing unit also contains of an Analog-to-Digital Converter (ADC). The analog signals produced by the sensors are digitized by ADC and sent to the processing unit for further processing.

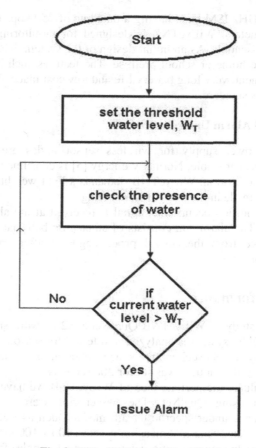

Fig. 3. WiEyeTNB Event Identification

3.2   Central Processing Unit

The Central Processing Unit (CPU) mainly consists of a microcontroller/microprocessor associated with a small storage unit including on-chip memory and flash memory. The processing unit is responsible for performing tasks, processing data and controlling the functionality of other components of the sensor node. A wireless system architecture demands the processor to do all the necessary computing capability coupled with low power consumption. Moreover the size of the processor should be compact in nature and thereby less costly. WiEyeTNB uses such a processor, an ARM 7 processor, in its design.

3.3   ZigBee Transceiver

The wireless sensor unit communicates with the alarm unit via a ZigBee wireless transceiver. The 802.15.4 standard specifies the physical layer and medium access control for low-rate. Low-cost wireless communications whilst protocols [7] like ZigBee is build upon this by developing the upper layers of the OSI Reference Model. Wireless sensor communications tend to operate in the RF industrial, scientific and medical (ISM) bands which are designed for unlicensed operation.

ZigBee in the 2.5 GHz ISM band having a data rate of 250 kbps offers an outdoor range close to 100 meters. WiEyeTNB is designed for monitoring children in the premises of homes or schools. As an initial design of the system, a ZigBee network is setup for covering the home or school premise. The features such as reliability, self healing, easy deployment, very long battery life and low cost made WiEyeTNB to use ZigBee as the wireless standard.

3.4   Powering and Alarm Units

The main type of power supply for wireless sensor nodes are batteries, either rechargeable or non-rechargeable. Normally energy [5] is consumed for sensing, data processing and communication. WiEyeTNB demands a light weight battery since the sensor node has to be made in the form of an ear- ring.

When an alarm condition occurs, the signal is received at the alarm unit through the ZigBee network. The alarm unit consists of an electric bell that is activated upon receiving the message from the central processing unit after analysing the data captured by the sensor.

4   System Performance

For the performance study of WiEyeTNB QualNet 5.0.2 network simulator has been used. Performance of the system is analyzed and tested for various terrains and path loss models. Path loss models such as free space, suburban, irregular terrain are used for simulation. The simulation time was set for 300 seconds.

In an effort to evaluate the performance of WiEyeTNB we have developed a few simulation scenarios using QualNet. These scenarios were designed to target WiEyeTNB performance under specific terrain models such as free space, path loss and irregular terrain.   The scenario dimension is set as 100 x 100 m^2. Fig. 4 shows the initial simulation setup having properties such as channel (single) frequency 2.4GHz, path loss model two-way type and non-fading model.

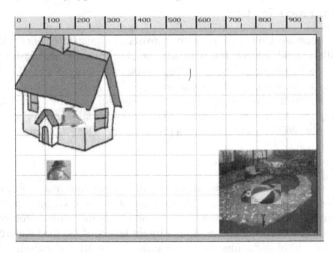

Fig. 4. Initial Simulation Setup Using QualNet 5.0.2

Fig. 5 shows the various stages of a specific simulation process. Image 1 shows a child moving towards a pool to pick her toy ball. Image 2 depicts the drowning event. The sensor unit identifies the event and issues the potential danger to the processing unit is shown in Image 3. The processing unit issues a warning alarm to the caregiver, shown in Image 4.

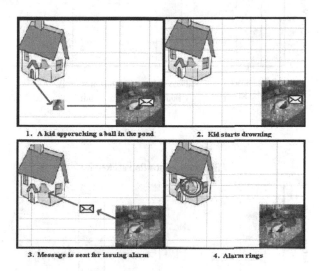

Fig. 5. Different Simulation Stages Using QualNet 5.0.2

The simulation results show that the system could issue a successful alarm, within an area close to 100 meters, even when the terrain is free space, path loss or irregular. The simulation is performed for a specific duration, 300 seconds, for the three different terrains.

Fig. 6 shows the packet analysis of the simulation of WiEyeTNB. Packets sent and received for three different terrains are analyzed. No considerable loss of packets are noticed when the terrain is changed from free space to path loss or irregular. Therefore WiEyeTNB performs well and issues an alert irrespective of the environment in which the system is deployed.

5 Challenges and Future Work

Being a wireless sensor related system WiEyeTNB has to overcome lot of challenges. Out of which the radio range of the wireless network has got prime importance. The child under monitoring should be inside the radio range of the wireless network. The ZigBee network provides an outdoor range close to 100 meters. This might serve the surveillance of the premises of homes better; repeaters must be used in case of schools with large premises to get additional range.

Increased vegetation in the environment has an effect on the received signal strength. That may sometimes cause no alarming or even false alarming. Apart from that multipath loss [6], absorption loss, diffraction loss and atmospheric loss have influence on the signal strength.

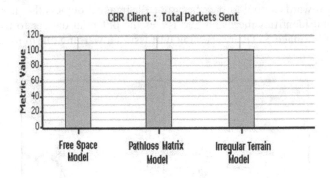

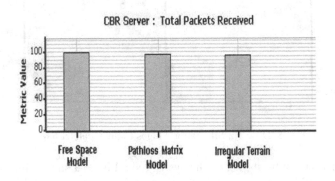

Fig. 6. Packet Analysis of WiEyeTNB Simulation

The most general empirical model for path loss is given as follows:

$$L_1(d) = L_0 + 10 \, c \, \log_{10}(d) \tag{1}$$

where L_0 is called reference point loss and represents the loss value at one meter distance away from the transmitter, c is the path loss component depending on the environment, d is the Euclidian distance (in m) from the transmitter. Parameters L_0 and c have been determined for various environments through empirical studies for possible values of L_0 and c in various environments.

Another major challenge associated with WiEyeTNB is the design of the compact sensor unit. The sensor unit is designed to be in the form of an ear-ring which is light-weight in nature. Various tradeoffs can be made in selecting suitable components for the sensor unit to make it compact. In wireless sensor networks although the average current consumption of a sensor unit is low, the instantaneous current can be high. This instantaneous or peak current consumption can have an adverse effect on the battery's actual capacity. In WiEyeTNB the sensor unit which is in the form of an ear-ring is made as a detachable device. It needs to be worn only when the child goes to places that need to be monitored. Therefore the battery can be recharged when the device is not in use. This helps in selecting light-weight battery that suits the compact design of the sensor unit.

An emergency alarm only need not avoid a potential casualty unless the location of the child is not known. Future work will be concentrating on having a simple user interface at home or school office so that the display helps the parents or caregivers to view the position of the child. A GPS module has to be included in the sensor unit to keep track of the child in the region.

By increasing the radio range of the network, WiEyeTNB can be used for monitoring children in large areas. ZigBee is a low tier, ad hoc, terrestrial, wireless standard in some ways similar to Bluetooth. The IEEE 802.15.4 standard is commonly known as ZigBee, but ZigBee has some features in addition to those of 802.15.4. It operates in the 868 MHz, 915 MHz and 2.4 GHz ISM bands. Even though ZigBee has features such as reliability, self healing, easy deployment, very long battery life, low cost etc, the range it offers is less compared to the other competitive standards. The maximum outdoor range of ZigBee is around 100 meters. Future work will be looking into wireless standards such as IEEE 802.11a/b/g/n in order to compensate the low outdoor range of ZigBee network.

A better range and an improved data rate will always enhance the effectiveness of any wireless system. Table 1 shows the comparative study of various IEEE 802.11 standards. Incorporating the advanced wireless standards like IEEE 802.11 g/n will widen the scope of WiEyeTNB. In future WiEyeTNB can be used for monitoring children in wide range of areas like parks and beaches.

Table 1. IEEE 802.11 Radio Classifications

Characteristics	IEEE 802.11 b	IEEE 802.11 a	IEEE 802.11 g	IEEE 802.11 n
Frequency	2.4 GHz	5 GHz	2.4 GHz	2.4GHz / 5 GHz
Data Rate	11Mbps	54Mbps	54Mbps	150Mbps
Indoor Range	38m	35m	38m	70m
Outdoor Range	140m	120m	140m	250m

6   Conclusions

WiEyeTNB is a system to aid the parents and caregivers to enhance the care given to children especially from drowning. The existing systems are purely based on surveillance cameras. Such systems need large number of monitoring cameras, high computing processors and huge storage space. WiEyeTNB is based on wireless sensor technology which is economical and does not demand high commutating processors. Moreover a single sensor replaces the need of any number of monitoring cameras which are costly in general. The system performance is analyzed for various terrain as well as path loss models. WiEyeTNB offers accurate alarming even in high vegetation environments. WiEyeTNB's range is limited to monitor a normal home or school premise. Incorporating wireless networks that offer high outdoor range can revolutionize the monitoring range of WiEyeTNB. Still WiEyeTNB resembles the quote "an ounce of prevention is worth a pound of cure".

Acknowledgments. We are grateful to Amrita University for providing an ambience where research and innovation are celebrated as a way of life. We are also thankful to our Chancellor Mata Amritanandamayi Devi who taught us the importance of doing research that aims to uplift the needs of the society.

References

1. WHO Website (2011),
   http://www.who.int/violence_injury_prevention/child/injury/
   world_report/en/index.html
2. Eng, H.-L., Toh, K.-A., Yau, W.-Y., Wang, J.: DEWS: A Live Visual Surveillance System for Early Drowning Detection at Pool. IEEE Transactions on Circuits and Systems for Video Technology 18(2) (February 2008)
3. Lu, W., Tan, Y.-P.: Swimmer Motion Analysis with Application to Drowning Detection. In: IEEE International Symposium on Circuits and Systems, ISCAS 2002 (May 2002)
4. Eng, H.-L., Toh, K.-A., Kam, A.H., Wang, J., Yau, W.-Y.: An automatic drowning detection surveillance system for challenging outdoor pool environments. In: Proceedings of the Ninth IEEE International Conference on Computer Vision, ICCV 2003 (2003)
5. Raghunathan, V., Schurgers, C., Park, S., Srivastava, M.: Energy Aware Wireless Sensor Networks. In: Wireless Sensor Networks. Kluwer Academic Publishers, Norwell (2004)
6. HARWAD University Website (2011),
   http://adsabs.harvard.edu/abs/2010AIPC.1285..509N
7. Karl, H., Willig, A.: Protocols and Architectures for Wireless Sensor Networks, pp. 15–329. John Wiley & Sons (2005)

An Effective Scheme for Detecting Articulation Points in Zone Routing Protocol

Tsung-Chuan Huang[1], Wei-Chung Cheng[2], and Lung Tang[3]

Department of Electrical Engineering, National Sun Yat-sen University
Kaohsiung, Taiwan
tch@mail.nsysu.edu.tw, freeze.bilsted@gmail.com,
D953010007@student.nsysu.edu.tw

Abstract. Zone Routing Protocol (ZRP) is a typical hybrid routing protocol used in Mobile Ad Hoc Networks (MANETs). Hybrid routing protocols are especially suitable for dynamic environments because they combine the best features of proactive and reactive routing protocols. The Gossip-based Zone Routing Protocol (GZRP) uses a gossip scheme, in which the node forwards a packet to some nodes instead of all nodes to further reduce the control overhead. However, GZRP does not perform well when the network includes articulation points since packets will be lost if an articulation node happens not to forward the packet or nodes happen not to forward packets to the articulation point. To raise the packet delivery ratio, the gossip probability of articulation points must be set to 1 and the packets to be forwarded must be sent to the articulation points in peripheral nodes. Accordingly, how to identify articulation nodes in the network becomes a critical issue. This paper proposes an effective scheme, called *articulation point detection* (APD), to find the articulation points. Simulation results show that the proposed APD-GZRP (GZRP with articulation point detection) can improve the packet delivery ratio and reduce both the control overhead and power consumption.

Keywords: Mobile Ad Hoc Network (MANET), articulation point, biconnected component, zone routing protocol, gossiping.

1 Introduction

A *Mobile Ad Hoc Network* (MANET) is a self-configuring network consisting of mobile devices (or nodes), where each mobile device is autonomous and connected through wireless links. In a MANET, the nodes are assumed to be free to move randomly and are able to communicate with each other by multi-hop links without the help of a fixed network infrastructure. With the proliferation of wireless devices, including cellular phones, personal digital assistants (PDAs), laptops, and microsensors, MANETs have become a challenging field of research.

In MANETs, *broadcasting* is a primitive way for a node to emit a message via wireless channels to its neighbor nodes. It is significant in terms of collecting global information and discovering neighbors. Most existing routing protocols,

P. Ren et al. (Eds.): WICON 2011, LNICST 98, pp. 521–533, 2012.
© Institute for Computer Sciences, Social Informatics and Telecommunications Engineering 2012

such as *Highly Dynamic Destination Sequenced Distance Vector Routing* (DSDV) [1], *Ad Hoc On-Demand Distance Vector Routing* (AODV) [2], *Dynamic Source Routing* (DSR) [3], and *Zone Routing Protocol* (ZRP) [4], rely on broadcasting for route and neighbor discovery. Additionally, broadcasting can also be used for paging a particular host, sending an alarm signal, or determining a route to a particular host [5].

Traditional broadcasting is called *blind flooding*; each node in the network re-transmits the message upon receiving the first copy of it or ignores the message if it is a duplicate one. Although blind flooding can obtain high reachability, it generates a large number of redundant messages. Transmitting more redundant messages will consume more system resources, such as bandwidth and battery power. Furthermore, the redundant messages will in turn induce packet collision, reduce the packet delivery ratio and increase the end-to-end delay. To lower re-dundant transmissions, several methods have been proposed. These methods can be identified as the *probabilistic* scheme, the *counter-based* scheme, the *distance-based* scheme, the *location-based* scheme and the *cluster-based* scheme [5]. These schemes restrain the redundant packet transmission such that the intermedi-ate nodes forward the received broadcasting packets only under specific condi-tions. In other words, the intermediate nodes do not retransmit the broadcasting packets blindly.

In general, the proactive routing protocol has little delay in data transmission because all routes are in the routing table, while the reactive routing protocol does not make extra overhead in maintaining the routing table but exhibits more delay time in data transmission and route discovery. Either proactive or reactive routing protocol is insufficient for all situations in terms of the node mobility, network size and traffic load. Therefore, the hybrid routing protocol is proposed to combine the advantages of proactive and reactive protocols. Zone Routing Protocol (ZRP) is a typical hybrid routing protocol which uses the proactive routing scheme, *IntrAzone Routing Protocol* (IARP) [6], within a zone domain and utilizes the reactive routing scheme, *IntErzone Routing Protocol* (IERP) [7], for inter-zone routing.

As large overlapping zone in ZRP will cause the maintenance of IARP to incur a high control overhead, Haas *et al.* [8] applied gossiping on ZRP by sending the route request to only part of the peripheral nodes rather than all of them to reduce the control overhead. However, the *Gossip-based Zone Routing Protocol* (GZRP) does not perform well when the network includes articulation points because packets will be lost if an articulation node happens not to forward the packet or nodes happen not to forward packets to the articulation point. In this paper, we propose an effective scheme to detect the articulation points by making use of the information in routing tables and link-state table of ZRP. After the articulation points have been identified, the packet delivery ratio can be enhanced, while the control overhead can be reduced by setting the gossip probability of articulation points to 1 and sending the forwarding packet to the articulation points in peripheral nodes.

The remainder of this paper is organized as follows. Section 2 introduces the related work, including gossiping, Zone Routing Protocol (ZRP) and traditional methods in dealing with the articulation points. Section 3 introduces our proposal for detecting the articulation point in ZRP. Simulation results are revealed and discussed in Section 4. Finally, we offer our conclusions in Section 5.

2   Related Work

2.1   Gossiping

Gossiping is an instance of percolation, which is a method employed to solve the broadcast storm. Gossiping forwards the control packets by a specific probability. Compared with flooding, gossiping has the advantage of broadcasting fewer control messages. The Gossiping scheme can be classified into the *static* gossip and *adaptive* gossip [8,9].

Static gossip, or pure gossip, sends packets with probability 1 for the source node, otherwise forwards packets with probability p for other nodes. The challenge of pure gossip, **GOSSIP1** (p, k), lies in the situation when the source node has only a few neighbors. The adaptive gossip schemes includes **GOSSIP2** (p_1, k, p_2, n), **GOSSIP3** (p, k, m) and **GOSSIP4** (p, k, k_0), which work depend on different factors of Ad Hoc Networks. The readers can refer to [8,9] for the details. **GOSSIP4** (p, k, k_0) is just like **GOSSIP1** (p, k), except that each node has k_0 as its zone radius.

Due to the mobility of MANETs, unpredictable articulation points will decrease the performance when using gossiping in ZRP.

2.2   Zone Routing Protocol (ZRP)

Zone Routing Protocol (ZRP) is a hybrid routing protocol in MANET, which combines proactive (IARP) and reactive (IERP) routing protocols together with the *Bordercast Resolution Protocol* (BRP) [10] with a query-control mechanism.

IARP is used to maintain the topology information of a limited scope, called *zone*. The zone radius of IARP is evaluated relying on how far the source node can propagate. This distance is measured by hops. When the minimum distance from a node to source node is equal to the zone radius, the nodes are called the *peripheral nodes*. Each node in a zone will broadcast routing information to its neighbors, so a larger zone radius may result in more routing traffic.

IERP is adopted to send data when destination nodes are outside the zone, which finds the route by initiating a route discovery process. Instead of flooding, this process uses "bordercasting" with a query control mechanism [11,12]. The query control mechanism can reduce the control traffic by Query Detection (QD1/QD2), Early Termination (ET) and Random Query Processing Delay (RQPD) [11,12].

BRP is a multicast service, which delivers packets efficiently to peripheral nodes. Using BRP in IERP can avoid redundant querying within a routing zone. This service sends the route request outward by the information which IARP provides, via multicast, to the surrounding peripheral nodes.

2.3   Articulation Point

In graph theory, a *articulation point*, also named *cutpoint* or *cut vertex*, is one whose removal increases the number of components [13]. Fig. 1 illustrates the articulation points u and v.

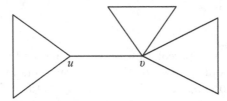

Fig. 1. A simple graph with articulation points u and v

In MANETs, the network topology can not avoid the existence of articulation points because of node mobility and random deployment. How to identify articulation points is an important issue in GZRP for the following reasons. The first is from the point of view of intrazone information. As shown in Fig. 2, the source node S wants to forward packets to nodes u and w via node v. Due to the characteristics of Gossip-based Zone Routing Protocol, if node v does not forward packets, nodes u and w will not receive the packet sent from source node S. This results in outdated local zone information, so the data transmission from one zone to another will be blocked because of wrong zone information.

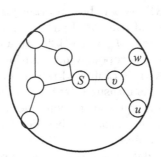

Fig. 2. Intrazone information with articulation point v

The second reason is from the viewpoint of interzone information. Let us look at Fig. 3. The source node S wants to broadcast the *RouteRequest* packet to nodes u and w, which are in other zones, through node v. The route request packets can not find the route in Gossip-based Zone Routing Protocol if v does not forward the packet. And the data transmission will be blocked with route failure.

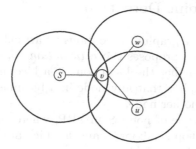

Fig. 3. Interzone information with articulation point v

The third reason comes from interzone routing. When a node sends *RouteRequest* packets to only part of peripheral nodes rather than to all peripheral nodes, the *RouteRequest* message will be blocked if the articulation points of peripheral nodes do not receive the *RouteRequest*. For the example in Fig. 4, since the node S is not an articulation point, it does not have to send *RouteRequest* packets to node v in gossip-based zone routing protocol. If node v does not receive the *RouteRequest* packet, the node S may not find nodes u and w; this also result in route failure.

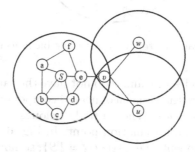

Fig. 4. Interzone routing with articulation point v

Depth-First Search (DFS) [14] is a traditional method to find the articulation point. However, this approach, such as Distributed Depth-First Search (DDFS) and CAM [15] require a communication cost of $O(dn^2)$ where n is the number of nodes and d is the maximum degree of node. In [16], Cut Vertex Detection (CVD) has been proposed for determining the articulation points in *static* Wireless Sensor Networks (WSNs). It needs only $O(dn)$ communication cost. However, it is not suitable for MANETs because the nodes in MANETs are free to move. In this paper, we propose a new method to detect the articulation point by taking advantage of the information in the routing table and link state table in IARP of ZRP. The communication complexity is also only $O(dn)$.

3   Articulation Point Detection

The biconnected graph is a graph that contains no articulation point [17]. Based on the concept, this paper proposes the *articulation point detection* (APD) algorithm to determine whether the local zone is a biconnected graph. The key point of biconnected graph is that any node in a biconnected graph must have more than one way to another node.

Fig. 5 shows a local zone of node S in ZRP, where the peripheral nodes, v and w, have the same 2-hop neighbors t and u which are in the local zone of S, and node v and w and their neighboers include cover all neighbors of node S. This means that all neighbors of node S are in the same biconnected component, so the local zone forms a biconnected graph. By the definition of a biconnected graph, the local zone of source node contains no articulation point.

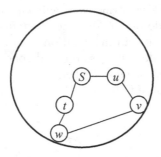

Fig. 5. A local zone topology with one biconnected graph

In Fig. 6, peripheral nodes w, v and y do not have the same neighbor except S. Hence, this graph has more than one biconnected components, $B_1 = \{x, y\}$, $B_2 = \{x, S\}$, and $B_3 = \{S, t, u, v, w\}$. When a node belongs to multiple biconnected components, this node is an articulation point. In Fig. 6, since node S belongs to two biconnected components, i.e. $B_2 \cap B_3 = \{S\}$, so node S is an articulation point.

Fig. 5 and Fig. 6 illustrate that the number of biconnected components in a local zone of S will determine whether S is an articulation point. In other words, the detection of articulation point depends on the number of biconnected components in a local zone.

The proposed APD algorithm is different from other articulation point detection scheme because APD does not build any tree in the local zone. Instead, we make use of the information in routing table and link state table of IARP, without extra overhead, to detect the articulation points. This articulation point detection (APD) consists of two phases: biconnected component identification and articulation point checking.

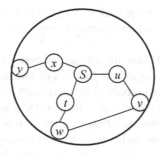

Fig. 6. A local zone topology with two components (connected graph with articulation point S)

Algorithm 1. Articulation Point Detection

Input: Node n, n's Routing Table, n's Link State Table, Zone Radius
Output: n is an articulation point or not

1: Arbitrarily choose two peripheral nodes of n, v and w
2: Let S be the set of the common neighbors of nodes v and w in the local zone of n
3: **if** $S - \{n\} = \emptyset$ **then**
4:         **return** n is an articulation point
5: **else**
6:         Let all the neighbors of n be in set N and all the neighbors of nodes v and w be in set P
7:         **while** $N - P \neq \emptyset$ **do**
8:               Arbitrarily choose a peripheral node u, $u \in N$, and let all the neighbors of u be in set T
9:               **if** $T \cap P = \{n\}$ **then**
10:                    **return** n is an articulation point.
11:              **end if**
12:              $P \leftarrow P \cup T$
13:         **end while**
14:         **return** n is not an articulation point.
15: **end if**

In the APD algorithm, the number of biconnected components in the local zone is determined first. (The details are described in the section of biconnected component identification below.) Then, the algorithm checks whether the node is in the same biconnected component. (The details are presented in the section of articulation point checking below.)

3.1 Biconnected Component Identification

Given the zone information of a node S, we put the neighbors of S into set N, called $N(S)$. We randomly chooses two peripheral nodes v, w from $N(S)$ to check whether the nodes, v and w, have common neighbor nodes which are in the local zone of S.

For example, in Fig. 5, nodes v and w have common neighbor nodes t and u, so the local zone only has one biconnected component, so the node S is not an articulation point.

In certain cases, the local zone might be divided into one *connected* components and one *biconnected* component instead of two *bioconnected* components. The connected component is consisted of biconnected component. If there are two biconnected components and their intersection is $\{S\}$, the node S is an articulation point. In other words, there are two connected components C_1, C_2 and two biconnected components in these two connected components, such that $B_1 \subset C_1$ and $B_2 \subset C_2$. If $C_1 \cap C_2 = \{S\}$, it means that only two biconnected components in these connected components have S as their intersection, i.e., $B_1 \cap B_2 = \{S\}$, so S is an articulation point.

In the example of Fig. 6, the biconnected component identification stage divides the graph into one biconnected component, $B_1 = \{S, t, u, v, w\}$, and one connected component, $C_1 = \{x, y, S\}$. C_1 consists of two biconnected components: $B_2 = \{x, y\}$ and $B_3 = \{x, S\}$. Because $B_1 \cap C_1 = \{S\}$ and $B_2 \cup B_3 = C_1$, the node S belongs to two biconnected components, $B_1 = \{S, t, u, v, w\}$ and $B_3 = \{x, S\}$, and $B_1 \cap B_3 = \{S\}$. So the node S is an articulation point. From this example, we can see that the APD algorithm can also the articulation point even if the graph is divided into two connected components, or one connected components and one biconnected component.

If the local zone has more than one biconnected component, node S is accordingly an articulation point. Otherwise, the next stage, articulation point checking, will be proceeded.

3.2   Articulation Point Checking

Given a biconnected component and unchecked peripheral nodes in the local zone, this stage is to confirm the articulation node. The unchecked peripheral nodes are examined one by one to see whether they are in the biconnected component. For each unchecked peripheral node x, let the neighbor nodes of x be $N(x)$. If there is a node in $N(x)$, except node S, belonging to the biconnected component, then x is also in the biconnected component. Otherwise node x is in another biconnected component. Since the two biconnected components only have one common node S, S is therefore an articulation point.

For example, in Fig. 6, the set of y's neighbor nodes is $N(y) = \{x, S\}$. $N(y)$ only has source node S in the biconnected component. As mentioned above, it is apparently to know that the node y is disconnected with the biconnected component and the source node S is an articulation point. By using the APD algorithm, the node S can determine it is an articulation point.

4   Performance Evaluation

We compare APD-GZRP, ZRP and GZRP by simulation using NS-2 [18]. In the simulation, the MANET environment consists of $50\backslash100\backslash150$ mobile nodes which are chosen from a uniform random distribution with initial positions in an area of 1300×1300 $meter^2$. The nodes move based on the *Random-Waypoint* model [19]; the movement starts from the initial position to a random destination with a random speed (uniformly distributed between $0 \sim 14$m/s). This simulation varies the pause time by $0\backslash80\backslash180s$. The pause time will affect the relative speeds of the mobile nodes. The transmission range of each mobile node is 250 meters. The simulation time is 180s and constant bit-rate (CBR) traffic sources are used. The source-destination pairs are chosen randomly over the network and data packet size for all is 512 bytes. The simulation parameters are listed in Table 1.

Table 1. Simulation Parameters

Simulator	NS-2
Simulation time	180 s
Simulation area	$1300 \times 1300m^2$
Number of nodes	$50, 100, 150$
Transmission range	250m
Transmission rate	100 kbps
Max speed	14 m/s
Pause time	$0, 80, 180$ s
Data packet size	512bytes
Movement model	Random-waypoint

The following performance metrics are measured: *packet delivery ratio, normalized routing overhead* and *power consumption*. The *packet delivery ratio* is the ratio of the number of data packets received at the final destination divided by the number of data packets originated from the source nodes. The *normalized routing overhead* is the number of total transmitted routing packets divided by the number of total delivered data packets. The *power consumption* is the total power consumed in the duration of simulation time. The power consumption will influence the lifetime of the wireless mobile node. With the same power energy, lower power consumption of nodes will extend the lifetime of the node and entire network.

4.1   Packet Delivery Ratio

Fig. 7 compares the packet delivery ratio of APD-GZRP, GZRP and ZRP. For articulation points ZRP and APD-GZRP forward the message with probability 1 but GZRP forwards with probability. So, ZRP and APD-GZRP outperform GZRP. The results reveal that APD-GZRP is nearly the same as ZRP in terms of packet delivery ratio.

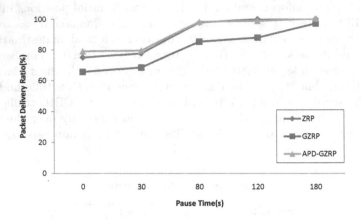

Fig. 7. Packet Delivery Ratio comparison with different pause time

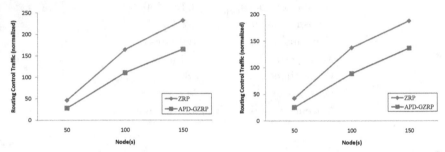

(a) Routing overhead with pause time 0 second.

(b) Routing overhead with pause time 80 seconds.

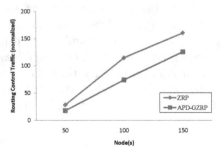

(c) Routing overhead with pause time 180 seconds.

Fig. 8. Routing overhead with different nodes and pause time

4.2   Normalized Routing Overhead

Fig. 8 illustrates the normalized routing overhead of APD-GZRP and ZRP at different pause time in different mobile nodes. These two methods are compared

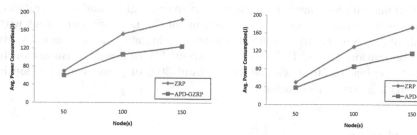

(a) Power consumption with pause time 0 second.

(b) Power consumption with pause time 80 seconds.

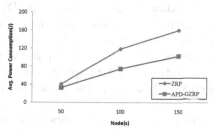

(c) Power consumption with pause time 180 seconds.

Fig. 9. Power consumption with different nodes and pause time

because their packet delivery ratios are about the same. Fig. 8 shows an obvious result that APD-GZRP has less routing overhead than ZRP in all situations.

4.3   Power Consumption

In comparing the power consumption of APD-GZRP and ZRP, the power model and parameters in NS-2 are set as in Table. 2. The initial power of each node is 200 joules (J). A node consumes 2 joules to receive one packet and 5 joules to transmit a packet. When a node is in idle mode, 0.05 joules are consumed.

Table 2. Power model and Parameters

Power Model	Simple
Initial power	200 Joules
Receiving power	2 Joules
Transmitting power	5 Joules
Idle power	0.05 Joules

The power consumptions of APD-GZRP and ZRP are compared in Fig. 9. From the comparison result in Fig. 8, it is reasonable that APD-GZRP consumed less power than ZRP because it incurs lower routing overhead. Both APD-GZRP and ZRP experience low power consumption in sparse regions and comparatively higher power consumption in the dense regions of the network, consistent with the result of Fig. 8 where more control overhead in higher condense network. By further observation, the APD-GZRP saves about 5% of power consumption in low density regions of 50 nodes and saves about 30% of power consumption in high density regions of 150 nodes.

5   Conclusion

This paper presents articulation point detection (APD) with GZRP (APD-GZRP). The proposed scheme utilizes the definition of an articulation point and local zone information to divide subgraphs and confirm the articulation nodes. The articulation nodes will now forward packets with probability 1 in APD-GZRP and general nodes must forward packets to articulation points. Thus, APD-GZRP can effectively improve the packet delivery ratio better than GZRP can.

In the simulation results, three different metrics are measured: *packet delivery ratio*, *normalized routing overhead* and *power consumption*. The packet delivery ratio of APD-GZRP and ZRP is almost equivalent but higher than GZRP. Moreover, the APD-GZRP has lower routing overhead and power consumption than ZRP in a similar packet delivery ratio. Because of that, the APD-GZRP outperforms GZRP and ZRP in MANETs.

Acknowledgments. This work was supported in part by the National Science Council, Taiwan, ROC, under Contract No. NSC98-2221-E-110-153.

References

1. Perkins, C.E., Bhagwat, P.: Highly dynamic destination-sequenced distance-vector routing (dsdv) for mobile computers. In: ACM Conference on Communications Architectures, Protocols and Applications, SIGCOMM 1994, pp. 234–244. ACM, London (1994), http://people.nokia.net/charliep/txt/sigcomm94/paper.ps
2. Perkins, C., Royer, E.: Ad-hoc on-demand distance vector routing. In: Proc. Second IEEE Workshop on Mobile Computing Systems and Applications, pp. 90–100 (February 1999)
3. Johnson, D.B., Maltz, D.A.: Dynamic source routing in ad hoc wireless networks. In: Mobile Computing, pp. 153–181. Kluwer Academic Publishers (1996)
4. Haas, Z.J., Pearlman, M.R., Samar, P.: The zone routing protocol (zrp) for ad hoc networks, Published Online, IETF MANET Working Group, INTERNET-DRAFT (July 2002), expiration: (January 2003), http://www.ietf.org/proceedings/02nov/I-D/draft-ietf-manet-zone-zrp-04.txt
5. Tseng, Y.-C., Ni, S.-Y., Chen, Y.-S., Sheu, J.-P.: The broadcast storm problem in a mobile ad hoc network. Wireless Networks 8, 153–167 (2002), http://dx.doi.org/10.1023/A:1013763825347, doi:10.1023/A:1013763825347

6. Haas, Z.J., Pearlman, M.R., Samar, P.: The intrazone routing protocol (iarp) for ad hoc networks, Published Online, IETF MANET Working Group, INTERNET-DRAFT (July 2002) expiration: (January 2003), http://www.ietf.org/proceedings/02nov/I-D/draft-ietf-manet-zone-iarp-02.txt

7. Haas, Z.J., Pearlman, M.R., Samar, P.: The interzone routing protocol (ierp) for ad hoc networks, Published Online, IETF MANET Working Group, INTERNET-DRAFT (July 2002) expiration: (January 2003), http://www.ietf.org/proceedings/02nov/I-D/draft-ietf-manet-zone-ierp-02.txt

8. Haas, Z.J., Halpern, J.Y., Li, L.: Gossip-based ad hoc routing. IEEE/ACM Trans. Netw. 14, 479–491 (2006)

9. Haas, Z., Halpern, J., Li, L.: Gossip-based ad hoc routing. In: INFOCOM 2002. Twenty-First Annual Joint Conference of the IEEE Computer and Communications Societies. Proceedings, vol. 3, pp. 1707–1716. IEEE (2002)

10. Haas, Z.J., Pearlman, M.R., Samar, P.: The bordercast routing protocol (brp) for ad hoc networks, Published Online, IETF MANET Working Group, INTERNET-DRAFT (July 2002) expiration: (January 2003), http://www.ietf.org/proceedings/02nov/I-D/draft-ietf-manet-zone-brp-02.txt

11. Haas, Z.J., Pearlman, M.R.: The performance of query control schemes for the zone routing protocol. IEEE/ACM Trans. Netw. 9(4), 427–438 (2001)

12. Haas, Z.J., Pearlman, M.R.: The performance of query control schemes for the zone routing protocol. In: SIGCOMM, pp. 167–177 (1998)

13. Harary, F.: Graph Theory, 3rd edn. Addison-Wesley, Reading (1972)

14. Cormen, T.H., Stein, C., Rivest, R.L., Leiserson, C.E.: Introduction to Algorithms, 2nd edn. McGraw-Hill Higher Education (2001)

15. Liu, X., Xiao, L., Kreling, A., Liu, Y.: Optimizing overlay topology by reducing cut vertices. In: Proceedings of the 2006 International Workshop on Network and Operating Systems Support for Digital Audio and Video, NOSSDAV 2006, pp. 17:1–17:6. ACM, New York (2006)

16. Xiong, S., Li, J.: An efficient algorithm for cut vertex detection in wireless sensor networks. In: Proceedings of the 2010 IEEE 30th International Conference on Distributed Computing Systems, ICDCS 2010, pp. 368–377. IEEE Computer Society, Washington, DC (2010)

17. Skiena, S.: Implementing discrete mathematics: combinatorics and graph theory with Mathematica. Addison-Wesley Longman Publishing Co., Inc., Boston (1991)

18. The Network Simulator NS-2, http://www.isi.edu/nsnam/ns/

19. Broch, J., Maltz, D.A., Johnson, D.B., Hu, Y.-C., Jetcheva, J.G.: A performance comparison of multi-hop wireless ad hoc network routing protocols. In: MOBICOM, pp. 85–97 (1998)

Demand-Matching Spectrum Sharing in Cognitive Radio Networks: A Classified Game

Shaohang Cui and Jun Cai

Department of Electrical and Computer Engineering
University of Manitoba, Winnipeg, Manitoba, Canada
{shaohang,jcai}@ee.umanitoba.ca

Abstract. Cognitive Radio (CR) has been proposed as a promising technique to solve spectrum scarcity problem in wireless communications. For the implementation of CR, one major challenge is to design distributed spectrum sharing, which needs to efficiently coordinate CRs in accessing the spectrum opportunistically based on only local information. To address this problem, in this paper, we make use of the heterogeneity among users in cognitive radio networks (CRNs) and propose a distributed cooperative game with classified players. A prioritized CSMA/CA technique is adopted so that CRs select channels and their priority to access channel based on their satisfaction history, a public signal for CRs to collaborate to achieve the Correlated Equilibrium (C.E.). A no-regret learning algorithm is adopted to learn the C.E. Simulation results show that the proposed C.E. based classified game (CECG) can achieve up to 40% better performance compared to the unclassified one.

Keywords: Cognitive radio, distributed spectrum sharing, classified game, correlated equilibrium, no-regret learning.

1 Introduction

With more and more wireless services emerging in the market, the spectrum scarcity problem arises as the bottleneck for the future development of wireless communications. However, based on Mitola's research [1], most fixed allocated spectrum is severely under-utilized. Cognitive Radio (CR) which smartly utilizes spectrum is thus proposed as a promising technology to alleviate the increasing stress on the fixed and limited radio spectrum. In such networks, CRs are secondary users to the spectrum. Namely, they must obey certain interference constraints so that its transmission will not interfere the communication of Primary Users (PUs), the licensed users of the spectrum. In this way, they are envisioned to be aware of the physical environment and capable to adjust their transmission accordingly.

In cognitive radio networks (CRNs), a major challenges is to achieve the coordination among CRs to share the spectrum effectively. However, centralized approaches are deemed to be impractical in CRNs, due to the complexity and cost to setup a Common Control Channel and to exchange control information.

P. Ren et al. (Eds.): WICON 2011, LNICST 98, pp. 534–546, 2012.
© Institute for Computer Sciences, Social Informatics and Telecommunications Engineering 2012

Distributed approaches are thus proposed. The key issue in designing distributed spectrum sharing is that the decisions of spectrum allocation should be made independently by each radio based only on its own information. Some research works have been done in literature. In [2], a biologically-inspired algorithm was proposed, which enabled the CR to eventually learn the appropriate spectrum band and adapt the probability to select a channel. In [3], a non-cooperative game model was used to obtain the spectrum allocation among a primary user and multiple secondary users. The problem was formulated as an oligopoly market competition, and Nash equilibrium (N.E.) is considered as the solution of the game. The Correlated Equilibrium (C.E.), which is more general than the Nash equilibrium, was considered for dynamic spectrum access in [4] and [5]. In [4] and [5], CSMA/CA was adopted as the sharing technique, which allocated channel to CRs equally. However, by considering the heterogeneity of CRNs, in terms of the channel conditions, the application-based channel requirements among CRs, and the time-varying channel availability, sharing channel equally may result in low resource utilization efficiency.

Inspired by prioritized CSMA in IEEE802.11e [6] [7], in this paper, we introduce a priority to classify CRs to improve the network performance, in terms of the number of satisfied CRs by allocating different portion of the channel to CRs based on their demands. A new algorithm to estimate the number of CRs in different priority levels is also proposed. In the channel allocation process, each CR jointly determine its channel selection and priority based on its possible satisfaction and the loss it may introduce to other CRs. Such tradeoff between satisfaction and cost results in a distributed cooperative game which can maximize the satisfaction of the whole network. No-regret learning algorithm is adopted to reach the C.E. of the proposed game. Simulation results show that the C.E. based classified game (CECG) can achieve up to 40% better performance compared to the unclassified game in highly heterogeneous networks.

The rest of this paper is organized as follows: In Section 2, we present the system model and utility function. In Section 3, we study the C.E. and an no-regret learning algorithm. Simulation results are shown in Section 4 and finally conclusions are drawn in Section 5.

2 System Model

Consider an overlay CRN. The primary users have a strict priority on the spectrum access while CRs can only access spectrum not being utilized by PUs. As we focus on the competition and collaboration among CRs in spectrum sharing, we ignore the cost and faults from spectrum sensing. Namely, each CR is equipped with a perfect spectrum sensing technique, which can alway detect the presence of PUs instantly. We consider a simple CR transceiver which can be tuned in a wide range of spectrum, but can operate only on one channel at any time. All CRs are in the interference range of each other, and thus have to compete for the idle channels. CSMA/CA is used as the sharing technique. To improve the efficiency by considering network heterogeneity, we introduce priority mechanism to differentiate users with respect to their specific transmission requirements and channel qualities. Since applying multiple (> 2) priorities may introduce high complexity with marginal improvement on performance, as shown in simulation results, we consider two priority levels in our algorithm.

2.1   Network Structure

Assume that there are N channels in the system, represented as a channel set $\{C_N\}$. Each channel is licensed to a PU and total I CRs seek for channel access opportunistically. CRs belongs to two different classes, i.e., class 1 and class 2, with low and high priority to access channels, respectively. Time is divided into slots and we label them as $t = 1, 2, \ldots$. In a slot, both PUs' activities and CRs' strategies keep unchanged. Each CR's action consists of tow parts: channel selection and priority selection. At the beginning of any slot t, each CR i, $i = 1, 2, \ldots, I$, knows the following:

1) $r_i^{req} \in R^+$: the demand of CR i (in bits per time slot) to satisfy its QoS requirements, where R^+ denotes the set of positive real numbers.

2) $C_{i,n}^t \in R^+$: the channel quality in terms of transmission rate in bits per time slot for CR i on channel n at time t.

3) $A_{i,n}^t \in \{0,1\}$: the availability of channel n for CR i at time t, which is determined by PUs' activities and the locations of both PUs and CR i. $A_{i,n}^t = 1$, if channel n is available for CR i at time t; otherwise, $A_{i,n}^t = 0$. $A_i^t = (A_{i,1}^t, \ldots, A_{i,N}^t)^T$ is the channel availability vector for CR i.

4) Ac_i^{t-1}: the action of CR i in the last slot $t - 1$. $Ac_i^{t-1} = (X_i^{t-1}, P_i^{t-1})$ is chosen from the action set

$$\Omega_i^{t-1} = S_i^{t-1} \times Sp_i^{t-1} \tag{1}$$

In (1), S_i^{t-1} is the channel allocation decision space and can be represented as

$$S_i^{t-1} = \{X_i^{t-1} \in (0,1)^c : X_i^{t-1^T}(1 - A_i^{t-1}) = 0, \sum_{n \in C_N} X_{i,n}^{t-1} \leq 1\} \tag{2}$$

where $X_i^{t-1} = (X_{i,1}^{t-1}, \ldots, X_{i,N}^{t-1})^T$ is the channel allocation decision of CR i. As indicated in (2), CR i can only select one available channel n with $X_{i,n}^{t-1} = 1$. Sp_i^{t-1} is the priority space of CR i

$$Sp_i^{t-1} = \{1, 2\} \tag{3}$$

We have $P_i^{t-1} \in Sp_i^{t-1}$. $P_i^{t-1} = 1$ stands for low priority, while $P_i^{t-1} = 2$ stands for high priority.

5) $r_i^{t-1} \in R^+$: the achieved average channel rate for CR i in the last slot $t - 1$, which is determined by the number of CRs in the allocated channel and their priorities in the last slot, i.e., by CR i's action Ac_i^{t-1} and all other users' actions, denoted as Ac_{-i}^{t-1}. This data can be acquired from the amount of data transmitted in the last time slot.

6) $N1_n^{t-1*}$ and $N2_n^{t-1*}$: the estimated number of users of class 1 and class 2 in the last slot $t-1$ on the selected channel n, respectively. An estimation method will be discussed later.

Based on the aforementioned information, each CR i makes its decision Ac_i^t for slot t. Note that CRs make their decisions based on local information only, which allows decentralized algorithms.

2.2 Prioritized CSMA/CA

CRs share channels using a prioritized CSMA/CA scheme. By allocating less waiting time on average to CRs with higher priority, these CRs have a higher chance to capture the channel than others.

We introduce following definitions for protocol description:

1) subslot: the time needed for a CSMA attempt. We assume K subslots constitute a slot which are denoted as $t_1, t_2, ..., t_K$. Note that the length of subslots are not equal and so is the length of slots.

2) minislot: the time needed by CR to determine whether another station has accessed the medium.

3) SIFS (Short Interframe Space): the smallest period between packets. It has a duration at least enough for CR to sense the channel clear and switch between receiving and transmitting modes.

4) AIFS (Arbitration Interframe Space): the smallest waiting time before sending a packet. It depends on the corresponding priority class and is larger than SIFS.

5) RTS/CTS: Request to Send frame/ Clear to Send frame.

6) DATA/ACK: Data frame/ Acknowledgment frame.

7) CW: Contention Window which depends on the corresponding priority class.

Fig. 1 shows the protocol of prioritized CSMA/CA. As illustrated in the figure, in any subslot t_k, for CR i wishing to send data, it generates its backoff time $\tau_i(t_k)$ according to a uniform distribution within the interval $(0, CW[P_i^t])$. The backoff counter starts decreasing after detecting that the channel is idle for an $AIFS[P_i^t]$. Upon expiry of the backoff counter, the CR sending an RTS to initiate its data transmission if the channel is still sensed clear. Only one radio with the smallest waiting time $WT_i = \tau_i(t_k) + AIFS[P_i^t]$ will transmit successfully on

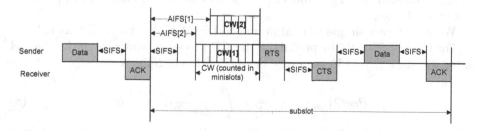

Fig. 1. Multiple backoff in Prioritized CSMA/CA

channel n in subslot t_k. The values of $AIFS$ and CW are set to guarantee that CRs in class 2 can have a smaller expectation of WT than those in class 1, so that they are more likely to take a smaller waiting time. Thus, CRs in class 2 have a higher priority to access the channel. The probability for CR i to catch channel n is

if $P_i^t = 2$

$$Prob_{i,n} = \frac{\delta}{CW[2]} \times \int_0^\delta \left(\frac{\tau}{CW[2]}\right)^{N2_n-1} d\tau + \int_\delta^{CW[2]} \left(\frac{\tau}{CW[2]}\right)^{N2_n-1} \left(\frac{\tau-\delta}{CW[1]}\right)^{N1_n} d\tau \tag{4}$$

if $P_i^t = 1$

$$Prob_{i,n} = \left(1 - \frac{\delta}{CW[2]}\right)^{N2_n} \times \int_0^{CW[1]} \left(\frac{\tau}{CW[1]}\right)^{N1_n+N2_n-1} d\tau \tag{5}$$

where $\delta = AIFS[1] - AIFS[2]$, and

$$N1_n^t = \sum_{i=1}^I \{X_{i,n}^t = 1\}\{P_i^t = 1\} \tag{6}$$

$$N2_n^t = \sum_{i=1}^I \{X_{i,n}^t = 1\}\{P_i^t = 2\} \tag{7}$$

Each CR will determine its own priority based on its utility, a function of its demand and satisfaction. The utility function will be discussed laster.

2.3   Decision-Feedback-Reaction Model

At the beginning of the t-th slot, each CR makes its decision based on the information about the network and its satisfaction, and hold this decision for the whole period of this slot. Note that channel catching probability and contention probability for CR i at slot $t-1$ are determined by all CRs on channel n, and they are known to CR i before slot t from channel catching results in the last slot. Hence, such probability can be seen as the feedback of CR i's action in the $(t-1)$-th slot. In realistic application, the number of subslots in a slot should be large enough to provide an accurate feedback. Based on this feedback, CR can make estimation of $N1_n^{t-1*} and N2_n^{t-1*}$, predict its future utility, and update its action in the next slot.

We introduce a simple estimation method for $N1_n^{t-1*}$ and $N2_n^{t-1*}$ as follows.

For CR i, if $P_i^t = 2$, the probability for CR i to successfully catch the channel after waiting a period in the range of $(AIFS[1], AIFS[2])$ is

$$Pcat21_{i,n} = \frac{\delta}{CW[2]} \times \int_0^\delta \left(\frac{\tau}{CW[2]}\right)^{N2_n-1} d\tau \tag{8}$$

Obviously, $Pcat21_{i,n}$ is only determined by $N2_n$, and could be acquired from CR i's competition results. Hence, $N2_n^*$ can be estimated from $Pcat21_{i,n}$ by, for example, maximum-likelihood estimation [8]. Then, substituting $N2_n$ in (4), we can have the estimated value of $N1_n$.

Similarly, if $P_i^t = 1$, the probability for CR i to contend on the channel after waiting a period in the range of $(AIFS[1], AIFS[2])$ is

$$Pcon11_{i,n} = 1 - (1 - \frac{\delta}{CW[2]})^{N2_n} \tag{9}$$

which is also only determined by $N2_n$. Thus we can similarly estimate $N2_n^*$ from $Pcon11_{i,n}$ and then estimate $N1_n$ by substituting $N2_n$ in equation (5).

In this paper, accurate estimates of $N1_n$ and $N2_n$ are considered, i.e., $N1_n^* = N1_n$ and $N2_n^* = N2_n$. However, as shown in the simulation, even up to 30% estimation error will not affect the performance of the proposed algorithm significantly.

3   Optimization Problem and Game Formulation

For a scenario with strict QoS requirement, for instance, voice transmission, a meaningful global system object should aim to guarantee as many CRs' satisfaction as possible. Here, the satisfaction means that the achieved average rate should be no less than the required one. Hence, we adopted a utility function different from the best effort utility functions in [5] to better match the scenarios with strict QoS requirements. As a decentralized scheme is required, a local utility function is defined to guide the allocation decision of each CR. In follows, we will first introduce the global optimization problem, and then discuss the distributed game and utility function in details.

3.1   Global Optimization Problem

The global object is to maximize the number of satisfied users. As the optimization problem is held for any time t, we ignore the index t for simplicity. Let $Ac = (Ac_1, ..., Ac_I)$ be the joint action of all radios. The optimization problem can be formulated as:

$$\max_{Ac} \sum_{i=1}^{I} (G(r_i, r_i^{req})) \tag{10}$$

s.t.

$$Ac \in \Omega = \Omega_1 \times ... \times \Omega_I \text{ (joint action set of all radios)} \tag{11}$$

where

$$r_i = \sum_{n \in C_N} X_{i,n} r_{i,n} \leq 1 \tag{12}$$

$$r_{i,n} = Prob_{i,n} A_{i,n} C_{i,n} \tag{13}$$

$r_{i,n}$ is the achievable rate for CR i on channel n. $Prob_{i,n}$ is the probability for CR i to catch channel n, as defined in (4) and (5). $G(a,b)$ is a logic function to check whether CR i is satisfied, i.e.,

$$G(a,b) = \begin{cases} 1 & , \quad a \geq b \\ 0 & , \quad a < b \end{cases} \tag{14}$$

Note that once CR's QoS is satisfied, it has no intention to further increase its achievable rate.

3.2   Distributed Game and Local Utility

Each CR tries to access channel to satisfy its QoS requirements, while at the same time such access may cause loss to other CRs on the same channel, as it decreases other users' probability to catch the channel. Intuitively, if each CR tries to satisfy itself, and at the same time limits the loss it causes to other CRs, more CRs in the system could be satisfied. That is to say, CRs should select channels with good channel condition and less users on it. Thus for a cooperative distributed game which aims to improve the global performance, the local utility for each CR should be a tradeoff between its satisfaction and other CRs' loss. Then, from the game theory point of views, the satisfaction acts as the income while other CRs' loss as the price.

Note that the local utility function is only an estimation from the last slot. For instance, since the reward of each CR's action is determined by other CRs' actions, the estimated achievable average rate calculated at the beginning of a slot may differ from the exactly achieved one. However, our simulation indicates that the proposed algorithm converges after a number of rounds.

We define a distributed game as follows:

CRs are players in the game. Ac_i^t, the action of CR i in slot t, is selected from action set Ω_i^t defined in (1). Since any CR's utility is determined not only by itself but by other CRs' actions, the local utility for CR i is defined as:

$$U_i(Ac_i^t, Ac_{-i}^t) = U_i^1(Ac_i^t) + \alpha U_i^2(Ac_i^t) \tag{15}$$

where Ac_{-i}^t represents all other CRs' action.

In (15)

$$U_i^1(Ac_i^t, Ac_{-i}^t) = G(r_i^t, r_i^{req}) \tag{16}$$

stands for the satisfaction, where r_i^t is defined in (12), and

$$U_i^2(Ac_i^t, Ac_{-i}^t) = -P_i^t(\alpha_1 N1_n^{t-1*} + \alpha_2 N2_n^{t-1*}) \tag{17}$$

stands for the cost, i.e., the loss of all other users in the channel n with $X_{i,n} = 1$. Since it is hard to learn the real decrement on the channel rates for other users, a rough estimation is adopted. Note that if CR i choses to act with higher priority, it may induce more loss to all other CRs in the same channel, and thus it should pay more. Thus, if a CR can be satisfied with low priority, there is no motivation for it to select the high priority in the same channel.

In (15) and (17), $\alpha, \alpha_1, \alpha_2$ are user-defined tradeoff factors. Since the actual effect of CR i's action on the global utility is unknown, these weights are adjustable.

4   Correlated Equilibrium and No-Regret Learning

In this section, we adopt the concept of C.E. and introduce a no-regret learning algorithm as a distributed adaptive learning algorithm to solve the optimization problem defined in the previous section.

4.1   Correlated Equilibrium (C.E.)

A C.E. is a solution concept that is more general than the well known N.E. [9]. Given a public signal (in this paper, that is the satisfaction history of CRs), a strategy consists of recommendatory actions to every possible observation of the public signal a player can make. Thus, strategies of users are related to the public signal. Players reach the C.E. if no player would want to deviate from a recommended strategy. Note that N.E. corresponds to the special case of a C.E. The C.E. considers the interaction among players to make decision and thus could achieve better performance than N.E..

In the proposed distributed game, the C.E. is defined as: if and only if, for all player i, with $Ac_i \in \Omega_i$ as its action, a probability distribution $Pr(Ac_i, Ac_{-i})$ satisfies

$$\sum_{\substack{Ac_{-i} \in \Omega_{-i} \\ \forall Ac_i', Ac_i \in \Omega_i}} Pr(Ac_i, Ac_{-i})[U_i(Ac_i', Ac_{-i}) - U_i(Ac_i, Ac_{-i})] \leq 0, \tag{18}$$

where $Pr(Ac_i, Ac_{-i})$ is the correlated strategy.

4.2   No-Regret Learning

No-regret learning (also called regret tracking, regret matching) is a kind of adaptive learning algorithms with fast convergence [10]. In no-regret learning, the probability to conduct an action is proportional to the regret for not having played other actions, and the stationary solution of the learning algorithm exhibits no regret. This algorithm will almost surely converge to C.E., as proved in [10].

For the action of CR i in slot t, $Ac_i^t \in \Omega_i^t$, we denote actions in the state space as $j \in \{0, 1, 2, ..., 2N\}$ for simplicity, i.e.: if $\exists X_{i,n}^t = 1$, $j = 2n + P_i^t - 2$; otherwise $j = 0$.

Each CR i executes the following steps:

1) Initialize arbitrarily probability of taking action for CR i. Set $\theta^{i,0} = 0$.

2) Generate regret matrix H^i with elements

$$H^i_{jk} = I\{Ac^t_i = j\} \times (U_{i,n}(k, Ac^t_{-i}) - U_{i,n}(j,, Ac^t_{-i})) \tag{19}$$

which stands for the regret of not using action k, other than the real action j, in slot t.

3) Set a regret value

$$\theta^{i,t+1}_{jk} = \theta^{i,t}_{jk} + \epsilon(H^i_{jk} - \theta^{i,t}_{jk}), 0 < \epsilon << 1 \tag{20}$$

which stands for the average gain that CR i would have received had he chosen action k in the past (from time 0 to t) instead of j. Here, ϵ is the learning rate.

4) Update action

CR i updates action $Ac^{t+1}_i = k$ with probability

$$P(Ac^{t+1}_i = k | Ac^t_i = j) = \begin{cases} \max(\theta^{i,t+1}_{jk}, 0)/\mu_i & , \quad k \neq j \\ 1 - \sum_{i \neq j} \max(\theta^{i,t+1}_{jk}, 0)/\mu_i & , \quad k = j \end{cases} \tag{21}$$

In (21), μ_i is an arbitrary updating rate that is sufficiently large, i.e.,

$$\mu_i > (N_{Ac_i} - 1)(u^{\max}_i - u^{\min}_i) \tag{22}$$

where N_{Ac_i} is the number of actions for CR i, $u^{\max}_i$ is the maximum achievable utility, and $u^{\min}_i$ is the minimum utility for CR i. In our work, we set $\mu_i = (N_{Ac_i} + 1)(u^{\max}_i - u^{\min}_i)$.

Note that the algorithm requires that CR i knows what utility it would have received for each action, even if that action was not taken. This puts a request to know the number of users of each class on each channel. In fact, a modified regret tracking algorithm can be used without such information [5] [11]. However, the convergence is far too slow.

5   Simulation Results

We focus on slightly congested systems, with total capacity of channels slightly less than the total user demand to highlight the effect of spectrum sharing algorithms on the resource utilization efficiency. For each CR, some randomly selected channels are set to be unavailable to reflect the occupation of PUs. For CRs' channel condition and required rate, we adopt randomly generated data following Gaussian distribution for simplicity to introduce heterogeneity among CRs.

In simulations, AIFS[1]=150, CW[1]=100, AIFS[2]=100, CW[2]=150, all in unit of minislots. In the case that there is only one user in each class on the same channel, the probability to catch channel for user in class 1 is 0.32, and for class 2 is 0.65. Learning rate $\epsilon = 0.1$, tradeoff factor $\alpha = 0.015$, $\alpha_1 = 1.1$ and $\alpha_2 = 2$ are obtained from simulation results.

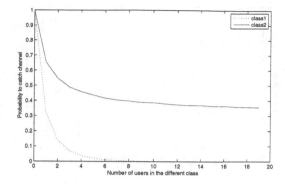

Fig. 2. Catching Probability vs. num of users of different class, with 1 user in the discussing class

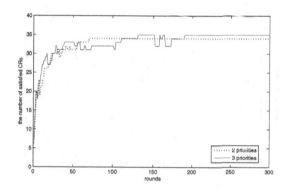

Fig. 3. $N = 3$, $I = 50$. Channel condition follow a Gaussian distribution with mean 30, variance 7. Required rate follow a Gaussian distribution with mean 3, variance 3.

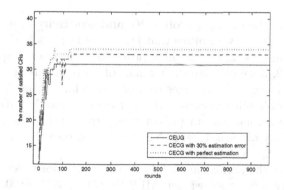

Fig. 4. $N = 3$, $I = 50$. Channel condition follow a Gaussian distribution with mean 30, variance 7. Required rate follow a Gaussian distribution with mean 3, variance 3.

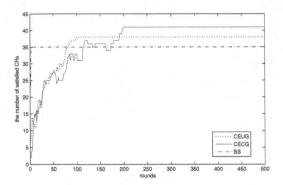

Fig. 5. $N = 15$, $I = 50$. Channel condition follow a Gaussian distribution with mean 15, variance 7. Required rate follow a Gaussian distribution with mean 7, variance 3.

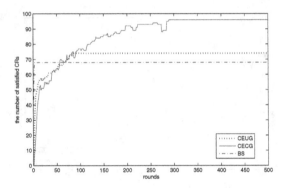

Fig. 6. $N = 25$, $I = 100$. Channel condition follow a Gaussian distribution with mean 15, variance 7. For 50 Users, the required rate follow a gaussian distribution with mean 7, variance 3, and other 50 Users with with mean 3, variance 3.

Fig. 2 compares the catching probability and sensitivity of users in different classes. From this figure, we can see that for a user in class 1, if we increase the number of users in class 2, the catching probability decreases rapidly; while for the user in class 2, if we increase the number of users in class 1, the probability decreases much slower and converges to a non-zero limitation. That is because, for the catching probability of class 2, the first part in equation (4) is not affected by $N1_n$, and the second part in (4) converges to 0 with large $N1_n$; while for catching probability of class 1, with $N2_n$ in the exponent, it decreases rapidly with increasing $N2_n$.

Fig. 3 compares the performance if 3 other than 2 priority levels are applied. For the 3-priority level case, we set AIFS[1]=150, CW[1]=100, AIFS[2]=125, CW[2]=125, AIFS[2]=100 and CW[2]=150. From this figure, we can see that with 3-level priority, the algorithm can only provide marginal performance improvement, but much slower convergence rate. That is because more priority levels will introduce a larger action set, which increases the complexity. Moreover, as in the proposed sharing algorithm, an unsatisfied CR can switch to the channel with better channel condition and lighter competition to increase its throughput other than continuously increasing its priority in the same channel, the improvement from more priorities becomes insignificant. This justifies our selection of 2 priority levels.

Fig. 4 shows the influence of estimation error. The performance of the C.E. based unclassified game (CEUG) in [5] is adopted as a comparison benchmark. From this figure we can see that for up to 30% estimation error, the performance of our algorithm is just affected slightly. The reason is that users are dispersed in all actions and the number of users with the same action is not large. Thus, the estimation error can only change the number of users with the same action slightly.

Fig. 5 compares the performance of the proposed CECG algorithm with CEUG in [5]. The best response (BS) algorithm with unclassified game in [12] is also adopted for comparison. In the BS algorithm, in every round each CR selects the channel with largest utility, and it has been proved in [12] that the N.E. of this unclassified game can be achieved. From the figure, performance improvement can be obviously observed in terms of the number of satisfied users. The introduction of C.E. brings in about 10% improvement comparing to the BS algorithm, as it considers the cooperation among CRs, at the cost of convergence rate. Note that if all CRs chose to be in the same class, our algorithm will degrade to that in [5]. Comparing to [5], since the proposed algorithm has a larger action set including those in CEUG, at least we can acquire a same performance as the CEUG algorithm.

Fig. 6 further demonstrates the influence of heterogeneity of users on the performance where two groups of CRs with difference in demands are applied. Comparing the results in Fig. 5 and Fig. 6, we can find that the improvement of CECG over CEUG (about 40%) is larger in the latter case than that in the former (about 10%). The simulation results further justify the necessity to apply the proposed algorithm for performance improvement in CRNs, especially when significant heterogeneity exists among CRs.

6   Conclusion

By taking into account the heterogeneity among users in CRNs, we proposed a distributed cooperative game with classified players in this paper for efficient spectrum sharing, where CRs select channel and their priority based on their satisfaction history. This satisfaction history is used as a public signal for CRs to collaborate with each other to achieve the C.E. A no-regret learning algorithm is adopted to learn the C.E. Simulation results show that the classified game has a better performance compared to the unclassified game, and the improvement is determined by the heterogeneity of the network.

Acknowledgment. This work is supported by the Natural Sciences and Engineering Research Council (NSERC) of Canada IRC and Discovery Grants.

References

1. Mitola III, J.: Cognitive radio: an integrated agent architecture for software defined radio. Ph.D. Thesis, KTH Royal Inst. Technology, Stockholm, Sweden (2000)
2. Atakan, B., Akan, O.B.: BIOlogically-inspired spectrum sharing in cognitive radio networks. In: Wireless Communications and Networking Conference, WCNC 2007, pp. 43–48. IEEE (2007)
3. Liu, J., Shen, L., Song, T., Wang, X.: Demand matching spectrum sharing game for non-cooperative cognitive radio network. In: International Conference on Wireless Communications & Signal Processing, WCSP 2009, pp. 1–5 (2009)
4. Zhu, H., Pandana, C., Liu, K.J.R.: Distributive Opportunistic Spectrum Access for Cognitive Radio using Correlated Equilibrium and No-Regret Learning. In: Wireless Communications and Networking Conference, WCNC 2007, March 11-15, pp. 11–15. IEEE (2007)
5. Maskery, M., Krishnamurthy, V., Qing, Z.: Decentralized dynamic spectrum access for cognitive radios: cooperative design of a non-cooperative game. IEEE Transactions on Communications 57(2), 459–469 (2009)
6. Mangold, S., Choi, S., May, P., Klein, O., Hiertz, G., Stibor, L.: IEEE 802.11e Wireless LAN for Quality of Service. In: Proc. IEEE European Wireless 2002, Florence, Italy (February 2002)
7. Blake, S., et al.: An Architecture for Differentiated Services, RFC 2475 (December 1998)
8. Weisstein, E.W.: Maximum Likelihood. From MathWorld–A Wolfram Web Resource, http://mathworld.wolfram.com/MaximumLikelihood.html
9. Aumann, R.J.: Subjectivity and correlation in randomized strategy. Journal of Mathematical Economics 1(1), 67–96 (1974)
10. Hart, S., Mas-Colell, A.: A simple adaptive procedure leading to correlated equilibrium. Econometrica 68(5), 1127–1150 (2000)
11. Hart, S., Mas-Colell, A.: A reinforcement procedure leading to correlated equilibrium. In: Economic Essays, pp. 181–200. Springer, Heidelberg (2001)
12. Pillutla, L.S., Krishnamurthy, V.: Game Theoretic Rate Adaptation for Spectrum-Overlay Cognitive Radio Networks. In: Global Telecommunications Conference, IEEE GLOBECOM 2008, November 30-December 4, pp. 1–5. IEEE (2008)

QoS-Based Spectrum Access Control
in MIMO Cognitive Radio Networks

Mei Rong and Shihua Zhu

Department of Information and Communication Engineering
Xi'an Jiaotong University, Xi'an, P.R. China

Abstract. Cognitive radio (CR) is a promising technique to solve the conflict between the scarcity and underutilization of spectrum. Underlay spectrum sharing is one of the most attractive schemes to increase the sum rate of cognitive users (CUs) as well as reduce the interference at primary users (PUs). However, the adoption of an empirical value as interference constraint may result in outage of PUs or degrade the performance of CUs. By introducing interference variables and calculating interference constraints according to the quality of service (QoS) of PUs with different transmission requirements in every slot, a QoS-based spectrum access control (QSAC) scheme for multi-input multi-output (MIMO) cognitive radio networks is proposed. Besides, CUs with larger signal-to-interference-ratio (SIR) are selected and block diagonalization (BD) is applied to enhance the sum rate of CR system. Performance analysis and simulation results show that, compared with previous methods, the QSAC scheme leads to improved performance of both achievable sum rate of CUs and outage probability of PUs with the same order of complexity, and the gain of achievable sum rate of CUs is about 33% when the total power of CR system is 100w.

Keywords: spectrum access control, cognitive radio, interference variable, quality of service.

1 Introduction

In the past decade there has been an explosive growth in spectrum demand due to the deployment of a wide variety of wireless services. On the other hand, the current utilization efficiency of the licensed radio spectrums could be as low as 15% on average [1]. Cognitive radio (CR), which can solve the conflict between scarcity and underutilization of spectrum [2], is a promising technique for the next generation mobile communication systems [3]. Generalized CR systems [4] have attracted extensive attention for cognitive users (CUs) can coexist with primary users (PUs) in the same band if the interference to PUs is constrained to be below a tolerable limit. Spectrum access control of CUs has become an important part of spectrum sharing strategies in order to exploit multiuser diversity to increase the sum rate of CUs and reduce the interference to PUs.

Access control algorithms of the traditional cellular networks prefer to select users with better channel condition to access [5], which have taken the advantage of multiuser diversity so as to maximize the sum rate of network or satisfy the quality of service (QoS) of users. In order to guarantee the transmission of PUs, interference to PUs has

P. Ren et al. (Eds.): WICON 2011, LNICST 98, pp. 547–557, 2012.
© Institute for Computer Sciences, Social Informatics and Telecommunications Engineering 2012

been considered in access control method [6], and hybrid priorities of users including the PUs with the highest priority has been established [7, 8]. The PUs' QoS has been taken into account in [7, 8], however, the absence of attention to the interference from primary (PR) system to the CR system degrades the performance of CUs. Considering the interaction between CR and PR systems, Hamdi et al. provided the spectrum access control schemes that chose CUs whose channels are less correlative with all PUs and other selected CUs to access [9–11].

Nevertheless, the varied QoS requirements of PUs, e.g., different QoS requirements between multiple PUs, or time-varying QoS requirements of each PU, leads to different interference tolerance. The adoption of an empirical value as interference constraint [10, 11] may result in outage of PUs in CR networks, where the QoS of PUs should be considered as a prerequisite. Therefore, a spectrum access control scheme based on the QoS of PUs is proposed in this paper. Interference variables are introduced and compared with interference constraint of each PU calculated according to its QoS, and the results control the access of CUs to guarantee the transmissions of PUs. Moreover, CUs with larger signal-to-interference-ratio (SIR) are pre-selected to enhance the sum rate of CUs. By exploiting multiuser diversity of CUs and setting the interference constraints more properly, the QoS-based spectrum access control (QSAC) scheme can provide larger sum rate of CUs as well as satisfy the QoS requirements of PUs. In the QSAC scheme, block diagonalization (BD) [12–15] is adopted to separate selected CUs, based on which, interference variables from CR system to PUs can be calculated. CUs satisfying interference constraints are permitted accessing, and parallel sub-channels are constructed for them by singular value decomposition (SVD). Analysis and simulation results confirm the performance gain of QSAC scheme over all the relevant schemes.

The rest of this paper is organized as follows. Section 2 describes the system model and formulates the problem of spectrum access control in the CR network. Section 3 puts forth the QSAC scheme. The signal-to-noise-ratio (SINR) and complexity performance of the QSAC scheme are evaluated in Section 4, which is followed by the simulation results and discussions in Section 5. Finally, Section 6 concludes the paper.

2   System Model and Problem Formulation

We consider the downlink of a single-cell multiuser system in underlay scenario, including K_p single-antenna PUs and K_c CUs each with N_c antennas. Two base stations are assumed in the cell, one primary base station (PBS) and one cognitive base station (CBS), both equipped with M antennas. The CR network is shown in Fig. 1.

Both PR and CR system are assumed to be OFDM systems, so the channels between users and BSs can be considered as quasi-static flat Rayleigh channels [16]. $\mathbf{H}_{c,k}$ and $\mathbf{G}_{c,k}$ are the channel matrices between the kth CU and the CBS and PBS. Meanwhile, $\mathbf{h}_{p,l}$ and $\mathbf{g}_{p,l}$ denote the channel vectors between the lth PU and the CBS and PBS, respectively. Their entries are independent complex Gaussian random variables with mean zero and variance one. The set of active CUs is called $\mathcal{A}$, and $|\mathcal{A}| = N_{ca}$. $\mathbf{x}_k$ and $\mathbf{s}_l$ denote the transmit signals to the kth CU and the lth PU, while $\mathbf{y}_k$ and $\mathbf{r}_l$ denote the receive signals at the kth CU and the lth PU, respectively. The equivalent channel

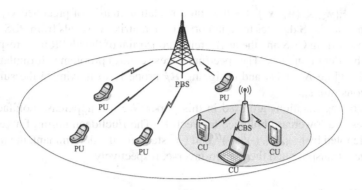

Fig. 1. Cognitive radio network

between PBS and PUs are assumed to be represented as a diagonal matrix Σ since the operations of PR system are beyond the scope of this paper. The equivalent channel gain between PBS and PU_l is σ_l. The signal model is

$$\mathbf{y}_k = \mathbf{H}_{c,k}\mathbf{x}_k + \mathbf{H}_{c,k} \sum_{\substack{i=1 \\ i\neq k \\ i\in\mathcal{A}}}^{N_{ca}} \mathbf{x}_i + \mathbf{G}_{c,k} \sum_{l=1}^{N_p} \mathbf{s}_l + \mathbf{z}_k, \tag{1}$$

$$\mathbf{r}_l = \sigma_l\mathbf{s}_l + \mathbf{h}_{p,l} \sum_{\substack{k=1 \\ k\in\mathcal{A}}}^{N_{ca}} \mathbf{x}_k + \mathbf{n}_l. \tag{2}$$

$\mathbf{z}_k$ and $\mathbf{n}_l$ are Gaussian noise vectors whose entries are assumed to be independent Gaussian random variables with mean zero and variance σ_0^2. CBS is aware of $\mathbf{h}_p$, $\mathbf{G}_c$, $\mathbf{H}_c$, and Σ as the assumption in [17].

In order to design the constraints satisfying different QoS requirements of multiple PUs and adapting to the time-variance of QoS requirements, we describe the spectrum access control problem as

$$\max_{\mathcal{A}, \mathbf{R}_k} C = \max_{\mathcal{A}} \sum_{\substack{k=1 \\ k\in\mathcal{A}}}^{N_{ca}} \max_{\mathbf{R}_k} \log_2 \left| \mathbf{I} + \frac{\mathbf{H}_{c,k}\mathbf{R}_k\mathbf{H}_{c,k}^H}{\mathbf{G}_{c,k}\mathbf{S}\mathbf{G}_{c,k}^H + \sigma_0^2\mathbf{I}} \right| \tag{3}$$

$$\text{s.t.} \sum_{\substack{k=1 \\ k\in\mathcal{A}}}^{N_{ca}} \text{Tr}\,(\mathbf{R}_k) \leq P$$

$$\sum_{\substack{k=1 \\ k\in\mathcal{A}}}^{N_{ca}} \text{Tr}\left(\mathbf{h}_{p,l}\mathbf{R}_k\mathbf{h}_{p,l}^H\right) \leq \delta_l, \qquad l = 1,\ldots,N_p$$

$$\mathbf{R}_k \geq 0, \qquad k \in \mathcal{A}, k = 1,\ldots,N_{ca},$$

where $\mathbf{R}_k = E[\mathbf{w}_{c,k}\mathbf{x}_k(\mathbf{w}_{c,k}\mathbf{x}_k)^H]$ is the autocorrelation matrix of precoded $\mathbf{x}_k$, and $\mathbf{w}_{c,k}$ is precoding matrix. $\mathbf{S}$ denotes the autocorrelation matrix of signals from PBS. P and δ_l are total power from CBS and the interference constraint of the lth PR user, respectively. $\mathbf{I}$ denotes the identity matrix. The spectrum access control problem is formulated as the process of finding N_{ca} CUs and designing $\mathbf{R}_k$ properly to maximize the sum rate C under all constraints.

The following notations are used in this paper. We use uppercase boldface letters for matrices and lowercase boldface for vectors. The Euclidean norm of a vector or a matrix is denoted by $\|\cdot\|$. $|\cdot|$, $(\cdot)^T$, $(\cdot)^H$ and $(\cdot)^\dagger$ stand for the determinant, the transpose, the conjugate transpose and the pseudo-inverse, respectively.

3   QoS Based Spectrum Access Control

The receiving SINR is considered as the measurement of QoS [18]. The power of CBS is assumed to be allocated to each antenna equally. As a result, SINR of the lth PU is

$$\mathrm{SINR}_{p,l} = \frac{P_{p,l}\sigma_l^2}{\frac{P}{M}\mathbf{h}_{p,l}\mathbf{w}_c\left(\mathbf{h}_{p,l}\mathbf{w}_c\right)^H + \sigma_0^2}, \tag{4}$$

where $\mathbf{w}_c = \left[\mathbf{w}_{c,1}^T \cdots \mathbf{w}_{c,N_{ca}}^T\right]^T$. Based on this observation, the following QoS based spectrum access control scheme is proposed.

First, the constraint δ_l is calculated from $\mathrm{SINR}_{p,l}$ as

$$\delta_l = \frac{P_{p,l}\sigma_l^2}{\mathrm{SINR}_{p,l}} - \sigma_0^2, \tag{5}$$

where $P_{p,l}$ denotes the power from PBS to the lth PU.

Second, $N_{ca} = \left\lfloor \frac{M}{N_c} \right\rfloor$ best CUs are selected satisfying $k = \arg\max_i \frac{\|\mathbf{H}_{c,i}\|}{\|\mathbf{G}_{c,i}\|}$ to exploit multiuser diversity. Then interference between selected CUs is canceled by BD. The complementary channel matrix of the kth CU is

$$\widetilde{\mathbf{H}}_{c,k} = [\mathbf{H}_{c,1}^T \ \mathbf{H}_{c,2}^T \ \cdots \ \mathbf{H}_{c,k-1}^T \ \mathbf{H}_{c,k+1}^T \cdots \ \mathbf{H}_{c,N_{ca}}^T], \tag{6}$$

and the singular value decomposition (SVD) of $\widetilde{\mathbf{H}}_{c,k}$ is

$$\widetilde{\mathbf{H}}_{c,k} = \widetilde{\mathbf{u}}_{c,k}\widetilde{\mathbf{s}}_{c,k}(\widetilde{\mathbf{v}}_{c,k} \ \widetilde{\mathbf{r}}_{c,k})^H, \tag{7}$$

where $\widetilde{\mathbf{r}}_{c,k}$ is composed by the columns of right singular vectors corresponding to the zero singular value. Precode $\mathbf{x}_k$ with $\widetilde{\mathbf{r}}_{c,k}$, i.e. project $\mathbf{x}_k$ onto the null-space of other CUs. This operation is repeated on each selected CU, and the interference between them is avoided. The equivalent channel matrices are

$$\hat{\mathbf{H}}_{c,k} = \mathbf{H}_{c,k}\widetilde{\mathbf{r}}_{c,k}. \tag{8}$$

After that, check whether each constraint is satisfied. The interference variables are described as

$$vio_l = \frac{P}{M} \mathbf{h}_{p,l} \widetilde{\mathbf{r}}_c \left(\mathbf{h}_{p,l} \widetilde{\mathbf{r}}_c \right)^H, \tag{9}$$

where

$$\widetilde{\mathbf{r}}_c = \left[\widetilde{\mathbf{r}}_{c,1} \ \widetilde{\mathbf{r}}_{c,2} \ \cdots \ \widetilde{\mathbf{r}}_{c,N_{ca}} \right]. \tag{10}$$

Then go to Step 3 unless $vio_l \leq \delta_l$, $l = 1, 2, \cdots N_p$, are all satisfied.

Third, harmful pre-selected CUs are removed. Compute the interference to each PU, and remove the most seriously interfering CU. Then go back to Step 2. If we cannot find N_{ca} CUs satisfying $vio_l \leq \delta_l$, reduce N_{ca} to $N_{ca} - 1$.

Fourth, to separate sub-channels, SVD for each accessing CU is carried out, such as

$$\hat{\mathbf{H}}_{c,k} = \hat{\mathbf{u}}_{c,k} \hat{\mathbf{s}}_{c,k} \hat{\mathbf{v}}_{c,k}^H. \tag{11}$$

Precode $\mathbf{x}_k$ at the transmitter side with $\hat{\mathbf{v}}_{c,k}$, and shape it at the receiver side with $\hat{\mathbf{u}}_{c,k}^H$, so the final equivalent channel matrices can be denoted by diagonal matrices as $\mathbf{H}_{c,k}^f = \hat{\mathbf{s}}_{c,k}$. The desired precoding matrices are $\mathbf{w}_{c,k} = \widetilde{\mathbf{r}}_{c,k} \hat{\mathbf{v}}_{c,k}$ and $\mathbf{w}_c = \left[\mathbf{w}_{c,1}^T \ \mathbf{w}_{c,2}^T \ \cdots \ \mathbf{w}_{c,N_{ca}}^T \right]^T$.

Algorithm 1. Procedure of QoS Based Spectrum Access Control

1. Calculate interference constraints according to PUs' QoS;
2. Select N_{ca} CUs and check whether the interference variables satisfy the interference constraints;
3. Remove harmful pre-selected CUs and go back to Step 2;
4. Construct parallel sub-channels for accessing CUs.

---

4   Performance Analysis

4.1   SINR Analysis

The QSAC method is compared with opportunistic spectrum sharing (OSS) method [11]. When our method is adopted, the SINR on the ith sub-channel of the kth accessing CU is

$$\text{SINR}_{c,i,k}^Q = \frac{P_{c,i,k} \hat{\mathbf{s}}_{c,i,k}^2}{\sum\limits_{l=1}^{N_p} P_{p,l} \left\| \hat{\mathbf{u}}_{c,k}^H \mathbf{G}_{c,k} \right\|^2 + \sigma_0^2}, \tag{12}$$

where $P_{c,i,k}$ denotes the power on the ith sub-channel of the kth accessing CU. The SINR of the lth PU is

$$\text{SINR}_{p,l}^Q = \frac{P_{p,l} \sigma_l^2}{\sum\limits_{\substack{k=1 \\ k \in \mathcal{A}}}^{N_{ca}} \sum\limits_{i=1}^{N_c} P_{c,i,k} \left\| \mathbf{h}_{p,l} \widetilde{\mathbf{r}}_{c,k} \hat{\mathbf{v}}_{c,k} \right\|_{i,i}^2 + \sigma_0^2}, \tag{13}$$

where $\|\mathbf{A}\|_{i,i}^2$ is the square of the ith diagonal element in matrix $\mathbf{A}$. Compared with the OSS method in [11], we can get

$$\frac{\text{SINR}^Q_{c,i,k}}{\text{SINR}^O_{c,i,k}} = \frac{P_{c,i,k}\hat{s}^2_{c,i,k}\left(\sum_{l=1}^{N_p}\|\mathbf{G}_{c,k}\|^2 P_{p,l} + \sigma_0^2\right)}{\left(\sum_{l=1}^{N_p}\|\hat{\mathbf{u}}^H_{c,k}\mathbf{G}_{c,k}\|^2 P_{p,l} + \sigma_0^2\right)\left(\|\mathbf{H}_S\mathbf{H}^\dagger_S\|^2_{n,n} P_{c,i,k}\right)}, \tag{14}$$

$$\frac{\text{SINR}^Q_{p,l}}{\text{SINR}^O_{p,l}} = \frac{P_{p,l}\sigma_l^2\left(\sum_{\substack{k=1\\k\in\mathcal{A}}}^{N_{ca}}\sum_{i=1}^{N_c} P_{c,i,k}\|\mathbf{h}_{p,i+(k-1)N_c}\|^2 + \sigma_0^2\right)}{\left(\sum_{\substack{k=1\\k\in\mathcal{A}}}^{N_{ca}}\sum_{i=1}^{N_c} P_{c,i,k}\|\mathbf{h}_{p,l}\tilde{\mathbf{r}}_{c,k}\hat{\mathbf{v}}_{c,k}\|^2_{i,i} + \sigma_0^2\right)P_{p,l}\sigma_l^2}, \tag{15}$$

where $\text{SINR}^O_{c,i,k}$ and $\text{SINR}^O_{p,l}$ denotes the SINR on the ith sub-channel of the kth CU and the lth PU when OSS method [11] is adopted, and $n = i + (k-1)N_c$.

Due to the elements of matrices are random variables, we compare the expectation of SINRs. Since $\sum_{i=1}^{N_c}|\hat{s}_{c,i,k}|^2 = \|\hat{\mathbf{H}}_{c,k}\|^2 = N_c^2 = 4$, $E\left(|\hat{s}_{c,i,k}|^2\right) = N_c^2/N_c = N_c = 2$, so

$$\frac{E\left(\text{SINR}^Q_{c,i,k}\right)}{E\left(\text{SINR}^O_{c,i,k}\right)} = E\left(\hat{s}^2_{c,i,k}\right) > 1. \tag{16}$$

Because $\tilde{\mathbf{r}}_{c,k}$ is a part of a unitary matrix, the multiplication of $\mathbf{h}_{p,l}$ and $\tilde{\mathbf{r}}_{c,k}$ is equivalent to projecting $\mathbf{h}_{p,l}$ onto a subspace of $\mathbb{C}^M$, $\|\mathbf{h}_{p,l}\tilde{\mathbf{r}}_{c,k}\| < \|\mathbf{h}_{p,l}\|$.

$$\frac{E\left(\text{SINR}^Q_{p,l}\right)}{E\left(\text{SINR}^O_{p,l}\right)} = \frac{E\left(\sum_{\substack{k=1\\k\in\mathcal{A}}}^{N_{ca}}\|\mathbf{h}_{p,l}\|^2 + \sigma_0^2\right)}{E\left(\sum_{\substack{k=1\\k\in\mathcal{A}}}^{N_{ca}}\|\mathbf{h}_{p,l}\tilde{\mathbf{r}}_{c,k}\|^2 + \sigma_0^2\right)} > 1. \tag{17}$$

So QSAC scheme has better performance than OSS method [11] in both PR and CR system.

4.2   Complexity Analysis

Here the complexity in terms of the time for a multiplication or an addition is analyzed. The time for calculating δ_l is $3N_p = 3M$, and for computing F-norm of CUs is $(2MN_c - 1)K_c$. Putting these norms in descend order costs K_c^2 times of a multiplication. In the selection step, we consider the worst case, i.e. there is no CU can access. The time includes two parts, called searching null-space and calculating interference variables, which is $\sum_{N_{ca}=1}^{M/N_c}(K_c - N_{ca} - 1)\left[N_c(N_{ca}-1)M^2 N_{ca} + MN_cN_{ca}\right]$ in all. It takes $MN_p/N_c = M^2/N_c$ times for comparing interference variables with constraints, and $N_{ca}N_c^3$ times for acquiring parallel sub-channels. For $K_c \gg M$, $K_c \gg N_{ca}$, $K_c \gg N_p$, $K_c \gg N_c$, the complexity of QSAC method is $O\left(K_c^2\right)$.

Table 1. The complexity of two methods

	Calculate δ_l	Select CUs	Compare	Separate
QSAC	$O(M)$	$O\left(K_c^2\right)$	$O\left(M^2/N_c\right)$	$O\left(N_{ca}N_c^3\right)$
OSS [11]	-	$O\left(K_c^2\right)$	-	$O\left(N_{ca}N_c^3\right)$

Table 2. The feedback quantity of three methods

	QSAC	OSS [11]	AUS [10]
$\mathbf{H}_c, N_c \times M$	K_c	K_c	K_c
$\mathbf{G}_c, N_c \times M$	K_c	-	-
$\mathbf{h}_p, 1 \times M$	N_p	N_p	N_p
$G_p, M \times 1$	1	-	-
Over All (in bits)	$4N_cMK_c + 2M(N_p + 1)$	$2N_cMK_c + 2N_pM$	$2N_cMK_c + 2N_pM$

OSS method has the complexity of $B_{\max} = MN_cK_c + K_c^2 + \xi\left(\sum_{i=1}^{J} |S(i)| + K_c\right)$ [11]. Because of the same relationship between M, N_{ca}, N_p, N_c and K_c, the complexity is $O\left(K_c^2\right)$. From Table 1 and the analysis above, we conclude that the QSAC method is in the same order of complexity with the OSS method [11].

4.3 Acquirement of Channel State Information (CSI) and Feedback Quantity Analysis

In academic research, perfect CSI is always assumed [4, 6, 7, 9–11, 15, 17]. Here we discuss the details. The channel matrices from PBS and CBS to CUs can be obtained by the feedback from CUs. On the other hand, the CBS can get the channel matrices form PBS and CBS to PUs through the feedback from PUs [17, 19]. In practice, for a fading environment, there are cases where it is difficult for the CBS to perfectly estimate instantaneous channels. In such cases, the results obtained in this paper provide capacity upper-bounds for the secondary transmission in a CR network [20]. Moreover, we give the quantity of feedback in Table 2.

From Table 2, we can note that the feedback quantity of the QSAC method is comparable to the other methods and acceptable.

5   Simulation Results and Discussions

A cellular system including a PBS and a CBS each equipped with 8 antennas, as well as 8 single-antenna PUs and 50 CUs each with 2 antennas is considered in this paper. The elements of channel matrices are independent complex Gaussian random variables with mean zero and variance one [10, 11]. The energy of noise is $\sigma_0^2 = 1$. For fair comparison, we set the near-orthogonal factors δ_p and δ_c to be 0.8 and 0.4, respectively, the same as in [11]. The QoS of the lth PU is assumed to be SINR $= l/4$, which is comparable with the QoS of 3G.

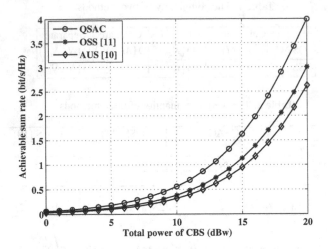

Fig. 2. Achievable rate of CR system

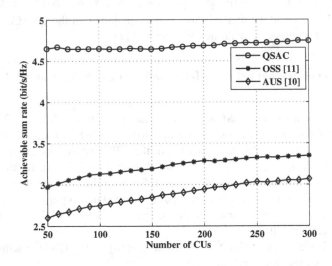

Fig. 3. Achievable rate of CR system with different K_c

The achievable sum rate of CR system in Fig.2 shows that the QSAC method provides the largest achievable sum rate of CUs because of the consideration of interference from PBS to CUs and the adoption of BD. In stead of choosing the CUs with larger channel gain [10, 11], we select CUs with larger SIR to exploit multiuser diversity more effectively. Moreover, the adoption of BD brings more spatial freedom of degrees than zero-forcing [10, 11], so as to enhance the performance of CR system. Since interference variables are introduced and compared with interference constraint of each PU calculated according to its QoS, the spectrum band is exploited more efficiently than the other two methods. The achievable rate of CR system with different

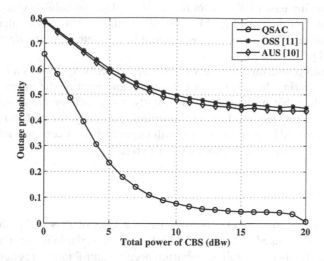

Fig. 4. Outage probability of PUs

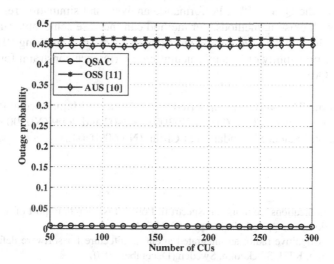

Fig. 5. Outage probability of PUs with different K_c

numbers of CUs is shown in Fig.3. In the simulation, we constrain both the total transmit power of PBS and CBS to be 40w. As shown in the figure, our method can achieve larger sum rate than the other methods by selecting CUs with larger SIRs to access and adopting BD.

Fig.4 and Fig.5 show the outage probability of PUs. The QSAC method calculates interference constraints for PUs according to their QoS. Compared with methods setting interference constraint as an empirical value, our method can alleviate the harm to PUs, and get less outage probability. From the outage probability of PUs with different K_c, it is evident that the increase of K_c cannot reduce the outage probability of PUs without changing the value of δ_l, δ_p and δ_c. Meanwhile, the figures show that calculating the interference constraints more properly, as adopted in our method, is an effective way to guarantee PUs' QoS.

To sum up, the combination of selected CUs in the QSAC method is a better trade-off between maximizing the sum rate of CR system and meeting the interference constraints of PUs than that of other methods. Firstly, we guarantee the transmission of PUs by properly setting the interference constraints. Secondly, the performance of CR system is also improved by permitting CUs with larger SIRs to access and adopting BD. So we obtain better performance than the other two schemes.

6   Conclusions

In this paper, the spectrum access control based on QoS of PUs in MIMO CR networks has been investigated. The concept of interference variable is introduced, based on which, an interference constrained spectrum access control method is developed for MIMO CR networks with heterogeneous QoS requirements of PUs. Through spectrum access control of CUs, the method can exploit diversity from multiuser CR system as well as guarantee the QoS of PUs. Performance analysis and simulation results show that compared with existing methods, our method can increase achievable sum rate of CR system by selecting the CUs with larger SIRs to access and adopting BD, as well as reduce outage probability of PUs by calculating interference constraint for each PU according to its QoS.

Acknowledgment. This work was supported by the National Major Special Projects in Science and Technology of China (2011ZX03003-001-02 and 2009ZX03003-008-02), the National Natural Science Foundation of China (No.60902043).

References

1. Federal Communications Commission Spectrum Policy Task Force, Report of the spectrum efficiency working group, Technical Report 02-135 (November 2002)
2. Mitola III, J.: Cognitive radio: an integrated agent architecture for software defined radio. PhD Dissertation, KTH, Stockholm, Sweden (December 2000)
3. Akyildiz, I.F., Lee, W.Y., Vuran, M.C., Mohanty, S.: NeXt generation/dynamic spectrum access/cognitive radio wireless networks: A survey. Computer Networks 50, 2127–2159 (2006)
4. Prasad, N., Wang, X.D.: Outage minimization and rate allocation for the multiuser gaussian interference channels with successive group decoding. IEEE Trans. Inf. Theory 55(12), 5540–5557 (2009)
5. Knopp, R., Jondral, P.A.: Information capacity and power control in single-cell multiuser communications. In: Proc. IEEE ICC 1995, Seattle, Washington, USA, pp. 331–335 (June 1995)
6. Hamdi, K., Zhang, W., Letaief, K.B.: Uplink Scheduling with QoS Provisioning for Cognitive Radio Systems. In: Proc. IEEE WCNC 2007, Hong Kong, pp. 2594–2598 (March 2007)
7. Li, J.Y., Xu, B.Y., Xu, Z.J., Li, S.Q., Liu, Y.: Adaptive packet scheduling algorithm for cognitive radio system. In: Proc. ICCT 2006, Guilin, China, pp. 1–5 (November 2006)

8. Zhu, P., Li, J.L., Wang, X.F.: Scheduling model for cognitive radio. In: Proc. 3rd International Conference on CrownCom, Singapore, pp. 1–6 (May 2008)
9. Hamdi, K., Zhang, W., Letaief, K.B.: Joint beamforming and scheduling in cognitive radio networks. In: Proc. IEEE GLOBECOM 2007, Washington D.C, USA, pp. 2977–2981 (November 2007)
10. Hamdi, K., Zhang, W., Letaief, K.B.: Low-complexity antenna selection and user scheduling in cognitive MIMO broadcast systems. In: Proc. IEEE ICC 2008, Beijing, China, pp. 4038–4042 (May 2008)
11. Hamdi, K., Zhang, W., Letaief, K.B.: Opportunistic Spectrum Sharing in Cognitive MIMO Wireless Networks. IEEE Trans. Wireless Commun. 8(8), 4098–4109 (2009)
12. Spencer, Q.H., Swindlehurst, A.L., Haardt, M.: Zero-forcing methods for downlink spatial multiplexing in multiuser MIMO channels. IEEE Trans. Signal Process. 52(2), 461–471 (2004)
13. Zhang, C., Guo, L.: BD Precoding schemes for cognitive MIMO system. In: Proc. IEEE ICNIDC, Shanghai, China, March 29-April 2, pp. 11–15 (2009)
14. Yi, H.Y., Hu, H.L., Rui, Y., Guo, K.Q., Zhang, J.: Null space-based precoding scheme for secondary transmission in a cognitive radio MIMO system using second-order statistics. In: Proc. IEEE ICC 2009, Dresden, Germany, pp. 1–5 (June 2009)
15. Bixio, L., Oliveri, G., Ottonello, M., Raffetto, M., Regazzoni, C.S.: Cognitive radios with multiple antennas exploiting spatial opportunities. IEEE Trans. Signal Process 58(8), 4453–4459 (2010)
16. Goldsmith, A.: Multicarrier modulation. In: Wireless Communications, ch.2, pp. 374–402. Cambridge University Press, Cambridge (2005)
17. Musavian, L., Aissa, S.: Capacity and Power Allocation for Spectrum-Sharing Communications in Fading Channels. IEEE Trans. Wireless Commun. 8(1), 148–156 (2009)
18. Choi, J.: Power allocation for two different traffics in layered MIMO systems. IEEE Trans. on Wireless Commu. 7(10), 3942–3950 (2008)
19. Zhang, L., Liang, Y.C., Xin, Y.: Joint beamforming and power allocation for multiple access channels in cognitive radio networks. IEEE J. Sel. Areas Commun. 26(1), 38–51 (2008)
20. Zhang, R., Liang, Y.C.: Exploiting multi-antennas for opportunistic spectrum sharing in cognitive radio networks. IEEE J. Sel. Topics Signal. Process. 2(1), 88–102 (2008)

A Tunable CMOS Continuous-Time Filter Designed for a 5.8 GHz ETC Demodulator

Hang Yu[*], Lai Jiang, Shengyue Lin, Yan Li, Rongchen Wei, and Zhen Ji

Shenzhen City Key Laboratory of Embedded System Design,
College of Computer Science and Software Engineering, Shenzhen University
518060, Shenzhen, P.R. China
{yuhang,jianglai,liyan,jizhen}@szu.edu.cn

Abstract. 5.8 GHz is specified as the operating frequency of the electronic tolling collection (ETC) system in the new national highway network in China. A low power, robust radio frequency receiver is the key design challenge in such a system. A 3rd order butterworth low-pass filter with tunable pass-band designed for the ETC receiver was presented in this work. The design is based on a single operational amplifier in order to reduce the overall power consumption. The filter was implemented in standard CMOS 0.18 μm technology. Simulation shows that the design achieves a maximum 3-dB bandwidth of 2 MHz with 0 dB insertion loss, while the power consumption is only ~200 μW.

Keywords: ETC receiver, Continuous-time filter, tunable pass-band, operational amplifier.

1 Introduction

Traffic congestion is becoming a problem in most major cities in China. One way to alleviate the traffic pressure is to construct urban intelligent traffic control system by employing information and wireless communication technologies. Among those, electronic tolling collection (ETC) system, which allows vehicles to pass through a toll booth without stopping, is one of the most effective methods. According to the Chinese standard of Dedicated Short Range Communications (DSRC) [1], the operating frequencies of the ETC system is set to be 5.8- 5.9 GHz.

A 5.8 GHz Radio Frequency (RF) low power receiver is essential for an ETC system, and the directional conversion architecture is generally adopted due to its simplicity and robustness. Currently, Shenzhen University is developing such a receiver. As shown in Fig.1, received signal is first down-converted to an intermediate frequency of 10 MHz. By using this method, the high DC offset generally presented at the receiver baseband, which is primarily caused by the leakage from the local oscillator to the receiver front-end, is avoided. A band-pass filter (BPF) and a log-amplifier / received signal strength

---

[*] The authors would like to thank the NSFC under grant No. 60901016, the project 10151806001000016 supported by Guangdong R/D Fund, the project JC201005280477A supported by Shenzhen city and the SRF for ROCS, SEM.

P. Ren et al. (Eds.): WICON 2011, LNICST 98, pp. 558–566, 2012.

indicator (Log-Amp/RSSI) are used to extract and amplify the IF signal, followed by a low-pass filter, an envelope detector, and a comparator with hysteresis for data recover. The receiver is required to recover data sequence up to 2 Mbit/s.

This work focuses on the low-pass filter in the ETC receiver. Because the maximum data rate (~2 Mb/s) is far below the 10 MHz IF frequency, a filter with 3rd order response is sufficient to isolate the recovered data from the down-converted signal. Butterworth type is chosen because it can provide the most flat in-band response, with a good compromise between gain, phase and signal delay [2]. The implemented filter is based on a single operational amplifier (OPAMP) in order to reduce the total circuit power consumption.

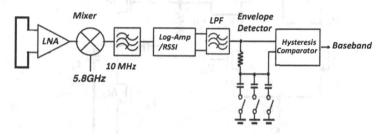

Fig. 1. Architecture of 5.8 GHz RF ETC receiver under developing in Shenzhen University

The paper is organized as follows: The CMOS operational amplifier design is presented in section 2, with discussion of design issues including the amplifier gain and bandwidth. The low pass filter was then implemented using the operational amplifier and several passive components, and the filter design procedure is presented in section 3. The filter is designed using standard CMOS 0.18 μm technology, and is validated under the Zeni IC design environment. The simulation results are presented in section 4, and the concluding remarks are given in Section 5.

2   Two-Stage OPAMP Design

Since the output signal from the Log-Amp/RSSI block is differential while a single-ended input is required for the envelope detector, a two-stage OPAMP that achieves both differential to single-ended conversion and signal amplification is implemented in this design. The first stage functions as a differential-to-single-ended converter, and only provides moderate gain. A common-source structure is added as the second stage for enhanced gain, and at the same time buffers the amplified signal. In addition, a R-C compensation network is added between the two stages in order to achieve a large unity-gain-bandwidth. The detailed schematic of the OPAM is given in Fig.2.

The first stage of the OPAMP consists of 5 transistors. M_5 provides the necessary DC bias current I_{SS}. M_3 and M_4 form the input pair, and M_1, M_2 make up of the active current loads. The input common mode voltage is defined as V_{in}. When V_{in} increases progressively and is larger than the threshold voltage of the M_3, M_4, they start to turn on and enter the active region. The minimum value of V_{in} that ensures all the transistors of the first stage operating in the active region is:

$$V_{in} = \sqrt{\frac{I_{ss}}{\mu_n C_{ox}(\frac{W}{L})_1}} + V_{TH3} + \sqrt{\frac{2I_{ss}}{\mu_n C_{ox}(\frac{W}{L})_5}}, \tag{1}$$

where V_{TH3} is the threshold voltage of M$_3$ and M$_4$, $(W/L)_1$ and $(W/L)_5$ represent the device sizes of M$_1$ and M$_5$, respectively.

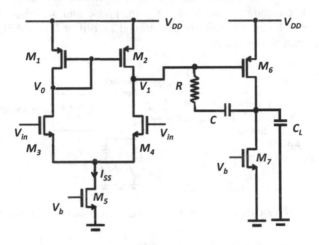

Fig. 2. Detailed schematic of the OPAMP

The outputs of the first stage, which are defined as V_0 and V_1, decrease with the increasing of V_{in}, and M$_3$ and M$_4$ can enter the triode region if V_{in} is too high. In order to maintain all transistors operating in the active region, the maximum V_{in} should satisfy equation (2).

$$V_{in} = V_{DD} - \sqrt{\frac{I_{ss}}{\mu_P C_{ox}(\frac{W}{L})_1}} - |V_{TH1}| + V_{TH3}, \tag{2}$$

where V_{TH1} is the threshold voltage of M$_1$ and M$_2$.

With V_{in} set to be between the limits defined as in (1) and (2), V_0 and V_1 are identical to the 1st order, and can be written as:

$$V_0 = V_1 = V_{DD} - |V_{GS1}| = V_{DD} - \sqrt{\frac{I_{ss}}{\mu_P C_{ox}(\frac{W}{L})_1}} - |V_{TH1}| \tag{3}$$

The common mode voltage gain of the first OPAMP stage under the proper bias condition can then be derived as in (4)

$$A_{CM} \approx \frac{-\frac{1}{2g_{m1,2}} \| \frac{r_{01,2}}{2}}{\frac{1}{2g_{m3,4}} + r_{05}} = -\frac{1}{1 + 2r_{05}g_{m3,4}} \frac{g_{m3,4}}{g_{m1,2}} \tag{4}$$

,where $r_{01,2}$ and r_{05} are the channel resistances of M_1/M_2 and M_5, $g_{m1,2}$ is the transconductance of M_1/M_2, and $g_{m3,4}$ is the transconductance of M_3 or M_4.

The differential small signal gain of the first stage can be estimated using (5),

$$A_{DM} = g_{m3,4}(r_{02} \parallel r_{04}),$$
(5)

where r_{02} and r_{04} are the channel resistance of M_2 and M_4, respectively.

Based on (4) and (5), the common mode rejection ratio (CMRR) can be written as

$$CMRR = \left| \frac{A_{DM}}{A_{CM}} \right| = (1 + 2r_{05}g_{m3,4})g_{m1,2}(r_{02} \parallel r_{04})$$
(6)

From (6), it indicates that the input pairs M_3 and M_4 should use large *(W/L)* ratio for high differential small signal gain and CMRR value. However, since the first stage output voltage, V_1, is also the DC bias voltage of the second stage, the device size of M_3 and M_4 can not be determined independently, and the *W/L* of M_5, thus the bias current I_{SS}, must be included in the design procedure in order for transistors in the second stage to operate properly in the active region.

An R-C compensation configuration is added between the two amplifying stages. This configuration moves the inter stage pole towards the origin and pushes away the output pole, which allows a much greater gain bandwidth product (GBW) than the structure that merely connects the compensation capacitor from one node to ground [3]. In addition, the resistor R in series with the capacitor C introduces a right half plane zero, $g_{m6}/(C+C_{GD6})$, which could be used to cancel the second system pole. The relation of R, C and C_L for pole-zero cancellation to occur is given in (7).

$$\frac{1}{C(g_{m6}^{-1} - R)} = \frac{-g_{m6}}{C_L},$$
(7)

where g_{m6} is the transconductance of M_6, and C_L is the load capacitor of the OPAMP.

With the R-C frequency compensation, the small signal gain of the completed operational amplifier can be written as

$$\frac{V_{out}}{V_{in}} = g_{m4}(r_{02} \parallel r_{04}) \frac{R + \dfrac{1}{SC} - g_{m6}}{\dfrac{1}{r_0} + \dfrac{1}{R + SC}}$$
(8)

3 OPAMP-Based 3rd Order Low-Pass Filter with Tunable Pass-Band

A butterworth architecture is used to implement the low pass filter because of its flat in-band response. In order to provide flexibility to the completed filter, tunability is introduced by integrating a programmable capacitor array. The proposed architecture of the low pass filter is given in Fig.3.

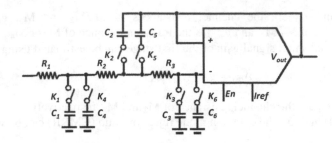

Fig. 3. Architecture of the OPAMP-based 3rd order low-pass filter

The design is based on the OPAMP discussed in the previous section, and totally 9 passive components, including a programmable capacitor array (C_1 and C_4, C_2 and C_5, C_3 and C_6) and three resistors (R_1, R_2, and R_3), are utilized. Using this scheme, the 3 dB cut-off frequency of the filter can be tuned by switches K_1 - K_6. When all switches are closed, the filter cut-off frequency is set to 1 MHz, and the cut-off frequency is set to 2 MHz if only K_1, K_2 and K_3 are open.

The frequency domain transfer function of the filter can be derived as (9).

$$H(\omega) = \frac{1}{S^3\alpha_3 + S^2\alpha_2 + S\alpha_1 + 1}$$
$$\alpha_3 = (C_{A1}C_{A2}C_{A3}R_1R_2R_3)$$
$$\alpha_2 = (C_{A1}C_{A3}R_1R_2 + C_{A1}C_{A3}R_1R_3$$
$$+ C_{A2}C_{A3}R_1R_3 + C_{A2}C_{A3}R_2R_3)$$
$$\alpha_1 = (C_{A1}R_1 + C_{A3}R_1 + C_{A3}R_2 + C_{A3}R_3)$$

(9)

, where C_{A1}, C_{A2}, and C_{A3} are defined as $K_1C_1+K_4C_4$, $K_2C_2+K_5C_5$, and $K_3C_3+K_6C_6$, respectively.

All required resistor and capacitor values can be determined from the 3rd order butterworth function [4]. Normalized pole positions are first derived based on the assumption that the low pass filter has unit cut-off frequency, and then the actual capacitor values are calculated by using the de-normalization factor, $C/(2f_cR)$, in which f_c is the actual cut-off frequency. In this design, resistor R_1, R_2, and R_3 are all fixed as 10K, and the resulting capacitor values for the two different cut-off frequencies are listed in Table I.

Table 1. Capacitor values of the 3rd low-pass filter

Cut-off frequency	C_{A1} (pF)	C_{A2} (pF)	C_{A3} (pF)
1 MHz	22.2	56.4	3.2
2 MHz	11.1	28.2	1.6

In order to reduce the silicon area required for the designed low pass filter, impedance multiplication technique discussed in [5] is used. As shown in Fig.4, the equivalent impedance seen from point A to the circuit ground is $1/g_m$, and the total impedance looking into the input (VI) is $Z+1/g_m$, in which the $1/g_m$ term can be neglected if M_8 is large enough. Because there exists a fixed $1:N$ ratio between M8 and M_9, the total current passing through the input is $N+1$ times of the current flowing through M_1. Thus, if Z is a capacitor C, an effective capacitance of $(N+1)C$ can be generated at the circuit input. The multiplication factor N in this design is chosen for the best power and area compromise.

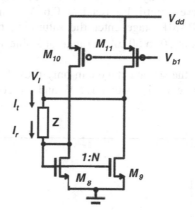

Fig. 4. Principe of impedance scaled down technique

4   Design Validation

The 3rd order butterworth low pass filter was implemented using standard CMOS 0.18 μm technology, and its functionality is fully validated under the Zeni IC design environment. Fig. 5 is the completed layout of the filter, and it occupies 250 x 460 μm^2 of silicon area.

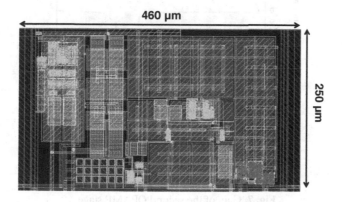

Fig. 5. Completed layout of the 3rd order butterworth low-pass filter

In order to find the proper DC bias condition to maximize the OPAMP small signal gain, under an stable bias voltage V_b, the first stage was simulated with various M_5 sizes (thus various DC bias current I_{SS}). The large signal common mode response of the OPAMP first stage with 4 different I_{SS} values (20 µA (A), 40 µA (B), 60 µA (C) and 80 µA (D)) is shown in Fig.6. Also, the common mode response of the second stage is simulated as shown in Fig.7.

For the first stage, the input common mode voltage varies from 0 to 1.8 V (Fig. 6). Complied with the theoretical analysis as shown in (3), as V_{in} increases from 0 V, the output voltage V_1 decreases, until V_{in} reaches 0.6 V. Under this condition, all transistors of the first OPAMP stage enter the saturation region and V_1 becomes stable. With I_{SS} varying from 20 to 80 µA, a range of stable V_1 from 1.1 to 1.3 V can be achieved.

Fig.7 demonstrates that the second stage can only provide small signal gain when its input voltage, in this case V_1, is around 1.2 V, and the corresponding I_{SS} is about 40 µA.

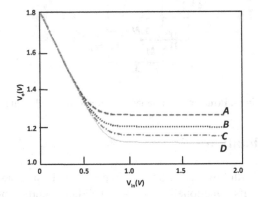

Fig. 6. Layout of the low-pass filter

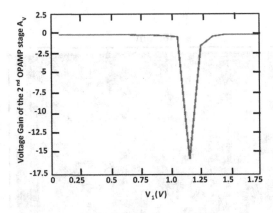

Fig. 7. Gain of the second OPAMP stage

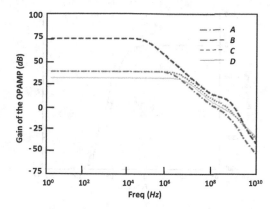

Fig. 8. AC small signal gain of the OPAMP

The response of the completed OPAMP in the frequency domain was estimated through AC simulation, and its gain with the 4 different bias current I_{SS} is plotted in Fig.8. Clearly, only when I_{SS} is set to 40 μA and V_1 is about 1.2 V, the OPAMP can achieve high gain. The simulated DC gain of the OPAMP in this bias condition is about 80 dB, and the 3-dB bandwidth is about 75 kHz.

The completed 3rd order butterworth low-pass filter was also characterized, and the gain and phase responses are given in Fig.9 and Fig.10. In the figures, curve E and F represents the cases when the filter cut-off frequency is set to 1 MHz and 2 MHz, respectively. The completed filter has 0 dB insertion loss, and the overall power consumption is only 200 μW with a stable 1.8 V power supply.

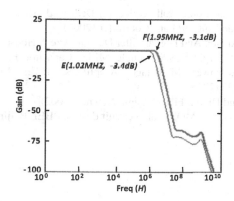

Fig. 9. Gain of the completed low pass filter

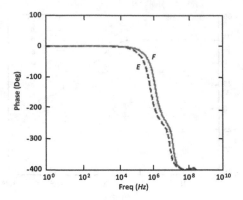

Fig. 10. Phase of the completed low pass filter

5   Conclusion

A 3rd order butterworth low-pass filter with tunable pass-band designed for the 5.8 GHz receiver is presented in this paper. The filter is based on a single two-stage OPAMP, and the tunability is achieved by digital-controlled capacitor array. The filter was implemented in standard CMOS 0.18 μm technology, and was fully characterized under the Zeni IC design environment. Simulation results show that the completed filter has 0 dB insertion loss, with configurable bandwidth of 1 MHz or 2 MHz, while consumes only 200 μW from a 1.8 V power supply.

References

1. GB/T 20851-2007, Electronic toll collection-Dedicated short range communication Interface with Roadside Unit and Lane Controller (2007)
2. Thede, L.: Practical Analog And Digital Filter Design. Artech House (2004)
3. Fan, X.H., Mishra, C., Edgar, S.S.: Single Miller Capacitor Frequency Compensation Technique for Low-Power Multistage Amplifiers. IEEE Journal of Solid-state Circuits 40(3), 584–592 (2005)
4. Winder, S.: Analog and Digital Filter Design. Newnes (2002)
5. Allen, P.E., Holberg, D.R.: CMOS analog circuit design. PHEI, Beijing (2002)

An Offset-Free 10 MHz Limiting Amplifier Designed for a 5.8 GHz ETC Receiver

Lai Jiang[*], Hang Yu, Rongchen Wei, Yan Li, Shengyue Lin, and Zhen Ji

Shenzhen City Key Laboratory of Embedded System Design,
College of Computer Science and Software Engineering,
Shenzhen University518060, Shenzhen, P.R. China
{jianglai,yuhang,liyan,jizhen}@szu.edu.cn

Abstract. Electronic tolling collection (ETC) system will be largely adopted in the next generation of Chinese highway network, and its operating frequency is specified to be 5.8 GHz. A limiting amplifier designed for the 5.8 GHz receiver of the ETC system is presented in this work. AC-coupled gain stage was realized to avoid additional offset cancellation mechanism. The trade-off between the small signal gain, number of stages, gain-bandwidth product, and power dissipation was studied by systematic analysis. Implemented using a standard CMOS 0.18 μm process, the simulation results show that the limiting amplifier achieves overall small signal gain of 81 dB, with 20 MHz bandwidth.

Keywords: Electronic tolling collection (ETC), limiting amplifier, received signal strength indicator (RSSI), offset-free section.

1 Introduction

This Electronic tolling collection (ETC) system adopts radio frequency identification (RFID) technology to facilitate tolling collection in a long range. Because a vehicle is allowed to be charged without slowing down, the ETC is thought to be an effective method to alleviate traffic congestion, and it will be largely adopted in the next generation of the highway network in China. The Standardization Administration of the People's Republic of China (SAC) has already released the Chinese standard of Dedicated Short Range Communications (DSRC), in which the ETC operating frequencies is defined to be 5.8 - 5.9 GHz [1].

The radio frequency (RF) signal processing components are crucial to improve the communication quality in an ETC system. Due to its simple, robust structure and low power consumption, direct conversion architecture is a good fit for an ETC receiver. The architecture of a typical direction conversion receiver is shown in Fig.1. The RF front-end is composed of a low noise amplifier (LNA) and a mixer. The RF input signal is first amplified by the LNA, and is then down-converted to an intermediate-frequency (IF) by

---

[*] The authors would like to thank the NSFC under grant No. 60901016, the project 10151806001000016 supported by Guangdong R/D Fund, the project JC201005280477A supported by Shenzhen city and the SRF for ROCS, SEM.

P. Ren et al. (Eds.): WICON 2011, LNICST 98, pp. 567–575, 2012.

the mixer, in order to prevent the high DC offset caused by the leakage from the local oscillator to the front-end input. A band-pass filter (BPF) following the mixer extracts the useful information, and a demodulator (Demod) together with the clock and data recovery circuit (CDR) is used to convert the received data into baseband for further processing.

In an ETC system, if multiple vehicles are presented at the tolling gate at the same time, an automatic communication channel selection mechanism should be used to assign a distinct communication channel for each one. This can be realized by inserting a received signal strength indicator (RSSI) into the receiver chain, as shown in Fig.1. The ETC receiver on a vehicle can first scan all the possible communication channels, and analyzes the received signal strength. The bi-directional communication link with the tolling gate will only be established if a vacant channel is found.

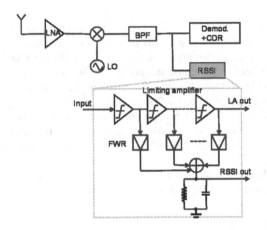

Fig. 1. Architecture of 5.8 GHz RF receiver

The RSSI circuit consists of a limiting amplifier, rectifiers, and a passive current summation network. In order to cover a wide input dynamic range, the limiting amplifier uses multiple cascaded gain stages to achieve a logarithmic character [2]. The output of each amplifying stage is sent to a rectifier, through which the input voltage of each gain stage is converted into an current. These currents are then summed together to indicate the power level of the input signal.

Generally in a RSSI, the random offset voltage appeared at the input of each gain stage will accumulate and deteriorate the overall performance of the limiting amplifier, and therefore additional offset cancellation mechanism is inevitable to ensure the system performance [3]. However, in a direction conversion receiver as shown in Fig.1, if a RSSI is targeted for the down-converted signal at the IF frequency, the gain stages in the limiting amplifier can be AC-coupled, and therefore the offset cancellation mechanism is not necessary.

This paper presents an offset-free limiting amplifier designed for the ETC receiver under developing in Shenzhen University. The paper is organized as follows: In section 2, a systematic level design process is presented to help determine the optimal circuit parameters, such as the number of stages, small signal gain required for each gain stage, and the overall power dissipation. Section 3 discusses the detailed design of the limiting amplifier. Implemented in a standard 0.18 μm CMOS process, the system is validated under the Zeni IC design environment. The simulation results are given in section 4. Finally, a conclusion is drawn in section 5.

2   Systematic Level Design

In order to prevent the random offset voltage presented at the input of each gain stage to accumulate along the amplifier chain, high pass networks implemented using passive components are added in between each gain stage. The systematic level diagram of an offset-free limiting amplifier is given in Fig.2.

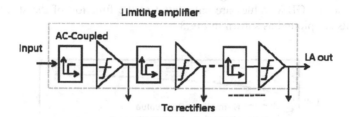

Fig. 2. Systematic level diagram of a limiting amplifier with AC-coupled gain stages

In our design, the required overall small signal gain is specified as 82 dB. In order to have a best compromise among small signal gain of each stage gain, bandwidth, and power dissipation, systematic level analysis is first performed to determine key parameters of each gain stage.

For simplicity, all gain stages are kept identical. For the 1st order approximation, the voltage transfer function of each gain stage can be estimated as

$$V_{out} = AV_{in}, \text{ for } V_{in} < V_S$$
$$V_{out} = V_L, \text{ for } V_{in} \geq V_S , \tag{1}$$

in which A is the small signal gain of each stage, Vs is the threshold voltage, above which a gain stage is saturated, and VL is the output voltage if the stage is saturated.

All gain stages operate in the linear region when the input signal is small enough. If the number of the stages is N, the output voltage of the limiting amplifier is then A^N x Vin. When the input signal strength increases progressively, the gain stages will be driven into saturation one by one starting from the last stage. Therefore, an approximated logarithmic relationship can be obtained between the input / output voltage of the limiting amplifier.

The linearity (in terms of dB) of the RSSI is determined by the gain of the each stage and the total number of stages consisting of the limiting amplifier. Although increasing the small signal gain and the stage number can improve the linearity, the required bandwidth of each gain stage, and the total power dissipation on the other hand will be deteriorated. The relationship among the stage gain, the overall bandwidth, and the power dissipation is studied by the normalization method presented in [2]. If the overall small signal gain and bandwidth of the limiting amplifier are noted as A_V and f_V, the normalized gain and bandwidth (A_C and f_C) for the identical single stage are given in the following:

$$A_C = A_V^{(1/N)-1} \tag{2}$$

$$f_C = \frac{f_V}{\sqrt{2^{1/N} - 1}} \tag{3}$$

From (2), although the voltage gain for each gain stage can be reduced when the cascading number of stages increases, but a large bandwidth is required in such condition, which is indicated by (3). Thus, the gain-bandwidth product (GBW) is used in the design procedure. Specifying the overall gain of 82 dB, the normalized gain, bandwidth, and the GBW values are calculated as the function of the stage number, and the results are plotted as shown in Fig.3.

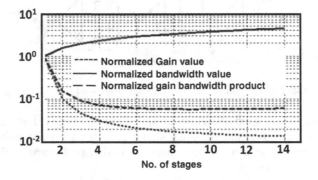

Fig. 3. Normalized gain, bandwidth and GBW of single gain stage for a limiting amplifier with 82 dB small signal gain

As shown in Fig.3, the bandwidth requirement tends to be stabilized when the stage number is larger than 10. However, a large number of gain stages will result in more power dissipation. If the power of the each stage gain is defined as P_C, the overall power consumption of the limiting amplifier P_V can be estimated by (4) [4]:

$$P_V = N \times P_C \propto N \times (GBW)^2 \tag{4}$$

In (5), the GBW is proportional to square root of the power consumption for each gain stage P_C, which is given in (5) :

$$GBW = \frac{g_m}{C} = \frac{\sqrt{2\mu C_{ox}(W/L)I_d}}{kWL} \propto \sqrt{\frac{I_d}{WL^3}} = \sqrt{\frac{P_C}{V_{DD}WL^3}} \tag{5}$$

, where I_d is the bias current of the identical gain stage, W and L are the width and length of the MOS transistor that provides the trans-conductance.

For 82 dB overall small signal gain, the normalized power consumption of the limiting amplifier is calculated for different stage numbers, as plotted in Fig.4. The total power consumption decreases as the number of stages becomes larger and remains stable when the stage number is larger than 4. Considering the requirements of logarithmic approximation [5], totally 9 stages are included in this design and the corresponding gain of each stage should be about 9 dB. In this case, the maximum error [5], defined as the maximum deviation of the implemented output-input voltage response from the ideal logarithmic function, is about 0.14 dB.

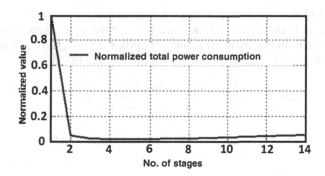

Fig. 4. Normalized total power consumption of a limiting amplifier with 82dB small signal gain

3   Circuit Implementation

The single gain stage employs a simple differential amplifier with NMOS input pair, and resistive load R_D. A source degeneration resistor $R3$ is added to improve the amplifier linearity. The AC-coupling between consecutive gain stages is realized by adding series capacitors $C1$ and $C2$ to the input, and therefore a passive high pass network is formed with the help of resistors $R1$ and $R2$. The input pair is also self-biased through $R1$ and $R2$, and therefore only a single bias voltage V_b is required to sustain the circuit operation. The detailed schematic of the gain stage is given in Fig.5.

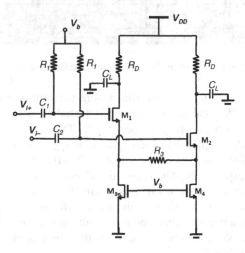

Fig. 5. Schematic of a single AC-coupled gain stage

Neglecting the gate-bulk capacitance of the input NMOS pair, the overall voltage gain of the identical gain stage can be written as:

$$A_V = \frac{G_m \times R_D \| C_L}{1 + sR_1C_1} = \frac{sG_m R_D R_1 C_1}{(1 + sR_1C_1)(1 + sR_D C_L)} \tag{6}$$

, where C_L is the load capacitance at the amplifier output.

Form (6), it is noted that the gain stage has a band-pass characteristic, and the passing band is determined by the two amplifier poles: $1/(R_1C_1)$ and $1/(R_DC_L)$.

The common mode rejection ration of the stage is given in (7),

$$CMRR = \frac{A_{vd}}{A_{cm}} = \frac{(g_m r + 1)(sR_D C_L + 1)}{g_m R_D (sC_L r_{1,2} + 1) + r_{1,2}}, \tag{7}$$

where $r_{1,2}$ is the channel resistances of M_1 / M_2, and r equals to $R_3/2$.

4   Design Validation

The 9-stage limiting amplifier was implemented using a standard 0.18 μm CMOS process. In this design, C_1, C_L, R_1 and R_D are selected as 950 fF, 400 fF, 71.5 KΩ and 3.76 KΩ, respectively. The finished layout of the limiting amplifier is shown in Fig.6. The complete design occupies 810 x 290 μm^2 of silicon area.

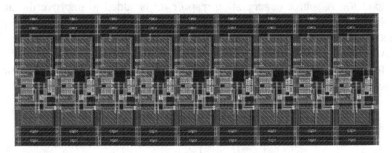

Fig. 6. Layout of the 9-stage offset-free limiting amplifier

Under Zeni IC design environment, the system performance is characterized. The performance of the identical gain stage is first studied under three different bias current I_{SS}, which were 5 μA, 10 μA, and 15 μA. The simulation results of the gain stage without the AC-coupled block are given in Fig.7. From Fig.7 (b), the 3 dB cutoff frequencies of the three cases are around 100 MHz, while the gains are 6.5 dB, 8.8 dB and 11 dB, respectively. The required DC bias voltage Vb can be obtained by the voltage transfer characteristics, which is around 0.9V as given in Fig.7 (a).

The AC performance of the single gain stage with the AC-coupled block is also simulated for the three bias currents, and the results are given in Fig.8. When the bias current is 15 μA, the block achieves a gain 8.8 dB, which is close to the optimization result discussed in section 2.

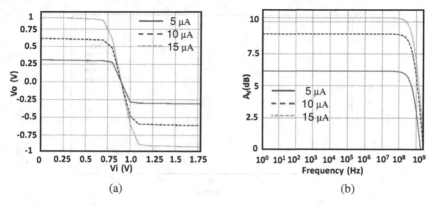

Fig. 7. Single gain stage performance under different bias currents: (a) voltage transfer characteristics; (b) gain and bandwidth

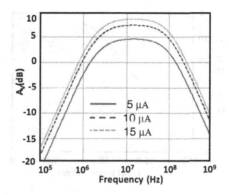

Fig. 8. Frequency response of the AC-coupled gain stage

The performance of the 9-stage limiting amplifier is studied through AC simulation, and the results are given in Fig.9. An overall small signal gain around 81 dB is achieved. The limiting amplifier presents a band-pass characteristcs with the center frequency at around 10 MHz, and the 3dB bandwidth is about 20 MHz (3.8 MHz - 23.55 MHz), approximately 1/5 of the bandwidth of an identical gain stage.

Varying the input signal strength from -100 dBm to 0 dBm (at 10 MHz carrier frequency), the -3 dB input sensitivity of the limiting amplifier is studied under different DC offset voltage, which vary from -50 mV to +50 mV. The results (as shown in Fig. 10) perfectly overlap, indicating the offset voltages at the input of each gain stage do not have noticeable impact on the system performance. The -3 dB input sensitivity of the finished limiting amplifier is about - 50 dBm.

The power consumption of the completed limiting amplifier is around 250 μW with a 1.8 V DC supply voltage.

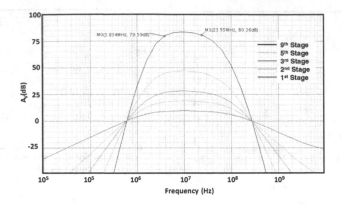

Fig. 9. Simulated gain at the outputs of various gain stages

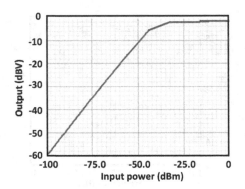

Fig. 10. The input-output transfer response of the limiting amplifier (with input DCoffset voltage ranging from -50 mV to 50mV)

5   Conclusion

A 9-stage limiting amplifier designed for the RSSI of a 5.8 GHz ETC receiver is presented in this work. Because the system is targeted for the down-converted signal at 10 MHz IF frequency, the offset cancellation mechanism generally included in the limiting amplifier designs is not required. Instead, the cascaded gain stages are AC coupled. The designed limiting amplifier consists of 9 identical gain stages in total, and the small signal gain is set to 9 dB for each stage. The optimized design is implemented in a standard 0.18 μm CMOS process, and validated under the Zeni IC design environment. Simulation results show that the limiting amplifier achieves the overall small signal gain of 81 dB at the center frequency of 10 MHz, and consumes about 250 μW from a single 1.8V power supply.

References

1. GB/T 20851-2007.: Electronic toll collection-Dedicated short range communication Interface with Roadside Unit and Lane Controller (2007)
2. Holdenried, C.D., Haslett, J.W., McRory, J.G.: A DC–4-GHz True Logarithmic Amplifier: Theory and Implementation. IEEE Journal of Solid-state Circuits 37(10), 1290–1299 (2002)
3. Kim, H.S., Ismail, M., Olsson, H.B.: CMOS Limiters with RSSIs for Bluetooth Receivers. In: MWSCAS, Dayton, OH, USA, vol. 2, pp. 812–815 (2001)
4. Huang, P.C., Chen, Y.H., Wang, C.K.: A 2-V 10.7-MHz CMOS Limiting Amplifier/RSSI. IEEE Journal of Solid-state Circuits 35(10), 1474–1480 (2000)
5. Barber, W.L., Brown, E.R.: A True Logarithmic Amplifier for Radar IF Applications. IEEE Journal of Solid-state Circuits SC-15(3), 291–295 (1980)

A Novel Miniature Four-Band CPW-Fed Antenna Optimized Using ISPO Algorithm

Huihui Li[1], Xuanqin Mou[1], Zhen Ji[2,*], Hang Yu[2], Yan Li[2], and Lai Jiang[2]

[1] School of Electronics and Information Engineering,
Xi'an Jiaotong University, Xi'an 710049, China
[2] College of Computer Science and Software Engineering, Shenzhen University,
Shenzhen 518060, China, Shenzhen Key Laboratory of Embedded System Design,
Shenzhen, China
lihuihui80@gmail.com, xqmou@mail.xjtu.edu.cn,
{jizhen,liyan,yuhang}@szu.edu.cn

Abstract. A novel four-band CPW-fed antenna simultaneously satisfied the requirement for Radio Frequency Identification (RFID) tag and WiMAX /WLAN applications is reported in this paper. Limited to 30×30 mm^2 area on a PCBoard with ε_r=4.4, the antenna has four U-shaped, two F-shaped and eight L-shaped slots as additional resonators to achieve multi-band operation. Intelligent Single Particle Optimization (ISPO) algorithm is used to determine the optimized slot configuration for the best return loss at 0.96 GHz, 2.5 GHz, 3.76 GHz and 5.8 GHz simultaneously. The performance of the designed antenna was validated through simulations using both the Finite Element Method and the Method of Moment.

Keywords: RFID, Four-band Antenna, Optimization, ISPO.

1 Introduction

Wireless communication applications such as Radio Frequency Identification (RFID) [1], Worldwide Interoperability for Microwave Access (WiMAX), and Wireless Local Area Network (WLAN) technologies are widely used nowadays. However, these applications operate at various frequency bands. For example, 0.86-0.96 GHz, 2.45 GHz and 5.8 GHz bands are allocated to RFID related applications, 2.5/3.5/5.5 GHz bands are allocated for WiMAX application, and 2.4/5.2/5.8 GHz bands are allocated for WLAN applications [2]. Recently, the need for multi-band antenna has gained attention since it is more desirable for a single system to support multiple application standards simultaneously. However, most of the reported multi-band antennas, such as [3], [4] and [5], can either only operate at two frequency bands, or require relatively large areas. To the authors' best knowledge, few antenna design covers the frequency bands of RFID/WiMAX/WLAN applications.

---

* The corresponding author is Prof. Zhen Ji. The authors would like to thank the NSFC under grant No. 60901016, the project 10151806001000016 supported by Guangdong R/D Fund, the project JC201005280477A supported by Shenzhen city and the SRF for ROCS, SEM.

P. Ren et al. (Eds.): WICON 2011, LNICST 98, pp. 576–581, 2012.

In this paper, we report a miniature four-band CPW-fed antenna for 0.96/2.5/3.76/5.8 GHz applications. Limited to 30×30 mm^2 area on a PCBoard with ε_r=4.4, the antenna geometric configuration was optimized by Intelligent Single Particle Optimization (ISPO) algorithm [6]. The return loss and the radiation patterns of the finalized design are verified by Finite Element Method (FEM) and Method of Moment (MOM) simulations.

This paper is organized as follows. In Section 2, the design methodology of proposed antenna is described in detail. Simulation results including the return loss, radiation patterns and gains of the proposed antenna are shown in Section 3. The paper is concluded in Section 4.

2   Design Methodology

The antenna is implemented on a low-cost FR-4 substrate with dielectric constant ε_r=4.4, loss tangent tanδ=0.02 and thickness h=1.6 mm (Fig.1). A 50 Ω CPW transmission line is used for the antenna feed. The width of the feeding line is fixed as S=2.6 mm, and the gap between the feeding line and the ground plane is G=0.2 mm. In order to achieve multiband resonance, the antenna has four U-shaped, eight L-shaped and two F-shaped slots. The slots, including the eight symmetric L-, two symmetric F- and the two larger U-shaped branches (9×4 mm^2) are introduced to increase the antenna electrical length at the two lower frequency bands (0.96 GHz and 2.5 GHz), and the two smaller U-shaped branches (5 × 1.5 mm^2) are utilized as refiners to slightly adjust the antenna frequency response [7].

In order to optimize the antenna input impedance within the targeted frequency bands simultaneously, the geometric configurations of the slots are determined using the ISPO algorithm. The ISPO method is based on an analogy with models of the social behavior of groups of simple individuals, and it is a method specialized for solving complicated multidimensional problems. Detailed discussion of the ISPO algorithm can be found in [6].

Previous work [8] has used Particle Swarm Optimization (PSO) to design a multi-band CPW-fed monopole antenna. In this work, the ISPO algorithm is utilized for antenna optimization. The ISPO is a method specialized for solving complicated multimodal problems [6]. Using this algorithm, the complete position vector is partitioned into sub-vectors with smaller number of dimensions, and the sub-vectors are updated repeatedly in sequence. Based on the information generated during the updating process, the velocity vector required for updating the position vector is adjusted intelligently. For instance, the velocity of the particle will be increased if the fitness value is improved; the velocity will be slowed down when the particle skips over the optimum; when the fitness value is not improved after several iterations in the sub-vector updating process, the particle will increase the diversity of velocity in order to escape from the local optimum. Detailed discussion of the ISPO algorithm can be found in [6].

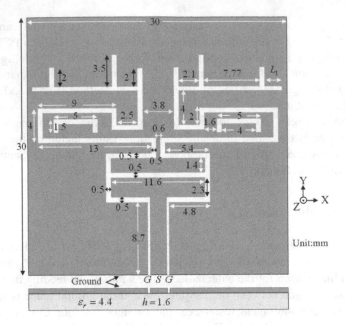

Fig. 1. Geometry of proposed four-band antenna

The target of the optimization process is set to achieve better-than- -10dB impedance matching at 0.96 GHz, 2.5 GHz, 3.76GHz and 5.8 GHz at the same time. For this purpose, totally nine physical dimensions (including L_1) of the antenna are defined as variables, which form the position vector described in the algorithm. To enhance the performance at 2.5 GHz, the weight right [9] of return loss at 2.5 GHz is a little larger than that at the other frequencies in the fitness function. The physical parameters of the finalized antenna are summarized in Fig.1. When L_1 equals to 1 mm, the antenna achieves the targeted frequency response.

3   Simulation Results

The ISPO-optimized multi-band antenna is verified using the FEM and MOM. As shown in Fig.2, the simulated return loss are -15.07 dB, -16.27 dB, -10.25 dB and -12.23 dB at the targeted frequency bands, all better than the design target. The bandwidth of the finalized antenna, which is defined as the frequency range within which the antenna achieves better than -10dB matching (VSWR $\leq$ 2), is 10 MHz at the 0.96 GHz band, 70 MHz at the 2.5 GHz band, 20 MHz at the 3.76 GHz band, and 480 MHz at the 5.8 GHz band. Calculated results obtained by two simulators are in a good agreement.

The radiation patterns of the antenna are also characterized, as shown in Fig.3 and Fig.4. It appears that the antenna radiates nearly omni-directionally in the xz plane, but the radiation patterns at all four bands show two nulls in the yz plane at $\theta=\pm90°$. Note that the antenna has relatively strong cross-polarized radiation (~20dB below the co-polarized radiation at upper frequencies and ~10dB below the co-polarized radiation at lower frequency), which is advantageous for RFID applications since the tag-reader orientation is not strictly limited. The antenna gain (Fig.5) obtained by MOM is -19.8 dBi, -2.55 dBi, 0.93 dBi and 4.03 dBi at the targeted frequency bands, respectively.

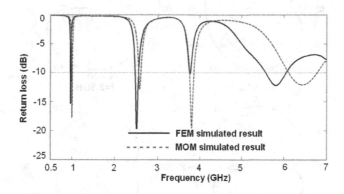

Fig. 2. Return loss of proposed four-band antenna obtained by FEM and MOM

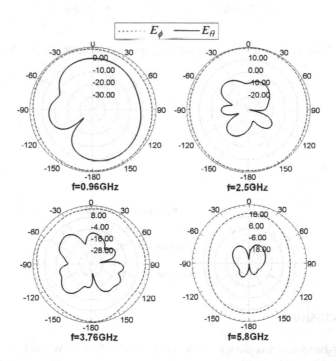

Fig. 3. Radiation patterns of proposed antenna in xz plane obtained by FEM

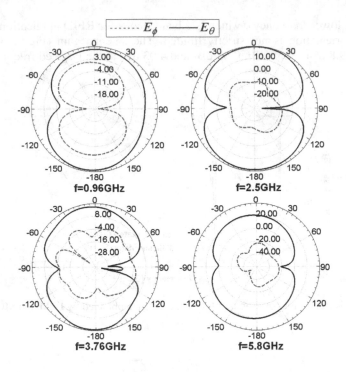

Fig. 4. Radiation patterns of proposed antenna in yz plane obtained by FEM

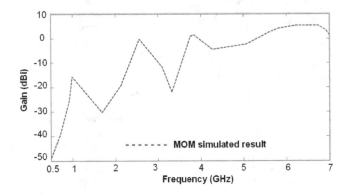

Fig. 5. Gain of proposed antenna obtained by MOM

4   Conclusion

A novel four-band antenna designed for RFID and WiMAX /WLAN applications is reported in the paper. Limited on a substrate of 30×30 mm^2 with ε_r=4.4, the antenna is resonated to multiple frequency bands by introducing four U-shaped, two F-shaped and eight L-shaped branches as additional resonators. To achieve impedance matching at 0.96 GHz, 2.5 GHz, 3.76GHz and 5.8 GHz simultaneously, the ISPO algorithm is utilized to help determine the slot geometric configurations. The performance of the ISPO-optimized antenna is characterized using the FEM method and the MOM method, and the simulation results show that the return loss within all the targeted frequency bands is better than -10dB.

Acknowledgments. The authors would like to thank the National Natural Science Foundation of China (NSFC) under grant numbers 60872125 and 60901016, Fok Ying-Tung Education Foundation, Guangdong Natural Science Foundation, Shenzhen City Foundation for Distinguished Young Scientists, SRF for ROCS, SEM and SZU R/D Fund.

References

1. Finkenzeller, K.: RFID Handbook: Fundamentals and Application in Contactless Smart Cards and Identification, 2nd edn. Wiley and Sons Inc., UK (2003)
2. Krishna, D.D., Gopikrishna, M., Aanandan, C.K.: A CPW-fed Triple Band Monopole Antenna for WiMAX/WLAN Applications. In: 38th European Microwave Conference, Amsterdam, The Netherlands, pp. 897–900 (2008)
3. You, B., Lin, B., Zhou, J., Xu, W.: Dual-frequency folded dipole antenna with PBG structure. Electronics Letters 45(12), 584–588 (2009)
4. Hu, S.M., Zhou, Y., Law, C.L., Dou, W.B.: Study of a Uniplanar Monopole Antenna for Passive Chipless UWB-RFID Localization System. IEEE Trans. Antennas and Propag. 58(2), 271–278 (2010)
5. Abu, M., Rahim, M.K.A., Suaidi, M.K., Ibrahim, I.M., Zhang, F.H.: A Meandered Triple-band Printed Dipole Antenna for RFID. In: Asia Pacific Microwave Conference, Singapore, pp. 1958–1961 (2009)
6. Ji, Z., Liao, H.L., Wang, Y.W., Wu, Q.H.: A Novel Intelligent Particle Optimizer for Global Optimization of Multimodel Functions. In: IEEE Congress on Evolutionary Computation, Singapore, pp. 3272–3275 (2007)
7. Wong, K.L.: Compact and Broadband Microstrip antennas. John Wiley and Sons Inc., New York (2002)
8. Liu, W.C.: Design of a Multiband CPW-fed Monopole Antenna Using a Particle Swarm Optimization Approach. IEEE Trans. Antennas and Propag. 53(10), 3273–3279 (2005)
9. Li, H.H., Mou, X.Q., Ji, Z., Yu, H., Li, Y., Jiang, L.: Miniature RFID Tri-band CPW-fed Antenna Optimised using ISPO Algorithm. Electronics Letters 47(3), 161–162 (2011)

Author Index